Human Communication in Society

5TH EDITION

Jess K. Alberts
Arizona State University

Thomas K. Nakayama
Northeastern University

Judith N. Martin
Arizona State University

Director, Portfolio Management: Karon Bowers
Content Producer: Barbara Cappuccio
Content Developer: Kate Tully
Portfolio Manager Assistant: Dea Barbieri
Product Marketer: Christopher Brown
Field Marketer: Kelly Ross
Content Producer Manager: Melissa Feimer
Content Development Manager: Sharon Geary
Managing Editor: Maggie Barbieri
Content Developer, Learning Tools: Amy Wetzel
Art/Designer: Kathryn Foot

Digital Studio Course Producer: Amanda Smith
Full-Service Project Manager: SPi Global
Compositor: SPi Global.
Printer/Binder: LSC Communications, Inc.
Cover Printer: Phoenix Color/Hagerstown
Cover Design: Lumina Datamatics, Inc.
Cover Credit: pixelfit/Getty Images; Klaus Vedfelt/
Getty Images; PamelaJoeMcFarlane/Getty Images;
LWA/Dann Tardif/Getty Images; Granger Wootz/
Getty Images

Acknowledgments of third party content appear on page 411, which constitutes an extension of this copyright page.

Library of Congress Cataloging-in-Publication Data

Names: Alberts, Jess K., author. | Nakayama, Thomas K., author. | Martin,
    Judith N., author.
Title: Human communication in society / Jess K. Alberts, Arizona State
    University, Thomas K. Nakayama, Northeastern University, Judith N. Martin,
    Arizona State University.
Description: 5th edition. | Hoboken, NJ : Pearson Education, [2019]
Identifiers: LCCN 2017033199| ISBN 9780134553726 | ISBN 0134553721
Subjects: LCSH: Communication--Social aspects.
Classification: LCC HM1206 .A43 2019 | DDC 302.2—dc23 LC record available at https://lccn.loc.gov/2017033199

Instructor's Review Copy:
ISBN-10:   0-13-455423-X
ISBN-13: 978-0-13-455423-5

Access Code Card:
ISBN 10:   0-13-456735-8
ISBN 13: 978-0-13-456735-8

à la carte Edition:
ISBN-10:   0-13-455424-8
ISBN-13: 978-0-13-455424-2

Student Rental Edition:
ISBN-10:   0-13-455372-1
ISBN-13: 978-0-13-455372-6

1   18

Brief Contents

Contents

Preface

As experienced researchers and instructors in the field of communication, we continue to be impressed by the breadth and depth of scholarship in our discipline; we also recognize that this scholarship presents challenges for students and instructors in the introductory survey course. For example, which research traditions should be covered: the traditional functionalist and psychological perspectives, the interpretive-qualitative perspectives, or the more recent critical perspectives? Which subfields should be covered: intercultural communication, communication technologies, nonverbal communication, or rhetorical studies? Should instructors focus primarily on helping students develop communication skills or should they focus primarily on theories and inquiry?

Our struggle to answer these questions led us to write the first edition of this text, which we believe met the goals we established early on: first, to expose beginning students to the breadth and depth of our discipline's scholarship, and second, to provide a balance between theory and application. Finally, our third goal was to present a lively overview of the discipline, to meet students "where they live," and to engage them in exploring the implications of communication in their daily lives.

Our overarching theme for the first edition was the interaction between the individual and society. In subsequent editions, we've enhanced the emphasis on this theme, adding new examples, illustrations, and pedagogical materials that connect the more traditional individual-centered, functionalist approach—that is, "who you are affects how you communicate"—with more contemporary critical approaches, which focus on the impact of societal structures and history on communication outcomes.

By highlighting this tension between individual and societal forces, we encourage students to recognize the value of multiple perspectives in understanding communication. Students need to be encouraged to think more reflexively about their individualism, as well as their and others social identities. Students often recognize that if they say the same thing as someone else, the message could be interpreted quite differently due to the differences in gender, age, sexuality, race and other societal forces. It is important for students to understand how to connect their individuality with larger societal forces that shape their communication experiences.

Human Communication in Society, Fifth Edition, like previous editions, covers the full range of topics addressed in existing textbooks but also introduces some useful innovations. We begin by describing the theoretical foundations of the study of communication, including models of communication, historical and contemporary approaches, and the role of identity in communication. We present the factors of perception, verbal and nonverbal communication, and listening and responding. We then explore communication in various contexts such as culture, close relationships, small groups, and organizations. Ours is the first book to provide comprehensive coverage of rhetoric (Chapter 12), and we devote full chapters to communication and mass media (Chapter 13) and to the increasingly important topic of interactive (social) media (Chapter 14). Overall, we discuss the full range of paradigmatic approaches in the field, offering a balance between theory and practice.

New to This Edition

Revel™

Revel is an interactive learning environment that deeply engages students and prepares them for class. Media and assessment integrated directly within the authors' narrative lets students read, explore interactive content, and practice in one continuous learning path. Thanks to the dynamic reading experience in Revel, students come to class prepared to discuss, apply, and learn from instructors and from each other.

Learn more about Revel

www.pearson.com/revel

Rather than simply offering opportunities to read about and study human communication, Revel facilitates deep, engaging interactions with the concepts that matter most. For example, students can complete a self-assessment to gauge their own communication style and explore ways to improve upon their skills. Students can respond to ethical issues in communication and see how their responses compare to others'. Students may interactively explore different theories of and approaches to communication, see how communication shapes identity, review the components of language and stages of listening, assess models for relationship development, and analyze group roles and communication structures in organizations. Students may interactively see how individual factors, cultural influences, and ethnocentric biases shape the way people perceive others and their world. By providing opportunities to read about and practice communication in tandem, Revel engages students directly and immediately, which leads to a better understanding of course material. A wealth of student and instructor resources and interactive materials can be found within Revel. Some of our favorites include:

- **Videos and Video Quizzes** Videos throughout the narrative show the various ways such factors as ethics, culture, language, and listening skills shape the act of communication to boost mastery. Many videos are bundled with correlating self-checks, enabling students to test their knowledge.

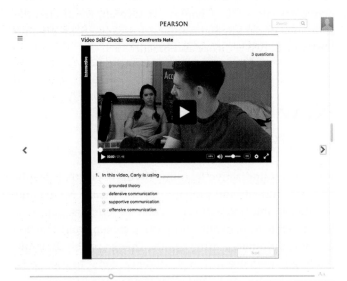

- **Critical Thinking Prompts** Fill-in applications allow students to answer questions that require them to apply their personal experiences to the concepts within the text.

- **New Animated Figures** Animated figures help students understand hard-to-grasp concepts through interactive visualizations.

- **Audio Narratives** In-text audio narratives bring the "It Happened to Me" stories to life, adding dimension and reinforcing learning in a way that a printed text cannot.

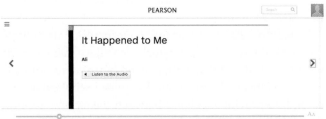

- **Integrated Writing Opportunities** To help students connect chapter content with personal meaning, each chapter offers two varieties of writing prompts: the Journal prompt, eliciting free-form topic-specific responses addressing topics at the module level, and the Shared Writing prompt, which encourages students to share and respond to one another's brief response to high-interest topics in the chapter.

For more information about all of the tools and resources in Revel and access to your own Revel account for the *Human Communication in Society*, Fifth Edition, go to www.pearson.com/revel.

In addition to the immersive learning experience offered by Revel, we've refined and updated the content in this new edition to create a powerful and contemporary resource for helping speakers connect to their audience. We've added several new features and revised features that both instructors and students have praised.

In this edition, general changes include new examples, theories, and applications, as well as updated photos that reflect the pervasiveness of social and other interactive media. Also, all chapters incorporate examples of studies and applications that include LGBT communicators.

New features in the fifth edition of *Human Communication in Society* include:

- Dynamic and new figures, including clearer images for the three communication models.

- More examples of specific research studies, particularly those that address LBGT as well as heterosexual relational communication—in all three major paradigms.

- A more explicit discussion of schemas and a new discussion on the influence of primacy and recency on selective attention.

- Updated videos that include speeches from notable celebrities and politicians, including Stephen Colbert, Donald Trump, and Michelle Obama.

- Chapters 13 and 14 ("Mass Media and Communication" and "Communicating Through Social and Other Interactive Media") have been updated and revised to more clearly differentiate between communication processes that occur in mass media and interactive media, respectively.

- References in each chapter have been updated to reflect the most recent available research on the topics addressed.

- Video self-assessments that ask students to respond thoughtfully to scenarios in video clips.

- Updated examples that address contemporary events and trends will help students connect the concepts to their personal experiences and concerns.

- Added review-based interactives that require students to interact with new concepts.

Chapter-By-Chapter Descriptions

Part 1

Chapter 1 explains the theme of this book—the interaction between the individual and society—as well as introducing important communication concepts and models. This chapter has been revised to include three new depictions of the linear, transactional and synergetic models of communication. The models are simpler and clearer to assist student comprehension. The Revel version includes interactive models of the new figures, allowing students to view the components in more depth. It also features an interactive survey that asks students to assess their communication skills and compare the results with their classmates.

Chapter 2 focuses on current research paradigms and methods. Additional research-based examples, including those focused on LGBT, as well as heterosexual communicators, have been added. In addition, the learning objectives and chapter material have all been streamlined; more mention of specific communication theories (previewing those covered in later chapters) and photos have been updated to better appeal to college age students. The Revel version includes an interactive version of The Synergetic Model for students to click through.

Chapter 3 explores the relationship between communication and identities. This edition includes updated examples with a focus on digital media, including apps, and the issue of how gender and sexualities are counted in various national census data. It also introduces cisgender and transgender, as well as the impact of DNA testing on racial attitudes. Revel content includes a multimedia gallery that shows how people perform their identities, along with a video and video quiz that delve into how race impacts perception and identity.

Chapter 4 focuses on communication and perception. Changes include a new discussion of schemas and the role of primacy and recency on selective attention as well as a clearer definition for attributional bias. Revel content includes several interactives that test the student's knowledge of the concepts, including a self-quiz on distinguishing between schemas, prototypes, and scripts, as well as a matching assessment that requires students to differentiate between physical, cognitive, and interpretive approaches to communicate.

Part 2

Chapter 5 outlines the elements of verbal communication. This edition includes a comparison of prescriptive and descriptive approaches to language use using French and German as examples. It also includes a discussion on US presidents and their knowledge of non-English languages, as well as anger at those who are not speaking English in public situations. The Revel version includes an interactive fill-in-the-blank exercise on "I" statements, along with an image gallery that demonstrates the functions of language.

Chapter 6 addresses issues of nonverbal communication. The discussion of nonverbal codes has been revised to clarify their meanings and to provide more concrete examples of the various codes. The Revel version includes interactive images with informational popups that delve into the nonverbal messages shown within.

Chapter 7 is devoted to listening and responding. The distinction is made early on between hearing and listening and other new material focuses on the role of listening in "civil dialogue." Civil Dialogue identifies effective listening strategies for dealing with the current political polarization and "echo-chambers"—where people listen/hear only views that support their own. This approach models how to speak honestly with each other without resorting to attack or criticism. Revel content delves into the four stages of listening, requiring students to properly identify the key components of each stage. It also features an interactive video self-assessment that asks students to listen to a problem, then respond appropriately.

Part 3

In Chapter 8, both Learning Objectives and text have been streamlined, and the chapter includes new material on intercultural empathy as well as updated statistics on US ethnic and racial demographics, migration patterns, refugee trends, tourism travel, and intercultural encounters. Revel videos showcase various scenarios that involve intercultural communication. Students are required to review these situations in video quizzes and video self-assessments, both of which require students to identify the communication patterns within.

Chapter 9 discusses communication in close relationships. The chapter has been streamlined, and a new feature entitled "The Truth about Hook-up Culture" has been added that addresses whether hook-up culture is as prevalent as has been reported and as undergraduate students often believe. The Revel version features an interactive model of Knapp's stages of romantic relational development. It also contains an interactive that shows students how they can reword hurtful messages into constructive ones.

Chapter 10 explores small group communication, and this edition includes updated material on communication technologies and small group communication (i.e., effective virtual teamwork, the role of technology tools in virtual teamwork). There are also new examples and description of symptoms of groupthink. Revel content includes interactives that delve into small group task roles, small group relational roles, and small group individual roles, with accompanying student audio.

Chapter 11 explores organizational communication. It has been revised to include a discussion of organizational climate and to include examples related to contemporary organization such as Uber. The Revel version includes an interactive simulation that asks students to put themselves in the mindset of a manager, presenting them with a series of workplace scenarios that require appropriate and ethical responses. Revel content also features several videos from prominent business executives who discuss concepts such as workplace bullying.

Chapter 12 covers the area of public communication. Rhetoric is presented with emphasis on its historical, theoretical, societal, and ethical aspects. This edition includes updated examples and introduces visual rhetoric and an updated discussion on rhetoric on the Internet. The Revel version includes several videos that provide rhetorical analysis on several prominent politicians and celebrities, including Oprah Winfrey, George W. Bush, and Donald Trump.

Chapter 13 discusses communication and mass media. We distinguish between mass media and interactive media. This chapter includes a discussion of watching mass media, such as television programming, on other devices such as laptops, tablets, and smartphones. We also discuss the perceived power of mass media and how people respond. We also introduce the ethical issues surrounding "fake news." Revel interactives delve into the evolution of popular media, explore how media use differs across cultures, and explores how high-power individuals – such as Stephen Colbert – can influence public opinion on current issues.

Chapter 14 covers interactive (social) media and communication. This chapter offers extensive new material, again focusing on the constant communication choices students make in deciding which medium to send messages and the consequences of these choices in both personal and professional contexts, as well as how media choices evolve to serve the needs of communicators. The chapter also includes new material on crowd-sourcing, crowdfunding and updated examples, statistics, and research findings reflecting current scholarship and trends in interactive media use, as well as guidelines for effective Twitter, email, and mobile phone use. The Revel version includes student testimony videos that explore how they use social media. Videos are accompanied by fill-in applications that ask Revel users to explore their own social and interactive media use.

Features

Key features retained in this new edition reflect our four goals for this textbook.

Accessible Presentation of Communication Theory

In addition to using a down-to-earth writing style and providing plenty of examples, *Human Communication in Society*, Fourth Edition, offers specific tools throughout the text to help students understand the theory and key concepts:

- **Key terms** are glossed in the margins of the page where the term is first used and defined, listed at the end of each chapter with the page number where the term and definition can be found, and compiled in a convenient Glossary at the end of the text.

KEY TERMS

paradigm p. 25	social penetration theory p. 28	ethnographic p. 34
theory p. 26	demand-withdrawal p. 30	cultural communication p. 35
methods p. 26	interpretive approach p. 32	rhetorical analysis p. 35
social science approach p. 27	rhetoric p. 32	member-checking p. 36
behaviorism p. 27	humanism p. 32	critical approach p. 36
hypothesis p. 27	qualitative methods p. 32	textual analysis p. 37
naturalistic p. 28	content analysis p. 33	
quantitative methods p. 28	defensive communication p. 33	

- **Chapter summaries** conclude each chapter.

SUMMARY

2.1 **Define the research concepts paradigm, theory, and method.**

- There are three research *paradigms* (belief systems) in communication research today. Each paradigm carries with it a set of assumptions about knowledge, the nature of reality, and human nature.
- *Theory* is a set of statements that explains a particular phenomenon.

Emphasis on Ethics in Communication

Each chapter includes one or more detailed sections discussing ethical issues relevant to that chapter's communication topic.

Opportunities to Apply What was Learned

We advocate a hands-on approach to the study of communication. For this reason, we've added features throughout the text that will help bring the theory home for students:

- **Skills improvement sections.** Chapters 4–14 conclude with a section providing practical guidelines for applying chapter material to everyday communication.
- **Exercises and activities.** "Apply What You Know" questions encourage students to work through challenging concepts.

Student Engagement

We like to think that we have translated our commitment to the field and our love of teaching into a text that will engage students. We encourage this involvement with the following pedagogical features:

- **"It Happened to Me"** boxes offer real-life accounts of student experiences that provide a "hook" to important communication concepts.
- **"Alternative View"** boxes offer perspectives that challenge mainstream thinking or offer an interpretation of a chapter-related topic counter to conventional wisdom.
- **"Communication in Society"** boxes serve to reinforce the connection between the individual and society as applied to chapter-related topics.
- **Critical Thinking Prompts,** placed in the margins at strategic intervals, encourage students to reflect on how major concepts connect with their everyday experiences.
- **"Did You Know?"** boxes offer examples of chapter-related material that students may find surprising or unfamiliar.

Instructor and Student Resources

Key instructor resources include an Instructor's Manual (ISBN 0-13-455414-0), TestBank, (ISBN 0-13-455431-0), and PowerPoint Presentation Package (ISBN 0-13-455417-5). These supplements are available on the catalog page for this text on Pearson.com/us (instructor login required). MyTest online test generating software (ISBN: 0-13-455422-1) is available at www.pearsonmytest.com (instructor login required). For a complete list of the instructor and student resources available with the text, please visit the Pearson Communication catalog, at www.pearson.com/communication.

Pearson MediaShare

Pearson's comprehensive media upload tool allows students to post videos, images, audio, or documents for instructor and peer viewing, time-stamped commenting, and assessment. MediaShare is an easy, mobile way for students and professors to interact and engage with speeches, presentation aids, and other files. MediaShare gives professors the tools to provide contextual feedback to demonstrate how students can improve their skills.

The best of MediaShare functionality, including student video submissions with grading and video quizzes, is now available to use and assign within Revel, making Revel an even more complete solution for Communication courses. By placing these key components of MediaShare within Revel, students have one all-inclusive space to practice and have their performance assessed while actively learning through interactive course content. Revel with MediaShare is an unparalleled immersive learning experience for the Communication curriculum.

- Set up assignments for students with options for full-class viewing and commenting or private comments between you and the student.
- Record video directly from a tablet, phone, or other webcam.
- Embed video from YouTube via assignments to incorporate current events into the classroom experience.

- Use MediaShare to assign or view speeches, video-based assignments, role plays, and more in a variety of formats including video, Word, PowerPoint, and Excel.
- Assess students using customizable, Pearson-provided rubrics or create your own around classroom goals, learning outcomes, or department initiatives.

- Set up quiz questions on video assignments to ensure students master concepts and interact and engage with the media.
- Import grades into most learning management systems.
- Ensure a secure learning environment for instructors and students through robust privacy settings.

A Word About Language

The text's commitment to presenting comprehensive coverage of the complex field of communication carries with it a responsibility to use language thoughtfully. We recognize the fact that, for complex historical and political relations, identity labels carry strong denotative meanings that may vary from person to person and across time. We have made an effort to use inclusive terms to represent the heterogeneity of opinions within various ethnic and racial groups.

For example, the term *Hispanic* was created and used in 1980 by the US government for the census and other purposes of collecting census statistics. However, many individuals of Spanish descent prefer Latina/o, as do we. We endeavor to use the latter to refer to US Americans of Spanish descent from a specific ancestral nation like Argentina, Mexico, or any country in Latin America or Spain. We also use Mexican American when referring to individuals coming more directly from Mexico, or Chicana/o to designate a more political consciousness among persons of Mexican descent.

Similarly, we use the inclusive term *Asian American* unless the context refers to individuals with a specific national origin (e.g., Japan or the Philippines). We use African American or Black interchangeably, recognizing that some individuals (often those from the Caribbean) prefer the more inclusive term *Black*, whereas others prefer *African American*. We also use Native American and American Indian interchangeably, recognizing that individuals are divided in their preferences for each of these terms.

We should also note that we use both White (which emphasizes race) and European American (which emphasizes ethnicity) to refer to US Americans of European ancestry. At the same time, we recognize that some individuals prefer to emphasize their more specific origins (Japanese American rather than Asian American, Yaqui rather than Native American, or German American rather than White).

Finally, we are learning to think more internationally in our use of language. Many of our neighbors in Latin and South America, as well as in Canada, find it offensive when we use the term *American* to refer to ourselves. (After all, these people are Americans as well.) Therefore, we prefer the term US American, in recognition of the fact that we are only one society out of many that make up the continents of North and South America.

Acknowledgments

We are once again grateful to all the students and instructors who have provided invaluable feedback to us as we wrote the five editions of *Human Communication in Society*. Unfortunately, we are unable to list here all of the students who participated, but we would like to acknowledge the instructors who have helped to shape and define all editions of our book.

Reviewers (First Edition)

Bob Alexander: University of Louisiana–Monroe
Isolde K. Anderson: Hope College
Jay Baglia: San Jose State University
Cheryl L. Bailey: Western Illinois University
John R. Baldwin: Illinois State University
E. Tristan Booth: Arizona State University
Joseph Bridges: Malone College
Lynn S. Cockett: Juniata College
Elisia L. Cohen: Saint Louis University
Lisa Coutu: University of Washington
Peter A. DeCaro: California State University–Stanislaus
Aaron Dimock: University of Nebraska–Kearney
Donald G. Ellis: University of Hartford
Larry A. Erbert: University of Texas at El Paso
Marty Feeney: Central College
Charles Feldman: George Washington University
Sarah L. Bonewits Feldner: Marquette University
Karen A. Foss: University of New Mexico
Kenneth D. Frandsen: University of New Mexico
John Gareis: University of Pittsburgh
Sonja M. Brown Givens: University of Alabama
    in Huntsville
Carroll Glynn: Ohio State University
Beryl S. Gutekunst: Chestnut Hill College
Thomas Edward Harkins: New York University
Carla Harrell: Old Dominion University
Brian L. Heisterkamp: California State University, San
    Bernardino
Dr. Patrick J. Hérbert: University of Louisiana–Monroe
Christine Courtade Hirsch: State University of
    New York–Oswego
John Katsion: Hannibal-LaGrange College
Joann Keyton: University of Kansas
Larry J. King: Stephen F. Austin State University

Thomas J. Knutson: California State University–Sacramento

Peter Lah: Saint Louis University

William A. Lancaster: Northeastern University

Sara McKinnon: Arizona State University

Jennifer Mease: Arizona State University

Diane Millette: University of Miami

Todd Norton: University of Utah

Shirley Oakley: Coastal Georgia Community College

Richard K. Olsen, Jr: University of North Carolina–Wilmington

Karen Otto: Florida Community College at Jacksonville–North Campus

Frank G. Pérez: University of Texas at El Paso

Linda Pledger: University of Arkansas–Little Rock

Steven B. Pratt: University of Central Oklahoma

Leanne Stuart Pupchek: Queens University of Charlotte

John C. Reinard: California State University–Fullerton

Brian Reynolds: State University of New York–Buffalo

Scott J. Robson: Washburn University

Pamela Schultz: Alfred University

David Schulz: California State University–Stanislaus

Kristina Horn Sheeler: Indiana University Purdue University Indianapolis

Deborah Shelley: University of Houston–Downtown

Nancy J. Street: Texas A&M University

Crispin Thurlow: University of Washington

Sarah Tracy: Arizona State University

April Trees: University of Colorado, Boulder

Kathleen J. Turner: Davidson College

Kyle Tusing: University of Arizona

Sam Wallace: University of Dayton

Toni S. Whitfield: James Madison University

Bill Yousman: University of Hartford

Reviewers (Second Edition)

Marcia S. Berry: Azusa Pacific University

Lynn S. Cockett: Juniata College

Larry A. Erbert: University of Colorado–Denver

Emma K. Gray: Portland Community College

Carla J. Harrell: Old Dominion University

Christine Courtade Hirsch: SUNY Oswego

Heather A. Howley: Cazenovia College

Thomas J. Knutson: Sacramento State University

Joanna Kostides: Holyoke Community College

Tema Milstein: University of New Mexico

Cynthia Ridle: Western Illinois University

Renee Beth Stahle: Aquinas College

Jenny Warren: Collin College

Reviewers (Third Edition)

Erin Baird: University of Oklahoma

Anthony Hurst: California State University–San Marcos

Vicki L. Karns: Suffolk University

Dan Lair: University of Denver

Valerie L. Manusov: University of Washington

Tema Milstein: University of New Mexico

Shane Semmler: University of South Dakota

Caitlin Wills-Toker: University of Georgia

Reviewers (Fourth Edition)

Becki Bowman: McPherson College

Kari Duffy: Carthage College

Mary Horner: St. Louis Community College

Gilberto Martinez: Texas A&M International University

Kerry Osborne: College of the Canyons

Leonard Schulze: Carthage College

Carl Thameling: University of Louisiana–Monroe

Reviewers (Fifth Edition)

Jessica Reeher-SUNY Oswego

Daryle Nagano-Los Angeles Harbor College

Sabeen Sheikh-Northern Virginia CC - Annandale

Farah Sanders-Utah Valley University

Emily Holler-Kennesaw State University

Karen Erlandson-Albion College

Carla Stevens-St. Ambrose University

William Price-Georgia Perimeter College

Additional Acknowledgments

We would also like to thank our colleagues and students for their invaluable assistance and moral support: a special thanks to Professor Pauline Cheong for providing foundational ideas for our revised chapter on computer-mediated communication, Professor Clark Olson who generously contributed his knowledge on small-group communication, and Professor Pauline Davies for her insightful feedback (and suggestions) regarding content, based on her extensive experience teaching the textbook material. Professor Karen Ashcraft (University of Utah) for her substantial assistance with the organizational communication chapter, and Professor Angela Trethewey for her support and help throughout this project.

And, of course, we need to thank the many, many students, at Arizona State University, Northeastern University, and elsewhere, who have good-naturedly provided invaluable feedback on the first, second, third, and fourth editions, and helping us to make the necessary changes in the fifth edition.

Thanks also to our editorial assistants, Ms. Lauren Mark, Dr. Marie Odile Hobeika, and Dr. Versha Anderson, who spent hours searching for (and finding) the most recent and relevant research articles, updated examples and contemporary margin material. We especially appreciate their assistance given that they had their own work to do, and the deadlines were very tight.

Thanks to the team at Pearson who made it all happen. Thanks to our Publisher, Karon Bowers. We could not have managed without Pearson's expertise, patience, and

practiced hand guiding us through the always complicated publishing process. Thanks also to Maggie Barbieri and Kate Tully, development editors, Ohlinger Publishing Services, for their enthusiasm, patience, and hard work. We want to acknowledge the work of project managers Annemarie Franklin, and Sasibalan "Sasi" Chidambaram at SPi Global, editorial assistant Dea Barbieri, and content development manager Sharon Geary.

Finally, to our partners—James LeRoy, David Karbonski, and Ronald Chaldu—who continue to tolerate our frequent absences with good grace. We give them our deepest thanks for their support throughout this and many other projects.

Jess Alberts is President's Professor in the Hugh Downs School of Human Communication at Arizona State University. She is an interpretive scholar who focuses on interpersonal communication and specializes in the study of conflict. **Thomas Nakayama** is a professor in the Department of Communication Studies at Northeastern University. He is a critical scholar who focuses on rhetoric and intercultural communication. **Judith Martin** is professor emerita in the Hugh Downs School of Human Communication at Arizona State University. She is a social scientist whose expertise is in intercultural communication.

Jess Alberts

Thomas Nakayama

Judith Martin

Introduction to Human Communication

LEARNING OBJECTIVES

1.1 Explain why it is important to study human communication.

1.2 Name and describe the seven primary components of communication.

1.3 Explain how the Synergetic Model of Communication differs from previous models.

1.4 Formulate your own communication ethic.

1.5 Articulate what makes a communicator competent.

CHAPTER TOPICS

The Importance of Studying Human Communication

What Is Human Communication?

A Model of Human Communication: The Synergetic Model

Communication Ethics

Putting It All Together: Communicating Competently

> *"If good communication skills were just common sense, then communication would not so often go awry."*

On her way to class, Charee called her dad to let him know what time she would arrive home; she then texted a friend to arrange to meet for lunch. While she waited for class to begin, she checked Facebook and Tumblr. When the professor arrived, she muted her phone and listened as the class began.

Most people, like Charee, exist in a sea of communication. They phone, email, and text message their friends and family; spend time on Facebook, Instagram, and Twitter; occasionally watch television; attend class lectures; and are inundated by media images as they shop for groceries or use public transportation. Given all of this, it is hard to imagine that just 25 years ago most communication occurred face to face, on landlines, or through the U.S. mail. But in fact, throughout much of human history, individuals lived close to the people they knew. They conducted commerce and maintained relationships primarily with the same small group of people throughout their lives. Today, people maintain relationships with individuals thousands of miles away, and they buy and sell products halfway around the globe on Amazon, eBay, and countless retail sites. This instant and widespread access to the world has its benefits, but it also has its costs.

With so many communication options, people need a wider range of communication knowledge and skills than ever before. Successful communicators must converse effectively face to face; determine what messages to send via email or Twitter; learn with whom it is appropriate to use text messaging; and absorb the norms and etiquette surrounding the use of social media, such as whether to communicate through a Facebook post or a private message. Becoming an effective communicator involves both understanding the components and processes of communication and putting them into practice. As you work in this course to improve your communication knowledge and skills, you may see positive changes in your relationships, your career, your engagement in civic life, and even your identity. How many other courses can claim all that?

The Importance of Studying Human Communication

1.1 Explain why it is important to study human communication.

As you begin this book, several questions may arise. First, you may wonder exactly how the study of human communication differs from other studies of humans, such as psychology. Communication differs from other social science disciplines because it focuses exclusively on the exchange of messages to create meaning. Scholars in communication explore what, when, where, and why humans interact (Emanuel, 2007). They do so to increase our understanding of how people communicate and to help individuals improve their abilities to communicate in a wide variety of contexts. In addition, unlike most social sciences, the study of communication has a long history—reaching back to the classical era of Western civilization when Socrates, Plato, and Aristotle wrote about the important role of communication in politics, the courts, and learning (National Communication Association [NCA], 2003; Rogers & Chafee, 1983). However, the ability to speak effectively and persuasively has been valued since the beginning of recorded history. As early as 3200–2800 BCE, the Precepts of Kagemni and Ptah-Hotep commented on communication (NCA, 2003).

Second, you may question why anyone needs to study communication; after all, most people have probably been doing a reasonably good job of it thus far. And isn't most communication knowledge just common sense? Unfortunately, it is not. If good communication skills were just common sense, then communication would not so often go awry.

ALTERNATIVE VIEW
Co-rumination: When Too Much Talk Is As Bad As Not Enough

Can you think of other occasions when people talk "too much"?

You have probably heard that to have good relationships, people need to "communicate more." However, sometimes communicating a lot can have negative effects. One type of "over-communication" that can cause harm is co-rumination. Co-rumination occurs when we talk—again—and again—and again—with others about a problem in our lives. It has been linked to negative outcomes such as depression, anxiety, binge eating, binge drinking, and self-harm (Nolen-Hoeksema, Wiscol, & Lyubomirsky, 2008).

Co-rumination often occurs among friends, because that is to whom we turn most often when we encounter problems. In an attempt to console or support each other, such as when a break-up occurs, friends often tolerate or even encourage each other to talk extensively about what happened and how they feel. Individuals are most likely to engage in co-rumination during adolescence and young adulthood. In addition, because women tend to talk more and offer more emotional and verbal support to their friends, they also are more likely to co-ruminate.

Why is co-rumination unhealthy? During co-rumination, participants' communication focuses on the issue and its negative effects rather than on solutions. Repeatedly discussing how bad something is and how horrible one feels about it does nothing to change the problem or to change how the person feels about it. In fact, such discussions may make one feel worse and helpless to do anything about it. Consequently, experts suggest that conversations that focus on solutions and suggest that the problem can be overcome offer a more effective approach.

SOURCE: Nolen-Hoeksema S., Wisco B., & Lyumbomirski S. Rethinking rumination. (2008). *Perspectives on Psychological Science*, 3, 400–424.

In fact, most people struggle with how to communicate well: they don't know how to listen so that other people feel heard; they aren't sure how to convince others to see their point of view, and they often aren't able to settle disagreements with people they care about deeply. Because communication is a complex activity, we need to learn skills that allow us to adapt our communication so others will hear, understand, connect with and care for us. Think of times when you felt others failed to communicate effectively with you. Have you ever felt that one of your teachers talked down to you? Have you had a relationship end because you and your partner had a misunderstanding? Or, have you failed to get what you wanted—a job, an invitation, your parents' support—because you couldn't figure out how to interact with others in specific contexts? In sum, talking is not equivalent to communicating. We can drown others in words, but if they do not understand, connect with and care about those words, then we have not communicated with them at all.

Now that we have so many ways to communicate and maintain relationships with others, some scholars have begun to ask if it is possible to have too much communication. Do you think this is possible or likely? To learn how some communication scholars answer this question, see *Alternative View: Co-rumination: When Too Much Talk Is As Bad As Not Enough*.

Finally, you may think of communication as a set of skills but believe that they are easily learned and wonder why there is an entire course (even a major!) that focuses on communication. Although it is true that every day people use communication to accomplish practical goals such as inviting a friend to see a movie, resolving a conflict with a colleague, or persuading the city council to install speed bumps in their neighborhood, communication is more than just a set of skills, like baking, that one can use in a variety of contexts and settings with little alteration. Rather, communication is an intricate process whose effective performance requires an in-depth understanding of how it works and the ability to apply one's critical thinking skills to communication experiences to learn from and improve them.

Critical Thinking: A Key to Successful Communication

Critical thinking requires that one become a critic of one's own thoughts and behavior. That is, rather than responding automatically or superficially, critical thinkers reflect on their own and others' communication, behavior, and ideas before responding

▲ If your romantic partner doesn't answer a text message, it could be because she is studying and has turned off her phone.

(Paul & Elder, 2008). Scholars have proposed various definitions of critical thinking; the one we advocate describes it as a process that involves the following steps (Passer & Smith, 2004):

1. Identify the assertion or action.
2. Ask, "what is the evidence for and against the assertion or action?"
3. Ask, "what does the bulk of evidence point to?"
4. Ask, "what other explanations or conclusions are possible?"
5. Continue to keep an open mind for new evidence and new ways of evaluating the assertion.

How might one apply this process to communication interactions? Let's explore this with a simple and common example, showing the steps in the process.

Step 1: Identify the action: Imagine that you send a text message to your romantic partner on a Friday evening, but hours later have not heard back. How should you interpret the lack of reply, and consequently, how should you respond? If you were thinking non-critically, you might interpret the behavior negatively (my partner is cheating on me!) even though you have little or no evidence to support this interpretation. You then might respond by dashing off an accusatory text.

Step 2: Evaluate your interpretations and beliefs: Critical thinkers evaluate their interpretations and beliefs before responding by asking themselves, "What evidence do I have for this belief or interpretation?" Thus, if their first impulse was to doubt their partner, they would ask themselves, "What evidence exists that my partner is cheating?" Does failing to return a text necessarily mean the partner is intentionally refusing to respond? Even if the partner is purposely refusing to respond to a text, does that mean the reason for refusing is unfaithfulness?

Step 3: What does the bulk of evidence point to? The critical thinker would then question whether this interpretation is supported by sufficient evidence and experience. A critical thinker would ask: What does the bulk of the evidence point to—for example, has my partner cheated before? Does my partner usually respond quickly to texts? Is my partner normally trustworthy?

Step 4: What other conclusions are possible? Next he or she would consider what other explanations are possible. For example, my partner's phone battery is dead; my partner fell asleep early and didn't receive my texts; my partner is studying and turned off her or his phone.

Step 5: Keep an open mind and evaluate new information as it is presented: Only after following this process would a critical thinker settle on a likely interpretation and response. Even then, the critical thinker would continue to keep an open mind and evaluate new information as it was presented. Thus, even if you decided there was no evidence that your partner was cheating, you might reevaluate your conclusion if your partner repeatedly failed to reply to texts on Friday nights.

Advantages of Studying Human Communication

There are many advantages to studying human communication. Individuals use communication to meet people, to develop professional and personal relationships, and to terminate dissatisfying ones. Communication scholar Steve Duck argues that relationships are primarily communicative (1994). Moreover, the relationships we have

Critical Thinking Prompt

Now that you have reviewed the steps involved in critical thinking, would you consider yourself high or low in critical thinking skills? What topics or situations are most likely to cause you to use your critical thinking skills? What can you do to improve these skills?

with others—including how we think and feel about one another—develop as we communicate. Through communication interactions, relationship partners develop shared meanings for events, explanations for their shared past, and a vision of their future together (Alberts, Yoshimura, Rabby, & Loschiavo, 2005; Dixon & Duck, 1993). So, if you tell your romantic partner, "I have never loved anyone as much as I love you, and I never will," you are simultaneously redefining your past romantic relationships, creating shared meaning for the present relationship, and projecting a vision of your romantic future together. Similarly, through communication with friends, coworkers, and acquaintances, we all define and redefine our relationships.

Perhaps most fundamentally, your communication interactions with others allow you to establish who you are to them (Gergen, 1982; Mead, 1934). As you communicate, you attempt to reveal yourself in a particular light. For example, when you are at work, you may try to establish yourself as someone who is pleasant, hardworking, honest, and competent. With a new roommate, you may want your communication behavior to suggest you are responsible, fun, and easygoing. However, at the same time that your communication creates an image of who you are for others, *their* communication shapes your vision of yourself. For example, if your friends laugh at your jokes, compliment you on your sense of humor, and introduce you to others as a funny person, you probably will see yourself as amusing. In these ways, communication helps create both our self-identities and our identities as others perceive them.

Communication has the potential to transform your life—both for the better and for the worse. (To read how one student's communication created a transformation, see *It Happened to Me: Chelsea*.) As many people have discovered, poor or unethical communication can negatively affect lives. How? Communicating poorly during conflict can end relationships, inadequate interviewing skills can result in unemployment, and negative feedback from conversational partners can lessen one's self-esteem. Sometimes communication can have even more significant effects. In 2005, singer Lil' Kim was sent to jail for perjury, or lying under oath (and thereby obstructing justice), when she testified that she had not noticed her manager's presence in the building with her when a gunfight occurred outside of a New York radio station where she gave an interview. However, security cameras revealed her manager opening the door for her as she left the station. Thus, she was imprisoned for a specific unethical (and illegal) communication act (CNN.com, July 7, 2005).

As you can see from Chelsea's story, developing excellent communication skills also can transform your life for the better. The three authors of this book have all had students visit months or years after taking our communication classes to tell us what a difference the classes have made in their lives. A student in a public speaking class reported that, because of her improved presentation skills, she received the raise and promotion she had been pursuing for years; another student in a conflict and negotiation class revealed that her once-troubled marriage became more stable once she learned to express disagreements better. A third student felt more confident after he took a persuasion class that taught him how to influence people.

Studying human communication may also benefit you by opening doors to a new career path. A degree in communication can prepare you for a wide variety of communication careers.

It Happened to Me
Chelsea

When the professor asked us to identify a time when communication was transformative, many examples came to mind. Finally, I settled on one involving a negative relationship. In high school there's usually one person you just don't get along with. Boyfriend drama, bad-mouthing, you name it. I remember dreading seeing this one girl, and I'm sure she felt the same about me. Graduation came and went, and I completely forgot about her. A year later, I came across her Facebook page as I was searching for old classmates online. As I thought about how petty our arguments were and how cruel we were to each other, I felt smaller and smaller. So I decided to end it. After friending her, I sent her a private message to apologize for my bad behavior. A couple days later I received a response from her saying she felt the same way and was also sorry for the way she acted. Next week we're going to have a cup of coffee together to really put the past behind us. Maybe to some people that doesn't seem all that life changing, but after hating this girl for two years, it's an amazing transformation for me.

Journal Prompt 1.1:
Studying Communication
Consider the following question:
How does the study of communication differ from other social science disciplines?

human communication

A transactional process in which people generate meaning through the exchange of verbal and nonverbal messages in specific contexts, influenced by individual and social forces, and embedded in culture.

What Is Human Communication?

1.2 Name and describe the seven primary components of communication.

Broadly speaking, human communication can be defined as a process in which people generate meaning through the exchange of verbal and nonverbal messages. In this book, however, we emphasize the influence of individual and societal forces and the roles of culture and context more than other definitions do. Because we believe these concepts are essential to understanding the communication process completely, we developed a definition of human communication that included them. Accordingly, we define **human communication** as a transactional process in which people generate meaning through the exchange of verbal and nonverbal messages in specific contexts, influenced by individual and societal forces and embedded in culture. In the following sections, we will illustrate our definition of human communication and explore the meaning of each of these concepts and their relationships.

Components of Human Communication

Consider the following scenario:

> Charee grew up in the United States and needed to talk to her father, Pham, who was reared in Vietnam, about her desire to attend graduate school out of state. She was worried; she was the first member of her family to attend graduate school and would be the first single family member to move so far away. She hoped to convince her father that it was a good idea for her to go away, while also displaying respect for him as her father and the head of the household. To ensure that things went well, she decided that they should meet at his favorite neighborhood café in the early afternoon so they could talk privately. She rehearsed how she would convey information that he might not be happy to hear and practiced responses to the objections she expected him to raise.

As this example reveals, communication is a complex process that can require considerable thought and planning. The complexity inherent in communication is a result of the variety of factors that compose and influence it. The seven basic components of communication to consider in planning an interaction are *message creation*, *meaning creation*, *setting*, *participants*, *channels*, *noise*, and *feedback*. Each of these features is central to how a communication interaction unfolds. To help you understand this process, we analyze Charee's experiences with her father.

messages

The building blocks of communication.

encoding

Converting ideas into messages.

decoding

Receiving a message and interpreting its meaning.

Message Creation **Messages** are the building blocks of communication, and the process of taking ideas and converting them into messages is called **encoding**. (Receiving a message and interpreting its meaning is referred to as **decoding**.) Depending on the importance of a message, people are more or less careful in encoding their messages. In our example, Charee was concerned with how she encoded her messages to her father. She particularly wanted to communicate to her dad that they would remain close, both to persuade him that she should go to graduate school out of state and to assure him that her leaving would not change their relationship. To accomplish this, she decided to encode her idea into this message: "I promise that I will call at least twice a week, I'll text you every day, and I'll come home for all holidays."

symbol

Something that represents something else and conveys meaning.

When we communicate, we encode and exchange two types of messages—verbal and nonverbal—and most of these messages are symbolic. A **symbol** is something that represents something else and conveys meaning (Buck & VanLear, 2002). For example, a Valentine's Day heart symbolizes the physical heart, it represents romantic love, and it conveys feelings of love and romance when given to a relational partner. The verbal system is composed of linguistic symbols (that is, words), whereas the nonverbal message system is composed of nonlinguistic symbols such as smiles, laughter, winks, vocal tones, and hand gestures.

When we say _communication is symbolic,_ we are describing the fact that the symbols we use—the words we speak and the gestures we use—are arbitrary, or without any inherent meaning (Dickens, 2003). Rather, their meaning is derived as communicators employ agreed-on definitions. For instance, putting up one's hand palm forward would not mean "stop" unless people in the United States agreed to this meaning, and the word _mother_ would not mean a female parent unless speakers of English agreed that it would. Because communicators use symbols to create meaning, different groups often develop distinct words for the same concept. For instance, the common word for a feline house pet is _cat_ in English, but _neko_ in Japanese. Thus, there is no intrinsic connection between most words and their meanings—or many gestures and their meanings.

▲ As this picture illustrates, communication is symbolic in that the words we use to communicate an idea such as "I love you" are arbitrary and are not inherently connected to the concept to which they refer.

Because human communication is predominantly symbolic, humans must agree on the meanings of words. Consequently, words can, and do, change over time. For example, the term _gay_ typically meant happy or carefree from the seventeenth century through much of the twentieth century. Although the term was occasionally used to refer to same-sex relationships as early as the 1800s, it has come to be used widely only since the late 1990s, when users agreed to this meaning and usage. Nonetheless, people may have different meanings for specific symbols or words, especially if they come from different ethnic or national cultures. Read about one student's difficulties communicating while on a trip to Europe in _It Happened to Me: Alyssa._

As Alyssa's experience reveals, though most people recognize that cultures vary in the words they use for specific ideas and items, they don't always realize that nonverbal gestures can have varied meanings across cultures as well. Creating messages is the most fundamental requirement for communication to occur, but it certainly is not enough. Messages also create shared meanings for everyone involved in the interaction.

It Happened to Me
Alyssa

Recently I traveled in Europe; I had no idea how difficult it would be to communicate, even in England. I spent the first few days navigating London on my own. It was so hard! People tried to help, but because of the differences in word choice and accents, I couldn't fully understand their directions. After London I went to Italy, where I had an even harder time communicating due to the language barrier. So I resorted to using nonverbal gestures such as pointing, smiling, and thumbs up and down. However, I ran into problems doing this. One night I ordered wine for a friend and myself. The bartender looked uncertain when he brought the two glasses of wine I'd ordered, so I gave him a "thumbs up" to mean okay, that he had it right. However, to him the gesture meant "one," so he thought I only wanted one glass, and he took the other away. It took us a while to get the order straight!

Meaning Creation   The goal of exchanging symbols—that is, of communicating—is to create meaning. The messages we send and receive shape meaning beyond the symbols themselves. We also bring to each message a set of experiences, beliefs, and values that help shape specific meanings. This is why people can hear the same message but understand it differently. Charee was aware of this as she planned the conversation with her father. She knew they didn't always have precisely the same meanings for every word. For example, the word "independent" carried positive meanings for her, but she knew it carried more negative and potentially upsetting meanings for her father. Therefore, when talking to her father, she would never argue that going away was good for her because it would make her more independent.

Meaning is made even more complex because, as the example suggests, each message carries with it two types of meaning—content meaning and relationship meaning. **Content meaning** includes denotative and connotative meaning. Denotative meaning is the concrete meaning of the message, such as the definition you would find in a dictionary. Connotative meaning describes the meanings suggested by or associated with the message and the emotions triggered by it. For example, denotatively the word *mother* refers to one's female parent, whereas connotatively it may include meanings such as warmth, nurturance, and intimacy. **Relationship meaning** describes what the message conveys about the relationship between the parties (Robinson-Smith, 2004; Watzlawick, Beavin, & Jackson, 1967). For example, if a colleague at work told you to "run some copies of this report," you might become irritated, but you probably wouldn't mind if your boss told you to do the same thing. In both cases the relationship message may be understood as "I have the right to tell you what to do," which is appropriate if it comes from your supervisor—but not if it comes from a peer.

Finally, communication helps create the shared meanings that shape families, communities, and societies. Specifically, the meanings we have for important issues including politics, civil behavior, family, and spirituality—as well as for less important concerns such as what food is tasty or what type of home is desirable—are created through people's interactions with one another. For example, if you were asked what your family "motto" is (that is, what is important in your family) what would you say? Some people might say it is "family first," whereas others declare it is "do the right thing." How do families come to have these shared beliefs and meanings? They do so through the countless interactions they have with one another; through these conversations and everyday experiences they create a meaning for what is important to their family. What do you think happens when two people marry, one of whom believes "family first" and another who thinks "do the right thing" is more important than even family? Like the families they grew up within, they will interact, live together, and jointly develop shared meanings for their family beliefs. A similar process occurs when people come together to form groups, organizations, communities, and societies. In sum, our relationships, our understanding of the world, and our beliefs about life and death are created through the interactions we have with others.

Setting The physical surroundings of a communication event make up its setting. **Setting** includes the location where the communication occurs, environmental conditions, time of day or day of the week, and the proximity of the communicators. Together these factors create the physical setting, which affects communication interaction.

Why do you think Charee chose to meet in mid-afternoon at her father's favorite café as the setting for their conversation? She did so for several reasons. First, her father would be more likely to feel relaxed and in a good mood in a familiar location that he liked. Second, she selected the middle of the afternoon so they would have more privacy and fewer interruptions. Finally, she chose a public setting because she believed her father would remain calmer in public than in a private setting, such as at home. As you can see, Charee carefully selected a comfortable setting that she believed would enhance her chances of being successful.

Participants During communication, **participants**—two or more people—interact. The number of participants, as well as their characteristics, will influence how the interaction unfolds. Typically, the more characteristics participants share (cultural, values, history), the easier they will find it to communicate, because they can rely on their common assumptions about the world.

As Charee planned her conversation, she recognized that she and her father shared a number of important characteristics—respect for elders in the family, a communal approach to relationships, and a desire for harmony. However, she also realized that

content meaning
The concrete meaning of the message and the meanings suggested by or associated with the message, as well as the emotions triggered by it.

relationship meaning
What a message conveys about the relationship between the parties.

setting
The physical surroundings of a communication event.

participants
The people interacting during communication.

they differed in important ways. Although she was close to her family, she desired more independence than her father would want for himself or for her. In addition, she believed it was acceptable for young, single women to live away from their families, a belief she was sure her father didn't share.

The type of relationship communicators have and the history they share also affect their communication. Whether communicators are family members, romantic partners, colleagues, friends, or acquaintances affects how they frame, deliver, and interpret a message. Because Charee was talking with her father rather than her boyfriend, she focused on displaying respect for his position as her father and asking (rather than telling) him about wanting to move away for college. As we have suggested already, the moods and emotions that communicators bring to and experience during their interaction influence it as well. Because Charee wanted to increase the likelihood that the conversation with her father would go well, she tried to create a situation in which he would be in a calmer and happier frame of mind.

▲ Text messaging is one channel of communication. What other channels do you often use?

Channels   For a message to be transmitted from one participant to another, it must travel through a channel. A **channel** is the means through which a message is conveyed. Historically, the channels people used to communicate with one another were first face to face, then written. Today, thanks to technology, we have many more communication channels—email, texting, social networks such as Facebook and Twitter, and Facetime, to name just a few.

channel
The means through which a message is transmitted.

The channel that a person selects to communicate a message can affect how the message is perceived and its impact on the relationship. For example, if your romantic partner broke up with you by changing his or her Facebook relationship status instead of by talking to you face to face, how would you respond? Because Charee was sensitive to the importance of the communication channel she used with her father, she elected to communicate with him face to face because it was a channel her father was familiar with and would find appealing.

Noise   **Noise** refers to any stimulus that can interfere with, or degrade, the quality of a message. Noise includes external signals of all kinds: not only loud music and voices, but also distracting clothing or hairstyles, uncomfortably warm or chilly temperatures, and so on. Noise can also come from internal stimuli, such as hunger or sleepiness. Semantic interference, which occurs when speakers use words you do not know or use a familiar word in an unfamiliar way, is another form of noise. If you have ever tried to have a conversation with someone who used highly technical language in a noisy room while you were sleepy, you have experienced a "perfect storm" of noise.

noise
Any stimulus that can interfere with, or degrade, the quality of a message.

Critical Thinking Prompt
How do you choose which channel to use when you communicate with others? Do you consider who they are, the topic, the importance of the message, or something else? Overall, do you think you pick the best channel most of the time? If not, what do you need to do to select more appropriately?

How did the noise factor affect Charee's choices? She chose to meet at a café in the middle of the afternoon, avoiding the crowded lunch and dinner hours. There would be fewer competing voices and sounds, and the wait staff would be less likely to interrupt with meal service, so there would be fewer distractions. By choosing a setting that minimized interference, she improved the chances that her message would be clear.

Feedback   Finally, the response to a message is called **feedback**. Feedback lets a sender know if the message was received and how the message was interpreted. For example, if a friend tells you a joke and you laugh heartily, your laughter serves as feedback, indicating that you heard the joke and found it amusing. Similarly, if you fall asleep during a lecture, you provide feedback to your professor that either you are tired or you find the lecture boring. Thus, your feedback serves as a message to the sender, who then uses the information conveyed to help shape his or her next message.

feedback
The response to a message.

Although Charee wasn't sure what type of feedback her father would provide or what type she would need to give him, she did spend time anticipating what they each would say. She also knew that she would need to be sensitive to his messages and be prepared to offer feedback that was both supportive and persuasive.

A Model of Human Communication: The Synergetic Model

1.3 Explain how the Synergetic Model of Communication differs from previous models.

To help people understand complex processes, scientists and engineers, among others, create visual models to show how all components of a process work together. Scholars of human communication have done the same. They have developed models to reveal how the seven components described work together to create a communication interaction.

The first such model of human communication depicted communication as a linear process that primarily involved the transfer of information from one person to another (Eisenberg, Goodall, & Trethewey, 2010; Laswell, 1948; Shannon & Weaver, 1949). In this model, communication occurred when a sender encoded a message (put ideas into words and symbols) that was sent to a receiver who decoded (interpreted) it. Then, the process was believed to reverse: The receiver became the sender, and the sender became the receiver (Laswell, 1948). This model (see Figure 1.1) also included the components of "noise" and "channel." A linear model assumes, for example, that your professor encodes her ideas into a lesson that she communicates to you via a face-to-face or video lecture (the channel) and that you hear her message and decode its meaning unless some noise interferes, such as the video failing to load or a loud noise outside drowning out her words. However, you can see some of the limitations of this model. It assumes that if a message is perfectly crafted its meaning will be clear to the audience, regardless of their own ages, experiences, and interpretations. You can probably think of times where this was not true. Because of these limitations, other, more complex models, such as our Synergetic Model, have been created to show a greater variety of factors that interact with one another to influence the communication process.

The **Synergetic Model** is a transactional model that, like most previous models, depicts communication as occurring when two or more people create meaning as they

Synergetic Model
A transactional model that emphasizes how individual and societal forces, contexts, and culture interact to affect the communication process.

Figure 1.1 A Linear Model of Communication

Early models depicted communication as a linear process that primarily involved the transfer of information from one person to another.

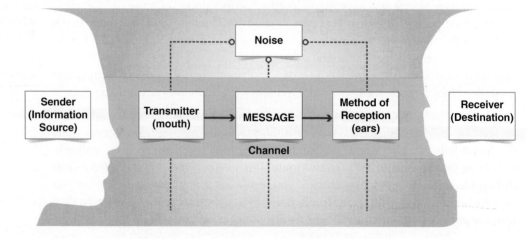

respond to each other and their environment. In addition, it is based on a belief in the important roles of individual and societal forces, contexts, and culture in the communication process. We call the model synergetic because synergy describes when two or more elements work together to achieve something either one couldn't have achieved on its own. For example, in the ubiquitous volcano science fair project, "lava" is created by adding vinegar to baking soda. Once the two products interact, something new is created. Similarly, when two people work together on a class project, often the outcome is better than either could have created on his own. Thus, our communication model is synergetic in that the different elements of communication work together to create something different, and greater, than just the sum of its parts. We discuss each of these elements, and to help clarify the concepts, we revisit Charee's interaction with her father once again to illustrate how they function during the communication process.

After carefully planning for the interaction with her father about her desire to leave home to go to graduate school, Charee engaged in the following conversation with him:

CHAREE: Purdue, Illinois, ASU, and Texas all let me in. *(While talking, Charee notices a quizzical look on her father's face.)*

CHAREE: I mean, all of them accepted me for graduate school.

DAD: Oh. How many did you apply to?

CHAREE: Just four. They all accepted me.

DAD: *(frowning, speaking uncertainly)* So where are you gonna go?

CHAREE: *(looking away, speaking hesitantly)* Uh, Texas, I think.

DAD: *(startled)* Texas?! Why not stay at ASU?

CHAREE: *(speaking patiently)* Because it's better for my career to go and study with other people. I'll be able to get a better job when I graduate if I can say that I studied with 12 people instead of 6, Dad. Plus, Texas is real high up there in the rankings. It's a good school.

DAD: *(shaking his head, speaking firmly)* Oh. Well, I think you can get a better job if you can show that you're loyal. If you stay at ASU, people will think, "Oh, she can stay at one place and do a good job. She has loyalty."

CHAREE: *(nodding her head, speaking carefully)* But I have been loyal to ASU for six years. People here know me and how I work. They also know that I can learn and grow somewhere else.

DAD: I guess I can see that. I just wish you didn't have to go.

Communication Is Transactional

To say that *communication is a transaction* (see Figure 1.2) captures the fact that (1) each participant is a sender and receiver *at the same time*, (2) meaning is created as people communicate together, (3) communication is an ongoing process, and (4) previous communication events and relationships influence its meaning (Warren & Yoder, 1998; Watzlawick, Beavin, & Jackson, 1967). What does this mean?

First, all participants in a communication event both receive and send messages simultaneously, even if those messages are sent only nonverbally. As you may have noted, when Charee explained that she was "let in" to four universities, she realized from her father's nonverbal behavior that he was confused. That is, she received his message even as she talked, and he sent a message even as he listened.

Second, a transactional model of communication assumes speakers collaborate through an exchange of messages with the goal of understanding one another. That

Figure 1.2 Communication Is Transactional

Transactional models express the idea that meaning is created as people communicate.

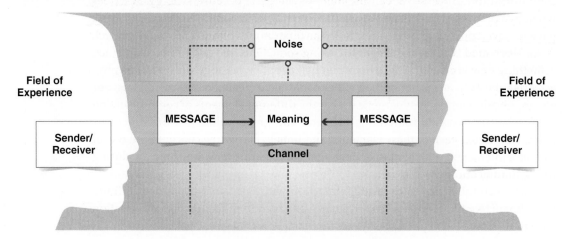

is, the purpose is not for receivers to perfectly understand the message senders have encoded, but that through working together participants can arrive at agreed upon meanings. Rather, similar to experiences you have had with your parents, meaning was created as Charee and her dad communicated together; she made a statement, he showed his lack of understanding, and Charee offered more information until they shared similar understandings or meaning.

Third, describing communication as ongoing highlights the fact that it is a process whose specific beginnings and endings can be difficult to discern. All of the interactions one has had with individuals in the past influence one's communication in the present, just as a person's current communication affects his or her expectations for and experiences of future interactions. For example, when you talk with your best friend you often can talk in short hand, because you can rely on shared communication and events you have had in the past. Similarly, Charee planned her interaction and communicated with her father based on her previous experiences with him. Specifically, she knew he would rather she stay close to home, so she was prepared to offer arguments for why leaving home for graduate school was best. Her experiences with her father, then, affected the messages she crafted for their conversation. In addition, she recognized that their conversation would influence how they communicated with each other in the future. If he became angry, he likely would communicate with her less or more negatively. This, in turn, would influence her future messages to him, and so on.

Finally, because communication is ongoing and interactive, when people communicate, they and their conversational partner(s) reaffirm or alter their identities and relationships. Thus, Charee's conversation with her father is likely to change how they see each other. He might see her as more adult and independent because of her desire to move away, or he may now perceive her as a less loving child. Similarly, she may view him as less of an authority figure and more of a peer, or she might believe he is more authoritarian and rigid than she previously thought.

Communication Is Influenced by Individual Forces

The individual is a primary focus in communication. Many separate individual forces or characteristics contribute to your identity, and these in turn affect your communication. Individual forces include your demographic characteristics such as age, race, ethnicity, nationality, gender/sex, sexual orientation, regional identity, and socioeconomic class, as well as such factors as personality and cognitive and physical ability. In addition, individual forces include your **field of experience**, such as your education and experiences.

field of experience
The education and experiences that a communicator possesses.

For example, Charee is female, 24, and a college graduate, whereas her father is a male in his late 40s who operates an automotive repair shop. Each of these individual factors influences the way they communicate as well the ways others communicate with them and about them. Because of her experiences as a college student, Charee knows what "let in" means and understands that universities often evaluate students who obtain all three degrees at one college negatively when they hire new professors. By contrast, her father is not aware of this information, and based on his culture and his experiences in the workforce, he understands that loyalty is often an important quality in an employee.

The combination of these individual characteristics is unique for every person, so people communicate in distinctive ways. However, every society places limits on the variations that are deemed acceptable. For example, not all men speak assertively, enjoy talking about sports, or "high five" one another. In mainstream U.S. culture, though, many people consider these behaviors as normal for males. Speaking in a more "female" style, such as speaking quietly or politely talking about fashion, or using nonverbal gestures that could be considered more stereotypically feminine, is typically considered inappropriate for men and boys. Those who veer somewhat from the norm may be seen as odd, or they might be shunned; those who veer too far from the norm may be labeled as mentally ill. So although we are each individuals, society places constraints on the range of our individualism, a topic we will explore later.

Communication Is Influenced by Societal Forces

As we suggested, individual differences are not value free. They are arranged in a hierarchy in which some individual characteristics are more highly valued than others. For example, being Caucasian is often advantageous in U.S. society, being young has advantages over being old, and being physically able is more advantageous than having a disability. How society evaluates these characteristics affects how we talk to—and about—people who display them.

The political, historical, economic, and social structures of a society influence this value hierarchy and affect how we view specific individual characteristics. The historical conditions under which many U.S. racial and ethnic groups arrived in the United States, for instance, continue to affect their identities, with many people making assumptions about individuals' occupation and/or social status based on their culture or ethnicity. For example, immigrants who move to the United States often are not fluent in English, so they create businesses of their own—as restaurant owners, shop keepers or service professionals. Consequently, many people fail to realize that immigrants also work as technology innovators, lawyers, professors, and physicians.

The values attributed to individual characteristics such as age, sexual orientation, and sex also come from these larger societal forces—whether communicated to us through the media, by our friends and family, or by organizations such as schools, religious institutions, or clubs. For example, the teachings of religious

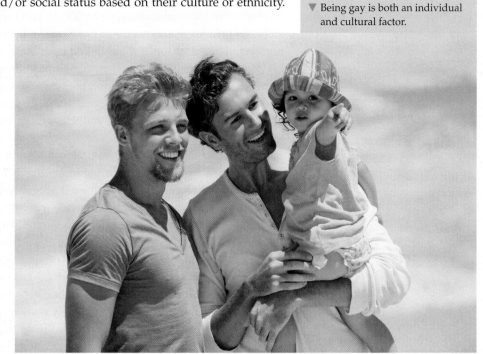
▼ Being gay is both an individual and cultural factor.

groups shape many people's views on sexual orientation, and because most societies historically have been patriarchal, they continue to value women in the public realm less than they do men.

In Charee's case, two societal forces were at work in her interaction with her father: how society views women and parent–child interactions. Pham was reared in a culture and time where males held considerably more power than females, and parents were assumed to know what was best for their children even when the children were grown. Consequently, he tends to hold the belief that fathers should have considerable decision-making power over their children, especially their unmarried female children. By contrast, Charee grew up in a culture and time where men and women are seen as more equal and parents exert less control over their children's lives as the children grow up.

Social hierarchies wherein men are more valued than women, or older people's opinions are considered more worthwhile than younger people's, arise from the meanings that societal structures impose on individual characteristics, and communication maintains these hierarchies. For example, cultures that value maleness over femaleness have many more stereotypes and negative terms for women than they do for men. Moreover, these cultures value certain types of communication over others. Thus, men in leadership positions are expected to communicate decisively and avoid appearing "weak" by apologizing or admitting mistakes, whereas the same is not usually true for women. We will explore social hierarchies in more detail in later chapters.

Communication Is Influenced by Culture

culture

Learned patterns of perceptions, values, and behaviors shared by a group of people.

Communication also is embedded in culture. **Culture** refers to the learned patterns of perceptions, values, and behaviors shared by a group of people. Culture is dynamic and heterogeneous (Martin & Nakayama, 2005), meaning that it changes over time and that despite commonalities, members of cultural groups do not all think and behave alike. You probably belong to many cultures, including those of your gender, ethnicity, occupation, and religion, and each of these cultures will have its own communication patterns.

When you identify yourself as a member of a culture defined by age, ethnicity, or gender, this culture-group identity also becomes one of your individual characteristics. For example, as people move from their teen years into young adulthood, middle age, and old age, they generally make a transition from one age-related culture to another. Because each cultural group has a unique set of perceptions, values, and behaviors, each also has its own set of communication principles. As you become an adult, then, you probably stop using language you used as a teenager. And even though changing your language is an individual decision, it is influenced by cultural and societal expectations as well.

Culture affects all or almost all communication interactions (Schirato & Yell, 1996). More specifically, participants bring their beliefs, values, norms, and attitudes to each interaction, and the cultures they belong to shape each of these factors. Cultural beliefs also affect how we expect others to communicate. As we discussed, because he is Vietnamese, Charee's father values family closeness, loyalty, and the role of the father as head of the family. Because she is Vietnamese American, Charee holds many of these same beliefs, but she also values independence and individuality in ways that her father does not.

In addition to participants' cultural backgrounds, the culture in which a communication event takes place influences how participants communicate. In the United States, politicians routinely mention religion in their public addresses and specifically refer to God; however, in France, because of a stricter separation between church and state, politicians typically do not mention religion or deities in their public communication and would be criticized if they did. Regional culture can also affect participants' expectations for appropriate communication behavior. For instance, southerners in the United States tend to be more nonverbally demonstrative and thus might hug others more than do northeasterners (Andersen, Lustig, & Andersen, 1990). Of course, other cultural differences (ethnic background, religious background) might influence these nonverbal behaviors as well.

Communication Is Influenced by Context

Each communication interaction occurs in a specific context. Context includes the setting, or aspects of the physical environment, in which an interaction occurs. It also includes which and how many participants are present, as well as the specific occasion during which the interaction unfolds (for example, a Sunday dinner or a birthday party). Context can exert a strong influence on how people communicate with one another. For example, you could argue with your close friend in private when just the two of you are present, during a social event when you are part of a group, during a staff meeting at work, on a television talk show about feuding friends, or on the sidewalk at campus. Can you imagine how each of these contexts would influence your communication? You might be more open if the two of you are alone and in private; you may try to get others involved if you are with friends; you could be more subdued in public on campus; you might refrain from mentioning anything too negative on television; or you might be more hostile in an email or text. It is because context strongly affects individuals' interactions that Charee arranged to talk with her father at his favorite café in the afternoon.

The tensions that exist among individual forces, societal forces, cultures, and contexts shape communication and meaning. To help clarify this tension, let's return yet again to Charee's conversation with her father. Their conversation was influenced by the context (a restaurant), multiple individual forces (each person's age, sex, cultural background, and education), multiple societal forces (the value placed on education, family, sex, and age) as well as their cultures (the meanings of independence, loyalty, and family). Thus, in the conversation between Charee and her father, the context in which the conversation occurred, their individual experiences with higher education, and the cultural meaning of the parent–child relationship all came together to influence the communication interaction. These components and their relationships to one another are depicted in Figure 1.3.

As we stated at the beginning of the chapter, and as is revealed in our model, for us, communication is a transactional process in which people generate meaning through the exchange of verbal and nonverbal messages in specific contexts, influenced by individual and societal forces and embedded in culture. This is the definition and model

---

Figure 1.3 The Synergetic Model

The Synergetic Model presents communication as a transactional process in which meaning is influenced by cultural, societal, and individual forces.

Journal Prompt 1.3:
The Synergetic Model
Consider the following question:
According to the Synergetic
Model, what are the individual and
social factors that influence the
communication process?

of communication that will guide you as you explore the remainder of this book. After you complete this course, we recommend that you return to this section to assess how your own understanding of the communication process has changed and deepened.

Our goal in developing this model is to provide a framework for students to organize, read, and understand this complex process we call communication. However, before moving on, we need to discuss one more essential concept that frames and guides all of your communication efforts—ethics.

Communication Ethics

1.4   Formulate your own communication ethic.

A diary study found that college students lied in one out of about every three social interactions, and over the course of a week only 1 percent of students said they told no lies at all (DePaulo, 2011). In another study, 74 percent of students admitted to cheating on exams and 84 percent to cheating on written assignments (McCabe & Trevino, 1996). And it isn't only college students who admit to deceiving others. In a survey conducted by the National Endowment of Financial Education (2011), 31 percent of respondents confessed to lying to their marital and living partners about money, often with disastrous consequences.

Given examples such as these, one may wonder if a communication ethic still exists. We strongly believe that it does. Even if unethical communication is widespread, and some people get away with their misbehavior, most people are still held responsible for the messages they create (Barnlund, 1962; Christians & Traber, 1997; Johannesen, 1990). If you spread gossip about your friends, lie to your employer, or withhold information from your family, justifying your behavior by pointing to the ethical failures of others will not excuse you. Those who know you and are close to you still expect you to meet basic standards for ethical communication.

Why are communication ethics so important? First, they sustain professional success. Yes, unethical people may prosper in the short run, but over time unethical practices catch up with the people who engage in them. To a great extent, your reputation as a person of integrity determines whether others want to hire you, work for you, or conduct business with you. Once that reputation is damaged, it can be difficult if not impossible to regain; consequently, communicating and behaving ethically is just good business.

Communication ethics are vital to personal relationships as well. Maintaining intimate and caring relationships can be difficult, but they become virtually impossible if one communicates unethically by lying, manipulating, or verbally abusing friends and lovers. Intimate relationships are grounded in trust. Without trust, people can't be open and vulnerable with one another, behaviors that are essential to intimacy. When one person abuses that trust by his or her unethical conduct, the other party often is deeply wounded and finds it difficult to ever again be intimate within the relationship. Far too many people have learned the hard way that a lack of ethics destroys relationships.

Critical Thinking Prompt
What are three specific communication
behaviors you believe are unethical?
What principles guide your decisions
regarding whether a given communication behavior is ethical or unethical?

As a communicator, you will face many ambiguous and difficult choices of both a professional and a personal nature. If you develop your own set of communication ethics, you will be better prepared to face these difficult choices. Therefore, in this section we provide some basic principles of ethical communication for you to consider as you critically review your own ethical standard.

Fundamentally, individuals, groups, and communities develop ethical codes to reflect their beliefs and values. Clearly the guidelines we offer reflect our own communication ethics. We do not expect you to adopt our beliefs wholesale. Rather, we present this information throughout this book so that you can analyze it critically to determine to what extent it reflects your own beliefs and behavior, what evidence supports it, and what other guidelines may be as useful or more useful for you. Thus, we want you to use your critical thinking skills specifically to critique our claims here and to use that analysis to form your own ethical code.

Defining Your Communication Ethic

Communication ethics describes the standards of right and wrong that one applies to messages that are sent and received. When you hear the term *communication ethics*, you might think we are simply referring to whether messages are truthful. Although truthfulness is one of the most fundamental ethical standards, communicating ethically requires much more than simply being truthful. It also involves deciding what information can and should be disclosed or withheld, and assessing the benefit or harm associated with specific messages. Individuals have a responsibility to evaluate the ethics of their own and others' communication efforts. Similarly, corporations ought to weigh the ethics of sharing or withholding information that might affect the value of their stock shares, and media companies should decide whether it is ethical to report private information about individuals. Let's look at some of the issues you need to reflect on as you develop your code of ethics.

communication ethics
The standards of right and wrong that one applies to messages that are sent and received.

Truthfulness   Truthfulness plays a fundamental role in ethical communication for two reasons: First, others expect messages to be truthful, and second, messages have consequences. Because people inherently expect speakers to be truthful, we actually may make it easier for them to deceive us (Buller & Burgoon, 1996). If an audience is not suspicious, they probably won't look for cues that the speaker is lying (McCornack & Parks, 1986). However, because of the implicit contract to be honest, discovery of deception can severely damage relationships. The more intimate the relationship, the greater the expectation people have that their partners will be truthful, and the more damaging any deception will be.

As we've implied, people rely on messages to be truthful because they have consequences. One's communication can influence the beliefs, attitudes, and behaviors of others. For example, an individual's communication could persuade a customer to purchase an item, a friend to lend money, or an acquaintance to become romantically involved with him or her. The more consequential the outcome of your message, the more likely you will be held accountable to the truth. You might not be criticized too harshly for exaggerating your salary during a flirtation with a stranger, but an employer will most likely consider it unethical if you lie about your salary on a job application.

Sharing or Withholding Information   A related fundamental principle of ethical communication concerns what information should be divulged and what can be withheld. When is withholding information a matter of legitimate privacy, and when is it a matter of inappropriate secrecy? Thus, you have to determine whether to tell your romantic partner how many sexual partners you have had; media organizations have to decide whether to reveal the identity of confidential news sources; and government officials decide what information to "leak" to the press.

In our view, a message can be considered legitimately private when other parties have no right to expect access to it. Inappropriate secrecy, by contrast, occurs when other parties might legitimately expect access to a message that is withheld. This distinction is important because it is generally ethical to maintain privacy, but it may be unethical to engage in secrecy.

What's the difference between privacy and secrecy? We believe communicators have an ethical responsibility to share information that other people require to make informed decisions. For example, if you have only dated someone once or twice, you may choose to keep private that you have a sexually transmitted disease. However, if the two of you consider becoming sexually intimate, you probably have an ethical obligation to reveal the information. Without this information, your partner cannot make an informed decision about whether to engage in sexual contact. What will happen to your relationship if you withhold the information and your partner contracts your disease—and finds

▲ Is it ethical to gossip or share others' private information?

out later that you withheld the information? Similarly, your friends may not need to know why you were fired from your last job, but your new boss may have a legitimate need for access to this information.

By contrast, revealing information can sometimes be unethical. For example, if you have agreed to maintain confidentiality about a topic, it could be considered unethical to reveal what you know. However, if you violate a confidence because of a higher ethical principle, most people would likely consider your behavior ethical. For example, if you have a duty of confidentiality to your employer, but your company engages in illegal toxic dumping, it likely would be more ethical to break this confidence. Here, the ethic of protecting the public health likely supersedes the ethic of keeping a confidence. These are not easy decisions, but they reflect the type of complex ethical choices that people have to make.

Now that you have read our guideline for differentiating secrecy and privacy, do you find yourself agreeing or disagreeing with it? Can you think of situations in which it would not apply? Can you think of a better principle one could use to make decisions about whether to withhold or reveal information? Again, it is not important that you adopt our guideline but that you think through and develop one that is in line with your own ethical code.

You can begin to think through your position on this issue by exploring an important trend in job searches—the growing use of Internet searches by corporations to gather information on potential or current employees as well as the practice of potential or current employees hiding Facebook information from employers. When individuals hide information on Facebook, do you believe they are engaging in secrecy or privacy attempts? How would you defend your position to someone who disagrees with you? That is, what evidence and examples would you use to argue for your belief? What arguments might someone make who disagrees with you? To what extent does the context of Facebook communication influence your response?

Benefit and Harm of Messages   To determine the most ethical choice, you also should consider the benefit or harm associated with your messages. A classic example concerns whether it is right to lie to a potential murderer about the whereabouts of the intended victim. A principle of honesty suggests that you should tell the truth. But in this case, once you evaluate the potential harm of sharing versus withholding the information, you might well decide to withhold the information.

More typically, issues of harm and benefit are less clear. For example, if you discover your best friend's romantic partner is being unfaithful, should you share that information? Will it result in more harm or more benefit? If you know that a relative cheated on her taxes, should you report her to the IRS?

Because many communication events are complex and the underlying ethical principles are not definitive, you will need to gradually develop your own philosophy of ethical communication and apply it on a case-by-case basis. This is one requirement of being an effective communicator. However, just as you develop your own ethical standards and decisions, others will do so as well, which means you and others in your life may not always agree.

Absolutism versus Relativism   A fundamental decision in communication ethics concerns how **absolute** or **relative** your ethical standards will be. Will you use the same

absolutism

The belief that there is a single correct moral standard that holds for everyone, everywhere, every time.

relativism

The belief that moral behavior varies among individuals, groups, and cultures and across situations.

absolute standards for every communication interaction, or will your ethical choices be relative and depend on each situation? The Greek philosopher Plato and the German philosopher Immanuel Kant conceptualized the absolutist perspective (Kant, 1949), and both believed there is a rationally correct, moral standard that holds for everyone, everywhere, every time. Relativists such as French philosopher Jean-Paul Sartre, by contrast, hold the view that moral behavior varies among individuals, groups, and cultures. They argue that because there is no universal standard of morality, there is no rational way to decide who is correct (Sartre, 1973).

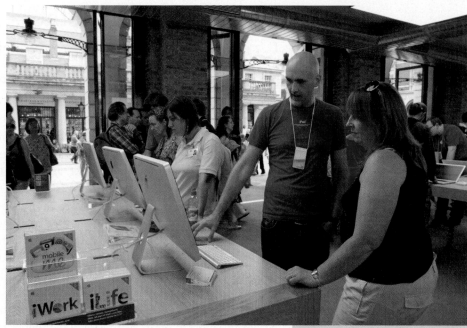

▲ Should a salesperson admit that a competitor's product might be as good as the product he or she is selling?

If you hold to the absolutist perspective that lying is always wrong, then in the previous example regarding the potential murderer, you would be obligated not to lie about the whereabouts of the intended victim. But if you adhere to a relativistic position regarding truth and deception, you would decide in the moment what the most ethical choice is based on the specific circumstances. You might tell a lie to save a life.

In reality, few people develop an ethical standard that is completely absolute or relative. Instead, absolutism and relativism are the opposite ends of a continuum, and most people's standards lie somewhere along that continuum.

The issue for you is to decide how absolute or relative your ethical standards will be. If you strongly believe that deception is wrong, you may choose the path of deception only when you believe the truth will cause great harm—a standard that falls toward the absolutist end of the continuum. However, if you favor a more relative view, you will consider a variety of factors, in addition to harm, as you make your decisions.

Communication Ethics in Practice

In this discussion of ethics, we have offered guidelines for creating your own communication ethics. However, in practice, many situations arise that are ambiguous, complex, and multilayered. At times you may not see how you can be ethical and accomplish important goals at the same time. For example, if you know that a friend and classmate has plagiarized a paper, what should you do? Should you keep quiet and maintain your friendship, or should you maintain your personal ethics and tell the instructor? Similarly, if you are a salesperson, how do you respond if a potential client asks whether a competitor's product is as good as yours, and you don't believe it is? Do you tell the truth and thus jeopardize a potential sale? People who tend toward an absolutist view say that you must always tell the truth, so you should only sell a product you truly believe is superior. Others may tell you that no one expects salespeople to be completely truthful in this context; therefore, you are not bound to share your opinion (Diener, 2002; Wokutch & Carson, 1981).

We believe that all communicators need to create an ethical stance based on their own beliefs, values, and moral training. Once *you've* established your ethical stance, you will be prepared to make thoughtful and deliberate communication choices.

**Journal Prompt 1.4:
Code of Ethics**
Consider the following question:
Why is developing one's own code of communication ethics important?

Putting It All Together: Communicating Competently

1.5   Articulate what makes a communicator competent.

The goal of this book is to help you improve your communication skills so that you can become a more successful, or competent, communicator. A competent communicator is one who is able to use communication to achieve his or her (realistic and appropriate) goals. More specifically, communicators are competent when they use their understanding of themselves, others, the context, and communication principles to adapt their communication to achieve their goals (Friedrich, 1994).

communication competence

The ability to adapt one's communication to achieve one's goals.

appropriateness

Following the rules, norms and expectations for specific situations or relationships.

effectiveness

Achieving one's goals successfully.

Communication competence is composed of two elements: **appropriateness**, which is defined as following the relevant rules, norms, and expectations for specific relationships and situations; and **effectiveness**, which involves achieving one's goals successfully. Speakers are competent when they understand the expectations regarding their behavior and are able to behave in a way that fulfills those expectations. For example, a best man offering a wedding toast is expected to be amusing, complimentary, and brief (as well as sober!). Failure to fulfill these expectations not only results in a poor toast, but it often also results in audience members negatively evaluating the speaker. If the toast seriously violates these expectations, the consequences may even include terminated relationships.

Effectiveness refers to the ability to achieve one's goals for an interaction without interfering with other, potentially more important goals. Taking the earlier example, a person giving a toast may have a goal of being humorous. However, if the best man makes jokes that are in poor taste, he might meet his goal of making the audience laugh, but he may fail another, more important goal of remaining friends with the bride and groom.

Generally, speakers have three types of goals that are important during an interaction: content, relationship, and identity. *Content* goals describe the concrete outcomes you would like to achieve during an interaction—to receive a job offer, earn a high grade on a speech, or to successfully initiate a new relationship. *Relationship* goals refer to your desire to change or maintain your relationship with another, for example, when you say "I love you" to your romantic partner in hopes of increasing your commitment to one another, or when you apologize so your romantic partner won't leave you. Finally, *identity* goals describe how we would like others to see us or help us see ourselves. When complaining about a grade, for instance, you likely want your grade changed (a content goal) but you probably also want your instructor to see you as deserving the higher grade (an identity goal).

Based on this definition, a communication behavior is judged to be competent only within specific situations or relationships (Cupach, Canary, & Spitzberg, 2009). That is, a behavior that might be appropriate or effective for one situation may not be so for another. For example, although "trash talking" may be competent (that is, appropriate and effective) in a sports context, is not likely to be appropriate during a discussion with one's romantic partner, even if it were effective. Communication competence requires that you understand yourself, your relationships and specific situations well enough that you can pull from your repertoire of communication skills exactly the right ones to use at this time, in this place, with this person, on this topic.

Journal Prompt 1.5:
Competent Communication
Consider the following question:
What does it mean to be a competent communicator?

If you think all of this sounds like a lot to do, you are beginning to understand why learning to communicate well is so complex. The good news is that we are here to help you develop the skills you need to be competent in a wide range of interactions. As you read through the remaining chapters in the book, reflect on how each concept can help you become a more competent communicator.

SUMMARY

1.1 Explain why it is important to study human communication.

- Studying human communication can enrich and transform your life professionally and personally.
- *Critical thinking*, which involves reflection and weighing evidence, is a key to successful communication.
- Communication skills are crucial in developing relationships, establishing identity, and opening career doors.

1.2 Name and describe the seven primary components of communication.

- The *process of communication* involves seven basic components: message creation, meaning creation, setting, participants, channels, noise, and feedback.

1.3 Explain how the Synergetic Model of Communication differs from previous models.

- The *Synergetic Model* views communication as a transactional process; it emphasizes that all communication interactions are influenced by the intersection of individual and societal forces, that they are embedded in culture, and that they occur in specific contexts.

1.4 Formulate your own communication ethic.

- Key aspects of communication ethics to consider as you make decisions include truthfulness, decisions regarding sharing or withholding information, and the benefit and harm associated with one's choices.
- Communicators' ethical choices are affected by their position on the continuum of absolutism versus relativism, which in turn influences their language use and how they receive and how they respond to others' communication efforts.

1.5 Articulate what makes a communicator competent.

- Understanding communication processes and the ethics of your own communication choices is the first step toward you becoming a more *competent communicator*.
- Competent communicators strive to be both effective and appropriate in their interactions with others.

KEY TERMS

human communication p. 6
messages p. 6
encoding p. 6
decoding p. 6
symbol p. 6
content meaning p. 8
relationship meaning p. 8

setting p. 8
participants p. 8
channel p. 9
noise p. 9
feedback p. 9
Synergetic Model p. 10
field of experience p. 12

culture p. 14
communication ethics p. 17
absolutism p. 18
relativism p. 18
communication competence p. 20
appropriateness p. 20
effectiveness p. 20

APPLY WHAT YOU KNOW

1. **Guidelines for Responding to Electronic Communication**

   Much debate has raged over whether it is appropriate to talk or text on one's cell phone in restaurants, in front of friends, or in the car. The Federal Aviation Administration is considering whether to allow airline passengers to use their cell phones during flights—and many people are already complaining about the possibility. The widespread use of instant text messaging and the ability to access our email almost anywhere have made the issues surrounding the appropriate use of electronic communication even more complex. To focus the discussion and guide your own decisions regarding your responses to these types of electronic communication, develop a list of rules for how, when, and with whom it is appropriate to use the various types of electronic communication.

2. **Creating a Communication Ethic**

   Interview three people and ask them to describe the underlying ethic(s) that guide their communication choices. Then write a brief statement that describes your own communication ethic.

EXPLORE

1. Make a list of all of the careers that you believe require good communication skills. Then, locate a list of careers from a university career center, such as North Carolina Wilmington's Career Center or Western Washington University Department of Communication's Career Information page, and examine the site's list of careers for which a communication degree prepares students. What careers did you list that are not listed on a university's career website? Why do you think the differences exist? Finally, create a list of careers you would post if you were responsible for creating such a site for your university.

2. Locate a website that discusses how to develop authentic communication skills, such as the site Authentic Communication or Hodu.com. After reading the suggestions and strategies described on the website, answer the following questions: When are you most likely to lie? What benefits do you think you will accrue if you lie? What can you do to increase how authentic you are when you communicate with others?

Perspectives on Human Communication

LEARNING OBJECTIVES

2.1 Define the research concepts paradigm, theory, and method.

2.2 Explain how behaviorism, causality, and quantitative methods influence the social scientific approach to studying communication.

2.3 Describe the role that humanism, description, and qualitative methods play in the interpretive approach to studying communication.

2.4 Discuss how a societal focus, emphasis on power and hierarchy, and textual analysis characterize the critical approach to studying communication.

2.5 Explain how the three research approaches influence the *Synergetic Model* of communication.

CHAPTER TOPICS

Contemporary Approaches to Studying Human Communication

The Social Science Approach: Assumptions, Theories, Methods, Ethical Issues, and Strengths and Limitations

The Interpretive Approach: Assumptions, Theories, Methods, Ethical Issues, and Strengths and Limitations

The Critical Approach: Assumptions, Theories, Methods, Ethical Issues, and Strengths and Limitations

A Multifaceted Approach

> *"Communication theories, then, are not just academic exercises; they explain and offer insight into one's own and others' communication."*

Charee and Mateo have been together for about 3 months. Although Charee likes Mateo a lot, she isn't sure exactly where she stands with him. He is generally caring when they are together, but he is unresponsive when she communicates with him via social media or even texting. For example, when she posts pictures of the two to Instagram, he never makes a comment, and if she texts a flirty emoji or to say that she misses him, he sends back brief messages that ignore her efforts to connect with him. This difference in their media behaviors upsets Charee, but when she tries to talk to Mateo about her feelings, he changes the topic, ignores her, or finds a reason to leave. Furthermore, she finds that the more she tries to get him to communicate with her about their differences, the quieter and more withdrawn he is. It's getting to the point where Charee wonders if they will ever be able to resolve their conflicts and sustain a satisfying relationship.

Charee is a communication major, and she's begun to worry about her and Mateo's pattern of conflict communication. Why doesn't Mateo express more in his text messages? Why does he get so quiet when she wants to talk about their relationship differences? Why does it bother her that he doesn't seem to engage in disagreements? Is it because they come from different family backgrounds and each learned different ways of dealing with relationships and conflict? Is it a reaction to Charee, specifically? Are they having more conflict because, with midterms coming up and no employment yet for summer, they both are having a lot of other stressors in their lives? Because Charee does not want her relationship with Mateo to end, she starts to think about the best way to approach this communication dilemma. She wonders if any communication experts and theorists have suggestions to help her and Mateo communicate more effectively.

Believe it or not, these are the types of real-life dilemmas that lead communication professors and scholars to develop theories about everyday communication. Theories are sets of statements that explain particular phenomena. In this case, as we'll see in this chapter, there are communication theories that can explain Mateo and Charee's relationship challenges and could ultimately help them work through their conflicts. In fact, research shows that learning how to manage conflict effectively leads to more satisfying relationships. Communication theories, then, are not just academic exercises; they can explain and offer insight into one's own and others' communication (Craig, 2013).

In this chapter, we will explore how communication scholars approach the study of communication and how this systematic study of communication differs from just making theories up out of thin air, or making generalizations from a few personal experiences. You will see that communication scholars do not all agree on how to best approach the study of communication! We'll also address larger questions, such as: How do we know what we know about communication? And how do communication scholars decide what to study in the first place? We want to introduce material that will show you the broad range of communication theories and lead to an exploration of the role of societal and individual forces in the communication process.

We'll explain three major approaches in the communication discipline: the social science, interpretive, and critical approaches. To help you understand these three approaches and how they arose, we'll also incorporate some description of the development of the communication discipline.

Contemporary Approaches to Studying Human Communication

2.1   Define the research concepts paradigm, theory, and method.

How might diverse communication experts investigate Charee's communication dilemmas? What do the experts tell us about differences in social media behavior and expressions of affection? Does expert information exist that explains Charee and Mateo's pattern of conflict communication or why they express themselves disparately? How can they find out what individual, context, and social forces affect their behavior? If you were Charee, what type of expert information would *you* trust to provide insight and guidance about interpersonal relationships? Would you trust information gathered from interviews with men and women about their Facebook and Instagram practices? Information gleaned from laboratory tests measuring male and female responses to conflict situations? Or would you rather learn about couples' differences from social critiques of male and female representations in popular culture products (e.g., films, music)?

It turns out that these ways of investigating represent three contemporary approaches to studying human communication: the social science approach, the interpretive approach, and the critical approach. Each of these approaches to understanding the situation is actually represented by contemporary scholars conducting real research. Each approach also reflects different assumptions about the nature of human behavior and the best way to obtain insights and build knowledge about human behavior. And each represents a particular historical tradition, some hundreds of years in the making.

Paradigms, Theories, and Methods

Before we discuss the various approaches to studying human communication, we need to answer a basic question: What do we mean by an *approach*? Each approach represents a belief system, much like a religious system or faith does. In the academic world we call these belief systems **paradigms** (Burrell & Morgan, 1988). Each approach or paradigm carries with it a set of assumptions about how we acquire knowledge, the nature of reality, and human nature. In turn, these assumptions guide research and theory development (Mumby, 1997). For example, most social scientists endorse a paradigm that assumes that knowledge should be acquired through "objective means," that reality is external to (or exists outside of) individuals, and that human behavior tends to be the same across time and groups. Therefore, social scientists believe knowledge can best be acquired through observing the behavior of a group of individuals and generalizing from that group to other groups of people. Using this approach, one might predict, for example, that specific types of people (e.g., males and females or U.S. Americans and Koreans) will consistently use different strategies to manage conflict across a variety of conflict situations.

Interpretivists, in contrast, assume that reality is socially constructed and, therefore, is specific to individuals, dyads, and groups; thus, behavior may not be consistent from person to person or group

paradigm

Belief system that represents a particular worldview.

▼ Communication researchers use various approaches and methods, including focus groups, to understand human communication.

to group. They believe we can best acquire knowledge by understanding the perspectives and experiences of individuals and groups, although such knowledge may not be generalizable for person to person or group to group. Each paradigm or approach involves preferences for particular theoretical ideas and also particular research methods.

theory
A set of statements that explains a particular phenomenon.

A **theory** is a set of statements that explains a particular phenomenon. Scholars develop theories in an attempt to explain why people communicate as they do. It is important that you understand in what sense we are using the word theory in this book. Here, theory refers to "a plausible or scientifically acceptable general principle or body of principles offered to explain phenomena" (Merriam Webster, 2017). Most of the scientific and social scientific theories with which you are familiar, such as the theory of evolution, are theories in this sense of the word. The other sense in which people use the term theory is to mean "an unproven assumption (or) conjecture" or, more commonly, an idea, hunch, or guess (Merriam Webster, 2017). For example, some people have a "theory" (or idea) that individuals behave more erratically during a full moon. However, there is no scientifically acceptable evidence or principles that this guess is accurate (Lilienfeld & Arkowitz, 2017). Although you might disagree with a specific scientific or communication theory, it is inaccurate to interpret the word theory in this context to mean that principle or principles are a tentative hypothesis or mere conjecture. That is, the scientific use of the word theory is very different from the speculative use of the term.

methods
The specific ways that scholars collect and analyze data, which they then use to support, prove, or disprove their theoretical claims.

Methods describe the specific ways in which scholars collect and analyze data, the results of which are used to support or disprove their theoretical claims. For example, they might ask a group of men and women to record the time they spend on social media over a period of a week and what kind of messages and other content they post. The researchers could then collect these time diaries and compare the amount of time spent by each gender group on various social media and what sorts of content they post. Researchers also use many other types of methods, including interviews, focus groups, and analyses of texts (such as speeches).

How do researchers decide which method to use? The method depends on their paradigm or approach to the study of human communication. For example, if they believe the best explanations (or theories) of communication behavior come from examining the behaviors of many people, a survey would be the most likely method, allowing them to collect information or data from a lot of people. Scholars often disagree about the virtues or faults of a particular method. Thus, some claim that survey studies have limited usefulness because they can only tell us how *most* people behave, and not much about an individual person. Others find interview methods inadequate because one cannot easily interview large numbers of people, making universal generalizations difficult. Like religious belief systems, these paradigms also include ethical beliefs about the right (and wrong) ways to study communication. For example, some scholars find it objectionable to conduct large-scale surveys because they feel that researchers are usually too distant and unfamiliar with the groups they are studying and often do not understand the individuals well enough to adequately interpret the results.

Why do communication experts disagree about the best way to study communication? Part of the reason lies in the fact that the communication discipline is interdisciplinary in nature—its paradigms, theories, and methods have been influenced by different disciplines over the years. The earliest influence was from the study of rhetoric (public speeches), whereas later influences came from the fields of sociology and psychology (see Table 2.1).

As a way of understanding the differences among the three contemporary approaches, let us examine how each might view Charee and Mateo's communication dilemma. Before we begin, however, we would like to offer an important caveat. Although we believe that by clearly differentiating each of these three paradigms from the others, we make it easier for you to understand them, the reality is a bit more complex and fluid. Many communication scholars' work does not fit neatly and precisely

Table 2.1 Major Contributions to the Study of Communication

Rhetorical Tradition	
Ancient Greeks	The power of persuasion
	Guidelines for effective public speaking
Middle Ages	Rhetoric established as liberal art
Renaissance	Humanism and Enlightenment: foundations of contemporary communication theory
Behaviorist Tradition	
Nineteenth Century	Rise of Behaviorism
	Elocution movement: study of proper public speaking
Twentieth Century	Establishment of the discipline of communication
	Humanism versus Behaviorism debate

into just one of the research paradigms; nor does it follow a single set of research methods. And although these paradigms may have been more clearly differentiated from one another in the early stages of their development, they have evolved over time. Scholars have borrowed from one another, their understanding of the research process has changed, and the differences among the paradigms have become less clearly defined. Some of the paradigms have more internal variations today than when they were originated. To highlight the underlying principles of these three paradigms in our discussion, let's look now at what each approach might have to offer Mateo and Charee.

The debates about the best way to approach the study of communication are nothing new! You might wonder how these debates got started and where contemporary communication scholars get their ideas about the varying approaches. The history of communication shows that the disagreements today are just a continuation of a discussion that started many, many years ago (Simonson, Peck, Craig, & Jackson, 2013).

Journal Prompt 2.1: Theories and Paradigms
Consider the following questions:
What is a theory? A research paradigm? Hypothesis?

The Social Science Approach: Assumptions, Theories, Methods, Ethical Issues, and Strengths and Limitations

2.2 Explain how behaviorism, causality, and quantitative methods influence the social scientific approach to studying communication.

The **social science approach** in communication originally focused on the individual or, less frequently, the dyad (a pair of people, like Charee and Mateo, who interact with each other). Because the social science approach grew out of the fields of psychology and sociology, communication scholars typically relied on some of the same research methods used by these social scientists.

social science approach
Contemporary term for the behaviorist approach.

Assumptions

Early social science researchers were oriented to **behaviorism**, which is a branch of psychology that focuses on observable behavior. They believed that the aim of communication research was to describe, predict, and explain human behavior with the ultimate goal of discovering universal laws that apply across situations and contexts. They believed predictions, or **hypotheses**, were possible because they saw reality as both observable and describable. So in Charee's case, the behaviorist view would involve making observations and then formulating predictions for why Mateo and Charee have conflicts and in discussing these conflicts why Mateo seems less than open. There are a number of social science theories that might explain their conflict patterns. Let's see how this works.

behaviorism
The focus on the study of behavior as a science.

hypothesis
A supposition or proposed explanation.

Theories and Methods

Social science researchers generally seek to determine what factors influence communication behavior. They make predictions (hypotheses) that came from theories or previous research findings, for example, that men and women communicate differently on social media, and then they test these predictions by gathering data through various methods. Common methods include observing subjects in either a laboratory or a **naturalistic** setting (that is, in everyday, real-life situations, such as a classroom, café, or shopping mall), using surveys, and conducting interviews.

Once social science researchers collect data, they use it to confirm or disconfirm their hypotheses about human communication behavior, most frequently through **quantitative methods**. These methods can be used to answer questions such as "how many?" and "what proportion?" That is, researchers convert their data into numerical indicators, and then analyze these numbers using statistics to establish relationships among the concepts.

Recent research shows that the majority of romantic couples' conversations, both gay and straight, use communication technologies (Ruppel, 2015), and there are several areas of communication research which might help explain Charee and Mateo's social media conflicts. For example, some theories argue that women's communication in general tends to be more emotional and relationship-focused than men's; thus, we might hypothesize that the same would be true for social media and text messages. And indeed some studies confirm this hypothesis. For example, one study hypothesized that young women's text messages would focus more on emotions than do young males' text messages, and this hypothesis was confirmed (Dunn & McLean, 2015). Using the same theoretical base, another study asked college students to complete a questionnaire about their social media participation, answering yes-or-no questions and providing other brief information (Do you use social networking sites to communicate with friends/family? How often do you communicate with friends/family?, etc.). The answers were converted to numerical data, submitted to statistical texts and the results, as predicted, showed that young women *are* more likely than men to use social media for maintaining relationships (Sponcil & Gitmu, 2013). Although Charee might expect that expressing her feelings for Mateo in text messaging and on Facebook would strengthen their relationship, communication researchers who have tested this hypothesis have found that this outcome depends on the stage of the relationship. Indeed, one theory, **social penetration**, discussed in more detail in Chapter 9, that might help Charee and Mateo, focuses on the role communication plays in various phases of satisfying romantic relationships.

For example, most U.S. Americans expect a degree of openness in their romantic relationship and assume that being open, disclosing, and sharing (private) information are important to the development of satisfying romantic relationships. Communication researcher Ruppel (2015) hypothesized that couples would use different communication channels in different phases of their relationship. She asked 64 gay and straight couples who were in romantic relationships for varying lengths of time about the types of information they would self-disclose using communication technologies (CT) or face-to-face communication, and the statistical results showed that her hypotheses were confirmed. Couples in newer relationships tended to prefer to self-disclose general information face to face or using text-based CT (i.e., text messages, FB). Couples in longer-term relationships felt freer to self-disclose through all forms of CTs and face to face. But all couples thought text-based CTs were inappropriate for intimate topics (Ruppel, 2015). It could be that Charee and Mateo have different perceptions about the appropriateness of certain topics to be discussed on social media or face to face at this stage of their relationship. Communication researchers Thompson and Vangelisti (2016) also used social penetration theory to determine how individuals, like Charee, handle a lack of openness and self-disclosure from their partner, that is, how might Charee handle the situation in a way that would strengthen and not negatively affect her relationship with Mateo?

naturalistic
Relating to everyday, real-life situations, such as a classroom, café, or shopping mall.

quantitative methods
Methods that convert data to numerical indicators, which are then analyzed using statistics to establish relationships among the concepts.

social penetration theory
Theory that proposes relationships develop through increases in self-disclosure.

They hypothesized that unmet expectations about openness would be stressful and negatively affect romantic relationships. So they asked 205 heterosexual undergraduate students who were in dating relationships to identify the degree of stress they felt when their partners were less open than they wished and how they coped with the stress. After gathering all these data, Thompson and Vangelisti conducted statistical analyses and found that their hypothesis about lack of openness causing stress was confirmed and also that certain coping strategies (punishing the other peron, exiting the relationship and reframing by making negative assumptions) were linked to higher stress and led to lower relational satisfaction. In contrast, reframing in a more positive way, for example, "setting an example of the behavior I expect from my partner" seemed to be more productive. In addition, clarifying the issues and using some types of humor were also associated with relational satisfaction. This study provides useful options for Charee as she considers how to deal with Mateo's seeming lack of openness.

▲ Meeting a partner's attempt to have a constructive discussion by refusing to listen or withdrawing decreases satisfaction in relationships.

COMMUNICATION IN SOCIETY
Can Communication Styles Predict Divorce?

The results of a national research project found that the patterns spouses use to communicate when a conflict arises may have a bearing not only on the quality of their relationship, but on whether the couple ends up divorcing early in the marriage.

Everyone assumes that aggressive conflict behaviors like yelling and insulting the other party can lead to divorce. However, Dr. Kira Birditt, a professor at the University of Michigan, wanted to see if less dramatic conflict behaviors (e.g., keeping quiet, leaving the argument) and even constructive behaviors (e.g., calm discussion, listening) might cause a marriage to end in divorce.

So she, along with a team of researchers, conducted a study examining the conflict communication patterns in the marriages of over 500 African American and White heterosexual couples over a period of 16 years. They asked the wives and husbands to describe their conflict behaviors during disagreements at different times during the 16 years. From time to time, the couples filled out questionnaires (separately) and were also interviewed by the researchers separately and together. The researchers also gathered divorce statistics on the couples.

They found that, indeed, conflict behaviors have important implications for divorce. As expected, husbands and wives reporting greater constructive conflict behaviors had lower divorce rates and those who used more destructive behaviors (e.g. shouting, insulting the other) had higher divorce rates.

However, they also found a particularly toxic pattern that, while seemingly less destructive, actually has damaging effects on the longevity of the marriage.

That is, when one spouse deals with conflict constructively (e.g. calmly discussing the situation, listening to their partner's point of view, or trying hard to find out what their partner is feeling) and other spouse withdraw—the end result is higher divorce rates. This is somewhat similar to the demand-withdrawal pattern described in this chapter.

It seems that if one spouse attempts to solve relationship problems with constructive behaviors, such as finding solutions, but the other spouse prefers to solve problems by leaving the situation, the spouse who uses constructive behaviors may perceive their partner's withdrawal as a lack of investment in the relationship and ultimately also loses interest.

Birditt and her team also found that conflict behaviors had similar effects on divorce for both Black and White couples, and that over time, wives were less likely to use destructive strategies or withdraw, whereas husbands' conflict behaviors remained stable. They speculate that it may be that relationships are more important to wives, who may realize over time that destructive and withdrawal behaviors are not good for the marriage, so they tend to accommodate and reduce their use of these unproductive behaviors.

SOURCE: Birditt, K. S., Brown, E., Orbuch, T. L., & McIlvane, J. M. (2010). Marital conflict behaviors and implications for divorce over 16 years. *Journal of Marriage and Family*, 72(5), 1188–1204.

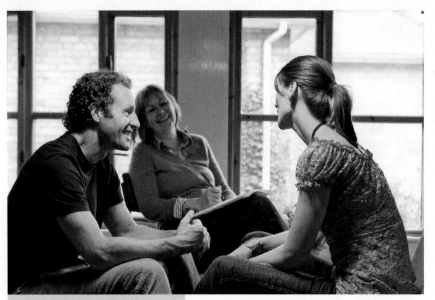

▲ Communication researchers interact with those being researched during the research process.

demand-withdrawal

An interaction pattern in which one partner criticizes or tries to change the other partner, who responds by becoming defensive and/or then disengaging—either psychologically or physically.

One other area of research that might help explain Charee and Mateo's conflict communication pattern is the **demand-withdrawal** interaction pattern, which communication researchers have investigated for more than 50 years. This pattern occurs when one partner criticizes or tries to change the other partner, who responds by becoming defensive and/or then disengaging—either psychologically or physically (Eldridge & Christensen, 2002).

Recently, researchers tried to better understand the demand-withdraw pattern by interviewing (individually) both partners in 75 gay, lesbian, and straight romantic relationships regarding two recent conflicts and then having them complete postinterview questionnaires (McGinn, McFarland, & Christensen, 2009). Based on previous research, they hypothesized, and the study confirmed, that more serious conflicts predicted greater demand/withdraw patterns, and these patterns predict less satisfaction with the outcome of the discussion. Additional research even suggests that negative communication patterns have larger societal implications in the form of higher divorce rates for heterosexual couples (see *Communication in Society: Can Communication Styles Predict Divorce?*). It will be interesting for researchers to discover if the same patterns also increase likelihood of divorce hold for gay married couples.

As you can see, researchers in the social science approach to understanding communication often use quantitative analysis of surveys and observation; they may also use experiments and focused interviews to gather data. However, they also sometimes use qualitative methods such as conversation analysis, where they examine naturally occurring conversation to understand better the sequences and functions of everyday talk, identify and count recurring themes, and then apply statistical analyses to these counts.

Ethical Issues

Researchers in all three approaches are concerned about the ethical issues involved in conducting communication research—although they may disagree on which issues are the most important. For example, communication researchers in the social science paradigm often follow the long-standing, specific ethical guidelines of the American Psychological Association, which in turn are based on ethical guidelines established by the medical profession. This code of ethics emphasizes that no harm should be done to research participants. Specifically, *all* participants must be informed about *all* aspects of the research process, including the expected duration of the research; the exact procedures; the right to decline (and all foreseeable consequences of declining); any potential risks, discomfort, or adverse effects of participating in the research; and any potential research benefit. They must also be informed that their privacy and confidentiality will be maintained; they must be told of any limits of confidentiality, if there are any incentives for participation, and who they can contact for additional information or clarification (http://www.apa.org/ethics/code/index.aspx).

For the most part, these guidelines are followed without any problems; however, there are some areas of communication research that involve challenges to these guidelines. For example, some communication researchers study deception in interpersonal relationships—why people choose to deceive their partners and the potential consequences for that deception. Imagine how difficult it is to study deception without deceiving participants involved in the study—something that is explicitly forbidden by the research code of ethics! In addition, researchers gathering data online face additional ethical challenges. Although it is easier to ensure complete anonymity and participants do not feel as much social pressure to complete the participation if uncomfortable, the researchers cannot provide immediate clarification if participants have questions and they cannot easily verify that participants are legally old enough (or fit other requirements) to take part in the study (Hargaittai & Sandvig, 2015).

Strengths and Limitations

Social science research can be useful in identifying and explaining communication patterns and predicting their effects. However, the social science approach—like other approaches—has its limits. As you probably have realized, human communication is not always predictable, and in particular, predictions based on laboratory research may not hold true outside the lab. Although surveys can provide insight into individuals, beliefs, and attitudes, survey questions cannot fully assess individuals' thoughts and feelings, which are based on a multiplicity of factors and influences, as we described in Chapter 1. In addition, answers to survey questions may be inadequate, particularly for complex issues because people often provide only short, superficial responses to predetermined questions. One might also argue that when surveys provide a set of answers from which respondents can choose, they are even less likely to tap into their true behaviors, beliefs, and emotions. Critics argue that researchers cannot obtain a full picture if they only measure behavior or if they assess thoughts and feelings only through survey questions.

The social science approach typically has focused on individual forces and their impact on communication without regard for societal forces. For example, social science research can provide useful information about effective strategies for

---

ALTERNATIVE VIEW
Sexting and Victimization of Women

Do you think that sexting increases chances of victimization of young women? Do you think sexting could ever be viewed as a positive way for young women to be empowered by producing their own images of women/girls? Could you agree that digital media practices can be viewed as both oppressive and empowering?

Amy Adele Hasinhoff, a professor in the Art History and Communication Department at McGill University, analyzes popular writings (discourse) about *sexting* (the act of sending [someone] sexually explicit photos or messages on a cell phone) and makes the argument that although sexting can lead to victimization of young girls, it can also be empowering.

Her argument goes like this: Most of societal concerns about mobile phones causing teens to make inappropriate sexual decisions (e.g., sexting) are directed exclusively to girls. Media stories focus on girls who sext and then turn up pregnant at an early age or describe girls posting photos and texts in which they appear to be "drunken sluts." There is no parallel discourse about technology causing boys to create sexual images or to be "provocative"—the assumption is that being sexually inhibited is not expected or desired for boys; in fact, accessing online pornography is usually seen as normal for them.

Hasinhoff promotes an alternative view of technology and teens. She suggests that the anonymity of digital media provides a source of support for some teenagers; those marginalized (some girls, gays) can communicate, gain confidence, and find romantic partners. Furthermore, she notes that digital communication offers important advantages for women and girls in romantic relationships; they can be more assertive in initiating, avoiding, and terminating relationships. By becoming producers of digital content, they can respond proactively to media messages that portray women as sexualized "objects" primarily useful to men for their pleasure (such as media images of unnaturally thin blonde models with unnaturally big breasts and lips). Her idea is that women can counteract these images by producing and promoting their own images. However, she asserts that mutual consent is key and that privacy rights must be protected.

She therefore recommends decriminalizing consensual texting, recognizing that eliminating sexting is impossible, and suggests that educators, policymakers, and scholars instead develop harm reduction models that account for privacy violations and harassment.

SOURCE: Adapted from Hasinhoff, A. A. (2015). *Sexting panic: Rethinking criminalization, privacy and consent.* Urbana, IL: University of Illinois Press.

communicating interpersonally, as shown by Ali's observations after attending a workshop on Dealing with Interpersonal Conflict at our university (see *It Happened to Me: Ali*). However, critics say that the social science approach tends to ignore the bigger picture, such as whether relational issues (e.g., interpersonal conflict) are related to particular contexts or are influenced by large societal issues, like structural inequalities (e.g., racism, sexism), socioeconomic issues, cultural differences, and forces of globalization, such as immigration.

It Happened to Me
Ali

Since I started learning about interpersonal communication, I have become a more assertive and effective communicator. I especially appreciate learning how to use better conflict skills. I know that I can change problems in my life and in other peoples' lives through better listening, which can lead to expressions of care and forgiveness. I think healthy and positive communication can have a huge influence on our day-to-day lives as individuals and as a community.

Journal Prompt 2.2: Social Science Approach
Consider the following question: How did behaviorism influence the social scientific approach?

The Interpretive Approach: Assumptions, Theories, Methods, Ethical Issues, and Strengths and Limitations

2.3 **Describe the role that humanism, description, and qualitative methods play in the interpretive approach to studying communication.**

Scholars who developed the **interpretive approach** were influenced by the ancient Greek tradition of **rhetoric**, (the art of persuasion), and by **humanism**, a branch of philosophy that celebrates human nature and its potential. Like the social science approach, the interpretive approach focuses on the individual, but interpretive communication researchers have goals and assumptions that differ from those who use the social science paradigm.

Assumptions

The goal of interpretive researchers is to understand and describe individual human communication behavior in specific situations, from the perspective of the communicator. As described in Table 2.1, originating with the ancient Greek rhetoricians, and then later with the humanists (during the Renaissance), the interpretive approach has emphasized the creativity, instead of the predictability, of human behavior. Interpretive researchers assume that humans construct their own reality and that researchers must tap into these constructions for a full understanding of human communication.

Theories and Methods

Interpretive researchers generally use qualitative methods for analysis. Rather than reducing data to numbers as quantitative researchers do, interpretivists use qualitative data or tests to understand how communicators and receivers understand a communication event (Lindlof & Taylor, 2011; Tracy, 2013). These methods—which can answer questions such as "What is it like?" and "How does it feel?"—are called **qualitative methods** because they assess the quality of communication interactions. And rather than manipulating the research situation as one might do in a lab, they tend to study naturally occurring communication.

What type of interpretive studies might help Charee and Mateo understand their communication patterns better? More in-depth studies investigating gender differences

interpretive approach
Contemporary term for humanistic (rhetorical) study.

rhetoric
Communication that is used to influence the attitudes or behaviors of others; the art of persuasion.

humanism
A system of thought that celebrates human nature and its potential.

qualitative methods
Methods in which researchers study naturally occurring communication rather than assembling data and converting it to numbers.

in social media use might help. For example, one group of communication researchers conducted focus groups in which they asked detailed questions about young people's social media use, the particular characteristics of each medium and which media they used at varying stages of a relationship (Yang, Brown, & Braun, 2014). To analyze the information, the researchers transcribed all the discussions. Unlike researchers in the social science paradigm who conduct statistical analyses to confirm (or disconfirm) their hypotheses, Yang and her colleagues searched for recurring themes and categories in the focus group discussion in an effort to understand more in depth the participants' views about their social media communication. This method of finding meaningful themes in research participants' communication is a type of **content analysis**—a technique for objectively and systematically identifying specified characteristics of communication messages. For Yang and her colleagues, it involved carefully reading and listening to the conversations over and over again, then developing a framework of categories which grouped, labeled, and summarized particular acts of communication in the data. The researchers systematically compared and contrasted the categories, continually refining them, always with the goal of capturing the actual experiences and views of the participants.

They found that women used social media, including text messaging, more than guys, and that their communication was more social and emotion-based than that of the males. As one male focus group participant said "I think one thing different for guys is that guys are less comfortable talking to each other on texts and Facebook. . . . It's like guys will go out with a bunch of people and have fun rather than like talk online. Yeah . . . it's just . . . different . . . I guess" (p. 17). However, the exception was for males in long-term romantic relationships; their use of social media was similar to the young women's. Also, there seemed to be a set sequence in social media use. "Individuals were expected to begin by contacting new acquaintances via Facebook, then move to text messaging and, as the relationship grew closer, proceed to cell phones. Violation of the sequence could undermine the development of a relationship" (p. 18). As you can see, this research confirms the social science study results discussed previously. A very similar study—focus groups with young people—found that Facebook has both positive and negative impacts on relationships; it can facilitate a relationship at the early stages, but it can become a burden in the romantic stage, especially if the couple experiences problems (Fox, Warber, & Makstaller, 2013). As with the studies cited previously, in the Fox study, men complained more than women about pressure from their partners and women were more expressive about their feelings on Facebook posts than men. As one young man said, "I'm kind of expected to show that affection back, so [. . .] I know I got in trouble once because she said she loved me on Facebook and I didn't reply back" (p. 785). Gay men in romantic relationships report similar challenges. Researcher Kathryn Macapagal and her colleagues, in an online survey, asked 323 gay and bisexual men in romantic relationships to describe their use of geosocial networking apps (e.g., Grindr, SCRUFF) and the effect of those apps on their relationships. Researchers reviewed the responses and came up with a list of themes. An analysis of the themes revealed that the men used these apps to chat, find potential partners, and meet up with friends, and many described their use as having positive impacts on their primary relationships, that is, promoted honest communication about emotional and sexual needs. However, some described negative impacts: conflicts, jealousy, reduction in trust, and decrease in interest and focus on partner. As one described it, "Hooking up with wrong characters can introduce short term turmoil" (Macapagal, Coventry, Puckett, Phillips, & Mustanski, 2016, p. 1520). All of these findings on gender differences could help Charee and Mateo understand their conflicts around social media behaviors.

Another recent study—that might also address Mateo and Charee's problematic communication patterns—investigated the nature of defensive communication in romantic relationships. As we will describe in Chapter 5, **defensive communication**

content analysis
Approach to understanding communication that focuses on specific aspects of the content of a text or group of texts.

defensive communication
Behavior that occurs when an individual perceives threat or anticipates threat from another individual.

occurs when an individual perceives a threat from another person perhaps as a result of feelings of inadequacy; the person who feels threatened then may lash out, criticize, and blame the other. In general, defensive communication is unproductive because it can lead to a cycle of conflict that results in unsatisfying personal relationships. To better understand defensive communication in romantic relationships, communication scholars Jennifer Becker, Barbara Ellevold, and Glen Stamp (2008) conducted in-depth interviews with 50 participants, asking them to recall a conversation with their romantic partner in which they became defensive. The researchers conducted individual interviews with each partner as well as joint interviews with both partners. Like Yang and Fox and their colleagues, they recorded and transcribed all the interviews (which resulted in 109 single-spaced typed pages!) and conducted a content analysis. Eventually, they developed a theory that outlined the components of defensive communication, as well as what contributes to, and resulted from, defensive communication, and the context of defensive communication. In this study, the researchers were trying to build a theory of defensive communication that would reflect the reality of the participants' everyday communication. This effort to build a theory based directly on participants' experiences and words is often used by interpretivists; it is called a *grounded theory approach* (Glaser & Strauss, 1967; Strauss & Corbin, 1998).

One of the most useful aspects of the Becker theory for Mateo and Charee (and anyone in close relationships) is a set of four suggestions for how to repair the potential damage caused by defensive communication. These strategies can be used uniquely or in combination:

1. Supportive communication (telling one another they understand, forgiving each other, intimacy/humor)
2. Apologizing and admitting wrongdoing
3. Focusing on preventive future defensive communication
4. A brief period of physical or verbal withdrawal

Here it is easy to see how theories are not just abstract notions but also sources of useful insights for improving everyday communication in important relationships.

ethnographic
Relating to studies in which researchers actively engage with participants.

Ethnographic, or field study, methods are common in interpretive research. In an ethnographic study, researchers actively engage with participants; methods include participant-observation and ethnographic interviewing. During participant observations, the researcher joins the group or community under study. These methods are often used by researchers who are investigating cultures different from their own. For example, communication expert Natalie Rybas (2012) spent a year investigating how people communicate their identity on social media. She spent many hours immersing herself in the "cybercontext." That is, she conducted in-depth interviews with people about their social media experiences, viewed videos produced by her students posted on Facebook, and kept a journal recording her own social media experiences. Her data, then, included her notes and transcriptions from the interviews and videos and her own journal material—all of which she analyzed (using content analysis) to discover the themes and categories that characterized how she and others presented themselves on social media sites. She found that although most people strive to present themselves in an authentic way on social media, that authenticity is somewhat more fluid than in face-to-face interaction (participants created or deleted information depending on who they thought the audience was, for example, friends, family, future employer)—a notion that we will discuss further in Chapter 14.

In contrast, during survey research, as in some of the studies described previously, the researcher maintains distance, simply observing participants or analyzing their reports or descriptions of their behavior (for example, couples' reports of conflict) without actually spending a lot of time with the couples.

Communication scholar Donal Carbaugh has conducted a number of interpretive studies in which he describes the **cultural communication** patterns of various communities: Finnish people, Blackfeet Indians, and U.S. residents in varying contexts. For example, using in-depth analyses of ethnographic observations and interviews, as well as discourse analyses, he describes the role of silence and listening in Blackfeet communication, the tendency of Finns to be reserved in communication, and the cultural value of nature and the local environment as a "place" held by hunters/residents in New England. More important, he shows how these communication patterns are inextricably tied to cultural identities in each community (Carbaugh, 2007; Carbaugh & Berry, 2001; Carbaugh & Cerulli, 2013).We'll see more examples of these types of cross-cultural studies in Chapter 8.

An important interpretive method is **rhetorical analysis**, in which researchers examine and analyze texts or public speeches as they occur in society. The earliest rhetorical scholars were interested in understanding how a speech affected audiences. These researchers sought to determine the best ways for speakers to construct and deliver speeches so they could affect their audiences in particular ways. Modern researchers also focus on interpreting what texts mean in the settings in which they occur. What do we mean by "the settings in which they occur"? We mean the physical space (e.g., classroom or place of worship) as well as broader environments (e.g., educational versus social; historical versus contemporary) in which the speech or text is delivered.

▲ Studying communication can help you to identify and understand employee–manager interactions.

cultural communication
Communication patterns within a specific community.

rhetorical analysis
Used by researchers to examine texts or public speeches as they occur in society with the aim of interpreting textual meaning.

Researchers who do rhetorical analysis typically do not interact with the speakers or authors of the texts they study, and therefore face different ethical concerns than do ethnographic researchers. Rhetoricians must be especially attentive to accuracy in their depictions of the text and the historical period in which the text occurred.

Although rhetoricians typically do not study interpersonal communication, some rhetorical studies address gender issues—rhetorical studies which analyze women's contributions through public communication, many of which were unnoticed at the time they were delivered (Borda, 2002; Campbell, 1994; Zaeske, 2002), and even critiqued on death. For example, rhetorician Palmer-Mehta (2016) analyzes the discourses about the passing of feminist Andrea Dworkin, well known for her outspoken condemnation of pornography and women's oppression, who died in 2005. Palmer-Mehta concludes that the discourses discussing her passing portray her as (1) emotional and irrational and (2) conflate her physical body ("fat, hairy, makeup-scorning, unkempt lesbian") (p. 298) with her work—both of which result in portraying her life's work as not worthy of respect and or affirmation and therefore making her death "ungrievable." Palmer-Mehta places these discourses in the larger societal hierarchy where women's connection to emotionality is a way of devaluing their contribution. You will have the opportunity to read more about rhetorical studies in Chapter 12. As you can see, the goal of all these interpretive studies is to describe and understand communication in specific locations and context. In contrast to social science studies, they are not overly concerned with predictions or universal generalizations.

Ethical Issues

For interpretive researchers, particularly those doing ethnographic research, ethical issues go beyond the concern for not harming research participants. Ethnographic researchers strive for equality and reciprocity, a mutual respect in their relationships with participants. Some researchers suggest that an ethical relationship with participants involves being friendly but at the same time maintaining sufficient scholarly distance and disengaging appropriately from participants after the research is completed. Others acknowledge that researchers and participants may become friends during the course of a study and that this relationship then involves a special set of "relational ethics"—a challenge to act in a "humane, nonexploitative way, while being mindful of our role as researchers" (Ellis, 2007, p. 5).

Another important ethical concern is presenting findings in a way that accurately reflects the views of the participants. To ensure this, researchers often share their interpretations and conclusions with the study participants, a procedure called **member-checking** (Lindlof & Taylor, 2011, p. 278). Some include their participants in various stages of the research and describe them as co-researchers, rather than subjects or participants (Tanno, 1997). Some suggest that to really protect the privacy of their participants, it's acceptable to fabricate quotes or represent the meaning of participants' words without quoting them exactly (Markham, 2012). Conducting research online brings additional ethical challenges. For example, are tweets and blog posts considered public data and fair game for researchers who want to study them, for example, to understand in depth the gender differences in social media communication? Even though the information is sent to many people and is relatively "public," should the senders be afforded informed consent if researchers want to analyze their written communication (Lindlof & Taylor, 2011)?

member-checking

Obtaining feedback from respondents to help improve the accuracy of research results.

Strengths and Limitations

The strengths of the interpretive approach include the in-depth understanding it provides of communication in specific situations and the insight it offers into the purposes of those messages. The limitation is that it usually involves few research participants—or none—as is the case in rhetorical analyses of texts. From a social science perspective, its utility is limited because researchers cannot generalize conclusions from such small samples. Thus, it does not help us discover broader laws about human behavior. A second limitation is that the researchers often are outsiders to the communities they study, which means that they may not accurately interpret the communication patterns they see. For example, some studies have concluded that the Amish avoid dealing with conflict, whereas an Amish person might explain that they do deal with conflict, but in a different way—by actively strengthening relationships so that they do not reach the point of open conflict (Kraybill, Nolt, & Weaver-Zercher, 2010).

Journal Prompt 2.3: Interpretive Approach
Consider the following question: Which elements of humanism are reflected in the interpretive approach to studying communication?

The Critical Approach: Assumptions, Theories, Methods, Ethical Issues, and Strengths and Limitations

2.4 Discuss how a societal focus, emphasis on power and hierarchy and textual analysis characterize the critical approach to studying communication.

Both the social science approach and interpretive approach focus on individual behavior, whereas the **critical approach** is much more concerned with how societal forces influence and interact with individual forces—with the ultimate goal of changing society.

critical approach

An approach used not only to understand human behavior but ultimately to change society also.

Assumptions

To reach the ultimate goal of changing society, critical researchers believe that one must understand the societal forces that shape how people come into contact and communicate. The roles that power and hierarchy play in these exchanges must be understood as well. For example, a critical scholar might consider the power differences that exist in everyday interactions between the school custodian and the principal, the refugee and the Red Cross worker, or the student and the professor. Critical scholars believe that by examining such interactions and writing about how power functions in them, people gain the awareness they need to resist societal forces of power and oppression. For one of our students, the critical perspective and its focus on uncovering power relations in communication are particularly appealing, as you'll see in *It Happened to Me: Kenneth.*

It Happened to Me
Kenneth

I had never heard of the critical approach, but I find it kind of interesting. I knew that people weren't treated equally, but it hadn't occurred to me that differences in, say, wealth, education, or attractiveness also can create inequalities and impact communication between people. This is something I intend to pay more attention to.

Like interpretivists, critical scholars believe that reality is subjective, or that we each construct our own reality. However, they also stress that these realities have corresponding material, or physical, consequences—meaning that they have real consequences in people's lives. For example, in the United States we socially construct a reality in which professional athletes are accorded high salaries and power, whereas schoolteachers are not. These social constructions result in real differences in how each group is treated, what each group can buy, and what sacrifices each group must make.

Theories and Methods

Cultural studies are one research approach that arises from the critical paradigm. This approach attempts to reveal the complexities of culture and the ways that people actively participate in their culture and resist its powerful influences. Cultural studies scholars believe such resistance might be expressed in a number of ways. For example, factory workers can resist the authority structure of management in many ways, some subtle (e.g., work slowdowns, extending their autonomy) and some more obvious (e.g., whistle-blowing) (Mumby, 2005).

Critical scholars generally use qualitative methods in their research, including both field observation, which we have discussed previously, and **textual analysis**, which is a method of analyzing cultural "products" such as media (TV, movies, journalistic essays) and public speeches or other texts (in which case they may be called *critical rhetoricians*). For example, communication scholar Anna Turnage (2013, 2016) analyzed metaphors found in employee email messages sent directly to former Enron CEO Ken Lay during the 2001 Enron crisis—when Lay was indicted for accounting and securities fraud

textual analysis
Similar to rhetorical analysis; used to analyze cultural "products," such as media and public speeches.

▼ The critical approach examines power differences, such as those between refugees and aid workers.

and the business declared bankruptcy. Enron, a huge corporation with 22,000 employees, was an oppressive organizational environment in which no dissent was tolerated. Turnage shows, however, that employees found a way, through emails, to resist the oppressive environment [e.g., "Thanks, Ken, you piece of sh**", "You load of bastards—you screwed us all and got fat on the profits of our sweat" (2013, p. 533)]. She argues that the metaphors that employees used represented "organizational resistance through technological means." Critical studies show that people find ways to meet their needs and struggle to make relationships and contexts more equitable.

Some critical researchers use ethnographic methods, similar to those used by interpretive scholars described in the previous section. With these analyses, critical scholars seek to understand the influence of societal forces such as the economic, government, and cultural institutions that produce, circulate, and profit from these cultural products. In addition, they may use ethnographic methods (observation, interviews) to understand how power and privilege affect people's lives. For example, one research project features collaboration between scholars and community members to raise awareness and find solutions to health disparities in minority communities (see *Did You Know? Engaging Through Art and Performance*).

How would critical scholars study interpersonal gender conflict? They would take a broad societal perspective and seek to understand Charee and Mateo's conflict within the larger context of gender roles. For example, they might suggest that a female-demand/male-withdrawal pattern is expected in heterosexual romantic relationships because straight men have traditionally occupied a more privileged position in society and in marriage relationships (responsible for fewer household

DID YOU KNOW?
Engaging Through Art and Performance

Communication scholar Olga Idriss Davis is part of a research team that works through partnership with community leaders and members with the goal of decreasing health disparities in minority communities in Arizona. Her responsibility is to engage the community in raising awareness and finding ways to promote better health.

Davis, who is trained in rhetoric and theatrical performance, saw an opportunity to combine her two fields of study into one educational and engaging event addressing the weighty issues of "cultural processes in risk and resilience" in minority groups. She put together an event that blended artists and performers (dancers, drummers, singers) with local health care professionals using visual and performance art. As she describes it, "The expression of public art is sometimes a better, or alternative, way of educating. Performance art has a way of dispelling boundaries of race, gender, sexuality, class. . . . It's a way of universally connecting humans to humans."

Davis worked closely with some of the artists who performed at this event, helping them to better understand both this concept and the interrelation of art and health. "I had them reflect on the social, political, and cultural issue of health disparities," she said. "Many of them connected through story. They're communicating their life experiences, their relationships, through their visual and performance talents."

In another research project, Davis showed how barbers in African American neighborhoods can serve as information and even intervention centers in the efforts to reduce high blood pressure and heart disease, which are often prevalent in minority communities. The Barbershop Hypertension Screening Program is designed to increase health literacy and knowledge of African American males through high blood pressure screening and referrals.

These projects are both good examples of how scholars, comingling knowledge and action, can work for social change at the grass-roots level.

SOURCES: "Engaging through Art and Performance." Retrieved April 20, 2011, from http://community.uui.asu.edu/features/art.asp. Davis, O. I., & Marsiglia, F. F. (2011, June). Cultural catalysts for community dialogues: Black barbers as interventionists in cardiovascular health of African American men. Poster presented at the annual meeting of the Society for Prevention Research, Washington, D.C" chores, child care, etc.) and therefore would be less likely than women to want to change (Jones, 2016).

Many critical scholars look to popular texts such as films, television, and digital media (e.g., social media and gaming) to understand male and female roles in society. For example, researchers investigated how men in nursing are portrayed in popular television shows. They conclude that while the goal was to expand images of nurses to include males, and to contradict common stereotypes, these characters were actually portrayed in ways that reinforced explicit and implicit stereotypes. The male characters were often subject to questions about their choice of career, masculinity, and sexuality, and their role usually was reduced to that of a prop, minority spokesperson, or source of comedy. The researchers note that these results have implications for better understanding of nursing practice and education and attracting more men to the profession (Weaver, Ferguson, Wilbourn, & Salamonson, 2014).

Similarly, Sal Humphreys and Karen Orr Vered (2014) analyze how gender is expressed and constructed in interactive media (blogs, games, social networking sites, mobile phones) but also reflects larger societal influences. They describe how digital media offer new ways of expressing gender. For example, in massively multiplayer online games (MMOGs) one can "choose" a gender, and women can now, more than ever before, exercise control on how they are viewed—by self-publishing, self-presenting in blogs, Twitter, and so on. However, Humphreys and Vered also caution that, at the same time, women are still constrained by societal norms and media power relations (men are still the hackers and the producers of most digital content), and women can be constrained by location services which enable others to track and surveil them. They describe the extreme hateful messages directed at a number of women who have drawn attention to sexist representations of women in gaming or to the sexist behavior of fellow technology workers at a recent professional conference. In each case, males unleashed a barrage of hate-filled messages, including threats of rape and death.

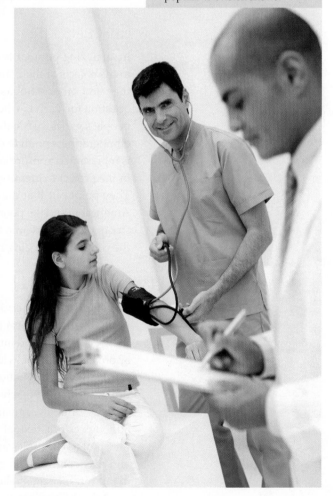

▼ Critical communication researchers investigate how men in nursing are portrayed in popular television shows.

Communication scholar Hillary Jones (2016) shows, through visual rhetorical analysis, how Pinterest, while professing to offer women new outlets for creative activities in digital scrapbooking, in actuality, ends up offering them only old forms of self and other-monitoring and exploitation. That is, browsing through Pinterest site is "like being assaulted by *Vogue, Shape, GQ, Better Homes & Gardens,* and hundreds of other magazines all at once" (p. 359) and creates yearning for unattainable ideal female accomplishments. The perfect woman constructed on Pinterest "plans perfect meals, custom cocktails for perfect parties (that she makes all the decorations for by hand, using repurposed materials), dresses a body honed by perfect workouts with the ideal outfit, dons perfect makeup and nail polishes, dresses her partner and children perfectly, welcomes guests into a perfectly designed home featuring perfect photos from perfect vacations and previous parties" (p. 359).

By contrast, communication researchers Paul Venzo and Kristy Hess (2013) showed how social media can be used to rapidly counteract the often negative and discriminatory media messages about lesbian, bisexual, gay, and transgender (LBGT) individuals. They conducted in-depth interviews with young workers in a community group that uses social media

Critical Thinking Prompt
Which of the three research approaches we've discussed—the social scientific, the interpretive, and the critical—do you believe is most likely to provide answers to the questions about communication you most would like to have answered? Why? Which do you believe would be least useful for answering your questions? Why?

to combat homophobia and negative portrayals of sexual diversity. In addition, they conducted textual analysis of the group's media activity and found that the group used Facebook as a primary means to distribute information about the group, provide an online support network, and rapidly counteract instances of homophobia in local media.

These critical scholars, unlike social science and interpretive scholars, are not interested in predicting communication or describing in-depth communication behavior. Rather, they hope to educate and illuminate communicators so that, ultimately, they might understand the larger societal impacts (such as media) on communicators' attitudes and practices and transform communication to become more just and equitable—a lofty goal for a scholar. Critical scholars look at the larger picture, attempting to see communication in the context of social, political, religious, and historical contexts. To do this, they use a variety of methods, but they often look to media texts. Unlike an interpretivist, who might focus on the specific communication patterns of men and women in various types of relationships and settings, or a social scientist, who might survey large groups of men and women as part of theoretical predictions, a critical scholar always explores the communication in the larger societal contexts.

What insights would these studies contribute to Charee and Mateo's dilemma? How could they help Charee and Mateo understand their relationship better? All these studies attempt to show the relationship between cultural gender roles as represented in popular culture and the political realities—focusing on the intersections of the individual and society. Perhaps Charee and Mateo might gain insights by stepping back and exploring how their own relationship is influenced by societal and cultural gender role expectations and pressures.

Ethical Issues

In analyzing popular texts, critical researchers may have a rather distant relationship to the objects of their study, but they are especially concerned about the way in which they and other scholars present the worldview of others (Krog, 2011). A key ethical question for them is whether they have the right to study, analyze, and represent other people's views, particularly when crossing racial/ethnic and class boundaries. Critical ethnographers point to ethical challenges of ensuring that the community under study is represented appropriately, that "the researcher is led by members of the community" in the project to identify and eliminate sources of oppression (Christians, 2011, p. 74). They point out that many cultural groups—such as indigenous groups (e.g., Native Americans) and the poor—have been exploited and misrepresented by researchers who stood to gain academic rewards by portraying them in certain ways. In the meantime, the communities being researched gained little from their participation.

Strengths and Limitations

The strength of the critical approach is its emphasis on the importance of economic, political, and historical forces in communication. These factors are largely ignored by the social science and interpretive approaches. A second strength inherent in the critical approach is its acknowledgment of the role of power in communication encounters.

However, a limitation of this approach is the lack of attention to face-to-face interaction by critical researchers who focus primarily on public and media communication such as film, TV, music videos, magazine advertisements, and digital media. So, although critical textual research may help us understand the historical and contemporary roots of sex roles and how contemporary gender images perpetuate stereotypes and may contribute to gender discrimination, it may not help us communicate better in our interpersonal relationships.

Like the interpretive approach, the critical approach relies on qualitative research methods and does not tend to generate generalizable conclusions. For example, in the popular cultural analyses described, the researchers did not measure viewers' reactions to the various movies, or try to measure individuals' online communication and then generalize about all individuals' attitudes toward gender roles. Rather, their essays present *their* analysis of the images and portrayals on the screen and in the digital media, and the validity of their conclusions is based only on the strength of their arguments.

**Journal Prompt 2.4:
Critical Approach**
Consider the following question:
What are characteristics of the critical approach to studying communication?

A Multifaceted Approach

2.5 Explain how the three research approaches influence the *Synergetic Model* of communication.

We hope that this review of the three major contemporary approaches gives you an idea of the varied viewpoints you will encounter within the field of communication studies. Rather than emphasizing one of the three in this text, we draw from all of them. This is our position: If you only view a sculpture from one perspective, you can never fully appreciate the work. The same goes for the field of communication studies.

Three Perspectives on Communication

If you want to be able to view the communication process, like a sculpture, from various perspectives, you need to understand and be able to recall the essential contributions each research approach offers. Here is a brief explanation of each approach:

- The social science approach seeks snapshots of certain communication phenomena and from them attempts to find universal laws that explain human communication.
- The interpretive approach uses content analysis, ethnographic field studies, and rhetorical analysis to take a more individualized, specific look at human communication.
- The critical approach seeks to uncover the element of power that exists in every interaction and to use communication analysis to effect social change.

Critical Thinking Prompt
If you were a communication scholar, which paradigm would you subscribe to? That is, which of the paradigms or approaches best fits your view of reality?

Figure 2.1 The Synergetic Model

According to the Synergetic Model of communication, what are some of the specific influences in the communication situation depicted here? In your answer, consider factors such as societal forces, culture, field of experience, relationship, context, and noise.

This review of the research paradigms illustrates the way that these three approaches have guided communication research. Our understanding of the communication process flows from all three research approaches, and from this we have formulated the *Synergetic Model* of communication, which we presented in Chapter 1. The Synergetic Model's focus on societal factors evolved from the critical approach, whereas its inclusion of individual forces reflects the influence of the social science and interpretive approaches.

Despite differences in the various communication models and research approaches, individual communicators play a key role in all of them. Therefore, like Charee and Mateo, to have a complete understanding of communication, communicators need to understand how individuals' identities influence and are influenced by communication. They also need to understand how individual and societal forces act together to affect identity development. Each communicator is unique because of the ways in which individual and social forces together create individual identities. In turn, these identities influence how individuals communicate and how others communicate with them. We explore the question of identity and communication in Chapter 3.

**Journal Prompt 2.5:
Combining Approaches**
Consider the following questions:
Why is it important to draw from all three research approaches in studying communication? What does each research approach contribute to the synergetic model of communication?

SUMMARY

2.1 Define the research concepts paradigm, theory, and method.

- There are three research *paradigms* (belief systems) in communication research today. Each paradigm carries with it a set of assumptions about knowledge, the nature of reality, and human nature.

- *Theory* is a set of statements that explains a particular phenomenon.

- *Methods* describe the specific ways in which scholars collect and analyze data, the results of which are used to test their theories.

2.2 Explain how behaviorism, causality, and quantitative methods influence the social scientific approach to studying communication.

- The social science approach emphasizes individual forces, seeks to predict human behavior, emphasizes universal theories, and generally uses quantitative research methods.

- Human communication is not always predictable, and in particular, predictions based on laboratory research may not hold true outside the lab.

2.3 Describe the role that humanism, description, and qualitative methods play in the interpretive approach to studying communication.

- Interpretive researchers generally use qualitative methods. The strengths of the interpretive approach include the in-depth understanding of communication in specific situations, but it is limited in that it usually involves few research participants—or none—as is the case in rhetorical analyses of texts.

- A second limitation is that the researchers often are outsiders to the communities they study, which means that they may not accurately interpret the communication patterns they see.

2.4 Discuss how a societal focus, emphasis on power and hierarchy, and textual analysis characterize the critical approach to studying communication.

- The critical approach is more concerned with how societal forces influence and interact with individual forces—with the ultimate goal of changing society. Critical researchers believe that one must understand the societal forces that shape how people come into contact and communicate.

- The strength of the critical approach is its emphasis on the importance of economic, political, and historical forces in communication and its acknowledgment of the role of power in communication encounters.

- Critical scholars generally use qualitative methods, often conducting textual analysis in which they analyze cultural "products" such as media (TV, movies, blogs, and other social media sites) and even speeches (in which case they may be called *critical rhetoricians*).

2.5 Explain how the three research approaches influence the *Synergetic Model* of communication.

- These three approaches combine to form the foundation for our Synergetic Model of communication.

- The Synergetic Model's focus on societal factors evolved from the critical approach, whereas its inclusion of individual forces reflects the influence of the social science and interpretive approaches.

KEY TERMS

paradigm p. 25
theory p. 26
methods p. 26
social science approach p. 27
behaviorism p. 27
hypothesis p. 27
naturalistic p. 28
quantitative methods p. 28

social penetration theory p. 28
demand-withdrawal p. 30
interpretive approach p. 32
rhetoric p. 32
humanism p. 32
qualitative methods p. 32
content analysis p. 33
defensive communication p. 33

ethnographic p. 34
cultural communication p. 35
rhetorical analysis p. 35
member-checking p. 36
critical approach p. 36
textual analysis p. 37

APPLY WHAT YOU KNOW

1. Identify a common communication topic (e.g., deception, teamwork, intimacy, credibility). How would researchers from the three different paradigms investigate this topic? What would be the general goal of each researcher? What would each emphasize in the investigation? What type of research methods might each use to conduct her or his investigation? What might be the ethical concerns of each?

2. Locate a journal article and a website/blog that report on the same communication issue from a social science perspective. How was the issue presented in each? What are the strengths and weaknesses of each article? What are the strengths and weaknesses of a social science approach to this topic?

Communicating Identities

LEARNING OBJECTIVES

3.1 Identify six reasons identity is important to communication.

3.2 Define *identity*.

3.3 Clarify how reflected appraisals, social comparisons, self-fulfilling prophecies, and self-concept contribute to identity development.

3.4 Identify examples of racial, national, ethnic, gender, sexual, age, social class, disability, and religious identities.

3.5 Discuss three ethical considerations for communicating in a sensitive manner to and about others' identities.

3.6 Explain three ways to communicate more effectively about identities.

CHAPTER TOPICS

The Importance of Identity

What Is Identity?

The Individual and Identity

The Individual, Identity, and Society

Ethics and Identity

Skills for Communicating about Identities

> *"We cannot separate our identities—as individuals or as members of society—from our communication experiences."*

When you think about identity, you may be pondering who you "really" are and how you got to be that way. When Charee thinks about her identity, sometimes she thinks about her national identity as a U.S. citizen (like when she applies for jobs and is asked if she is eligible to work in the United States). Other times she thinks about her ethnic identity as an Asian American from an immigrant family. As mentioned in the first chapter, her father is an immigrant from Vietnam and she sees herself as a Vietnamese American. Sometimes she thinks about her gender identity in other contexts. Can you choose to be whomever you want, or do your background and social environment determine who you are? In this chapter, we address these identity questions as well as the important role communication plays in them.

As we discussed in Chapter 1, communication is a deeply cultural process. In this chapter, we explore how individual characteristics, such as gender and age and the societal meanings associated with them, interact to create cultural identities—and the important role communication plays in that development. Within cultures, communication patterns, habits, values, and practices develop around specific individual characteristics such as race, gender, sexuality, age, social class, and religion. For example, in the United States, people commonly understand that it is not acceptable to tell racist or sexist jokes, particularly in the workplace, at job interviews, and in other formal settings. This understanding exists because people are aware of the impact of this type of communication on people's identities. We all possess many cultural identities because we identify with genders, races, ethnicities, religions, organizational affiliations, schools, and so on. Some of these identities affect our communication experiences more than others. We explain which identities are most influential and why. We also examine how societal forces influence identity and discuss ethical issues associated with communication and identities. We conclude by looking at some skills for communicating about identities.

The Importance of Identity

3.1   Identify six reasons identity is important to communication.

Identity has a tremendous impact on the communication process in a number of ways. How we communicate, as well as how our communication is received by others, can be shaped by our identities and the identities of others. Let's look at some of the ways that identity influences communication. First, because individuals bring their self-images or identities to each communicative encounter, every communication interaction is affected by their identities. For example, when elderly people converse with teenagers, both groups may have to accommodate for differences in their experiences and language use.

Second, communication interactions create and shape identities (Hecht, 1993). If older adults treat teenagers with respect and admiration during their conversations, these young people may view themselves as more mature and more valuable than they did previously. Conversely, communication can also be used to denigrate other identities and create tension between groups. It is always important to think about the impact of communication on various identity groups.

Third, identity plays an important role in intercultural communication, which is something that has become increasingly common in our global, technology-based world. As more and more businesses have international branches and subsidiaries, workers are increasingly likely to have contact with people from other cultures. The more familiar they are with the values related to identity in these cultures, the better prepared they will be to succeed in today's society.

Fourth, understanding identity is useful because so much of U.S. life is organized around and geared toward specific identities (Allen, 2004). In the United States, we have television stations such as *Black Entertainment Television* and *Telemundo* and magazines like *Ebony* and *Out*, which are targeted to groups based on their race, age, gender, or sexuality. We also have entertainment venues such as Disneyland and Club Med that are developed specifically for families, romantic couples, and singles. In this identity-based climate, individuals often communicate primarily with others who share their identities. Consequently, learning how to communicate effectively with individuals whose identities vary from yours may require considerable thought and effort.

Fifth, identity is a key site in which individual and societal forces come together to shape communication experiences. Although we each possess identity characteristics such as social class or nationality, the society where our communication takes place will define the meanings of those characteristics. For example, depending on whether you are in the United States or visiting a country where anti-American sentiment is common, what it means to be an "American" can have different nuances. Moreover, we cannot separate our identities—as individuals or as members of society—from our communication experiences.

Finally, identity is an important part of how we send and receive messages. When someone wants to speak for or against a proposed change in restaurant regulations at a city council meeting, he or she may preface the remarks by noting that they are an owner of a restaurant in the city and then make their arguments. In other situations, people may identify themselves as parents, consumers, fans, and other identities. Sometimes identities are used to mobilize people to act, such as the Women's March held on January 21, 2017. Not all women agreed with the protest, but we are a complex set of interconnected identities. Identity is vital to how meaning is created in communication (Hecht, 1993). We explain this interaction more fully throughout this chapter.

**Journal Prompt 3.1:
Communication and Society**
Consider the following question:
What are six advantages to understanding the relationship between communication and identity?

What is Identity?

3.2 Define *identity*.

When you enrolled in college, you were most likely required to provide a piece of identification, such as a birth certificate, passport, or driver's license. Identity is tied closely to identification; it refers to who you are and the specific characteristics that make you different from other individuals. In communication studies, *identity* includes not only who you are but also the social categories you identify yourself with and the categories that others identify with you. Society creates social categories such as *middle aged* or *college student*, but they only become part of one's identity when one identifies with them or others identify you in these categories. For example, you may think of yourself as short, but others may classify you as being of average height. Many young people in their late teens and early twenties identify with the category *college student*, but a growing number of people in their thirties, forties, and even older are also returning to school and identifying with this category. The many social categories that exist can be divided into two types: *primary* and *secondary identities* (Loden & Rosener, 1991; Ting-Toomey, 1999). Primary identities are those that have the most consistent and enduring impact on our lives, such as race, gender, and nationality. Secondary identities, such as college major, occupation, and marital status, are more fluid and more dependent on situation.

To help define the term **identity**, let's examine its essential characteristics. The first characteristic is that identities exist at the individual and the societal levels. Jake Harwood (2006) explains this concept: "At the individual (personal identity) level, we are concerned with our difference from other individuals, and the things that make us unique as people.

identity
Who a person is; composed of individual and social categories a person identifies with, as well as the categories that others identify with that person.

▲ Our communication with others helps us understand who we are and how others perceive us.

At the collective (social identity) level, we are concerned with our group's differences from other groups, and the things that make our group unique" (pp. 84–85). For example, if you are an athlete, and you are thinking about how you are different and unique from others who are not athletic, then you are focusing on part of your individual identity. If you are focusing on how your sports team is different and unique from other sports teams, then you are focusing on your social identity.

We should note that identities are not necessarily only individual or social; they can be both, depending on the situation. How is this contradiction possible? Let's look at an example. Many readers of this text are U.S. Americans, and their national identity is part of their social identity. Because they are surrounded by others from the United States, they may not be conscious of this as being part of their individual identity. But if they travel abroad, their national identity becomes part of their individual identity because this significant characteristic will differentiate them from others.

A second important aspect of identity is that it is both fixed and dynamic. Again, this seems like a contradiction. If you think about it, however, you will realize that certain aspects of our identities, although stable to some extent, actually do change over time. For instance, a person may be born male, but as he grows from an infant to a boy to a teenager to a young man to a middle-aged man and then to an old man, the meanings of his male identity change. He is still a male and still identifies as a male, but what it means to be male alters as he ages, and social expectations change regarding what a boy or a man should be (Kimmel, 2005).

A third characteristic of identity is that individual and social identities are created through interaction with others. The relationships, experiences, and communication interactions we share with others shape how we see ourselves. For example, people who travel abroad and then return home may experience stress, but they also experience growth and change—and communication with those they meet as they travel plays a key role in both (Martin & Harrell, 1996).

A fourth consideration is that identities need to be understood in relation to historical, social, and cultural environments. The meaning of any identity is tied to how it has been viewed historically and how people with that identity are situated in a given culture and society (Hecht, Jackson, & Ribeau, 2003; Johnson, 2001). For instance, throughout history, we have had varied notions of what it means to be female (Bock, 1989).

Although Cleopatra was an Egyptian Pharaoh and Joan of Arc led the French army into battle in the fifteenth century, these individual women were significant exceptions to the rule. In their times and for much of history, women have been perceived as intellectually inferior, physically delicate, or morally weak when compared to men. Because of these beliefs, in many cultures women were denied voting and property rights and even custody of their children in the event of divorce.

Thus, a hierarchy exists across cultures in which one identity (male) is preferentially treated over another (female). You can probably think of other examples in which preferential treatment was given—or denied—based on race, sexuality, religion, social class, or age (Allen, 2004).

In sum, identity is key to understanding communication, and communication is key to understanding identity. As Abrams, O'Connor, and Giles have stated, "identity and communication are mutually reinforcing" (2002, p. 237).

Journal Prompt 3.2: Understanding Identity
Consider the following prompt:
Describe the four characteristics that are important in understanding identity.

The Individual and Identity

3.3 Clarify how reflected appraisals, social comparisons, self-fulfilling prophecies, and self-concept contribute to identity development.

Although it can be tempting to boil a person's identity down to one word—say, *nerd, jock,* or *sorority girl*—in reality, everyone is more complex than that. If you had to pick only one word to describe yourself and you had to use it in every situation—personal and professional—what word would you choose? For most people this task is impossible, for we all see ourselves as multidimensional, complex, and unique. People in the United States, especially, are invested in the notion that they are unique. Twins often go to great lengths to assure people that they are *not* the same. Perhaps the most famous example of this is the Olsen twins, Mary-Kate and Ashley. Mary-Kate dyed her hair dark so she would look less like her sister, and when the sisters received a star on Hollywood's Walk of Fame, they requested that they be given separate stars (a request that was denied). Like almost everyone, they recognize and value their uniqueness—and they would like others to do so as well.

How is it possible that people who are as much alike as twins can still have distinct identities? It is possible because of the ways in which identities are created and how these identities are "performed" in daily life.

Identity Development through Communication

In communication, our understanding of identity development arises out of a theory called symbolic interactionism (Blumer, 1969; Mead, 1934). According to this theory, individuals' meanings for the objects, actions, and people around them arise out of social, or symbolic, interaction with others. What you define as beautiful, ethical, and even edible is based on what you have heard and experienced during your interactions with others. You likely learned through observing and communicating with others that eating lobster is a luxury but that eating bugs is disgusting. We develop and reveal identities through communication interactions in much the same way. In this section, we describe three communication processes involved in identity development—*reflected appraisals, social comparison,* and *self-fulfilling prophecies*—and explore how they shape one's sense of self, or self-concept.

reflected appraisals
The idea that people's self-images arise primarily from the ways that others view them and from the many messages they have received from others about who they are.

looking-glass self
The idea that self-image results from the images others reflect back to an individual.

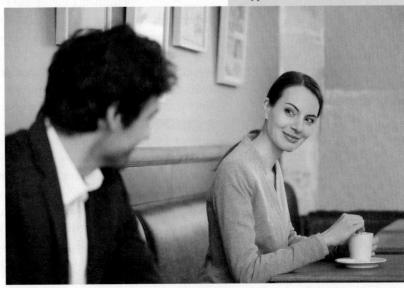

▼ Our self-images arise from how others communicate and interact with us. If others flirt with you, your notion of how others see you may be influenced by that type of communication.

Reflected Appraisals   A primary influence on identity development is a communication process called **reflected appraisals** (Sullivan, 1953). The term describes the idea that people's self-images arise primarily from the ways that others view them and from the many messages they have received from others about who they are. This concept is also often referred to as the **looking-glass self** (Cooley, 1902; Edwards, 1990), a term that highlights the idea that your self-image results from the images others reflect back to you.

The process of identity development begins at birth. Although newborns do not at first have a sense of self (Manczak, 1999; Rosenblith, 1992), as they interact with others, their identities develop. How others act toward and respond to them influences how infants build their identities. For example, as infants assert their personalities or temperaments, others respond to those characteristics. Parents of a calm and cheerful baby are strongly drawn to hold and play with the infant, and they describe the child to others as a "wonderful" baby. By contrast, parents who have a tense and irritable baby may feel frustrated if they cannot calm their child and might respond more negatively to the infant. They may engage in fewer positive interactions with their baby and describe the child as "difficult." These interactions shape the baby's identity for himself or herself and for the parents, as well as for others who have contact with the family (Papalia, Olds, & Feldman, 2002).

The reflected appraisal process is repeated with family, friends, teachers, acquaintances, and strangers as the individual grows. If as a child you heard your parents tell their friends that you were gifted, your teachers praised your classroom performance, and acquaintances commented on how verbal you were, you probably came to see yourself those ways. However, if family, friends, and acquaintances commented on how you couldn't "carry a tune in a bucket" and held their ears when you sang, then over time you likely came to view yourself as someone who couldn't sing. Through numerous interactions with other people about your appearance, your abilities, your personality, and your character, you developed your identities as a student, friend, male or female, or singer, among others. To read about one student's experiences with reflected appraisals, see *It Happened to Me: Bianca*.

It Happened to Me
Bianca

I really relate to the concept of reflected appraisals. I was born in Brazil with an Italian mother and a Brazilian father. When I attended an all-girls private school in Cleveland, Ohio, I had a very difficult time blending in. After spending so much time with these other students, however, I gradually began feeling like one of them. I was speaking English all the time, even at home with my parents (whose first language is not English). I felt like I was an American. People communicated to me as an American. In my junior year, I moved back to Brazil. Being Brazilian and speaking Portuguese fluently, their reflections of me made me feel completely Brazilian and I began to lose my sense of American identity. Even today, at a U.S. college, I feel confused about my selfhood because of the different ways I am reflected off of people depending on which nationality group I am hanging out with.

particular others

The important people in an individual's life whose opinions and behavior influence the various aspects of identity.

generalized other

The collection of roles, rules, norms, beliefs, and attitudes endorsed by the community in which a person lives.

Interaction with two types of "others" influences this process of identity development. George Herbert Mead (1934) described them as *particular others* and the *generalized other*. **Particular others** are the important people in your life whose opinions and behavior influence the various aspects of your identity. Parents, caregivers, siblings, and close friends are obvious particular others who influence your identity. Some particular others may strongly influence just one of your identities or one aspect of an identity. If you perceive that your soccer coach believes you have no talent, then you may see yourself as a poor soccer player even if friends and family tell you otherwise.

Your sense of yourself is also influenced, however, by your understanding of the **generalized other**, or the collection of roles, rules, norms, beliefs, and attitudes endorsed by the community in which you live. You come to understand what is valued and important in your community via your interactions with significant others, strangers, acquaintances, various media such as movies, books, and television, and the social institutions that surround you. For example, if you notice that your family, friends, and even strangers comment on people's appearances, that the media focus on people's attractiveness, that certain characteristics consistently are associated with attractiveness, and that people who look a certain way seem to get lighter sentences in criminal proceedings, get more attention at school, and are hired for the best jobs, then you develop an internalized view of what the generalized other values and rewards with regard to appearance. You then will compare yourself to others within your community to see if you fulfill the norms for attractiveness, which then affects how this aspect of your identity develops.

Gradually, you begin to see yourself in specific ways, which in turn influences your communication behavior, which further shapes others' views of you, and so on. Thus, individual identities are created and re-created by communication interactions throughout one's life.

However, reflected appraisals aren't the only type of communication interaction that shapes identity. Each of us also engages in a process called *social comparison*, which influences how we see and value our identities.

▲ Children's self-images are affected by their teachers' reflected appraisals. The teachers in your life are particular others.

Social Comparisons Not only do we see ourselves as possessing specific characteristics, we also evaluate how desirable those characteristics are. As we discussed, the generalized other becomes the basis for our understanding of which characteristics are valued. For example, Amish children learn through their interactions with family, friends, the church, and their community that aggression is a negative trait that one should minimize or eliminate (Kraybill, 1989). In contrast, in gangs, aggression is valued and encouraged, and community members learn this as well (Sanders, 1994).

Once we understand what characteristics are valued (or disdained) in our communities, we assess whether we individually possess more, or less, of them than do others in our communities. We compare ourselves to others to determine how we measure up, and through this social comparison, we evaluate ourselves. In this way, the groups we compare ourselves to—our reference groups—play an important role in shaping how we view ourselves.

We compare ourselves to others in our identity group and decide how we rate. A woman might say, "I look good for my age," comparing herself to others in her reference group, which in this case is other women her age. Similarly, classmates often want to know each other's test scores and grades so that they can decide how to view their own performances. For example, how would you feel if you earned a 78 on an exam and your grade was the highest in the class? What if 78 were the lowest grade in the class? Thus, your evaluation of yourself and your abilities is shaped not only by a specific trait but also by how it compares to the traits of others in your reference group. However, your self-evaluation can vary depending on what you use as a reference group. If you compare your appearance to that of your friends, colleagues, and classmates, you may feel pretty good. However, if you use the idealized images of actors and models in magazines and movies, you may not feel as positively about your attractiveness.

The website and app "Hot or Not" allows you to upload photos of yourself to be judged by others. You can then post your rating to Facebook or other social media sites (Creighton, 2014). This kind of new media experience adds to the way that social comparison works because you are rated on a scale of 1 to 10 and can see where others place your appearance. Is this technological development a positive or negative influence on our identities?

Self-Fulfilling Prophecy Communication interactions can also influence one's identity through a process known as the **self-fulfilling prophecy**, meaning that when an individual expects something to occur, the expectation increases the likelihood that it

self-fulfilling prophecy
When an individual expects something to occur, the expectation increases the likelihood that it will, as the expectation influences behavior.

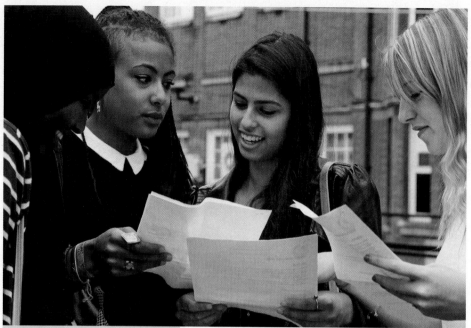

▲ We compare ourselves with others in our reference group and decide how we measure up.

will because the expectation influences behavior. For example, if you believe you can perform well on an exam, you are likely to study and prepare for the exam, which typically results in your doing well. Others also have expectations for you that can influence your behavior. For example, if your sales manager believes you are a poor salesperson, she may assign you to a territory where you won't have access to big accounts, and she may refuse to send you to sales conferences where your skills could be honed. If you still succeed, she may believe that you just got lucky. However, because you have a poor territory, don't have the opportunity to enhance your sales skills, and receive no rewards for your successes, you probably will not be a very good salesperson.

Thus, the belief in a particular outcome influences people to act and communicate in ways that will make the outcome more likely; in turn, the outcome influences how we perceive ourselves. For example, parents often unwittingly influence how their children perform in math and how their children perceive themselves as mathematicians. If a child hears her mother complain about her own poor math skills and how unlikely it is that her child will do better, the child is unlikely to succeed in math classes. When the child encounters difficulty with math, the messages she heard from her mother may increase the likelihood that she will give up and say, "Well, I'm just not good at math." By contrast, if a child hears messages that she is good at math, she is more likely to keep trying and work harder when faced with a difficult math problem. This, in turn, will influence her to see herself as a competent mathematician.

Self-fulfilling prophecies can have a powerful effect on an individual's performance, especially when they are grounded in stereotypes of one's identity. For example, stereotypes exist that Asian students excel at math, that African American students are less verbally competent than white students, and that females are worse at math and spatial reasoning than males. Studies have shown that even subtly or implicitly reminding individuals of these stereotypical expectations can impact their performance, a concept called **stereotype threat**.

stereotype threat

Process in which reminding individuals of stereotypical expectations regarding important identities can impact their performance.

In one study, African Americans who were simply reminded of race performed significantly worse on a verbal exam than when the issue of race was not mentioned (Steele & Aronson, 1995); and in another study, Asian American students performed better on a math test when reminded of their race (Shih, Pittinsky, & Ambady, 1999). In a similar study, females who were cued to think about gender performed worse on math and spatial ability tests than when the issue of gender was not raised (McGlone & Aronson, 2006). Yet another study found that white male engineering students solved significantly fewer problems when told that they were part of a study to examine why Asian Americans perform better in math than when told it was simply a timed test (Smith & White, 2002).

These studies reveal that individuals' performances can be enhanced or hampered when they are reminded, even implicitly, of expectations related to important identities. This is true not only of sex and gender but also has been shown to be true of socioeconomic status (Croizet & Claire, 1998) and age. These findings remind us that we need to be careful about creating self-fulfilling prophecies for others and allowing others' expectations to become self-fulfilling prophecies for us.

Through repeated communication interactions such as reflected appraisals, social comparisons, and self-fulfilling prophecies, we come to have a sense of who we are. This sense of who we are is referred to as one's *self-concept*.

Self-Concept   As we have suggested, identity generally continues to evolve, as people age and mature, and, at the same time, individuals also have some fairly stable perceptions about themselves. These stable perceptions are referred to as self-concept. **Self-concept** includes your understanding about your unique characteristics as well as your similarities to, and differences from, others. Your self-concept is based on your reflected appraisals and social comparisons. However, reflected appraisals only go so far. When someone describes you in a way that you reject, they have violated your self-concept. For example, if you think of yourself as open and outgoing, but a friend calls you "a very private person," you are likely to think the friend doesn't know you very well. Thus, your self-concept is an internal image you hold of yourself. It affects the external image you project to others, and in turn, your self-concept influences your communication behavior. If you think of yourself as ethical, you may correct others or assert your views when they behave in ways you believe are unethical.

Self-esteem is part of an individual's self-concept. It describes how you evaluate yourself overall. It arises out of how you perceive and interpret reflected appraisals and social comparisons. Like identity, self-esteem can alter over time. It functions as a lens through which we interpret reflected appraisals and social comparisons, which may make it hard to change. For example, if you have relatively high self-esteem, you may discount negative reflected appraisals and overgeneralize positive ones. So, if a student with high self-esteem fails an exam, he may attribute the failure to external factors (e.g., the test was unfair) rather than to himself. On the other hand, a person with low self-esteem may see negative reflected appraisals where none exist and may consistently compare herself to unrealistic reference groups. In addition, this person is more likely to attribute a failure to the self (I'm not smart enough) than to external factors.

Because self-esteem is such a powerful lens through which you see the world, your self-concept may not be entirely consistent with how others see you. Several additional factors can create a mismatch between how you see yourself and how others do. First, your self-image and the feedback you receive may be out of sync because others don't want to hurt your feelings or because you respond negatively when faced with information that contradicts your self-image. Few people tell their friends and loved ones that they are not as attractive, talented, smart, or popular as they themselves think they are. Why? They don't want make others feel bad or they don't want to deal with the recipient's feelings of anger or sadness.

Second, if you hold onto an image of yourself that is no longer accurate, you may have a distorted self-image—or one that doesn't match how others see you. For example, if you were chubby in grade school, you may still think of yourself as overweight, even if you are now slim. Similarly, if you were one of the brightest students in your high school, you may continue to see yourself as among the brightest students at your college, even if your GPA slips.

Finally, people may not recognize or accept their positive qualities because of modesty or because they value self-effacement. If

self-concept
The understanding of one's unique characteristics as well as the similarities to, and differences from, others.

self-esteem
Part of one's self-concept; arises out of how one perceives and interprets reflected appraisals and social comparisons.

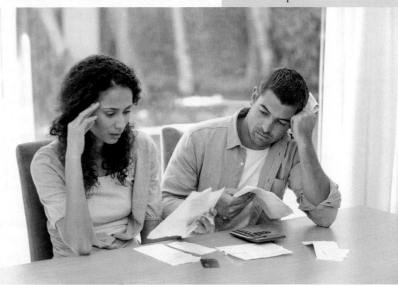

▼ Communication plays an important role in how we develop our self-concept.

your social or cultural group discourages people from viewing themselves as better than others, you may feel uncomfortable hearing praise. In such cases, the individual may only compare himself to exceptionally attractive or talented people or may refuse to acknowledge his strengths in public settings. In Japanese culture the appearance of modesty (*kenkyo*) is highly valued (Davies & Ikeno, 2002). A similar trait of "yieldedness to others" (*glassenheit*) leads the Amish to downplay their accomplishments (Kraybill, 1989). As you can see, both culture and identity are deeply embedded in our communication.

Yet another aspect of self-concept is self-respect. Whereas self-esteem generally refers to feeling good about one's self, **self-respect** describes a person who treats others—and expects themselves to be treated—with respect (Rawls, 1995). Self-respect demands that individuals protest the violation of their rights and that they do so within the boundaries of dignity and respect for others. However, people with high self-esteem may not necessarily have self-respect (Roland & Foxx, 2003). For example, some people with high self-esteem may not treat others with respect or respond to violations of the self with dignity. Many atrocities, such as those committed by Saddam Hussein against his people, have been waged by those who, because of their sense of superiority, thought they had the right to dominate and harm others.

Throughout this discussion of identity development, we have focused on four separate constructs: reflected appraisals, social comparison, self-fulfilling prophecy, and self-concept. However, identity development is a circular process in which these constructs are interrelated. For example, reflected appraisals influence your self-concept, which affects your communication behavior, which in turn shapes how others see you and, ultimately, what they reflect back to you. Then the process starts all over again. The issue of identity goes beyond this complex process of development, however. In everyday life, we enact or "perform" these identities. Let's see how this process works.

Performance of Individual Identity

The **performance of identity** refers to the process or means by which we show the world who we think we are and is related to **self-presentation**—the notion that in performing identity we try to influence others' impressions of us, by creating an image that is consistent with our personal identity. For example, many Green Bay Packers fans express their identity by wearing team colors, calling themselves Cheeseheads, and wearing plastic cheese wedges on their heads. In contrast, Pittsburgh Steelers fans often wave "the terrible towel" to cheer on their team. People also perform their identities in more subtle ways every day—with the type of clothing or jewelry (including wedding rings) that they choose to wear or the name they use. Some celebrities have taken stage names that the public is more familiar with than their legal birth names. For example, Charlie Sheen's name is Carlos Estevez. Lady Gaga's real name is Steffani Germanotta. What do these different names communicate to the public? How do these names help these celebrities perform their public identities?

Communication style is another way people perform, or enact, their identities. For example, do you speak to your mother in the same way that you speak with your friends? If you bring a friend home, do you feel like a different person as he watches you communicate with your family? If so, you're not alone. Most people adapt their communication to the identity they wish to perform in a given context.

In fact, the branch of communication studies called performance studies focuses on the ways people perform, or communicate, their various roles. In other words, people **enact identities** by performing scripts that are proper for those identities. In their analysis of how men use body size as a positive identity, communication scholars Tony Adams and Keith Berry (2013) analyze the performance of a heavy size as a positive identity on FatClub.com. On the one hand, "members explicitly reframe weight gains and bigger

self-respect
Treating others, and expecting to be treated, with respect and dignity.

performance of identity
The process or means by which we show the world who we think we are.

self-presentation
Influencing others' impressions by creating an image that is consistent with one's personal identity.

enacting identities
Performing scripts deemed proper for particular identities.

DID YOU KNOW?
Rising Intolerance

Why do different identities come into conflict? What might be triggering these conflicts?

In less than a week after Donald Trump's election to the presidency of the United States, "More than three hundred incidents of harassment or intimidation" were reported by the Southern Poverty Law Center (2016). Some of these attacks referenced President Trump, while others did not. When he was told of these attacks, President Trump said, "If it helps, I will say this, and I will say right to the cameras: Stop it" (qtd. in Yan et al., 2016). What do you think is fueling this conflict between identities? Why are some people intolerant of others? What can and should be done to help us all live together peacefully?

SOURCE: Bailey, C. (2016, November 14). Hundreds of hate crimes reported since election: SPLC. *NBC News*. Retrieved February 10, 2017 from http://www.nbcnews.com/news/us-news/hundreds-hate-crimes-reported-election-splc-n683761.

Yan, H. et al. (2016, December 22). "Make America White Again": Hate speech and crimes post-election. *CNN*. Retrieved February 10, 2017 from http://www.cnn.com/2016/11/10/us/post-election-hate-crimes-and-fears-trnd/.

bodies as desirable and erotic," but they also know that "affirming performances and relationships do not proceed without the possibility for criticism" (p. 321). Here the question of identity and what that identity means is answered through communication. The members of this website use communication to recreate different meanings about what a large size body means, but they also recognize that they are open to negative criticism of their body size by others in a culture that generally looks down on large bodies. Their performances reject dominant images of attractiveness and perform different identities as their "orientations toward and uses of bigger bodies are creative, and the community offers a pedagogical space in which to imagine distinct and often-devalued ways of relating"(p. 322). Performing their identities becomes a way to resist the dominant negative view of large bodies.

Nadene Vevea (2008) analyzed how people use tattoos and body piercing to perform their identities. In her interviews, she found that people use body art for many different reasons, to communicate many different feelings. For example, "some of the fraternity brothers who responded to my survey all got matching tattoos to signify their membership but use body art as a positive connection between friends to show loyalty to one another" (p. 22).

We show the world who we think we are through the performance of identity—in this case, these sports fans are enacting their enthusiasm for soccer and performing their Polish identity.

role expectations

The expectation that one will perform in a particular way because of the social role occupied.

mutable

Subject to change.

Journal Prompt 3.3: Identity Development

Consider the following questions: What are the key concepts in identity development? How is identity performed?

Sometimes we enact family roles; other times we enact occupational roles. The enactment of identity is closely tied to one's movements into and out of different cultural communities and one's expectations regarding particular roles. Police officers, physicians, and teachers also enact particular roles in performing their occupations. If one of these professionals—say, a teacher—steps out of the appropriate role and tries to be the best friend of her students, problems can arise. In Minnesota, a physician "has been reprimanded for allegedly touching 21 female patients inappropriately during what were described as 'unconventional' medical exams" (Lerner, 2008). In this case, "Dr. Jed E. Downs, 51, reportedly would close his eyes and make 'unusual sounds or facial expressions' while examining female patients, according to an investigation by the Minnesota Board of Medical Practice" (Lerner, 2008). In this case, we expect physicians to communicate—verbally and nonverbally—in professionally appropriate ways. When the physician does not do this, problems can arise.

Thus, we perform various roles and communicate with others based on **role expectations**. If you are pulled over for a traffic violation, you expect the police officer to perform in a particular way. In turn, you communicate with the officer based on a prescribed script. If you do not enact the expected role or if the police officer does not enact the prescribed role, then confusion—or worse—can occur. Everyone carries many scripts with them into all kinds of interactions. For example, the authors of this book are all pet owners. When we speak to our pets, we sometimes repeat communication patterns that our parents used with us when we were children. Pets are not children, yet we often communicate to them as if they were because the script is familiar to us.

As we noted previously, identities are **mutable**, or subject to change. When people change identities, they also change the way they perform them. For example, as people age, if they perform the "grown-up" role appropriately, they hope others will treat them more like adults. If they don't change the way they behave, then they might be told to "stop acting like a child."

Because identities are not fixed, sometimes you see mismatches between the performance of identity and any single identity category. Sometimes the difference between identity performance and identity category can be rather benign. For example, if we say that someone is young at heart, we are saying that we perceive that person's identity performance to resemble that of someone much younger in years. Thus, two people may be the same chronological age, but one may listen to contemporary music, watch current films and television shows, and dress according to the latest fashion trends. The other may listen to oldies radio stations and dress as he or she did years ago.

Sometimes this disconnect is viewed much more negatively. When people enact a gender identity at odds with the cultural identity category, such as when males perform identity scripts that are typically female, they may be ridiculed, ostracized, or worse. Still, how do particular identity categories, or ways of performing them, acquire meaning? How do you know what a particular category is supposed to "look like" or how it is to be performed? The answer has to do with societal forces, the subject we take up next.

The Individual, Identity, and Society

3.4   Identify examples of racial, national, ethnic, gender, sexual, age, social class, disability, and religious identities.

The development of individual identities is influenced by societal forces. Therefore, you cannot understand yourself or others without understanding how society constructs or defines characteristics such as gender, sexuality, race, religion, social class, and nationality. For example, as a child, you were probably told (some of) the differences between boys and girls. Some messages came from your parents, such as how boys' and girls' clothing differs or how girls should behave as compared with boys. Other messages came from your schoolmates, who may have told you that "they" (either boys or girls) had "cooties." You may also have picked up messages about gender differences, or about any of the identity categories mentioned, from television or other media. By combining messages from these various sources, you began to construct images of what is considered normal for each identity category.

Communication scholars are particularly interested in how identities are communicated, and created, through communication. For example, in his work focusing on communication interactions, Donal Carbaugh (2007) is particularly interested in studying intercultural encounters, and he focuses on how communication interaction reveals insights into cultural identities.

When people enact identities that are contrary to social expectations, they may be pressured to change their performance. Thus, boys and girls who do not perform their gender identities in ways prescribed by society might be called "sissies" or "tomboys." People who do not perform their racial identities in ways that are expected are sometimes called "oreos," "apples," "coconuts," "bananas," or "race traitors." Although the Church of Jesus Christ of Latter-Day Saints has banned the use of alcohol, those Mormons who do drink are sometimes called "Jack Mormons."

Those who do not conform to expected social communication or performance patterns may become victims of threats, name calling, violence, and even murder (Sloop, 2004). These aggressive responses are meant to ensure that everyone behaves in ways that clearly communicate appropriate identity categories. For example, after a lengthy lawsuit, Shannon Faulkner became the first woman to enroll at the Citadel, South Carolina's formerly all-male military college. During the time that she attended the school, she received death threats and had to be accompanied by federal marshals (Bennett-Haigney, 1995). Thus, some groups in society have strong feelings regarding how identities should be performed, and they may act to ensure that identities are performed according to societal expectations.

In this section of the chapter, we will look at a range of primary identity categories. Note that each is a product of both individual and societal forces. Thus, whatever you think your individual identity might be, you have to negotiate that identity within the larger society and the meanings society ascribes to it.

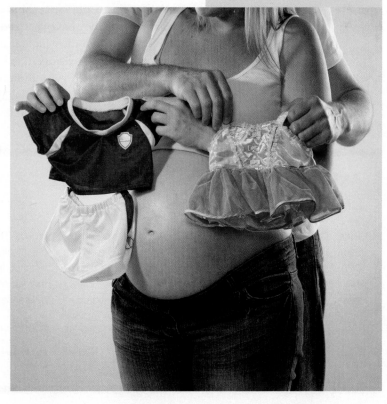

▼ Many parents choose clothes that communicate the gender of their babies.

Racial Identity

Despite its frequent use, the term *race* is difficult to define. Historically, races were distinguished predominantly by physical aspects of appearance that are generally hereditary. A race was defined as a group with gene frequencies differing from those of other groups. However, many physical anthropologists and other scholars now argue that because there is as much genetic variation among the members of any given race as between racial groups, the concept of race has lost its usefulness (Hirschman, 2003). For more on this contemporary view of race, based on the new tools of DNA analysis, refer to *Alternative View: DNA Testing and Racism*.

Despite the difficulty in accurately delineating the various races, race is still a relevant concept in most societies, and individuals still align themselves with specific racial groups, which we discuss next.

racial identity

Identification with a particular racial group.

Racial identity, the identification with a particular racial group, develops as a result of societal forces—because society defines what a race is and what it is called. This means that racial categories are not necessarily the same from country to country. For example, the 2001 census in the United Kingdom did not include Chinese in the "Asian/Asian British" category, but the 2011 census "re-positioning of the 'Chinese' tick box from 'Any other ethnic group' to Asian/Asian British" shows that these racial categories are fluid (Office for National Statistics, 2012). Their census includes the "Irish Traveller" category that the U.S. census does not.

Even within the United States the categorization of racial groups has varied over time. The category *Hispanic* first appeared on the U.S. census form as a racial category in 1980. In the 2000 census, however, Hispanic was categorized as an ethnicity, which one could select in addition to selecting a racial identity. Therefore, one could be both *Asian* (a race) and *Hispanic* (an ethnicity), or one could be both *white* (a race) and *Hispanic* (again, an ethnicity). Similarly, as Susan Koshy (2004) has noted, people from India were once labeled "non-white Caucasians," but today are categorized with Asian Americans on the U.S. census. These categorizations are important because historically they have affected the way people are treated. Although discrimination based on race is no longer legal, we continue to live with its consequences. For example, although slavery ended almost 150 years ago in the United States, many churches, schools, and other social institutions remain racially segregated (Hacker, 2003).

What do you think you would do if a total stranger began making racist or other bigoted comments to you? How would you react?

Although people often think of racial categories as scientifically or biologically based, the ways they have changed over time and differ across cultures highlight their cultural rather than their biological basis. How cultures describe and define specific races affects who is considered to belong to a given race and, consequently, how those individuals are treated. As anthropologist Gloria Marshall explains: "Comparative studies of these popular racial typologies show them to vary from place to place; studies of these popular racial classifications also show them to vary from one historical period

ALTERNATIVE VIEW
DNA Testing and Racism

There are a number of DNA testing kits available for purchase. Some of these include Ancestry DNA, 23andMe, and Family Tree DNA. DNA testing has become quite popular today, but what is their impact on racial attitudes about other racial groups? In their research on this question, Sasha Kimel and Jonah Kunst studied the effect of finding that someone is or is not part of another racial or ethnic group. They note that "ancestry results are actually based on much less than 0.1 percent of our genes." Yet it is most common to find that you are not related to a number of other groups. Their research found that when people are not connected genetically to another group, they are more inclined to support violence toward that other group. They tie this tendency to the rhetoric of genocide which is often based on genetic, biological differences from other groups.

SOURCE: Kimel, S., & Kunst, J. (2016, May 26). Can DNA ancestry testing make you more racist? *Scientific American*. Retrieved February 10, 2017 from https://blogs.scientificamerican.com/guest-blog/can-dna-ancestry-testing-make-you-more-racist/.

to another" (1993, p 117). Moreover, communication is a strong factor in furthering, affecting, or altering racial categories and identities to serve different social needs. For example, Guzman and Valdivia (2004) studied the media images of three Latinas—Salma Hayek, Frida Kahlo, and Jennifer Lopez—to see how gender and Latinidad are reinforced through the media (see Chapter 11). Face-to-face communication also influences peoples' ideas about racial identities. If individuals have little contact with people of a different racial group, it is especially likely that one or two encounters may lead them to draw conclusions about the entire group.

Beginning with the 2000 census, the U.S. government has allowed people to claim a **multiracial identity** (Jones & Smith, 2001). This category recognizes that some people self-identify as having more than one racial identity. So, how should we categorize Barack Obama? Although "there is much to celebrate in seeing Obama's victory as a victory for African Americans," writer Marie Arana (2008) also thinks that "Obama's ascent to the presidency is more than a triumph for blacks." She feels that "Barack Obama is not our first black president. He is our first biracial, bicultural president." What difference does it make if we see Obama as our first African American president or as our first biracial president? As you think through this issue, you can see the complexities of race and racial politics within a culture.

multiracial identity
One who self-identifies as having more than one racial identity.

Multiracial identities have arisen as a result of history as well. The Dutch colonization of Indonesia led to many mixed race children who were known as "Indische Nederlanders," or Dutch Indonesians. The actor Mark-Paul Gosselaar is an example of a Dutch Indonesian. There is even a Facebook page devoted to the Dutch Indonesian community. What other multiracial identities have resulted from the many ways that people have migrated around the world (e.g., through colonization, slavery, wars, invasions, and so on)?

National Identity

Racial identity can often be confused and conflated with **national identity**. We often misuse the notion of nationality when we ask someone "What's your nationality?" but what we really want to know is their ancestry or ethnic background. *Nationality* or national identity refers to a person's citizenship. In other words, Lady Gaga's nationality is not Italian, but U.S. American because she holds U.S. citizenship. John F. Kennedy's nationality was not Irish; he was a U.S. citizen. Many U.S. Americans did not actively choose their national identity; they simply acquired it by being born in the United States. Although many of us have not actively chosen our national identity, most of us are content with—or even proud—of it.

national identity
A person's citizenship.

Like our other identities, the importance placed on national identity can vary, depending on many factors. At the 2014 Winter Olympics in Sochi, Russia, the U.S. women's hockey team came up with the hashtag #dawnsearlylight to promote the U.S. men's hockey game against Russia which aired at an early hour in the United States. As *Sporting Times* noted, "Sound familiar? Hopefully, since it's the second line of the national anthem" (Negley, 2014). The Olympics are one context that tends to draw on national identities.

In a recent study on Iranian American and Iranian Canadian children, M. Razavi found that they use the Internet in developing what she calls "New National Identities" (2013). These youths use the Internet to gather information about the United States or Canada and incorporate this new information into their sense of their national identity. She distinguishes this new national identity from local co-ethnic cultures to highlight the role of the Internet.

Ethnic Identity

Although race and ethnicity are related concepts, the concept of ethnicity is based on the idea of social (rather than genetic) groups. Ethnic groups typically share a national

ethnic identity

Identification with a particular group with which one shares some or all of these characteristics: national or tribal affiliation, religious beliefs, language, and/or cultural and traditional origins and background.

or tribal affiliation, religious beliefs, language, or cultural and traditional origins and background. A person's **ethnic identity** comes from identification with a particular group with which they share some or all of these characteristics. Thus, some U.S. citizens say that they are Irish because they feel a close relationship with Irish heritage and custom, even though they are no longer Irish citizens—or perhaps never were. Likewise, in the United States many U.S. Americans think of themselves as Italian, Greek, German, Japanese, Chinese, or Swedish even though they do not hold passports from those countries. Nonetheless, they feel a strong affinity for these places because of their ancestry. Unlike national identity, ethnic identity does not require that some nation's government recognizes you as a member of its country. It is also unlike racial identity, in that any racial group may contain a number of ethnic identities. For example, people who are categorized racially as white identify with a range of ethnic groups, including Swedish, Polish, Dutch, French, Italian, and Greek.

In other parts of the world, ethnic identities are sometimes called *tribal identities*. For example, "in Kenya, there are 50 tribes, or ethnic groups, with members sharing similar physical traits and cultural traditions, as well as roughly the same language and economic class" (Wax, 2005, p. 18). Tribal identities are important not only across Africa, but also in many nations around the world, including Afghanistan (Lagarde, 2005). In some societies, tribal or ethnic identity can determine who is elected to office, who is hired for particular jobs, and who is likely to marry whom. In Malaysia the three major ethnic groups are Malay, Indian, and Chinese. Because the Malay are in power and make decisions that influence all three groups, being Malay gives one an important advantage. In the United States, however, the ethnic identities of many white Americans are primarily symbolic because they have minimal influence in everyday life (Waters, 1990). Even if ethnic identity does not play an important role in your life, it can carry great significance in other parts of the world.

Gender Identity

Similar to race, gender is a concept constructed through communication. *Gender* refers to the cultural differences between masculinity and femininity, whereas *sex* refers to the biological differences between males and females. Gender describes the set of expectations cultures develop regarding how men and women are expected to look, behave,

---

ALTERNATIVE VIEW
Counting Gender and Sexual Identities

As the official record of a nation's population, what information should any census seek? What categories should the census use?

The United States is just one of many countries that conduct a census at regular intervals. Census forms typically ask for basic identity information such as age, race, and gender.

In 2011, the census in India made history because its new census form gave respondents three gender identity options: "Male," "Female," and "Other." The 2011 census "[gave] India a firm count for its 'third-gender' hijra community—the origins of which go back millennia to a time when transsexuals, eunuchs and gays held a special place in a society backed by Hindu myths of their power to grant fertility" (Daigle, 2011).

In planning for the 2021 census for England and Wales, the Office of National Statistics is currently studying whether to ask people about their gender and sexual identities. The ONS is concerned about the "'public acceptability' of asking a question on the topic in 2021" ("Next UK census," 2016). Census officials believe it is important to know more about sexual minorities and transgender people in order to assess discrimination and public policies, but if the social stigma remains high, the data collected may not be accurate.

How should the United States handle these issues? Should questions about sexual and gender identity be on the next census in 2020?

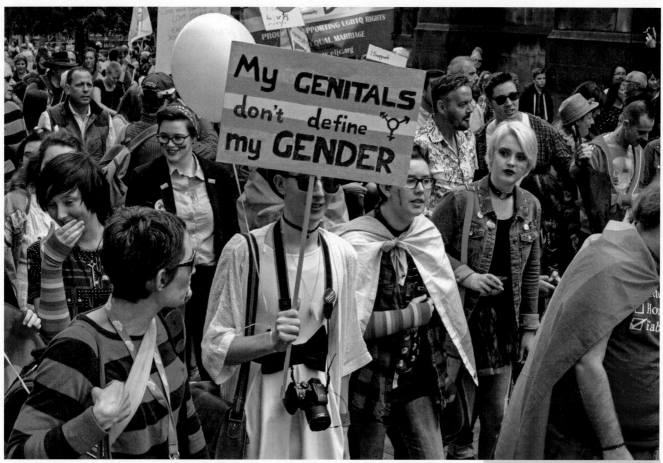

▲ People can perform gender identity in many different ways; there is no right or wrong way to perform gender identity.

communicate, and live. For example, in U.S. culture women (who are biologically female) are expected to perform femininity (a cultural construction) through activities such as nurturing, crossing their legs and not taking up too much room when sitting, speaking with vocal variety and expressivity, and wearing makeup. How do people respond to women who cut their hair in a flattop, sit sprawled across the couch, speak in an aggressive manner, and refuse to wear makeup? Often, they call them names or ridicule them; occasionally they even mistake them for males because these behaviors are so culturally attached to notions of masculinity.

Gender identity refers to how and to what extent one identifies with the social construction of masculinity and femininity. Gender roles and expectations have changed enormously over the centuries, and cultural groups around the world differ in their gender expectations. How do we develop our notions of gender, or what it means to be masculine or feminine? We learn through communication: through the ways that people talk about gender, through the media images we see, and through observing the ways people communicate to males and females. For example, although crying is acceptable for girls, young boys receive many messages that they are not supposed to cry.

A leading scholar on gender, Judith Butler (1990, 1993) was one of the first to argue that gender identity is not biological but based on performance. She asserted that people's identities flow from the ways they have seen them performed in the past. In other words, a man's performance of male identity rests on previous performances of masculinity. Because the performances of traditional masculinity have been repeated for so long, individuals come to believe that masculine identity and behaviors are natural. However, some people choose to enact their identity in nontraditional ways, and their performances will be interpreted against the backdrop of what is considered acceptable and appropriate.

Sometimes people distinguish between cisgender and transgender as ways of thinking about gender identity. **Cisgender** refers to a matching between one's gender

gender identity
How and to what extent one identifies with the social construction of masculinity and femininity.

cisgender

Someone whose gender identity matches their biological sex.

transgender

Someone whose gender identity does not match their biological sex.

sexual identity

Which of the various categories of sexuality one identifies with.

gender fluid

Someone whose gender identity is not fixed, but is dynamic and changes in different contexts, at different times.

identity and their biological body. A cisgender man is someone who identifies as male and was born into a male body. In contrast, **transgender** refers to someone who identifies with a different gender than their biological body. A transgender man is someone who identifies as a man, but was born into a female body.

The complexity of how people identify with gender is reflected in Facebook's 2014 change to the gender options. "Facebook offers 56 options. You can use up to 10 of them on your profile" (Weber, 2014). Yet, even this array of choices may not capture the diversity of gender identifications possible in people's everyday lives (see *Alternative View: Gender Fluidity*).

Sexual Identity

Sexual identity refers to which of the various categories of sexuality one identifies with. Because our culture is dynamic, it has no set number of sexual identity categories, but perhaps the most prominent are heterosexual, gay or lesbian, and bisexual. Although most people in our culture recognize these categories today, they have not always been acknowledged or viewed in the same ways. In his *History of Sexuality*, French historian and theorist Michel Foucault (1988) notes that over the course of history, notions of sexuality and sexual identities changed. In certain eras and cultures, when children were born with both male and female sexual organs, a condition referred to as *intersexuality*, they were not necessarily operated on or forced to be either male or female.

Many people think of sexuality or sexual identity as private, but it frequently makes its way into the public arena. In everyday life, we often encounter people who will personally introduce us to their husbands or wives, a gesture that shares a particular aspect of their sexual identity. However, our society often exposes an individual's sexual identity to public scrutiny. For example, Brian Boitano, the 1988 gold medalist from the Olympics, revealed that he is gay when he was chosen by President Obama to attend the 2014 Winter Olympics in Sochi, Russia. He said, "I don't feel that I can represent the country without revealing this incredible side of myself" (qtd. in "Brian Boitano," 2014). In contrast, former congressman Anthony Weiner sending a link to a sexually explicit photo to a twenty-one-year-old woman led to other issues about his sexuality and his need to engage in sexting: "I went from not really thinking through

ALTERNATIVE VIEW
Gender Fluidity

Although many people identify with the categorization of cisgender and transgender, there are other people who identify in more **gender fluid** ways. These people may feel more feminine at some times and more masculine at others. Cisgender and transgender do not capture the dynamic and fluid nature of how they identify with gender. Sometimes the term genderqueer is used, but there are other terms that try to capture the complexity of gender.

very much to having everything just blow up in such a monumental way, that you'd have to be really blind to not realize there must be some things that I need to resolve here and understand a little better. Therapy wasn't something that came naturally to me. I am this middle-class guy from Brooklyn, the men in our family don't hug each other, we don't talk about our feelings" (qtd. in Van Meter, 2013).

Because identity categories are social constructions, there is not always agreement about what they mean. Clearly, in the public arena, people manipulate these identity categories to help retrieve their reputations when their sexual activities become public.

In daily life, a person's sexual identity plays a role in such mundane matters as selecting which magazines to read and which television shows and movies to watch, as well as choosing places to socialize, people to associate with, and types of products to purchase. Television shows, magazines, books, Internet sites, and other cultural products are targeted toward particular sexual identities, or they assume a certain level of public knowledge about sexual identities and groups. For example, *The Bachelor/ Bachelorette, Millionaire Matchmaker,* and *Real Housewives of Orange County* presume an understanding of U.S. heterosexual culture. In contrast, the Logo cable channel is specifically geared to gay and lesbian viewers. *Modern Family* includes gay characters, whereas *Looking* centers gay characters in its storyline. *Glee* and *Orange is the New Black* include transgender characters. These communication texts can reinforce, confirm, or challenge our notions of various categories of sexual identity.

Age Identity

Age, when thought of strictly as the number of years you've been alive, is an important identity for everyone. But your **age identity** is a combination of how you feel about your age as well as what others understand that age to mean. How old is "old"? How young is "young"? Have you noticed how your own notions of age have changed over the years? When you were in first grade, did high school students seem old to you? Although *age* is a relative term, so are the categories we use for age groups. Today, for example, we use the terms *teenager, senior citizen, adult,* and *minor,* but these terms have meaning only within our social and legal system. For example, the voting age is 18, but people have to wait until they are 21 to buy liquor. Someone who commits a heinous crime can be charged as an adult, even if he or she is not yet 18. Still, whether a person feels like an adult goes beyond what the law decrees and comes from some set of factors that is far more complex.

Other age-related concepts are culturally determined as well. For example, the notion of "teenager" has come into use only relatively recently in the United States, and it is certainly not a universal category (Palladino, 1996). The notion that people have "midlife" crises is not a universal cultural phenomenon, either. Moreover, these age categories are relatively fluid, meaning that there are no strict guidelines about where they begin and end, even though they do influence how we think about ourselves (Trethewey, 2001). For example, because people today generally live longer, the span of years thought of as middle age comes later in our lives. These changes all illustrate the dynamic nature of age identity and the categories we have for it.

The use of terms for generations tries to group people by age groups, such as the Greatest Generation, Baby Boomers, or Millennials. There are stereotypes that go along with these age groups that influence how we think about them. What are some stereotypes about your generation?

Social Class Identity

Social class identity refers to an informal ranking of people in a culture based on their income, occupation, education, dwelling, child-rearing habits, and other factors (Online Glossary, 2005). Examples of social classes in this country include working class,

age identity
A combination of self-perception of age along with what others understand that age to mean.

social class identity
An informal ranking of people in a culture based on their income, occupation, education, dwelling, child-rearing habits, and other factors.

middle class, upper-middle class, and upper class. Most people in the United States identify themselves as middle class (Baker, 2003). However, there is no single agreed-on definition for each of the classes. For example, "the 'middle class' income range has been described as between $32,900 and $64,000 a year (a Pew Charitable Trusts study), between $50,800 and $122,000 (a U.S. Department of Commerce study), and between $20,600 and $102,000 (the U.S. Census Bureau's middle 60% of incomes)" (Horn, 2013).

For Ken Eisold, social class "is really more about identity" (qtd. in Horn, 2013). In other words, the amount of money that people earn is only one part of identifying as middle class.

In his work on social class, French sociologist Pierre Bourdieu (1984) found that people of the same social class tended to view the world similarly: They defined art in similar ways, and they enjoyed similar sports and other aspects of everyday life. Moreover, based on his study of social class, Paul Fussell (1992) noted that U.S. Americans communicate their social class in a wide variety of ways, some verbal and some nonverbal. For example, middle-class people tend to say "tuxedo," whereas upper-class people are more apt to say "dinner jacket." In the category of nonverbal elements that express social class identity, he included the clothes we wear, the way we decorate our homes, the magazines we read, the kinds of drinks we imbibe, and the ways we decorate our automobiles. We will discuss more about class and verbal and nonverbal communication in the next two chapters.

Those in occupations such as nursing, teaching, and policing soon may no longer be considered middle class. What other occupations have fallen or might fall from middle-class status? In their study *The Fragile Middle Class*, Teresa Sullivan and her colleagues noted the increasing numbers of bankruptcy filings (2001), especially among those in occupations that we consider securely middle class, such as teachers, dentists, accountants, and computer engineers. In the wake of the recent recession, there has been increasing public discussion about income inequality and its toll on the middle class. The recession has drawn attention to the very wealthy and the increasing wealth they are amassing while unemployment remains stubbornly high. These discussions may portend a new focus on social class identity.

One reason people in the United States avoid discussing social class is because they tend to believe that their country is based on *meritocracy*, meaning that people succeed or fail based on their own merit. This idea leads to claims such as "anyone can grow up to be president." However, this has not proven to be true. For example, until the election of Barack Obama in 2008, every president in the United States has been white, male, and, in all cases but one, Protestant. Social identity and class have a powerful impact on one's life because they can determine where you go to school (and what quality of education you receive), where you shop (and what quality of resources you have access to), which leisure activities you participate in (on a scale from constructive and enriching to destructive and self-defeating), and who you are most likely to meet and with whom you are mostly likely to socialize. In this way, social class identity tends to reproduce itself; the social class one is born into is often the

Critical Thinking Prompt
How does your own speech reveal your social class background and identity? Can you identify aspects of your family's home, yard, interior decorating, and clothing that reveal social class identity?

▼ Social class identity is an important influence in the ways that people socialize and engage in leisure activities.

same as the social class one dies in. People who are working class tend to live around other working-class people, make friends with working-class people (who influence their expectations and behavior), and attend schools that reinforce working-class values. In an early study that showed how communication was used to perform social class identity in conjunction with gender and race, Gerry Philipsen (1992) noted that men tended to speak much less than women and rarely socialized outside their working-class community, which he called "Teamsterville." More recently, Kristen Lucas (2011) studied how family is an important site for communication messages that "both encourage and discourage social mobility" (p. 95). By examining how families reproduce their working-class identity, we can see how there are contradictory messages sent to the children about social class and moving toward white-collar occupations.

In our previous example of the 2011 census in India, the census form does not ask people about their caste. In that cultural context, "census officials worried the sensitive subject of caste in multicultural and secular India could upset the results of the population count" (Daigle, 2011). Social class can be a sensitive topic in many cultures.

It Happened to Me
Melinda

My parents went through a divorce when I was two, and my mother has worked hard so we could have a comfortable life. Throughout my life, I've gone to private schools and universities with other students whose families had much more money than mine. I've always tried to fit in with the other students. Recently my mother has gone into debt, and I am having trouble adjusting to this change. I haven't told any of my upper-class friends because I am afraid they won't understand my situation. It can be a struggle to be honest with people you don't think will understand your situation, but it is a struggle that I have to overcome. People should accept each other for who they are, not what social class they fit into.

Disability Identity

People can identify with or be identified as disabled for many different reasons. **Disability identity** is often defined as having an impairment of some kind. Some people experience differences in hearing, sight, or mobility. Not all disabilities are visible or evident to others. In 1990, the United States passed the Americans with Disabilities Act, which recognized disability as an important identity that needed federal protection from discrimination. This act also defines "disability" in Section 12102:

> The term "disability" means, with respect to an individual:

(A) a physical or mental impairment that substantially limits one or more major life activities of such individual;

(B) a record of such an impairment; or

(C) being regarded as having such an impairment. (Americans with Disabilities Act, 1990, 2008)

disability identity
Identification with physical or mental impairment that substantially impact everyday life.

Although this legal definition may be helpful to some, it does not tell us what this identity means and how it is performed by those who identify as disabled, nor does it tell us how disability is viewed by others.

It is through communication that "disability" as an identity gains its meaning in our society. As Deanna Fassett and Dana L. Morella explain:

> while someone might have a medical or physical condition that structures her/his experience, it is in her/his interactions with others that that condition takes on meaning and becomes what our collective social environment would consider disability, with all the punishments and privilege that entails. We build this social environment in our own mundane communication, in classrooms and faculty meetings; we learn and reiterate, often unknowingly, as institutional members, what is normal and what is not and what that means. (p. 144)

If we are swimming in a sea of communication, the many meanings that we generate in everyday communication give meaning to disability.

Like other identities, disability is performed; it is "always in the process of becoming, then disability is something we do, rather than something we are" (Henderson and Ostrander, 2008, p. 2). Disability, in this view, is about how it is enacted and lived; it is not about a fixed state of being. For example, in his study on disabled athletes who play wheelchair rugby, Kurt Lindemann found that "performances of disability, especially in a sport context, can subvert the stigma associated with physical disability in surprisingly effective ways" (2008, p. 113). By focusing on athletic activities, disabled people attempt to challenge stereotypical views of those with disabilities. More recently, disabled actors have complained about media productions that feature able-bodied actors portraying disabled characters, such as Kevin McHale's portrayal of Artie Abrams in *Glee*. Some question whether there is a stereotype that disabled actors can't perform and work as well on studio sets as able-bodied actors.

People who are not disabled can become disabled and then develop this new identity as a part of their larger configuration of identities. For example, many people, as they grow older, may experience increasing hearing loss, reduced visual acuity, or other physical or mental impairments that can render them disabled. But disability, of course, is not limited to older people. How we talk about disability, see it in media images, and experience it in everyday life are all part of how we communicate about and construct the meanings of disability as an identity. In her study on autobiographical narratives of those growing up with chronic illness or disability, Linda Wheeler Cardillo found that "communication at all levels has a powerful impact on these persons and their experiences of difference. A deeper understanding of this experience and how it is shaped by communication can lead to more sensitive, respectful, affirming, and empowering communication on the part of health-care providers, parents, teachers, and others" (2010, p. 539).

Religious Identity

religious identity
Aspect of identity defined by one's spiritual beliefs.

In the United States today, **religious identity** is becoming increasingly important. Religious identity is defined by one's spiritual beliefs. For example, although Jim hasn't been to a Catholic church in decades, he still identifies himself as Catholic because of his upbringing and the impact the religion has had on his outlook. Most researchers and writers agree that "religion is certainly one of the most complex and powerful cultural discourses in contemporary society, and religion continues to be a source of conflict between nations, among communities, within families, and . . . within one's self" (Corey, 2004, p. 189). Although you may believe that your religious identity is part of your private life and irrelevant outside your family, this is not true. For example, in the aftermath of the 2001 September 11 attacks, Muslim identity has been viewed with particular suspicion. A 2004 study done by researchers in the Department of Communication at Cornell University found the following attitudes about Muslim Americans:

Critical Thinking Prompt
How would you describe your religious identity? How do you communicate it to others? Do you ever conceal it? If so, when and why?

About 27 percent of respondents said that all Muslim Americans should be required to register their location with the federal government, and 26 percent said they think that mosques should be closely monitored by U.S. law enforcement agencies. Twenty-nine percent agreed that undercover law enforcement agents should infiltrate Muslim civic and volunteer organizations to keep tabs on their activities and fund-raising. About 22 percent said the federal government should profile citizens as potential threats based on the fact that they are Muslim or have Middle Eastern heritage. In all, about 44 percent said they believe that some curtailment of civil liberties is necessary for Muslim Americans (Cornell University, 2004).

Religious identity also takes on public significance because it correlates with various political views and attitudes (Corey & Nakayama, 2004). For example, the 2004 Cornell study found that Christians who actively attend church were much more likely to support differential treatment of Muslim Americans. In contrast, the nonreligious, or those less active in their churches, were less likely to support restrictions on civil liberties of Muslim Americans.

ALTERNATIVE VIEW
Islamophobia

What responsibilities do we have to use communication to work against Islamophobia, or the fear of Muslims?

High-profile terrorist attacks in a number of countries has created significant fear of Muslims and prejudicial attitudes against them. A number of hateful acts have been committed against Muslims and mosques in recent years. In January 2017, a lone gunman entered a mosque in Quebec City and opened fire, killing six and injuring 19 people. A number of politicians have spoken out against this type of violence against the Muslim community, including Joël Lightbound, a member of the Canadian Parliament representing this area. In his speech, he explains the role of communication. In part, he said:

"Today, I also want to apologize to them. I apologize for having observed stigmatization and ostracization over the past few years, having seen the mistrust, the fear, and the hatred among my peers. And having tried to respond, but not having done enough.

Silence also has consequences. Never again."

SOURCE: Lum, Z.-A. (2017, February 2). Joël Lightbound urges no more silence over Islamophobia after Quebec City mosque attack. *Huffington Post Canada*. Retrieved February 10, 2017 from http://www.huffingtonpost.ca/2017/02/02/joel-lightbound-quebec-shooting_n_14575968.html.

However one responds to other people's religious beliefs, most U.S. Americans feel a strong need to embrace and enact personal religious identities (Corey & Nakayama, 2004). In 2000, for example, 46 percent of U.S. Americans belonged to religious groups, and approximately 40 percent of U.S. Americans claimed to attend religious services regularly (Taylor, 2005). Thus, in their article on "Religion and Performance," Frederick Corey and Thomas Nakayama (2004) write that individuals feel a "tremendous need to embody religious identities and reinforce those identities through spirited, vernacular performances" (p. 211). To understand how one student's religious identity affects her life, read *It Happened to Me: Elizabeth*.

It Happened to Me
Elizabeth

If I meet someone in a college class, I don't tell them that I'm involved in a church or that I'm a Christian unless they bring it up or it's obvious they are, too. I do not want to appear to be a religious nut waiting to shove my belief system down their throat. My belief in Christ is really at the core of who I am, though. When I meet people through work who are in churches, I am open with them about my work, my life, and even my challenges. This is because they are my brothers/sisters in Christ, and that's the culture of what we do—care for, and about, one another.

The virtual environment has also been influenced by, and influences, religious identity. Sometimes people find religious communities online, and some people even use their iPhones for prayer and other religious purposes. Others resist the Internet for fear it would compromise or challenge their religious beliefs. Communication scholar Heidi Campbell notes: "Digital religion as a concept acknowledges not only how the unique character of digital technology and culture shapes religious practice and beliefs, but also how religions seek to culture new media contexts with established ways of being and convictions about the nature of reality and the larger world" (p. 4).

We've shown throughout this chapter that aspects of our personal identity such as race, nationality, ethnicity, gender, age, social class, and religion develop through the tension between individual and societal forces. Although we may assert a particular identity or view of ourselves, these views must be negotiated within the larger society and the meanings that the larger society communicates about that identity. See *Alternative View: Islamophobia* for an example of how communication can be used to deal with religious differences and the dangerous role of silence. In the next section, we discuss the role of ethics in communication about identity.

Journal Prompt 3.4:
Identify Categories
Consider the following question:
What are the primary identity categories? Define each and give an example of how identity might be performed for each primary identity category.

Ethics and Identity

3.5 **Discuss three ethical considerations for communicating in a sensitive manner to and about others' identities.**

As you are probably aware, a person's sense of identity is central to how he or she functions in the world. Moreover, because identities derive their meanings from society, every identity comes with values attached to it. The ways we communicate may reflect these values. If you wish to be sensitive to other people's identities, you should be aware of at least three key ethical issues that can impact your communication with others.

One issue you might consider is how you communicate with people whose identities are more, or less, valued. What do we mean by more or less valued? You probably already know. In the United States, for example, which of the following identities is more highly valued: White or multiracial? Male or female? Lawyer or school bus driver? Still, these rankings are not necessarily consistent across cultures. In Denmark, for example, work identities do not follow the same hierarchical pattern as those in the United States (Mikkelsen & Einarsen, 2001). Thus, Danes are more likely to view street sweepers and doctors as social equals because they don't place as high a value on the medical profession nor as low a value on service jobs as many U.S. Americans do. In the United States, in contrast, many service workers complain that most of the people they serve either ignore them or treat them rudely—even with contempt. Consequently, you might ask yourself, "Do I communicate more politely and respectfully with high- versus low-status people?" If you find yourself exhibiting more respect when you communicate with your boss than you do with the employees you manage, then you might want to consider the impact of your communication on your subordinates' identities.

The second ethical point to reflect on involves language that denigrates or puts down others based on their identities. Such language debases their humanity and shuts down open communication. Examples of unethical communication and behavior related to identity occur if men yell sexual slurs at women on the street, or straight people harass individuals they believe are gay, or when white people are disrespectful to people of color. Although you probably don't engage in such obvious insults to people's identities, do you denigrate them in other, more subtle ways? For example, have you ever referred to someone as "just a homemaker" or "only a dental assistant"?

Third, think about whether you tend to reduce others to a single identity category. As we pointed out previously, each of us is composed of multiple identities, and even within a specific identity group, individuals may differ widely from one another. Thus, individuals may be offended when others respond to them based on only one of their identities, especially one that is not relevant to the situation at hand. For example, managers in some organizations will not promote mothers of small children to highly demanding positions. They justify this by claiming the women won't be able to fulfill both their family and their professional roles competently. Although these women may be mothers, their identities as mothers likely are not relevant to their workplace identities and performances—just as men's identities as fathers are rarely seen as relevant to their jobs. Each person is a complex of identities, and each person desires others to recognize his or her multiple identities. You are more likely to communicate ethically if you keep this fact in mind.

Journal Prompt 3.5: Ethics and Identity
Consider the following question:
What are three key ethical concerns related to identity?

Skills for Communicating about Identities

3.6 **Explain three ways to communicate more effectively about identities.**

Related to our discussion about ethical issues, we offer three guidelines for communicating more effectively about identities. The first guideline concerns the self-fulfilling

ALTERNATIVE VIEW
Catfishing

Sometimes people invoke identities that are not their own to gain something from others. Sometimes called "catfishing," people will engage others into their fabricated network of identities and social relationships to get them into a relationship. Manti Te'o, who played football at Notre Dame, and Thomas Gibson, an actor on "Criminal Minds," were both purported to have been snared in catfishing games. Both are believed to have been in lengthy online relationships with women that they had never met.

In *Digital Trends*, Molly McHugh identifies five different types of catfish:

> There's the Revenge Catfish: This catfish feels he or she was wronged by you (or someone or something you're tied to) and is pathologically creating this online romance simply to get back at you.

> There's the Bored Catfish. This catfish has an Internet connection and too much time on his or her hands.

> There's the Secretly-in-love-with-you Catfish. This catfish harbors an unrequited crush on you, and for some reason doesn't find him- or herself good enough in real life to go for it.

> There's the Scary Catfish. This catfish is simply out to break hearts and cause chaos.

> There's the Lonely Catfish. This catfish usually has some sort of sob story and needs someone to talk too, and with a pretty picture and a Facebook profile, you've become that person.

Although the motives for engaging in catfishing may be even more complex than these five categories, what are the ethics of catfishing? McHugh raises an important challenge for all of us when she asks:

> Really, we're all catfish. Have you ever edited your profile picture to look a little better? Do you untag? Have you ever faked a location check-in? We're all guilty of bending the truth with our profiles to some degree—hell, it's what all these platforms want us to do. Social media is a very aspirational beast and it's not very surprising that it's led to a catfishing epidemic.

SOURCE: McHugh, M. (2013, August 23) It's catfishing season! How to tell lovers from liars online, and more. *Digital Trends*. Retrieved March 3, 2014, from http://www.digitaltrends.com/web/its-catfishing-season-how-to-tell-lovers-from-liars-online-and-more/#ixzz2uvnrrkOx. Read more: http://www.digitaltrends.com/web/its-catfishing-season-how-to-tell-lovers-from-liars-online-and-more/#ixzz2uvnL1KoP.

prophecy we discussed previously: How you communicate *to* someone and *about* someone can influence how they perform their identity or how it develops. If a parent continually communicates with the child as if she were irresponsible, then the child is likely to act irresponsibly. To communicate effectively, be aware of the ways you create self-fulfilling prophecies through your own communication.

Second, there are many ways to perform a particular identity. You can improve your ability to communicate if you are tolerant of the many variations. For example, even if you believe that "real men" should act in certain ways, you are likely to communicate more effectively if you do not impose your beliefs on others. For example, you should not assume that because someone is male, he enjoys watching football, baseball, and other sports; wants to get married and have children; or eats only meat and potatoes. If you do, you are likely to communicate with some men in ways they will find less interesting than you intend.

Third, remember that people change over time. If you have been out of touch with friends for a period of time, when you encounter them again you may find that they have embraced new identities. Sometimes people change religious identities, or sometimes they change occupations. You can increase your communication effectiveness if you recognize that people change and that their new identities may be unfamiliar to you.

**Journal Prompt 3.6:
Communicating Identity**
Consider the following question:
What are three strategies you can use to communicate more effectively with regard to identities?

SUMMARY

3.1 Identify six reasons identity is important to communication.

- We bring our identities to each communication interaction.
- Communication interactions create and shape identities.
- Identity plays a key role in intercultural communication.
- Much of our life is organized around specific identities.
- Identity is a key site in which individual and societal forces come together.
- We invoke our identities to help others understand our communication.

3.2 Define *identity*.

- Primary identities (race, ethnicity, age) are the focus in this chapter and have the most consistent and enduring impact on our lives.
- Secondary identities, such as occupation and marital status, are more changeable over the life span and from situation to situation.
- Our identities exist at both the individual and social level, are both fixed and dynamic, and are created through interaction.
- Identities must be understood within larger historical, social, and cultural environments.

3.3 Clarify how reflected appraisals, social comparisons, self-fulfilling prophecies, and self-concept contribute to identity development.

3.4 Identify examples of racial, national, ethnic, gender, sexual, age, social class, disability, and religious identities.

- Individuals perform their identities, and these performances are subject to social commentary. Straying too far from social expectations in these performances can lead to disciplinary action.

3.5 Discuss three ethical considerations for communicating in a sensitive manner to and about others' identities.

- Learning to value and respect people within all identity groups.
- To avoid using denigrating language or reducing people to a single identity category.
- Avoid reducing people to a single identity category.

3.6 Explain three ways to communicate more effectively about identities.

- Being aware of the ways you create self-fulfilling prophecies through your communication.
- Being tolerant of different ways of enacting various identities.
- Being aware that people's identities may change over time.

KEY TERMS

identity p. 47
reflected appraisals p. 49
looking-glass self p. 49
particular others p. 50
generalized other p. 50
self-fulfilling prophecy p. 51
stereotype threat p. 52
self-concept p. 53
self-esteem p. 53
self-respect p. 54

performance of identity p. 54
self-presentation p. 54
enacting identities p. 54
role expectations p. 56
mutable p. 56
racial identity p. 58
multiracial identity p. 59
national identity p. 59
ethnic identity p. 60
gender identity p. 61

cisgender p. 62
transgender p. 62
sexual identity p. 62
gender fluid p. 62
age identity p. 63
social class identity p. 63
disability identity p. 65
religious identity p. 66

APPLY WHAT YOU KNOW

1. List the identities that are most important to you. Some of these identities may not have been discussed in this chapter. Note some situations in which the identities not discussed in the chapter become most relevant and some situations in which other identities dominate.

2. Which of your identities are shared by a majority of people in society? What are some of the stereotypes of those identities? To answer this question, you may need to ask people who do not share that identity.

Communicating, Perceiving, and Understanding

LEARNING OBJECTIVES

		CHAPTER TOPICS
4.1	Explain why understanding perception is important.	The Importance of Perception
4.2	Describe the three processes people use to understand information collected through the senses.	What Is Perception?
4.3	Name three individual factors that affect one's perceptual processes.	Perception and the Individual
4.4	Articulate how power, culture, social comparisons, and historical time period influence perception.	The Individual, Perception, and Society
4.5	Explain why ethics is relevant to the perception process.	Ethics and Perception
4.6	Identify three ways you can improve your perception skills.	Improving Your Perception Skills

> *"No one should assume that what he or she perceives*
> *is the same as what others perceive."*

After the first meeting of their research methods class, Charee and Mateo went out for coffee. They soon found themselves sharing their impressions of the instructor.

CHAREE: What did you think of Professor Wolfe?

MATEO: I suppose she's okay. She made the class seem kind of hard, and I am worried she will be difficult to talk to if I need help.

CHAREE: Really? I liked her a lot. I thought she was funny and would be really easy to talk to. I think I am going enjoy taking this class.

MATEO: She seemed kind of unapproachable to me. I guess we'll have plenty of chances to find out what she is really like during the semester.

As the conversation between Charee and Mateo illustrates, our perceptions of others strongly influence how we respond to and communicate about them. If we perceive people as friendly and similar to ourselves, we tend to be drawn toward them and want to communicate with them. If we view individuals as distant and quite unlike ourselves, we may try to minimize contact. However, not everyone perceives and responds to people and events the same way. Our perceptions are affected by individual factors, such as age, gender, genetics, and experience, as well as by societal forces including culture, historical events, and social roles.

For instance, on average, females experience pain more intensely than do males (Hurley & Adams, 2008), so a touch that feels uncomfortable to a man may feel painful to a woman. (It can be helpful to remember this difference when we are shaking hands with others.) But how can societal forces affect perception? Among other things, societies teach us what foods and beverages are tasty and how they should be served. One example of this is the difference in how soft drinks are served in the United Kingdom versus how they are served in the United States. In most parts of the United Kingdom, cold beverages include a few pieces of ice, whereas in the United States a glass of soda may be half ice. Because of this, people in the two cultures have different perceptions of what a "good" cold drink should taste like.

In this chapter, we will first explore the importance of perception and the perception process. Next, we'll examine how individuals' attributes and experiences affect their perceptions, and we will consider societal influences on perception. We also will discuss how people can evaluate their perceptions through an ethical lens. Finally, we will end with suggestions for sharpening your perception skills.

The Importance of Perception

4.1 Explain why understanding perception is important.

How individuals respond to people, objects, and environments depends largely on the perceptions they have about them. For example, when we perceive people as being polite, we are more likely to agree to their requests (Kellerman, 2004). When we communicate, we don't just respond to others' words; we respond to our perceptions of the way they look, sound, smell, and sometimes how they feel. For example, considerable research has established that when people perceive others as attractive, they treat them better than those viewed as less attractive (Chaiken, 1986; Wilson & Nias, 1999).

In addition, research suggests that sexual attraction is influenced by the body odor of a potential partner (McCoy & Pitino, 2002; Singh & Bronstad, 2001). Some studies indicate that people are sexually attracted to others whose body odor they find most attractive and that this attraction serves to help them locate mates likely to be a good genetic match.

So, the next time someone breaks off a relationship by saying, "It's not you; it's me," they may be telling the truth. You just may not smell right to that person! Interestingly, women may be more likely to make this statement than are men because a variety of research has found that on average women have a keener sense of smell than do men (Estroff, 2004; Herz & Inzlicht, 2002). Overall, women may be more positively influenced by smells they find attractive and negatively by smells they dislike. For more information on the influence of smell on perception, see *Communication in Society: Sex Differences in Smell.*

As we noted in Chapter 3, identities play an important role in communication. They also influence and are influenced by perception. Thus, just as our perceptions of others impact how we communicate with them, our perceptions and communication impact how they see themselves. Let's take our previous scenario as a case in point. How might Mateo's or Charee's perceptions affect Professor Wolfe's perception of herself? If most people perceive Professor Wolfe as Charee does—as amusing and open—and, therefore, respond to her by laughing and spending time with her, then she probably sees herself positively. On the other hand, if most people respond as Mateo did, and consequently choose to have little contact with her, Professor Wolfe may perceive herself more negatively.

As you might expect, then, perception and identity are powerfully intertwined. On the one hand, Mateo's perceptions of Professor Wolfe affect her identity. At the same time, how the professor views herself and others impacts how she perceives and responds to the world around her. If she has a positive self-image, Professor Wolfe may perceive that others like her, she might be more optimistic and see the positive aspects of a situation more readily, and she could be less aware of others' negative reactions to her.

As you read this chapter, you are receiving considerable sensory input. An air conditioner or heater might be running, people may be moving past you, and the temperature where you sit likely fluctuates over time. In addition, you may feel hungry or tired, you might detect the scent of cleaning products, and the chair you are sitting on could be uncomfortable. How are you able to manage all the information your senses bring to you so that you can focus on your reading? How are you able to make sense of all this sensory input? The answer is that you continuously engage in a variety of processes that limit and structure everything you perceive (Kanizsa, 1979; Morgan, 1977). Let's look at how this works.

▲ Research reveals that when people perceive others as attractive, they treat them better than those viewed as less attractive.

Journal Prompt 4.1: Perception and Communication
Consider the following question: Why is perception important to the communication process?

COMMUNICATION IN SOCIETY
Sex Differences in Smell

Have you noticed a difference in sense of smell between the sexes? Why do you think women typically have a keener sense of smell?

Did you know that scientists often use all-female panels when they look for objective descriptions of food based on sensory perception, such as taste, smell, and appearance? They do so because on standard tests of smelling ability—including odor detection, discrimination, and identification—women consistently outscore men. One researcher has claimed that this difference is evident even in newborn babies.

Age also influences an individual's sense of smell. A study that tested 3,282 participants found that, overall, one's sense of smell was most acute between the ages of 19 and 35 and was the least acute when one is older than 55. However, in all of the three tests conducted, women out performed men. Other studies have shown that women also rate the sense of smell as being more important to them than do men.

Experiments that have examined men's and women's scent ability reveal that both sexes are able to recognize others from their body odor alone. In an experiment at Hebrew University, Jerusalem, childless women held an unrelated baby in their arms for an hour. When tested later to see if they could recognize the

baby they had held by scent, most of them were successful. This study did not test men, so it isn't clear if men possess similar smell recognition ability for unfamiliar others. However, other tests have determined that men and women both can recognize their own children or spouses by their scent. Typically in these studies, participants' children or spouses wore a T-shirt for several days, and then the participants were asked to use scent to recognize the T-shirt belonging to their family member.

SOURCES: Croy I., Buschhüter D., Seo H. S., Negoias S., & Hummel T. (2010) Individual significance of olfaction: Development of a questionnaire. *Eur Arch Otorhinolaryngol*, 267(1), 67–71. doi: 10.1007/s00405-009-1054-0.

Hummel T., Kobal G., Gudziol H., & Mackay-Sim, A. (2007). Normative data for the "Sniffin' Sticks" including tests of odor identification, odor discrimination, and olfactory thresholds: An upgrade based on a group of more than 3,000 subjects. *Eur Arch Otorhinolaryngol, 264*(3), 237–243.

Korneliussen, I. (2012). Women smell better than men. *Science Nordic*. Retrieved May 14, 2014, from http://sciencenordic.com/women-smell-better-men.

Maccaby, E. E., & Jacklin, C. N. (1978). *The psychology of sex differences*. Palo Alto, CA: Stanford University Press.

What Is Perception?

4.2 Describe the three processes people use to understand information collected through the senses.

perception
A sense-making procedure in which we attempt to understand our environment so we can respond to it appropriately.

selection
The process of choosing which sensory information to focus on.

organization
The process by which one recognizes what sensory input represents.

interpretation
The act of assigning meaning to sensory information.

Perception refers to a sense-making procedure where we attempt to understand our environment so we can respond to it appropriately. For example, if you see a small animal, before you reach down to pet it, you will seek to determine what type of animal it is and whether it is friendly. Perception is composed of three processes: **selection**, **organization**, and **interpretation**. We use these processes to understand the information we collect through our senses—what we see, hear, taste, smell, and touch. The sensory data we select, the ways we organize them, and the interpretations we assign to them affect the ways we communicate (Manusov & Spitzberg, 2008). Although these processes tend to happen concurrently and unconsciously, researchers separate them to better explain how they function.

Selection

selective attention
Consciously or unconsciously attending to just a narrow range of the full array of sensory information available.

Because people experience more sensory information than they can process, they selectively focus on and remember only part of it. In every interaction, each communicator has a field of perception. In this field, some objects, symbols, or words are at the center, others are on the periphery, and still others are outside the field altogether. Consciously or unconsciously, we attend to just a narrow range of the full array of sensory information available and ignore the remainder. This process is called **selective attention**.

Suppose your friend is telling you an interesting story about a mutual acquaintance while the two of you are seated in a crowded restaurant. Most likely, your friend will have your full attention. Peripherally you may notice the sights and sounds of the other people in the room, the smells of food, and the glare of sunlight coming through the window; however, none of this will distract your focus. You probably will not even notice who is sitting at the table next to you, the color of the walls, or the storm clouds gathering in the sky. Your attention will be devoted to the center of your field: your friend.

The sensory input we select, however, is not random (Goldstein, 2010; Greenough, Black, & Wallace, 1987). When a range of sensory experiences accost you, various factors affect your selection, including your identity, features of the person or object you have encountered, and your experiences and values. For example, at large social events you are likely to attend to only one or a few people because you cannot focus on everyone at once. Who captures your focus depends on:

- aspects of your identity (e.g., if you are Native American, you may find your attention drawn more to participants who also are Native American)
- features of the person (e.g., someone dressed differently from everyone else will likely attract your attention)
- your goals (e.g., if you would like to meet a potential romantic partner, you may pay special attention to attractive men or women in your age range)

Researchers also have found that people are most likely to pay attention to and remember information based on when it is heard and whether it is positive or negative. Specifically, our opinions may be influenced more by information we learn first, called the **primacy effect**, or most recently, which is referred to as the **recency effect**. The primacy affect occurs when we evaluate a person, source, or event based on the first information we hear about her/it. Thus, if your professor is engaging, funny, and energetic during the first week of class, you will probably be more forgiving of him when he has a bad day. Recency operates similarly, except in this case our judgment is influenced more significantly by something we have learned recently. If you have seen three films by the same director, for instance, the likelihood that you will see her fourth movie typically is influenced more by how much you liked her third film than your reactions to her previous ones.

primacy effect
The tendency to form a judgment or opinion based on the first information received.

recency effect
The tendency to form a judgment or opinion on the most recent information received.

In addition, individuals are more attentive to and remember information that is negative, violates their expectations, and is made in situations that are important to them (Siu & Finnegan, 2004). For example, a comment such as "What on earth did you do to your hair?" is more likely to remain prominent in your mind and to influence your mood than "Nice haircut." Similarly, when an instructor says, "This will be on the test," students usually pay close attention to what the instructor says next. Comments that violate our expectations also become more salient and gain more attention. Suppose you meet someone new and ask "How are you?" Instead of the expected, "Fine, thanks," the person explains in detail all the misfortunes that have befallen him or her in the past year. You not only will be surprised, you will remember the event. You may even decide that this new person is highly negative, or strange, and that you should avoid future interactions with him or her.

Organization

After selecting the sensory input we will attend to, we need to be able to recognize *what* it represents. To do this, we must organize the information into a recognizable picture that has meaning. If you are awakened in the middle of the night by a loud noise, you will certainly attend to that noise and little else. However, you also must be able to make sense of the sound to respond. Is it a mechanical sound or an animal one? Is it human? You can make judgments such as these because you possess organizational structures or templates that tell you what information belongs together and how to "read" or understand what you perceive (Kanizsa, 1979). How does this work? In this section we examine two primary cognitive principles—cognitive representation and categorization—which help people organize and respond to their perceptions.

▲ Schools and workplaces have fire drills to help people create cognitive maps that are familiar and enable them to act appropriately in an emergency.

cognitive representation
The ability to form mental models of the world.

schemas
Cognitive structures that help us organize information.

prototype
A representative or idealized version of a concept.

▼ Nikki Haley is a conservative politician who conforms to a feminine prototype.

Cognitive Representation   The term **cognitive representation** describes the human ability to form mental models, or cognitive maps, of the world we live in (Levinthal & Gavetti, 2000; Weick, 1995). We create these maps and then refer to them later when circumstances call for them. For example, people know that a fire alarm communicates danger; furthermore, they know how to respond to a fire alarm because they have a cognitive map for alarms. Schools and workplaces have fire drills, in fact, to help people create cognitive maps that are familiar and enable them to act appropriately in an emergency. And research has shown that people who rehearse a plan—or develop a cognitive map—for specific crises are more likely to survive (Sherwood, 2009).

People also develop and use cognitive maps when they communicate. As we grow up, we learn cognitive maps or models for engaging in many types of communication acts, such as complaining, apologizing, and asking for a favor. Many people learn quite early that it is useful to be nice to someone before asking them for a favor, and this information becomes part of the map for requesting favors. Remember that maps are *representations* of things, not the things themselves. Thus, cognitive maps consist of general outlines; they are not fixed sets of utterances that are memorized. Three specific types of cognitive representations, or maps, that individuals use to organize their perceptions about people and communication are schemas, prototypes, and interpersonal scripts.

Schemas are cognitive structures that help us organize information. These structures are composed of preconceived ideas and frameworks representing an aspect of the world. People have more complex schema for topics they know a lot about. Schemas are important because they influence both what we pay attention to and how well we retain and integrate new knowledge. That is, we are more likely to notice things that fit into our schema. In addition, we tend to reinterpret contradictions to the schema by viewing them as exceptions or by distorting the contradictions so they fit the schema. For instance, if you are afraid of dogs, you probably have developed a schema that positions them as dangerous, unpredictable, and perhaps repellent. As a result, you probably are more aware of dogs in your environment, even if they are some distance away. If you happen to meet a friendly dog, you may believe the dog is an exception to the general rule that dogs are dangerous, or you may decide that the dog is friendly now, but that does not mean it won't be vicious at any moment.

Communication behavior is strongly influenced by idealized maps called prototypes. A **prototype** is the most representative example of a person or concept. For example, many people's prototypical idea of a professor is a person who is male, has white hair (and perhaps a beard), and wears a tweed jacket with leather patches. Although a few professors fulfill this prototype, many more do not. (Just look around your campus.) Nonetheless, this prototype persists, in part because of how media depict college professors. We also possess prototypes for "ideal" best friends, romantic partners, and family members.

Prototypes are important because people compare specific individuals to their prototypes and then respond to them based on the degree to which they perceive that the individual conforms to that prototype. This often happens when it comes to the issue of gender. People have prototypical ideas of what a "man" or a "woman" is. These prototypes represent idealized versions of masculinity and femininity. The degree to which an individual resembles one's prototype influences how one perceives and communicates with that person. One study found that for conservative voters, how feminine a female political candidate appears is associated with how likely she is to win an election (Hehman, Carpinella, Johnson, Leitner, & Freeman, 2014). For these voters, then, women who display traditionally feminine characteristics reflect their idealized version or prototype of women and they, therefore, favor them. Sarah Palin and Nikki Haley are both conservative politicians who display feminine characteristics and have been successfully elected to public office.

An interpersonal **script** is a relatively fixed sequence of events expected to occur; it functions as a guide or template for how to act in particular situations (Burgoon, Berger, & Waldron, 2000; Pearce, 1994). We develop scripts for activities we engage in frequently (Fehr, Baldwin, Collins, Patterson, & Benditt, 1999). Most people have a script for how to meet a new person. For example, when you first encounter a student you'd like to get to know, you probably introduce yourself, tell the person a basic fact about yourself such as "I live across the hall from you," and then ask a question such as "How do you like living on campus?" "What is your major?" or "Where is your home town?" Thus, you follow a routine of sorts.

script
A relatively fixed sequence of events that functions as a guide or template for communication or behavior.

We enact scripts because we find them comfortable, they are efficient, and they keep us from making too many social mistakes. Although many of the scripts we use will be familiar to others, we also tailor them to fit our own expectations for a situation. Our choice of script or the way we alter a script depends on our perceptions of others. We may use a different script to initiate a conversation with someone we perceive as friendly, attractive, and fun than with someone we perceive as shy, quiet, and withdrawn.

As this discussion suggests, cognitive representations help people navigate through the physical and social world. These maps provide guidelines that shape how we communicate with others through the schemas, prototypes, and interpersonal scripts we develop as we grow up and mature.

categorization
A cognitive process used to organize information by placing it into larger groupings of information.

▼ How do you perceive these two people? Do any stereotypes come to mind?

Categorization   Another type of cognitive process we use to organize information is **categorization**. Categorization is inherent to all languages. The linguistic symbols (or words) we use represent the groupings we see around us. Because it is impossible to remember everything, we use groupings that represent larger categories of information or objects (Goldstein, 2010; Lakoff, 1987).

For example, we lump a lot of information under the category of *restaurant*. What did you think of when you read the word *restaurant*? You probably envisioned a subcategory, such as a café or a pancake house. However, the concept of *restaurant* has certain features that apply to all subcategories, so that you know what is meant and what to expect when you go to one. You understand that *restaurant* refers to a place to eat and not a place to worship or attend classes. Forming and using categories allows us to understand and store information and makes us more efficient communicators.

Although grouping is a natural cognitive and perceptual process, it also can lead to misperceptions. Categorizing can cause one to reduce complex individuals to a single category or to expect them to behave in ways consistent with the category, regardless of the circumstance. For instance, you might categorize an individual based on your perception that the person is either smart and interesting or dull and boring. Once you reduce people to a category, you may communicate with them as if they possess no other characteristics. If you categorize one of your coworkers as dull and boring, you may only interact with her over tasks and never invite her to join you after work, where she might be able to show you that she actually is interesting and fun.

label

A name assigned to a category based on one's perception of the category.

When people categorize others, they typically also assign them a **label**. The two activities tend to go hand in hand. Thus, groups of people and the individuals within those groups may be labeled or described as jocks, sorority girls, hipsters, or nerds. Although labeling others can function as a useful shortcut, it also can lead to negative outcomes (Link & Phelan, 2001). When we label people, we run the risk of viewing them only through the lens of the label. The label also influences our expectations, evaluations, and responses to them. Labeling can cause problems even when the labels are positive, as was the case in *It Happened to Me: Lin Sue.*

When you were growing up, did your family have a label they used to describe you? Were you the smart one, the well-behaved one, or the goof-up? If you were labeled the goof-up, you may not have been given many opportunities to disprove the label, and your ideas may have been discounted even when they were valid. Because of such a label, you may have come to discount the value of your own ideas. This effect can be magnified when entire groups of people are labeled in ways that create problems, such as the labeling of British people as snobbish or Muslims as terrorists.

stereotyping

Creating schemas that overgeneralize attributes of a specific group.

As you may have guessed, labeling is related to stereotyping. **Stereotyping** occurs when schemas overgeneralize attributes of a group to which others belong (Cox, Abraham, Devine, & Hollon, 2012; Operario & Fiske, 2003). A stereotype is an assumption that every member of the group possesses certain characteristics. For example, you may assume that most females enjoy talking about fashion trends, so, you initiate a conversation with an unfamiliar woman by discussing *Vogue*. But not every member of a group fits the stereotype—if you use the fashion opener with every woman you meet, you may encounter some women who give you a blank stare in response.

Although grouping individuals makes it easy to remember information about them, it often leads to inaccurate beliefs and assumptions. Overgeneralizing a group's attributes makes it difficult to see the individuality of the people we encounter. Thus, a reliance on stereotypes can get those who use them into trouble.

It Happened to Me
Lin Sue

Because I am Chinese American, people often assume that I am some kind of whiz kid in academics. Well, I'm not. I was hit by a car when I was little, and I have residual brain impairment because of it. I have to study hard just to make passing grades. I get both angry and embarrassed when people assume I am this great student and imply that I will surely go to graduate school. I will feel fortunate if I just get out of undergraduate school. I really wish people wouldn't do this to me. They think they are being nice and complimentary, but they are still stereotyping me.

Interpretation

As we perceive and organize sensory information, we assign meaning to it (Goldstein, 2010). Returning to our previous example, imagine that you are awakened late at night. You hear a loud noise, which you determine is caused by a banging on your bedroom window. You now have to interpret what this means. Is it a tree branch? A loose shutter? Is it someone trying to break in?

We all assign meaning to the information we perceive, but we do not all necessarily assign the same meaning to similar information. One of the factors that influences how we interpret information is the frame through which we view it.

frame

Assumptions and attitudes that we use to filter perceptions to create meaning.

Frames The assumptions and attitudes we use to filter perceptions to create meaning are called **frames**. An individual's understanding of an event depends on the frame used to interpret it (Dillard, Solomon, & Samp, 1996). For example, if you are someone who frames the world as a dangerous place rife with criminals, you are likely to interpret that banging on your window as an indication of someone trying to break in. Similarly, if your friend frames the world as a place full of rude people, he may interpret your failure to say hello as a deliberate snub, whereas if his view is that people are nice, he may interpret your behavior as a failure to see him. In essence, individuals view the world through interpretive frames that then guide how they make sense of events (Dijk, 1977; Durfeel, 2006).

Individuals' frames develop over time, based on experience, interaction with others, and innate personality (Neale & Bazerman, 1991; Putnam & Holmer, 1992). Because we cannot perceive every aspect of an experience, frames also direct our attention toward some features of an episode and away from others. A bad mood, for example, directs attention to the negative aspects of an event. Usually, people don't become aware of frames until something happens to force them to replace one frame with another. If a friend points out that you are focusing only on the negative, you will become more aware of how your mood is framing, or focusing, your perceptions and interpretations. Your frame can change, then, as new information is introduced.

How should you use this information about framing? Now that you are aware that interpretations of people, events, and objects are influenced by an individual's specific frames, you should be more critical of your own interpretations. It is helpful to recognize that your interpretations (as well as others') do not necessarily represent the "truth"—but simply represent a particular way of viewing the world.

Frames are important elements of interpretation because they function as lenses that shape how observers understand people and events. But bear in mind that interpretation involves more than just framing; when individuals interpret events, they also offer explanations for them. When we develop explanations for our own and others' behaviors, we are engaged in making attributions. Let's see how this process works.

Attribution   How often do you wonder "why did she (or he) do that?" As we observe and interact with others, we spend considerable energy attempting to determine the causes of the behavior. For example, if your friend ignores you before class, you try to figure out why. At heart, most of us are amateur psychologists who search for the reasons people behave as they do. How confident are you regarding your attributions about specific others, such as your best friend or one of your parents?

Attribution theory explains the cognitive and verbal processes we use to judge our own and others' behavior (Manusov & Spitzberg, 2008). Fritz Heider (1958, 2013), a psychologist and professor, said that attribution is the process of drawing inferences. When individuals observe others, they immediately draw conclusions that go beyond mere sensory information. When someone cuts you off in traffic, what conclusion do you usually draw? What attribution would you make if you called your romantic partner at 3 A.M. and he or she wasn't home? Although we're constantly being told we shouldn't judge others, attribution theory says we can't help it (Griffin, 1994).

One attribution we often make is whether the cause of an individual's behavior is internal or external. An *internal* cause would be a personality characteristic, whereas an *external* cause would be situational.

We are particularly likely to make internal attributions when the behavior is unexpected—that is, when it is something that most other people would not do (Kelley, 1973). For instance, if someone laughs during a sad scene in a movie, people are more likely to attribute this unexpected reaction to a personality trait—for example, rudeness or insensitivity. But when the behavior fits our expectations, we are likely to attribute it to external causes. Therefore, if someone cries during a sad movie scene, people are likely to attribute the behavior to the movie.

In addition to expectations, attributions may also depend on whether we are the actor or observer of the behavior. A common mistake that occurs when we make

Critical Thinking Prompt
Are you an optimist or a pessimist? Do you think people are inherently generous or self-serving? The answers to these questions, and others like them, reveal how your beliefs help shape the frames you use and how, in turn, those frames influence the way you see—and respond to—the world. What other frames do you use that influence your perceptions?

attribution theory
Explanation of the processes we use to judge our own and others' behavior.

attributional bias

A cognitive bias that refers to the systematic errors made when people evaluate or try to find reasons for their own and others' behaviors.

self-serving bias

The tendency to give one's self more credit than is due when good things happen and to accept too little responsibility for those things that go wrong.

fundamental attribution error

The tendency to attribute others' negative behavior to internal causes and their positive behaviors to external causes.

overattribution

Selecting an individual's most obvious characteristic and using it to explain almost anything that person does.

ascriptions about behavior is called **attributional bias**. Attributional bias describes the systematic errors people make when they evaluate or try to find reasons for their own and others' behaviors. For example, we are more likely to attribute our own negative behavior to external causes and our positive actions to internal states (Harvey & Martinko, 2010). This is referred to as a **self-serving bias**. If you are polite, it is because you have good manners; if you are rude, it is because others mistreated you. Operating under this bias, we tend to give ourselves more credit than is due when good things happen, and we accept too little responsibility for those things that go wrong.

Most individuals are harsher judges of other people's behavior than they are of their own. We tend to attribute others' negative behavior to *internal* causes (such as their personality) and their positive behavior to *external* causes (such as the situation). This tendency is referred to as the **fundamental attribution error** (Schwarz, 2006). For example, when you are driving during rush hour traffic and someone cuts in front of you abruptly as two lanes merge, what attribution do you make about the other driver? According to fundamental attribution error, people are more likely to attribute the behavior to some trait internal to the other driver ("That driver is a jerk and is deliberately trying to get ahead of me") rather than to something external ("That driver is distracted by a child in the car and doesn't realize the lane is merging"). But if the other driver slows down to let you enter the merged lane first, most people might assume the driver was simply following the rules of the road rather than deliberately attempting to be thoughtful.

A third type of attribution error people engage in is called **overattribution**. Overattribution occurs when you select one or two obvious characteristics (such as an individual's sex, ethnicity, or age) and use them to explain almost anything that person does (Olivier, Leyens, Yzerbyt, & Walther, 1999). If your professor forgets a meeting with you and you attribute it to the fact that he is an "absent-minded professor," you likely are engaging in overattribution. Overattribution occurs because we use mental "shortcuts" to understand events around us. However, doing so has consequences. For example, you may remember that in 2012 George Zimmerman shot and killed teenager Trayvon Martin as he was walking back from a convenience store. What you may not remember is that Zimmerman saw Martin, an African American youth wearing a hoodie, and made an attribution that likely contributed significantly to what happened later. Before he confronted Martin, Zimmerman called 911 and said that Martin looked like "a real suspicious guy;" then he said "This guy looks like he's up to no good, or he's on drugs or something. It's raining, and he's just walking around." This utterance exemplifies how the over attribution operates—we see a person, we select one characteristic and make attributions about that person based on our preconceived, often stereotyped, beliefs about that characteristic. In this case, it appears that Zimmerman's attribution, or more properly his overattribution, about a young African American man wearing a hoodie, led to an encounter that ended with Zimmerman injured and Martin dead.

Typically, our attributions don't result in such dire consequences. However, when people who have power make overattributions about people of color, women, or those with disabilities, among others, it can result in unemployment, housing discrimination, and even violence for members of those groups.

▼ You are likely to attribute an internal cause to unexpected behavior—such as laughter during a sad movie.

When we make overattributions about others, we can hurt others even if we don't intend to.

Attributional biases have implications for the way people communicate and conduct relationships. For example, the types of attributions spouses make are linked to their feelings of marital satisfaction (Sillars, Roberts, Leonard, & Dun, 2000; 2002). Those in unhappy relationships tend to assume the spouse's negative behaviors are internal, or personality based, and difficult to change. Unfortunately, they also tend to view their spouse's positive behaviors as situational and temporary (Bradbury & Fincham, 1988). Thus, unhappy spouses often feel helpless to change their partner's negative characteristics. This pessimistic outlook can then increase negative communication within the relationship.

Interestingly, when people make attributions about others, they tend to trust the negative information they hear more than

It Happened to Me
Danika

I was at a party recently when I went up to this attractive guy and stood next to him. When he didn't seem to notice me, I introduced myself and tried talking to him. But he completely ignored me! I was so put off that I stomped away and started complaining to my friend Amira. I told her that the guy might be good looking, but he sure was full of himself. She looked puzzled. "Oh, were you standing on his left side?" she asked. When I told her yeah, she explained that he was deaf in his left ear and probably hadn't heard me. I felt bad that I had jumped to a negative attribution so quickly. Later, I approached him on his right side and talked to him; I found out he was a really nice guy.

the positive information (Lupfer, Weeks, & Dupuis, 2000). If you hear both positive and negative information about a classmate, you tend to remember and rely on the negative rather than the positive information to formulate your attributions. However, you are not confined to these faulty attributional processes; you can work to overcome them.

First, remember that none of us is a mind reader and that the attributions we make are not always accurate. Remain aware that attributions are really just guesses (even if they are educated guesses). It also helps if one remains aware of the self-serving bias and works to minimize it. Recognize that we all have a tendency to attribute our own positive actions to ourselves and others' negative actions to themselves. Look for alternative explanations for your own and others' behavior. Last, avoid overemphasizing the negative. People have a tendency to remember and to highlight the negative, so try to avoid the negative in your own comments and balance the positive against the negative in your evaluations of others. For an example of a mistaken attribution, see *It Happened to Me: Danika*.

**Journal Prompt 4.2:
Perception and
Interpretation**
Consider the following questions: How important is the role of interpretation in the perception process? What factors most influence how individuals interpret events?

Perception and the Individual

4.3 Name three individual factors that affect one's perceptual processes.

Thus far, we have explained how perceptions are formed: Individuals engage in selective attention, use a variety of organizational processes, and assign meaning to their perceptions. Thus, if you hear a loud noise in the street, you will turn your attention to the street; and if you see a car stopped and a person lying in the road with her motorcycle, you will categorize the event as an accident. Finally, you likely will decide (interpret) that the car hit the motorcycle rider. However, a variety of individual factors influence people's perceptual processes and affect their selection, organization, and interpretation of sensory input. For example, those who often ride motorcycles may attribute fault for the accident to the car driver (because they have frequently experienced inattentive auto drivers), whereas people who only drive cars may attribute blame to the motorcyclist (because they observed cyclists driving between lanes of cars on the road). The individual factors that influence our perceptual processes generally fall into three categories: physical, cognitive, and personality characteristics. Let's begin with the physical factors.

DID YOU KNOW?
The Ringtone Adults Cannot Hear

Are you familiar with Mosquito Ringtones? What are the implications of the Mosquito Teen Repellent and Mosquito Ringtone for communicating, perceiving, and understanding?

The Mosquito Ringtone is based on technology created by Britain Howard Stapleton, who developed a device described as the Mosquito Teen Repellent. The device emitted a high-pitched frequency tone that adults could not hear but that teenagers found annoying. It was used by shopkeepers to disperse teenagers from public spaces where they congregated.

Later, inventive students converted the same technology into a ringtone that adults could not hear. This allowed them to receive phone calls and text messages while in class without their teachers being aware of it—that is, provided their teachers were old enough.

To test your ability to hear Mosquito Ringtones at different frequency levels, go to http://www.freemosquitoringtone.org.

Physical Differences

Each person's unique physical capabilities affect what they perceive and how they understand it. Some people have more acute hearing than others, whereas some have more acute sight or taste. For example, professional wine tasters have a highly developed sense of taste, pilots are required to have 40/40 vision, and musicians must possess the ability to identify various pitches and notes. As mentioned previously, age can influence perception, and an individual's sex can affect the sensory input they notice.

Personality and Individual Characteristics

Each person's unique mix of personality, temperament, and experience also influences how they interpret and respond to sensory information. Elements that make up this mix include emotional state, outlook, and knowledge.

Emotional State If you are feeling happy or optimistic, you will tend to interpret and respond to sensory input differently than if you are feeling depressed, angry, or sad (Planalp, 1993). For instance, if you feel angry, you may perceive music, other people's voices, or background noise as irritating. By contrast, if you are in a positive mood, you may behave more helpfully toward others. In one experiment, researchers tested 800 passersby (Gueguen & De Gail, 2003). In half of the cases, researchers smiled at the passersby, and in half they did not. A few seconds after this interaction, the passersby had the opportunity to help another researcher who dropped his or her belongings on the ground. Those who were exposed to the smile in the first encounter were more likely to be helpful in the second. Thus, even a small impact on your emotional state can influence how you perceive and interact with others.

Outlook One's outlook refers to a tendency to view and interpret the world in consistent ways. Research shows that people tend to have a natural predisposition to either optimism or pessimism, based on genetics and experience (Seligman, 1998). People who are optimistic by nature may expect more positive experiences and make fewer negative attributions. These positive expectations can have an influence on their behavior—but not always for the best. For example, young people with an optimistic bias tend to believe that they are less likely than others to experience negative consequences from health behaviors. Therefore, they may be more likely than others to engage in sexual risk-taking (Chapin, 2001).

Knowledge People frequently interpret what they perceive based on what they know of an event. If you know that your friend has a big exam coming up, you may interpret his or her irritability as the result of nervousness. Our knowledge of specific topics also influences our perceptions, communication, and decision making. For instance, a study on organ donation revealed that members of families that discussed the subject were twice as likely to donate their organs as were members of other families (Smith, Kopfman, Lindsey, Massi, & Morrison, 2004). The researchers concluded that once people communicate and know more about the topic of organ donation, they perceive it in a more positive light.

Cognitive Complexity

As we discussed previously, the process of categorization helps us to organize information. Scientists refer to the categories we form as **constructs**. **Cognitive complexity** refers to how detailed, involved, or numerous a person's constructs are (Burleson & Caplan, 1998; Granello, 2010). But how does cognitive complexity affect perception?

First, people tend to be more cognitively complex about—and have more constructs for—those things that interest them or with which they have had experience. If you enjoy music, you likely have a wide range of constructs regarding types of music, such as rap, hip-hop, alternative, progressive, and neocountry, and these are constructs that others may not possess at all. This high number of constructs affects your perceptions of music. As you listen, you can distinguish between multiple forms of music, and you recognize when an artist is employing a specific form or fusing two or more.

One important purpose of education is to help you expand your constructs related to specific topics. As you progress through the chapters in this book and attend to your instructor's lectures and discussions, you will develop more constructs for communication. When you began this course, you may have had just one broad construct that you labeled "communication" that included all types of communication in which you engaged. By the time that you finish this course, you will have many categories or constructs to describe different types of communication, such as rhetoric, small group communication, interpersonal communication, and intercultural communication. Once you have these constructs, you will then be able to more easily develop them and increase your understanding of them and, ultimately, the communication process as whole. As you acquire new information about each of these constructs, you will have a structure in which to place and organize new information, which in turn will help you understand and remember that information. It might be helpful for you to think of constructs as folders that you use to organize information, and to which you refer later to help you understand a topic better.

In addition to these sets of personal constructs that help you interpret the world, you also possess *interpersonal constructs* that you use to make decisions and inferences about other people (Deutsch, Sullivan, Sage, & Basile, 1991). From an early age, everyone possesses simple constructs that help them organize their perceptions of others. These constructs tend to be bipolar, or based on opposing categories of characteristics, such as funny or serious, warm or cold, and responsible or careless. One's age, intellectual ability, and experiences influence how complex or detailed such constructs are. For example, very young children typically describe others with only a few constructs, such as nice or mean; most adults, however, have a much more involved set of constructs that allows them to describe others in more varied and specific ways, such as thoughtful, amusing, argumentative, or kind.

When you have cognitively complex construct systems, you tend to have many ways of explaining and understanding interpersonal interactions. Suppose, for example, that your friend Laura was almost an hour late meeting you for a dinner date. If you are cognitively complex, you might come up with a number of reasons to explain this behavior: Laura (a) was in a traffic accident, (b) forgot about the date, (c) was detained by an unforeseen event, (d) decided not to keep the date, and so on. These are all plausible explanations; without further information you will not know which one is correct. The point is that cognitively complex individuals can develop a large set of alternative explanations while they wait for more information to clarify the situation.

constructs
Categories people develop to help them organize information.

cognitive complexity
The degree to which a person's constructs are detailed, involved, or numerous.

Critical Thinking Prompt
Do you wonder how cognitively complex your interpersonal constructs are? To find out, think of a person you know well. Then for the next sixty seconds, write down as many terms as you can think of to describe that person. How many terms were you able to generate? How many different categories of terms were you able to list? (For example, *nice, kind, thoughtful* would group into one category as would athletic, physically fit, sporty.) Typically, the more terms and categories of terms you can generate, the more cognitively complex your interpersonal constructs are believed to be.

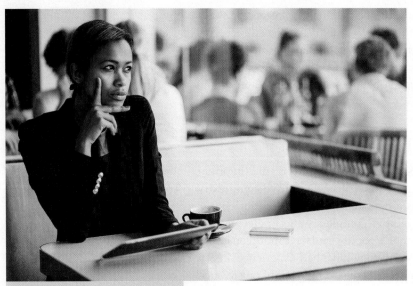

▲ Cognitively complex individuals can develop a large number of explanations for the late arrival of a dinner date.

**Journal Prompt 4.3:
Cognitive Complexity**
Consider the following question:
What is cognitive complexity, and how does it influence the perception process?

In turn, your degree of cognitive complexity influences your perceptions and thus your communication behavior. For example, if you can only explain Laura's lateness by deciding that she is thoughtless, you will likely perceive her negatively and use a hostile communication style when you meet. Individuals' levels of complexity influence a broad range of communicative issues, such as how many persuasive messages they can generate (Applegate, 1982) and how well they can comfort others (Holmstrom & Burleson, 2010; Samter & Burleson, 1984).

Your perceptions strongly shape your communication and your actions. If you strike up a conversation with someone new who looks physically attractive but whose voice reminds you of someone you dislike, you may choose to end the conversation and move on. However, if you meet someone who reminds you of someone you like, you might invest energy in getting to know that person. If you interpret a new friend's teasing as a sign of affection, you may decide to increase your involvement with her. In these ways, your perceptual processes influence your interactions and relationships. In addition, broader societal factors also play a role in what you perceive, how you organize it, and the meanings you attach to it.

The Individual, Perception, and Society

4.4 Articulate how power, culture, social comparisons, and historical time period influence perception.

How do societal factors affect perception? As we will explain in this section, the position individuals hold in society and the cultures in which they live affect what they perceive and how they interpret these perceptions. As you read this section, we encourage you to consider the societal forces that affect your perceptions as well as how they might affect the perceptions of others.

The Role of Power

Every society has a hierarchy, and in a hierarchy some people have more power than others. Your relative position of power or lack of power influences how others perceive you, how you perceive others, and how you interpret events in the world. Moreover, those in power largely determine a society's understandings of reality. For example, in the United States, the dominant perception is that everyone can move up in society through hard work and education ("Middle of the Class," 2005). However, individuals who are born poor and who live in deprived areas with few resources can find upward mobility to be difficult, no matter how hard they try to follow the path to "success" as defined by mainstream U.S. culture. Thus, the perceptual reality of these people is likely to differ from that of those higher in the power hierarchy. Nonetheless, a specific view of reality dominates U.S. culture because it is communicated both explicitly and implicitly through media messages, public speeches, schools, and other social institutions.

One's individual experiences within that hierarchy may lead one to accept or reject that dominant perception. For example, middle-class people may believe that if they work hard they will get ahead in society, whereas poor people may perceive that it takes a lot more than hard work and education (Ehrenreich, 2001). Similarly, if you grew up relatively wealthy, you may believe that your admission to a highly selective college is largely as a result of your intelligence, hard work, and skills, whereas someone who grew up relatively poor may believe that social connections and family money better explain this achievement (Douthat, 2005).

Your position in the racial hierarchy also influences your perceptions, such as about the reality of racial bias. It is well documented that white Americans and African Americans have different perceptions regarding the role of race in the United States (Hacker, 2003). A study conducted after Hurricane Katrina devastated the Gulf Coast revealed a broad divergence in perceptions: When asked whether racial inequality remains a major problem, 71 percent of African Americans replied yes, compared to only 32 percent of whites (Pew Research Center for the People and the Press, 2005).

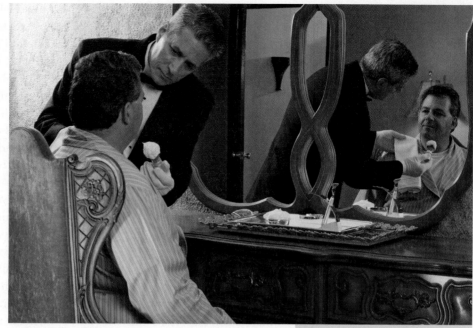

▲ Power differences affect people's perceptions of how easy or difficult it is to attain financial success.

The Role of Culture

Culture strongly influences individual perception. One way it does so is through its *sensory model*. Every culture has its own sensory model, which means that each culture emphasizes a few of the five senses (Classen, 1990). Moreover, what a culture emphasizes affects what its members pay attention to and prefer. People in the United States, for example, tend to give primacy to the visual; thus, we have sayings such as "seeing is believing," and students almost demand that professors use PowerPoint slides in the classroom. By contrast, people living in the Andes Mountains of South America tend to place more emphasis on what they hear than on what they see. In their culture, important ideas are transmitted through characters in stories and narratives (Classen, 1990). Knowing this, how do you think students in the Andes prefer to learn? You might imagine that they would prefer elaborate stories rather than a list of brief terms and concepts on PowerPoint slides.

A culture is composed of a set of shared practices, norms, values, and beliefs (Brislin, 2000; Shore, 1996), which in turn helps shape individuals' thoughts, feelings, perceptions, and behaviors. For example, individuals in East Asian cultures often are highly interdependent and emphasize the group over the individual. Consequently, they don't approve of bragging and encourage greater self-criticism than some other cultures. By encouraging self-criticism (and then working on self-improvement), the thinking goes, they are contributing to the overall strength of the group (Heine & Lehman, 2004; Markus, Mullally, & Kitayama, 1997). In the United States, however, the emphasis is often on the individual, and most people are encouraged to distinguish themselves from others. For example, current books on dating and work success teach U.S. Americans how to "brand" themselves like a product. The dominant culture in the United States also encourages people to talk about their success and to refrain from self-criticism. As a result, someone from East Asia may see U.S. Americans as braggarts, whereas a person from the United States may see East Asians as overly modest (Kim, 2002).

Cultural background also influences how people expect to talk to one another (Scollon & Wong-Scollon, 1990). In some Native American cultures, for example,

▲ Some travelers become upset when their cultural expectations about what is "food" are not fulfilled.

individuals perceive strangers as potentially unpredictable, so they may talk little—if at all—until they have established familiarity and trust with the newcomer (Braithwaite, 1990). This approach differs considerably from the customs of some European American cultures, in which people view strangers as potential friends and strike up conversations to become acquainted with them (Krivonos & Knapp, 1975).

Now imagine a Native American and a European American from these different communication cultures meeting for the first time. How is each likely to behave? The Native American may remain relatively quiet while observing the new person. The European American will most likely try to engage in a lively conversation and may ask a number of questions to draw the other person out. As a result, the Native American may view the European American as nosy, pushy, and overly familiar, whereas the European American may see the Native American as unfriendly or shy (Braithwaite, 1990). Each perceives or evaluates the other based on expectations that were shaped by his or her own cultural perceptions, values, and the meanings typical for his or her own culture (Scollon & Wong-Scollon, 1990).

Cultural norms, values, and expectations provide a backdrop of familiarity. When we travel or when we meet people from other cultures close to home, we can learn from exposure to our differences. However, sometimes these differences are upsetting, frustrating, or baffling. For example, one of our students, Simone, was taken aback when she was offered *chapulines* (fried grasshoppers) during her trip to Oaxaca, Mexico. Take a look at some foods common in other parts of the world that most people in the United States likely consider strange, if not simply disgusting, such as haggis or head cheese. How much does your own ethnocentrism factor into your personal reaction to each of these foods? Interestingly, most of us not only value the ways of our own culture, we often feel that others' cultural norms are less desirable—or even wrong—an issue we discuss next.

The Role of Social Comparison

As we discussed previously, categorizing groups of objects, information, or people is a basic quality of perception. *Social* categorization—or categorizing people—leads us to specific expectations about how others should or should not behave. These social categories and the expectations associated with them typically arise out of our culture and where we are positioned in the culture. Every culture has rules and expectations that its members take for granted. Because we become socialized to our culture and its rules at a very young age—so much so that most of it is absorbed subconsciously—we are not aware that our rules and expectations are learned. Instead, we feel as if they are simply "right" and that other rules and expectations are "wrong." For example, in the United States, people in different social classes have varying expectations or understandings for why people receive government subsidies for food or housing. Individuals who are middle and upper-middle class often perceive those who receive these subsidies as people who do not want to work hard, and they may therefore categorize them as lazy or dependent. However, people who are in the working class or among the working poor may have different perceptions, asserting that those who rely on these government subsidies work hard but are underemployed or have to live on a salary that is not a living wage ("Middle of the Class," 2005; Ehrenreich, 2001). Similarly, in the United States, youth is typically valued over age so older people may be seen as less competent or valuable. As a result, elders often are perceived as poor job candidates and as a burden on families and societies. In other cultures, such as Korean, Greek, and Native American, aging is celebrated and elders are respected. If you are from one of these cultures, you may perceive that U.S. Americans are misguided or even wrong in their treatment of the elderly. As you can see, the perceptions and categories that we develop tend to be tied to stereotypes and prejudice, which both flow from ethnocentrism, the perceptual concept at the core of social comparison.

Ethnocentrism   Most people view their own group as the standard against which they evaluate others. Thus, one's own ethnic, regional, or class group is the one that seems right, correct, or normal. This tendency to view one's own group as the standard against which all others are judged is described as **ethnocentrism**. It comes from the Greek words *ethnos*, which means nation, and *kentron*, which refers to the center of a circle (Ting-Toomey, 1999). People behave ethnocentrically when they view their own values, norms, or modes of belief and behavior as better than those of other groups.

ethnocentrism

The tendency to view one's own group as the standard against which all other groups are judged.

Although it is normal to be proud of one's national, cultural, racial, or ethnic group, one becomes ethnocentric when he or she engages in polarized thinking and behavior. This occurs when people believe that if "we" are right, correct, normal, and even superior, then "they" must be wrong, incorrect, abnormal, and inferior. Such thinking can seriously interfere with our ability to communicate effectively with those outside our group.

Stereotypes   Previously we described stereotypes as broad generalizations about an entire class of objects or people, based on some knowledge of some aspects of some members of the class (Brislin, 2000; Stephan & Stephan, 1992). When you stereotype computer programmers as smart but socially inept, you likely are basing your beliefs on your interactions with a few programmers—or perhaps on no interactions at all. Stereotypes may be based on what you have read, images in the media, or information you have obtained from others, as you'll see was the case with one college student in *It Happened to Me: Damien*.

If you develop a stereotype, it tends to influence what you expect from the stereotyped group. If you believe that someone is a lesbian, you may also believe she engages in specific types of communication behavior, dress, or interests. When you hold these types of beliefs and expectations, they tend to erase the stereotyped person's individual characteristics. In addition, you are likely to communicate with her as if your stereotypes were accurate rather than basing your messages on her actual interests and behavior (Snyder, 1998).

Stereotyping is an understandable and natural cognitive activity; in fact, stereotypes can serve as useful shorthand to help us understand the world. If you are interviewing for a job in the southern United States, it may be helpful for you to know that many Southerners prefer to engage in social interaction before getting down to business (though this is certainly not always true). However, when stereotyping leads to polarized understandings of the world as "between me and you, us and them, females and males, blacks

It Happened to Me
Damien

Shortly after school started, I decided to join a fraternity and began going to parties on the weekends. Often when people heard me mention that I was a part-time computer programmer, they would first look shocked and then crack some kind of joke about it, like, "Bill Gates, Jr., eh?" I guess it surprises people that I don't have glasses, that I am a person of color, and that I engage in some social activities! I realize that their preconceived notions about "techies" have come from somewhere, but, since at least half of my fellow "computer geeks" are far from the nerdy stereotype, it would be nice if people would recognize that we aren't all pale, glasses-wearing, socially awkward nerds!

and whites," then it can cause problems (Ting-Toomey, 1999, p. 149). In turn, polarized thinking frequently leads to a rigid, intolerant view of certain behavior as correct or incorrect (Ting-Toomey, 1999). For example, do you believe it is more appropriate for adult children to live on their own than with their parents before they marry? People with polarized thinking assume that their own cultural beliefs regarding this issue are right or correct instead of recognizing that cultures differ in what is considered appropriate.

prejudice

Experiencing aversive or negative feelings toward a group as a whole or toward an individual because she or he belongs to a group.

Prejudice   Stereotypes and feelings of ethnocentrism often lead to prejudice. **Prejudice** occurs when people experience aversive or negative feelings toward a group as a whole or toward an individual because she or he belongs to a particular group (Rothenberg, 1992). People can experience prejudice against a person or group because of his or her physical characteristics, perceived ethnicity, age, national origin, religious practices, and a number of other identity categories.

Given the negative associations most people have with the concept of prejudice, you may wonder why it persists. Researchers believe that prejudice is common and pervasive because it serves specific functions, the two most important of which are *ego-defensive functions* and *value-expressive functions* (Brislin, 2000). Let's explore these concepts.

ego-defensive function

The role prejudice plays in protecting individuals' sense of self-worth.

The **ego-defensive function** of prejudice describes the role it plays in protecting individuals' sense of self-worth. For example, an individual who is not financially successful and whose group members tend not to be financially successful may attribute blame to other groups for hoarding resources and preventing him or her from becoming successful. The less financially successful individual may also look down on groups that are even less financially successful as a way to protect his or her own ego. These attitudes may make people feel better, but they also prevent them from analyzing reasons for their own failure. Moreover, they negatively affect the ways people talk to and about the targeted groups. People who look down on groups that are less financially successful may describe them and talk to them as if they were lazy, incompetent, or not very bright.

value-expressive function

The role played by prejudice in allowing people to view their own values, norms, and cultural practices as appropriate and correct.

Prejudice serves its **value-expressive function** by allowing people to view their own values, norms, and cultural practices as appropriate and correct. By devaluing other groups' behavior and beliefs, people maintain a solid sense that they are right. Unfortunately, this same function causes group members to denigrate the cultural practices of others. You may have seen many examples of the value-expressive function of prejudice, as when individuals engage in uncivil arguments and personal attacks over issues such as men's and women's roles, abortion, and politics.

The Role of Historical Time Period

In addition to a person's place in the power hierarchy, his or her culture, and his or her awareness of social comparison, the historical period in which one grows up and lives influences perception and communication (U.S. National Research Council, 1989). For example, anyone living in the United States who was older than five or six on September 11, 2001, likely has had their perceptions altered by events of that day. They may feel less safe, perceive air travel as riskier, and feel more patriotic than they did before the terrorist attacks on that day. These perceptions may in turn influence how they talk about the United States, or how they communicate, for example, with individuals who are Muslim.

Other historical events have affected the perceptions of individuals who lived through them. For instance, people who lived through the Great Depression may perceive resources as being scarcer than others do; those who were young during the Vietnam War likely believe that collective action can influence political policy; and those who grew up watching "The Real World" and other reality TV programs probably view privacy differently than do prior generations. As you might expect, these perceptions influence how, and about what, the various generations communicate, a process called the **cohort effect**. Thus, those who came of age after 2000 may feel comfortable discussing a wide range of topics previously considered taboo, such as sexual conduct or family dysfunction. Similarly, women who grew up when sexual discrimination was more prevalent might object to the use of "girls" when referring to women.

cohort effect
The process by which historical events influence the perceptions of people who grew up in a given generation and time period.

Social Roles

The roles one plays socially also influence one's perception, and consequently, communication. **Social role** refers to the specific position or positions that an individual holds in a society. Social roles include job positions, familial roles (such as mother or father), and positions in society. For example, Teri holds a variety of roles, including mother, religious leader, soccer coach, and community activist. The fact that she holds these social roles affects how people perceive and communicate with her in several ways. First, society defines specific expectations for her various social roles (Kirouac & Hess, 1999). Many people, for example, expect that religious leaders will be especially moral, selfless, and well intentioned. In turn, these expectations affect the ways that religious leaders interact with others. If you expect Teri, as a religious leader, to be highly moral, she may work to communicate with you in ways that fulfill your expectations.

social role
The specific position or positions one holds in a society.

Second, the education, training, and socialization Teri undergoes for her social roles influence her perceptions. In much of U.S. culture, it is expected that women will become mothers and that they will behave in specific ways as they fulfill that role. As they grow up, girls are socialized and taught—by both word and example—how mothers are supposed to communicate. Because Teri is a parent, she may perceive different issues as important. For example, she may be more concerned with the quality of schools, the safety of her neighborhood, and access to health care than a nonparent might. Similarly, when individuals receive education and training, their perceptions of the world around them are affected. A person trained as a police officer, for example, may perceive the world as populated with more criminals than the average person does; whereas a person trained as a nurse may be more aware of how to prevent illnesses and injuries.

Each individual's perceptions are unique, based on his or her own roles and characteristics. However, individuals also share certain perceptual realities with others in their power position in society's hierarchy as well as with others in their cultures and social role groups. Because of these differing realities and power positions, your perceptions may lead you into prejudicial and intolerant thinking and communication. In the concluding section of this chapter, we suggest strategies for improving your perception processes and communication.

Journal Prompt 4.4: Social Comparison
Consider the following questions: What is social comparison? How is it related to ethnocentrism and prejudice?

Ethics and Perception

4.5 Explain why ethics is relevant to the perception process.

As we've discussed throughout this chapter, the ways people communicate to and about others are connected to their perceptions and cognitions about them. That is, what we select to attend to, what categories we put people in, and the attributions we make about them all strongly influence what we believe, say, and do. For example, Tara was driving home late one night and stopped at a traffic light when she noticed a young man of color in the car next to hers. She reached over and locked her door. As she looked up, she saw the man smile slightly then lean over and lock *his* door. In this case, Tara was responding based on stereotypical perceptions and cognitions, and the other driver was gently reminding her of that fact.

A common example of a time when perception, ethics, and communication intersect occurs when speakers perceive and label other groups of people negatively and then use derogatory terms to refer to them. Unfortunately, using such terms can reinforce and even intensify one's own, as well as others', negative responses to these groups. In addition, if what individuals attend to and perceive about people first is their skin color, their sex, or their relative affluence, they may find themselves communicating with those people stereotypically and failing to recognize other roles they fulfill. Doing so may lead one to assume and communicate as if all adult women are mothers (or there is something wrong with them if they are not) or to refer to a physician as nurse because she happens to be female. Each of these behaviors is problematic in that it denies others their right to legitimate identities. Consequently, such behaviors are ones that are usefully examined through an ethical lens. That is, when tempted to create stereotypes of others and to communicate with them based on that stereotype, it helps to ask yourself if doing so fits within your own ethical framework.

Although social factors such as power and position can impact many aspects of your life, you do have control of, and responsibility for, your perceptions and cognitions. Even though your social circle and your family may engage in problematic perceptual, cognitive, and communicative processes, once you become an adult you are responsible for how you interpret the world. To help you think about your perceptions and cognitive processes through an ethical lens, we discuss some guidelines to assist you in this process.

Journal Prompt 4.5: Ethics in Perception
Consider the following question: How are ethics relevant to the perception process?

Improving Your Perception Skills

4.6   Identify three ways you can improve your perception skills.

You probably realize now that perceptions are subject to variance and error because of the variety of steps one goes through in forming them (selection, organization, and interpretation) and the range of factors that influence the perception process (individual characteristics, cognitive complexity, power, culture, historical time period, and social roles). However, certain cognitive and communication behaviors can improve one's ability to perceive and understand the world.

▼ One communication act that can improve your perception skills is checking with others to see if their perceptions are similar to yours.

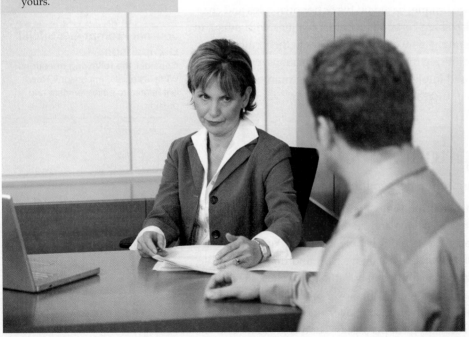

First, one can engage in *mindfulness* to improve perception and understanding. Mindfulness refers to a clear focus on the activity one is engaged in, with attention to as many specifics of the event as possible (Langer, 1978). People tend to be most mindful when they are engaged in a new or unusual activity. Once an activity becomes habitual, we are likely to overlook its details. Mindfulness requires that one bring the same level of attention and involvement to routine activities as one does to novel ones.

In addition, before assuming your perceptions are accurate, you might ask yourself a few questions to help you check those perceptions:

- Have you focused too narrowly and missed relevant information as a result of selective attention? For example, did you focus on what the person was wearing rather than what he or she was saying?
- What type of organizational pattern did you use? For example, just because two people are standing next to one another does not mean they are together.
- To what extent have you considered all possible interpretations for the information you perceived, using the full range of your cognitive complexity? For example, if you did poorly on a test, was it as a result of poor test construction, your lack of sleep, the teacher's failure to prepare you, or your own failure to study sufficiently?
- How might your physical condition have influenced your perceptions? For example, are you tired, hungry, or frightened?
- How has your cultural background influenced your perceptions? For example, are you perceiving politeness as deception?
- How has your social role influenced your perception? For example, have you begun to perceive all elderly people as infirm because you work in a nursing home?
- How has your social position influenced your perception? For example, have you considered how others with different positions might perceive the same issue?

Another way to improve one's perception and understanding is to clearly separate *facts* from *inferences*. Facts are truths that are verifiable based on observation. Inferences are conclusions that we draw or interpretations we make based on the facts. Thus, it may be a fact that Southerners speak more slowly than do people from other regions of the United States, but it is an inference if you conclude that their slow speech indicates slow thought processes.

Finally, one communication act in particular will greatly improve anyone's perception skills: *perception checking*. You engage in perception checking by communicating with others to determine if their perceptions match your own. If they do not, you may need to alter your perceptions. Perception checking is a way of communicating that allows you test your assumptions about what another person has said or done. When you engage in second-person perception checking, you seek feedback directly from the person you have spoken with or observed. In this situation, you may find this four-step procedure to be helpful:

- Describe the other person's behavior as you saw it. *When I texted you yesterday, you didn't respond.*
- State your interpretation of that behavior. *It made me wonder if you are angry with me.*
- Ask if your interpretation is accurate. *Are you mad at me?*
- If not, ask why your interpretation was inaccurate. *Why didn't you respond?*

Another type of perception checking occurs when you ask one or more people how they perceive a third party or an event. For example, Rosario once had an extremely negative reaction to a job candidate who interviewed at her company. She perceived him as arrogant and sexist. However, when she talked with her colleagues she discovered that no one else had a similarly strong negative response to the candidate. She decided that her perceptions must have been influenced by something in her own background; for example, he may have reminded her of someone she had once known who did display those negative traits. In revising her opinion of the candidate, Rosario demonstrated a well-developed sensitivity to the perception side of communication. All of us can benefit from greater awareness of the assumptions and attributions we make.

**Journal Prompt 4.6:
Perception Skills**
Consider the following questions:
What one skill could you develop that would most improve your perception processes? Why would it help?

SUMMARY

4.1 Explain why understanding perception is important.

- Perception plays an important role in everyday communication.

4.2 Describe the three processes people use to understand information collected through the senses.

- People use three perceptual processes to manage the vast array of sensory data in their environments: selection, organization, and interpretation.

4.3 Name three individual factors that affect one's perceptual processes.

- The sensory data we select to attend to, how we organize it, and the interpretations we assign are all influenced by our individual characteristics, such as physical abilities and differences, cognitive complexity, and personality and individual differences.

4.4 Articulate how power, culture, social comparison, and historical time period influence perception.

- Perception processes are affected by one's position in the power hierarchy, culture, social comparisons, historical events during one's lifetime, and social roles.

4.5 Explain why ethics is relevant to the perception process.

- Perception, ethics, and communication intersect when speakers perceive and label other groups of people negatively and then use derogatory terms to refer to them.
- Using such terms can reinforce and even intensify one's own as well as others' negative responses to these groups.

4.6 Identify three ways you can improve your perception skills.

- You can improve your perception skills by engaging in mindfulness, separating facts from inferences, and concentrating on perception checking.

KEY TERMS

perception p. 74
selection p. 74
organization p. 74
interpretation p. 74
selective attention p. 74
primacy effect p. 75
recency effect p. 75
cognitive representation p. 76
schemas p. 76
prototype p. 76

script p. 77
categorization p. 77
label p. 78
stereotyping p. 78
frame p. 78
attribution theory p. 79
attributional bias p. 80
self-serving bias p. 80
fundamental attribution error p. 80
overattribution p. 80

constructs p. 83
cognitive complexity p. 83
ethnocentrism p. 87
prejudice p. 88
ego-defensive function p. 88
value-expressive function p. 88
cohort effect p. 89
social role p. 89

APPLY WHAT YOU KNOW

1. **Examining Stereotypes** For each of the words, write down your beliefs about the group represented. In other words, provide a list of specific characteristics you believe are typically displayed by members of these groups.

   a. fraternity members
   b. politicians
   c. models
   d. rap stars
   e. body builders
   f. religious leaders

   After you have done so, compare your list to the lists created by other members of your class. What characteristics for each group did you have in common? What characteristics differed? Can you think of at least one person from each group who does not display the characteristics you listed? What information and perceptions helped shaped your stereotypes? How valid do you think your stereotypes are?

2. **Attributional Biases** As this chapter explains, people have a tendency to attribute their own positive behavior to internal traits and their negative behavior to external factors. However, they are also more likely to attribute others' positive behavior to external conditions and others' negative behavior to internal traits. In this exercise we want you to indicate how the attributional bias would cause you to describe each of the following behaviors, depending on who had performed it.

   Example: Forgetting to make a phone call
   I'm busy. You're thoughtless.
   Example: Earning a good grade
   I'm intelligent. You were lucky.
   Do the exercise for each of the following behaviors/events:

   a. Receiving a raise
   b. Breaking a vase
   c. Arriving late
   d. Winning an award
   e. Burning a meal
   f. Making a group laugh

   Compare your responses with those of others in your class. What terms were used to describe one's own experiences? What terms were used to describe others' experiences? What is it about the perception process that makes attributional bias so common?

   Although this is just an exercise, remember that attributional bias is quite common. Pay attention to your own thoughts and comments the next time something bad happens to you or others.

3. **Ethics and Perception** The authors argue that ethics is relevant to our perceptual processes. To what extent do you agree or disagree with this statement? Provide three arguments for each position. Now that you have considered arguments for both positions, is your opinion the same as it was before or has it altered?

EXPLORE

1. Go to a website that features perception exercises and information, such as the Hanover College Sensation and Perception Tutorials or the Encyclopedia of Psychology's Sensation and Perception tutorial. After experiencing at least two of the tutorials, write a paragraph in which you explain what you have learned about perception.

2. Go to a website such as Gestalt Laws or Perceptual Grouping and read the information regarding the Gestalts laws of grouping. In a brief paper, provide an explanation of the Gestalt laws, then describe how these laws might influence how we view and communicate with others.

Verbal Communication

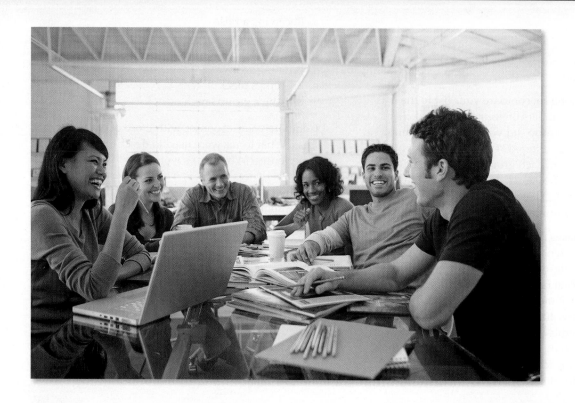

⌄ LEARNING OBJECTIVES

5.1 Identify three reasons for learning about verbal communication.

5.2 Describe the functions and components of language.

5.3 Identify and give examples of several major influences on verbal communication.

5.4 Describe the relationships between language, perception, and power.

5.5 Identify and give examples of confirming communication, disconfirming communication, and hate speech.

5.6 Discuss ways to improve your own verbal communication skills.

CHAPTER TOPICS

The Importance of Verbal Communication

What Is Verbal Communication? Functions and Components

The Individual and Verbal Communication: Influences

The Individual, Verbal Communication, and Society: Language, Perception, and Power

Ethics and Verbal Communication

Improving Your Verbal Communication Skills

> *The verbal elements of communication are the foundation*
> *on which meaning is created.*

When Charee texts her friends, she knows that her verbal communication changes from when she speaks to them face to face. She uses "lol" and other such "Netspeak" abbreviations, and she makes sure that she doesn't use complete sentences. This is true as well when she is using Twitter, which limits her to 140 characters. Even with other social media sites, she keeps her messages brief. But when she writes a paper for class, she knows that she needs to change the way she uses her verbal communication skills. She needs to use complete sentences and formal language, without using Netspeak.

When we think of "communication," we tend to think about the verbal elements of communication: the words people choose, the accents they speak with, and the meanings they convey through language. We frequently don't consider the ways in which verbal communication assists or hinders relationship development, the technology we use, or its effect on the creation of identities.

In this chapter we will explore the verbal elements of communication and how people use verbal communication to accomplish various goals. First we discuss the importance of verbal communication and its value as a topic of study. We then describe how individuals use verbal communication, including the functions it serves and the components of language that make it possible. Next we explore individual characteristics that influence verbal communication, such as gender, age, regionality, ethnicity and race, and education and occupation. We investigate the societal forces that influence verbal communication by examining the relationships among language, perception, and power. Finally, we provide suggestions for communicating more ethically and more effectively.

The Importance
of Verbal Communication

5.1   Identify three reasons for learning about verbal communication.

Although the nonverbal aspects of communication are important, the verbal elements of communication are the foundation on which meaning is created. If you doubt that this is the case, try this simple test. Using only nonverbal communication, convey this message to a friend or roommate: "I failed my exam because I locked my keys in my car and couldn't get my textbook until well after midnight." How well was your nonverbal message understood? If you have ever traveled in a country where you didn't speak the language, no doubt you already knew before trying this experiment that nonverbal communication can only get you so far. Similarly, although you may try to incorporate emoticons or other devices to mimic nonverbals, the verbal elements of messages are vital in texting, email, and many social networking sites. We will touch on the

▲ Children from families who converse and eat meals together on a regular basis have higher self-esteem and interact better with their peers.

importance of nonverbal communication here and discuss it in depth in Chapter 6. In this section we propose that to be a highly effective communicator you need to understand the verbal elements of communication.

Verbal communication is also important because of the role it plays in identity and relationship development. As you might remember from our discussion in Chapter 3, individuals develop a sense of self through communication with others. More specifically, the labels used to describe individuals can influence their self-concepts and increase or decrease their self-esteem. People's verbal communication practices also can impede or improve their relationships, which is a topic we will discuss further in Chapter 9. Research by four psychology professors at Emory University supports our claims about the relationship between verbal communication and an individual's identity development and relationship skills. These scholars found that families that converse and eat meals together on a regular basis have children who not only are more familiar with their family histories but also tend to have higher self-esteem, interact better with their peers, and are better able to recover from tragedy and negative events (Duke, Fivush, Lazarus, & Bohanek, 2003).

It Happened to Me
Cristina

I was teaching an adult education class composed primarily of Mexican immigrants when I first noticed that the language people speak affects how they behave. I'm bilingual, so even though we normally spoke English in my class, sometimes we switched to Spanish. Over time, I noticed that several male students were respectful and deferential when we spoke English; however, when we switched to Spanish, they became more flirtatious and seemed less willing to treat me as an authority figure. Now I understand that these differences probably were related to how men and women interact in the two cultures.

Journal Prompt 5.1: Studying Verbal Communication
Consider the following question:
What are three reasons for learning about verbal communication?

In addition, the very language people speak is tied to their identities. Studies of bilingual and multilingual speakers show that their perceptions, behaviors, and even personalities alter when they change languages (Ramírez-Esparza, Gosling, Benet-Martínez, Potter, & Pennebaker, 2006). Why does this occur? The answer is that every language is embedded in a specific cultural context, and when people learn a language, they also learn the beliefs, values, and norms of its culture (Edwards, 2004). So speaking a language evokes its culture as well as a sense of who we are within that culture. Thus the language you use to communicate verbally shapes who you are, as you will see in *It Happened to Me: Cristina.*

What Is Verbal Communication? Functions and Components of Language

5.2   Describe the functions and components of language.

Verbal communication generally refers to the written or oral words we exchange; however, as our opening example shows, verbal communication has to do with more than just the words people speak. It includes pronunciation or accent, the meanings of the words used, and a range of variations in the way people speak a language, which depend on their regional backgrounds and other factors.

Language, of course, plays a central role in communication. Some argue that it is our use of language that makes us human. Unlike other mammals, humans use symbols that they can string together to create new words and with which they can form infinite sets of never-before-heard thought, or read sentences.

This ability allows people to be creative and expressive, such as when they take ordinary words and use them in new ways. For example, the word robo sapiens—nominated by the American Dialect Society as one of the most creative words for 2013—refers to a class of robots with human intelligence. This is a play on the words homo sapiens for humans and robo for robot. Even small children who are unschooled in grammar create their own rules of language by using innate linguistic ability together with linguistic information they glean from the people around them. For example, young children often say "mouses" instead of "mice" because they first learn, and apply broadly, the most common rule for pluralizing—adding an *s*.

To help you better understand the role of language in the communication process, the next section explores seven communicative functions of language as well as four components of language use.

Functions of Language

We all use language so automatically that we usually don't think about the many roles it plays. However, language helps us do everything from ordering lunch to giving directions to writing love poems. Moreover, a single utterance can function in a variety of ways. For example, a simple "thank you" not only expresses gratitude, it also can increase feelings of intimacy and liking. Consequently, understanding the ways language functions can help you communicate more effectively. As we discuss next, language can serve at least seven functions: instrumental, regulatory, informative, heuristic, interactional, personal, and imaginative.

- The most basic function of language is **instrumental**. This means we can use it to obtain what we need or desire. For instance, when you send an e-vite to your friends to a party to celebrate a birthday, the invitation is instrumental in that you want your friends to come to the party and the invitation helps make that happen.

- A second (and closely related) language function is **regulatory**, meaning that we can use it to control or regulate the behaviors of others. In your invitation, you may ask your friends to bring a bottle of wine or a dessert to the party, as a way of regulating their behavior.

- Another basic function of language is to **inform**—to communicate information or report facts. When you invite your friends to the party, you usually include the date and time to inform them of when you want them to come.

- We also use language to acquire knowledge and understanding, which is referred to as a **heuristic** use. When you want to invite friends, you may ask them to respond to indicate if they are available at that date and time to learn if your party is going to occur as scheduled or if you need to make some changes.

- When language is used in an **interactional** fashion, it establishes and defines social relationships in both interpersonal and group settings. Thus, when you invite your friends to a celebration, you engage in a behavior that helps maintain your relationship with them as friends.

- **Personal language** expresses individuality and personality and is more common in private than in public settings. When you invite your friends to the party, you might jokingly add a private message to one, "Don't bring a cheap bottle of wine, like you did last time." In this way, you use language to express your sense of humor.

- A final way you can use language is imaginatively. **Imaginative** language is used to express oneself artistically or creatively, as in drama, poetry, or stories. Thus, if your e-vite says "Screw cake, let's drink!" or "Let Them Eat Cake," you would be using the imaginative function of language.

As our discussion thus far indicates, language has seven basic functions, and speakers use them to accomplish specific goals or tasks. Note that these functions overlap and that one utterance can accomplish more than one function at the same time.

instrumental
Use of language to obtain what you need or desire.

regulatory
Use of language to control or regulate the behaviors of others.

informative
Use of language to communicate information or report facts.

heuristic
Use of language to acquire knowledge and understanding.

interactional
Use of language to establish and define social relationships.

personal language
Use of language to express individuality and personality.

imaginative
Use of language to express oneself artistically or creatively.

Critical Thinking Prompt
As a student, which functions of language do you use most frequently? Which do you use most often in your professional life? If you use different functions in each of these roles, why do you think this is true?

For example, when inviting your friends to a party, if you jokingly said, "James, our butler, will be serving bubbly and cake promptly at eight, so don't be late!" your utterance would both be imaginative (unless you actually have a butler named James) and regulatory. That is, you would be using language creatively while also attempting to regulate your guests' behavior to ensure they arrived on time.

Now that we have summarized the essential functions that language can serve, let's examine the basic components that allow us to use language as a flexible and creative tool of communication.

Components of Language

Scholars describe language use as being made up of four components: *phonology* (sounds), *syntax* (structure or rules), *semantics* (meaning), and *pragmatics* (use). Every language has its own rules of **grammar**—the structural rules that govern the generation of meaning in that language. See *Did You Know? Prescriptive vs. Descriptive Approaches to Language* to read about the different ways that French and German deal with these issues. In this section, we examine the role each plays in the communication process.

grammar

The structural rules that govern the generation of meaning in a language.

Phonology: Sounds   **Phonology** is the study of the sounds that compose individual languages and how those sounds communicate meaning. Basic sound units are called *phonemes*. They include vowels, consonants, and diphthongs (pairs of letters that operate as one, such as *th*). Different languages can use different phonemes. For example, French does not have the *th* sound. As a result, many native French speakers find it difficult to pronounce "this" or "that." Similarly, in Japanese, a phoneme that is between *r* and *l* is the closest equivalent to the English *r* sound. For more information about phonology, see https://www.internationalphoneticassociation.org, the home page of the International Phonetic Association.

phonology

The study of the sounds that compose individual languages and how those sounds communicate meaning.

Syntax: Rules   **Syntax** refers to the rules that govern word order. Because of the English rules of syntax, the sentences "The young boy hit the old man" and "The old man hit the young boy" have different meanings, even though they contain identical words. Syntax also governs how words of various categories (nouns, adjectives, verbs) are combined into clauses, which in turn combine into sentences. Whether or not we are conscious of them, most of us regularly follow certain rules about combining words—for example, that the verb and subject in a sentence have to agree, so people say "the pencil *is* on the table," not "the pencil *are* on the table." Because of these rules, people combine words consistently in ways that make sense and make communication possible.

syntax

The rules that govern word order.

Semantics: Meaning   **Semantics** is the study of meaning, which is an important component of communication. To illustrate the effect of syntax compared with the effect of meaning, Noam Chomsky (1957), an important scholar in the field of linguistics, devised this famous sentence: "Colorless green ideas sleep furiously" (p. 15). This sentence is acceptable in terms of English grammar, but on the semantic level it is nonsensical: Ideas logically cannot be either colorless or green (and certainly not both!), ideas don't sleep, and nothing sleeps furiously (does it?).

semantics

The study of meaning.

As you remember from Chapter 1, a central part of our definition of communication is the creation of shared meaning. For any given message, a number of factors contribute to the creation of its meaning. Perhaps most important are the words the speaker chooses. For example, did you have a friend in high school who always gave the right answer in class, got excellent grades, and always seemed to have a wealth of information at his fingertips? What word would you use to describe this friend: *kind, generous, considerate, thoughtful,* or *compassionate*? Because each word has a slightly different meaning, you try to choose the one that most accurately characterizes your friend. However, in choosing the "right" words, you have to consider the two types of meaning that words convey: *denotative* and *connotative*—terms that we also discussed in Chapter 1.

DID YOU KNOW?
Prescriptive versus Descriptive Approaches to Language

As you read the following description of how different languages approach the question of how to properly use each language, decide what you think of each approach. Do you prefer the prescriptive or descriptive approach? Can the approaches be combined?

French and German require different approaches to understanding the proper use of each language. A prescriptive approach guides the use of French in France. This means that the rules for correct usage are prescribed, or rigidly formalized and dictated.

In France, the French language is guided by the Académie française (or French Academy). This institution is the authority on the French language and determines what is and is not proper French. In 2016, a number of changes to the French language were rolled out in schools that created an uproar in France. Although these changes were voted on in 1990 by the French Academy, they were largely unnoticed at the time. About 2,400 French words have changed their spelling. For example, onion can now be spelled "ognon" or the more traditional "oignon." The circumflex (^) is also being dropped from many words, such as in *paraître,* which becomes *paraitre* (to appear), and some hyphens disappear in words such as *porte-monnaie,* which becomes *portemonnaie* (wallet).

Part of their charge is to guard the French language against the intrusion of other languages, especially English, but also Arabic, German, Tahitian, and others. So instead of saying, "un restaurant en self-service" (a self-service restaurant), the correct French is "un restaurant en libre-service" as posted on February 2, 2017.

In contrast, German in Germany takes a *descriptive approach* to language. The Duden dictionary is published every four or five years and describes the changes to the German language as it has been changed by German speakers. Thus, Duden has added "blog" to their dictionary as German speakers use that word, instead of the more German equivalent: digitale Netztagebücher. Although the German Language Society was upset that so many new words borrowed from English appeared in Duden, others see the German language changing as it incorporates these new terms. For Duden, how German speakers use language should determine which terms it includes. Duden takes a descriptive approach because it attempts to describe common usage instead of dictating what usage is correct. German speakers prefer to say "apps" rather than "Anwendungen für mobile Endgeräte," and so Duden recognizes this difference by including the English word.

SOURCES: Académie française. (2017, February 2). Self-service. Retrieved February 20, 2017, from: http://www.academie-francaise.fr/dire-ne-pas-dire.

Sauerbrey A. (2013, September 25). How do you say "blog" in German? *New York Times.* Retrieved March 6, 2014, from: http://www.nytimes.com/2013/09/26/opinion/how-do-you-say-blog-in-german.html?_r=0.

Willsher, K. (2016, February 5). Not the oignon: Fury as France changes 2,000 spellings and drops some accents. *The Guardian.* Retrieved May 28, 2017, from https://www.theguardian.com/world/2016/feb/05/not-the-oignon-fury-france-changes-2000-spellings-ditches-circumflex.

The **denotative meaning** refers to the dictionary, or literal, meaning of a word and is usually the agreed-on meaning for most speakers of the language. Referring back to our description of your friend, a denotative definition might describe *kind* as benevolent and *considerate* as empathy for another's emotions or circumstances. Does either word exactly capture how you would describe your friend? If not, which word does?

denotative meaning
The dictionary, or literal, meaning of a word.

Words also carry **connotative meanings**, which are the affective or interpretive meanings attached to them. Using the previous example, the connotative meaning of the word *wise* implies an older person with long experience, so it might not be the best choice to describe your young friend.

connotative meaning
The affective or interpretive meanings attached to a word.

Pragmatics: Language in Use   Just like phonology, syntax, and semantics, the field of **pragmatics** seeks to identify patterns or rules people follow when they use language appropriately. In the case of pragmatics, however, the emphasis is on how language is used in specific situations to accomplish goals (Nofsinger, 1999). For example, scholars who study pragmatics might seek to understand the rules for communicating appropriately in a sorority, a faculty meeting, or an evangelical church. They would do this by examining communication that is successful and unsuccessful in each setting. The three units of study for scholars of pragmatics are *speech acts, conversational rules,* and *contextual rules.* Let's examine what each contributes to communication.

pragmatics
Field of study that emphasizes how language is used in specific situations to accomplish goals.

speech act theory
Branch of pragmatics that suggests that when people communicate, they do not just say things, they also *do* things with their words.

Speech Acts   One branch of pragmatics, **speech act theory**, looks closely at the seven language functions described previously and suggests that when people communicate, they do not just say things, they also do things with their words. For example, speech act theorists argue that when you say, "I bet you ten dollars the Yankees win the World Series," you aren't just saying something, you actually are doing something. That something you are doing is making a bet, or entering into an agreement that will result in an exchange of money. You are also performing the act of challenging the other person to engage in the bet, or put their money where their mouth is.

One common speech act is the request. A recent study examined one type of request that occurs primarily in U.S. family contexts—the common practice of "nagging" (Boxer, 2002). Nagging (repeated requests by one family member to another) often concerns household chores and is usually a source of conflict. The researcher found that nagging requires several sequential acts. First, there is an initial request, which is usually given in the form of a command ("Please take out the garbage") or a hedged request ("Do you think you can take out the garbage this evening?"). If the request is not granted, it is repeated as a reminder (after some lapse of time), which often includes an allusion to the first request. ("Did you hear me? Can you please take out the garbage?") When a reminder is repeated (the third stage), it becomes nagging and usually involves a scolding or a threat, depending on the relationship—for example, whether the exchange is between parent and child ("This is the last time I'm going to ask you, take out the garbage!") or between relational partners ("Never mind, I'll do it myself!").

The researcher found that men were rarely involved in nagging, and she suggests that this is because men are perceived as having more power and are therefore able to successfully request and gain compliance from another family member without resorting to nagging. She also notes that children can have power (if they refuse to comply with a request despite their lack of status) and a parent can lack power despite having status. The researcher also found that nagging mostly occurs in our intimate relationships. She concludes that, by nagging, we lose power—but without power, we are forced into nagging; thus it seems to be a vicious cycle! The study shows that what we *do* with words affects our relationships.

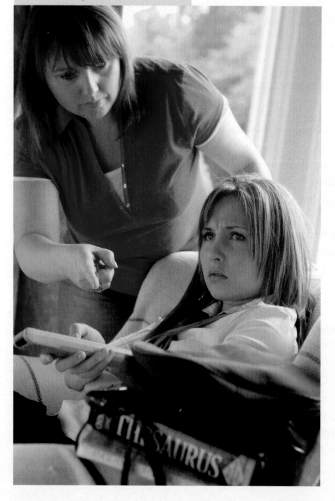

▼ Nagging is one common type of speech act that occurs in U.S. family contexts.

Understanding the meaning of various speech acts often requires understanding context and culture (Sbisa, 2002). For this reason, people may agree on what is *said* but disagree on what is *meant*. For example, the other day Katy said to her roommate Mike, "I have been so busy I haven't even had time to do the dishes." He replied, "Well, I'm sorry, but I have been busy, too." What did he think Katy was "doing" with her utterance? When they discussed this interaction, Katy explained that she was making an excuse, whereas Mike said he heard a criticism—that because *she* hadn't had time to do the dishes, *he* should have. Thus, messages may have different meanings or "do" different things, from different persons' viewpoints. This difference lies in the sender's and receiver's interpretations of the statement. Most misunderstandings arise not around what was said—but around what was done or meant.

As we have seen, speech acts may be direct or indirect. That is, speech acts such as requests can be framed more (or less) clearly and directly. Let's suppose that you want your partner to feed the dog. You may directly ask: "Would you feed the dog?" Or you could state an order: "Feed the dog!" On the other hand, you may communicate the same information indirectly: "Do you know if the dog was fed?" or "I wonder if the dog was fed." Finally, you may make your request indirectly: "It would be nice if someone fed the dog," or "Do you think the dog looks hungry?"

Which do you think is better—to communicate directly or indirectly? This is actually a trick question. The answer is: It depends—on the situation and the cultural context. Consider what you do with words to get someone else to act. Although direct requests and questions may be clearer, they also can be less polite. Ordering someone to feed the dog makes one's desire clearly and unequivocally known, but at the same time, it can be seen as rude and domineering.

Recent research shows that U.S. Americans tend to be more indirect in their requests, when compared to Mexicans (Pinto & Raschio, 2007), but probably not as indirect as many Asians (Kim, 2002). However, when expressing disagreement, most U.S. Americans tend to be more direct than most Asians. A recent study investigated how Malaysians handled disagreements in business negotiation and concluded that the Malays' opposition was never direct or on record, but always indirect and implied. Despite their disagreements with the other party, they honored the other, always balancing power with politeness (Paramasivam, 2007). A pragmatic approach reminds us that how language is used always depends on the situation and cultural context. We'll discuss more cross-cultural differences in communication practices further in Chapter 8.

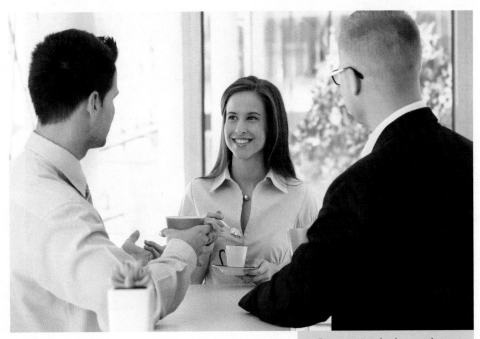

▲ Conversational rules—such as turn-taking—govern the way we communicate and vary somewhat from context to context.

Conversational Rules Conversational rules govern the ways in which communicators organize conversation. For example, one rule of conversation in U.S. English is that if someone asks you a question, you should provide an answer. If you do not know the answer, others expect you to at least reply, "I don't know" or "Let me think about it." However, in some cultures and languages, answers to questions are not obligatory. For example, in some Native American cultures, such as that of the Warm Spring Indians of Oregon, questions may be answered at a later time (with little reference to the previous conversation) or not answered at all (Philips, 1990).

Perhaps the most researched conversational rules involve turn-taking. The most basic rule for English language speakers, and many others, is that only one person speaks at a time. People may tolerate some overlap between their talk and another's, but typically they expect to be able to have their say without too much interruption (Schegloff, 2000). Still, as a refinement of this point, Susanna Kohonen (2004) found in her cross-cultural study of turn-taking that conversationalists were more tolerant of overlaps in social settings, such as at parties or when hanging out with friends, than in more formal settings. Also, in computer-mediated communication, turn-taking is influenced by face-to-face interactions, but uses strategic pauses more to regulate speech (Anderson Beard, & Walther, 2010). In other words, although computer-mediated communication is not face to face, the communication interaction rules mimic face-to-face interactions; however, the different context results in slightly different rules. Different cultures may recognize different turning points, or appropriate places for another speaker to resume communication. Whereas English speakers focus on grammatical stops, Korean speakers focus on a lexical boundary where action completion occurs (Park, 2016). Thus, sometimes the context influences conversational rules. We discuss contextual rules next.

▲ Pragmatics involves understanding the implicit communication rules that apply in one setting or another.

Other rules for turn-taking determine who is allowed to speak (Sacks, Schegloff, & Jefferson, 1978). For example, if you "have the floor" you can generally continue to speak. When you are finished, you can select someone else. You can do this either by asking a question, "So Sue, what is your opinion?" or by looking at another person as you finish talking. If you don't have the floor but wish to speak, you can begin speaking just as the current speaker completes a turn.

The turn-allocation system works amazingly well most of the time. Occasionally, however, people do not follow these implicit rules. For example, the current speaker could select the next speaker by directing a question to her, but someone else could interrupt and "steal" the floor. Also, some speakers are quicker to grab the talk turn, which allows them more opportunities to speak. Then, speakers who are slower to begin a turn or take the floor have fewer opportunities to contribute to the conversation. They may feel left out or resent the other speakers for monopolizing the conversation.

Contextual Rules   No matter what language or dialect you speak, your use of language varies depending on the communication situation (Mey, 2001). For example, you probably wouldn't discuss the same topics in the same way at a funeral as you would in a meeting at your workplace, in a courtroom, or at a party. What would happen if you did? For example, telling jokes and laughing at a party is typically acceptable, whereas those same jokes and laughing might be interpreted negatively in a courtroom or at a funeral. One challenge for pragmatics scholars, then, is uncovering the implicit communication rules that govern different settings. As noted previously, communication pragmatics also vary by culture. For example, in some houses of worship, appropriate verbal behavior involves talking quietly or not all, acting subdued, and listening without responding—but in others, people applaud, sing exuberantly, and respond loudly with exclamations like "Amen!" Neither set of communication rules is "right"; each is appropriate to its own setting and cultural context.

As you can see, verbal language is far more than the words people use; it also includes the sounds and meanings of those words, and the rules individuals use for arranging words and for communicating in particular settings. Moreover, speakers differ in the ways they use language to communicate. They also differ in the ways they enunciate their words and how they present their ideas. For example, Southerners "drawl" their vowels, whereas New Englanders drop the *r* after theirs; some speakers are extremely direct, and others are not. What accounts for these differences? We explore the answers in the next section.

Journal Prompt 5.2:
Functions of Language
Consider the following question: What are the seven functions of language? Give an example that illustrates how each works.

The Individual and Verbal Communication: Influences

5.3   Identify and give examples of several major influences on verbal communication.

As we saw in Chapter 3, our communication is influenced by our identities and the various cultures to which we belong. In turn, our communication helps shape these identities. When identities influence several aspects of language, we say that speakers have a distinct **dialect**, a variation of a language distinguished by its **lexical choice** (vocabulary), grammar, and pronunciation. In other instances, the influence of identity is less dramatic, and speakers vary only in some pronunciations or word choices. In this section we examine how identities related to gender, age, regionality, ethnicity and race, and education and occupation shape language use.

dialect
A variation of a language distinguished by its vocabulary, grammar, and pronunciation.

lexical choice
Vocabulary.

Gender

Growing up male or female may influence the way you communicate in some situations, because men and women are socialized to communicate in specific ways. In fact—as exemplified in the popularity of books like *Men Are from Mars, Women Are from Venus* (Gray, 2012)—many people believe that English-speaking men and women in the United States speak different dialects. These beliefs are reinforced by media depictions that tend to present stereotypical depictions of men and women in magazines, on television, and in movies. For example, one team of researchers reviewed how journal articles talked about gender differences in the past fifty years and found that because people are more interested in hearing about differences than similarities, shows and books that emphasize these differences tend to sell better and receive wider recognition (Sagrestano, Heavey, & Christensen, 1998).

Even scholarly research tends to focus on, and sometimes exaggerate, the importance of sex differences; some researchers have reported that women's verbal style is often described as supportive, egalitarian, personal, and disclosive, whereas men's is characterized as instrumental, competitive, and assertive (Mulac, Bradac, & Gibbons, 2001; Wood, 2002), and as we saw in Chapter 2, there is some evidence that differences exist in social media "talk." But other research refutes this claim. A recent review of studies comparing males and females on a large array of psychological and communication differences, including self-disclosure and interruptions, revealed few significant differences (Hyde, 2006). How can these contradictory findings be explained? To begin, many studies of gender differences ask participants to report on their perceptions or ask them to recall men's and women's conversational styles (e.g., Aylor & Dainton, 2004). This approach can be problematic because people's perceptions are not always accurate. For example, Nancy Burrell and her colleagues (1988) argue that persistent, stereotypical, gender-based expectations likely influence people's perceptions that men and women behave or communicate differently even when few behavioral differences exist. More recently, Heilman, Caleo, and Halim (2010) found that gender stereotypes were invoked even more strongly when workers were told they would communicate using computer-mediated communication rather than face to face.

How do these faulty perceptions arise about communication differences between men and women? Two important contributors are a person's perceptions of his or her own gendered communication and media representations of men's and women's

▼ Televisions shows, such as *The Real Housewives of Orange County*, tend to present stereotypical depictions of men and women.

communication. Experts assert that gender-based perceptions are hard to change, whether or not the perceptions are true. For example, the negative stereotype of the talkative woman is persistent. In one recent study, students were shown a videotaped conflict between a man and a woman and were asked to rate the two on likability and competence. In different versions of the video, the researchers varied how much the man and woman each talked. As the researchers expected, viewers rated the couple as less likable when they saw the woman doing more of the talking. And the man who talked more was rated as most competent (Sellers, Woolsey, & Swann, 2007). Even though this negative stereotype persists, many studies have shown that not only do women generally *not* talk more than men, actually the opposite is true—men tend to be more talkative in many situations (Leaper & Ayres, 2007). In addition, the stereotype persists that women are more "kind, helpful, sympathetic, and concerned about others," whereas men are seen as "aggressive, forceful, independent, and decisive" (Heilman, 2001, p. 658). Furthermore, these gender stereotypes can create differential treatment in the workplace and in social situations.

When people adapt to a specific audience, they are often adjusting to the communication style of the more powerful members of that audience. Thus, if powerful members of the audience use more direct or task-focused language, so might the speaker. In addition to adapting their communication style, people also often use more deferential or tentative language when communicating with more powerful people. Both men and women adapt to these power differences; thus both groups are more likely to use tentative language with their bosses than with their siblings. Women use language that is more tentative overall because generally they have lower status, and people with lower status are not typically expected to make strong, assertive statements (Reid, Keerie, & Palomares, 2003). Similarly, women tend to use more "filler words" (such as *like* or *well*) and more conditional words (*would, should, could*) (Mehl & Pennebaker, 2003).

Researchers have wondered whether gender differences in conversations are a consequence of interacting with a partner who uses a particular style of communication. For example, if you encourage another person to talk by nodding your head in agreement, asking questions, etc., you are using a facilitative style of communication. To explore this question, social psychologists Annette Hannah and Tamar Murachver assigned male and female partners who were strangers to each other to meet and talk several times. After the first conversation, their communication styles were judged by outside observers to be either facilitative or nonfacilitative; and the researchers found that, regardless of gender, participants responded to each other in ways that mirrored their partner's style (Hannah & Murachver, 2007).

Over time, however, in subsequent conversations, the women and men shifted their speech toward more stereotypically gendered patterns; that is, the men talked more, for longer times, whereas women increased their use of minimal responses, reduced the amount they spoke, and asked more questions. In other words, the women increased their facilitative style of speech while the men decreased theirs. Discussing their findings, the researchers pose several questions: Why are women more facilitative in their speech? Why do they talk less when talking with men? Do they feel threatened or insecure? Are they less comfortable in talking more than men? Perhaps women feel that dominating conversations with men has negative social consequences and, therefore, they encourage men to do the talking—an explanation that would be confirmed by the previous study we mentioned, where students negatively evaluated couples in which the women talked more than the men. The researchers provide no definitive explanation, but note, as do we, that gender differences are complicated (Hannah & Murachver, 2007).

In conclusion, women and men do show differences in their communication styles, and much of this difference likely is attributable to differences in power, status, and expectations in communication situations.

Age

You may not think of age as affecting language use, but it does, particularly when it comes to word choice. For example, you might have talked about "the cooties" when you were a child, but you probably don't now. Moreover, children have a whole vocabulary to describe "naughty topics," especially related to bodily functions. Yet, most adults do not use those words. Adolescents also develop vocabulary that they use throughout their teenage years and then drop during early adulthood. Adolescents have described highly valued people and things as "cool," "righteous," "bad," "hot," and "phat," depending on the generation and context. This distinct vocabulary helps teenagers feel connected to their peers and separate from their parents and other adults. For other examples of teen slang terms, see *Did You Know? Contemporary Slang.*

The era in which you grew up also influences your vocabulary. As you age, you continue to use certain words that were common when you were growing up, even if they have fallen out of use. This is called the **cohort effect** and refers to common denominators of a group that was born and reared in the same general period. For example, your grandparents and their contemporaries may say "cool" or "neat" and your parents may say "awesome" when referring to something they really like. What do you say? Recent research suggests that young girls (particularly young, urban, upwardly mobile) are the trendsetters in language use both for their own and other cohorts. The most recent examples are their use of "I can't even . . ." and the "vocal fry" or "creaky voice" (made by compressing the vocal chords and reducing the airflow through the larynx, makes speech to sound rattled or "creaky"). Zooey Deschanel and Kim Kardashian slip in and out of this register, as does Britney Spears, but it has been observed in college-aged women across the country. Women have long tended to be the linguistic innovators. Linguists say that if you want to see the future of a language find a young, urban woman. We have women to thank for "up-talk"—the rising intonation at the end of a sentence that has spread into mainstream speech—the discourse marker "like," and now, vocal fry (Arana, 2013; Cohen, 2014).

People's communication skills and the meanings they attribute to concepts also vary because of their age. Why? Older people are more cognitively developed and have had more experiences; therefore, they tend to view concepts differently than do younger people, especially children (Pennebaker & Stone, 2003). For example, children typically engage in egocentric speech patterns (Piaget, 1952). This means that they cannot adapt their communication to their conversational partners nor understand that others may feel or view the world differently. Children lack the number of constructs adults have. For example, young children have little concept of future or past time, so understanding what might happen next week or month is difficult for them. Consequently, parents usually adapt their communication when trying to help children understand some event in the future.

cohort effect

The influence of shared characteristics of a group that was born and reared in the same general period.

DID YOU KNOW?
Contemporary Slang

While we are accustomed to hearing many of the new slang words that appear as abbreviations in texting and other Internet usage, there are many others that that we might not recognize. For example, you are probably familiar with bff or "best friends forever. Or "kk" for "okay" or "it's cool." But have you ever seen 770880? In Chinese, this is equivalent to XOXO. What about AMHA? This is the French equivalent to IMHO or "in my humble opinion." Different languages have developed different slang to communicate with others, and these slang terms may not be distinguishable beyond their language group. Other languages have adapted to new technological environments, just as English has.

Regionality

Geographical location also strongly influences people's language use. The most common influence is on pronunciation. For example, how do you pronounce the word "oil"? In parts of New York it is pronounced somewhat like "earl," whereas in areas of the South it is pronounced more like "awl," and in the West it is often pronounced "oyl" as in "Olive Oyl." Sometimes regionality affects more than just accent, leading to regional dialects. Why do these differences arise?

Historically, verbal differences developed wherever people were separated by a geographical boundary—whether it was mountains, lakes, rivers, deserts, oceans—or some social boundary, such as race, class, or religion (Fromkin & Rodman, 1983). Moreover, people tended to speak similarly to those around them. For example, in the eighteenth century, residents of Australia, North America, and England had relatively little contact with one another; consequently, they developed recognizably different dialects even though they all spoke the same language. Typically, the more isolated a group, the more distinctive their dialect.

In the United States, dialectical differences in English originally arose because two groups of English colonists settled along the East Coast. The colonists who settled in the South, near present-day Virginia, primarily came from Somerset and Gloucestershire—both western counties in England—and they brought with them an accent with strongly voiced *s* sounds and with the *r* strongly pronounced after vowels. In contrast, the colonists who settled in the north, what we now call New England, came from midland counties such as Essex, Kent, and London, where people spoke a dialect that did not pronounce the *r* after vowels, a feature still common to many New England dialects (Crystal, 2003). See Figure 5.1 for an interesting outgrowth of U.S. local dialects.

Figure 5.1 Generic Names for Soft Drinks by County

The terms we use to refer to soft drinks also vary by region in the United States.

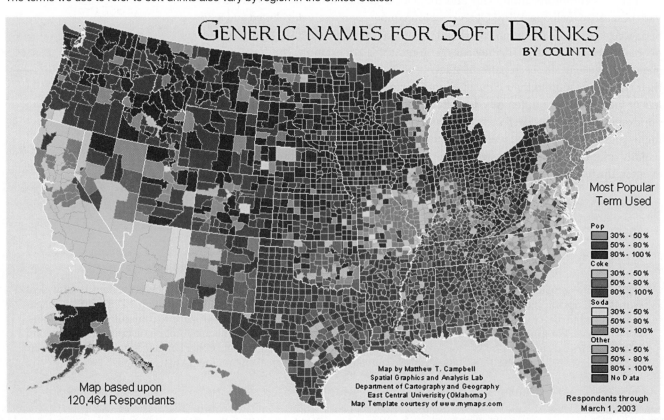

Other waves of immigration have occurred over the past four hundred years, increasing dialectical diversity in the United States. Each group of immigrants brings a distinctive way of speaking and culture-specific communication rules. Some groups, especially those who have remained somewhat isolated since their arrival, maintain much of their original dialect; an example is the inhabitants of Tangier Island in the Chesapeake Bay (Crystal, 2003). Other groups' dialects have assimilated with the dialects of their neighbors to form new dialects. Thus, the seventeenth-century "western" English dialect of Virginia has become the southern drawl of the twenty-first century.

Today the world is a global village, so people all over the country (and, for that matter, all over the world) are able to speak frequently with one another and have access to similar media. Nonetheless, according to a recent comprehensive study, local dialects are stronger than ever (Labov, 2005; Preston, 2003). Language professor Julie Sedivy (2012) notes that: "It may seem surprising, but in this age where geographic mobility and instant communication have increased our exposure to people outside of our neighborhoods or towns, American regional dialects are pulling further apart from each other, rather than moving closer together." Do you have a recognizable regional linguistic dialect?

Ethnicity and Race

One's ethnicity can influence one's verbal style in a number of ways. In the United States, English is a second or colanguage for many citizens. This, of course, influences syntax, accent, and word choice. For example, if one is Latino or Latina and learns Spanish either before or at the same time as one learns English, one may use the same syntax for both. Thus, Spanish speakers may place adjectives after nouns (*the house little*) when they are speaking English because that is the rule for Spanish. The reverse can also occur: When English speakers speak Spanish, they have a tendency to place adjectives before nouns (*la pequeña casa*), which is the rule for English but not for Spanish.

Speakers' ethnicity can also influence their general verbal style. For example, Jewish Americans may engage in a style of talking about problems that non-Jews perceive as complaining (Bowen, 2012); some Native American tribes use teasing as a form of public rebuke (Shutiva, 2012); and some Chinese Americans who live in the southern United States are particularly likely to let other speakers choose conversational topics (Gong, 2012). When two ethnic or racial groups speak the same language but use different syntax, lexical items, or verbal style, one or both of the groups may view the other's verbal style as incorrect, as a failed attempt at proper speech rather than as a dialect with its own rules (Ellis & Beattie, 1986).

These views can have important real-life implications—political and monetary. Take the controversy about **African American Vernacular English**—a version of English that has its roots in West African, Caribbean, and U.S. slave languages. There is no agreed-on definition of African American Vernacular English; some linguists emphasize the international nature of the language (as a linguistic consequence of the African slave trade); others stress that it is a variety of English (e.g., the equivalent of Black English) or as different from English and viewed as an independent language. Yet we should also keep in mind that "there is no single and correct way to be 'African American.' These identities are negotiated in context and situationally emergent" (Hecht, Jackson, & Ribeau, 2003, p. 2).

In his book, *"You are an African American, so why are you talking like a white person,"* Jeffrey Walker (2010) encourages African Americans to practice **code switching**—or change the way that they speak in different situations. Code switching is an important linguistic practice that helps speakers of different languages and dialects to change the way that they speak to communicate more effectively in mainstream culture, while also demonstrating cultural group membership in other situations. For example, some

African American Vernacular English

A version of English that has its roots in West African, Caribbean, and U.S. slave languages.

code switching

The practice of changing language or dialect to accommodate to the communication situation.

It Happened to Me
Jessica

My parents immigrated from Lebanon to the United States and opened a family restaurant. When I worked there, my family communicated in Arabic, and we spoke it publicly in front of customers. Once in a while, a customer would express their upset that my parents were not adapting their kid to an American way of life. Some even felt entitled to know what we were talking about. Often, we were communicating about a private matter, and in truth, the restaurant was only a semi-public space. Those who did not feel comfortable with our code switch could, and probably did, choose another establishment. To this day, my family and I still code switch here. It is an integral part of our identity, which is provisional in a predominantly white, middle-class suburb. But we also code switch to English when we go back to Lebanon. That's how we planned grandma's surprise birthday party!

African Americans may use African American Vernacular English when speaking in social settings with other African Americans to demonstrate their community membership, but use a more standard English when speaking in a professor context.

Education and Occupation

We will discuss education and occupation together because they are often mutually influencing. For example, medical doctors speak a similar language because they share a profession, but also because they were educated similarly. Typically, the more educated people are, the more similarly they speak (Hudson, 1983). Thus, larger dialect differences occur between Easterners and Midwesterners if they have not been to college than if they have doctoral degrees. This does not mean that all lawyers talk the same or that all professors speak similarly; rather, it suggests that differences become less pronounced as people receive more education.

Education affects dialect in part because any given university or college attracts people from different parts of the country. Therefore, college students have contact with a variety of dialects. At the same time, as students attend college they develop similar vocabularies from their shared experiences and learn similar terms in their classes. For example, you may never have used the term *dyad* to refer to two people before you went to college, but this is a term you might encounter in a range of courses, including psychology, sociology, anthropology, and communication.

Your occupation also influences the specialized terms you use to communicate. The specialized terms that develop in many professions are called **jargon**. Lawyers routinely speak of *torts, depositions*, and *ex parte*. Physicians speak of *contusions* (bruises), *sequelae* (results), and *hemorrhagic stroke* (a stroke where a blood vessel bursts). In fact, most occupations have their own jargon. In addition to influencing your lexical choices, your occupation may also influence your overall communication style—including tone of voice and some nonverbal behaviors. For example, nursery school teachers are often recognizable not only by their vocabulary but also by the rhythm, volume, and expressivity of their communication style.

To sum up, then, various features of language—phonology, syntax, semantics, and pragmatics—contribute to the development of meaning in verbal communication. These features combine with individual influences in language use, such as gender, age, and level of education, to create one's specific communication style. However, we have not yet covered every aspect of verbal communication. We now turn to the influence of societal forces on verbal communication.

jargon
The specialized terms that develop in many professions.

Journal Prompt 5.3: Influences on Dialect
Consider the following question:
How do our region, gender, age, ethnicity and race, and education and occupation influence the way we speak?

▼ Physicians, like members of other professions, develop specialized terms called jargon.

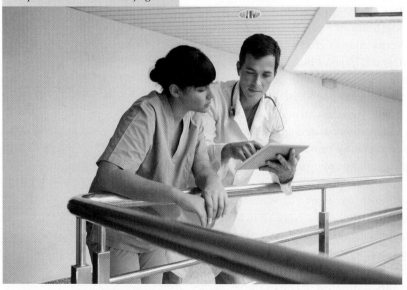

The Individual, Verbal Communication, and Society: Language, Perception, and Power

5.4 Describe the relationships between language, perception, and power.

How do societal forces influence verbal communication? Culture and power are two of the most important influences. Culture impacts verbal communication primarily through its influence on language and perception. As we saw in Chapter 4, perception plays a key role in communication. Power is connected to verbal communication because within society, some language styles are viewed as more powerful, with consequences for both the powerful and the powerless.

Language and Perception

Scholars have long argued about the influence of language and culture on perception. The central issue they have debated is whether the words a culture has available to it influence how its members see and perceive the world around them. For example, the English language expresses action in the past, present, and future. Thus, English speakers may say "Alan went to the library" (past), "Alan is at the library" (present), or "Alan will be going to the library" (future). In contrast, Japanese makes no distinction between the present and future. Although the verb for "went" is *ikimashita*, the verb used for both "is" and "will be going" is the same, *ikimasu*. Because English and Japanese have two different verb structures, scholars have questioned whether English speakers and Japanese speakers think about present and future actions in different ways. Scholars who have debated this relationship between language and perception generally fall into two camps: the *nominalists* and the *relativists.*

Nominalists claim that any idea can be expressed in any language and that the structure and vocabulary of the language do not influence the speaker's perception of the world. According to nominalists, English and Japanese may express present and future in different ways, but English speakers and Japanese speakers still understand the distinction.

In contrast, the **relativists** argue that language serves not only as a way for us to voice our ideas but that, in addition, it "is itself the shaper of ideas, the guide for the individual's mental activity" (Hoijer, 1994, p. 194). This idea is the basis for the **Sapir-Whorf hypothesis**. The Sapir-Whorf hypothesis argues that the language people speak deter-mines the way they see the world. Adherents to this hypothesis believe language is like a prison because it constrains the ways individuals can perceive the world (Deutscher, 2010). According to this hypothesis, the distinction between the present and the future is not as clear-cut for Japanese speakers as it is for English speakers. As another example, surfers have many more words for the types of waves in the ocean than do nonsurfers (Scheibel, 1995); the Sapir-Whorf hypothesis argues that, because of this, surfers perceive more types of waves than do others.

So how much does language influence perception? The Sapir-Whorf hypothesis position has been challenged by a number of scholars who investigate the connection

nominalists

Those who argue that any idea can be expressed in any language and that the structure and vocabulary of the language do not influence the speaker's perception of the world.

relativists

Those who argue that language serves not only as a way for us to voice our ideas but "is itself the shaper of ideas, the guide for the individual's mental activity."

Sapir-Whorf hypothesis

Idea that the language people speak determines the way they see the world (a relativist perspective).

▼ Surfers have many more words for the types of waves in the ocean than do nonsurfers.

between language and how we think. They represent a modified relativist position on the relationship between language and perception. For example, Steven Pinker (2007), a renowned cognitive scientist, cautions against assuming a simplistic connection between language and thought, and rejects the Sapir-Whorf assumption that the particular language we speak compels us to perceive the world in a particular way or prevents us from thinking in different ways. By looking at language from the perspective of our thoughts, Pinker shows that what may seem like arbitrary aspects of speech (such as "hunk" vs. "goo") aren't arbitrary at all, but rather that they are by-products of our evolved mental machinery. In sum, all languages have the formal and expressive power to communicate the ideas, beliefs, and desires of their users. From this vast range of possibilities, human communities select what they want to say and how they want to say it. This view allows for more freedom than indicated by the Sapir-Whorf hypothesis.

Critical Thinking Prompt

Which viewpoint makes more sense to you—nominalist or relativist? Why?

Language and Power

In many ways, language and power are inextricably connected. People in power get to define what languages and communication styles are appropriate. In addition, people who use language and communication according to the rules of the powerful may be able to increase their own power. This view of the relationship between language and power is explained by *cocultural theory*. **Cocultural theory** explores the role of power in daily interactions using the five following assumptions:

cocultural theory

Explores the role of power in daily interactions.

1. In each society, a hierarchy exists that privileges certain groups of people; in the United States, these groups include men, European Americans, heterosexuals, the able-bodied, and middle- and upper-class people.

2. Part of the privilege these groups enjoy, often subconsciously, is being able to set norms for what types of communication are acceptable or not acceptable (Orbe, 1998). Consequently, communication patterns of the dominant groups (in the United States, rich, male, White, educated, straight) tend to be more highly valued. For example, the preferred communication practice in many large corporations is that used by White males—direct, to the point, task oriented, and unemotional (Kikoski & Kikoski, 1999).

3. Language maintains and reinforces the power of these dominant groups, again, mostly subconsciously. Thus, people whose speech does not conform to what is valued in society may be excluded or negatively stereotyped. As we noted previously, commentators sometimes characterize women's speech as sounding more tentative than male speech. Because society values male speech styles at work, women aspiring to corporate leadership positions may undertake a special effort to make their speech direct or tough enough, or to avoid being too cooperative or nurturing in their communication practices.

4. In the relationship realm, society tends to value a more female communication style, and men may be criticized for failing to communicate appropriately with their intimates. Remember that none of these language variations is inherently good or bad, powerful or powerless; it is the societal hierarchies that teach us how to view particular communication practices. Of course, not every White male is direct, to the point, and task oriented, nor does every woman speak tentatively at work. Nor is every woman supportive and self-disclosive and every man distant and terse in close relationships. These generalizations can help explain communication practices, but they should not solidify into stereotypes.

5. These dominant communication structures impede the progress of persons whose communication practices do not conform to the norms. For example, what are the consequences for women who do not conform to "male" communication norms in a corporation? Or for African Americans who do not conform to "White"

communication norms of the organizations in which they work? Or for students who do not conform to the "middle-class" communication norms at a university? They may risk being labeled negatively ("not serious enough," "soft," "doesn't have what it takes") and marginalized.

We explore these ideas further in Chapter 8. Now, let's look at how these societal hierarchies affect attitudes toward words, accents, and dialects, and how they impact identity labels.

Power and Words

Attitudes about power can be built into language by certain roots or by the structure of the language. Consider words such as *chairman, fireman,* or the generic use of *he* and *man* to refer to people. In the past it was widely believed that it didn't matter whether we used masculine words to mean *human*, but in recent decades researchers discovered that people didn't think *human* when someone mentioned the word *man*—they thought about a man. Similarly, awareness of the inequality inherent in terms such as *Mr.* (not designating marital status) and *Mrs.* (which does) has resulted in the use of new, more equal terms such as *Ms.* and *he* or *she*. More recently, some have argued for the use of "they" instead of "he or she" to be more inclusive of all gender identifications (see Table 5.1), including the *Washington Post* and the American Dialect Society (Hess, 2016).

Although some languages, such as Japanese or Korean, are strongly gendered (meaning that traditionally, men and women used almost a separate language), English is somewhat gendered, or androcentric. **Androcentrism** is the pairing of maleness with humanity and the consequent attribution of gender difference to females—often to women's disadvantage. Scholars recently reviewed 50 years of psychology articles for androcentric bias. Although they found few uses of *he* for *human*, information was still portrayed in a way that emphasized male as the norm. Male data was placed first in tables, and gender differences were often described as female—subconsciously assuming that male is the norm and female is different. Researchers point out that being different is not necessarily harmful but probably reflects some of the underlying stereotypes (and societal hierarchies) we have discussed previously (Hegarty & Buechel, 2006).

androcentrism

The use of male experience as normative for humanity and female experience as emphasizing gender difference.

What are the implications for students? We argue that it's not about freedom of speech or being overly politically correct, but rather about audience and awareness. Gender-neutral language has gained support from most major textbook publishers, and from professional and academic groups, as well as major newspapers and law journals. As an English professor suggested, "You need to be able to express yourself according to their guidelines, and if you wish to write or speak convincingly to people who are influenced by the conventions of these contexts, you need to be conscious of their expectations."

Table 5.1 Gender-Neutral Language

Gender-based	Gender-neutral
he/she	they
congressman/congresswoman	member of Congress
policeman	police officer
mankind	humanity
Miss, Mrs.	Ms.
freshmen	first-year students
man the controls	take control
male nurse	nurse

Power and Accent

Where did people learn that an English accent sounds upper crust and educated? Or that English as spoken with an Asian Indian accent is hard to understand? Why do communicators often stereotype Black English as sounding uneducated? Although these associations come from many sources, they certainly are prevalent in the media. People have become so accustomed to seeing and hearing these associations that they probably don't even question them. In fact, William Labov, a noted sociolinguist, refers to the practice of associating a dialect with the cultural attitudes toward it as "a borrowed prestige model." For example, until the 1950s, most Americans thought that British English was the correct way to speak English (Labov, 1980); even today, people continue to think that an English accent sounds refined and educated. By contrast, Southern drawls and Black English have become stigmatized so that today, people who speak them are often perceived negatively. For similar reasons, people often find the English accent of people from India (where English often is a first language) difficult to understand—as reported by our student in *It Happened to Me: Bart*.

Such language stereotypes can be "set off" in one's head before a person even speaks, when one *thinks*, generally because of the person's appearance, that she or he will not speak Standard English (Ruben, 2003). This is probably what happened to our student, Bart. Once he adjusted to the Indian English accent, he found he could understand his Indian professor just fine. (For examples of accents from many different language backgrounds, go to http://accent.gmu.edu/index.php.)

How does language cause one group to become elevated and another denigrated? The answer lies partly in understanding the social forces of history and politics. The positive and negative associations about African American, White, and British English developed during the nineteenth and twentieth centuries when European Americans were establishing themselves as the powerful majority in the United States, while passing legislation that subjugated African Americans and other minority groups. Thus, it is not surprising that the languages of these groups were viewed so differently. Similarly, the English spoken by people from India was negatively stereotyped as the aberrant language of the colonized because England was the colonial power in India until the mid-twentieth century. Similar attitudes can be seen toward immigrant groups today; their accented English is often stigmatized, sometimes leading to language discrimination and lawsuits, as illustrated in *Did You Know? Language Discrimination*.

Power and Identity Labels

The language labels that refer to particular identities also communicate important messages about power relations. Members of more powerful groups frequently invoke labels for members of other groups without input from those group members. For example, straight people label gays but rarely refer to themselves as straight. White people use ethnic and racial labels to refer to others (*people of color, African American*, or *Black*) but rarely refer to themselves as *White*. This power to label seems "normal," so most people don't think twice about specifying that a physician is a "woman doctor," but never describing one as a "male doctor." Or they might identify someone as a gay teacher but not a white teacher (even if this teacher is both). People usually don't think about the assumptions that reflect societal power relations; in sum,

It Happened to Me
Bart

I recently had a course taught by an Asian Indian professor, and it took me some time to understand his accent and form of speaking. Sometimes I thought he was mumbling, and sometimes his speech sounded so fast that I couldn't understand it. After a couple of classes, my hearing disciplined itself to understand him better. In the end, I realized he was a fine teacher.

DID YOU KNOW?
Language Discrimination

Should language discrimination be illegal? Are there jobs where speaking English with an accent would impair someone's ability to do the job? Does language discrimination happen outside of employment as well?

Language discrimination includes interlanguage discrimination and intralanguage discrimination. Interlanguage discrimination happens when people are treated differently because of the languages that they speak. In countries with an official language, discrimination can occur against those who do not speak the official language(s). Intralanguage discrimination happens when people are treated differently because they speak in a way that is not considered "proper" or the dominant language. In the United States, for example, someone who speaks Hawaiian pidgin or African American Vernacular English, may be treated differently than someone who speaks standard American English. Both kinds of discrimination can happen in job situations where someone is not hired or promoted because of an accent or is treated differently from other employees. Language discrimination can also happen in schools when students are forbidden to speak certain languages. In the United States, for example, some schools require students to speak English, not only in class but also outside of class. Language discrimination can also happen in social settings when someone is rebuffed because of the way they speak.

In the United Kingdom, there is no "British accent" but many different accents. Much more than in the United States, these accent differences reflect people's social class backgrounds. In 2017, the Social Mobility Commission, a British government organization, released a report that showed that people from working class background are paid an average of £6,800 (approximately $8,500 USD), or 17 percent less than similar professionals from more privileged backgrounds. This social class pay gap exists across the workforce, but the pay gap is highest in "finance (£13,713), medicine (£10,218) and IT (£4,736)" (or over $17,000 USD, $12,700 USD and $5,900 USD, respectively). The chair of the commission noted that this study "provides powerful new evidence that Britain remains a deeply elitist society."

When we discriminate against people who speak in certain ways or speak certain languages, we are discriminating against the individuals, not just the accents or languages.

Source: Social Mobility Commission. (2017, January 26). New research uncovers "class pay gap" in Britain's professions. Retrieved February 20, 2017 from https://www.gov.uk/government/news/new-research-uncovers-class-pay-gap-in-britains-professions.

---

individuals feel the need to mark minority differences, but they tend not to identify majority group membership.

Not only do the more powerful get to label the less powerful, but they may also use language labels to stigmatize them. However, the stigma comes from the power relations, not from the words themselves. For example, in the Polish language, the word *Polack* simply means "a man from Poland," but the stigma associated with the term comes from the severe discrimination practiced against Eastern Europeans in the early twentieth century, which led to jokes and stereotypes that exist to this day. The term *Oriental* originated when Western countries were attempting to colonize, and were at war with, Asian countries—and the connotative meaning was *exotic* and *foreign*. Today, many Asians and Asian Americans resent this label. Read about one of our student's opinions on the topic in *It Happened to Me: Hiroko*.

This resentment can make communication more difficult for Hiroko and those who use this term to refer to her. As this example reveals, understanding the dictionary meanings of words does not always reveal the impact of identity labels. Members of minority communities are the best informants on the communicative power of specific labels.

Not everyone in an identity group has the same denotative meaning for a particular label. For example, some young women

Critical Thinking Prompt
Think about labels and terms we have for males and females. Why do you think so many more negative terms exist for females than for males?

It Happened to Me
Hiroko

I get really tired of people referring to me as "Oriental." It makes me sound like a rug or a cuisine. I refer to myself as Asian American or Japanese American. I know people probably don't mean anything negative when they use it, but it makes me uncomfortable. If it's somebody I know well, I might ask them not to use that word, but usually I just don't say anything.

ALTERNATIVE VIEW

Changing Whitehouse.gov

When Donald Trump was inaugurated as the 45th president of the United States, the new, revised White House webpage dropped the Spanish language parts of the website. The United States does not have an official, legal language. English is the most widely spoken language and Spanish is the second most spoken language in the nation. Throughout its history, many languages have been spoken in the United States, including indigenous languages, as well as the languages of immigrants, for example, German and Italian. Many of our presidents understood and/or knew other languages. Both Roosevelt presidents spoke French and German. Many presidents knew Greek and Latin. George W.

Bush knows Spanish, Barack Obama speaks Indonesian, and Bill Clinton knows German. Donald Trump, in contrast, is proudly an English monolingual. He also attacked Jeb Bush in the Republican primary for speaking Spanish. How should the United States deal with multiple languages? Should we embrace being a multilingual society? Or should we insist on an English-only monolingual approach? What's best for business, educational institutions, high tech industries, and other parts of the nation?

Source: Stavans, I. (2017, January 30). Trump, the wall and the Spanish language. *New York Times.* Retrieved from https://www.nytimes.com/2017/01/30/opinion/trump-the-wall-and-the-spanish-language.html?_r=0.

do not like to be called "girl"; they find it demeaning. Others are comfortable with this term. Some people view these calls for sensitivity in language as nothing more than unnecessary political correctness.

Moreover, the power of labels can change over time. In an earlier age, many viewed the term *WASP* (White, Anglo-Saxon, Protestant) as a descriptor or even a positive label; now, however, it is seen as rather negative (Martin, Krizek, Nakayama, & Bradford, 1999). The shift probably reflects the changing attitudes of Whites, who are now more aware of their ethnicity and the fact that they are not always the majority. Similarly, the term *Paddy* as in "paddy wagon" (a term for a police wagon) originally was a derogatory term; some older Irish Americans may still find it offensive. It reflected a stereotype, widely held one hundred years ago, of Irish men as drunks who had to be carted off to jail. Now that discrimination (and stereotyping) against the Irish has all but disappeared, this term has lost much of its impact.

In summary, language, power, and societal forces are closely linked. The societal environment profoundly influences the way people perceive the world and the language choices available to them. Those in power set the language and communication norms, often determining what verbal communication style is deemed appropriate or inappropriate, elegant or uneducated. They frequently get to choose and use identity labels for those who are less powerful. Those whose language does not fit the standard, or who are the recipients of negative labels, may feel marginalized and resentful, leading to difficult communication interactions.

Journal Prompt 5.4: Language and Power
Consider the following questions: How does power influence language, words, accent, and labels? Can you give examples of the role of power in language, words, accent, and labels?

Ethics and Verbal Communication

5.5 Identify and give examples of confirming communication, disconfirming communication, and hate speech.

We have already discussed a number of ethical issues related to verbal communication in this book. In Chapter 1, we argued that ethical communicators consider the benefit and/or harm associated with their messages. In this section, we examine one specific type of language whose use may harm individuals or relationships.

Hate Speech

In the United States, we place a high value on freedom of speech. We have codified this value into our legal system, beginning with the First Amendment to the Constitution.

However, freedom of speech is always balanced by competing societal interests. As the familiar saying goes, freedom of speech does not include the right to shout "fire!" in a crowded theater. But what about the right to express negative opinions about others? In the 1980s and 1990s, as U.S. society became more aware of the ethics of minority rights, the term *hate speech* began to be used (ACLU, 1994). **Hate speech**, or the use of verbal communication to attack others based on some social category such as race, ethnicity, religion, or sexuality, is seen as threatening an entire group or inciting violence against members of these groups. In the United States, the First Amendment guarantee of free speech is generally used to protect against laws that would make hate speech illegal (Liptak, 2008). However, many argue that even if hate speech is legal, it is unethical.

▲ Hate speech is legal in the United States, but many argue that it is unethical.

hate speech
Use of verbal communication to attack others based upon some social category.

Many countries view the use of verbal communication to attack, demean, and degrade other groups of people as not only unethical but also illegal. Canada's criminal code, for example, forbids speech, writing, and Internet postings that advocate genocide or that publicly incite hatred (Media Awareness Network, n.d.). As another example, in some European countries it is illegal to deny that the Holocaust occurred. In February 2017, an Austrian woman was found guilt of denying the Holocaust happened when she criticized a Facebook posting of the German soccer team commemorating the liberation of Auschwitz which called "spreading lies" ("Austrian woman," 2017). Also in February 2017, Amazon came under attack for selling books that deny the Holocaust in countries where it is illegal to do so, but later took down the books from their sites in France and Germany; they are still available in the United Kingdom and the United States (Gamp, 2017; Holmes, 2017).

Sometimes even speaking another language from others can invoke anger and, sometimes physical aggression. In November 2016, a man was punched in the face several times on a Metro Transit bus in Minneapolis because he was speaking Somali to a friend. The bus video shows the attack was unprovoked and the attacker yelled "speak English" (Jany, 2016). A month earlier, in October 2016, a British man grabbed a plank of wood and hit a Spanish man in the face and yelled at him to "speak English" (Duncan, 2016). Although people are free to speak in any languages they wish, sometimes negative feelings and attitudes arise when people are not speaking the dominant language.

Whether illegal or unethical, the use of verbal communication to attack others based on their group membership is often seen as an attack on the whole group, not just the person who is the receiver of such messages. See *Did You Know? Cyberbullying* for another example of using verbal communication to attack others.

Critical Thinking Prompt
As ethical communicators, where should we draw the line between free speech and unethical verbal communication?

Confirming and Disconfirming Communication

Although hate speech may be obviously unethical, there are other, less obvious types of communication that can be unethical because of the harm they can cause. One of these is *disconfirming communication*. **Disconfirming communication** occurs when people make comments that reject or invalidate a self-image, positive or negative, of their conversational partners (Dance & Larson, 1976). Consider the following conversation:

disconfirming communication
Comments that reject or invalidate a positive or negative self-image of our conversational partners.

TRACEY: Guess what? I earned an A on my midterm.

LOU: Gee, it must have been an easy test.

DID YOU KNOW?
Cyberbullying

Does the rapid pace of new technology development make cyberbullying difficult, or even impossible, to stop?

Cyberbullying has emerged as a serious problem as communication technologies have developed. The consequences can be as severe as the victims of the cyberbullying committing suicide. Cyberbullying is defined by the U.S. Department of Health and Human Services as:

> bullying that takes place using electronic technology. Electronic technology includes devices and equipment such as cell phones, computers, and tablets as well as communication tools including social media sites, text messages, chat, and websites.

As technology continues to develop, new apps become available that some people use for cyberbullying. Although the underlying intent behind creating new apps might not be to allow new venues for cyberbullying, people often use apps for their own goals. One app that has gained popularity in cyberbullying is Yik Yak. This app has become popular among young people because it is perceived as beyond the surveillance of parents and educators, unlike Facebook or other social media sites. As new apps are developed, parents and educators might not be able to keep up with these new apps. As the technological landscape changes, cyberbullies will find new routes to harass others.

Although particular apps can be identified, is it possible to stay on top of all of the new communication technology and apps that are being developed?

SOURCE: U.S. Department of Health and Human Services. (n.d.). What is cyberbullying? Retrieved March 7, 2014, from: http://www.stopbullying.gov/cyberbullying/what-is-it/.

Lou's response is an example of disconfirming communication because it suggests that Tracey could not have earned her A because of competence or ability. Consequently, his message disconfirms Tracey's image of herself. You can disconfirm people either explicitly ("I've never really thought of you as being smart") or implicitly (as Lou did).

How can messages such as these cause harm? Imagine that you received numerous disconfirming messages from people who are important to you. How might it affect you? Such messages not only can negatively influence your self-image, but they also can impair your relationships with the people who disconfirm you. For instance, Harry Weger Jr. (2005) and John Caughlin (2002) have found that when couples engage in disconfirming behavior, their marital dissatisfaction increases. Disconfirming messages can harm both individuals and relationships and may be considered unethical as well as ineffective because they focus on the person.

If you want to avoid sending disconfirming messages, what should you do instead? You can provide others with confirming messages. Confirming messages validate positive self-images of others, as in the following example of **confirming communication**.

confirming communication
Comments that validate positive self-images of others.

TRACEY:	Guess what? I earned an A on my midterm.
LOU:	That's great. I know it's a tough class; you deserve to be proud.
OR LOU MIGHT SAY:	Congratulations! I know you were studying very hard and you deserve that grade.

Confirming messages are not only more ethical, they are usually more effective. Most people enjoy communicating with those who encourage them to feel good about themselves. Although engaging in confirming communication will not guarantee that you will be instantly popular, if you are sincere, it will increase the effectiveness of your communication and ensure that you are communicating ethically. If using confirming communication does not come naturally to you, you can practice until it does.

You might be wondering how you can provide negative feedback to people without being disconfirming. We discuss how to do this in the next section.

Journal Prompt 5.5: Types of Communication
Consider the following question:
What are examples of confirming communication, disconfirming communication, and hate speech? Give at least one example of each type of communication.

Improving Your Verbal Communication Skills

5.6 Discuss ways to improve your own verbal communication skills.

When considering the ethics of language use, you should think about the effectiveness of your verbal choices. What are some guidelines for engaging in more effective verbal communication? We describe two ways in which you might improve: You can work on using "I" statements and also become more aware of the power of language.

"I" Statements

One type of disconfirming message involves making negative generalizations about others. Although you recognize that people are complex and variable, have you nevertheless found yourself making negative generalizations such as those listed here?

> "You are so thoughtless."

> "You are never on time."

As you can see, negative generalizations (which also are called "you" statements) are typically disconfirming. But, in the real world everyone lives in, some people *are* thoughtless, and some *are* consistently late. So is there an ethical and effective way to make your dissatisfaction known? Yes. You can use a type of message called an "I" statement. "I" statements allow you to express your feelings (even negative ones) by focusing on your own experiences rather than making negative generalizations (or "you" statements) about others.

"I" statements are conveyed through a three-part message that describes

1. the other person's behavior,
2. your feelings about that behavior, and
3. the consequences the other's behavior has for you.

Taking the examples just given and rewriting them as "I" statements, you could come up with:

> "When you criticize my appearance (behavior), I feel unloved (feeling), and I respond by withdrawing from you (consequence)."

> "I think I must be unimportant to you (feeling) when you arrive late for dinner (behavior), so I don't feel like cooking for you (consequence)."

"You" statements often lead recipients to feel defensive or angry because of the negative evaluation contained in the message and because the listener resents the speaker's position of passing judgment. "I" statements can lead to more constructive resolution of conflicts because they arouse less defensiveness. They also are more effective than "you" statements because the receiver is more likely to listen and respond to them (Kubany, Bauer, Muraoka, Richard, & Read, 1995). In addition, to make "I" statements, speakers have to explore exactly what they are dissatisfied with, how it makes them feel, and what the consequences of the other person's behavior are. "I" statements prevent speakers from attacking others to vent their feelings.

Although many communication scholars believe in the value of "I" statements, a recent study found that people reacted similarly to *both* "I" and "you" statements involving negative emotions. However, the authors point out that their study involved written hypothetical conflict situations. They admit that their results might have been different if they had studied real-life conflict situations (Bippus & Young, 2005).

Although "I" statements can be effective in a variety of contexts, this does not mean they are *always* appropriate. Situations may arise where others' behavior so violates what you believe is decent or appropriate that you wish to state your opinions strongly. Thus, if your friend abuses alcohol or takes illicit drugs, you may need to say, "You should not drive a car tonight" or "You need to get help for your addiction." The effectiveness of one's verbal communication must always be evaluated in the context of the situation, the relationships one has with others, and one's goal.

Become Aware of the Power of Language

As we noted in Chapter 1, language is a powerful force that has consequences and ethical implications. Wars have been started, relationships have been ruined, and much anger and unhappiness has resulted from intentional and unintentional verbal messages. The old adage "Sticks and stones can break my bones, but words will never hurt me" is not always true. Words *can* hurt.

When a speaker refers to others by negative or offensive identity terms, the speaker not only causes harm, he or she also denies those labeled individuals their identities—even if it isn't intentional. For example, one of our students, Cynthia, told us how bad she felt when she realized that some of her gay coworkers were offended by her use of the term homosexual (instead of gay). They explained that homosexual was used as a description of a psychiatric disease by the American Psychiatric Association's list of mental disorders until 1973 and has a connotation of this sexual orientation as a cold, clinical "condition." Using her embarrassment as a learning experience, she initiated an enlightening discussion with her coworkers. She learned that often the best way to discover what someone "wants to be called" is to ask. However, a conversation of this nature can only occur in the context of a mutually respectful relationship—one reason to have a diverse group of friends and acquaintances.

Journal Prompt 5.6: Improving Verbal Communication
Consider the following question:
What are two ways you can improve your verbal communication skills?

SUMMARY

5.1 Identify three reasons for learning about verbal communication.

- Verbal communication plays a significant role in people's lives, assisting in relationship development, creating identities, and accomplishing everyday tasks.

5.2 Describe the functions and components of language.

- Language is the foundation of verbal processes and it functions in at least seven ways: instrumental, regulatory, informative, heuristic, interactional, personal, and imaginative.

- The four components of language study are *phonology*, the study of sounds; *syntax*, the grammar and rules for arranging units of meaning; *semantics*, the meaning of words; and *pragmatics*, the rules for appropriate use of language.

5.3 Identify and give examples of several major influences on verbal communication.

- Individual influences on language include speakers' memberships in various identity groups (gender, age, regionality, ethnicity and race, education and occupation).

- When identities influence several aspects of language (vocabulary, grammar, and pronunciation), these speakers have distinct dialects. In other instances identity groups' language variations may be minor, involving only some pronunciation or word choices.

5.4 Describe the relationships between language, perception, and power.

- Societal forces affect verbal processes because they shape our perceptions and the power relationships that surround us.

- The language used in a given society influences its members' perceptions of social reality, whereas power relationships affect how its members' verbal patterns are evaluated.

5.5 Identify and give examples of confirming communication, disconfirming communication, and hate speech.

- Communicating ethically means avoiding *hate speech* (verbally attacking someone based on race, ethnicity, religion, or sexuality).

- *Disconfirming communication* rejects or invalidates self-image, while *confirming communication* validates positive self-image.

5.6 Discuss ways to improve your own verbal communication skills.

- Learn to use *"I" statements* when expressing dissatisfaction.

- Recognize the power of language. Words can hold deeper meaning and ethical implications, so use them thoughtfully.

KEY TERMS

instrumental p. 97
regulatory p. 97
informative p. 97
heuristic p. 97
interactional p. 97
personal language p. 97
imaginative p. 97
grammar p. 98
phonology p. 98
syntax p. 98

semantics p. 98
denotative meaning p. 99
connotative meaning p. 99
pragmatics p. 99
speech act theory p. 100
dialect p. 103
lexical choice p. 103
cohort effect p. 105
African American Vernacular
    English p. 107

code switching p. 107
jargon p. 108
nominalists p. 109
relativists p. 109
Sapir-Whorf hypothesis p. 109
cocultural theory p. 110
androcentrism p. 111
hate speech p. 115
disconfirming communication p. 115
confirming communication p. 116

APPLY WHAT YOU KNOW

1. For each scenario, write a paragraph describing a typical communication exchange. For each, think about the various elements of verbal communication: sounds, grammar, meaning (word choice), conversational rules, and contextual rules.

   - an informal family outing
   - a meeting with your advisor
   - a bar, where you are trying to impress potential partners

   Hint: Working in a small group, see whether you and your classmates can come up with some shared contextual rules for communication in these various situations. Give some reasons why you can or cannot come up with shared rules.

2. Take three sheets of paper and write one of the following words on each sheet: *garbage, milk, mother*. Take the first piece of paper and crumple it up and then stomp on it. Do the same with the second and third pieces. How did you feel crumpling up and stomping on the first piece of paper? The second? The third? What does this say perhaps about the difference between denotative and connotative meanings?

3. For each of the examples that follow, create an "I" statement that expresses your feelings about the situation:

   - Once again, your roommate has borrowed some of your clothes without asking and has returned them dirty or damaged.
   - For the third time this semester, your instructor has changed the date of an exam.
   - Your good friend has developed a habit of canceling plans at the last moment.
   - Your romantic partner embarrasses you by teasing you about personal habits in front of friends.

   Form a group with two or three of your classmates. Take turns reading your "I" statement for each situation. Discuss the strengths and weaknesses of each statement. As a group, develop an "I" statement for each situation that best expresses the group's feelings without encouraging defensiveness in the receiver.

4. Locate five people who either grew up in different parts of the United States or who grew up in different countries. Try to include both men and women and people of different ages in your sample. Ask each person to answer the following questions:

   - What do you call a carbonated beverage?
   - How do you pronounce "roof"?
   - What expressions do you use that some other people have had trouble understanding?
   - What does the term *feminist* mean?
   - Who do you think talks "different"?

Nonverbal Communication

LEARNING OBJECTIVES

CHAPTER TOPICS

6.1 Describe the important role of nonverbal communication in social interaction.

The Importance of Nonverbal Communication

6.2 Define *nonverbal communication*.

What Is Nonverbal Communication?

6.3 Define five nonverbal codes and explain the five functions of nonverbal messages.

Nonverbal Communication and the Individual

6.4 Explain how nonverbal communication can both trigger and express prejudice and discrimination.

The Individual, Nonverbal Communication, and Society

6.5 Explain how nonverbal communication can be used to communicate unethically.

Ethics and Nonverbal Communication

6.6 Explain how you can improve your ability to interpret nonverbal behavior.

Improving Your Nonverbal Communication Skills

Humans express a wide array of nonverbal behaviors, many of which can be quite subtle. Consequently, understanding nonverbal communication requires knowledge and skill.

Charee took her four-year-old sister with her to a group project meeting at which some members argued about how to present their class paper. After observing the interaction for a few minutes, her sister Anna whispered, "When it's your turn to talk, you have to make your mad face."

Even though Anna is only four years old, she is sensitive to the nonverbal behavior of others. She readily reads others' facial expressions and assigns meaning to them. Children learn the basics of nonverbal communication quickly (Boone & Cunningham, 1998); in fact, infants from an early age imitate others' nonverbal behavior. For example, when newborns observe caregivers sticking out their tongues, they do the same (Als, 1977; Meltzoff & Prinz, 2002).

In this chapter, we take a close look at the intricacies of nonverbal communication and the many factors that shape nonverbal messages and their interpretation. First, we describe the importance of nonverbal communication, provide a definition, and explore how it differs from nonverbal behavior. We then give you an overview of the various types of nonverbal codes, and we examine the functions that nonverbal messages serve. We next explore how societal forces intersect with individuals' nonverbal communication. We conclude the chapter by discussing ethical issues in nonverbal communication and providing you with suggestions for improving your nonverbal communication skills.

The Importance of Nonverbal Communication

6.1   Describe the important role of nonverbal communication in social interaction.

Nonverbal communication plays an important role in social interaction. It helps us express and interpret verbal messages, navigate everyday life, and make policy decisions.

First, nonverbal communication allows us to communicate more complex messages—such as when we:

- smile to *reinforce* an expression of thanks;
- use the "OK" sign to *substitute* for saying "I am all right";
- laugh flirtatiously to *contradict* the words, "I hate you";
- put your fingers close together to *illustrate* how thin your new computer is.

Second, nonverbal communication influences how individuals interpret messages, especially those related to feelings, moods, and attitudes. Nonverbal cues are important to the expression of emotion because communicators are often more comfortable expressing their feelings nonverbally (such as by smiling or glaring) than they are stating them more explicitly through words (Mehrabian, 2007). For example, how often do you flatly tell a friend or colleague, "I am mad at you"? If you are like most people, this is a relatively rare event; instead, you probably rely on some type of nonverbal cue to indicate your dissatisfaction. The ability to decode others' nonverbal communication effectively helps you interpret the nuanced meanings in others' messages as well as how they feel—and how they feel about you. It also helps you respond better to those messages and feelings. This ability is particularly important in close relationships. For instance, a study of nonverbal communication and marital satisfaction found that couples' ability to correctly decode their partner's nonverbal communication affect was connected to their relational satisfaction, especially for husbands (Koerner & Fitzpatrick, 2002).

Nonverbal communication can be complex and ambiguous—both for senders of messages to convey and for receivers of messages to interpret. Even though we begin learning nonverbal communication as children, we often have difficulty interpreting others' nonverbal communication. Why is this so? One reason is the fact that humans express a wide array of nonverbal behaviors, many of which can be quite subtle. Consequently, understanding nonverbal communication requires knowledge and skill.

However, beware of books, websites, and magazine articles that promise to teach you to "read a person like a book": there is no such thing as a key to decoding or interpreting every **nonverbal behavior** in every context. Why not? Because understanding nonverbal communication requires interpreting behavior and assigning meaning to it, and we don't always have the information we need to do that. If you are sitting in the library and notice a stranger staring at you, what does the stare mean? Does the person think he knows you? Is he interested in meeting you? Is he being aggressive? Or is the person simply lost in thought and only *appearing* to be gazing at you? Nonverbal cues can be ambiguous. Because the meaning of nonverbal behavior is determined by a variety of factors, including context, culture, and even intentionality, it can be tricky to interpret a specific behavior.

In addition, nonverbal cues are continuous, meaning that people exhibit nonverbal behaviors virtually all the time they are conscious, and multiple behaviors act in concert to create a given message—or different messages, even unrelated ones. For example, imagine that Joan is talking to her husband about their need to spend time together to strengthen their marriage. Just as her husband asks, "What do you want to do about our marriage?" Joan happens to look over his shoulder at her computer screen and sees it displaying an error message. In frustration, she throws up her hands and sighs heavily. Joan was responding to her computer failure, but her husband thought she was responding to his question. He became upset, assuming she was expressing a wish to give up on their marriage.

Nonverbal communication also can be difficult to interpret because nonverbal cues are multichanneled; that is, they can be transmitted in a variety of ways simultaneously. Speakers can convey nonverbal messages through their facial expressions, voice qualities, eye gaze, posture, and gestures, among other ways. Moreover, because a variety of cues may occur at the same time, it can be difficult and confusing to keep up with everything (Schwartz, Foa, & Foa, 1983). If, for example, you are focusing on someone's face, you may miss important messages conveyed by the body.

"Pop psychology" treatments of nonverbal communication typically assume that each behavior has one meaning regardless of the context or who is performing it. Such explanations don't distinguish between nonverbal behavior and nonverbal communication; nor do they consider context, culture, individual variations in behavior, or the relationship that exists between the people being observed. All of these factors, and more, can influence the meaning of a nonverbal behavior in a specific instance. So don't believe that just because someone has her arms crossed over her body it means she is closed off to you. It may simply mean she needs a sweater.

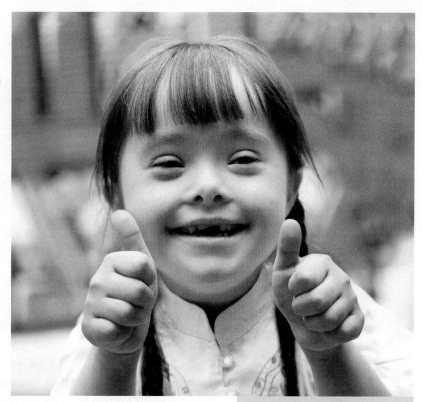

▲ Even young children understand and use nonverbal communication.

nonverbal behavior
All the nonverbal actions people perform.

▲ Public policy seeks to regulate nonverbal expression, such as what type of clothing people can wear.

Third, nonverbal skills can help individuals navigate everyday life. For example, humans rely on nonverbal cues to determine whether other humans are a threat. In the television show *Going Tribal*, journalist Bruce Parry visited the remote Suri tribe in Ethiopia. As he approached the first tribal member, Parry carefully observed the tribesman thrust his bow and arrow at him and pace quickly back and forth while averting his eye gaze. Although many of the Suri's nonverbal behaviors communicated belligerence, the fact that he did not stare aggressively influenced Bruce to approach him slowly with a gift—which was accepted.

Similarly, on a daily basis people need to be able to read subtle nonverbal behaviors to assess how friendly or hostile others may be. This is especially true for individuals whose identities are less valued culturally or whose societal position makes them more vulnerable. Because of this vulnerability, such individuals tend to become quite adept at reading and interpreting nonverbal communication. For example, if Gary's boss walks into the office frowning and shaking her head, Gary may interpret this as meaning that she is in a bad mood; consequently, he may try to be especially helpful and avoid doing anything to provoke her. In a study that compared African Americans' and White Americans' ability to read the nonverbal behaviors of Whites, researchers found that African Americans were far better at detecting prejudicial attitudes as expressed in subtle nonverbal behavior than were Whites (Richeson & Shelton, 2005). Similarly, a study of heterosexual and gay men found that gay men were better able to identify the sexual orientation of unfamiliar men when watching videos of them (Shelp, 2002).

Finally, nonverbal communication also is important because it can affect public policy decisions. For example, after several years of allowing students to wear just about anything they wished to school, many public schools now institute dress codes. Although some schools primarily regulate clothing that they see as "inappropriate" or too revealing, others require school uniforms. The supporters of this latter policy argue that school uniforms "help erase cultural and economic differences among students" (Isaacson, 1998) and improve student performance and attendance. Regulating school dress rests on the assumption that one form of nonverbal communication—attire— should be regulated because it can be distracting or even disruptive. Other examples of public policy attempts to regulate nonverbal expression include efforts to ban flag burning and to forbid the wearing of Muslim headscarves. Countries would not engage in efforts to control nonverbal expression if it were not so important.

Journal Prompt 6.1: Interpreting Nonverbal Communication
Consider the following question:
What features of nonverbal communication make it challenging for us to interpret it easily?

What Is Nonverbal Communication?

6.2 Define *nonverbal communication*.

The nonverbal components of communication include all the messages that people transmit through means other than words. More specifically, communication scholar Valerie Manusov and psychologist Miles Patterson define **nonverbal communication** as "encompassing the sending and receiving of information through appearance, objects, the environment and behavior in social settings" (Manusov & Patterson, 2006, p. xi).

nonverbal communication
The sending and receiving of information through appearance, objects, the environment, and behavior.

Thus, they argue that we communicate nonverbally when we blow a kiss, scratch our arm, or wear clothing that signals our group membership. Even more frequently, nonverbal and verbal aspects of communication combine to convey messages, as when we indicate anger by turning our backs and saying, "I don't want to talk with you right now."

However, not every scholar believes that all nonverbal behavior is communicative. These researchers argue that nonverbal communication occurs only when nonverbal behavior has symbolic meaning and is communicated intentionally (Burgoon, Buller, & Woodall, 1996). That is, they believe nonverbal communication stands for something, whereas nonverbal behavior may not. For example, from this perspective, scratching one's arm usually isn't intended by the scratcher, nor understood by the observer, to convey a particular message. Although it may provide information (that one's arm itches), it doesn't necessarily signal an *intentional* message. Rather, it would be considered an involuntary bodily "output." However, these scholars would argue that in baseball when a manager scratches his arm to signal that a runner on base should steal home, scratching the arm is symbolic and, therefore, an instance of nonverbal communication.

Nonetheless, these scholars acknowledge that some nonverbal communication does lack the element of intentionality. For example, a smile may be understood as an expression of pleasure even if the smiler is unaware that he is smiling. Thus, if a behavior typically is used communicatively, then that behavior is understood to be part of our nonverbal "vocabulary" and will be interpreted as such, regardless of one's own conscious use of it (Burgoon, Buller, & Woodall, 1996).

However, scholars who prefer a broader definition of nonverbal communication argue that many actions one might consider just a "bodily output" can still convey messages nonverbally. For example, people usually cough because of a scratchy throat or yawn because they are tired, and when they engage in these behaviors others interpret their meaning. Of course, they also believe that when a person coughs as a signal to capture someone's attention or deliberately yawns to indicate he is bored, he is engaging in nonverbal communication.

As our discussion thus far suggests, most nonverbal behaviors have a variety of meanings—just as scratching one's arm can have multiple meanings. Therefore, neither we, nor anyone else, can provide you with interpretations for specific nonverbal actions. Perhaps in part because of this difficulty, we cannot accurately estimate the amount of meaning that nonverbal communication contributes to the overall meaning in an interaction. This inability is revealed in *Did You Know? How Much Does Nonverbal Communication Contribute to Meaning?* where you can see why it can be difficult to estimate how much meaning nonverbal components convey in any message.

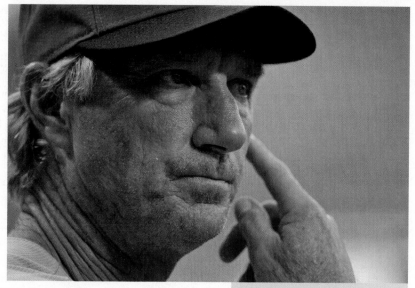

▲ Baseball coaches often develop nonverbal signals that have specific symbolic meaning known only to their teammates.

Critical Thinking Prompt
Which of these two positions regarding nonverbal communication/nonverbal behavior seems more reasonable to you, and why? What evidence or reasoning influenced your decision? Finally, what difference does this distinction make?

Journal Prompt 6.2: Defining Nonverbal Communication
Consider the following questions: What is nonverbal communication? How do some scholars differentiate nonverbal behavior from nonverbal communication?

Nonverbal Communication and the Individual

6.3 Define five nonverbal codes and explain the five functions of nonverbal messages.

If a smile is viewed as communicating pleasure even when the smiler doesn't intend to do so, then why don't all behaviors that are part of our nonverbal vocabulary always

DID YOU KNOW?
How Much Does Nonverbal Communication Contribute to Meaning?

How much of the meaning of a message do you think is conveyed by its nonverbal components? Fifty percent? Seventy-five percent? One of the most common beliefs about communication is that more than 90 percent of the meaning of a message is transmitted by its nonverbal elements. However, in truth, we do not know! So where did this belief originate?

In 1967, psychologist Albert Mehrabian (along with Morton Wiener) wrote that 93 percent of the meaning of the utterances he examined was conveyed through the nonverbal aspects of communication. Specifically, he argued that 38 percent of meaning in his study was derived from paralinguistic cues (tone of voice, etc.) and 55 percent from facial expressions, leaving only 7 percent of meaning to be provided by the verbal message. After he published his findings, other people, researchers and nonresearchers alike, began to generalize his claims about his one study to all communicative interactions.

However, a variety of scholars have contradicted this claim, either arguing for a different percentage (Birdwhistell, 1985) or suggesting that one cannot accurately determine how much words, context, nonverbal messages, and other factors actually contribute to the meaning of an utterance. Those who critique Mehrabian's analysis argue that his study exhibited several problems. First, it examined how people interpreted the meaning of single tape-recorded words, which is not how we naturally communicate. Second, he combined the results of two studies that most scholars believe should not be combined. Further, he did not consider the contributions to meaning made by gestures and posture. Also, he tried to estimate the contribution of particular nonverbal behaviors—for example, gesture versus facial expression. In practice, however, no one behavior is particularly useful in determining meaning. In other words, inferences made about the meaning of any given action are not all that reliable, nor are estimates of what percentage of the total message a single nonverbal cue communicates.

SOURCES: Birdwhistell, R. L. (1985). *Kinesics and context: Essays in body motion communication.*

Philadelphia: University of Philadelphia Press.Mehrabian, A. (1971). Nonverbal communication.

Chicago: Aldine-Atherton.Mehrabian, A. (2007). Nonverbal communication. Chicago, IL: Aldine de Gruyter.

convey the same meaning? The answer is that assigning one simple meaning to a nonverbal behavior ignores the multiple meanings that may exist, depending on the context in which the behavior occurs. For example, you will read in this chapter that when a person leans toward another (called *forward body lean*), this is often a sign of interest or involvement. Does that mean that forward body lean always indicates interest? Absolutely not! A person might lean forward for a variety of reasons: her stomach hurts, the back of her chair is hot, or her lower back needs to be stretched.

To understand the meaning of a nonverbal behavior you have to consider the entire behavioral context, including what the person might be communicating verbally (Jones & LeBaron, 2002). Therefore, interpreting others' nonverbal behavior requires that you consider a variety of factors that can influence meaning. To interpret nonverbal communication, you also need to know the codes, or symbols and rules, that signal various messages. Finally, you will benefit from a familiarity with the variety of ways that nonverbal messages function. These are topics we take up next.

Influences on Nonverbal Communication

Four factors that play a significant role in how we interpret nonverbal communication are: *culture, relationship, familiarity, and gender. Culture* is one of the more important factors that influence the meaning of nonverbal communication. This is not to say that many nonverbal cues and signals aren't shared; in fact, research shows that gaze is used to communicate aggression, dominance, and power as well as connection and nurturance across cultures and even species (Matsumoto, 2006); however, the specific manner in which gaze is used to communicate these messages can vary. For example, in many Arabic cultures, eye gaze during social interaction is more direct than is typical in the United States (Watson & Graves, 1966); thus, eye gaze that might be interpreted as friendly and involved in an Arabic culture could be perceived as somewhat aggressive by a U.S. American. Similarly, within the United States, gaze and visual behavior differ across sexes and ethnic groups, with women tending to gaze more than men (Briton & Hall, 1995) and African Americans often using more continuous eye gaze while talking and less while listening than do many Whites (Samovar & Porter, 2004).

Some nonverbal cues are used widely across cultures, such as nodding to mean yes. However, many nonverbal gestures have vastly different meanings in different cultures. In the United States, for instance, the "thumbs up" signals success and the "hitchhiker's thumb" asks for a ride, but these nonverbal signs carry potentially vulgar meanings in several other cultures. In East Africa, instead of pointing with fingers, people often point with their lips—a gesture that is completely unfamiliar to most people in the United States. Differences in gestures also occur across ethnic groups in the United States. For example, Korean Americans historically tended to reserve smiling, shaking hands, and saying hello for friends and family; however, many immigrants changed this pattern of behavior once they recognized its meaning and importance in the United States (Young, 1999). Thus, the meaning of any nonverbal behavior is defined by the cultures of those interacting (Axtell, 1993; Segerstrale & Molnár, 1997).

▲ This gesture of support for the University of Texas Longhorns might be misinterpreted in Norway, where it is a sign of Satan.

In addition to culture, *the relationship between the people interacting* affects the meaning of nonverbal behaviors (Manusov, 1995). If a husband takes his wife's arm as they are crossing the street, the meaning likely is viewed as some mixture of care and affection; if a police officer were to do so, one probably would interpret it as an aggressive or controlling gesture. However, if a boss were to do the same with a subordinate, the meaning is more complex and potentially confusing or troubling. One might wonder whether she is being friendly, controlling, affectionate—or maybe too affectionate? How we interpret others' nonverbal behavior, then, is highly dependent on the type of relationship we have with them.

Third, the meaning we attribute to someone's nonverbal behavior varies based on *familiarity or how well we know the communicator.* For example, if a stranger smiles at you, you might interpret it as a gesture of friendliness because that is the meaning most often associated with this facial expression. However, if you know your best friend tends to smile when she is angry, then you will be more accurate at interpreting that her smile is a sign of her displeasure than would someone who did not know her well. Once we know people, then, we can usually read their nonverbal behavior and interpret its associated messages with more accuracy, as Abbad explains in *It Happened to Me: Abbad.* Finally, we tend to

It Happened to Me
Abbad

I am from the Middle East, and I arrived in the United States in 2000 with a couple of my friends. On a school break, we decided to travel to Washington, DC. On the road, we stopped at a McDonald's to eat and to pray. As Muslims, we have to pray five times a day, and during the prayer we cannot talk at all. While in the middle of our prayer, a McDonald's employee approached and asked what we were doing. Since we could not talk, one of my friends used a hand gesture that in our culture means "wait for a minute." This hand gesture is expressed by holding all of one's fingers and thumb together sort of like a cup. For some reason, the employee understood the gesture as an invitation for a fight. I guess this is what it means in some parts of the United States. That's when the employee called 911. By the time the police officer arrived, we were done with our prayer. We explained we were new to this country and that the hand gesture we used means something else in our culture. We apologized to the employee for the misunderstanding and continued on our trip.

interpret individuals' nonverbal behavior based on their sex. For example, when women toss their hair, the behavior often is read as flirtatious—and therefore communicative. However, if a man does the same, we are more likely to believe he is just trying to get his hair out of his eyes—a nonverbal behavior that is not necessarily communicative. As we discuss throughout this book, sex differences in nonverbal and verbal communication are as a result of biological as well as social and cultural influences.

Nonverbal Codes

nonverbal codes

Distinct, organized means of expression that consists of symbols and rules for their use.

Nonverbal codes or signals are distinct, organized means of expression that consist of both symbols and rules for their use (Cicca, Step, & Turkstra, 2003). For example, when you place your hand palm up and then curl your fingers toward yourself, you are using a symbol that in the United States is understood to mean "come here." Rules for the use of that symbol include that the palm is face up and the arm is straight in front of you. This symbol is part of larger set of symbols that belong to the nonverbal code of kinesics.

Although we describe a range of codes in this section, we do not mean to imply that any one code occurs in isolation. Generally, a set of behaviors or codes together determines the meaning or significance of an action. For example, if people are smiling, can we interpret that they are happy? As you know, sometimes people smile when they are angry, to be polite, or to conceal their feelings. To better understand what a smile means, we typically pay attention to how tense or relaxed a person's body is, whether the person's eyes are also "smiling," how physically close or distant the other person is to us, and whether her voice sounds "happy" or "angry." Thus, we interpret others' nonverbal communication by looking at many types of codes. However, here we discuss the codes individually, because it is easier to understand them that way. In the real world, without access to a variety of nonverbal codes and the context of the interaction, interpretations about any behavior may be questionable or even wrong (Patterson, 1983). In this section, we'll look at five types of nonverbal codes—*kinesics, paralinguistics, time and space, haptics,* and *appearance and artifacts*—to see how this system of nonverbal codes works.

kinesics

Nonverbal communication sent by the body, including gestures, posture, movement, facial expressions, and eye behavior.

Kinesics **Kinesics** is perhaps the largest nonverbal code; it describes a system of studying nonverbal communication sent by the body, including gestures, posture, movement, facial expressions, and eye behavior. For clarity, we group kinesics communication into two general categories, those behaviors involving the body and those involving the face.

gestures

Nonverbal communication made with part of the body, including actions such as pointing, waving, or holding up a hand to direct people's attention.

illustrators

Signals that accompany speech to clarify or emphasize the verbal message.

emblems

Gestures that stand for a specific verbal meaning.

adaptors

Gestures used to manage emotions.

regulators

Gestures used to control conversations.

The Body Our bodies convey many nonverbal messages. For example, we use **gestures** such as pointing, waving, and holding up our hands to direct people's attention. Communicators use four types of nonverbal gestures: *illustrators, emblems, adaptors,* and *regulators.* **Illustrators** are signals that accompany speech to clarify or emphasize the verbal messages. Thus, when people come back from a fishing trip they hold their hands far apart to indicate the size of the fish that got away. **Emblems** are gestures that stand for a specific verbal meaning; for example, raising one's hand in class indicates one wishes to speak and placing a finger parallel to one's lips signifies that others should be quiet. **Adaptors** are gestures we use to manage our emotions. Many adaptors are nervous gestures such as tapping a pencil, jiggling a leg, or twirling one's hair. Finally, people use **regulators** to control conversation; for example, if you want to prevent someone from interrupting you, you might hold up your hand to indicate that the other person should wait. In contrast, if you wish to interrupt and take the floor, you might raise a finger to signal your desire.

Gestures contribute a lot to our communication efforts; even their frequency can signal meaning. For instance, how much gesturing we do while speaking can indicate how involved we are in a conversation. Many people who are excited indicate their involvement by using many and varied gestures; those who have little involvement may indicate their lack of interest by their failure to gesture.

We also use our bodies to convey meaning through **posture and movement**. In general, posture is evaluated in two ways: by how *immediate* it is and by how relaxed it appears (Mehrabian, 1971; Richards, Rollerson, & Phillips, 1991). **Immediacy** refers to how close or involved people appear to be with each other. For example, when people like someone they tend to orient their bodies in the other person's direction, lean toward them, and look at them directly when they speak. How do people act when they wish to avoid someone? Typically, they engage in the opposite behavior. They turn their backs or refuse to look at them, and if they are forced to stand or sit near the person they dislike, they lean away from them. To understand this, imagine how you would behave if you were attempting to reject an unwanted amorous advance.

Relaxation refers to the degree of tension one's body displays. When you are at home watching TV, for instance, you probably display a relaxed posture: lounging in a chair with your legs stretched out in front of you and your arms resting loosely on the chair's arms. However, if you are waiting at the dentist's office, you may sit hunched forward, your legs pressed tightly together, and your hands firmly grasping the chair arms.

The way you walk or move also can communicate messages to others, particularly about your mood or emotional state. Sometimes you use movement deliberately to communicate a message—such as when you stomp around the apartment to indicate your anger. At other times, your movement is simply a nonverbal behavior—that is, you move naturally and unconsciously without any clear intentionality. Even when your movement is not intentional, observers can and do make judgments about you. One study found that observers could identify when pedestrians were sad, angry, happy, or proud, just from the way they walked (Montepare, Goldstein, & Clausen, 1987). However, some emotional states (anger) were easier to identify than others (pride), and some individuals were easier to classify than others. So although people consciously communicate a great deal with their body movements and gestures and observers interpret others' movements, some messages are more clearly transmitted than others. It should also be noted that many of the same factors discussed previously, such as culture, context, background knowledge, and gender, can affect the ability to interpret kinesic behavior.

The Face   *Facial expressions* communicate more than perhaps any other nonverbal behavior. They are the primary channels for transmitting emotion, and the eyes, in particular, convey important messages regarding attraction and attention. Some research suggests that facial expressions of happiness, sadness, anger, surprise, fear, and disgust are the same across cultures and, in fact, are innate (Ekman & Friesen, 1969, 1986), although not all scholars agree. Through observations of deaf, blind, and brain-damaged children, researchers have concluded that commonality of facial expressions among humans is not the result of observation and learning but rather to genetic programming (Eibl-Eibesfeld, 1972; Ekman, 2003).

The ability to accurately recognize others' emotions gives individuals an edge in their interpersonal actions. For example, people with greater emotional recognition accuracy are effective in negotiations and are able to create more value for all parties and to achieve more favorable outcomes (Elfenbein, Maw, White, Tan, & Aik, 2007). If you are not adept at recognizing others' emotions, however, you can improve your ability to do so. A variety of studies show that individuals who are trained in emotion recognition and then receive feedback on their performance can improve their ability to recognize others' emotional expressions, especially if their targets are from different cultures than their own (Elfenbein, 2006).

Of course, people don't display every emotion they feel. Individuals learn through experience and observation to manage their facial expressions, and they learn which expressions are appropriate to reveal in what circumstances. In many cultures expectations of appropriateness differ for men and women. For example, in the United States, males are often discouraged from showing sadness, whereas females are frequently

posture and movement
Kinesics behaviors that communicate messages by how immediate or relaxed they are.

immediacy
How close or involved people appear to be with each other.

relaxation
The degree of tension displayed by the body.

▼ What nonverbal messages might be understood from this photo? Remember that a nonverbal behavior can have multiple meanings.

▲ The face and the eyes are particularly important for conveying emotion.

criticized for showing anger. In addition, women are routinely expected to smile, no matter how they feel, while relatively few men receive the same message. Whether or not they are conscious of such cultural expectations, many men believe they shouldn't feel strong emotions or don't want others to see them express strong emotions.

Eye behavior is especially important in conveying messages for humans as well as animals. For example, both humans and dogs use prolonged eye gaze (a stare) to communicate aggression, and they avert their gaze when they want to avoid contact. Furthermore, eye behavior interacts with facial expressions to convey meaning. Thus, most people believe a smile is genuine only when the eyes "smile" as well as the lips. Actors such as Viola Davis and Bradley Cooper are particularly gifted at this; they can, at will, express what appears to be a genuine smile.

Like other types of nonverbal communication, context and culture shape the meanings people attach to eye behavior. For example, cultures differ significantly in how long one is supposed to engage in eye contact and how frequently. Many Native Americans such as Cherokees, Navajos, and Hopis engage in minimal eye contact and many Arabic people maintain more intense and prolonged eye contact when they are listening compared to most White U.S. Americans (Chiang, 1993). Swedes tend to gaze infrequently but for longer periods of time, whereas southern Europeans gaze frequently and extensively (Knapp & Hall, 1992, 2001). Your relationship with others also affects how you interpret their eye behavior. Thus, you may find it appealing when a romantic partner gazes into your eyes but find the same behavior threatening when exhibited by a stranger. For an example of how differences in eye contact and facial expression can affect communication, see *Communication in Society: When You Smile on the Job.*

paralinguistics

All aspects of spoken language except for the words themselves; includes rate, volume, pitch, and stress.

Paralinguistics   The vocal aspects of nonverbal communication are referred to as **paralinguistics**. Paralinguistics are those aspects of language that are *oral* but not *verbal*.

COMMUNICATION IN SOCIETY
When You Smile on the Job

Do you think it is reasonable for a retail store to require women cashiers to smile and make eye contact with all customers? Why or why not? Why do you think the female Safeway employees believed their smiles were the cause of the men's attention?

Have you noticed the smiles and greetings you receive when you shop at major grocery store chains such as Walmart and Safeway? Grocery stores weren't always such welcoming places. This friendly behavior, often called the "supermarket mandatory smile," began in the United States in the late 1990s. Although many stores encouraged this behavior, Safeway actually required its employees to greet customers with a smile and direct eye contact. However, some female employees lodged complaints over this policy because they argued that male customers repeatedly propositioned them and asked them out on dates when they acted so friendly. Although

Safeway denied that their policy was the cause of the men's behavior, they did eventually end it. If the organization had consulted nonverbal research on flirting, they might never have instituted the policy in the first place. One of the most common behaviors women use to signal their interest in men is a smile combined with eye contact and a slight tilt of the head (Trost & Alberts, 2009).

SOURCE: Trost, M. R., & Alberts, J. K. (2006). How men and women communicate attraction: An evolutionary view. In D. Canary & K. Dindia (Eds.), *Sex, gender and communication: Similarities and differences* (2nd ed.; pp. 317–336). Mahwah, NJ: Lawrence Erlbaum.

That is, paralinguistics describe all aspects of spoken language except the words themselves. For example, typically you recognize other speakers' voices in large part through their paralinguistics, or how they sound, rather than the specific words they say. For this reason, when you call a close friend or relative, you may expect them to recognize you just from hearing your voice on the telephone. If someone close to you fails to recognize your voice, you may feel hurt or offended, because their failing to do so suggests that perhaps they don't know you as well as you think they do. Paralinguistics are composed of two types of vocal behavior—*voice qualities* and *vocalizations*.

Voice Qualities   **Voice qualities** include *speed, pitch, rhythm, vocal range*, and articulation; these qualities make up the "music" of the human voice. We all know people whose voice qualities are widely recognized. For example, Former President Barack Obama's vocal qualities were frequently remarked on. One critic (Dié, 2008) described it as resembling that used by preachers, arguing that if you listen only to how the former president speaks (rather than what he says), you would feel as if you were sitting in a small church in any Black neighborhood in the United States. He uses the same "ebb and flow," or rhythms and intonations, that are common to ministers' rhetorical style. To compare the vocal qualities of various presidents, go to **www.presidentsusa.net/audiovideo.html** and listen to audio and video recordings of many presidents.

> **voice qualities**
>
> Qualities such as pitch, rhythm, vocal range, and articulation that make up the "music" of the human voice.

Speakers whose voices vary in pitch and rhythm seem more expressive than those whose voices do not. For example, actor Kristen Stewart is criticized by some as boring and inexpressive because they perceive her delivery as monotonous and her face as blank—in both movies and in real life. Speakers also vary in how they articulate sounds, some pronouncing each word distinctly and others blurring their words and sounds. We tend not to notice this paralinguistic feature unless someone articulates very precisely or very imprecisely. If you have difficulty understanding a speaker, usually the fault lies not with how fast the person talks but with how clearly he or she articulates. When combined, the qualities of pitch and rhythm make your voice distinctive and recognizable to those who know you.

Critical Thinking Prompt
Think back to the last time you encountered someone you could tell was truly happy to see you. How could you tell? What nonverbal behaviors communicated the other person's happiness to you?

Vocalizations   **Vocalizations** are the sounds we utter that do not have the structure of language. Tarzan's yell is one famous example. Vocalizations include vocal cues such as laughing, crying, whining, and moaning, as well as the intensity or volume of one's speech. Also included are sounds that aren't actual words but that serve as fillers, such as "uh-huh," "uh," "ah," and "er."

> **vocalizations**
>
> Uttered sounds that do not have the structure of language.

The paralinguistic aspects of speech serve a variety of communicative purposes. They reveal mood and emotion; they also allow us to emphasize or stress a word or idea, create a distinctive identity, and (along with gestures) regulate conversation.

Time and Space   How people use time and space is so important to communication that researchers have studied their use and developed specialized terms to describe them. **Chronemics**, from the Greek word *chronos*, meaning "time," is the study of the way people use time as a message. It includes issues such as punctuality and the amount of time people spend with each other. **Proxemics** refers to the study of how people use spatial cues, including interpersonal distance, territoriality, and other space relationships. Let's see how these factors influence communication and relationships.

> **chronemics**
>
> The study of the way people use time as a message.
>
> **proxemics**
>
> The study of how people use spatial cues, including interpersonal distance, territoriality, and other space relationships, to communicate.

Chronemics   People often interpret others' use of time as conveying a message, which removes it from the realm of behavior and places it in the realm of communication. For example, if your friend consistently arrives more than an hour late, how do you interpret her behavior? Culture strongly influences how most people answer this question (Hall & Hall, 1987). In the United States, time typically is valued highly; we even have an expression that "time is money." Because of this, most people own numerous clocks and watches. Events are scheduled at specific times and typically begin on time. Therefore, in the United States, lateness can communicate thoughtlessness, irresponsibility, or selfishness. A more positive or tolerant view might be that the perpetually late person is carefree.

Not all cultures value time in the same way, however. In some Latin American and Arab cultures, if one arrives 30 minutes or even an hour after an event is scheduled to begin, one is "on time." When people come together from cultures that value time differently, it can lead to conflict and a sense of displacement. This happened when one of our colleagues taught a class in Mexico. On the first class day, she showed up at the school shortly before the class was scheduled to begin. She found the building locked and no one around. And even though she knew that people in Mexico respond to time differently than she did, during her stay she never was comfortable arriving "late," and routinely had to wait outside the building until someone showed up to let her in.

The timing and sequencing of events convey a variety of messages. For example, being invited to lunch carries a different meaning than being invited to dinner, and being asked to dinner on a Monday conveys a different message than being asked to dinner on a Saturday. Events also tend to unfold in a particular order; so we expect informal interaction to precede intimate interaction and small talk to precede task talk. When these expectations are violated, we often attribute meaning to the violations, as shown in *Did You Know? Expectancy Violations*.

monochronically

Engaging in one task or behavior at a time.

polychronically

Engaging in multiple activities simultaneously.

In addition, some people use time **monochronically**, whereas others use it **polychronically**, and the differences can be perceived as transmitting a message (Hall, 1983; Wolburg, 2001). Individuals who use time monochronically engage in one task or behavior at a time—one reads *or* participates in a conversation *or* watches a movie. If you engage in multiple activities at the same time, you are using time polychronically. Historically in the United States, people have used time monochronically; however, now that technology is so pervasive, more people are using time polychronically as they send text messages, post pictures on Instagram, or read a few tweets as they interact with others. Unfortunately, people who use time monochronically may be insulted by those who use it polychronically, leading to comments such as, "Put down that phone and pay attention to me when I talk to you!"

Whenever an individual's use of time differs from that of others, miscommunication is possible. If you tend to value punctuality more than others do, you may arrive at events earlier than expected and irritate your host, or you may be perceived as too

DID YOU KNOW?

Expectancy Violations

Think of a time when someone violated your expectations for nonverbal behavior. How did you interpret the behavior? Did you see it as a positive or negative violation? Why? How did you respond? How can a person use expectancy violation theory to increase liking?

Our expectations are one factor that influences our interpretations of others' nonverbal behavior. *Expectancy violation theory* states that when people violate our expectations, we tend to notice, become aroused, and attribute meaning to the violation, resulting in increased scrutiny and appraisal of the violator's behavior. For example, if you expect a stranger to shake your hand on being introduced, you likely will search for an explanation if she or he hugs you instead.

However, we don't necessarily interpret and respond to these violations negatively. Judee Burgoon and her colleagues repeatedly have shown that responses to another's violation of our expectations are influenced by how we perceive the violator. In other words, we judge a violation as positive or negative

depending largely on whether we view the violator as someone with whom we'd like to interact. Thus, if the stranger who hugs you is attractive and you are single, you may evaluate this violation positively. This judgment shapes your response to the violation; in this case, if you interpret the hug positively, you may respond by hugging back (Burgoon & Hale, 1988; Burgoon & LePoire, 1993).

SOURCES: Burgoon, J. K., & Hale, J. L. (1988). Nonverbal expectancy violations: Model elaboration and application to immediacy behaviors. *Communication Monographs*, 55, 58–79.

Burgoon, J. K., & Le Poire, B. A. (1993). Effects of Communication expectancies, actual communication, and expectancy disconfirmation on evaluations of communicators and their communication behavior. *Human Communication Research*, 20(1), 67–96.

eager. Similarly, if you don't value punctuality, you may discover that others won't schedule activities with you or are frequently annoyed with you for disrupting their plans. Relationships and communication benefit when the people involved understand how others value and use time.

Proxemics   As we mentioned previously, proxemics is the study of how one uses space. People use variance in distance from others for two purposes: to create a sense of safety and comfort and to signal intimacy and closeness. First, individuals need to maintain sufficient space from others to feel safe in their surroundings. The more unfamiliar or uncomfortable one is with another person, the more space one requires. This is one reason we often feel uncomfortable riding on crowded buses or trains. In these cases, we are forced to maintain minimal space between ourselves and people we don't know. Interestingly, this psychological and physical need for safety results also occurs in virtual space. An individual's avatar responds to space violations the same way a person would in real life (Phillips, 1998).

Individuals' use of space also serves a communicative function. The distance people stand or sit from one another symbolizes physical or psychological closeness. For example, if you were sitting in an almost vacant theater and a stranger entered and proceeded to sit right next to you, how would you feel? If you are like many people in the United States, you might feel uncomfortable. By contrast, if a longtime friend or your romantic partner walked into the theater and chose to sit rows away from you, how would you respond? You probably would be perplexed, perhaps even hurt or angry.

We respond to how close others sit or stand to us, because how much space we require to feel comfortable with others suggests how close or intimate we are them. That is, our physical closeness with others typically communicates our psychological closeness with them. Research by Edward T. Hall, a well-known anthropologist, has delineated four spheres or categories of space that reflect people's comfort and closeness with others (Hall, 1966). Let's take a look at each.

Intimate distance (zero to eighteen inches) tends to be reserved for those whom one knows very well. Typically, this distance is used for displaying physical and psychological intimacy, such as lovemaking, cuddling children, comforting someone, or telling secrets. **Personal distance** (eighteen inches to four feet) describes the space we use when interacting with friends and acquaintances. People in the United States often use the nearer distance for friends and the farther one for acquaintances, but cultures

intimate distance
(zero to eighteen inches) The space used when interacting with those with whom one is very close.

personal distance
(eighteen inches to four feet) The space used when interacting with friends and acquaintances.

and personal preference strongly influence this choice. When others prefer closer distances than you do, you may find their closeness psychologically distressing; comedian Jerry Seinfeld has referred to these people as "close talkers." One of our students details her encounters with such a person in *It Happened to Me: Katarina.*

It Happened to Me
Katarina

I have a friend whom I like very much but who makes me really uncomfortable sometimes. She tends to lean in very close when she talks, especially if she has been drinking. One night, we were sitting together at a party. I sat in the corner of a couch while she leaned in to talk with me; I kept trying to pull my face away from hers while she talked until I was almost leaning over the back of the couch.

Social distance (four to twelve feet) is the distance most U.S. Americans use when they interact with unfamiliar others. Impersonal business with grocery clerks, sales clerks, and coworkers occurs at about four to seven feet, whereas the greatest distance is used in formal situations such as job interviews. **Public distance** (12 to 25 feet) is most appropriate for public ceremonies such as lectures and performances, though an even greater distance may be maintained between public figures (such as politicians and celebrities) and their audiences.

One's culture, gender, relationship to others, and personality all influence whether one feels most comfortable at the near or far range of each of these spheres. In the

social distance
(four to twelve feet) The distance most U.S. Americans use when they interact with unfamiliar others.

public distance
(twelve to twenty-five feet) The distance used for public ceremonies such as lectures and performances.

United States, two unacquainted women typically sit or stand closer to each other than do two unacquainted men, whereas many men are more comfortable sitting or standing closer to unknown women than they are even to men they know (Burgoon & Guerrero, 1994). However, people in other cultures may prefer the closer ranges. Cultural disparities can result in a comedic cross-cultural "dance," where one person tries to get closer to the other and that person, made uncomfortable by the closeness, moves away.

What does the space between interactants in a given culture reveal? It can communicate intimacy or the lack of it; it also can communicate power and dominance. If person A feels free to enter person B's space without permission but refuses to allow B the same privilege, this lack of reciprocity communicates that A is dominant in the relationship. This situation is common between supervisors and subordinates and may exist in some parent–child relationships as well.

All humans, as well as animals, have strong feelings of territoriality. We exhibit territorial behavior when we attempt to claim control over a particular area. A primary way we attempt to claim and maintain control of a space is through personalization or marking, especially by use of artifacts. Thus, we alter spaces to make them distinctly our own through activities such as placing a fence around a residence or displaying family photos in an office. These markers are a form of nonverbal communication that specifies territorial ownership or legitimate occupancy (Becker, 1973). Markers function mainly to keep people away, thereby preventing confrontational social encounters. An unexpected manifestation of territoriality is described in *Did You Know? Space Invaders.*

DID YOU KNOW?
Space Invaders

What do road rage, street harassment, and mob violence have in common? They all are responses to perceptions that one's space has been invaded.

Most articles on nonverbal communication and territory focus on how people "mark" their private and public spaces, such as when homeowners use fences to delineate their property lines or when students leave jackets on the seats they regularly occupy. Less often do we examine how invasions of space lead to antisocial behavior. However, like other animals, humans may respond aggressively when they believe their territory has been invaded.

A common type of space violation in the United States occurs when one driver cuts off another driver. When an individual pulls into the lane ahead and causes them to slow down, some drivers become angry. They may engage in acts of road rage, such as chasing after the offender, driving them off the road, or pulling a gun. Why would someone respond violently to a behavior that usually is only a minor inconvenience? People who do so typically have a strong sense of ownership over their cars and the spaces they occupy. They are likely to perceive that they have been disrespected and that the other person has willingly and arbitrarily invaded their territory. As a result, they feel the need to establish dominance over "their" space by responding aggressively.

Another regularly occurring response to perceived territory invasion is street harassment. Street harassment is a form of verbal or nonverbal harassment that has a sexual component.

It is typified by debasing, objectifying, or threatening behavior designed to intimidate. Most women, and some gay men, have experienced it. How is this behavior a response to space invasions? Social control theory argues that street harassment is, at least in part, an effort on the part of many men to mark the public domain as their territory. In these cases, women without male partners are seen as violators of men's territory, and street harassment is viewed as a way to discourage them from intruding into this space alone (Lord, 2009). This behavior appears to be successful. A majority of women report that they have changed where they walk or live to avoid street harassment.

Yet another response to space intrusions is mob violence. You may have wondered why peaceful protests so often devolve into aggression. In part, they do so because as the group becomes more crowded, each person's zone of personal space become smaller, and as a result, people began to feel hostile. As the group continues to grow and personal space is rendered nonexistent, individuals grow angrier and less civil, which can lead to violence. Even peaceful demonstrations can become disruptive, and angry ones can become lethal.

SOURCE: Lord, T. L. (2009). *The relationship of gender-based public harassment to body image, self-esteem, and avoidance behavior.* Unpublished dissertation. Ann Arbor, MI: ProQuest.

Primary territories (areas under private control, such as houses and the bedrooms within them) serve as extensions of the owner's sense of identity, so markers there often include personally meaningful symbols reflecting the owner's style and taste (name plates, art objects, flower gardens). Public territories are less central to our self-concepts and, therefore, we tend to mark them with objects that are less personalized or that represent explicit claims to the space (for example, "reserved parking" signs). When someone violates a public territory, we tend to react with verbal retaliation, for example, asking the violator to leave. In contrast, we are likely to react strongly when someone violates our primary territory, for example, by seeking physical retaliation and legal sanctions (Abu-Ghazzeh, 2000).

Haptics Although researchers in communication know that touch, or **haptics**, is important, it is among the least studied forms of nonverbal communication. Nonethe-less, research does indicate that infants and children need to be touched to be physically and psychologically healthy (Field, 2002). Also, although people vary considerably in how much or what type of touch they prefer, most enjoy being touched by those they care about. To understand how differences in preferences for touch affect relationships, see *It Happened to Me: Alondra.*

haptics
The study of the communicative function of touch.

It Happened to Me
Alondra

I grew up in upper Michigan, where people rarely touch unless they know each other very well. Then I started working with a guy from the South. From the beginning, he touched me whenever we talked; he touched my arm, put his hand on my shoulder, or even put his arm on the back of my chair. This infuriated me! I thought he was being condescending and too familiar. Later, I realized that he does this with everybody. I understand he doesn't mean anything by it, but I still don't like it.

Touch can be categorized into several general types (Givens, 2005), but people rarely notice the types unless a discrepancy occurs between their expectations and their experience. **Professional touch**, or **functional touch** is the least intimate; people who must touch others as part of their livelihood, such as medical and dental caregivers, hairstylists, and tailors, use this type of touch. Because touch often conveys intimacy, people who must use professional touch have to be careful of their interaction style; for example, they may adopt a formal or distant verbal communication style to counteract the intimacy of their touch. **Social-polite touch** is part of daily interaction. In the United States, this form of touch is more intimate than professional touch but is still impersonal. For example, many U.S. Americans shake hands when greeting acquaintances and casual friends, though in many European countries, such as France and Italy, hugging and kissing are appropriate forms of social touch. Even within the United States, people have different ideas about what types of touch are appropriate socially.

Friendship touch is more intimate than social touch and usually conveys warmth, closeness, and caring. Although considerable variation in touch may exist among friends, people typically use touch that is more intimate with close friends than with acquaintances or strangers. Examples include brief hugs, a hand on the shoulder, or putting one's arm loosely around another's waist or shoulders. **Love-intimate touch** most often is used with one's romantic partners and family. Examples are the long kisses and extended hugging and cuddling we tend to reserve for those with whom we are closest.

As is true of other forms of nonverbal communication, sex, culture, and power strongly influence patterns of touch. In the United States, heterosexual males are more likely to reserve hand-holding for their romantic partners and small children, whereas females touch other women more frequently and hold hands with older children, their close female relatives, and even female friends. In general, women tend to touch other women more frequently than men touch other men, and in cross-sex interactions, men are more likely to initiate touch than do women (Hall & Hall, 1990). However, in cross-sex interactions, the nature of the relationship influences touch behavior more than does

professional touch
Type of touch used by certain workers, such as dentists, hairstylists, and hospice workers, as part of their livelihood; also known as *functional touch.*

functional touch
The least intimate type of touch; used by certain workers such as dentists, hairstylists, and hospice workers, as part of their livelihood; also known as *professional touch.*

social-polite touch
Touch that is part of daily interaction in the United States; it is more intimate than professional touch but is still impersonal.

friendship touch
Touch that is more intimate than social-polite touch and usually conveys warmth, closeness, and caring.

love-intimate touch
The touch most often used with one's romantic partners and family.

▲ Demand touching is often used to establish dominance and power.

the sex of the participants. Across all stages of heterosexual romantic relationships, partners reciprocate touch, so they do not differ in amount of touch (Guerrero & Andersen, 1991). However, men respond more positively to their partners' touch than do women (Hanzal, Segrin, & Dorros, 2008). In addition, men initiate touch more in casual romantic relationships, whereas women do so more often in married relationships (Guerrero & Andersen, 1994).

Each form of touch we have discussed thus far has a "positive" quality; but, of course, people also use touch to convey negative messages. For example, one study revealed that individuals (especially parents) use aggressive touch and withdrawal of affectionate touch with children to signal their displeasure (Guerrero & Ebesu, 1993). Aggressive touch can include grabbing, hitting, and pinching, whereas withdrawal of affection involves rejecting the touch attempts of others, as when one pushes another's arm away or refuses to hold hands. Both children and adults use aggressive touch with their peers as well, though in none of these instances is aggressive touch considered an appropriate or competent way to communicate.

demand touching

A type of touch used to establish dominance and power.

Another type of touch that can be perceived negatively is **demand touching**, which is a type of touch used to establish dominance and power. Demand touching increases in hierarchical settings, such as at work. One significant characteristic of demand touching is that touchers typically have higher status and have more control over encounters than do receivers; this allows them more freedom of movement and more visual contact. An everyday example of demand touch occurs when a supervisor stands behind a subordinate and leans over to provide directions, placing his or her hand on the subordinate's shoulder. The subordinate can't move easily or look directly at the supervisor, and the subordinate may feel both physically and psychologically constrained (Kemmer, 1992).

artifacts

Physical objects including cars, clothing, and other material items.

Appearance and Artifacts   In all cultures, individuals' appearance matters, as do their **artifacts**, or the clothing and other accessories they choose. Let's first consider appearance and how it operates as a nonverbal code.

In general, people's looks are believed to communicate something about them, and people develop expectations based on how others look. Hairstyle, skin color, height, weight, clothing, accessories such as jewelry, and other aspects of appearance all influence how we are perceived and how we perceive others. And in the United States, appearance is seen as especially important (Newport, 1999).

What is considered attractive, however, is influenced by one's culture and the time period in which one lives (Grammer, Fink, Joller, & Thornhill, 2003). Many people find it hard to believe that the Mona Lisa was considered a great beauty in her day, and even more people wonder who could ever have liked the clothes and hairstyles their own parents wore when they were young. Although the global village we live in now means the media transmit images that can be seen all over the world, cultures still vary in what they consider most attractive. The current ideal body type for women in the United States, as portrayed in the media, for example, is considered too thin and unfeminine by many African Americans (Duke, 2002). Although some American women get collagen injections to achieve full lips, our Japanese students tell us that such thick lips are not considered attractive in Japan. Some Europeans also dislike the defined musculature favored for males in magazines and television ads in the United States.

In the United States, people invest considerable time, money, and energy adapting their appearance to cultural ideals of attractiveness. They diet, color and style their hair, frequent gyms and tanning booths, and even undergo extreme makeovers to be more attractive. People engage in all these efforts because the U.S. culture generally equates beauty with happiness, success, goodness, and desirability.

Although people face certain limits in reshaping their bodies and other physical attributes, they also have great flexibility in using clothing and other artifacts to convey important messages about themselves. In most business contexts, a suit is perceived to be authoritative and an indication of status.

▲ Ideals of what constitutes beauty differ according to time period, culture, class, and other factors.

This is especially true of men; evaluations of their status often are based on their appearance and clothing (Mast & Hall, 2004). People also use artifacts to signal their occupations and identities. Nurses, flight attendants, and police officers wear uniforms to help others identify them and to send specific messages about their jobs (Gundersen, 1990). Thus, police officers wear paramilitary uniforms not only to allow us to easily identify them but also to reinforce their role in maintaining social order.

Individuals also choose their accessories and artifacts, such as purses, watches, jewelry, sunglasses, and even cars, to communicate specific messages about status, personality, success, or group membership. A student who carries a leather briefcase on campus creates a different image than one who carries a canvas backpack. On a typical college campus, it is fairly easy to differentiate the communication professors from the business professors and the engineering students from the theater majors based on their dress and artifacts. We might argue that in the United States, where it is not considered polite to announce one's status or success, people often use artifacts to make those announcements for them (Fussell, 1992).

As you can see from the preceding discussion, multiple categories of nonverbal behavior influence communication; these include kinesics, paralinguistics, chronemics and proxemics, haptics, and appearance and artifacts. These categories are, in turn, influenced by multiple individual and cultural factors. In the next section, we explore how these categories work together to influence how we send and interpret messages.

Critical Thinking Prompt
What artifacts are important to you in terms of communicating your identity or status? If you had only one means of communicating high status, would you drive an expensive car, wear designer clothes, or live in an upscale neighborhood? What do you think your choice reflects about you?

The Functions of Nonverbal Messages

As mentioned previously, when people interpret nonverbal behaviors they don't isolate kinesics from haptics or proxemics from appearance; rather, they observe an integrated set of behaviors, consider the context and the individual, and then attribute meaning. If you see two people standing closely together in a public place, you wouldn't necessarily assume they were being intimate. Rather, you would examine how relaxed or tense their bodies appeared, evaluate their facial expressions and eye gaze, and consider the appropriateness of intimate displays in this public space (for example, a bar versus a church). Only then might you make an attribution about the meaning or function of the couple's behavior.

In general, scholars have determined that nonverbal behaviors serve five functions during interaction (Patterson, 1982, 2003). Those five functions are: communicating information, regulating interaction, expressing and managing intimacy, establishing social control, and signaling service-task functions. The most basic function is to communicate information, and this is the one we examine first.

communicating information

Using nonverbal behaviors to help clarify verbal messages and reveal attitudes and motivation.

Communicating Information   Most fundamentally, nonverbal messages are used to **communicate information**. From the receiver's point of view, much of a sender's behavior is potentially informative. For example, when you meet someone for the first time you evaluate the pattern of the sender's behavior to assess a variety of factors. First, you might evaluate the sender's general disposition to determine if it is warm and friendly or cool and distant. You likely will also assess her more fleeting nonverbal reactions to help you decide if she seems pleased to meet you or is just being polite. Finally, of course, you evaluate the person's verbal message. For example, does the speaker say, "I've really been looking forward to meeting you," or does she say, "I'd love to chat, but I've got to run"? You then combine all these pieces of information to ascribe meaning to the encounter.

Nonverbal communication helps individuals convey and interpret verbal messages. They can do this in five ways:

1. By repeating a message (winking while saying "I'm just kidding");
2. By highlighting or emphasizing a message (pointing at the door while saying "Get out!");
3. By complementing or reinforcing a message (whispering while telling a secret);
4. By contradicting a message (saying "I love your haircut" while speaking in a hostile tone and rolling one's eyes);
5. By substituting for a message (shaking one's head to indicate disagreement).

As these examples illustrate, using nonverbal communication effectively can make you a better *verbal* communicator.

regulating interaction

Using nonverbal behaviors to help manage conversational interaction.

expressing and managing intimacy

Using nonverbal behaviors to help convey attraction and closeness.

establishing social control

Using nonverbal communication to exercise influence over other people.

Regulating Interaction   Nonverbal communication also is used to **regulate interaction**. That is, people use nonverbal behaviors to manage turn-taking during conversation. Thus, if you want to start talking, you might lean forward, look at the current speaker, and even raise one finger. To reveal that you are finished with your turn, you may drop your volume and pitch, lean back, and look away from and then back toward the person you are "giving" your turn to. The regulating function tends to be the most automatic of the five, and most of us rarely think about it. The behaviors you use in this way include the more stable ones such as interpersonal distance, body orientation, and posture, as well as more fluid behaviors like gaze, facial expression, volume, and pitch, which are important in the smooth sequencing of conversational turns (Capella, 1985).

▼ Various nonverbal behaviors regulate the interaction that occurs in a conversation.

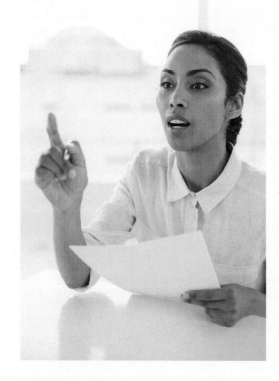

Expressing and Managing Intimacy   A third function of nonverbal communication, and the most studied, involves **expressing and managing intimacy**. The degree of your nonverbal involvement with another usually reflects the level of intimacy you desire with that person. If you meet someone new and notice your partner is leaning toward you, gazing into your eyes, nodding his head, and providing many paralinguistic cues such as "uh huh" as you talk, he is revealing a high degree of nonverbal involvement, which often signals attraction and interest. Of course, people can manipulate these behaviors to suggest attraction and involvement even if they are not experiencing these feelings. For example, in the workplace when subordinates talk with their supervisors, they often display fairly high levels of nonverbal involvement, regardless of their true feelings for their bosses.

Establishing Social Control   People also use nonverbal communication to exert or **establish social control**, or to exercise influence over other people. Individuals engage in the social control function when they smile at someone they want to do them a favor or when they glare at noisy patrons in a theater to encourage them to be quiet. You can use either

ALTERNATIVE VIEW

Nonverbal Reciprocity or Nonverbal Complementarity?

Which of the following explanations seems more accurate to you? In what situations do you believe people are more likely to engage in nonverbal reciprocity? In nonverbal complementarity?

Nonverbal Reciprocity

Numerous studies provide evidence that many people unconsciously mimic their partner's postures, gestures, and other movements in social settings. Furthermore, this mimicry, or reciprocity, seems to increase liking and rapport between speakers. In turn, increased liking and rapport lead to more frequent mimicry. However, status or dominance affects who is likely to mimic whom. Lower status individuals are more likely to reciprocate the behaviors of higher status people, which may be unconsciously designed to increase liking and rapport (Chartrand & Bargh, 1999; Dijksterhuis & Smith, 2005).

Nonverbal Complementarity

A set of studies found that people respond to another's nonverbal power moves with complementary responses; that is, they respond to dominant behaviors with submissive ones and submissive behaviors with dominant ones (Tiedens & Fragale, 2003). Thus, if one person stares aggressively at another (a dominant behavior), the recipient of the stare is likely to look away (a submissive behavior). Furthermore, participants reported feeling comfortable with complementarity.

These studies specifically examined how people negotiate status in relationships with no prior hierarchy. Thus, in groups and relationships in which everyone is on equal footing, the first dominant or submissive display by an individual may result from a random movement or a tactical strategy. Whatever the cause of the display, a hierarchical relationship can then result if an observer responds in a complementary fashion. Moreover, because people prefer to complement dominance with submissiveness, and vice versa, they are likely to promote that differentiation. Thus, nonverbal complementarity and the comfort associated with it may encourage hierarchical relationships and help maintain them. This phenomenon, then, may be one reason why hierarchies are so common and widespread.

SOURCES: Chartrand T. L., & Bargh J. A. (1999). The chameleon effect: The perception-behavior link and social interaction. *Journal of Personality and Social Psychology, 76,* 893–910.

Dijksterhuis, A., & Smith, P. K. (2005). What do we do unconsciously? And how? *Journal of Consumer Psychology 15*(3), 225–229.

Tiedens, L. Z., & Fragale, A. R. (2003). Power moves: Complementarity in dominant and submissive nonverbal behavior. *Journal of Personality and Social Psychology, 84,* 558–568.

---

positive or negative behaviors (or both) in your efforts to control others. People who are "charming" or very persuasive typically are extremely gifted at using nonverbal behavior to influence others.

When expressing and managing intimacy people tend to respond in similar, or reciprocal, ways to one another's nonverbal behavior. On the other hand, when engaging in social control, people tend to respond in complementary ways to one another's nonverbal behavior. To better understand the role of these responses in nonverbal interactions, see *Alternative View: Nonverbal Reciprocity or Nonverbal Complementarity?*

Signaling Service-Task Functions Finally, nonverbal communication has a **service-task function**. Behaviors of this kind typically signal close involvement between people in impersonal relationships and contexts. For example, golf pros often stand with their arms around a novice golfer to help her with her golf swing, and massage therapists engage in intimate touch as part of their profession. In each of these cases, the behavior is appropriate, necessary, and a means to a (professional) end.

Accurately interpreting nonverbal messages is a complex endeavor, requiring

service-task functions

Using nonverbal behavior to signal close involvement between people in impersonal relationships and contexts.

▼ Exercise trainers often use the service-task function of nonverbal communication.

Journal Prompt 6.3:
Nonverbal Communication Functions
Consider the following question:
What five functions does nonverbal communication serve?

awareness of a number of elements—factors that influence individuals' communication patterns, nonverbal communication codes and signals, and the communicative functions that nonverbal messages fulfill. However, in some senses, we have only shown you one piece of the picture, as we have thus far focused primarily on nonverbal communication as performed by individuals. In the next section, we expand the frame to explore how societal forces influence both the performance and interpretation of nonverbal messages and behavior.

The Individual, Nonverbal Communication, and Society

6.4   Explain how nonverbal communication can both trigger and express prejudice and discrimination.

Nonverbal communication, like all communication, is heavily influenced by societal forces and occurs within a hierarchical system of meanings. One's status and position within the societal hierarchy, as well as one's identity, are all expressed nonverbally. However, the more powerful elements in society often regulate these expressions. In addition, nonverbal communication can trigger and express prejudice and discrimination. Let's see how this operates.

Nonverbal Communication and Power

Nonverbal communication and power are intricately related—especially via the nonverbal codes of appearance and artifacts. In the United States, power is primarily based on an individual's access to economic resources and the freedom to make decisions that affect others. Economic resources are typically revealed or expressed through nonverbal codes. In spring 2014, style blogs commented on the $3,800 Chanel "graffiti" purse that Gwyneth Paltrow sported. Stylists found the beat up, deconstructed bag to be "hideous." So why would Paltrow carry an expensive bag that most people agree is ugly? She likely did so because people display wealth through the clothing and accessories they wear (as well as the quality of their haircuts, and the value of their homes and cars). What better way is there to signal wealth than by showing that one has so many purses that one can afford to carry an expensive, unattractive bag on occasion? Whether one can afford to buy the latest designer fashions, or only to shop in discount stores, communicates clearly one's social class and power. English professor Paul Fussell (1992) provides an extensive description of how nonverbal messages communicated in our everyday lives reveal class standing. Consider, for example, the messages communicated by one's home. Fussell notes that the longer the driveway, the less obvious the garage, and the more manicured the grounds, the higher is one's socioeconomic class.

People use nonverbal cues to communicate their own status and identities, and to evaluate and interpret others' status and identities. Based on these interpretations, people—consciously and unconsciously—include and exclude others, and approve or disapprove of others. For example, in wealthy communities, people who don't look affluent may be stopped and questioned about their presence. (This practice was taken to its furthest extent when George Zimmerman confronted Trayvon Martin about his presence in his future stepmother's community.) More overtly, gated communities offer clear nonverbal messages about who belongs and who does not belong to a community. Of course, it isn't just the wealthy who use artifacts to convey their identity and belonging. Gang members, NASCAR fans, football fans, and many others also use attire as well as gestures to signal their individual and group identities.

The use of nonverbal cues to communicate social class extends beyond the use of appearance and artifacts. For example, psychology professors Michael Kraus and

Dach Keltner (2009) examined individuals' use of non-verbal communication while interacting with a stranger. In these interactions they found that people with high socioeconomic status were more likely to display non-verbal signs of disengagement, such as doodling, and fewer signs of engagement, such as smiling and nod-ding, than people with lower socioeconomic status. In addition, people who observed these interactions could correctly guess the participants' social class from their nonverbal behavior. Thus, nonverbal communication reproduces—or recreates—the society and social classes in which we live.

Although all groups use nonverbal communication to convey identity, more powerful segments of society typically define what is allowed. For example, many corporations have dress codes designed to communicate a particular pro-fessional image to the public. For the same reason, they may also have rules that regulate nonverbal expression of men's facial hair. The military and many police organizations have policies on tattoos as well (Zezima, 2005). Because these organizations are hierarchical, the decisions made by those in power in the organization must be followed by those who wish employment there.

In 2005, the National Basketball Association issued rules governing the off-court dress of NBA players: They are to dress in "business casual" whenever engaged in team or league business, and they are specifically excluded from wearing sleeveless shirts, shorts, T-shirts, headgear of any kind, chains, pendants, and sunglasses while indoors.

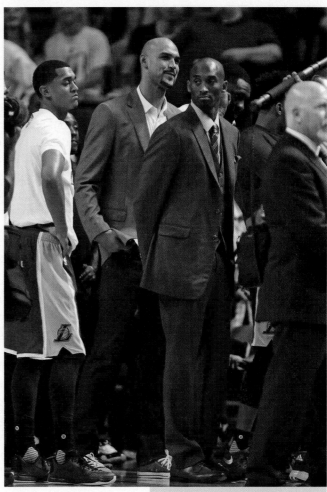

▲ The NBA issued rules governing NBA players' off-court dress to help shape the images they present to the public.

Through these dictums, the organization is attempting to regulate not only the players' clothing, but also their expression of their identities. Of course, not all players support these regulations (Wise, 2005). Some NBA players feel that the ban on chains and other jewelry was racially motivated. In short, this new policy "called attention to a genera-tional chasm between modern professional athletes, many of whom are Black, and their mostly White paying customers" (Wise, 2005, p. A-1).

The number and range of dress codes and regulations on appearance underscore the powerful impact that nonverbal cues can have. The more powerful segments of soci-ety also define what is most desirable and attractive in our culture. For example, cos-metic corporations spend $231 billion annually on the development of beauty products and advertising to persuade consumers to buy them. The largest cosmetic companies have expanded to China where the nation's 451 million women are of great interest to the cosmetics market (Carvajal, 2006). The media broadly communicate to us the defini-tions of beauty. This is why many U.S. Americans believe that blonde hair is better than brown, thin is better than fat, large breasts are better than small, and young is better than old—beliefs that are not shared universally. Messages promoting a specific type of youth and beauty might seem rather harmless, until one considers the consequences for those who are not thin and blonde, especially those who have no possibility of meeting the dominant standards of beauty.

Aspects of dress are important in the United States at cultural events, particularly for women. The outfits worn to the Academy Awards and other "show business" honor ceremonies are reviewed and evaluated and are a topic of great interest for many people. Similarly, what the president's wife wears on Inauguration Day and at subsequent parties is a subject of conversation; in fact, the First Lady's wardrobe is discussed and critiqued every day on TV, in blogs, and in magazines. The interest (and evaluation) of

Critical Thinking Prompt
How does this hierarchy of attractiveness affect communication with others? Do people respond to others negatively because of their appearance? Might they feel marginalized and resentful—even before they interact with others who more clearly meet the dominant standards?

these nonverbal expressions, such as clothing, is driven by societal forces. In all of these cases, women know that their nonverbal messages will be carefully scrutinized and evaluated.

Nonverbal Communication, Prejudice, and Discrimination

At the intersection of societal forces and nonverbal communication are prejudice and discrimination. Both can be triggered by nonverbal behavior and are also expressed through nonverbal behavior. Let's look at how this works. First, one's race and ethnicity, body shape, age, or style of dress—all of which are communicated nonverbally—can prompt prejudgment or negative stereotypes. How often do people make a snap judgment or generalization based on appearance? Second, prejudice and discrimination are expressed nonverbally. In some extreme cases, nonverbal signals have even triggered and perpetrated hate crimes. For example, one night in Phoenix, Arizona, Avtar (Singh) Chiera, a small-business owner and a Sikh, waited outside his business for his son to pick him up. Two White men pulled up in a small red pickup truck, yelled at him, and then opened fire on him. Because of anger over the events of 9/11, the two men likely targeted him as an Arab because of his turban and beard, even though Sikhs are neither Arab nor Muslim (Parasuram, 2003). In this encounter, nonverbal messages were the most important; the words spoken (if any) were of minimal impact.

Although the example of the shooting of Chiera is extreme, there are many other more subtle ways that prejudice can be communicated nonverbally—for instance, averting one's gaze or failing to reciprocate a smile. It can be as subtle as shifting your gaze, leaning your body away, or editing your speech. Sociologist A. G. Johnson (2001, pp. 58–59) gives a list of specific nonverbal behaviors that can be interpreted as prejudicial. These are mostly noticed only by the person experiencing them and often happen unconsciously and unintentionally:

- Not looking at people when we talk with them;
- Not smiling at people when they walk into the room, or staring as if to say, "What are you doing here?" or stopping the conversation with a hush they have to wade through to be included in the smallest way;
- Not acknowledging people's presence or making them wait as if they weren't there;
- Not touching their skin when we give them something;
- Watching them closely to see what they're up to; and
- Avoiding someone walking down the street, giving them wide berth, or even crossing to the other side.

Journal Prompt 6.4: Power and Nonverbal Communication
Consider the following questions: How does power influence nonverbal communication norms? How does status influence a person's nonverbal communication?

Given the potential consequences of nonverbal communication, you may find it helpful to consider how your nonverbal communication reflects your own ethical stance. To guide you in making appropriate and ethical choices, in the next section we explore the ethics of nonverbal communication.

Ethics and Nonverbal Communication

6.5   Explain how nonverbal communication can be used to communicate unethically.

The ethics of nonverbal communication are actually quite similar to the ethics of communication in general. When people engage in behavior such as deceiving or threatening others or name-calling, their nonverbal behavior typically plays a central role in their messages. For instance, liars use nonverbal behavior to avoid "leaking" the deception, and they may also use it to convey the deceptive message. Moreover, deceivers may feel that lying nonverbally—for example, by remaining silent—is less "wrong" than lying with words. In the Old Testament, Joseph's brothers were jealous of their father's affection for him, so they sold Joseph into slavery. When they returned without him, however, they didn't "tell" their father what happened; instead they gave him Joseph's bloody coat and let their father draw the conclusion that wild animals had killed Joseph. In this way, they deceived their father without actually speaking a lie. What do you think? Is it better, or less unethical, to lie nonverbally than it is to do so verbally?

When communicators use nonverbal cues that ridicule, derogate, or otherwise demean others, they run the risk of their behavior being viewed by others as unethical. For example, if someone speaks in a patronizing vocal tone, screams at the less power-ful, or touches others inappropriately, would you view this behavior as unethical? What if people respond to others' communication in a way that misrepresents how they actu-ally feel? For instance, if they laugh at a racist or sexist joke even though they dislike it, would you see that behavior as unethical?

Because these are the types of decisions you have to make routinely throughout your life, here are some guidelines for ethical nonverbal communication to help you make those decisions. Consider whether:

- your nonverbal behaviors reflect your real attitudes, beliefs, and feelings;
- your nonverbal behaviors contradict the verbal message you are sending;
- your nonverbal behaviors insult, ridicule, or demean others;
- you are using your nonverbal behavior to intimidate, coerce, or silence someone;
- you would want anyone to observe your nonverbal behavior; and
- you would want this nonverbal behavior directed to you or a loved one.

Although there is no litmus test for evaluating the ethics of every nonverbal message in every situation, if you keep these guidelines in mind, they will help you make better, more informed decisions.

Improving Your Nonverbal Communication Skills

6.6   Explain how you can improve your ability to interpret nonverbal behavior.

By now you may be wondering how to decide what a set of behaviors means. How do you decide, for example, if your sports coach's touch is appropriately intimate (service-task) or just intimate? In the workplace, how can you determine whether your subordi-nate genuinely likes you and your ideas (nonver-bal involvement) or is merely trying to flatter you (social control)?

One way you can assess your own and others' nonverbal communication is to examine how it interacts with verbal messages (Jones & LeBaron, 2002). That is, how congruent (similar) are the two sets of messages? When the two types of messages are **congruent**, they are often genu-ine (or we assume them to be so). For example, a positive verbal message ("I like you") combined with a positive nonverbal message (smile, for-ward body lean, relaxed posture) usually conveys a convincing positive message. However, it is also

Journal Prompt 6.5: Unethical Nonverbal Communication
Consider the following question: What are some ways in which it is possible for people to engage in unethical nonverbal communication?

congruent
Verbal and nonverbal messages that express the same meaning.

▼ The meaning of this nonverbal behavior is strongly affected by the context.

contradicting
Verbal and nonverbal messages that send conflicting messages.

possible that people who are good at deception are able to offer congruent messages while lying, and those who are less adept at communicating may unintentionally offer contradictory messages when telling the truth. Given all of this, what other factors could you rely on to help you decide whether a congruent message is truthful?

Of course, verbal and nonverbal messages can also purposely **contradict** one another. When using sarcasm, people intentionally combine a positive verbal message ("what a nice pair of shoes") with a contradictory or negative nonverbal message (a hostile tone). However, at other times people offer contradictory messages unintentionally or carelessly. Caretakers often confuse children (and encourage misbehavior) by telling a child to stop a particular behavior while smiling or laughing. How does a child interpret this message? Most children will accept the nonverbal aspect of the message and ignore the verbal (Eskritt & Lee, 2003).

In addition to assessing the congruence of the verbal and nonverbal components of a message, you improve your comprehension of nonverbal messages by analyzing the context, your knowledge of the other person, and your own experiences. For example, if you are playing basketball and a teammate slaps you on the rear and says, "good going," the message may be clear. Given the context, you may read it as a compliment and perhaps a sign of affection or intimacy. But what if the slap on the rear occurs at work after an effective presentation? Given that such behavior is generally inappropriate in a business context, you probably will (and should) more closely assess its meaning. You might ask yourself whether this person simply lacks social skills and frequently engages in inappropriate behavior. If so, the message may be inappropriate but still be meant in a positive fashion. In contrast, if the person knows better and has touched you inappropriately at other times, the behavior may be intentionally designed to express inappropriate intimacy or social control.

Here are a few more suggestions to keep in mind:

- Recognize that others' nonverbal messages don't always mean the same as yours.
- Be aware of individual, contextual, and cultural factors that influence meaning.
- Ask for additional information if you don't understand a nonverbal message or if you perceive a contradiction between the verbal and nonverbal messages.
- Remember that not every nonverbal behavior is intended to be communicative.
- Don't place too much emphasis on fleeting nonverbal behaviors such as facial expression or vocal tone; rather, examine the entire set of nonverbal behaviors.

Journal Prompt 6.6: Improving Nonverbal Communication
Consider the following question:
What are some specific strategies you can use to improve your ability to communicate nonverbally?

SUMMARY

6.1 Describe the important role of nonverbal communication in social interaction.

- It helps us express and interpret verbal messages and, in doing so, helps us more effectively navigate everyday life.

6.2 Define *nonverbal communication*.

- Nonverbal communication is defined as all the messages that people transmit through means other than words.

6.3 Define five nonverbal codes and explain the five functions of nonverbal messages.

- Nonverbal communication occurs through five codes or types of signals: kinesics, paralinguistics (vocal qualities), chronemics and proxemics (time and space), haptics (touch), and appearance and artifacts

- These codes can combine to serve one of five functions, including communicating information, regulating interaction, expressing and managing intimacy, exerting social control, and performing service-task functions.

6.4 Explain how nonverbal communication can both trigger and express prejudice and discrimination.

- Race and ethnicity, body shape, gender, age, or style of dress—all of which are communicated nonverbally—can prompt prejudgment or negative stereotypes.

- Prejudice and discrimination are expressed nonverbally through behaviors such as eye rolling, ignoring, smirking, and turning one's back on others.

6.5 Explain how nonverbal communication can be used to communicate unethically.

- You communicate unethically when you use nonverbal cues to demean others by speaking in a patronizing tone, screaming at the less powerful, and touching others inappropriately.

6.6 Explain how you can improve your ability to interpret nonverbal behavior.

- You can improve your ability to interpret nonverbal messages by assessing the congruence of the verbal and nonverbal components of a message; analyzing the context; asking for additional information if you don't understand a nonverbal message; and remembering that not every nonverbal behavior is intended to be communicative.

KEY TERMS

nonverbal behavior p. 123
nonverbal communication p. 124
nonverbal codes p. 128
kinesics p. 128
gestures p. 128
illustrators p. 128
emblems p. 128
adaptors p. 128
regulators p. 128
posture and movement p. 129
immediacy p. 129
relaxation p. 129
paralinguistics p. 130

voice qualities p. 131
vocalizations p. 131
chronemics p. 131
proxemics p. 131
monochronically p. 132
polychronically p. 132
intimate distance p. 133
personal distance p. 133
social distance p. 133
public distance p. 133
haptics p. 135
professional touch p. 135
functional touch p. 135

social-polite touch p. 135
friendship touch p. 135
love-intimate touch p. 135
demand touching p. 136
artifacts p. 136
communicating information p. 138
regulating interaction p. 138
expressing and managing
    intimacy p. 138
establishing social control p. 138
service-task functions p. 139
congruent p. 143
contradicting p. 144

APPLY WHAT YOU KNOW

1. **Waiting Times** How long is the "appropriate" amount of time you should wait in each of the following situations? Specifically, after how long a period would you begin to feel angry or put out? Estimate waiting times for:

    a. your dentist
    b. a checkout line in a department store
    c. a movie line
    d. a friend at lunch
    e. a friend at dinner
    f. being on hold on the telephone
    g. your professor to arrive at class
    h. a stop light
    i. your romantic partner at a bar
    j. your professor during office hours.

    Do you see any patterns in your expectations for waiting times? What influences your expectations most—your relationship with the other party? The comfort of the waiting area? Your ability to control events? Compare your waiting times with others' to see how similar or different they are.

2. **Violating Norms for Proximity** For this exercise we would like you to violate some of the norms for spacing in your culture. Try standing slightly closer to a friend or family member than you normally would, then note how they react. If you have a romantic partner or very close friend, sit much farther from them than you normally would. For example, in a theater, sit one seat away from him or her, or sit at the opposite end of the couch if you would typically sit closer. Pay attention to the reactions you elicit. Finally, when talking with an acquaintance, increase the distance between you each time the other person tries to decrease it and see how the other person responds. What do these responses to your space violations reveal to you regarding the importance of spacing norms in the United States?

    NOTE: Be careful in your selection of people with whom you violate norms of space, and be prepared to explain why you are behaving so oddly.

EXPLORE

1. Go to a website such as Michigan State University's Presidential Audio Recordings or Archer Audio Archives and compare the vocal qualities of four presidents—two presidents who served before the widespread use of television and two who have served since. What role do you think vocal versus visual cues played in the popularity of each president? Are there presidents whose appearance you find more appealing than their vocal qualities? Are there presidents whose vocal qualities you find more appealing than their appearance?

2. The study of facial expressions of emotion is complex and ongoing. Recently, researchers have begun studying the effect of Botox (which paralyzes facial muscles) on facial expressions and emotional response. Go to a website such as PsychCentral's *Facial Expressions Control Emotions* or WebMD's *Botox May Affect Ability to Feel Emotions* and read the articles. Based on what you read, write a brief paper in which you hypothesize how the use of Botox could affect interpersonal interaction.

Listening and Responding

 LEARNING OBJECTIVES

CHAPTER TOPICS

7.1 Identify six reasons why listening is important.	The Importance of Listening
7.2 Describe the four stages of listening.	What is Listening? Four Stages
7.3 Describe the influences on listening and barriers to effective listening.	Listening and the Individual: Influences and Barriers
7.4 Understand the role of societal forces (hierarchy, contexts, and community) in listening.	The Individual, Listening, and Society: Hierarchy, Contexts, and Community
7.5 Describe ethical challenges in listening.	Ethics and Listening
7.6 Discuss two ways to improve your own listening behavior.	Improving Your Listening Skills

> *"Listening retains its position as the most widely used daily communication activity."*

Charee wonders if her listening skills are deteriorating. After taking a class in communication and learning about both bad listening habits and effective strategies for listening, she realized that she often doesn't listen to what others are saying because she's busy thinking of the next thing she's going to say. She also started thinking about the impact of what her professor calls "chronic earbud attachment syndrome"—the "addiction" that she and many of her fellow students have to their earbuds. Although this doesn't impact their *ability* to listen, she thinks it probably affects their *opportunities* to listen, perhaps meaning she misses out on little things that humans hear throughout the day that help make sense of the world and maybe also sends a negative message to others. She thinks about the fact that when she's in an elevator with her professor, she doesn't have to converse or stand in silence; she can avoid the interaction. She says it was hard, and it took conscious effort, but she's been trying to take more listening opportunities and also to listen to what others say and acknowledge their thoughts before she responds. She thinks it's helped because now she even finds the discussions in classes more productive and interesting.

Listening may be the single most important skill in the communication process because communication doesn't exist without a listener! (Lacey, 2013, p. 168) But most of us, like Charee, don't really think about it very much. Why is this? Perhaps it's because we confuse hearing and listening. As we will discover later in this chapter, hearing is passive; it occurs when listeners pick up the sound waves directed at them. Listening, however, like speaking or writing, is a more active communication process and involves understanding and evaluating messages. Or perhaps we think that listening can't be taught or learned. After all, few college courses teach listening theory and practice. However, as we'll discover in this chapter, a great deal of academic research focuses on the listening process, which includes not only hearing what others say, but also critically evaluating messages and responding. Communication experts have shown that by being aware of the dynamics of listening and working on being better listeners, we can become better communicators overall.

In this chapter, we will first identify six important reasons for improving listening and responding skills. We will then describe the process of listening as well as some of the influences and barriers to effective listening. Finally, we'll discuss the role of societal forces in listening, ethical issues related to listening, and suggestions for becoming a more effective listener.

The Importance of Listening

7.1   Identify six reasons why listening is important.

You might not understand why it is important to learn about listening. After all, it seems rather automatic, something we don't think about often. As this section shows, however, improving our listening skills can lead to many personal and professional benefits.

The first important reason for learning more about listening is that we spend so much time doing it! Listening is the primary communication activity for college students (Janusik & Wolvin, 2009), and experts estimate that they spend 55 percent of their total average communication day listening. About half that time is spent in interpersonal listening (class, face-to-face conversations, phone, listening to voice messages) and the other half in media listening (Emanuel et al., 2008).

In fact, media listening, in the broadest sense, encompasses a variety of online activities, including social media such as Facebook and Twitter—which provide a steady stream of messages (Greenwood, Perrin, & Duggan, 2016).

Second, having better listening skills can improve your memory, give you a broader knowledge base, and increase your attention span (Pasupathi & Billitteri, 2015). The brain is like any other muscle; you have to use it to improve it. The more you exercise it, the better you'll be able to process and remember information. The first step in exercising the brain is to pay better attention when others are speaking. You can't remember something if you never learned

▲ Learning to be a better listener can boost academic performance.

it, and you can't learn something—that is, encode it into your brain—if you don't pay enough attention to it.

A third, related reason to learn more about listening is that good listening skills can enhance academic performance. Not surprisingly, a number of research studies have shown that college students who have good listening skills are better students than those who are less effective listeners (Cooper & Buchanan, 2010). The most recent research shows that one of the most important outcomes of classes on listening is that students become more aware of what constitutes good listening (Ferrari-Bridgers et al., 2017). Although this indicates that a college course can help you identify the skills needed to be a good listener, you may need a lot of practice and attention to skill building on your own to become an effective listener. This is what Charee, in the opening vignette, realized.

Better listening is also linked to enhanced personal relationships—a fourth reason to learn more about listening. In earlier chapters, we have discussed how effective communication skills can lead to enhanced personal relationships. This is also true for listening skills. It's easy to understand how better listening can lead to fewer misunderstandings, which in turn can lead to greater satisfaction, happiness, and a sense of well-being for us and those we care about (Floyd, 2014; Pasupathi & Billitteri, 2015).

A fifth reason to improve listening skills is because leaders in many professions have long emphasized that effective listening is a highly desirable workplace skill; in fact, the ability to listen effectively is still one of the top three skills sought in job applicants (Janusik, 2010, p. 193). Poor listening skills can be costly: the consequences include wasted meeting time; inaccurate orders/shipments; lost sales; inadequately informed, misinformed, confused, or angry staff and customers; unmet deadlines; unsolved problems; wrong decisions; lawsuits; and poor employee morale (Battell, 2006). In contrast, people with good listening skills are perceived to be more trustworthy, which is important to a variety of work relationships, including physician–patient, salesperson–customer, and supervisor–employee (Lloyd, Boer, Kluger, & Voepel, 2015). People who are perceived to be good listeners in work settings are likely to be perceived as having leadership qualities (Kluger & Zaidel, 2013), and listening seems to play an interesting role in career advancement as well. One study showed that as workers move into management positions, listening skills become more important (Welch & Mickelson, 2013), particularly critical and comprehensive listening—listening that involves close attention to the verbal and nonverbal aspects to the message. In fact, there is some evidence that listening competence can actually promote a sense of well-being at work (Ala-Kortesma & Isotalus, 2015).

Finally, good listening can actually lead to improved health. Some studies show that when we listen attentively, heart rate and oxygen consumption are reduced, which leads to increased blood and oxygen to the brain—a healthy cardiovascular condition (Diamond, 2007). Health psychologist James J. Lynch (1985) conducted pioneering research showing that human interaction (or the lack of it) can dramatically affect cardiovascular systems. He found that when the patients talked about their own problems, their blood pressure increased to high levels. However, when the patients listened to a nonthreatening personal story or the reading of a passage from a book, the patients' blood pressure dropped to much lower levels because they momentarily focused on something outside themselves (cited by Shafir, 2003, p. 241). These results suggest that listening—an important aspect of personal connectedness—can improve human health.

Now that we've discussed the importance of learning about listening, the next section describes the process of listening, which shows that listening is much more than just hearing what others are saying.

Journal Prompt 7.1:
Listening and Responding
Consider the following questions:
What are six reasons for learning about listening and responding? Why are good listening and responding skills so important in professional contexts?

What Is Listening? Four Stages

7.2 Describe the four stages of listening.

The first step in striving to improve listening skills is to understand exactly what we mean when we talk about listening. Thus, we first provide a definition and then describe the process of listening.

Although there are various definitions for **listening**, the one we'll use is provided by the International Listening Association. Listening is "the process of receiving, constructing meaning from, and responding to spoken and/or nonverbal messages" (ILA, 1995, p. 4; Wolvin, 2013, p. 104). As you can see, this definition includes the concept described in Chapter 1 as the decoding phase of the communication process. It involves four stages: *hearing, understanding, evaluating,* and *responding* (Rosenfeld & Berko, 1990).

Let's see how this might work. **Hearing** occurs when listeners pick up the sound waves directed toward them. Suppose you're sitting in your apartment deep into Facebook and you hear sounds in the kitchen; it's your roommate, Josie, returning from her job as a server in a restaurant near campus. She yells out, "Guess what happened at work today?" For communication to occur, you must first become aware that information is being directed at you. In other words, you have to hear the sounds. But of course, hearing something is not the same as understanding or evaluating the information—the next steps. This means that hearing is not the same as listening. Hearing is really only the first step.

Once you sense that sounds are occurring, you have to interpret the messages associated with the sounds—that is, you have to **understand** what the sounds mean. The meaning you assign affects how you will respond—both physiologically and communicatively. In the example of your roommate, Josie, you understand her words—she's asking you to guess what happened at her work that day.

After you understand (or at least believe you understand) the message you have received, you **evaluate** the information. When you evaluate a message, you assess your reaction to it. For example, what do you think Josie is really asking you? Did

listening
The process of receiving, constructing meaning from, and responding to spoken and/or nonverbal messages.

hearing
The stage when listeners pick up the sound waves directed toward them.

understanding
Interpreting the messages associated with sounds or what the sounds mean.

evaluating
Assessing your reaction to a message.

something incredibly important happen to her at work? Or does she ask you this every time she returns from work, so that you know it doesn't matter what you answer because she is going to tell you some long, drawn-out story about people she works with whom you don't know? Or is she trying to engage you in conversation because you have both been busy and haven't seen each other much lately? As you can see, critical thinking skills are important in evaluating what you have heard—what are the possible interpretations of the message sent? What are the logical interpretations?

Finally, you **respond** to messages. Maybe you decide that you really want to hear what Josie's going to tell you or at least want to have a conversation with her and you tell her so—"no, I can't imagine what happened at work today, tell me!" Your response provides the most significant evidence to others that you are listening. Responding means that you show others how you regard their messages. For example, you could have responded to Josie in a sarcastic tone, letting her know that you'll listen but you're not really interested; or you could have just said "hmmm," telling her you don't even want to engage in a conversation. Even failing to respond is a type of response! Not answering a text message or not replying to a Tweet or Facebook message is a response of sort. You can respond in numerous ways; however, your response will be influenced by *how* you listen.

In addition to these phases of listening, we need to recognize that the total process of listening as a communication process is complex, involving motivations (we have to want to listen), cognitions, emotions, and behaviors (Bodie, Worthington, Imhof, & Cooper, 2008). In addition, some communication experts expand the definition of listening to include lurking—following Tweets, blog and Facebook posts—without responding (see *Alternative View: Lurkers as Listeners*).

Now that you understand the process of listening, the next section shows how an individual's personal characteristics influence listening and responding. We also describe how different situations require different types of listening skills.

responding
Showing others how you regard their message.

Critical Thinking Prompt
Think of a recent conflict you had, and describe how listening behaviors might have influenced the outcome. How might it have been different if those involved had spent more time listening instead of talking?

Journal Prompt 7.2: Defining Listening
Consider the following questions: What is a definition of listening? What are the four stages of listening?

ALTERNATIVE VIEW
Lurkers as Listeners

The work summarized here suggests a new way of defining listening—suggesting that just by attentiveness to the many new messages we attend to each day, we are listening, even if we don't respond. What do you think? Does listening only occur in face-to-face settings? Do we have to respond explicitly to be a listener?

Some communication scholars have suggested that we broaden our definition of listening—given all the new communication technologies. For example, they suggest that participation in various online activities—reading blogs, streaming videos, lurking on social media sites, attending to messages in Facebook, following tweets or RSS feeds—all constitute listening. They argue that even though the lurkers or "listeners" may not respond by posting messages, they directly contribute to the community by acting as a "gathered audience" who are engaged as listeners and are necessary to provoke the senders to keep speaking.

Furthermore, they note that listening to several (or several hundred) Twitter users or Facebook friends requires a real skill: "One needs to inhabit a stream of multilayered information, often leaping from news updates to a message from a friend experiencing a stressful situation, to information about what a stranger had for lunch, all in the space of seconds. Some will require attention; many can be glimpsed and tuned out" (Crawford, 2009, p. 529).

SOURCES: Crawford, K. (2009). Following you: Discipline of listening in social media. *Continuum: Journal of Media & Cultural Studies, 23*(4), 525–535.

Lacey, K. (2013). *Listening Publics: The Politics and Experience of Listening in the Media Age*. Cambridge, UK: Polity.

Listening and the Individual: Influences and Barriers

7.3 Describe the influences on listening and barriers to effective listening.

Do you have any friends who are especially good listeners? Any who are not so good? Do you find it easier to listen in some situations than in others?

Although some studies have identified general listening skills (see *Communication in Society: The "Big Five" of Listening Competency*), there are many factors that influence whether listening in any particular situation is easier or more difficult. In this section, we describe some of these factors, including individual listening styles and individual characteristics such as gender, age, and nationality. Finally, we discuss physical and psychological barriers to listening.

Influences on Listening

Not everyone listens in the same way; our personal listening habits may be influenced by gender, age, ethnicity, or even certain idiosyncratic patterns. These influences can then affect how we respond to others. Let's look first at the various listening styles and then turn to other characteristics that may influence how we listen and respond.

listening style
A set of attitudes, beliefs, and predispositions about the how, where, when, who, and what of the information receiving and encoding process.

Listening Styles   According to experts, a **listening style** is a set of "attitudes, beliefs, and predispositions about the how, where, when, who, and what of the information reception and encoding process" (Watson, Barker, & Weaver, 1995, p. 2). To put it more simply, it is "the way people prefer to receive oral information" (Watson et al., 1995, p. 9). Researchers have identified four listening styles used in various situations (Bodie & Worthington, 2010; Watson et al., 1995) and find that a given individual will tend to prefer to use just one or two of these styles (Barker & Watson, 2000).

Each listening style emphasizes a particular set of skills that are useful for responding to others in particular situations. The point of this is not that you should strive to develop a particular style or that having a particular style ensures you will be a good listener, but that your listening style should vary somewhat by context or situation. And, indeed, studies have shown that most people do vary their listening style from situation to situation (Imhof, 2004).

action-oriented listening style
Listening style that reflects a preference for error-free and well-organized speaking.

Action-Oriented Listening Style   The **action-oriented listening style** reflects a preference for error-free and well-organized speaking, with an emphasis on active

COMMUNICATION IN SOCIETY
The "Big Five" of Listening Competency

A recent online questionnaire asked 1,319 students to describe what it means to be an effective listener. The results revealed the following top or "Big Five" dimensions of effective listening.

Notice how each of these dimensions is associated with the phases of listening (hearing, sensing, and so on). Are there other skills that you would add?

1. Openness or willingness to listen
2. Ability to read nonverbal cues
3. Ability to understand verbal cues

4. Ability to respond appropriately
5. Ability to remember relevant details

Although these skills are important and confirm findings from previous studies, the authors of the study note that other factors, such as age, maturity, and personal experiences, influence an individual's listening competence. In addition, they note that the study design did not address the influence of context or interpersonal relationship.

SOURCE: Cooper, L. O., & Buchanan, T. (2010). Listening competency on campus: A psychometric analysis of student listening. *International Journal of Listening, 24*(3), 141–163.

responding. People using this style focus more on the content of the message than on the person delivering it, and they want to not only hear the message, but also to do something with it. They may get impatient if a speaker is not direct or concise enough.

The action-oriented style requires **informational listening** skills, useful in situations requiring attention to content. For example, at work you probably listen primarily for content, to make sure you understand the instructions of your boss, supervisor, or coworkers. Informational listening skills are also useful at school, during course lectures, or when professors give detailed instructions about assignments. How can you improve your informational listening skills? Here are some suggestions:

1. Attend to what the speaker is saying: Maintain eye contact, face the person, and lean toward him or her.

2. Don't judge the speaker prematurely: Making mental judgments can prevent you from understanding the content of the speaker's message.

3. Paraphrase: Reflect the speaker's words back to make sure you understand and let the speaker know you are listening—for example, if your professor is describing instructions for an assignment, you might say, "You're saying that the five-page paper needs to cite at least ten different research sources."

4. Clarify: Ask questions to clear up any confusion or seek more information. For example, if you don't completely understand your professor's instructions about a paper assignment, you might ask, "Can we email it to you or do you want us to hand it to you in class?"

5. Review and summarize: Summarizing captures the overall meaning of what has been said and puts it into a logical and coherent order, but should not add any new information. After your summary, you might also ask, "Is that correct?"

Content-Oriented Listening Style The **content-oriented listening style** reflects an interest in detailed and complex information, simply for the content itself. People using this style prefer debate or argument content over simpler speech; they attend to details and are interested in the quality of the speech. Critical thinking skills are particularly important in this style.

This style involves the informational listening skills detailed previously and an additional set of **critical listening** skills (Mooney, 1996), which go hand in hand with critical thinking skills. These skills are useful in a wide variety of situations, particularly those involving persuasive speaking—for example, when you are listening to a political speech or a sales pitch—or even in more informal settings, such as when friends or acquaintances try to persuade you to see their point of view about an issue or activity. Here are some suggestions for developing critical listening skills:

1. Consider the speaker's credibility. Is this speaker qualified to make these arguments? Is this speaker trustworthy?

2. Listen between the lines. Are the words and the body language consistent? Are the content and the emotion in harmony?

3. Evaluate the messages being sent and their implications. Ask yourself, "What conclusions can be drawn from what is being said? Where is this leading?"

4. Weigh the evidence. Does what is being said make sense? Are the opinions presented supported by fact?

5. Periodically review and summarize. As with informational listening, you need to periodically check to make sure you understand the message. Ask yourself, "Do I have it straight? Do I understand the speakers' arguments and main points?"

People-Oriented Listening Style People using this style are interested in hearing about others' experiences, thoughts, and feelings and finding areas of common interest. The

informational listening
Listening skills that are useful in situations requiring attention to content.

content-oriented listening style
A listening style that reflects an interest in detailed and complex information, simply for the content itself.

critical listening
Listening skills that are useful in a wide variety of situations—particularly those involving persuasive speaking.

▲ People-oriented listening involves listening not only to words but also to others' feelings.

people-oriented listening style
A listening style that is associated with friendly, open communication and an interest in establishing ties with others.

supportive listening
Listening skills focused not only on understanding information but also "listening" to others' feelings.

people-oriented listening style is often associated with friendly, open communication and an interest in establishing ties with others rather than in controlling them (Villaume & Bodie, 2007). The people-oriented style is useful in many different contexts as a recent study found that most people prefer empathic, person-centered listeners who are sensitive to their emotions (Itzchakov et al., 2014).

People-oriented listening involves **supportive listening** skills, focused not only on understanding information but also "listening" to others' feelings—which they may communicate nonverbally (Bodie & Jones, 2012; Bodie, Vickery, & Gearhart, 2013), as we've seen in Chapter 6. Consider the following suggestions for effective supportive listening (Fowler, 2005). Notice also how many of them involve nonverbal behaviors on the listener's part, and also the overlap with informational listening skills:

1. Put the other person at ease. Give space and time and "permission to speak." Do this by showing that you *want* to hear the speaker. Look at him or her. Nod when you can agree. Encourage the speaker to talk.

2. Remove distractions. Be willing to take out your earbuds, close a door, and stop texting, checking Facebook, or surfing on your iPad. Let the speaker know he or she has your full attention.

3. Empathize with the other person, especially if he or she is telling you something personal or painful; take a moment to stand in the other person's shoes, to look at the situation from his or her point of view. Empathy can be expressed by allowing the person to talk while maintaining a nonjudgmental, noncritical manner; don't discount the person's feelings (e.g. "it's not really that bad" or "you'll feel better tomorrow") ; and paraphrase what you think the person really means or feels, to communicate that you understand the emotions and feelings involved.

4. Be patient. Some people take longer to find the right word, make a point, or clarify an issue.

5. Be aware of your own emotions. Being supportive can sometimes be challenging and may cause stress on the part of the listeners (Jones, 2011). As we'll discuss later in the chapter, emotions can be a barrier to effective listening.

time-oriented listening style
A listening style that prefers brief, concise speech.

Time-Oriented Listening Style   The **time-oriented listening style** prefers brief, concise speech. Time-oriented listeners don't want to waste time on complex details; they just want the aural equivalent of bullet points. They may check their email or send a text when they think someone is taking too long to get to the point. They may also state how much time they have for an interaction to keep the interaction concise and to the point. No specific set of skills accompanies this style; in fact, this style seems to involve rather ineffective listening behavior, except in cases where time is of the essence and concise information is imperative (e.g., emergency situations). If you find yourself using this style in many situations, you may want to consider which of the other three styles may be more effective.

In conclusion, to become a more effective listener in a variety of personal and professional contexts, identify your preferred style(s) and then work on developing the skill sets that accompany the other styles. For example, if you tend to be a people-oriented listener, you might improve your informational and critical listening skills. On the other hand, if you tend to prefer the content-oriented style, you might work to develop your supportive listening skills.

Individual Identity Characteristics   Now let's turn to other individual influences on listening behaviors. How do individual identity characteristics such as gender, age, and ethnicity affect listening behaviors? Do males and females tend to listen differently? Do older people listen in a different way than do younger people? And a related set of questions: Should we adapt our listening behaviors depending on who we are listening to? For example, should we listen to children differently from adults? Let's look at how the experts weigh in on answers to these questions.

Gender   Some scholars think that in general men and women not only differ in their listening styles, but that women tend to be better listeners than men. Other researchers have found no gender differences in listening behavior (Pearce, Johnson, & Barker, 2003; Imhof, 2004). Before looking at the research on this topic, let's discuss the issue of gender stereotypes—that is, the common perceptions people have concerning gender and listening.

Two communication scholars have identified common gender-based listening stereotypes: Men, they say, are supposedly logical, judgmental, interrupting, inattentive, self-centered, and impatient; whereas women are stereotyped as emotional, noninterrupting, attentive, empathetic, other-centered, responsive, and patient (Barker & Watson, 2000). And there is some evidence suggesting that individuals with strong feminine orientation prefer a person-centered listening style, and more masculine individuals prefer a more task-oriented style (Johnston, Weaver, Watson, & Barker, 2000).

For example, a recent study, asking five hundred staff workers and managers in a variety of industries to rate themselves on a Listening Competency Scale, found some gender differences: Both female staff and managers rated themselves as more competent at therapeutic (supportive) listening, and overall, female managers scored higher than the male managers (Welch & Mickelson, 2013). As we've discussed in earlier chapters, most behavioral scientists believe that although some innate gender differences may exist, most behavioral differences between men and women are influenced more by cultural norms than biology. To sum it up, there do seem to be a few gender differences in listening behaviors, but both men and women can demonstrate feminine and masculine listening behaviors (Bodie & Fitch-Hauser, 2010). Remember, too, that gender differences are not fixed and given; people of both genders can learn to be effective listeners.

Age   Do you listen differently to your parents than to your younger siblings? The fact is that people have different communication capacities and skill levels during various life stages, which means that we often adapt our listening behaviors depending on the age of the speaker (Brownell, 2012). We can and should adapt our listening behaviors for children (Clark, 2005). Because young children are in the process of developing their communication skills, we need to be patient when they "break" conversational rules or are struggling to say something; children have more to say than they can express. Give them your undivided attention, maintaining eye contact when they're speaking and asking questions; in other words, be a good listening role model (Brownell, 2012).

As we get older, listening may become more difficult if

Critical Thinking Prompt
Consider the various listening styles and think about which style(s) you tend to use. Which are you less likely to use? Which sets of skills might you need to work on to become a more effective listener?

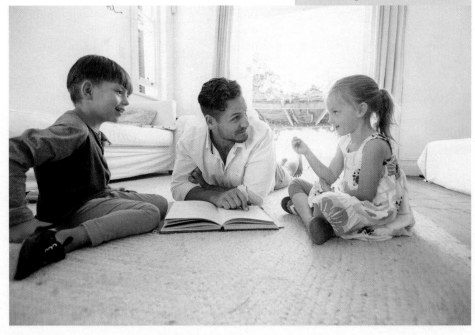

▼ Listening to children involves adjusting one's listening style and being tolerant of children's "breaking" conversational rules.

hearing ability is an issue. We'll discuss hearing disability in the next section, under barriers to listening. However, not everyone who is old is deaf or has diminished mental abilities. Assuming that they are—that is, yelling or treating listeners like children—can be hurtful and insulting (Froemming & Penington, 2011).

Nationality   Do people in all cultures consider listening equally important? The answer is no. Generally speaking, people in Western countries (the United States and Europe) tend to place more emphasis on speaking skills, whereas many Asians consider listening to be the most important communication skills and are taught early that they *must* be good listeners (Beall, 2010, p. 233). In addition, there are cultural differences in what people consider appropriate nonverbal expressions of listening and responding (Imhof & Janusik, 2006). In most Western cultures, good listening is demonstrated by eye contact, head nods, and some back-channeling vocalizations such as "hmmm" and "oh." However, in some countries, such as Vietnam and Thailand, good listening behavior (listening respectfully) involves avoiding eye contact. In other countries, such as Japan, good listening may involve responding with lots of head nods, back-channeling, and even saying "yes, yes," which actually means, "I hear you," not "I agree with you" (Fujii, 2008). We'll explore more cross-cultural differences in communication patterns in the following chapter.

Here, however, to summarize, factors that can influence an individual's listening behavior include gender, age, ethnicity, and nationality, as well as one's own listening style preferences and the particular situation. Still, one cannot assume that an individual will listen in a particular way just because she or he belongs to a certain gender, age, or nationality group. Listening is a complex behavior, and numerous factors beyond these kinds of identity characteristics can serve as barriers, the topic we turn to next.

Barriers to Listening

Like Charee in the opening vignette, people have many reasons for not listening to others. Some typical ones include physical and physiological barriers, psychological barriers, conflicting objectives, and poor listening habits (Robertson, 2005). Let's explore in more detail how these factors can interfere with effective listening.

Physical and Physiological Barriers   Physical barriers to listening include a noisy environment or physical discomforts that make it difficult to concentrate. We have all had the experience of trying to listen to someone in a noisy bar or in a room with

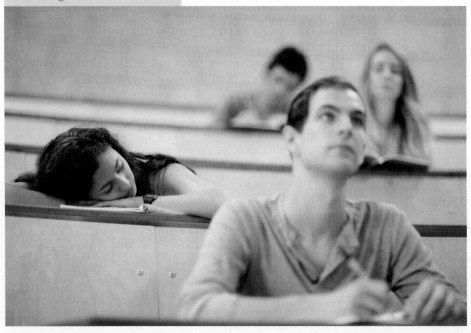

▼ Fatigue is a common barrier to listening.

a loud television, or while standing outside with traffic whizzing by on a busy highway. Physical barriers are the most elemental; if we can't hear because of the noise around us, it doesn't matter how refined our listening skills are.

Another physical barrier is fatigue. Whether a listener is tired from lack of sleep or from high stress, it can be a barrier to good listening. For example, it's difficult for students to listen effectively in class when they are exhausted; and it's difficult for parents to listen to children when they are stressed out from working hard and managing their many responsibilities. As we hope you understand by now, listening well takes effort and requires alertness and focus—both of which may be absent when one is tired.

Another type of listening barrier is physiological—for example, a hearing disability. Good listening is a skill, but it is also strongly affected by a person's physical ability to hear. The Hearing Loss Association of America estimates that more than 35 million people in the United States have a hearing loss that could be treated and, in fact, an increasing number of younger people have hearing problems associated with Personal Media Players (PMP) (Johnson-Curiskis, 2012). (See *Did You Know? Statistically, How Many People Are Deaf or Hard of Hearing?*) Unfortunately, many people with hearing loss do not treat it—whether because of vanity (not wanting to wear a hearing aid), lack of funds, or lack of knowledge about the disability. Getting over this barrier may mean recognizing and treating the disability or, in the case of mild impairment, asking people to enunciate more clearly and use adequate speech volume.

Psychological Barriers   Common psychological barriers that prevent us from listening effectively are boredom and preoccupation. The human mind can process information at a rate of about 600 words per minute, about three times faster than the typical speaker can talk. This phenomenon is sometimes labeled the "thought-speech differential" (Brownell, 2012, p. 81). Consequently, as Charee discovered, your mind has plenty of time to wander, and you can easily become distracted or bored, which will certainly undermine the amount that you listen to and retain.

Preoccupation, or distracted listening, is a related psychological barrier. During an interaction, people often think of other things and, thus, do not listen to what is being said. Preoccupation can be caused by many things. For example, many students

DID YOU KNOW?
Statistically, How Many People Are Deaf or Hard of Hearing?

How often do you assume that the person listening to you has good hearing? How might this assumption influence how you respond and, ultimately, the outcomes of your communication encounters? How might you modify your way of speaking if you knew you were speaking to someone with a hearing loss?

Statistically, how many people are deaf or hard of hearing? It is actually difficult to estimate because some people may not wish to identify themselves as having a hearing loss, or the questions may not ask directly if a person has a hearing loss. People who are hard of hearing refers to people with hearing loss ranging from mild to severe. They usually communicate through spoken language and can benefit from hearing aids, captioning, and assistive listening devices. People who are deaf mostly have profound hearing loss, which implies very little or no hearing. They often use sign language for communication.

Here are some interesting facts about hearing loss:

- About 2 to 3 out of every 1,000 children in the United States are born with a detectable level of hearing loss in one or both ears. More than 90 percent of deaf children are born to hearing parents.
- One in eight people in the United States (13 percent, or 30 million) aged 12 years or older has hearing loss in both ears.
- Hearing loss increases with age. About 2 percent of adults aged 45 to 54 have disabling hearing loss. The rate increases to 8.5 percent for adults aged 55 to 64 and nearly 25 percent of those aged 65 to 74 and 50 percent of those who are 75 and older have disabling hearing loss.
- Men are more likely than women to report having hearing loss.
- Approximately 15 percent of Americans (26 million people) between the ages of 20 and 69 have high frequency hearing loss due to exposure to noise at work or during leisure activities.

Hearing loss can have important academic, social, and emotional impacts. Hearing loss can delay spoken language development and academic performance. Hearing loss affects an individual's ability to communicate and can lead to of loneliness, isolation, and frustration, particularly among older people with hearing loss.

SOURCES: (2014, February). *World Health Organization Media Center Fact Sheet.* Retrieved February 17, 2017, from http://www.who.int/mediacentre/factsheets/fs300/en/.

(2016, December 15). National Institute on Deafness and Other Communication Disorders (NIDCD) Quick Statistics. Retrieved February 24, 2017 from https://www.nidcd.nih.gov/health/statistics/quick-statistics-hearing.

▲ Strong emotions can interfere with listening by making people defensive, overly sensitive, or hostile.

are preoccupied with cellphones and other digital devices, leading scholars to investigate the phenomenon of "distracted students" and how professors cope with students who are not really listening to classroom discussions (Cheong et al., 2016). Of course, the same distraction can occur in informal conversations.

Another source of preoccupation comes from strong emotions. For example, some older Americans identify emotional triggers that cause them to tune out (e.g., "false familiarity," for example, someone calling them by their first names) (Froemming & Penington, 2011). By contrast, even joy, for example, can make a person too preoccupied to listen and can also influence how he or she understands and reacts to messages, so if something wonderful has just happened to you, you may be concentrating on your good news and how you are going to celebrate, rather than focusing on the speaker. Thus, a wide variety of emotions can distract you and influence how you listen and respond in communicative interactions (Nichols, 2009).

Emotions can also make people defensive and thus impair their listening abilities. Defensive listening occurs when someone perceives, anticipates, or experiences a threat (Nichols, 2009). In such cases, the listener often puts up a "wall" for protection. These walls can distort incoming messages, leading to misinterpretation. For example, one of our colleagues described how her emotional reactions to her father hindered her ability to listen to him: "We had such a rotten relationship that every time he even opened his mouth to speak, I was so defensive, so sure he was going to criticize me or yell at me that I never even heard a word he said." Some people are more defensive than others; their personalities and experiences have influenced them to respond defensively to many messages. However, certain types of messages are more likely to elicit defensive listening. Preconceived ideas about issues or participants can also trigger strong emotions. For example, sometimes we allow negative past experience with a person to interfere; that is, if you expect your sibling (or father) to be angry at you, you will likely interpret any comment as hostile—as was the case with our colleague and her father. The psychological barriers discussed here can act as "filters that allow only selected words and ideas into our consciousness . . . [they can also] screen out the less comfortable and uncomfortable messages, [so that] only pieces of the message are received—the comfortable pieces" (Shafir, 2003, p. 46). The end result is that these barriers can stifle the potential for developing meaningful relationships and new ideas.

Conflicting Objectives   A third barrier to listening involves conflicting objectives. How people understand and react to others' communicative attempts depends in part on their objective(s) for the conversation. For example, how do you listen to a lecture when your instructor announces, "This will be on the midterm"? How do you listen when told the material will *not* be on a test? Your different objectives for these situations are likely to influence how well you listen.

Sometimes participants to a conversation differ in their objectives for an interaction. For example, during a business meeting Ignacio's objective was to explain a new procedure for evaluating employees, whereas Roberta's objective was to get a raise. Consequently, the two focused on different aspects of their conversation, assigned

COMMUNICATION IN SOCIETY
Listening and Civil Dialogue

The extreme polarization of political views during and after the 2016 presidential campaign reveals that people increasingly live in echo chambers, where those inside only hear the expressions of opinions that agree with their own and mistake those echoes as majority views. This polarization has resulted in fracturing of family and personal relationships leading experts to call for communication strategies that enable people to be able to speak honestly with each other without resorting to attack or criticism. For example, see "When Your Loved Ones Voted the Other Way https://www.nytimes.com/video/us/politics/100000004881605/family-conversations-on-trump.html.

Civil Dialogue®, developed by Clark Olson and colleagues at Arizona State University, is a structured method of public conversations designed to engage people with differing opinions on a controversial topic (see http://www.civil-dialogue.com/). Civil Dialogue has been used to build bridges between individuals on divergent sides of topics, including climate change, evolution, sexual violence, presidential elections and more. It has been used in both local communities and in the classroom, engaging communities as diverse as homeless populations to Arab communities.

In a "Civil Dialogue," groups of citizens or students are invited to describe their positions from "strongly agree" to "strongly disagree" on a topic while seated in front of an audience. The participants (and later audience members) are encouraged to communicate their personal opinions and experiences without trying to change each other's minds or demonize one another. A core element of these dialogues is *active* or *intentional* listening and facilitators stress the importance of letting voices be heard, the impact of narrative story in listening to the "other" point of view, and the opportunity to model civility.

The reasoning behind this is while it's easy to shoot down an opinion or a position alone, *listening* to someone's life experience can help us see how, even if we don't agree, a formative experience is never wrong. It's just another shade of reality.

SOURCES: Genette, J., Olson, C. D., & Linde, J. (2017). *Hot topics, cool heads: A handbook on Civil Dialogue®*. Dubuque, IA: Kendall Hunt.

Olson, C. D., Genette, J., & Linde, J. (n.d.). Civility in urban spaces: The use of Civil Dialogue® in urban controversies. Available at http://www.civil-dialogue.com/civil-dialogue-in-urban-controversies.html

Jensen, T. (2017, January 22). When Your Loved Ones Voted the Other Way. https://www.nytimes.com/video/us/politics/100000004881605/family-conversations-on-trump.html.

different meanings to what occurred, and remembered different aspects of their meeting. Of course, people may have multiple objectives for an interaction, each of which will influence how they listen and respond.

Poor Listening Habits As it turns out, people can more easily define poor listening than effective listening. Similarly, people can more easily identify the listening habits and flaws of others than they can their own. In our opening story, Charee saw other students' poor listening behaviors—although she also recognized her own.

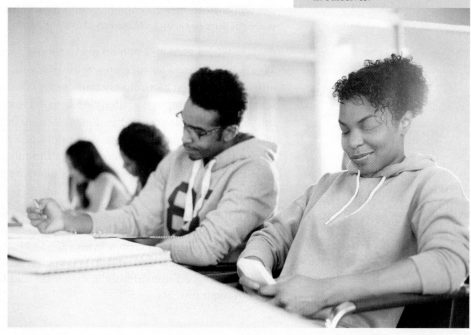

▼ It is easier to identify poor listening habits in others than in ourselves.

Here are five common ineffective listening behaviors, which result in not really getting the speaker's message.

1. **Wandering:** Probably the most common. The listener's mind wanders from time to time, not really focused on what the speaker is saying. The words go in one ear and out the other.

2. **Rejecting:** The listener "tunes out" the speaker at the beginning of the message, often because of a lack of respect or dislike for the speaker.

3. **Judging:** The listener focuses on what the speaker says, but makes a hasty evaluation of the speaker's message, ignoring the remainder of the message.

4. **Predicting:** So common—the listener gets ahead of the speaker and finishes her thoughts; again, missing at least some of the speaker's message.

5. **Rehearsing:** The listener is thinking about what she is going to say next.

Journal Prompt 7.3:
Listening Styles
Consider the following questions:
Which of the four listening styles do you find the most challenging? Which of the four common barriers do you encounter most often?

Are there other annoying habits you would like to add to this list? Are you guilty of any of these? Most of us are. Perhaps the most important way to avoid these bad habits is to first become more aware of our own listening behavior and to really focus on the speaker rather than on our own thoughts, feelings, and what we're going to say next. As we've mentioned, however, societal factors can have an important impact on one's ability to listen effectively, and this is the subject we turn to next.

The Individual, Listening, and Society: Hierarchy, Contexts, and Community

7.4   Understand the role of societal forces (hierarchy, contexts, and community) in listening.

As emphasized throughout this book, communication behaviors do not exist solely on the individual level but are a complex interaction of individual and societal factors, reflected in our Synergetic Model of communication. Let's examine listening as it's affected by three levels of societal forces: social hierarchy, context, and community.

Social Hierarchy

Societal norms and social hierarchy influence much of our communication behaviors, and listening is no exception. Let's look more closely at how this works. Every society transmits messages about who is most powerful and important, and these are the people who set the communication norms. How do these messages affect our listening and responding?

Each time we meet someone for the first time, we immediately evaluate whether that person is worth listening to. We mentally go through our personal (influenced by society's) criteria. If the person doesn't meet the criteria, the person's words "become fainter and fainter until only our thoughts fill our attention" (Shafir, 2003, p. 57). Some of the most crucial information to be gained as listeners—like people's names—gets lost while we process acceptability checklists. Three important "filters" are social status, physical appearance, and vocal cues.

Social Status   One criterion on many people's acceptability checklist is social status. We ask ourselves: Is this person worthy of my time and attention? Most of us are more attentive and listen more closely to those we consider equal to us or higher in society's hierarchy. For example, we listen closely to the words of physicians, teachers, successful business people, and celebrities. Rebecca Z. Shafir (2003), a renowned speech pathologist and listening expert, recounts the story of a manager of a large department who, as part of his power trip, ordered his staff to follow him down the hall as they asked questions or presented ideas (like the demanding boss, Miranda Priestly, in the movie *The Devil Wears Prada*):

> He rarely made eye contact with his subordinates and walked past them as they spoke. Yet, when conversing with his peers or those higher on the administrative ladder, a dramatic change in his voice and body language took place. He looked them in the eye and smiled, nodding his head at any comment or suggestion. He laughed uproariously at their jokes and thanked them profusely for their unique insights. (p. 53)

Critical Thinking Prompt
Review the listening barriers described in the chapter. Which do you think are the most common in your own life? Which do you think are the most difficult to overcome? What is the evidence for your answers to these questions?

Shafir goes on to say that this manager's attention to status overrode his ability to gain the voluntary cooperation of his staff and resulted in ineffective management, low staff morale, and high turnover. Regardless of the positions we hold, most of us are similarly influenced by systems of hierarchy, and these systems are sometimes tinged with prejudice. For example, do we listen with as much attention to people who have less education? Perhaps not, as Danny found out in *It Happened to Me: Danny*.

Physical Appearance One of the most common obstacles to listening relates to physical appearance. Societal forces set the norms for physical attractiveness, which include being physically able-bodied, having symmetrical features, and embodying certain weight and height norms. This means that many people hold stereotypes about people with disabilities or physical challenges and they often find it difficult to listen to them, avoiding eye contact or ignoring the person entirely. One of our colleagues, Tanya, had a stroke as a young adult and uses a walker or wheelchair. She describes a common situation she encounters:

It Happened to Me
Danny

Being in college, I'm a part of a culture that's very different from the culture where I grew up. In college, people value talking about ideas, learning new information, and working toward becoming more "educated." When I go home, however, I have to remember that not everyone in my family, and not all of my friends, went to college. They don't understand a lot of the jargon I use, and they don't know about the things I've studied. I try to be mindful of this when I visit; I don't want to sound condescending. I also try to remember that their opinions are equally valid and that I need to listen as attentively to them as I do to my college friends.

> It really irritates me sometimes when I'm in public and people avoid looking at me, look at my husband instead and ask him what I want. Why can't they listen to what *I'm saying* and respond to *me*?

In sum, social hierarchies can act as a filter that, in turn, influences people's listening behaviors.

Vocal Cues In addition to social status and appearance, vocal cues (the *way* a person talks) can also be a filter that influences how people listen to others. Sometimes these judgments are factually accurate. For example, people can often tell by hearing someone's voice whether the speaker is male or female, young or old. However, a recent study showed that people make other judgments about a person, in addition to gender and age, based on the pitch and sound of their voice (Imhof, 2010). In this study, the researchers found that people with higher pitched voices were judged by others to be more outgoing and open, but less conscientious and less emotionally stable. The judgments stem from societal cues and assumptions that link people's vocal cues to personality. Another study found that job applicants with a U.S. Midwestern accent were evaluated more positively than those with a foreign accent (Deprez-Sims & Morris, 2010).

The important question is, how do we listen to people we consider "less conscientious" or "less emotionally stable" or foreign? Something to keep in mind is whether we are making unwarranted judgments that then influence how we listen.

The point here is that these "filters," based on social hierarchy, can prevent us from listening to others with openness and in a nonjudgmental manner that is usually thought of as part of effective listening. However, several experts have pointed out that it is probably not really possible to "set aside prejudices" and "consider all people as equal," so that setting these goals as a necessary and sufficient condition for effective listening means almost certain failure. Rather, they suggest that we see them as ideals—goals to strive *toward*. In so doing, certainly becoming aware of our "filters" is a first step (Bodie, 2010; Floyd, 2010).

Listening in Context

As discussed previously, different contexts may call for different listening styles and behaviors. For example, in professional contexts we generally focus on content or action listening, whereas in social contexts we generally focus more on people and relationship affirmation. With friends, we are often called on to listen sympathetically and with little judgment, establishing empathy and communicating a recognizable *"feeling* of being heard" (Shotter, 2009, p. 21).

In professional contexts, too, whether one is working on an assembly line or as a manager, listening with empathy is important because it enables people to understand each other and get the job done (Battell, 2006; Imhof, 2001). At the same time, employees must be cautious about letting their work relationships get too personal. For example, when Donna's new boss, Lena, asked Donna to be Facebook friends, Donna was flattered. However, when Lena posted nasty messages about her divorce and aired problems she was having with her children, and continued these conversations at work, Donna soon found that Lena's personal issues were taking lots of time and keeping her from getting work done. In addition, she discovered that her coworkers were critical of her for being unable to keep things on a professional level. The lesson, then, is that colleagues need to balance task and relational listening skills (Nichols, 2009).

Societal forces may affect listening behavior in any context. For example, some individuals are the victims of prejudice, discrimination, or even bullying in social or workplace contexts because of gender, age, race, ethnicity, or sexual orientation. When this happens, they may not be able to easily adapt their listening behavior. Others' bullying or discriminatory reactions to them may completely undermine their attempts to demonstrate good communication skills. Deborah Tannen's (1994) influential work showed how women's contributions in office meetings were often not listened to, and similarly, a disabled person might display good listening skills in a conversation by making eye contact, leaning forward, and paying close attention, but these good communication skills can be undermined if the speaker expresses prejudice toward the listening disabled person by *avoiding* eye contact in return, or by ignoring the disabled person's contribution by not listening when that person becomes the speaker. We'll address the role of prejudice and discrimination in communication further in Chapter 8.

Listening and Community

soundscape
The everyday sounds in our environments.

Communication scholar David Beard (2009) reminds us that in addition to all the voices in various hierarchies and contexts we listen to every day, we also listen to **soundscapes**—the everyday sounds in our environments. Together these sounds establish a community identity. For example, in many small towns, church bells—or in some countries, the imam calling Muslims to prayer five times daily—help define the boundaries of regional or religious communities and shape a community identity.

Community-specific soundscapes can also vary with generational differences. Contrast the technological soundscapes of your parents' and grandparents' generation—the hiss of the needle on a record player, the sound of rotary phone dialing (and perhaps even a live operator's voice), the chimes of the NBC logo, the screech of dial-up Internet access—with your own soundscapes. What were the soundscapes of the neighborhood where you grew up? What sounds do you hear every day that may represent your generational identity and communities? Perhaps more importantly, how do these affect you? Are they comforting? Irritating? Are there some that you tune out? Perhaps they are so much a part of the sound "background" that we don't consider their effect on us.

Although, as you've seen, the quality of one's listening is subject to powerful social forces as well as individual factors such as listening style, gender, and age, we do have some latitude for making choices about our own behavior. In other words, we do make ethical decisions about listening—the topic we turn to next.

Ethics and Listening

7.5 Describe ethical challenges in listening.

People have several ethical decisions to make about listening. These decisions include choosing what you will listen to and when, as well as how you will respond when listening to other people or to the soundscapes that surround you.

To begin, choosing to listen or not is an ethical decision, in both face-to-face and mediated communication contexts (Beard, 2009; Lacey, 2013; Stoltz, 2010). Just because someone wants to tell you something doesn't mean you have to listen. And sometimes the act of listening—or refusing to—means taking a moral stand. For example, let's say a friend of yours tweets a vicious rumor about another person or tells a racist joke. You have an ethical decision to make. How are you going to respond? Are you going to retweet it? Ignore it?

You can tell your friend you don't want to hear any more or even gently explain why you don't want to. Or you can do nothing, sacrificing honesty to avoid making yourself (and others) feel uncomfortable. What are the consequences of each of these decisions? If you listen to something offensive and pass it on, you are in effect agreeing with the tweet. It may be awkward to tell your friend (either at the moment or later) that you don't want to listen to such remarks, but the friend may think twice before sending similar tweets in the future. Obviously, there are no easy answers; you need to consider the consequences and possible outcomes in each situation as you make these ethical decisions.

Let's say you overhear some information or see a text message not intended for you. What are some guidelines for dealing with this information? As we suggested in Chapter 1, you might first consider the expectations of the individual who sent the message. Perhaps this person has made it clear that he or she wants this information kept private. Or you might consider that if you were in this person's position, you would want the information to be kept private. Or perhaps you know that the sender does not mind if the information is shared more widely—but what about the person to whom the message is addressed? You need to consider his or her wishes, too. Depending on the privacy expectation, the ethical decision might be to listen to or read the message—or not. Would the sender or addressee feel harmed? Would any benefit result from your listening to the message? The answer to these questions probably depends a great deal on your relationships with the sender and addressee.

Journal Prompt 7.4:
Listening and Context
Consider the following question:
How do contexts affect how we listen and respond to others?

▼ Ethical listening involves knowing how to handle confidentiality if you receive a message not intended for you.

A close friend may not mind your listening in on messages; someone you don't know very well may object strenuously.

Mediated communication contexts also can pose ethical issues with regard to listening. Communication expert Kate Lacey says we need a special set of listening skills to help us cope with this barrage of messages and to be selective in our listening choices; we train in "public speaking," but not "public listening" (p. 190). She notes that on the one hand, we have an ethical responsibility to "grant right of audience" to those who would otherwise not be heard because they present opportunities to expand our horizons, and of course we need to balance openness with critical thinking. On the other hand, much of our social media listening is increasingly narrowed—device settings/apps that program what we hear (music, talk, TV, newsites) to our idiosyncratic preferences (Gottried & Shearer, 2016; Lacey, 2013). Here are some choices we make, as listeners, to become more or less ethical beings, in our mediated world:

1. The choice to cut ourselves off from listening to our immediate environments: As Charee discussed in the chapter opening, we can choose to listen alone (putting on the headset/earbuds), which sometimes might be a positive, self-constructive act. At other times, however (e.g., in a work situation or at home when our relational partner wants to talk), doing so can be isolating and damaging to relationships.

2. The choice to listen selectively: For example, we can choose to listen to media "candy" or to media that enhance and inspire us as people. We can choose to listen to a friend's choice of media, so we can discuss it together, or we can listen only to our own choices.

3. The choice not to listen: For example, in the public arena, we can decide to listen (or not listen) to a political speaker who espouses ideas we oppose. Our choice has a potential impact on us and our thinking because listening implies the possibility of change in attitudes and behavior. Listening to a political speaker (or even a friend) promoting ideas and beliefs that we disagree with may open us up to ideas previously unexplored or may reinforce our own beliefs. Choosing never to listen to opposing views ensures that we won't alter our beliefs or learn to defend them in a logical and constructive way.

4. The choice to listen together: For example, when we attend a music concert or a political rally, we open ourselves to being part of a community of music fans or political sympathizers (Beard, 2009). The consequences of the decision to listen with a particular community may open up opportunities for new experiences that may alter our future thinking or behavior.

The point is that all these choices are just that—choices. Although we don't usually consider these types of choices when we think of listening, the decisions we make regarding them do influence our communication life—influencing our communication identity and relationships with those important to us.

**Journal Prompt 7.5:
Ethical Listening**
Consider the following question:
What are some ethical choices you have encountered in listening and responding?

Improving Your Listening Skills

7.6 Discuss two ways to improve your own listening behavior.

As we have shown in this chapter, listening (including responding appropriately) is an important communication skill. As is the case with all communication skills, however, there are no surefire, easy recipes for becoming a more effective listener. Still, two guidelines might help you improve.

Identify Poor Habits

As noted, most people have some poor listening habits, particularly in our close and intimate relationships, where partners often develop irritating practices such as finishing the other person's sentences, interrupting, and "tuning out" the other person. These irritating behaviors crop up especially if you are an action- or time-oriented listener. Ask yourself, then: What keeps you from really listening? Which filters block your ability to hear and understand what others are saying? Overcoming listening barriers—especially those that are reinforced by social hierarchies—can be challenging.

Perhaps one way to overcome those societal messages is through awareness that our listening behaviors play an important role in the outcome of communication encounters. A number of research studies have shown that when people listen attentively to one another, the speaker is more likely to speak coherently. On the other hand, when listeners

▲ Interrupting or completing other people's sentences are barriers to listening that we can all learn to overcome if we try.

do not pay careful attention, speakers tend to be less coherent, less engaged, and may even feel undervalued (Pasupathi & Billitteri, 2014). Put another way, regardless of who they are or their social location, when speakers feel they are listened to with respect and attentiveness, they become better communicators and vice versa.

Strive for Mindful Listening

Applying the concept of mindful listening, described by renowned listening expert Rebecca Z. Shafir (2003), can help. We defined mindfulness in Chapter 4. Mindful listening, which is a specific kind of mindfulness, is based on Eastern philosophy and Zen Buddhism; it is defined by focus, concentration, and compassion, and it can bring health, peace, and productivity to our everyday lives. This holistic approach requires that we listen with the heart, body, and mind, and for most of us, that means a major change in attitude. Mindful listening focuses on the *process* of listening versus the *payoff*.

Shafir suggests that to be a better listener to each of our friends, family, and acquaintances, we need to understand their "movie." What does that mean? Shafir compares listening to movies with listening to people. Most of us don't have trouble focusing on and paying attention while watching a movie; we get caught up in the plot, the emotion, and the characters. Why, she asks, should listening to people be any different? To continue the comparison, if we approach a listening opportunity with the same self-abandonment as we do a movie, think how much more we might gain from those encounters (Shafir, 2003).

Being a mindful listener requires three elements:

1. the desire to get the whole message,
2. the ability to eliminate the noisy barriers discussed previously, and
3. the willingness to place your agenda lower on the priority list than the speaker's.

Mindful listening is based on empathy—the ability to identify with and understand someone else's feelings. As listening expert Michael Nichols states it, listening is not just taking in information; it is also "bearing witness" to, validating, and affirming another's expression. The core of listening, he says, is "to pay attention, take an interest in, care about, validate, acknowledge, be moved . . . appreciate" (2009, p. 14).

Journal Prompt 7.6: Improving Listening
Consider the following question:
What are two ways you can improve your own listening behavior?

SUMMARY

7.1 Identify six reasons why listening is important.

- Listening is considered to be one of the most important communication skills, partly because we spend so much time doing it!

- Better listening skills can lead to improved cognition, improved academic performance, enhanced personal relationships, enhanced professional performance, and better health.

7.2 Describe the four stages of listening.

- *Listening* is defined as "the process of receiving, constructing meaning from, and responding to spoken and/or nonverbal messages" and occurs in four stages: hearing, understanding, evaluating, and responding.

7.3 Describe the influences on listening and barriers to effective listening.

- Our own personal listening habits may be influenced by our gender, age, ethnicity, or even our own predominant listening style.

- There are four listening styles: *action-oriented style* involves informational listening skills; *content-oriented style* involves informational and critical listening skills;

people-oriented style involves supportive listening skills; and *time-oriented style* is rather ineffective and involves quick hurried listening.

- People have many reasons for not listening to others, but some typical ones include physical or physiological barriers, psychological barriers, conflicting objectives, and poor listening habits.

7.4 Understand the role of societal forces (hierarchy, contexts, and community) in listening.

- Listening habits and preferences are influenced by societal forces: contexts, and hierarchies.

7.5 Describe ethical challenges in listening.

- Ethical decisions with respect to listening behavior include choosing what to listen to and when, how to respond when listening to other people or to the soundscapes around us, including media.

7.6 Discuss two ways to improve your own listening behavior.

- Although we can offer no surefire, easy recipes for becoming a more effective listener, two guidelines might help: identify your poor listening habits or barriers and practice mindful listening.

KEY TERMS

listening p. 150
hearing p. 150
understanding p. 150
evaluating p. 150
responding p. 151

listening style p. 152
action-oriented listening style p. 152
informational listening p. 153
content-oriented listening style p. 153
critical listening p. 153

people-oriented listening style p. 154
supportive listening p. 154
time-oriented listening style p. 154
soundscape p. 162

APPLY WHAT YOU KNOW

1. When you are in class or in a large group, notice how people listen to each other and respond. Reflect on what you think is more or less effective about others' listening skills. Then apply what you observed to your own listening skills.

2. Ask someone to observe your listening skills over a period of time. This person can be a parent, friend, teacher, or romantic partner. Ask the observer to give you constructive feedback on how you can improve your listening skills. Try to implement those suggestions.

Communication across Cultures

LEARNING OBJECTIVES

8.1   Explain why it is important to learn about intercultural communication.

8.2   Define intercultural communication and describe three types of border dwellers.

8.3   Describe how cultural values influence communication.

8.4   Explain the roles that politics, history, and power play in communication between people from different cultural backgrounds.

8.5   Give three guidelines for communicating more ethically with people whose cultural backgrounds differ from your own.

8.6   Discuss ways to improve your own intercultural communication skills.

CHAPTER TOPICS

The Importance of Intercultural Communication

What Is Intercultural Communication?

Intercultural Communication and the Individual: Cultural Values

The Individual, Intercultural Communication, and Society: Politics, History, and Power

Ethics and Intercultural Communication

Improving Your Intercultural Communication Skills

> *"Many, if not most, of your daily interactions are intercultural in nature."*

Charee has become good friends with Kaori, a Japanese exchange student. Kaori's English is really good, but sometimes they misunderstand each other when they text. For example, Charee recently learned that when she used terms like brb and ttyl or made sarcastic remarks such as "what a great idea, Einstein!" Kaori didn't understand. Kaori didn't tell Charee that she didn't understand, but just didn't respond to the messages. She only explained later when Charee became concerned about the lack of response and pressed Kaori to tell her if something was wrong.

Kaori's story illustrates several points about intercultural communication. First, intercultural contact is a fact of life in today's world; and second, although intercultural contact can be enriching, it can also bring challenges and misunderstanding, especially in mediated communication such as text messaging. In Kaori's case, communicating in English in text messages is especially challenging because of the lack of nonverbal cues. She explained to Charee that she doesn't always feel comfortable telling people when she doesn't understand. She said that in Japan, people generally avoid direct communication and prefer to be more indirect, as we will discuss later. Kaori is an example of someone living "on the border"—between two cultures—having to negotiate sometimes conflicting sets of languages and cultural values.

In today's world, we typically have many opportunities to meet people from different cultures. You may sit in class with students who are culturally different from you in many ways—in nationality, ethnicity, race, gender, age, religion, sexual orientation, and physical ability. In addition, today's widespread access to communication technologies and foreign travel provides many opportunities for intercultural encounters beyond the classroom. On the other hand, the increasing number of terrorist attacks in many countries, the tightening of national borders in response to global migration, conflicts between police and communities of color in the U. S., and the racist and hateful content posted on social media may inspire doubt about the ability of people from different cultures to coexist peacefully and may lead to belief that cultural differences necessarily lead to insurmountable problems. However, we believe that increased awareness of intercultural communication can help prevent or reduce the severity of problems that arise due to cultural differences.

In this chapter, we'll first explore the importance of *intercultural communication* and define what we mean when we use this term. Next, we will describe the increasingly common experience of individuals who must negotiate different cultural realities in their everyday lives. Then we'll examine how culture influences our communication and discuss how society affects communication outcomes in intercultural interactions. Finally we provide suggestions for how one can become a more ethical and effective intercultural communicator.

The Importance of Intercultural Communication

8.1 Explain why it is important to learn about intercultural communication.

How many reasons for studying intercultural communication can you think of? If you are like many students, entering college has given you more opportunities than ever before for intercultural contact, both domestically and internationally. You will communicate better in these situations if you have a good understanding of intercultural communication. In addition, increased knowledge and skill in intercultural communication can improve your career effectiveness, intergroup relations, and self-awareness. Let's look at each of these reasons more closely.

Increased Opportunities for Intercultural Contact

Experts estimate that more than a billion people travel each year. People leave their countries for many reasons, including national revolutions and civil wars (Syria and Sudan) and natural disasters (floods in Europe and India, earthquakes and avalanches in Italy). Experts estimate there are now a record number of displaced people in the world, 63.5 million, and almost 1 percent of the earth's population is displaced (United Nations High Commissioner for Refugees [UNHCR], 2016). Sometimes, in a process called **diaspora**, whole groups of people are displaced to new countries as they flee genocide or other untenable conditions or are taken forcefully against their will. Diasporic groups often attempt to settle together in communities in the new location while maintaining a strong ethnic identity and a desire to return home. Historically, diasporic groups include slaves taken from Africa in the 1700s and 1800s, Jews persecuted throughout centuries and relocating around the world, Chinese fleeing famine and wars in the nineteenth and twentieth centuries, and Armenians escaping Turkish genocide in early 1900s (Pendery, 2008; Waterston, 2005). More recent diasporas in the 1990s include Eritreans from Ethiopia, Albanians from Kosovo, and Chechens from Russia (Bernal, 2005; Koinova, 2010). Some experts refer to the current Latino diaspora, the increasing numbers of Latin Americans who settle outside their homelands, or the Syrian diaspora, the thousands of who have fled civil war in that country. Some migrants travel to new lands voluntarily for economic opportunities (to make a better life for themselves or their families) or personal reasons (to join family or friends abroad).

diaspora
The movement, migration, or scattering of a people away from an established or ancestral homeland.

Increasing numbers of people travel for pleasure, more than a billion in 2016 (UNTWO PR 16085, 2016). Many people, like the student Kaori in the opening story, also travel for study. According to the Institute of International Education, more than a million international students study in the United States each year and more than 300,000 U.S. students study overseas (*Open Doors*, 2016). Many students study

---

DID YOU KNOW?

Meeting Other Travelers Adds Depth to Argentina Visit

Have you had experiences with people from other cultures that changed how you saw the world or the United States? If so, what was it about those interactions that changed your views? If you could change other countries' views of the United States, what would you want to tell them?

Allison, from the United States, is an exchange student in Argentina. Here's an excerpt from her travel blog:

We went to the North West last week; four of us stayed in a youth hostel there. I felt like I had discovered a secret that had been hidden from me all my life. I IMMEDIATELY felt at home. It was just a bunch of kids all traveling from all parts of the world just hanging out and meeting people and sharing all their stories. Our first friends we met were two Canadian kids who had been backpacking through South America the past two months. We spent a lot of time with them drinking mate (the traditional Argentine tea) and chatting about all their experiences in South America. There was a Venezuelan girl and a Japanese girl. It was a pleasure sharing a room with them. In talking to everyone I became even more aware of how misinformed about international news we are in America and how uncommon it is for us to actually be interested enough to really be concerned about what's going on in the rest of the world.

I had a really intriguing conversation with an Israeli soldier who had been traveling through South America during his time off. Hearing his stories was absolutely heartbreaking . . . all that he was forced to see and to do was absolutely awful! No one of any age should have to endure those things, and he's been doing it since he was 18. I guess that's how it is for people that live in countries where that's just their reality. They become accustomed to falling asleep with gun shots outside their window and getting up to go to work not having any idea what their day will hold and whether or not they'll die. It's awful and such a foreign concept to us; maybe we should make it more of a reality. . . .

SOURCE: Allison Nafziger Travel Blog. Reprinted by permission of Allison Nafziger.

abroad because of the exciting opportunities that exist for intercultural encounters, as exchange student Allison describes in *Did You Know? Meeting Other Travelers Adds Depth to Argentina Visit*.

Another source of increased opportunity for intercultural contact exists because of the increasing cultural diversity in the United States. According to U.S. census figures, there are continuing dramatic increases in ethnic and racial diversity, and in the next several decades the United States will become a "plurality nation" in which no group is in the majority (Cooper, 2012). In fact, there are now four states—Hawaii, California, New Mexico, and Texas—that are "majority-minority"—where there is no one majority ethnic group, and minority groups account for more than 50 percent of the population. Nevada and Maryland should gain this status by 2020 (Kayne 2013; Teixeira, Frey, & Griffin, 2015).

As shown in Figure 8.1, the Hispanic population will more than double in size and constitute approximately 30 percent of the population by 2060; in the same time period, the Asian American population will also double in size and will constitute about 9 percent of the total population. African Americans will remain approximately the same in numbers and compose almost 13 percent of the population; Whites will continue to be a smaller majority as minority populations increase in number. The group that will increase the most is the "two or more races" category, which is projected to more than double. The nation's elderly population will increase considerably from 2014 through 2060, as the baby-boom generation enters the traditional retirement years. The number of working-age Americans and children will grow more slowly than the elderly population and will shrink as a share of the total population (Colby & Ortman, 2015).

Of course, communication technologies also provide increased opportunity for intercultural encounters. You can play video games with students in China, get acquainted with a former exchange student's friends and family on Facebook, debate rock climbing techniques with climbers from Norway to New Zealand on a sports blog, or collaborate with students from around the country for a virtual team project in one of your classes. In the next sections of this chapter, we will discuss the opportunities that these types of contacts offer—and the benefits to be had from learning more about the intricacies of intercultural communication.

Critical Thinking Prompt

How multicultural is your circle of friends? How many of your friends differ from you in nationality, religion, class, gender, age, sexual orientation, or physical ability?

Figure 8.1   Population by Race and Ehnicity, Actual and Projected Percentages: 2014 and 2060

AIAN = American Indian and Alaska Native; NHPI = Native Hawaiian and other Pacific Islander

SOURCE: U.S. Census Bureau projections, 2012.

Enhanced Business Effectiveness

Studying intercultural communication can lead to greater success in both domestic and international business contexts. In the domestic context, the U.S. workforce is becoming increasingly diverse as the general population does the same. In fact, a growing number of research studies show that being around people who are different can make us more creative, more diligent, and make us work harder, especially for groups that value innovation and new ideas. Specifically, these types of organizations that have gender and racial diversity have more diverse ideas and outperform less diverse groups (Phillips, 2014). Furthermore, virtual communication makes global business communication faster and cheaper to collaborate with overseas vendors and customers. A primary cause for international business failures is still lack of attention to cultural factors. For example, eBay, the successful American Ecommerce giant copied its American model to China and got completely destroyed by local competitor *Taobao*. Why? Because *Taobao* understood that in China, shopping is a social experience and people like talking and even haggling with sellers and building relationships with them. *Taobao* had a chat feature that allowed customers to easily talk to sellers (Custer, 2015).

Improved Intergroup Relations

Although we cannot blame all the world's political problems on ineffective intercultural communication, the need for better communication and understanding between countries and ethnic groups is clear. Sometimes tensions can be created by (and be the result of) world events and government policies. After the recent devastating terror attacks in France, Germany, and the United States, people and governments had heightened concerns about security posed by Middle Eastern refugees moving into Europe and the United States. For some, this concern translated to anti-immigrant/refugee attitudes and legislation. While immigrants in the United States have generally more easily assimilated into the larger U.S. society, tensions between communities of color and police and anti-immigrant attitudes, particularly directed at Muslims, have led some to question our ability to realize a peaceful multicultural society. For example, the statements of 31 governors that Syrian refugees were not welcome in their states in 2015 and President Trump's attempt to ban some immigrants in 2017 reflect the tension and conflict regarding the issue of immigration in the United States and overseas (Fantz & Brumfield, 2015; Townsend, Walters, & Otten, 2017).While some feel that these are reasonable measures, others feel that it paves the way for increased prejudice and discrimination against foreigners, particularly those from the Middle East and Latin America. One Pew poll found that older adults were far more likely than young people to view the large number of refugees from Iraq and Syria as a major threat (Smith, 2017).

Intercultural communication expertise can facilitate interethnic relations, which have frequently involved conflict. Consider the ethnic struggles in Bosnia and the former Soviet Union; the continued unrest in the Middle East; and the racial and ethnic struggles and tensions in neighborhoods of many U.S. cities. These conflicts often call for sophisticated skills of intercultural communication and **peacebuilding**, or working toward equilibrium and stability in a society so that disputes do not escalate into violence and war. For example, communication scholar Benjamin Broome (2004, 2014) has successfully facilitated interethnic relations on the island of Cyprus, which was one of the most heavily fortified regions in the world. Through his efforts and implementation of intergroup dialogues over many years, small groups of Greek and Turkish Cypriots have worked together to identify communication barriers and propose suggestions for improved relations between their two groups (Broome, 2013 Broome & Jakobsson, 2006). It should be acknowledged, however, that even with sophisticated intervention, miscommunication

peacebuilding
Working toward stability in a region to prevent conflicts from escalating into war.

▲ Intercultural contact is a fact in today's world. Many, if not most, of our daily interactions are intercultural in nature.

and intercultural conflicts can persist: witness the long-standing conflicts in the Middle East, where peacebuilding efforts have long been part of the attempts at resolution. In some cases, people are not motivated to resolve these "intractable conflicts," which are "exceptionally complex, usually involving issues of identity, meaning, justice, and power, often resisting even the most determined attempts at resolution" (Broome & Collier, 2012, p. 1). Although we must admit that there is no easy cure-all for intercultural tensions and misunderstandings, intercultural communication skills are certainly valuable in this area.

Enhanced Self-Awareness

The final reason for studying intercultural communication is to increase self-awareness. This may seem like a contradiction, but it is not. Intercultural exploration begins as a journey into the cultures of others but often results in increased self-knowledge and understanding (Braskamp, Braskamp, & Merrill, 2009). People often learn more about themselves and their own cultural background and identities by coming into contact with people whose cultural backgrounds differ from their own, as our student discovered during her stay in South Africa (see *It Happened to Me: Susan*).

What you learn about intercultural communication may depend on your social and economic position. For example, individuals from minority racial and ethnic groups in the United States may learn to be a bit wary of intercultural interactions and expect some slights, such as a Chinese American colleague who is sometimes approached at professional meetings by White communication professors who assume she is a waitress and ask her to take their drink order!

It Happened to Me
Susan

I rarely ever thought about being White or an American until my family and I spent a year in South Africa. Then, I thought about both every day, especially about my being White. The official language of South Africa is English, but even though we technically spoke the same language as the South Africans, my family and I had problems. It started when we were to be picked up from the airport in a *combie*, but I didn't know what that was. It turned out to be a van! Small pick-up trucks were *bakkies*, traffic signals were *robots*, and friends wanted to collect my *contact details*, which meant that they simply wanted the number of my *mobile*, better known as a cell phone, and our address. I felt that every time I opened my mouth, everyone *knew* I was American. The Black/White thing was even more pronounced. When we went down to the flea market or to the Zulu mass at the church we attended, we stood out like "five white golf balls on a black fairway" as my husband liked to say. I wondered if the self-consciousness I felt being White was the same as an African American has walking down the street in America.

By contrast, White and middle-class individuals may find that intercultural learning includes an enhanced awareness of privilege, such as a White colleague who tells of feeling uncomfortable staying at a Caribbean resort, where he was served by Blacks whose ancestors were brought there as slaves by Europeans colonizers. Although he realized that it was his relative privilege that allows him to travel and experience new cultures and places, he also wondered whether this type of travel simply reproduces those same historical postcolonial economic patterns.

With these reasons for studying intercultural communication in mind, we need to define precisely what we mean by intercultural communication and culture, and give examples of intercultural interaction, the subjects we turn to next.

What Is Intercultural Communication?

8.2 Define intercultural communication and describe three types of border dwellers.

Generally speaking, **intercultural communication** refers to communication that occurs in interactions between people who are culturally different. This contrasts with most communication studies, which focus on communicators in the same culture. Still, in practice, intercultural communication occurs on a continuum, with communication between people who are relatively similar in cultural backgrounds on one end and people who are extremely different culturally on the other. For example, your conversations with your parents would represent a low degree of "interculturalness" because you and your parents belong to two different cultural (age) groups and you probably have much in common—nationality, religion, and language. On the other hand, an interaction with a foreign teaching assistant who has a different nationality, language, religion, age, socioeconomic status, and gender would represent a high degree of interculturalness. Although these two examples represent different ends on the continuum, they are both intercultural interactions. So you can see that many, if not most, of your daily interactions are intercultural in nature.

The two essential components of intercultural communication are, of course, culture and communication. Having read this far in your text, you should have a good understanding of communication. However, we think it is worthwhile to review our definition of **culture**. In Chapter 1, we defined culture as *learned patterns of perceptions, values, and behaviors shared by a group of people*. As we also mentioned, culture is dynamic (it changes), **heterogeneous**, and operates within societal power structures (Martin & Nakayama, 2014, p. 32) and we can explore how features of culture impact individuals' intercultural interactions. With a cautionary note—not all cultural differences have equal impact on one's interactions. For example, although your parents may sometimes seem to come from a different culture, age differences generally have a less dramatic effect on people's interactions than do ethnic and national differences.

Because of increased opportunities for cultural contact, many people today are **border dwellers**, who engage in intercultural communication on a daily basis and often experience contradictory cultural patterns, as they move between ethnicities, races, religions, languages, socioeconomic classes, or sexual orientations. One can be a border dweller in three ways: through travel, through socialization (co-cultural groups), and through participation in an intercultural relationship. Let's look at each in turn.

Border Dwellers through Travel   Individuals travel between cultures both voluntarily and involuntarily, and for both long and short periods. Voluntary travelers include study-abroad students, corporate personnel, missionaries, and military people and immigrants who settle in other locations, usually seeking what they perceive is a better life, as is the case for many immigrants who come to the United States. Involuntary travelers include refugees forced into cultural migration because of war, famine, or unbearable economic hardship or those who are forced to permanently migrate to a new location, including the many diasporic groups referred to previously.

When people think of traveling or living in a new culture, they tend to think that learning the language is key to effective intercultural interaction; however, intercultural communication involves much more than language issues. Most sojourners find there are two types of challenges: (1) dealing with the psychological stress of being in an unfamiliar environment (feeling somewhat uncertain and anxious) and (2) learning how to

Journal Prompt 8.1: Studying Intercultural Communication
Consider the following questions:
What are four reasons for studying intercultural communication? Of the reasons given, which do you think are most important? Can you think of other reasons?

intercultural communication
Communication that occurs in interactions between people who are culturally different.

culture
Learned patterns of perceptions, values, and behaviors shared by a group of people.

heterogeneous
Diverse.

border dwellers
People who live between cultures and often experience contradictory cultural patterns.

behave appropriately in the new culture, both verbally (e.g., learning a new language) and nonverbally, for example, bowing instead of shaking hands in Japan (Kim, 2005).

The first of these two challenges is often called *culture shock*. **Culture shock** is a feeling of disorientation and discomfort resulting from the unfamiliarity of surroundings and the lack of familiar cues in the environment. Sometimes people even experience culture shock when they move from one region of the United States to another (e.g., relocating from Boston to Birmingham or from Honolulu to Minneapolis). When travelers return home, they may experience similar feelings, known as **reverse culture shock or re-entry shock**, which is a sort of culture shock in one's own home location (Pitts, 2016). After being gone for a significant amount of time, aspects of one's own culture may seem somewhat foreign, as the student Maham discovered on his return home to Pakistan after living in the United States for four years (see *It Happened to Me: Maham*).

There are many reasons why an individual may be more, or less, successful at adapting to a new culture. Younger people who have had some previous traveling experience seem to be more successful than older people and first-time travelers. By contrast, if the environment is hostile or the move is involuntary, adaptation may be especially difficult and the culture shock especially intense. For example, Asian, African, and Latino students in the United States tend to have a more difficult adaptation because of experiences of discrimination and hostility based on their race/ethnicity (Hanasono, Chen, & Wilson, 2014; Lee & Rice, 2007). Although we may think that anti-immigrant attitudes are a recent phenomenon in the United States because of the number of immigrants or where they come from, historians remind us that today's immigrants have much in common with previous immigrants—including anti-immigrant attitudes (Jaret, 1999).

culture shock

A feeling of disorientation and discomfort as a result of the lack of familiar environmental cues.

reverse culture shock/re-entry shock

Culture shock experienced by travelers on returning to their home country.

It Happened to Me
Maham

I would say that I experienced culture (re-entry) shock when I visited Pakistan after moving away from there four years ago. In those four years, I had basically forgotten the language and became very unfamiliar with the culture back home. Even though I enjoyed my visit to Pakistan a lot, I had problems adjusting to some of the ways of life. I was not familiar with the bargaining system . . . where people can go to the store and bargain for prices. I felt very out of place . . . . As I spent more time there, I got adjusted and used to how people did things there.

Critical Thinking Prompt

How important is it to reject your own home culture in adapting to a new culture? How can immigrants use their own cultural traditions to help make a smooth transition to the new culture? What could we in the host country do to help immigrants transition successfully to the United States?

For diasporic groups, whether relocated within their own country or in a foreign country, the culture shock and disorientation can be complicated and even extended because of their strong desire to return home and a feeling of rootlessness. As one Iraqi refugee said, after fleeing war and terrible violence, only to encounter unemployment and poverty in the United States, "We came to this country for the future of our children. We have no future" (Yako & Biswas, 2014, p. 143).

One thing that can ease culture shock is having a social support network. This can come from organizations such as an international student office or a tourist bureau that can assist with housing, transportation, and so forth. Close relationships with other travelers or host-country acquaintances, as in the case of Charee and Kaori, can also provide support in the form of a sympathetic ear; through these relationships sojourners can relieve stress, discuss, problem solve, acquire new knowledge, or just have fun (Geeraert, Demoulin, & Demes, 2014; Sobré-Denton, 2011). The role of social support is even more crucial for immigrants. Diasporic individuals often maintain strong relationships with other members of their group, providing for each this much needed social support, sometimes through cyber communities or in face-to-face interaction (Kim & McKay-Semmler, 2013). If there is little social support or the receiving environment is hostile, immigrants may resist assimilation, finding that their culture is "a source of comfort and strength, a source of rational survival, persistence, and positive self-identity" (De La Garza & Ono, 2015, p. 281).

ALTERNATIVE VIEW
Immigrants

Some people seem to think that the key to successfully adapting to a new culture is to completely reject one's home culture. However, some experts suggest that maintaining a strong connection to one's original language and culture actually facilitates a smooth transition to the new culture. Scholar Lucas Torres asked immigrants themselves, in focused interviews as well as quantitative survey questionnaires, what they thought were the knowledge and skills that lead to successful cultural adaption of Latinos to the United States. Although some of his findings are expected—ambition, perseverance, hard work, good communication/ relational skills—they also answered that it was important to maintain the traditional Latino culture (cultural practices such as celebrating holidays, keeping up language skills, strong connections with family and cultural values of respect). They explained that these practices actually serve as strong motivators to successfully adapt—as one said "Competent Latinos embrace their cultures, and because they do. . . . I think they derive some sort of, I guess, motivation for them to pull forward" (p. 587).

SOURCE: Torres, L. (2009). Latino definitions of success: A *cultural model of intercultural competence. Hispanic Journal of Behavioral Sciences, 31*, 576–593.

Another option for immigrants is to adapt in *some* ways to the new culture, which means accepting some aspects, such as dress and outward behavior, while retaining aspects of the old culture. For many recent immigrants to the United States, this has been a preferred option and seems to lead to less stress. For example, Asian Indians constitute one of the largest immigrant groups in the United States. Many have successfully adapted to U.S. life both professionally and socially. Still many retain viable aspects of their Indian culture in their personal and family lives—continuing to celebrate ethnic or religious holidays and adhering to traditional values and beliefs (Hegde, 2012). Some experts suggest that this integration of two cultures is a model for successful cultural adaptation (see *Alternative View: Immigrants*).

However, this integration of two cultures is not always easy, as we'll see later in the chapter. Families can be divided on the issues of how much to adapt, with children often wanting to be more "American" and parents wanting to hold on to their native language and cultural practices (Ward, 2008).

Border Dwellers through Socialization   A second group of border dwellers is composed of people who grow up living on the borders between cultural groups. Examples include ethnic groups, such as Latinos, Asian Americans, and African Americans, who live in the predominantly White United States, as well as people who grow up negotiating multiple sexual orientations or religions. In addition to those who must negotiate the two cultures they live within, the United States has increasing numbers of multiracial people who often grow up negotiating *multiple* cultural realities (Parker, Morin, Horowitz, Lopez, & Rohal, 2015).

▼ Border dwellers through socialization include many multiracial individuals and families. How might the concept of border dwellers change as these many children grow up?

There are many famous multiracial U.S. Americans, including singers Rihanna (Afro-Bajan, Irish, and Afro-Guyanese) and Nicki Minaj (East Indian and

▲ Americans are now more accepting of interracial and gay marriages.

Afro-Trinidadian), and actors Dwayne Johnson (also known as The Rock), who is Black and Samoan, and Wentworth Miller (father is African American, Caucasian, and Native American and mother is Middle Eastern and Caucasian). Members of minority groups sometimes find themselves in a kind of cultural limbo—not "gay" enough for gay friends, not "straight" enough for the majority; not Black enough or White enough. However, many recognize their unique positions, in limbo between, but also potential bridges between, two cultures. For example, children raised in biracial homes find they are often able to, as adults, relate easily with individuals of both races. They can fit in with both Whites and Blacks and often have diverse friendship networks.

Border Dwellers through Relationships   Finally, many people live on cultural borders because they have intimate partners whose cultural background differs from their own. Within the United States, increasing numbers of people cross borders of nationality, race, and ethnicity in this way, creating a "quiet revolution" (Root, 2001). In fact, by 2015, almost 15 percent of all new marriages in the United States were between spouses of a different race or ethnicity—more than double the number in 1980 (Parker et al., 2015). Overall, partners in interethnic and interracial romantic relationships have faced greater challenges than those establishing relationships across religions, nationalities, and class groups.

Did you know that until June 12, 1967, it was illegal in Virginia (and 13 other states) for Whites and Blacks to marry? As shown in the recent movie *Loving*, this ban against miscegenation (interracial sexual relationships) was challenged in Virginia by Mildred and Richard Loving, who had been married in 1958 in Washington, DC (where interracial marriages were permitted). In 1967, the Supreme Court declared Virginia's anti-miscegenation ban unconstitutional, thereby ending all race-based legal restrictions on marriage in the United States. Attitudes toward intercultural relationships have changed significantly in the ensuing decades, particularly attitudes toward interracial relations. For example, in a 2013 Gallup Poll, more than two-thirds of Americans said they approved of interracial marriage (Newport, 2013). However, in another recent study when respondents were asked directly how they feel when a close relative wants to marry outside their own race, only 54 percent of Blacks and 26 percent of Whites responded favorably (Djamba & Kimuna, 2014).

Intercultural relationships are not without their challenges. The most common challenges involve negotiating how to live on the border between two religions, ethnicities, races, languages, and, sometimes, value systems. A recent study of intercultural marriages, some based on religious and some on racial and ethnic differences, found that communication played an important role in the success of these relationships. That is, open communication about the differences helped promote relationship growth. If partners were able to understand, appreciate, and integrate each other's similarities and differences, they would be able to use these in an enriching manner (Reiter & Gee, 2009).

The balancing act between cultures can be especially challenging when friends, family, and society disapprove. A Jewish professor who married a Muslim woman reflects on how people would react if he decided to convert to Islam:

Journal Prompt 8.2: Defining Intercultural Communication
Consider the following questions: What is a definition of intercultural communication? What is meant by the phrase "culture is dynamic, heterogeneous, and operates within societal power structures"?

> What a scandalous action! My family would be outraged and my friends startled. What would they say? How would I be treated? What would colleagues at the university do if I brought a prayer rug to the office and, say, during a committee meeting, or at a reception for a visiting scholar, insisted on taking a break to do my ritual prayers? (Rosenstone, 2005, p. 235)

Intercultural Communication and the Individual: Cultural Values

8.3 **Describe how cultural values influence communication.**

The Influence of Cultural Values on Communication

In Chapters 5 and 6, we described how culture influences verbal and nonverbal communication. You might think that these differences would be important to understanding intercultural communication, however, just as important is understanding **cultural values**, which are the beliefs that are so central to a cultural group that they are never questioned. Cultural values prescribe what *should* be. Understanding cultural values is essential because they so powerfully influence people's behavior, including their communication. Intercultural interaction often involves confronting and responding to an entirely different set of cultural values. Let's see how this works.

Social psychologist Geert Hofstede (1998, 2010) and his colleagues conducted a massive study, collecting 116,000 surveys about people's value preferences in approximately 80 countries around the world. Psychologist Michael Bond and his colleagues conducted a similar, although smaller, study in Asia ("Chinese Culture Connection," 1987). Although these studies identify value preferences of national cultural groups, they can also apply to religious and ethnic or racial groups, socioeconomic class groups, and gender groups. For example, anthropologists Florence Kluckhohn and Fred Strodtbeck (1961) conducted a study that identified the contrasting values of three cultural groups in the United States: Latinos, Anglos, and American Indians. Recently, communication scholars have identified cultural values of other racial groups: African Americans and Asian Americans. Together, all these studies identified a number of cultural values.

As you read about these cultural value orientations, please keep three points in mind. These guidelines reflect a common dilemma for intercultural communication scholars—the desire to describe and understand communication and behavior patterns within a cultural group and the fear of making rigid categories that can lead to stereotyping:

1. The following discussion describes the *predominant* values preferred by various cultural groups, not the values held by *every person* in the cultural group. Think of cultural values as occurring on a bell curve: Most people may be in the middle, holding a particular value orientation, but many people can be found on each end of the curve; these are the people who *do not go along* with the majority.

2. The following discussion refers to values on the cultural level, not on the individual level. Thus, if you read that most Chinese tend to prefer an indirect way of speaking, you cannot assume that every Chinese person you meet will speak in an indirect way in every situation.

3. The only way to understand what a particular individual believes is to get to know the person. You can't predict how any one person will communicate. The real challenge is to understand the full range of cultural values and then learn to communicate effectively with others who hold differing value orientations, regardless of their cultural background.

Now that you understand the basic ground rules, let's look at seven key aspects of cultural values.

Individualism and Collectivism   One of the most central value orientations identified in this research addresses whether a culture emphasizes the rights and needs of the individual or that of the group. For example, many North American and northern European cultural groups, particularly U.S. Whites, value individualism and

cultural values

Beliefs that are so central to a cultural group that they are never questioned.

▲ In individualistic cultures, the nuclear family household is most common [just parent(s) and children]: children are raised to be autonomous and to live on their own by late adolescence, whereas parents are expected to not "be a burden" on their children when they age.

individualistic orientation

A value orientation that respects the autonomy and independence of individuals.

collectivistic orientation

A value orientation that stresses the needs of the group.

Critical Thinking Prompt
As you were growing up, in what ways were you reared to be individualistic? Collectivistic? Which orientation was the predominant cultural value of your family?

independence, believing that one's primary responsibility is to one's self (Bellah, Madsen, Sullivan, Swidler, & Tipton, 2007; Hofstede et al., 2010). In relationships, those with this **individualistic orientation** respect autonomy and independence, and they do not meddle in another's problems unless invited. For example, in cultures where individualism prevails, many children are raised to be autonomous and to live on their own by late adolescence (although they may return home for short periods after this). Their parents are expected to take care of themselves and not "be a burden" on their children when they age (Triandis, 1995).

In contrast, many cultures in South America and Asia hold a more **collectivistic orientation** that stresses the needs of the group, as do some Hispanic and Asian Americans in the United States (Ho, Rasheed, & Rasheed, 2004). Some argue that working-class people tend to be more collectivistic than those in the middle or upper class (Dunbar, 1997). For collectivists, the primary responsibility is to relationships with others; interdependence in family, work, and personal relationships is viewed positively. Collectivists value working toward relationship and group harmony over remaining independent and self-sufficient. For example, giving money to a needy cousin, uncle, or aunt might be preferable to spending it on oneself. Or sharing belongings, such as cars, computers, mobile phones may be expected in collectivist communities. In many collectivist cultures, too, children often defer to parents when making important decisions, like accepting a new job or choosing a spouse (McGoldrick, Giordano, & Garcia-Preto, 2005).

As noted previously, however, not all Japanese or all Indians are collectivistic, nor are all U.S. Americans individualistic. A recent book by journalist Colin Woodard (2012) maintains that there are significant regional differences here in the degree of commitment to individual freedom or conversely, sacrifice for the good of the community. In addition, generational differences may exist within countries where collectivism is strong. For example, some Japanese college students show a strong preference for individualism whereas their parents hold a more collectivistic orientation—which sometimes leads to intercultural conflict (Matsumoto, 2007). Young people in many Asian countries (e.g., Korea, Vietnam) are increasingly influenced by Western capitalism and individualism and are now making their own decisions regarding marriage and career, rather than following their family's wishes—a practice unheard of 50 years ago (Shim, Kim, & Martin, 2008). In addition, not all cultures are as individualistic as U.S. culture or as collectivistic as Japanese culture. Rather, cultures can be arranged along an individualism–collectivism continuum (Ting-Toomey, 2010) based on their specific orientations to the needs of the individual and the group.

preferred personality

A value orientation that expresses whether it is more important for a person to "do" or to "be."

Preferred Personality   In addition to differing on the individualism–collectivism spectrum, cultural groups may differ over the idea of the **preferred personality**, or whether it is more important to "do" or to "be" (Kluckhohn & Strodtbeck, 1961). In the United States, researchers have found that *doing* is the preferred value for many people, including European Americans, Asian Americans, and African Americans (Ting-Toomey, 1999). In general, the "doing mode" means working hard to achieve material gain, even if it means sacrificing time with family and friends. Other cultural groups, for example, many Latinos, prefer the *being* mode—which emphasizes the importance of experiencing life and the people around them fully and "working to live" rather than "living to work" (Hecht, Sedano, & Ribeau, 1993).

Some scholars suggest that many African Americans express both a doing mode, fighting actively against racism through social activity for the good of the community, and a being mode, valuing a sense of vitality and open expression of feeling (Hecht, Jackson, & Ribeau, 2002). Cultural differences in this value orientation can lead to communication challenges. For example, many Latinos believe that Anglos place too much emphasis on accomplishing tasks and earning money and not enough emphasis on spending time with friends and family or enjoying the moment.

▲ In many collectivist cultures, adult children often defer to parents when making important decisions.

Human Nature A third value difference concerns the **view of human nature**—in particular, whether humans are considered fundamentally good, evil, or a mixture. The United States, for example, was founded by the Puritans who believed that human nature was fundamentally evil (Hulse, 1996). In the years since the founding of the country, a shift occurred in this view, as evidenced in the U.S. legal and justice systems. It emphasizes rehabilitation, which suggests a view of humans as potentially good. In addition, the fact that the U.S. justice system assumes people are innocent until proven guilty indicates that people are viewed as basically good.

In contrast, cultural groups that view humans as essentially evil, such as some fundamentalist religions, emphasize punishment over rehabilitation. Some evidence indicates that U.S. Americans in general are moving again toward this view of human nature. For example, state laws such as the "three-strikes rule" emphasize punishment over rehabilitation by automatically and significantly increasing the prison sentences of persons convicted of a felony who have been previously convicted of two or more violent crimes or serious felonies. Also, incarceration rates in the United States have increased by more than 500 percent since the early 1970s, and among developed countries, the United States now has the highest percentage of incarcerated individuals—more than China, Cuba, and Russia (Mahapatra, 2013). As you might imagine, people who differ on the question of human nature can have serious disagreements on public policies concerning crime and justice.

Human–Nature Relationship A fourth value that varies from culture to culture is the perceived relationship between humans and nature, or the **human–nature value orientation**. At one end of this value continuum is the view that humans are intended to rule nature. At the other extreme, nature is seen as ruling humans. In a third option, the two exist in harmony. Unsurprisingly, the predominant value in the United States has been one of humans ruling over nature, as evidenced in the proliferation of controlled environments. Phoenix, Arizona, for example, which is in a desert, has more than 200 golf courses—reflecting the fact that Arizonans have changed the natural environment to suit their living and leisure interests. In other parts of the United States, people make snow for skiing, seed clouds when rain is needed, dam and reroute rivers, and use fertilizer to enhance agricultural production. Such interventions generally reflect a belief in human control over nature (Trompenaars & Hampden-Turner, 2012).

Critical Thinking Prompt
What kinds of communication problems might occur when members of a diverse work team hold different value orientations toward being and doing? How might someone who usually uses a being mode view someone with a doing mode, and vice versa?

view of human nature
A value orientation that expresses whether humans are fundamentally good, evil, or a mixture.

human–nature value orientation
The perceived relationship between humans and nature.

In contrast, many in the Middle East view nature as having predominance over humans. This belief that one's fate is held by nature is reflected in the common Arabic saying "*Enchallah*" ("Allah willing"), suggesting that nature will (and should) determine, for example, how crops will grow. A comparable Christian saying is "God willing," reflecting perhaps a similar fatalistic tendency in Christianity. Interestingly, many Spanish-speaking Christians express the same sentiment with the word "*Ojalá*," which is rooted in "*Enchallah*" and originates from the centuries when southern Spain was a Muslim province.

Many American Indians and Asians value harmony with nature. People who hold this cultural orientation believe that humans and nature are one and that nature enriches human life. For many traditional American Indians, certain animals such as buffalo and eagles are important presences in human activity (Porter, 2002). For example, the use of feathers can be an important part of the sundance, a religious ceremony practiced by many different American Indian groups. In this ceremony, the eagle is viewed as the link between humans and creator. When people see an eagle in the sky during a ceremony, they are especially thankful because the eagle flies highest of all birds and the moment it disappears into the skies, people's prayers are heard. These traditions show high regard and utmost respect for these animals and reflect a belief in the close and important relationship between humans and nature ("Eagle aviary allows American Indians to continue heritage," 2005).

In the United States, differences arise between real estate developers, who believe that humans take precedence over nature, and environmentalists and many Native American groups, who believe that nature is as important as humans. This conflict has surfaced in many disagreements; for example, in controversies over water rights in Oregon between Indian tribes who want to maintain water levels for endangered fish they traditionally harvest, denying water to farmers downstream (Barboza, 2013) and between loggers and environmentalist over the endangered spotted owl, which are now also threatened by the more aggressive barred owl in the southwestern United States (Sahagun, 2014).

power distance

A value orientation that refers to the extent to which less powerful members of institutions and organizations within a culture expect and accept an unequal distribution of power.

Power Distance   **Power distance**, the fifth value orientation, refers to the extent to which less powerful members of institutions and organizations within a culture expect and accept an unequal distribution of power (Hofstede et al., 2010). In Denmark, Israel, the United States, and New Zealand many people value small power distances. Thus, most people in those countries believe that inequality, although inevitable, should be minimized, and that the best leaders emphasize equality and informality in interactions with subordinates. In many situations, subordinates are expected to speak up and contribute.

Societies that value large power distance—for example, Mexico, the Philippines, and India—are structured more around a hierarchy in which each person has a rightful place, and interactions between supervisors and subordinates are more formal (Hofstede et al., 2010). Seniority, age, rank, and titles are emphasized more in these societies than in small power distance societies. In addition, a preference for informal communication tends to go along with small power distance orientation.

People who are used to large power distances may be uncomfortable in settings where hierarchy is unclear or ambiguous

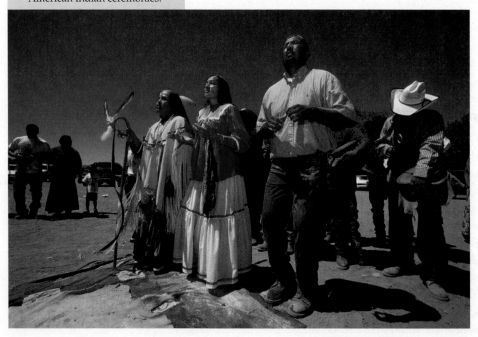

▼ Reverence for nature plays an important role in many American Indian ceremonies.

and communication tends to be informal. For example, international students who come from countries where a large power distance value predominates may initially be uncomfortable in U.S. college classrooms, where relations between students and teachers are informal and characterized by equality, especially in online classes, a situation described in *It Happened to Me: Nagesh*.

In contrast, U.S. Americans abroad often offend locals when they treat subordinates at work or home too informally—calling them by their first names, treating them as if they were friends. For example, when former President George W. Bush visited Europe, he referred to the Belgian Prime Minister by his first name, Guy. This surprised and amused many Belgians, who are accustomed to more formality.

Note that value orientations often represent a cultural ideal rather than a reality. Although

It Happened to Me
Nagesh

I was amazed when I took my first online class at an American university. The students seemed very disrespectful toward the teacher and toward each other. In discussions, they addressed the teacher very informally, just like "hey, I have a question!" They didn't address the professor by title, and they would openly disagree with each other. In my country (India), students would never behave this way toward a teacher. I found it difficult to speak up in this kind of online classroom situation.

many Americans say they desire small power distance, the truth is that rigid social and economic hierarchies exist in the United States. Most Americans are born into and live within the same socioeconomic class for their whole lives (Moving on up, 2013).

Long-Term versus Short-Term Orientation   The research identifying the five values we've described has been criticized for its predominately Western European bias. In response to this criticism, a group of Chinese researchers developed and administered a similar, but more Asian-oriented, questionnaire to people in 22 countries around the world ("Chinese Culture Connection," 1987). They then compared their findings to previous research on value orientations and found considerable overlap, especially on the dimensions of individualism versus collectivism and power distance. These researchers did identify one additional value dimension that previous researchers hadn't seen—**long-term versus short-term orientation**.

This dimension reflects a society's attitude toward virtue or truth. A **short-term orientation** characterizes cultures in which people are concerned with possessing one fundamental truth, as reflected in the **monotheistic** religions of Judaism, Christianity, and Islam. Other qualities identified in the research and associated with a short-term orientation include an emphasis on quick results, individualism, and personal security and safety (Hofstede et al., 2010).

In contrast, a **long-term orientation** tends to respect the demands of virtue, reflected in Eastern religions such as Confucianism, Hinduism, Buddhism, and Shintoism, which are all **polytheistic** religions (belief in more than one god). Other qualities associated with a long-term orientation include thrift, perseverance, and tenacity in whatever one attempts, and a willingness to subordinate oneself for a purpose (Bond, 1991, 2010).

Indulgence versus Restraint   Based on recent research by Michael Minkov, one of Hofstede's associates, there is now a seventh value dimension, **Indulgence versus Restraint** (Hofstede, Hofstede, & Minkov, 2010). This dimension is related to the *subjective* feelings of happiness. That is, people may not actually *be* happy or healthy but they report that they *feel* happier and healthier. National cultures that are categorized as more indulgent (Mexico, Nigeria, Sweden, Australia) tend to allow relatively free gratification of needs related to enjoying life and having fun. They report that having lots of friends is important (e.g., Facebook), active participation in sports and there is less moral regulation. Societies that emphasize restraint (Russia, Egypt and other Islamic countries, China, India) tend to suppress gratification of needs and regulate it by means of strict social norms. Having many friends is reportedly less important, there is more watching of sports, but less

long-term versus short-term orientation
The dimension of a society's value orientation that reflects its attitude toward virtue or truth.

short-term orientation
A value orientation that stresses the importance of possessing one fundamental truth.

monotheistic
Belief in one god.

long-term orientation
A value orientation in which people stress the importance of virtue.

polytheistic
Belief in more than one god.

indulgence versus restraint orientation
A value orientation that reflects a subjective feeling of happiness. The indulgence orientation emphasizes relatively free gratification of basic and natural human drives related to enjoying life and having fun. Restraint emphasizes suppressing gratification of needs and regulates it by means of strict social norms.

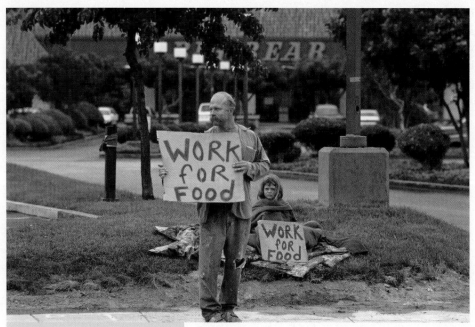

▲ Although being white involves cultural advantages, being poor involves disadvantages.

dialectical approach
Recognizes that things need not be perceived as "either/or," but may be seen as "both/and."

dichotomous thinking
Thinking in which things are perceived as "either/or"—for example, "good or bad," "big or small," "right or wrong."

**Journal Prompt 8.3:
Cultural Values**
Consider the following questions:
What are seven common core values that differentiate various cultural groups? How might these values influence intercultural communication?

participation, and a strong work ethic. Countries with a predominant indulgent orientation emphasize freedom of speech over maintaining order; countries with more restraint orientation tend to value maintaining order over allowing freedom of speech.

Although knowing about these value differences can help you identify and understand problems that arise in intercultural interactions, you might be concerned that this approach to the study of intercultural communication leads to generalizing and stereotyping. One strategy for counteracting this tendency is the **dialectical approach**. Dialectics has long existed as a concept in philosophical thought and logic. In this book we introduce it as a way to emphasize simultaneous contradictory truths. Thus, a dialectical approach helps people respond to the complexities of intercultural communication and to override any tendencies to stereotype people based on cultural patterns. This concept may be difficult to understand because it is contrary to most formal education in the United States, which often emphasizes **dichotomous thinking**, in which things are "either/or"—good or bad, big or small, right or wrong. However, a dialectical approach recognizes that things may be "both/and." For example, a palm tree may be weak *and* strong. Its branches look fragile and weak, and yet in a hurricane it remains strong because the "weak" fronds can bend without breaking. Similar dialectics exist in intercultural communication and emphasize the fluid, complex, and contradictory nature of intercultural interactions. Dialectics exist in other communication contexts such as relationships, which we explore in Chapter 9.

This dialectical approach helps us resist making quick, stereotypical judgments about others and their communication behavior. One individual can have individualistic and collectivistic tendencies, can be both culturally similar and different from us, and can be culturally privileged in some situations and culturally disadvantaged in others (Ting-Toomey, 2010). We provide more specific detail on how the dialectic approach can be used to avoid stereotyping others later in the chapter.

The Individual, Intercultural Communication, and Society: Politics, History, and Power

8.4 Explain the roles that politics, history, and power play in communication between people from different cultural backgrounds.

As you have probably gathered by now, intercultural communication never occurs in a vacuum, but must be understood in the context of larger societal forces. In this section, we first focus on social, political, and historical forces; second, we turn our attention to the role of power in intercultural communication.

Political and Historical Forces

That societal forces can affect intercultural encounters is exemplified by the varying reactions toward some immigrant groups after the attacks at the Boston Marathon, San

Bernardino and the Orlando night club, Pulse, in 2016. Research by scholar Sunil Bhatia (2008) seems applicable here. She found, through interviews with Asian-Indian Americans, after 9/11, that these immigrants experienced reactions from others that caused them to question their "American" identity. Before 9/11, they considered themselves well-adapted to U.S. culture. However, after 9/11, people treated them differently. Their neighbors, who knew them well, were much friendlier and sympathetic. However, some strangers were more hostile to them (sometimes mistaking non-Muslims for Muslims). Thus, they were reminded that they were different; they were not completely accepted as Americans by the U.S. majority. The same sentiments and actions seem to occur now as hate crimes against American Muslims have increased (Lightblau, 2016), and interaction between Muslims (or those who are perceived as Muslims) and other Americans can be difficult.

Historical forces also can influence contemporary intercultural interaction in a dialectical relationship. For example, although slavery is long gone in the United States, one could not understand contemporary Black–White relations in this country without acknowledging its effect. Author James Loewen (2010) describes the twin legacies of slavery that are still with us: (1) social and economic inferiority for Blacks brought on by specific economic and political policies from 1885 to 1965 that led to inferior educational institutions and exclusion from labor unions, voting rights, and the advantage of government mortgages; (2) cultural racism instilled in Whites. Some thought that the election of Barack Obama as the first African American U.S. president demonstrated significant progress in interracial relations (Dyson, 2009). However, the intense political and social conversations that have occurred since then, often centering on race (e.g., the killing of unarmed black men by police, including Michael Brown, Alton Sterling, Freddie Gray, Walter Scott, Eric Garner, Laquan McDonald, and the Black Lives Matter movement) might also demonstrate that the historical legacies of racism impact interracial encounters even today.

Current demographic statistics also indicate that Americans remain fairly racially segregated in their schools and neighborhoods (Massey, 2016; Scott, 2016) and results in interactions between Whites and Blacks in the United States that are often limited and sometimes challenging. For example, a recent Pew poll found that 70–80 percent of both Black and White Americans report that all or most of their close friends are of the same race (Parker et al., 2015). As a society, which institutions or contexts now promote the best opportunities for interracial contact? Neighborhoods? Educational institutions? Churches, synagogues, and other places of worship? The workplace? Neighborhoods and workplaces do not seem to provide opportunities for the *type* of contact (intimate, friendly, equal-status interaction) that facilitates intercultural relationships (Johnson & Jacobson, 2005). By contrast, it appears that *integrated* religious institutions and educational institutions provide the best opportunities for intercultural friendships and the best environment to improve interracial attitudes (Johnson & Jacobson, 2005). For example, a study of six California State University campuses found that the students on these campuses interacted equally, in interracial and intraracial encounters (Cowan, 2005). These campuses are diverse; no single ethnic or racial group is a majority. However, a more recent study cautions that sometimes students in multicultural campus assume that they have intercultural relationships just by virtue of being surrounded by cultural diversity and may not make the effort to actually pursue intercultural friendships (Halualani, 2008).

Intercultural Communication and Power

As we noted in Chapter 5, the more powerful groups in society establish the rules for communication, and others usually follow these rules or violate them at their peril (Orbe, 1998). A number of factors influence who is considered powerful in a culture. For example, being White in the United States has more privilege attached to it than being Latino. Although most Whites do not notice this privilege and dominance, most minority group members do (DiAngelo, 2011; Moon, 2016). Being male also has historically been more valued than being female, and being wealthy is more valued than being poor.

COMMUNICATION IN SOCIETY
African American TV Families: Diverse Enough?

This author writes about the debate over the role of reality television shows reflecting or shaping our views on racial and economic diversity. How important do you think it is that television shows, especially reality TV, reflect or critique social reality?

Does diversity matter in reality TV? Tamar Braxton of *Braxton Family Values*, on WEtv, explained why her family chose to do a reality show: she noted that it was important "especially for our black community" to show audiences people to whom they could relate. And it makes sense for the network's bottom line—attracting a large diverse audience.

[However,] it should also be noted that the families on some reality television can't be used to generalize about families of any race; they're really rich: for example, *Braxton Family Values*, where one sister is singer Toni Braxton, and *The Real Housewives of Atlanta*, part of a franchise where affluence is the common experience.

So although there may be racial diversity, is the lack of socioeconomic diversity of African American TV families, scripted and unscripted, a problem? As Cynthia Bailey, of *The Real Housewives*

of *Atlanta*, says, she couldn't identify with the *Cosby Show* when she was growing up. "That wasn't what my family was like," she says. "In my mind, that was almost a rich black family."

Some experts think this is a problem. Communication professor Catherine Squires, author of *African Americans and the Media*, says that because television shows, especially reality television, are supposed to reflect reality, "[l]ooking at rich, black people acting out after you've looked at rich, white people acting out, does that give people who aren't rich and black any sense of what the black people closer to their lives are like?" And even a show like *Real Housewives*, which is relatively diverse across the franchise, represents each racial group as largely cut off from the others. Squires says that, while the monoracial nature of television does reflect ongoing segregation everywhere from schools to Hollywood, such mirroring means it's all the more important to notice.

SOURCE: Rothman, L. (2012, July 8). Essence Fest 2012: Is reality TV still not diverse enough? *Time.com*. Retrieved March 22, 2014, from http://entertainment.time.com/2012/07/08/essence-reality-tv-family-panel/.

Further, being able-bodied is traditionally more valued than being physically disabled (Allen, 2011; Johnson, 2017). Every society, regardless of power distance values, has these kinds of traditional hierarchies of power. Although the hierarchy is never entirely fixed, it does constrain and influence communication among cultural groups.

How do power differences affect intercultural interaction? They do so primarily by determining whose cultural values will be respected and followed. For example, even though the United States is increasingly diverse culturally, faculty, staff, and students in most U.S. universities adhere to the values and communication norms set by the White, male-dominant groups. These values and communication norms emphasize individualism. Thus, although group work is common in many courses, professors usually try to figure out how to give individual grades for it, and most students are encouraged to be responsible for their own work. Moreover, the university is run on monochronic time (see Chapter 6), with great emphasis placed on keeping schedules and meeting deadlines—and these deadlines sometimes take precedence over family and other personal responsibilities. The communication style most valued in this culture also is individual-oriented, direct and to the point, and extremely task-oriented, as is the case in many organizations in the United States (Sanchez-Burks, Lee, Choi, Nisbett, Zhao & Koo, 2003).

What is the impact for those who come from other cultural backgrounds and do not fit into this mold—say, for those who have collectivistic backgrounds and value personal relationships over tasks and homework assignments? Or for those, like Kaori, whose preferred communication style is more indirect? They may experience culture shock; they also may be sanctioned or marginalized—for example, with bad grades for not participating more in class, for not completing tasks on time, or for getting too much help from others on assignments.

To more fully consider these problems we need to introduce the concept of the **cocultural group**, meaning significant minority groups within a dominant majority that do not share dominant group values or communication patterns. Examples include some Native American, Mexican American, and Asian American individuals who choose not to assimilate to the dominant, White U.S. culture. Researcher Mark Orbe (1998) suggests that cocultural group members have several choices as to how they can

cocultural group

A significant minority group within a dominant majority that does not share dominant group values or communication patterns.

relate to the dominant culture: They can assimilate, they can accommodate, or they can remain separate. He cautions that each strategy has benefits and limitations. For example, when women try to assimilate and "act like men" in a male-oriented organization, they may score points for being professional, but they also may be criticized for being too masculine. When African Americans try to accommodate in a largely White management, they may satisfy White colleagues and bosses, but earn the label "oreo" from other African Americans. In contrast, resisting assimilation or remaining apart may result in isolation, marginalization, and exclusion from the discussions where important decisions are made (Orbe & Roberts, 2012).

Journal Prompt 8.4: Politics, History, and Power
Consider the following question: What roles do politics, history, and power play in communication between people from different cultural backgrounds?

Ethics and Intercultural Communication

8.5   Give three guidelines for communicating more ethically with people whose cultural backgrounds differ from your own.

How can you communicate more ethically across cultures? Unfortunately, no easy answers exist, but a few guidelines may be helpful.

First, remember that everyone, including you, is enmeshed in a culture and, thus, communicating through a cultural lens. Recognizing your own cultural attitudes, values, and beliefs will make you more sensitive to others' cultures and less likely to impose your own cultural attitudes on their communication patterns. Although you may feel most comfortable living in your own culture and following its communication patterns, you should not conclude that your culture and communication style are best or should be the standard for all other cultures. Such a position is called **ethnocentrism**, which you learned about in Chapter 4. Of course, appreciating and respecting other cultures does not mean you don't still appreciate and respect your own.

ethnocentrism
The tendency to view one's own group as the standard against which all other groups are judged.

Second, as you learn about other cultural groups, be aware of their humanity and avoid the temptation to view them as an exotic "other." Communication scholar Bradford Hall (1997) has cautioned about this tendency, which is called the "zoo approach."

When using such an approach, we view the study of culture as if we were walking through a zoo admiring, gasping, and chuckling at the various exotic animals we observe. One may discover amazing, interesting, and valuable information by using such a perspective and even develop a real fondness of these exotic people, but miss the point that we are as culturally "caged" as others and that they are culturally as "free" as we are (Hall, 1997, p. 14). From an ethical perspective, the zoo approach denies the humanity of other cultural groups. For example, the view of African cultures as primitive and incapable led Whites to justify colonizing Africa and exploiting its rich resources in the nineteenth century.

Third, you will be more ethical in your intercultural interactions if you are open to other ways of viewing the world. The ways that you were taught about the world and history may not be the same as what others were taught. People cannot engage in meaningful communication if they are unwilling to suspend or re-examine their assumptions about the world. For example, some Europeans believe that the United States becomes involved in other countries' affairs so that it can control its oil interests, whereas many U.S. Americans believe that concern over human rights is the motivation. If neither group will consider the opinion of the other, they will be unlikely to sustain a mutually satisfying conversation.

Journal Prompt 8.5: Ethical Intercultural Communication
Consider the following question: What three strategies can you use to help you respond ethically during intercultural interactions?

Improving Your Intercultural Communication Skills

8.6   Discuss ways to improve your own intercultural communication skills.

How can you communicate more effectively across cultures? As with ethics, no magic formula exists, but here are several suggestions.

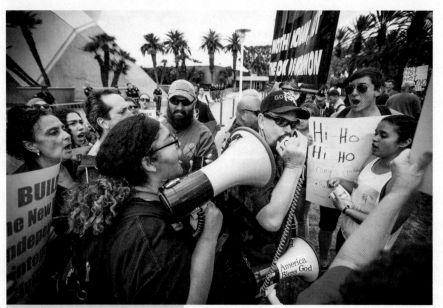

▲ It is difficult to engage in meaningful communication if people are unwilling to suspend or re-examine their deeply held assumptions.

Increase Motivation

Perhaps the most important component is *motivation*. Without the motivation to be an effective communicator, no other skills will be relevant. Part of the problem in long-standing interethnic or interreligious conflicts—for example, between the Israelis and the Palestinians—is the lack of interest, on both sides, in communicating more effectively. Some parties on both sides may even have an interest in prolonging conflict. Therefore, a strong desire to improve one's skills is necessary. Perhaps a review of the first section of this chapter can provide some motivation by reminding you of the benefits gained by learning more about intercultural communication.

Increase Your Knowledge of Self and Others

In addition to being motivated, you become a more effective intercultural communicator if you educate yourself about intercultural communication. Having some knowledge about the history, background, and values of people from other cultures can help you communicate better, both face to face and online. When you demonstrate this type of knowledge to people from other cultures, you communicate that you're interested in them and you affirm their sense of identity. Obviously, no one can know everything about all cultures; nonetheless, some general information can be helpful, as can an awareness of the importance of context and a dialectical perspective.

Self-knowledge also is important. If you were socialized to be individualistic and direct in your communication style, you may initially have a hard time understanding collectivistic tendencies or indirect communication. Once you become aware of these differences, however, you can more easily communicate with someone who holds a different perspective. Growing up in a middle-class family may also influence your perceptions. Many middle-class people assume that anyone can become middle class through hard work. But this view overlooks the discrimination faced by people of color, members of religious minorities, gays, lesbians, and transgender individuals. How can you increase your cultural self-awareness? Perhaps the best way is to cultivate intercultural encounters and relationships.

Developing facility in intercultural communication occurs through a cyclical process. The more one interacts across cultures, the more one learns about oneself, and then the more prepared one is to interact interculturally, and so on. However, increased exposure and understanding do not happen automatically. Being aware of the influence of culture on oneself and others is essential to increasing one's intercultural experience and competence (Ting-Toomey, 2010).

Where should you start? You can begin by examining your current friendships and reach out from there. Research shows that individuals generally become friends with people with whom they live, work, and worship. So your opportunities for intercultural interaction and self-awareness are largely determined by the type of people and contexts you encounter in your daily routine.

Avoid Stereotypes

Cultural differences may lead to stereotyping and prejudices. As we discussed in Chapter 4, normal cognitive patterns of generalizing make our world more manageable.

However, when these generalizations become rigid, they lead to stereotyping and prejudices. Furthermore, stereotyping can become self-fulfilling (Guéguen, Lourel, Charron, Fischer-Lokou, & Lamy, 2009). That is, if you stereotype people and treat them in a prejudiced or negative manner, they may react in ways that reinforce your stereotype.

On the other hand, we must note, overreacting by being "sweet" can be equally off-putting. African Americans sometimes complain about being "niced" to death by Whites (Yamato, 2001). The guideline here is to be mindful that you might be stereotyping. For example, if you are White, do you only notice bad behavior when exhibited by a person of color?

▲ The Washington Redskins' team name is controversial. To some it's offensive and racist, to others, it's not. How might we respond to a similar label for African Americans or Whites?

As we noted earlier, taking a dialectical approach is a useful strategy to avoiding stereotyping others. Here are six dialectics that can assist you in communicating more effectively in intercultural interactions.

1. **CULTURAL–INDIVIDUAL**

   What it is: It emphasizes that some behaviors are determined by our culture, whereas others are simply idiosyncratic, or particular to us as individuals. Taking this approach means that one does not immediately assume that someone's behavior is culturally based.

   Example: *Robin twists her hair while she talks.* This idiosyncratic personal preference should not be mistaken for a cultural norm. She doesn't do it because she is female, or young, or Protestant, or African American.

2. **PERSONAL–CONTEXTUAL**

   What it is: This dialectic focuses on the importance of context or situation and the personal in intercultural communication. Reducing an interaction to a mere meeting of two individuals means viewing intercultural communication too simplistically.

   Example: *A Greek and a German exchange student strike up a conversation in a gym where they are both exercising.* The immediate situation has an impact, so their conversation would probably differ dramatically if it occurred at a party or at a funeral service. The larger situation, including political and historical forces, also plays a role. The two might be wary of engaging in conversation due to recent events surrounding the economic problems in Greece. Some Germans felt that the Greek government and people were irresponsible in their failed financial policies and resented having to "bail out" the Greek economy again. Likewise, many Greeks felt that the Germans were unfair, that these demands were an expression of longstanding German prejudice toward Greeks. At the same time, the characteristics of the specific individuals also affect the exchange. Some Greeks (or Germans) would ignore the larger situation and reject the antipathy toward the other group. Others would attach great importance to the larger context and view the other student negatively.

3. **DIFFERENCES–SIMILARITIES**

   What it is: Real, important differences exist between cultural groups; we've identified some of these in this chapter. However, important commonalities exist as well.

   Example: One of our students summed up this point nicely in *It Happened to Me: Angelina.*

4. **STATIC–DYNAMIC**

What it is: Although some cultural patterns remain relatively stable and static for years, they also can undergo dynamic change. A static–dynamic dialectic requires that you recognize both traditional and contemporary realities of a culture.

Example: Many people form impressions about American Indians from popular films such as *Smoke Signals*—or even children's movies like *Pocahontas* or *The Indian in the Cupboard*, which portray Indians living the rural life they lived centuries ago—even though the majority of Indians in the United States today live in urban areas (American Indians, 2010).

5. **HISTORY/PAST–PRESENT/FUTURE**

What it is: This dialectic focuses on the present and the past.

Example: One cannot fully understand contemporary relations between Arabs and Jews, Muslims and Christians, or Catholics and Protestants without knowing something of their history. At the same time, people cannot ignore current events. For example, the conflict over where Yasser Arafat was to be buried in the autumn of 2004 flowed from a complex of historical and contemporary relations. His family had resided for generations in Jerusalem and wanted him laid to rest there. Israel, having current control of Jerusalem and viewing Arafat as a terrorist leader of attacks against Israel, refused.

6. **PRIVILEGE–DISADVANTAGE**

What it is: In intercultural interactions, people can be simultaneously privileged and disadvantaged (Johnson, 2017).

Example: Although U.S. Americans may be privileged in having more money and the luxury of travel, they can also feel vulnerable in foreign countries if they are ignorant of the local languages and customs. Poor Whites in the United States can be simultaneously privileged because they are White and disadvantaged because of their economic plight (Engen, 2012). As a student, you may feel privileged (compared to others) in that you are acquiring a high level of education, but you may also feel economically disadvantaged because of the high cost of education.

Strive for Empathy

In addition to being motivated, learning about others and avoiding stereotypes, striving for intercultural empathy can also increase your cross-cultural competence. Empathy refers to the ability to know what it's like to "walk in another person's shoes." However, empathic skills are culture bound, meaning that we cannot really view the world through another person's eyes without knowing something about his or her experiences and life (DeTurk, 2001). Communication scholar Broome (1991) stresses that, rather than trying to achieve absolute accuracy in predicting someone else's thoughts (which is impossible), people should forge strong relationships and strive for the creation of shared meaning in their intercultural encounters—accepting that understanding another's point of view and their feelings is not an all or nothing proposition—it is a *process* and relational empathy is a goal one strives for in intercultural encounters.

It Happened to Me
Angelina

In my first year of college, I had the most memorable friendship with a person from the Middle East. Through this friendship I learned a lot about the way people from the Middle East communicate with friends, family, and authority. My new friend and I differed in many ways—in religion, culture, nationality, race, and language. However, we were both female college students, the same age, and we shared many interests. She dressed like I did and styled her hair similarly, and we shared many ideas about the future and concerns about the world.

Navigating the Borderlands

If you are one of those individuals who lives on the borderlands and engages in intercultural communication in everyday life (e.g., through travel or an intercultural relationship, or circumstances), how can you improve your intercultural competence? How can you successfully negotiate the tensions between often-contradictory systems of values, language, and nonverbal behavior of two or more cultures? In some cases, people in such situations can feel caught between two systems; feeling as if one were swinging on a trapeze, a metaphor that captures the immigrant's experience of vacillating between the cultural patterns of the homeland and the new country, or between two ethnic or religious groups (Hegde, 1998). Typically, cultural minorities are socialized to the norms and values of both the dominant culture and their own; they may be pressured to assimilate to the dominant culture and embrace it, yet those in the dominant culture may still be reluctant to accept them as they try to do so. As one Black woman expressed, "Immediately when I step into a setting where I'm the only Black, I'm feeling like all eyes are upon me, for my entire race, especially Black women. My tone changes, the way I speak, following the rules of language—not that I don't do it anyway, but I'm more alert, making sure that I don't stumble over certain words" (Scott, 2013, p. 319).

Managing these tensions while living on the border and being multicultural can be both rewarding and challenging. Based on data from interviews she conducted, Janet Bennett (1998) described two types of border dwellers or, as she labeled them, "marginal individuals": *encapsulated marginal people* and *constructive marginal people*.

Encapsulated marginal people feel disintegrated by having to shift cultures. They have difficulty making decisions and feel extreme pressure from both groups. They try to assimilate but never feel comfortable or at home.

In contrast, **constructive marginal people** thrive in their "border" life and, at the same time, recognize its tremendous challenges. They see themselves as choice makers. They recognize the significance and potential of being "in between." For example, communication scholar Lisa Flores (1996) shows how Chicana feminist writers and artists acknowledge negative stereotypes of Mexican and Mexican American women—illiterate Spanglish-speaking laborers, passive sex objects, servants of men and children—and transform them into images of strength—as strong, clever bilinguals, reveling in their dual Anglo-Mexican heritage. In so doing, they also gain strength by reaching out to other women (women of color and immigrant women), and together strive to achieve more justice and recognition for women who live "in the middle" between cultural worlds.

Although border dwelling can be challenging and frustrating, it also can lead to cultural insights and agility in navigating intercultural encounters.

encapsulated marginal people
People who feel disintegrated by having to shift cultures.

constructive marginal people
People who thrive in a border-dweller life, while recognizing its tremendous challenges.

Journal Prompt 8.6: Improving Intercultural Communication
Consider the following questions: What are three suggestions for communicating more effectively across cultures? Which do you think is the most important? Why?

SUMMARY

8.1 Explain why it is important to learn about intercultural communication.

- Four reasons for learning about intercultural communication are increased opportunity, increased business effectiveness, improved intergroup relations, and enhanced self-awareness.

8.2 Define intercultural communication and describe three types of border dwellers.

- *Intercultural communication* is defined as communication between people from different cultural backgrounds.
- Increasing numbers of individuals today live on cultural borders—through travel, socialization, or relationships.
- *Culture* is defined as learned patterns of perceptions, values, and behaviors shared by a group of people. It is dynamic and heterogeneous, and operates within power structures.

8.3 Describe how cultural values influence communication.

- Seven core cultural values differentiate various cultural groups, and these value differences have implications for intercultural communication.

8.4 Explain the roles that politics, history, and power play in communication between people from different cultural backgrounds.

- Power is often an important element in that those who hold more powerful positions in society set the rules and norms for communication. Those individuals who do not conform to the rules because of differing cultural backgrounds and preferences may be marginalized.
- Societal forces, such as political and historical structures, play an important role in intercultural communication because intercultural encounters never occur in a vacuum.

8.5 Give three guidelines for communicating more ethically with people whose cultural backgrounds differ from your own.

- To ensure that you are communicating ethically during intercultural interactions, avoid ethnocentric thinking, recognize the humanity of others, and remain open to other ways of understanding the world.

8.6 Discuss ways to improve your own intercultural communication skills.

- You can become a more effective intercultural communicator in at least five ways: increase your motivation, acquire knowledge about self and others, avoid stereotyping, strive for intercultural empathy, and navigate the borderlands.
- There are six dialectics that can help you improve your intercultural communication: cultural-individual, personal-contextual, differences-similarities, static-dynamic, history/past-present/future, and privilege-disadvantage.

KEY TERMS

diaspora p. 169
peacebuilding p. 171
intercultural communication p. 173
culture p. 173
heterogeneous p. 173
border dwellers p. 173
culture shock p. 174
reverse culture shock/re-entry
    shock p. 174
cultural values p. 177
individualistic orientation p. 178

collectivistic orientation p. 178
preferred personality p. 178
view of human nature p. 179
human–nature value
    orientation p. 179
power distance p. 180
long-term versus short-term
    orientation p. 181
short-term orientation p. 181
monotheistic p. 181
long-term orientation p. 181

polytheistic p. 181
indulgence versus restraint
    orientation p. 181
dialectical approach p. 182
dichotomous thinking p. 182
cocultural group p. 184
ethnocentrism p. 185
encapsulated marginal
    people p. 189
constructive marginal
    people p. 189

APPLY WHAT YOU KNOW

1. **Cultural Profile** List all the cultural groups you belong to. Which groups are most important to you when you're at college? When you're at home? Which groups would be easiest to leave? Why?

2. **Intercultural Conflict Analysis** Identify a current intercultural conflict in the media. It can be conflict between nations, ethnic groups, or gender. Read at least three sources that give background and information about the conflict. Conduct an analysis of this conflict, answering the following questions:

   - What do you think are the sources of the conflict?
   - Are there value differences?
   - Power differences?
   - What role do you think various contexts (historical, social, and political) play in the conflict?

Communicating in Close Relationships

CHAPTER
9

 LEARNING OBJECTIVES

> *"Communication is the foundation on which all relationships are built."*

Charee and her friend Cristina were at a club one weekend when Charee spotted a man who had hit on her earlier in the evening. As he walked toward the two women, Charee leaned over to Cristina and said, "There's that jerk I was telling you about." Eighteen months later, Cristina and the "jerk" were married.

How is it that one person's jerk is another person's ideal mate? On more than one occasion, you may have wondered why your friends pick the romantic partners they do. Or perhaps you even have questioned your own choices. Though relationship researchers haven't unraveled all the mysteries of love and friendship, they have made considerable progress in explaining how and why relationships develop, are maintained, and sometimes fail—and the role communication plays at each stage.

To help you understand communication in close relationships, we begin by describing the importance of these relationships and providing a definition for them. Next, we address the role of the individual in close relationships and explore the factors that increase the likelihood that you will become involved with another person. We then examine five theories and two models that explain how communication influences relationship development between friends and romantic partners. We conclude our focus on individuals in relationships by discussing problems that can occur in friendship and romance, such as aversive communication, jealousy, aggression, and sexual coercion. Finally, we explore the societal forces that influence relationships and the communication within them and present you with guidelines for communicating more ethically and effectively in your own relationships.

The Importance of Communication in Close Relationships

9.1   Describe the importance of close relationships.

Friends play an important role in people's lives. Close relationships are a source of much happiness (and some distress) and serve as a significant context within which a person's interactions take place (Donaghue & Fallon, 2003). As is illustrated in *It Happened to Me: Olivia*, friends can come to the rescue in a crisis by providing both emotional and physical support. Relationships with friends, lovers, and family members also offer a sense of belonging, help alleviate loneliness, and are central to psychological and physical health.

Researchers have found that loneliness, or a lack of close relationships, is associated with psychological disorders such as depression and anxiety (Miller, 2002). People with even a few close relationships experience greater well-being than those who are lonely (Gierveld & Tilburg, 1995). People with satisfying relationships also experience

It Happened to Me
Olivia

I was at a friend's house, eating junk food and watching TV, when someone knocked on the door. Standing there in the rain, with tears running down her face and sobbing, was one of our friends. She told us that her mom had hit her and thrown her things out her bedroom window. We sat with her for ages until she calmed down; then, we asked her to stay the night. Without us, she would have had nowhere to go and no one to talk to.

▲ Friends are an important source of comfort.

better physical health. For example, an examination of 148 studies found that the quantity and quality of individuals' social relationships were linked both to their mental health and to their longevity. The authors found that high-quality social relationships were associated with a 50 percent increased likelihood of living longer (Holt-Lunstad, Smith, & Layton, 2010).

Similarly, studies of marital relationships reveal that people in happy marriages are less likely to experience high blood pressure and serious heart episodes (Holt-Lunstad, Birmingham, & Jones, 2008). Thus, close relationships can improve not only our satisfaction with life but also our health.

The relationships we develop with friends, family, and romantic partners are qualitatively different from other types of interpersonal relationships, such as those people have with their mail carriers or Starbucks's barista (LaFollette, 1996). Close relationships are distinguished by their frequency, intensity, and diversity of contact (Kelley et al., 1983) as well as their level of intimacy, importance, and satisfaction (Berg & Piner, 1990).

People in close relationships see each other as unique and irreplaceable. They are more open in their communications with each other than with other people, and they tend to disclose more personal details (Janz, 2000). In addition, the communication in these relationships is influenced more by individual factors (as opposed to social factors) than is usually true of casual relationships. That is, people in close relationship know each better and share more experiences, so they are better able to adapt their own communication and more effectively interpret their partner's communication. This can lead to greater ease in communicating as well as increased understanding and intimacy. For these reasons, people in close relationships expect their relationships to endure over time because they are committed to them (Wright, 1999).

Casual relationships, in contrast, involve little disclosure or affection and are perceived as interchangeable because they are usually role-based, as between a salesperson and a customer (Janz, 2000). For example, although you might like your mail carrier and would miss seeing her if she quit her job, you probably would be perfectly content to receive your mail from someone new. But if your fiancé or best friend terminated your relationship, it's unlikely that you would be content with a substitute. Because these relationships are not based on the participants' knowledge of each other as individuals, the communication that occurs within them tends to be influenced more by social norms for interacting and, therefore, are less personal and more superficial.

Journal Prompt 9.1: Close Relationship Communication
Consider the following question:
How does the communication in close relationships differ from communication in casual relationships?

Close Relationships and the Individual

9.2   Explain five communication theories of relationship development.

Because relationship development is an important aspect of life and because the process sometimes goes awry—for example, approximately one-third of first marriages end in divorce or separation within 10 years (Bureau of Labor Statistics, October 2013)—scholars have devoted considerable effort toward creating theories and models to explain it. No single theory can explain how all human relationships develop; however, the following theories offer insight into how relationships develop and change over time as people communicate with one another.

Theories of Relationship Development

Do you ever question why you form friendships and romantic relationships with some people but not others? Many social science scholars have, so they studied close relationships extensively and, based on those studies, they have developed a variety of theories to explain why we choose whom we choose. Why should you be interested? As we discussed in Chapter 2, theory helps explain and pre-

▲ Close relationships can be a source of happiness, comfort, and even distress.

dict behavior. When you understand the factors that predict and explain the successful initiation and development of relationships, you can use that knowledge to help you begin relationships and communicate in them so they are more successful and enduring. Here we discuss several communication theories that help explain why some interactions lead to relationships and some don't, as well as why some of those relationships last longer than others.

Attraction Theory   For any romantic or platonic relationship to develop, you must first notice that a particular person exists and be interested enough to initiate contact. Charee still remembers meeting Mateo during their first year of college. A mutual friend introduced them, and she became interested when she saw him (tall, good looking, and muscular!) and learned that he was also studying communication. She spent most of the evening talking to him, even though thirty other people were at the party.

Attraction theory explains the three primary forces that draw people together to form relationships. These three forces—*proximity, interpersonal attractiveness*, and *similarity*—were all operating the evening Charee and Mateo met. They were students at the same university, they found each other attractive, and they discovered that they had similar career interests.

Of course, proximity, attractiveness, and similarity don't guarantee a lasting friendship or romance, but they do set the stage for relationships to develop. Let's see how these three factors influence relational development and the role that communication plays in each.

Proximity   Most people are not aware of it, but **proximity**—how close you are to others—plays an important role in relationship development. Historically, proximity referred to physical closeness between people. Typically, people became friends with or dated those who lived in their apartment complexes, neighborhoods, or dorms; those who were in their classes; or those with whom they worked (Sias & Cahill, 1998; Sprecher, 1998). Now, however, technologies such as Facetime, Snapchat, and social networks have made it easier for people to create the feeling of proximity even with individuals who are not physically nearby.

Proximity has a strong impact, at least initially, on individuals' interactions and relationships. One of the ways proximity affects relationship development is that it facilitates informal, relatively unplanned communication that provides the opportunity for people to notice others' attractive qualities, learn about their similarities, and develop a relationship (Berscheid & Reis, 1998).

attraction theory
Theory that explains the primary forces that draw people together.

proximity
How physically close one is to others.

Once people graduate from college, however, they often find their romantic options dwindle significantly because proximity to other young, single individuals decreases. In response, companies such as Tinder have developed apps that make it easier for users to find potential romantic partners in their area without having to rely on chance proximity. We discuss the influence of social media and dating apps on interpersonal relationship in more detail in Chapter 14.

Usually, the easier it is to interact with someone, the easier it will be to develop and sustain a relationship. Of course, some people do develop and maintain long-distance relationships, though this may be more common for romantic relationships than friendships. Recent statistics suggest that approximately 3 million married couples live apart for reasons other than dissatisfaction with their relationship and that up to 75 percent of college students will engage in long-distance relationships at some time during college (Stafford, 2010). Most of these people, however, likely were physically close to one another at some point in their relationships.

attractiveness

The appeal one person has for another, based on physical appearance, personalities, or behavior.

Attractiveness   Obviously, proximity is not enough to launch a relationship. Most of us have daily contact with dozens of people. How is it that you form relationships with some and not others? One of the more obvious answers is **attractiveness**. Although most of us are attracted to those we find physically appealing (Buss, Shackelford, Kirkpatrick, & Larsen, 2001), we also tend to develop relationships with people who are approximately as attractive as we are. This tendency is called the **matching hypothesis**. Interestingly, researchers have found that the matching hypothesis applies to friendships (Bleske-Rechek & Lighthall, 2010), romantic relationships (Sprecher & Hatfield, 2009), marriage (Hinsz, 1989), and even roommates (Kurt & Sherker, 2003).

matching hypothesis

The tendency to develop relationships with people who are approximately as attractive as we are.

Fortunately, attractiveness is a broad concept. It is composed of physical attractiveness, social attractiveness, and task attractiveness (McCroskey, McCroskey, & Richmond, 2006). Social attractiveness refers to how friendly, outgoing, warm, and sociable one is perceived to be, whereas task attractiveness refers to how desirable people are as coworkers or task partners (Burgoon & Bacue, 2003). People are attracted to others not only because of their physical appearance but also for their contributions to mutual tasks, wonderful personalities, or charming ways. Most of these qualities are revealed through communication; therefore, individuals with good communication skills are often perceived as more attractive than they might be otherwise (Burleson & Samter, 1996). Consequently, improving your communication skills can increase others' desire to form relationships with you.

similarity

Degree to which people share the same values, interests, and background.

Similarity   It may be equally obvious that most people are attracted by **similarity**; they like people who are like them, who enjoy the things they enjoy, who value what they value, and with whom they share a similar background (Byrne, 1997). In many cases opposites *do* attract, but when it comes to background, values, and attitudes, "birds of a feather [more often] flock together." For example, Buss (1985) found that the more similar the participants in his study were, the more likely they were to report increased levels of attraction. This makes sense. If you like to socialize, enjoy the outdoors, and are involved in a religious community, you may find it difficult to develop a relationship with someone who is introverted, prefers to stay home to read and listen to music, and avoids organized religion. However open-minded you are, you probably view your orientation to the world as preferable, especially concerning values such as religion, politics, and morality.

You may wonder how individuals determine whether they are similar in values, attitudes, and background. Generally, they discover this during the early stages of conversational interaction either in face-to-face or online contexts (Berger & Calabrese, 1975; Berger & Kellerman, 1994). Researchers also have found that individuals are attracted to people, especially friends, whose communication skills are similar to their own (Burleson & Samter, 1996). This is true whether one possesses low or high levels of communication skills. It's important to note that friendship pairs who have low levels of communication skills are just as satisfied with their friendships as are those who have high levels of skills. All of these findings suggest that the type of people who might be attracted to you are people who are similar to you in terms of communication skills, interests, and attractiveness and that spending time with them can provide opportunities for friendship or romance to develop. This is why the best advice for meeting compatible others is to engage in activities you enjoy and make the effort to attend these activities regularly.

▲ We are attracted to people who like the same activities we do.

Attractiveness and similarity in communication competence as well as similarity in attitudes and values are revealed through communication. You can see, then, why communication is considered the foundation on which all relationships are built.

Uncertainty Reduction Theory One communication theory that examines how communication impacts relationship development is uncertainty reduction theory. According to **uncertainty reduction theory** (Berger & Calabrese, 1975), when we first meet someone much of our interaction is dedicated to reducing uncertainty and determining whether we wish to interact with the person again. This theory argues that relationship development is facilitated or derailed by participants' efforts to reduce their uncertainty about each other. It assumes that people are uncomfortable with uncertainty about others and seek to reduce it to decide if the other person is safe, interesting, and desirable—or dangerous, boring, and undesirable.

uncertainty reduction theory
Theory that argues relationship development is facilitated or derailed by participants' efforts to reduce their uncertainty about each other.

Uncertainty reduction theory explains much of the behavior we engage in when we first meet people. For example, if you are introduced to someone new at a party, what do you do? If you are like most people, you probably provide a bit of information about yourself or ask questions about the other person. You might ask how your new acquaintance knows the host, what he or she does for a living, or whether he or she likes the music that is playing. If you like the other person based on this relatively superficial interaction, you will probably continue to talk with him or her. If, however, you find the person strange or uninteresting, you're likely to excuse yourself and find someone new with whom to talk.

This explains why our initial interactions with others are so important. To initiate new relationships, we have to be able to communicate in a way that helps others reduce their uncertainty about us in a positive and pleasant manner. If we find others desirable based on our initial attempts to reduce uncertainty and continue to have opportunities to interact, we tend to increase our levels of disclosure and to solicit more personal disclosure from the other person. This process continues until the two participants either form a relationship or cease to have opportunities to interact. An important assumption of uncertainty reduction theory, however, is that as we reduce our uncertainty about someone, we like the person more because we dislike uncertainty. Although uncertainty reduction is central to forming relationships, there is a least one type of romantic relationship in which couples may be willing to tolerate uncertainty. To understand how this process works, read about one woman's experience in *Communication in Society: Why Can't Couples Talk about Their Friends with Benefits Relationships?*

Predicted Outcome Value Theory Have you ever liked someone initially but over time, as you learned more about the person, you discovered you didn't like the person after all? How can this be explained by uncertainty reduction theory? According to

predicted outcome theory
Theory that attempts to explain how reducing uncertainty can lead to attraction or repulsion.

communication researcher Michael Sunnafrank, it can't. Consequently, he developed **predicted outcome theory** (1986), an adaptation of uncertainty reduction theory that attempts to explain how reducing uncertainty can lead to **attraction** *or* repulsion. Sunnafrank argues that during initial conversations with others we attempt to determine whether continuing to interact with another person is of value, that is, whether it is worth our time and energy. If we predict that future interactions will be valuable, we continue to talk with the person, and if we continue to predict positive outcomes, we will form a relationship. However, if at any point we begin to predict negative outcomes for our interactions, then we will de-escalate or end the relationship.

What do these theories tell us about developing our own relationships? First, they can help us to better understand why some relationship can catch fire—or die out—quickly. From our first moments of meeting someone, both we and the other party are attempting to determine how safe, competent, and interesting the other is. If something goes wrong at the beginning—a mistimed joke, a comment that suggests we are boastful, or nonverbal behaviors that indicate disinterest—the interaction can immediately end and cut off any potential relationship. Second, all of us make quick assessments of others based on their conversations, and if we want to attract others we need to communicate in ways that suggest we will be interesting, fun, or even useful to know. If you have difficulty developing relationships, you might want to pay attention to your initial interactions with others to see if you are unintentionally communicating a negative image.

Social Exchange and Equity Theories   The three theories we have discussed thus far focus on the earliest stages of relationship development; the next two, social exchange and equity theories, examine the characteristics of relationships as they develop past the initial stages. Social exchange and equity theories are similar in that they both propose that relationship development, satisfaction, and longevity are related to how

---

COMMUNICATION IN SOCIETY
Why Can't Couples Talk about Their Friends with Benefits Relationship?

Have you or anyone you know been in a friends with benefits (FWB) relationship? How hard was it for you or your friend to communicate about the relationship? Do you think that communicating clearly about boundaries and expectations would have improved the relationship?

We all have been told many times that communication is essential for good relationships. However, one relationship most people don't want to talk about is their FWB relationship. Most FWB relationships would benefit from a good talk, yet according to communication professor Kendra Knight, such communication is rare. Why? The college students she interviewed offered four reasons why they don't feel comfortable talking about their FWB relationships.

1. **Talking about the relationship is at odds with the view that FWBs are casual and easy.** Maintaining relationships can be effortful and emotional, which is what many participants want to avoid. FWBs are supposed to be fun and not carry the baggage of a "real" relationship.

2. **Talking about the relationship can be face-threatening.** A basic premise of FWBs is that the partners are not exclusive or committed to one another. Even talking about the relationship suggests one wants more from the relationship, which some feel makes a person look needy.

3. **Talking about emotions in the relationship violates the rules of the relationship.** Though FWBs are supposed to be "just friends," in reality many people have strong emotions about their relationships. They may feel jealousy, possessiveness, and insecurity—feelings that are antithetical to a FWB relationship.

4. **Talking about the relationship threatens the status quo.** Even when one person is willing to discuss the relationship, the other partner may be fearful that talking about the relationship will disrupt it or change it somehow. Not talking about the relationship, then, is seen as a way to maintain the relationship as it is.

SOURCE: Knight, K. (September, 2014). Communicating dilemmas in adults' friends with benefits relationships: Challenges to relational talk. *Emerging Adulthood*. Retrieved http://eax.sagepub.com/content/early/2014/09/19/21676968 14549598 November 25, 2014.

"rewarding" individuals find their relationships to be. **Social exchange theory** (Thibault & Kelley, 1959) argues that in U.S. society, people attempt to maximize the rewards and minimize the costs of their friendships and romantic relationships. The rewards of such relationships include companionship, being cared for, and in some cases, sex. The "exchange" part of the theory argues that in exchange for these rewards, people provide similar rewards to their relationship partners. Of course, providing rewards for others counts as a "cost," so the belief is that people seek relationships where perceived rewards outweigh perceived costs. Based on this theory, individuals are satisfied in and committed to their relationships when they feel they are receiving sufficient rewards and not too many costs. Although the fundamental ideas of social exchange may make sense, many people object to it because they see as it as calculating and unromantic.

Equity theory (Walster, Berscheid, & William, 1973) offers a refinement of social exchange theory. It argues that rather than focusing purely on rewards and costs, people are most interested in achieving fairness in their relationships. That is, individuals are satisfied when they perceive their relationships as equitable and dissatisfied when they perceive them as inequitable. Equity describes the desire for one's costs (or inputs) to be balanced by one's rewards (or outputs). According to equity theory, both people who are **underbenefitted** (those whose inputs exceed their outputs) and those who are **overbenefitted** (those whose outputs exceed their inputs) may feel dissatisfied with their relationships. Underbenefitted people may feel angry or taken advantage of, whereas overbenefitted people often feel guilty. According to this theory, dyads are happiest when fairness occurs, that is, each person gets out what she or he puts into the relationship.

Equity is not the same as equality; the theory doesn't argue that each partner should receive the same amount of rewards for satisfaction to occur. Instead, it suggests that whoever contributes more should benefit more from the relationship. Some research supports this theory. For example, a study of 200 couples found that satisfaction was highest for people who perceived their relationship to be equitable. Overbenefitted partners were the next-most satisfied, followed by those who felt underbenefitted (Canary & Stafford, 1992). If the ratio of costs and rewards is dissatisfying for one or both partners, then the two of you should discuss how you can change that ratio. If, for example, you feel angry and underbenefitted, you could reduce your costs. This happened to Aaron. He and his roommate Matt became friends during their first semester living together, and Aaron really enjoyed hanging out with him. Over time, he realized that he was picking up the tab far more often when they went out and that Matt never returned favors that he routinely granted, such loaning Matt his car and taking him to the airport. Eventually Aaron decided that he wasn't enjoying their friendship anymore, so he decided to cut his costs and get a new roommate for sophomore year.

The five theories that we have discussed describe the relationship development process as a fairly rational one based on judgment and choice. For a more controversial, and biological, take on romantic relationship development, see *Alternative View: An Evolutionary Theory of Relationship Development.*

Models of Relationship Development

Thus far, we have discussed five theories that attempt to explain why and how voluntary relationships such as romantic relationships and friendships develop. Because they are theories, these explanations tend to be somewhat general and do not focus on the particular types of interactions that occur during relationship development. Therefore, several scholars have developed models of relationship development that seek to explain more specifically the ways that communication promotes or inhibits relationship development and maintenance.

Stage Models of Relationship Development   The best-known stage model was developed in 1978 by Mark Knapp, a communication scholar (Knapp, 1978; Knapp &

social exchange theory
Theory that explains the development and longevity of relationships as a result of individuals' ability to maximize the rewards and minimize the costs of their relationships.

equity theory
Theory that argues that people are more satisfied in relationships they perceive as fair, that is, where their costs are balanced by their rewards.

underbenefitted
Underbenefitted people perceive that their costs exceed their rewards.

overbenefitted
Overbenefitted people perceive that their rewards exceed their costs.

equity
Perception that one's costs (or inputs) are balanced by one's rewards (or outputs).

ALTERNATIVE VIEW
An Evolutionary Theory of Relationship Development

What courtship behaviors does the evolutionary model of relationships explain well? What courtship behaviors does it fail to explain? How would an evolutionary model explain the phenomenon of "hooking up"—or could it?

Evolutionary theories of relationship development come to us from studies in anthropology and social psychology. These theories assume that the primary (though unconscious) motivating factor for most species, including humans, is to reproduce—and that this need influences how and why people form what is typically referred to as romantic relationships. Psychologist Davis Buss, an important scholar in the field of evolutionary psychology, argues that heterosexual relationship development or mating is not, in fact, a romantic or particularly civilized process; rather, he claims that even among humans, mate selection and retention involves competitive, conflictual, and even manipulative processes.

Evolutionary theory posits that because males and females make different contributions to reproduction, they behave differently during relationship development (Buss, 2003; Kenrick & Trost, 1996). More specifically, Buss suggests that females and males communicate and behave during relationship development in ways designed to aid them in achieving their goals and maximizing their outcomes. The female's goal is generally to attract a mate who is reliable, trustworthy, and committed to the relationship because she will need help rearing her children. The male's goal may be to have a number of relationships (because

his parental investment is less) or to find one mate he can trust because he does not want to invest time and energy in a child who is not his own.

This model of relationship development also suggests that because we can always be certain who a child's mother is, whereas fatherhood is not certain in the same way, men and women behave differently in relationships. For example, this view is used to explain men's greater promiscuity, expressions of jealousy, and lesser willingness to forgive acts of infidelity as adaptive mechanisms that help men achieve their reproductive potential (Buss, 2003).

To better understand this theory, consider the amount of time and energy each parent invests in his or her offspring. The mother's investment is inherently greater than the father's. Women generally need to invest at least two years (nine months of pregnancy and the remainder of the time to nurture an infant), whereas men must invest only a short time—theoretically, only a few minutes—to father a child. The evolutionary model argues that these differences explain why men may try to have sex earlier in a relationship and require less commitment than women typically do (Buss, 2003; Trost & Kenrick, 1993).

Knapp's stage model
Model of relationship development that views relationships as occurring in "stages" and that focuses on how people communicate as relationships develop and decline.

initiating
Stage of romantic relational development in which both people behave so as to appear pleasant and likeable.

experimenting
Stage of romantic relational development in which both people seek to learn about each other.

intensifying
Stage of romantic relational development in which both people seek to increase intimacy and connectedness.

integrating
Stage of romantic relational development in which both people portray themselves as a couple.

bonding
Stage of romantic relational development characterized by public commitment.

Vangelisti, 1997). **Knapp's stage model** conceptualizes relationship development as a staircase. The staircase depicts relationship development as being composed of five steps that lead upward toward commitment: **initiating**, **experimenting**, **intensifying**, **integrating**, and **bonding**. It also portrays relationship dissolution as occurring in five steps that lead downward: **differentiating**, **circumscribing**, **stagnating**, **avoiding**, and **terminating**. In this model, couples at the relationship maintenance level of development move up and down the staircase as they move toward and away from commitment as a result of the fluctuation of their relationships.

Knapp's stage model is a *communication* model because it explores how individuals' communication practices affect relationship development and decline. For example, *circumscribing* is identified by the fact that couples' conversations focus mostly on "safe" topics, such as household tasks, whereas *experimenting* is defined by couples' communication efforts to learn more about one another. This stage model assumes one can determine what stage a couple is in by observing what the two people say and do. For example, if couples spend most of their communication interactions discussing the ways in which they are different, they are at the *differentiating* stage. As Table 9.1 reveals, each stage is based on the types of communication couples perform within it.

As you might have noticed, Knapp's model includes a *termination* stage. This does not suggest that all relationships end, but it does recognize that many relationships do (Weber, 1998). Relationships that end are often treated as "failures," and the people who experience them often feel that they have done something wrong. But, in fact, as people grow and mature, it is not unusual for them to change their social networks (Dainton, Zelley, & Langan, 2003). This is not to say that you won't have long-lasting or permanent relationships, but not every relationship termination should be viewed as a mistake.

Table 9.1 Knapp's Stages of Romantic Relational Development

Stage	Goal	Example
Initiating	Appear pleasant, likeable	"Hi! I sure like your car."
Experimenting	Learn about each other	"Do you like to travel?"
Intensifying	Increase intimacy, connectedness	"I can't imagine being with anyone else."
Integrating	Establish dyad as a couple	"I love you. I feel like you are a part of me."
Bonding	Public commitment	"Will you marry me?"
Differentiating	Increase interpersonal distance	"I'm going; you can come if you want to."
Circumscribing	Discuss safe topics	"Did you pick up the dry cleaning?"
Stagnating	Prevent change	"Let's not talk about it right now, okay?"
Avoiding	Decline to interact with partner	"I'm too busy now. I'll get back to you later."
Terminating	Ending the relationship	"It's over."

SOURCE: Knapp, M. L., & Vangelisti, A. (1997). Interpersonal communication and relationships (2nd ed.). Boston: Allyn & Bacon.

Critics of Knapp's stage model point out that people don't move from one stage to the next in an orderly fashion, and many couples experience a "repair" stage where they try to improve their relationship prior to moving on to termination (which he does not mention). Importantly, critics also argue that people who meet online may not move through the stages he details or may do so in a different order. The potential romantic partners one meets in a public place, they argue, may reveal their goals and preferences gradually over the course of multiple dates, but users of online sites often reveal personal information early in their interactions to avoid over-investing time and energy in pursuit of less-than-ideal matches (Lever, Groy, Royce, & Gillespie, 2008).

Knapp has responded to this critique by arguing that dyads can skip stages but that they have to go back at some point and move through the skipped stages. For example, when two people "hook up," they may move from initiation to integration in a matter of hours. However, if they go on to form a relationship and stay together, they will have to go back and experience the experimenting and intensifying stages. Knapp also argues that over the course of a relationship, dyads move up and down the staircase as people and events change.

As you read about Knapp's stage model of relationship development, you may have thought that this model doesn't describe your own experiences very well. If so, you are not alone. Indeed, some researchers believe that relationships can follow a number of paths: Some may be fairly straight like a sidewalk, whereas others may be like winding mountain paths, as described by **relational trajectory models** (Baxter & Bullis, 1986; Surra, 1987).

Turning Point Model of Relationship Development The most popular model that emerged from research on relational trajectory research is the **turning point model** (Baxter & Bullis, 1986). It is a non-linear model that best captures the fact that relationship development can be bidirectional—that is, that couples move both toward and away from commitment over the course of their relationship. The original model proposed that romantic couples engage in approximately 14 types of "turning points" that influence the direction of their relationship trajectory (see Table 9.2). For example, the turning point "passion" (first kiss or saying, "I love you") tends to be an event that increases couples' commitment to their relationship,

differentiating
Stage of romantic relational dissolution in which couples increase their interpersonal distance.

circumscribing
Stage of romantic relational dissolution in which couples discuss safe topics.

stagnating
Stage of romantic relational dissolution in which couples try to prevent change.

avoiding
Stage of romantic relational dissolution in which couples try not to interact with each other.

terminating
Stage of romantic relational dissolution in which couples end the relationship.

▼ The bonding stage of romantic relationships is characterized by public commitment, such as moving in together or becoming engaged.

Table 9.2   Turning Points in Developing Relationships

Turning Point	Description	Effect on Relationship
Get-to-know time	Events and time spent together learning about one another	Increases commitment
Quality time	Special occasions for appreciating the other or the relationship	Increases commitment
Physical separation	Time apart as a result of school breaks, etc.	Little effect on commitment
External competition	Competing for partner's time/attention because of others or events	Decreases commitment
Reunion	Coming back together after physical separation	Increases commitment
Passion	Physical/emotional expression of affection	Increases commitment
Disengagement	Ending the relationship	Decreases commitment
Positive psychic change	Acquiring a more positive outlook on partner/relationship	Increases commitment
Exclusivity	Decision to date only each other	Increases commitment
Negative psychic change	Acquiring a more negative outlook on partner/relationship	Decreases commitment
Making up	Getting back together after a breakup	Increases commitment
Serious commitment	Moving in with one's partner or getting married	Increases commitment
Sacrifice	Providing support or gifts to one's partner	Increases commitment

SOURCE: Baxter, L. A., & Bullis, C. (1986). Turning points in developing romantic relationships. Human Communication Research, 12, 469–493.

relational trajectory models

Relationship development models that view relationship development as more variable than do stage models.

turning point model

Model of relationship development in which couples move both toward and away from commitment over the course of their relationship.

whereas the turning point "external competition" (such as a rival lover) decreases commitment to the relationship.

A slightly different turning point model of friendship also has been developed (Baxter & Bullis, 1986; Becker et al., 2009). Here, turning points most often associated with increased closeness between friends include participating in activities together, taking a trip together, sharing living quarters, self-disclosing, hanging out with mutual friends, and sharing common interests. Decreased closeness most often occurred when friends stopped living together, had conflicts, experienced interference from one person's romantic partner, moved so that they no longer lived near one another, or underwent change (Johnson, Wittenberg, Haigh, & Wigley, 2004).

Although we know more about heterosexual relationships than we do about gay and lesbian relationships, what we do know suggests that these two types of relationships may follow different relational development paths. In heterosexual relationships, friendship and romantic sexual involvement traditionally have been mutually exclusive; therefore, the termination of romantic intimacy usually meant the end of the friendship as well (Nardi, 1992, 2007). In contrast, gay male friendships often start with sexual attraction and involvement but evolve into friendship with no sexual/romantic involvement, whereas lesbian relationships may begin with friendship and evolve into romantic relationships (Nardi, 1992, 2007; Peplau, 2009). However, this difference between heterosexual and gay and lesbian couples may be less true than it once was; more heterosexual young people appear to be combining the categories of friendship and sexual involvement.

How does understanding stage and relational trajectory models help you understand your relationships? First, they explain the types of interactions that lead to and reflect where you are in your relationships with others. Second, they can help you understand your own relationship patterns by letting you see where your relationships commonly terminate, where they are strongest, and how you can change patterns that aren't working for you.

▼ One turning point in romantic relationships is the presence of external competition.

In the next section, we will examine the specific communication processes that individuals use to develop, maintain, and terminate their relationships.

Communicating in Friendships and Romantic Relationships

9.3   Identify tactics for initiating, maintaining, and terminating friendships and romantic relationships.

People tend to see friendship as being a different type of relationship than a romance. If that is true, how do you think communication differs between friendship pairs and romantic couples?

In the following, Jeff describes how he sees the difference between friendship and romantic relationships:

> You're more likely to let your friends see you warts and all. There's no fear of rejection, for me anyway. . . . In a romantic relationship, you don't want them to see you at your worst. . . . You want them to think you're very well adjusted. And your friends know that's a total crock so there's no use even pretending. (Reeder, 1996)

As Jeff's description illustrates, friendships can differ markedly from romances in how much we reveal, especially in the early stages. But other differences exist as well. For example, we typically expect exclusivity from our romantic partners but not from our friends. Also, people often have higher expectations for their romantic partners, especially with regard to physical attractiveness, social status, and a pleasing personality (Sprecher & Regan, 2002). And we may require greater expressions of commitment and caring from romantic partners than from friends (Goodwin & Tang, 1991). In the following sections, we explore in more detail the similarities and differences between friendships and romances.

Initiating Relationships

An individual's ability to begin a conversation is essential to the development of any relationship. Although many people disparage small talk, there can be no "big talk" if small talk does not precede it. But even before you engage in small talk, you need to be able to signal your interest to others.

Initiating Romantic Relationships   Meeting romantic partners and establishing relationships can be a problem for many people for a variety of reasons. LGBTQ individuals, for example, may find it difficult to identify and meet potential partners in their day-to-day lives. In addition, dating anxiety is pervasive among almost all adolescents and young adults—regardless of sexual orientation (Essau, Conradt, & Petermann, 1999).

How can people initiate interaction to show they are interested in a potential relationship? Frequently, budding partners "test the waters" by flirting. Considerable research has been conducted on flirting in heterosexual relationships, both because of its crucial role in the initiation of romantic relationships and because of its ambiguity. Much flirting

Journal Prompt 9.2: Relationship Theories and Models
Consider the following questions: What are the five theories of relationship development discussed in this section? What are two models of relationship development?

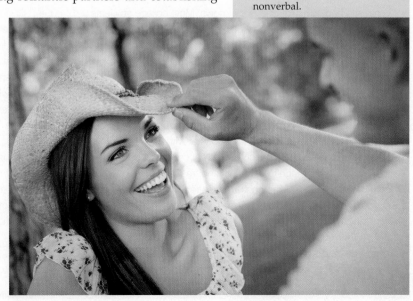

▼ Most flirting, though not all, is nonverbal.

(though not all) is nonverbal, because nonverbal communication entails less risk: if the other person does not respond, you can pretend you weren't flirting after all.

When initiating a potential heterosexual romantic/sexual relationship, women are typically more active than men; they use more eye contact, smiles, brief touches, and grooming behavior to signal interest and attraction. Although men do use gazing, smiling, and grooming behaviors, the only behavior they engage in more than women do is intimate touching (hugging, hand holding). Thus, in heterosexual relationships, women engage in more flirtation at the onset of the interaction; then, men tend to escalate the relationship through touch (McCormick & Jones, 1989). Visit the website for the Social Issues Research Centre at http://www.sirc.org/publik/flirt2.pdf if you would like to learn more about the "science of flirting."

The problem of initiating romantic relationships can be challenging for LGBTQ individuals. It is not just a matter of fear of rejection or anxiety. Gay men have been assaulted or killed because heterosexual men believed they were being flirted with. This is one reason that more LGBTQ individuals use social networking sites (e.g., Moovz, Tumblr) and dating apps (e.g., Grindr for gay and bisexual men; Her for lesbians) created specifically for them to meet potential romantic partners.

Once couples successfully convey their interest and initiate a conversation in person or online, if their interest continues they may begin dating. Or do they? Some scholars, journalists, and college students suggest that dating no longer exists. They argue that traditional dating has been replaced by group dates, hook-ups, friends with benefits, and celibacy. To explore this idea further, see *Communication in Society: The Truth about Hookup Culture on Campus.* Initiating romantic and dating relationships is not always easy. People often lack confidence in their social and communication skills. Many people aren't sure how or where to approach others, and they worry about being rejected.

In general, successful relationship development appears to be related to effective communication skills. For example, individuals who self-disclose a little as they initiate relationships are more successful than those who disclose a lot or none at all. Competent daters know that one should disclose primarily positive information early in relationships. They also act interested in what others have to say, help others out, and are polite and positive. Finally, those who successfully initiate relationships are more

---

Critical Thinking Prompt

Think back to the last time you were aware that someone was interested in you romantically. How did you know? What verbal and nonverbal behaviors suggested that romance was a possibility?

COMMUNICATION IN SOCIETY
The Truth about Hookup Culture on Campus

What is a hook-up? No one really knows. Most college students have their own definition of the term, and according to Dr. Kathleen Bogle, author of *Hooking Up: Sex, Dating, and Relationships on Campus*, it's deliberately vague. "The point is that it involves sexual activity, ranging from kissing to intercourse, outside of an exclusive relationship," she tells *Teen Vogue*. The hook-up is nothing new—Bucknell sociologist William Flack has been studying it since 2001, and casual sex has been happening on campus for decades—but the dominance of explaining your encounter with a romantic venture as "hooking up" has become widely accepted as something that everyone in college does, but it's not really as campus-wide as most people think. The hook-up culture, is in fact, more of a subculture. It hasn't replaced dating, it's just changed how we think about it.

"When I go out and visit colleges and talk to students, they'll all say the date is dead and hardly anyone dates here, but in reality if we just look at seniors, most of them have been on a number of dates," Dr. England says. Her research shows that while the average college senior has hooked up with eight people over four years, they have also gone on an average of seven dates and had an average of two relationships. Sixty-nine percent of college seniors also report being in a relationship lasting more than six months. And while 67 percent of respondents told Dr. England that they hooked up and dated before their most recent relationship became a "relationship," 26 percent dated without hooking up beforehand.

But because of the widespread myth that everyone is hooking up all the time, it sometimes seems like the date is dead. It's pretty safe to say that society's ideas about dating have changed since the age of the dance card, but nowadays, there is no universally accepted norm—we just think there is.

SOURCE: Adapted from Dwyer, L. (September 9, 2015). The surprising reality of hook-up culture on campus. *Teen Vogue.* Retrieved March 22, 2017, from http://www.teenvogue.com/story/hookup-culture-myth-dating-college.

able to plan and ask for dates. In contrast, ineffective behaviors include trying too hard to make an impression, disclosing too much information too soon, being passive (waiting for the other person to initiate conversation and activities), and acting too self-effacing or modest (Young, 1981).

At times, initiating a romantic relationship may seem like a rather complicated dance. Each person has a part, but the dance steps vary from one couple to the next. Fortunately, initiating friendship can seem a bit more straightforward.

▲ Do you think dating is dead?

Initiating Friendships   In any relationship, even friendships, initiating conversation can be difficult because people may fear rejection. In fact, many people assume that the other person's failure to initiate a conversation is because of a lack of interest (Vorauer & Ratner, 1996). If everyone felt this way, however, no relationship would ever begin! Therefore, you may need to begin the conversation if you wish to meet new people.

What is the best way to approach a new person? A nonthreatening comment such as "This sure is an interesting class" usually works, as does a question expressing interest in the other person, such as "Are you a communication major?" If the other person is receptive, you will feel more comfortable continuing the conversation. And if the person doesn't respond in a way that furthers the conversation, you can easily move on.

Once you begin the conversation, you can keep it going by asking a broad, open-ended question. For example, you could ask, "Why did you choose this university?" or "What do you enjoy doing when you're not working?" The idea is to ask questions that can't be answered with a yes or no or with only a brief response. Your goal is to get the other person talking and to learn more about him or her.

Of course, initiating a conversation isn't enough to move you from meeting someone to having an established relationship. A key skill for successfully moving a relationship forward is the ability to share and elicit communication that is appropriate for the stage of your relationship—neither revealing all the intimate details of your life nor withholding all of your thoughts, values, and experiences. Both of these approaches can lead to problems as we try to develop and maintain relationships. **Social penetration theory** describes how the process of disclosing, or revealing, ourselves through communication shapes relationships (Altman & Taylor, 1973, 1987). According to this theory, people gradually increase their self-disclosure as they get to know one another and, through a process of reciprocal disclosure, strangers become friends or lovers. The authors propose that self-disclosure occurs across three dimensions: breadth, depth, and frequency:

social penetration theory
Theory that proposes relationships develop through increases in self-disclosure.

- *Breadth* describes the number of different topics dyads willingly discuss. For example, you probably discuss only a few general topics with strangers, such as movies, what you do for a living, or hobbies; however, as you become more intimate with others you likely discuss a wider range of topics, including how you feel about the people in your life or dreams you have for the future.

- *Depth* refers to how deep or personal communication exchanges are; people tend to provide superficial disclosures to strangers (e.g., I like Thai food) and reserve more personal revelations for their intimates (e.g., I am disgusted if the different foods on my plate touch each other). The depth of your conversations increases as you learn more about others.

- *Frequency* is how often self-disclosure occurs; individuals usually share more disclosures with people with whom they are close.

Altman and Taylor propose that through increases in communication breadth, depth, and frequency people become more familiar with and trusting of one another, and as they become closer, they feel comfortable revealing more of themselves. Through this circular process, relationships of increasing intimacy are developed. This process seems relatively clear and possibly easy, so why do some people have difficulty forming relationships? Often, the problem these people encounter is that they either don't understand that disclosure is a process that occurs over time or they do not understand the norms of disclosure for their relationships.

As discussed in Chapter 8, what is considered "disclosure" can differ across cultures. In the United States, for example, people may disclose problems in their families or personal stories about their lives. In China, by contrast, revealing that a relative is ill or that one is not fond of one's sibling is considered impolite in any but the closest of relationships. If you don't know the norms for disclosure you might reveal more than others are comfortable hearing, and they may consider you odd, inappropriate, or someone to avoid. Similarly, if you are in a culture that discloses a lot of information easily, and you don't reciprocate that disclosure, you may be seen as secretive, unfriendly, or hard to talk with. Learning how much disclosure is appropriate at different times in the relationship affects how people perceive strangers and acquaintances and how likely they will be to strike up a relationship with them.

If you and your partner successfully navigate the process of meeting and developing a relationship, you will then need to develop a way to maintain your relationship.

Maintaining Relationships

Effective communication is, of course, essential to developing and maintaining relationships. In fact, a strong association exists between peoples' communication skills and their satisfaction with their relationships, particularly romantic ones (Emmers-Sommers, 2004; Noller & Fitzpatrick, 1990). It appears that effective communication and relationship satisfaction operate in a circular process in which effective communication increases couples' happiness with their relationships, and satisfaction with the relationship leads to more effective communication. Communication also is essential to developing friendships. Most of the important functions that friends serve—providing companionship and a sense of belonging, offering emotional and physical support as well as reassurance, and giving feedback on self-disclosures—are communication-based (Duck, 1991).

Although initiating friendships and romances can produce anxiety, it can also be exhilarating and fun. When relationships are new, we tend to focus on their more positive aspects. However, as relationships endure, we have a harder time ignoring their shortcomings. Consequently, maintaining relationships over time can be challenging. However, communication can help us meet these challenges in two essential ways: through helping us manage common tensions that arise in our relations and by allowing us to engage in interactions that sustain our connections to each other.

▼ A strong association exists between people's communication skills and their satisfaction with their relationships.

Maintaining Romantic Relationships through Communication   Communication professor Leslie Baxter and her colleagues have proposed relationship dialectics to explain how relationships develop and are maintained. As you may remember from Chapter 8, *dialectic* refers to the tension people experience when they have two seemingly contradictory but connected values or needs. As you will see, developing close relationships is associated with the ability to manage these contradictory but connected desires.

For example, perhaps you feel lonely when you are separated from your romantic partner, but sometimes you feel suffocated when you're together. You want to be able to tell your best friend anything, but also sometimes you feel the need for privacy. These types of feelings arise when you experience a dialectical tension, and they are common in all types of relationships. How you respond to and manage these tensions

It Happened to Me
Laurel

I started seeing this guy a few weeks ago, and finally I understand why I've been feeling the way I do. Although I enjoy being with him, I have started to feel smothered. He wants to talk on the phone several times a day, he texts me constantly when we are apart, and he wants to spend more evenings together than I do. I enjoy hanging out with my friends and being alone; he wants to be with me all the time. I was beginning to think there was something wrong with him, and then I read Baxter's article on relationship dialectics. Now I think we just have different needs for autonomy. However, I don't know if we will be able to manage this so that we'll both be happy.

impacts how successfully you can develop and maintain relationships.

Three primary dialectical tensions exist in relationships: autonomy/connection, expressiveness/privacy, and change/predictability (Baxter, 1988). Autonomy/connection refers to one's need to connect with others and the simultaneous need to feel independent or autonomous. For example, early in relationships people typically have a high need to feel connected to their romantic partners and can barely tolerate being separated from them. But as the relationship develops, most people need time away from their partners so they don't feel stifled or overwhelmed. Once this occurs, they are faced with managing the autonomy/connection dialectic both as individuals and as members of a dyad. That means that if they have too much connection, one person may feel overwhelmed and withdraw from the relationship (see *It Happened to Me: Laurel*).

The second tension, expressiveness/privacy, builds on social penetration theory. It describes the need to be open and to self-disclose while also maintaining some sense of privacy. For example, although Warren may reveal his feelings about his romantic partner to his closest friend, he may not disclose that he was fired from his first job. To maintain their relationships, dyads need to manage this tension effectively. As we mentioned in our discussion of social penetration theory, if you reveal too much information too early, others may find your communication behavior inappropriate and may shy away from you. On the other hand, if you fail to open up and express yourself, others may perceive you as aloof or cold and may not continue the relationship. Thus, this dialectical tension is important to relationships in the initiating stage of development as well as during the development and maintenance stages.

Finally, the change/predictability tension delineates the human desire for events that are new, spontaneous, and unplanned while simultaneously needing some aspects of life to be stable and predictable. For example, you probably want your partner's affection for you to be stable and predictable, but you might like your partner to surprise you occasionally with a new activity or self-disclosure. Relationships that are completely predictable (that is, certain) may become boring, but those that are totally spontaneous are unsettling; either extreme may render the relationship difficult to sustain.

Dialectics are constantly in process. Each day, couples and friends manage their individual and relationship needs for autonomy/connection, expressiveness/privacy, and change/predictability; the manner in which they manage these tensions influences the continuance of their relationships. Understanding dialectical tensions is useful because it can help you respond to the competing feelings you may experience in relationships.

relational maintenance

Behaviors that couples perform that help maintain their relationships.

To understand more specifically how couples maintain successful relationships, communication researchers Dan Canary and Laura Stafford conducted some of the earliest studies of how couples strategically keep their relationships satisfying. Based on their research, they created a typology of **relational maintenance** behaviors that heterosexual, gay, and lesbian couples use (Canary & Stafford, 1994; Haas & Stafford, 1998; see Table 9.3).

More recently, scholars have examined the nonstrategic, routine behaviors couples perform that help maintain their relationships. They determined that individuals use twelve types of conversational behaviors in their daily lives, including humor/joking, self-report (or self-disclosure), positivity (attempts to make interactions pleasant), and talking about television. Moreover, these couples tended to engage in more conflict, humor, household task talk, and planning on weekends than during the work week (Alberts, Yoshimura, Rabby, & Loschiavo, 2005).

Maintaining Friendships through Communication   Conversation plays an important role in friendship as well. One study determined that many conversations with friends last only about three minutes and that these conversations were mostly small talk. Nonetheless, people rated these conversations as highly significant (Duck, 1991). Thus, intimate disclosures may be important, but so are daily, routine interactions, which connect friends and reaffirm or maintain their relationships.

▼ Couples maintain their relationships through routine as well as strategic behaviors.

Interestingly, scholars have found that friends are most satisfied with each other when they possess similar levels of communication skills (Burleson & Samter, 1996). It is not how skillful friends are overall that predicts their satisfaction with each other, but whether they possess "similar or different degrees of communication skill (or lack of skill)" (Dainton, M. A., Zelley, E., & Langan, E. (2003). Maintaining friendships throughout the lifespan. In D. J. Canary & M. Dainton (Eds.), Maintaining relationships through communication (pp. 79–102). Mahwah, NJ: Erlbaum.).

Table 9.3   Couples' Relationship Maintenance Behaviors

Behavior	Description	Example
Positivity	Acting cheerful, positive; upbeat; doing favors for one another	Giving compliments, speaking positively about the future, running errands for one's partner
Openness	Sharing one's feelings and encouraging one's partner to do the same; talking about one's concerns and listening to one's partner	Expressing one's love and affection as well as fears and worries—and encouraging one's partner to do the same
Assurances	Reminding a partner about one's love and commitment to the relationship	Saying I love you, talking about the future, stressing one's commitment to the relationship
Sharing tasks	Helping equally with tasks, performing household responsibilities	Offering to do things that aren't one's responsibility, such as walking a partner's dog
Social networks	Spending time with friends; engaging in routine events and rituals	Inviting friends over to socialize; celebrating birthdays and holidays
Joint activities	Spending time with one another	Watching television together, going to movies, hiking with each other
Cards/letters/calls	Using mediated communication	Texting, telephoning, emailing each other
Avoidance	Spending time apart; refusing to discuss particular issues	Spending time with friends instead of one another; changing the topic when unwanted issues arise
Anti-social	Engaging in behaviors that seem unfriendly or unpleasant	Acting temperamental, moody, or critical to create distance in the relationship
Humor	Being funny in positive or negative ways	Making jokes, teasing, and being sarcastic

SOURCE: Canary, D., Stafford, L., Hause, K., & Wallace, L. (1993). An inductive analysis of relational maintenance strategies: Comparisons among lovers, relatives, friends, and others. *Communication Research Reports*, 10, 5–14.

What are some maintenance behaviors that friends use to keep their relationships alive? Not surprisingly, they use: assurances (indicating the importance of the friendship), positivity, open discussion, and listening as well as simply spending time together and keeping in touch though face-to-face or online messages (Fehr, 2000; Johnson, 2000; Messman, Canary, & Hause, 2000). Furthermore, it has been found that absence of interaction is often given as the reason for a friendship ending (Dainton et al., 2003).

Although research shows that straight, gay, and lesbian couples use similar strategies to maintain their romantic relationships and friendships, this does not mean that straight and gay dyads face similar issues regarding maintenance of their relationships. Although it is true that some heterosexual romantic couples start out as friends or maintain a friendship after the romance is over, gays and lesbians typically have much more crossover between their friendship and romantic relationships for several reasons. First, because gay male and lesbian communities often are small, individuals may experience pressure to remain friends with former romantic partners to preserve harmony within their social circles (Peplau, 2009). In addition, partners in gay and lesbian relationships often receive significantly less social and practical support from their families, so their friends are major providers of support and more central to their lives. Consequently, when couples break up, they likely are more invested in their joint friendships and have a stronger desire to maintain some of the social support they have developed as a couple (Fingerhut & Peplau, 2013). Finally, because their networks are smaller, lesbians and gay men have smaller pools from which to select friend and romantic partners. For these reasons, gay men and lesbian women may have stronger incentives and more need to maintain their relationships.

As you can see, communication is essential to both friendship and romantic relationship maintenance. However, sometimes we find ourselves unable, or unwilling, to invest energy in maintaining previously valued friendships or romances.

Ending Relationships

Not all relationships endure. When couples consistently engage in behaviors that are not satisfying, one or both partners likely will exit the relationship. Some courtship relationships end after the first date, whereas others end after months or years. Friendships end as well. Relatively few people retain all the friends they make over the course of their lives (Rawlins, 1992). Despite this, relationship termination can be an awkward stage—both to experience and to study.

People generally are much more willing to answer questionnaires and speak with researchers about developing or maintaining a relationship than about ending one. Studying this process is also difficult because relationship de-escalation and termination typically occur over an extended period, with no easy way to say when exactly the process began. Some relationships do end abruptly and decisively, however. The two basic trajectories for ending romantic relationships as well as friendships are called *sudden death* and *passing away* (Duck, 1982; Hays, 1988).

Sudden death refers to relationships that end without prior warning (at least for one participant). Some people are shocked to discover their partners are leaving. Although unexpected for the one partner, the other may have been thinking about his or her departure for some time. Occasionally an event occurs, such as

sudden death

Process by which relationships end without prior warning for at least one participant or due to a betrayal.

▼ Communication is key to maintaining friendships.

▲ Romantic relationships may end due to a lack of autonomy, compatibility, and supportiveness, as well infidelity.

passing away
Process by which relationships decline over time.

infidelity or betrayal, that so damages the relationship that the partners terminate the relationship relatively quickly.

More typically, relationships experience a **passing away**, or decline over time, and the partners are aware that problems remain unresolved. During this period, the partners may vacillate between attempts to improve the relationship and efforts to de-escalate it. Over months or even years, romantic couples may seek counseling, take trips together, or try other methods to improve the relationship, whereas friends may sporadically try to renew their friendship. At the same time, they may develop outside interests or friends as they withdraw from the relationship. It can be a difficult period, especially for romantic couples.

To help you understand this often-confusing stage of relationship development, we next explore the reasons that relationships end and the communication strategies people use to terminate them.

Reasons and Strategies for Courtship Dissolution When asked why their relationship terminated, gay and heterosexual couples provide similar reasons: lack of autonomy, lack of similarity/compatibility, lack of supportiveness, and infidelity. Heterosexual couples also indicated that insufficient shared time, inequity, and the absence of romance contributed to the demise of their relationships (Baxter, 1991; Kurdek, 1991).

People also terminate relationships because characteristics they thought they liked in a partner become less appealing over time. One study determined that in almost one-third of the courtship relationships examined, the qualities individuals initially found attractive became the qualities that led to the end of the relationship (Felmlee, 1995), a concept called *fatal attractions*. For example, one woman liked her relational partner because he had a "don't-care" attitude and liked to have fun, but later she found him irresponsible (Felmlee, 1995).

When relationships end, everyone looks for explanations. People blame themselves, they blame the other person, and they may even blame people outside the relationship. Sometimes no one is to blame (Duck, 1991). For example, relationships may end because the partners live too far apart or the timing is wrong. You might meet Ms. or Mr. Right, but if you meet immediately following a painful breakup or just as you are beginning a new and demanding job, you won't have the emotional stability or time needed to develop a successful relationship. In sum, relationship termination is normal, though it can be difficult.

Researchers have identified five general categories of disengagement strategies for dissolving romantic relationships (Cody, 1982):

negative identity management
Communicating in ways that arouse negative emotions to make the other person upset enough to agree to break off the relationship.

de-escalation strategies
A broad category that includes promising some continued closeness and suggesting that the couple might reconcile in the future.

1. Surprisingly (or perhaps not), the most frequent strategy romantic couples use to end their relationships is **negative identity management**, which means communicating in ways that arouse negative emotions to make the other person upset enough to agree to break off the relationship, e.g., criticizing one's romantic partner or conveying indifference to his or her feelings and desires.

2. **De-escalation strategies**, a broad category, were next used most often and included behaviors such promising some continued closeness ("we can still be friends") and suggesting that the couple might reconcile in the future—conversations that attempt to reframe or change the definition of the relationship.

3. **Justification strategies** occurred third most frequently. As the label implies, justification strategies attempt to provide a reason or excuse for why the relationship has failed and should end, for example, explaining the positive consequences of ending the relationship ("we can devote more time to our careers") or the negative consequences of not ending the relationship ("we will come to hate each other"), or addressing the feelings and concerns of the partner ("I care for you, but you deserve someone who can commit to you").

4. **Positive tone strategies** were next most often used. These strategies expressed caring, sadness about the termination of the relationships, and a desire to be fair.

5. **Behavioral de-escalation** strategies occurred least frequently and involved avoiding the partner. Behavioral de-escalation strategies likely are the least common because it is difficult to avoid a person with whom you have a romantic relationship. If Richard doesn't return Jamie's phone calls or avoids the classes they have together, Jamie most likely will track him down to find out why.

justification strategies
Providing a reason or excuse for ending the relationship.

positive tone strategies
Communicating concern for the rejected partner and trying to make the person feel better.

behavioral de-escalation
Avoiding the partner.

Reasons and Strategies for Friendship Dissolution Why do friendships end? Friendships are particularly vulnerable to termination because few societal pressures encourage their continuance (Blieszner & Adams, 1992) and because friends may not expect to have consistent contact. Some friendships decline without either person being aware of it. Once the friends recognize the decline, it may no longer be possible for the relationship to recover. Thus, friendships, unlike romantic relationships, can end without either person being dissatisfied with the relationship.

Friendships end for a range of reasons, based on how close the friendship was. Casual friends are more likely to report that their relationships ended because of a lack of proximity, whereas close and best friends more often state that their relationships terminated because of decreased affection. In addition, best and close friends report that their friendships dissolved as a result of interference from other relationships, such as one person's romantic partner (Johnson et al., 2004).

Scholars have identified five specific factors that can contribute to the termination of a friendship: lack of communication skills, rule-breaking, deception, boredom, and other reasons (Duck, 1988). With regard to the first factor, if you wish to maintain relationships you must display appropriate communication skills. We know that poor conversationalists tend to be lonely (Duck, 1988) and that lonely people are not perceived to be competent communicators (Canary & Spitzberg, 1985).

Friendships also end because one or both members violate fundamental, often unspoken, rules of the relationship that have been established over the course of the friendship (Argyle & Henderson, 1984; Bowker, 2004). For example, most friends believe that good friends don't gossip about each other, flirt with each other's romantic partners, or lie to each other. Successful relationship partners discern the rules of the relationship and adhere to them.

Because friendships are generally less formal than romantic relationships, the termination strategies used in them may be more subtle and less obvious (Hays, 1988). For example, a friend's permission is not required to end a friendship, and one can simply stop contacting a friend, which happens only rarely in romantic relationships.

When friends desire relationship dissolution, they are likely to use one or more of the following disengagement strategies: withdrawal/avoidance, Machiavellian tactics, positive tone, and openness (Baxter, 1982). As with behavioral de-escalation among romantic couples, when friends engage in **withdrawal/avoidance** they spend less time together, don't return phone calls, and avoid places where they are likely to see the other. **Machiavellian tactics** involve a different type of avoidance; they use a third party to communicate one's unhappiness about the relationship and one's desire to de-escalate or end it. **Positive tone strategies** are similar to positive tone tactics used by romantic couples; they communicate concern for the rejected friend and try to make the person

Critical Thinking Prompt
What rules do you have for close friendships? That is, what could a friend do that would be such a significant violation of your expectations that you would terminate your friendship?

withdrawal/avoidance
Friendship termination strategy in which friends spend less time together, don't return phone calls, and avoid places where they are likely to see each other.

Machiavellian tactics
Having a third party convey one's unhappiness about a relationship.

openness

Straightforwardly explaining why the relationship is ending.

feel better. Thus, you might tell a friend that you wish to end your friendship because school and work take up too much time, rather than admitting you do not enjoy his or her company any more. Finally, **openness** means that one straightforwardly explains to one's friend why the relationship is ending.

Although this section has focused on how and why friendships and romances end, relationship termination isn't the only difficulty friends and romantic partners face. Individuals face relationship problems at all stages. In the next section, we discuss some of the communication challenges that can occur in close relationships.

Aversive Communication Behaviors in Relationships

Although relationships can provide love, companionship, and joy, they also can be the source of some of our greatest suffering. Once we open ourselves to intimacy and commitment, we also open ourselves to the possibility of hurt and betrayal. Not all communication behaviors are associated with successful or satisfying relationships; some have negative effects on relationships, the topic we discuss next.

Close relationships are often marked by the presence of aversive, or negative, behaviors. According to Miller (1997), 44 percent of us are likely to be annoyed by a relational partner on any given day, and young adults have 8.7 annoying experiences with their romantic partners weekly. In the context of our close relationships, we "criticize, nag, betray, lie, disappoint, ostracize, embarrass, and tease one another, to name just a few behaviors" (Kowalski, Valentine, Wilkinson, Queen, & Sharpe, 2003, p. 473). Whatever the intention of the perpetrator, these negative actions are likely to hurt their victims. In turn, victims often respond with even more negative behaviors, which can lead to a cycle of blame and criticism (Kowalski et al., 2003), and if these behaviors occur too frequently or the cycle escalates, they can devastate close relationships.

deception

Concealment, distortion, or dishonesty in communication.

Deception   Some types of **deception** can impair relationships, though not all. For example, a person may withhold information because it is too private to share or because it might cause pain. For example, one might tell a friend "Dinner was wonderful," even if it was a bit burned and bitter; however, individuals who discover they've been deceived about an important issue become resentful, disappointed, and suspicious (Bok, 1978; Sagarin, Rhoads, & Cialdini, 1998).

Although relationship partners consider deception to be a rare occurrence, research indicates that concealment and distortion of information are integral to many conversations and relationships. As many as 80 to 90 percent of people admit to deceiving their partners (Turner, Edgley, & Olmstead, 1975), and the most frequent issue individuals deceive their partners about is competing relationships.

The findings about deception in dating relationships are especially interesting for two reasons: First, research has established that people are not good at detecting deception (Burgoon et al., 2014) and second, most people assume that those they love tell the truth (Buller & Burgoon, 1996). This strong tendency to not suspect

▼ Close relationships are often marked by the presences of aversive, or negative, behaviors.

our intimates is called the **truth bias** and research shows that people generally do not look for cues that a partner is deceiving them (McCornack & Parks, 1986). However, once suspicion has been introduced, romantic partners' deception detection improves (Stiff, Kim, & Ramesh, 1989). Thus, you probably have a fairly good chance of deceiving your partner *unless* she or he is suspicious; in that case, you are more likely to get caught.

Lying can be devastating to friendships. College students report being as distressed by a friend's betrayal of their confidences as by a romantic partner's infidelity (Cauffman, Feldman, Jensen, & Arnett, 2000). Some people expect their friends to be even more honest and open with them than are their romantic partners, and the failure to be truthful is one of the primary reasons friends give for terminating their friendships.

Jealousy Given the findings about deception, it is not surprising that one of the more problematic types of communication for dating couples is the expression of jealousy. **Jealousy** is a complex and often painful emotion that frequently leads to ineffective communication. The feeling combines anger, sadness, worry, embarrassment, and disappointment (Guerrero, Trost & Yoshimura, 2005). Jealousy occurs when a person perceives a threat to an existing relationship. Jealousy seems to flow from feelings of insecurity about the relationship or the ability to cope with a change in it (Rydell & Bringle, 2007).

Men and women often differ in the ways they express and manage jealousy. Men are more likely to consider leaving the relationship and to become involved with other partners in an attempt to repair their self-esteem; women are more likely to focus on repairing the relationship (Buss, 1988; White & Mullen, 1989).

One problematic aspect of jealousy concerns the manner in which couples communicate about their jealous feelings (Bevan, 2013). Communication researchers have discovered that how couples deal with and communicate about jealousy has a stronger impact on the relationship than the jealous feelings themselves (Andersen, Eloy, Guerrero, & Spitzberg, 1995). Paradoxically, jealous people tend to seek proof to justify their feelings. In some relationships, an individual can dispel the partner's fears, but this requires trust. Unfortunately, jealousy often arises because one partner has little trust in the relationship. Thus, jealous people may reject all assurances and even escalate their accusations (White & Mullen, 1989).

Regrettably, some communication interactions about jealousy lead to physical violence (Harrusm, 2003). A study of 138 jealous subjects determined that almost 80 percent had acted aggressively because of their jealousy, and more than 50 percent had actually assaulted their partners (Mullen & Maack, 1985). What types of communication are more likely to escalate interactions about jealousy to these dangerous levels?

Overt rejection or the expression of disdain by an accused partner during an argument can precipitate relationship violence (Psarska, 1970). For example, a partner accused of infidelity may angrily reply, "I've never been involved with anyone else, but who knows why, since you are such a lousy partner." The feelings of jealousy themselves give rise to strong passions, but the hostile response of the loved one may influence expressions of jealousy to explode into violence (White & Mullen, 1989).

Although jealousy may be more common in romantic relationships, it does exist within friendships (Lavallee &

truth bias
The tendency to not suspect one's intimates of deception.

jealousy
A complex and often painful emotion that occurs when a person perceives a threat to an existing relationship.

▼ Jealousy often arises because one partner has little trust in the relationship.

Parker, 2008). For example, if a person is becoming close to a second friend and fails to include his first friend in their joint activities, the first may feel the relationship is threatened and experience jealousy.

Individuals are often jealous of their friends' romantic partners as well. When people fall in love, they often focus intently on their romantic partners, to the detriment of their friendships (Roth & Parker, 2001). However, the friend who communicates those feelings of insecurity and jealousy poorly can damage the friendship. Criticizing the third party, engaging in aggression toward the third party, or complaining repeatedly to the friend can lead to increased conflict and rejection (Grotpeter & Crick, 1996).

interpersonal violence

Physical violence against a partner or child.

Interpersonal Violence **Interpersonal violence**—physical violence against a partner or child—is a serious problem in the United States. Research indicates that current or former boyfriends or girlfriends commit most domestic violence. This is true for both females (39 percent) and males (30 percent), although the majority of domestic violence is committed against females (76 percent), compared to males at 24 percent (Bureau of Justice Statistics, 2014).

Research indicates that domestic violence among same-sex couples occurs at similar rates as domestic violence among straight couples. (Rohrbaugh, 2006). Same-sex domestic violence also is similar in many ways to that in heterosexual couples. Both experience the following: patterns of abuse that include physical, emotional, and psychological harm; the abuser sufferers from mental illness or suffered abuse as a child; the abuser blackmails his or her partner into silence, and physical abuse and sexual abuse co-occur. However, there are notable differences. Gay and lesbian abusers may threaten to "out" their partners, which can have negative consequences for their family lives, friendships, and employment status. Similarly, gay and lesbian targets may be more reluctant to contact law enforcement because doing so will reveal their sexual orientation. In addition, in gay and lesbian relationships, abusers can threaten to take away their partners' children because in some states a non-birth parent has no legal parental rights. Another difference is that gay and lesbian victims are more likely to fight back than are heterosexual women (Center for American Progress, 2011).

Two types of interpersonal aggression can occur in gay, straight, and lesbian romantic relationships: battering and situational couple violence. *Battering* describes relationships in which one individual uses violence as a way to control and dominate his or her partner (though most batterers are male). *Situational couple violence* is characterized by less intense forms of violence and tends to be more mutual in its performance, although women usually suffer more serious injuries than do men. During situational couple violence, couples may engage in pushing, shoving, slapping, or throwing objects, but they typically don't engage in beating one another severely or using weapons, in contrast to battering

Research reveals that couples who engage in situational couple violence lack fundamental communication and problem-solving skills, and they appear unable to let even small matters slide (Lloyd, 1990). These couples are more likely than nonabusive couples to attack each other's character, curse, and threaten their partners. They also make few attempts to de-escalate the conflict or facilitate their conversations calmly (Cordova, Jacobsen, Gottman, Rushe, & Cox, 1993; Sabourin, 1996). In addition, husbands in aggressive relationships attribute hostile intent to their wives' communication and behavior and respond negatively when their wives attempt to influence them (Anglin & Holtzworth-Munroe, 1997). Thus, the communication of couples who engage in situational violence appears to contribute significantly to their hostility and abuse.

Situational violence is also present in friendship and peer relationships. Aggressive behavior among friends includes: physical aggression (pushing, shoving, or hitting), verbal aggression (intimidating others as well as engaging in malicious teasing, taunting, and name-calling), and indirect aggression (gossiping, spreading cruel rumors, and encouraging others to reject or exclude someone). Situational violence among peers can also take place in the form of online harassment and bullying—which is discussed further in Chapter 14.

Sexual Coercion   Sexual coercion is another type of negative, potentially violent, interaction in which the participants' communication is of importance (Willan & Pollard, 2003). People often find it difficult to discuss sexual coercion. Part of the problem arises from lack of clarity on what it is. **Sexual coercion** is most effectively defined as "the act of using pressure, alcohol or drugs, or force to have sexual contact with someone against his or her will, (including) persistent attempts to have sexual contact with someone who has already refused" (Struckman-Johnson, C. J., Struckman-Johnson, B. L., & Anderson, B. (2003). Tactics of sexual coercion: When men and women won't take no for an answer. Journal of Sex Research, 40(1), 76–86.). Some people believe that a person who "gives in" to such pressure is equally to blame; however, sometimes people engage in unwanted sex because of concern for the relationship, difficulty with resisting pressure, or real concern for personal safety (Spitzberg, 1998).

> **sexual coercion**
> Physically nonviolent pressure to engage in unwanted sex.

Individuals of all sexes and sexual orientations experience unwanted sexual behaviors, though the degree to which groups experience it differs. One of the more comprehensive studies on unwanted sex was conducted by the Centers for Disease Control and Prevention in 2010. Researchers there found that over their lifetimes: approximately 18 percent of women and 1.4 percent of men report being raped; 13 percent of women and 6 percent of men experienced sexual coercion, and 27 percent of women and 12 percent of men were subjected to unwanted sexual contact, such as hugging, kissing, touching (Black et al., 2011).

Other studies have determined that lesbians and bisexual women experienced unwanted sex at rates similar to heterosexual women. However, the unwanted sex experienced by gay and bisexual men is markedly different from that of heterosexual men (Menning & Holtzman, 2014). In one study, 11.6 percent of gay men and 13 percent of bisexual men reported being raped (Balsam, Beauchaine, & Rothblum, 2005).

As these studies suggest, sexual assault is pervasive, and men as well as women suffer from abuse. How is sexual assault a communication issue? Although some sexual assaults are perpetrated by strangers, the majority of them are committed by friends, acquaintances, and romantic partners. In these cases, communication can play a significant role, especially when sexual coercion occurs. Perpetrators of sexual coercion use a variety of verbal tactics to pressure individuals into sexual acts. Some badger the person or beg until he or she relents; other use bribes, persuasion, or the threat of withdrawing their affection or themselves from the relationship. In addition, the targets of coercion often are people who have difficulty defending themselves and their positions or who have been taught to be compliant and overly considerate of others.

What can you do to prevent yourself from becoming a target—or a perpetrator? The ability to discuss consent is one important way. The ability to talk about what each party wants and would willingly participate in needs to be articulated and respected. Don't discount your partner's refusal. That is, don't assume that your partner is using *token resistance*, that is, saying no then giving in (Muehlenhard & Hollabough, 1988); any indication of reluctance or refusal should be honored. If anyone tries to persuade you into sexual contact that you do not want, do not engage in arguing or explaining your position. Once you begin to explain your position, you provide information for the other party to use to persuade you that your "reasons" are not valid. You are better off simply stating what your position is (No, I don't want to . . .). When asked why you won't do something, simply say "because I don't want to." Here are some specific ways you can respond to sexual pressure (McCoy, K., & Oelschlager, J. 2011):

- "I really like you. I'm just not ready to have sex."
- "If you really care about me, you'll respect my decision."
- "I said no. I don't owe you an explanation."

Other ways you can protect yourself from being a target or a perpetrator is to avoid drinking or being around people who are drinking or not isolating yourself from other people in your environment. Most importantly, be clear to yourself about what you want. Indecisive people can be coerced or persuaded to engage in behavior they will later regret.

How can you tell if you are being coerced? If your partner makes comments such as "If you value me and our relationship, you'll have sex with me" or "We've had sex before, so you can't say no" or attempts to make you feel that you "owe" him or her sex because of money your partner has spent, then you are probably experiencing sexual coercion (McCoy, K., & Oelschlager, J. 2011). If you would like additional information on preventing unwanted sex, the health clinics and security departments of most colleges and universities can provide pamphlets, books, and other resources.

The effectiveness of individuals' communication plays an important role in how enduring and rewarding their relationships are. Thus, individuals are at the center of relationships, and what they say and do affects their relationships at every stage. However, societal norms and pressures shape relationships as well. In the next section, we examine relationships within this broader frame.

Journal Prompt 9.3: Flirting and Communication
Consider the following questions:
What strategies do women use to initiate a relationship through flirting? How do men and women compare in their understanding and interpretation of women's flirting communication?

The Individual, Relationship Communication, and Society

9.4   Explain the role that society plays in the formation and maintenance of interpersonal relationships.

Most heterosexuals are unaware of the effect of cultural norms on their romance choices (O'Brien & Foley, 1999) and on how they express affection and commitment in them. Until 50 years ago, partners of different races could not legally have intimate relationships in the United States; until the year 2000, Alabama still had a law against interracial marriages (Root, 2001; Sollors, 2000). Unsurprisingly, the vast majority of marriages in the United States are still racially homogeneous. Moreover, they occur primarily between people of similar religious backgrounds (Watson, Klohnen, Casillas, Simms, Haig, & Berry, 2004), economic status (Kalmijin, 1994), age (Watson, Klohnen, Casillas, Simms, Haig, & Berry, 2004), education (Bennhold, 2012), weight (Schafer & Keith, 1990), and appearance (Little, Burt, & Perrett, 2006). Such a high degree of similarity, or **homogeneity**, suggests individual preference is not the only factor influencing our choices.

Commonly held stereotypes also influence choices about whom one should or should not date and marry. For example, some interracial pairings are more common than others. In 75 percent of Black–White marriages, the husband is Black, and in 75 percent of White–Asian couples, the husband is White (Sailer, 2003). The frequency of these pairings reflects strong societal norms about who is attractive (and who is not).

homogeneity
High degree of similarity.

▼ People are drawn to others who are highly similar to themselves.

As discussed earlier (in Chapter 8), communication norms vary across cultures, and the romance context is no exception. For example, in some cultures (e.g., Japan, Indonesia, Kuwait), romantic couples rarely express their feelings or affections in public (Chung, 2016). Other cultures prohibit public expressions of affection, as in Indonesia, where it is illegal to kiss in public (MSNBC News, 2004). Thus, every relationship is situated within a set of societal and cultural norms and expectations, and what occurs within that relationship is likely to be affected by those norms.

Cultural norms and legal policies also impact the ways in which LGBTQ individuals can communicate with and about their romantic partners. They often can't express affection in public without fear of negative, even violent, responses. For this reason, they may refer to their lovers as "friends" or "roommates" or attempt to conceal their romantic partner's sex by never using pronouns such as *him* or *her*. Having to alter one's verbal and nonverbal behavior to conform to society's norms may seem a small matter if you are heterosexual. But imagine what life would be like if in many contexts you could never acknowledge your partner or you had to pretend that you were "just friends." Not only would this be exhausting, it would significantly inhibit your ability to be close to others. Unfortunately, this is the life that many gays and lesbians live.

The practices of specific institutions (e.g., religions) impact our communication and relationships. For example, many faiths have long prescribed whom their members should marry, how many spouses they could have, and even if they should date. For example, the Mormon faith once permitted men to have more than one wife (although it no longer does); Muslim men are instructed to marry Muslim women; and Hindus often discourage young people from dating and selecting their own marital partners. Although over time religions can and do alter their positions on these issues (e.g., the Church of Jesus Christ of Latter Day Saints' position on polygamy), they may be slower to change than other social institutions. For example, a recent Pew Research survey found that although some Catholics are open to nontraditional families, 9 in 10 U.S. Catholics still believe that a household headed by a married mother and father is ideal for child-rearing. In these ways, religious institutions and beliefs influence how we view relationships as well as how we act within them and communicate about our relationships.

Similarly, business organizations create policies and practices that affect the types of relationships and communication practices their employees can have, for example, bans against "affectional relationships," fraternization—or relationships that cross the organizational hierarchy—in the military, and limits on nepotism (hiring one's family members. They express their views on same-sex relationships by providing, or not providing, domestic-partner benefits or even firing employees who marry same-sex partners. Organizations often create rules that attempt to control and influence employees' communication, through sexual harassment policies, secrecy clauses, and dictates on what can be communicated to others outside the organization.

In addition to shaping relationships in the ways already

> **Critical Thinking Prompt**
> What cultural factors – whether familial, religious, social, or organizational – have the greatest influence on your relationships?

▼ Societal institutions such as synagogues influence our communication and relationships.

discussed, societal factors influence negative aspects of romantic relationships, such as violence and rape. For example, most talk about violence in romantic relationships focuses on the behavior of individual aggressors rather than on the social structures that allow abuse (Payne & Smith, 2013). Most people assume that men and women experience equity in their relationships (Ferraro, 1996; Lloyd & Emery, 2000) and that men are not abused by their partners. However, the facts are that women typically earn less money than men, are more responsible for children than men, and often are physically weaker than men. These factors seriously compromise how equal women can be in heterosexual relationships and likely account for the fact that far more women are severely injured and murdered by their partners than vice versa (NCADV, 2015).

At the same time, little conversation occurs about violence against men; in fact, men who are abused are often ridiculed and stigmatized so that they have few places to turn for help and support (Kimmel, 2002).

In addition, the ways we talk about romance can encourage acceptance of aggression in relationships. For example, U.S. media frequently portray male aggression as normal and acceptable, as in romance novels, where male aggression is often a central, and recurrent, plot point. The popular image that men have urgent and difficult-to-control sexual drives implies that women are responsible for controlling sexual contact. Thus, more attention is paid to how *women* behave during unwanted sexual encounters than how men behave.

Finally, people frequently blame the victim. For example, people often ask "What was she doing out late at night by herself?" When we blame victims, we ask what they could have done to prevent the violence rather than focusing on what we should do as a culture to minimize relational aggression. Lloyd and Emery argue that how we define aggression is important; when we make statements such as "He just slapped her around a bit," we diminish the real emotional and physical trauma associated with assault. Overall, these researchers propose that if we truly wish to reduce the violence in relationships, we must examine and alter the ways we talk about relational aggression.

Unlike marriage, friendships are not governed by laws and institutions. However, social norms still affect our choice of friends or our behavior within friendships. Take a moment to think about your closest friends over the past five years. How similar are they to you? Do you have any friends who are decades older than you? How many of your friends are from a different ethnic group than you are? Clearly some people do have friends who differ from themselves on demographic factors such as race, age, income, and education, but this is more often the exception than the rule (Aboud & Mendelson, 1996). As we discussed in Chapter 8, these multicultural relationships, though potentially rewarding, sometimes take more "care and feeding" than relationships in which two people are similar. Intercultural friends may receive pressure from others, particularly from majority group members, to stick with people who are similar to them (Pogrebin, 1992).

Thus, friendship is not only an individual matter, but it also is a social event that occurs in contexts that exert a powerful influence on its development (Allan, 1977). In the United States, it is understood that friendships play an extremely important role in the lives of adolescents. In this culture, parents are encouraged to understand that their adolescent children will turn away from talking and spending time with them (Rawlins, 1992). By contrast, married adults are expected to place their romance partners and families before their friends (Dainton et al., 2003).

Journal Prompt 9.4: Society and Relationships
Consider the following questions: What are some ways in which society affects individuals' romantic relationships? How does society influence individuals' friendships?

Ethics and Close Relationships

9.5   Explain how to ensure that interactions with close others are authentic.

Although communicating ethically is important in all contexts and relationships, it is nowhere more important than in the context of close relationships. If we communicate unethically with our friends, family, and romantic partners, the consequences may be severe. Certainly relationships have ended as a result of deception, secrecy, and even the truth, too harshly expressed. All the ethical considerations we have discussed throughout this book are important in close relationships, but here we will focus on authentic communication.

Authentic communication is particularly important in close relationships for two reasons: We expect our closest friends and family members to be authentic, or "real," with us, and authentic communication is connected to intimacy. Why is authenticity in communication an ethical issue? Because inauthentic communication attempts to manipulate the interaction or the other person for one's own goals, it can be considered a type of deception, given that during inauthentic communication, one hides how one really feels and misrepresents one's feelings and beliefs. In addition, inauthentic communication denies people the information they need to make an informed choice about their relationships with others.

▲ To maintain an authentic relationship, you need to confront issues that are important to the relationship.

For most people, intimacy is based on the feeling that one knows and is known by another. When we feel intimate with others, we believe that we are connecting with their "true" selves and that we are able to be our truest selves in the relationship. However, when people are not authentic in their communication with those close to them or deny them the right to communicate authentically, it can decrease intimacy and even lead to termination of the relationship. And if we discover that an intimate friend or partner was being inauthentic and manipulative, we may feel not only deceived but betrayed. For example, if you discover that your friend has been pretending to like your romantic partner while making negative remarks about her on the sly, you might feel angry and betrayed. In addition, if you want to continue the relationship, you now have to deal not only with your friend's feelings about your romantic partner but also with your friend's deceit.

How can we ensure that our interactions with close others are authentic? We can do so by being open to others' communication efforts, being open in our own communication, taking responsibility for what we say, and respecting the rights of others to speak. In effect, we need to avoid the three "pitfalls" of inauthentic communication: topic avoidance, meaning denial, and disqualification.

1. **Topic avoidance.** To maintain an authentic relationship with another, it is vital to confront issues that are important to the relationship and to the other person. If one or both people in a relationship prohibit the other from discussing issues that are important to either of them, it can be difficult for them to maintain intimacy and commitment. For example, if a good friend wishes to discuss his or her sexual identity and one refuses to do so, she risks damaging the closeness and relationship with the other person by shutting down communication on this topic.

2. **Meaning denial.** In addition, authentic communication involves taking responsibility for what we say and mean. If one is angry and teases a friend harshly because of it, it is inauthentic to deny that one is angry and trying to be hurtful. Even worse, if one puts the onus on the friend for being "too sensitive," he may

be compounding the problem. Repeated interactions such as this can undermine trust and intimacy.

3. **Disqualification.** Finally, authentic communicators allow others to speak regardless of their own position or experience. If a single friend attempts to give relationship support and advice, she may feel disqualified if her friend refuses to listen because she isn't married. We also can disqualify a romantic partner by denying him or her the right to speak on a topic because of his or her sex or because we perceive ourselves to be more expert on the topic. If a person finds herself saying, "What could you know about this?" then she may be disqualifying the other party and potentially engaging in inauthentic communication.

Engaging in authentic communication can help people develop and maintain their relationships more effectively. To help you begin the process, we conclude this chapter with suggestions for how you can more effectively engage in an important but difficult type of relationship communication—hurtful messages.

Journal Prompt 9.5: Authenticity in Communication
Consider the following questions: What is authentic communication? Why is authenticity considered an ethical issue? What communication strategies can you use to ensure you engage in authentic communication?

Improving Your Relationship Communication Skills

9.6   Articulate how to deliver hurtful messages effectively.

Of the many communication skills that are important to the development and maintenance of close relationships, perhaps none is more difficult to enact than effectively offering negative feedback to one's friends, family, and romantic partners. The closer people are to one another and the more regularly they interact, the more often they may feel the need to express their dissatisfaction with the other person or the relationship.

Unfortunately, many people (unintentionally, and some perhaps intentionally) wound others when they attempt to express dissatisfaction (Vangelisti, 2007). When we do this, we are conveying hurtful messages. **Hurtful messages** occur when a person criticizes, teases, rejects, or otherwise causes an emotional injury to another (Folkes, 1982). Such messages often critique another person's behavior, appearance, abilities, personality, or identity. In general, they suggest the other party is deficient in some way. These messages are painful because they convey negative feelings and rejection (Vangelisti, 1994). The most upsetting messages tend to be those that convey dissatisfaction or a lack of regard for the relationship. Comments such as "I don't think we have anything in common anymore" or "I think we should start seeing other people" are perceived as the most distressing because they signal a fundamental shift in a partner's feelings.

Hurtful messages can be intentional or unintentional. Intentional messages are those that are perceived as being designed specifically to cause harm to the recipient. When people make hurtful comments to one another when angry, their messages typically are seen as intentional. Hurtful messages also can be unintentional, that is, not intended to hurt the recipient. People can utter unkind comments accidentally, out of thoughtlessness or insensitivity (Myers, Schrodt, & Rittenour, 2006). For example, small children are well known for making hurtful comments (e.g., "Why are you so fat?") because they lack awareness and perspective-taking abilities. Although unintentional hurtful messages may be somewhat less painful than those perceived as intentional (Mills, Nazar, & Farrell, 2002), both can wound the recipient and the relationship.

Of course, recipients' interpretations aren't based only on their perceptions of the other person's intentions. The way a message is framed also influences how it affects the recipient. The intensity and hurtfulness of the message impact the degree to which the recipient feels injured. Intensity refers to the degree of emphasis with which a speaker makes his or her claim (McEwen & Greenberg, 1970). For example, "I am miserable in our relationship" is more intense than "I am not as happy as I once was in our relationship." In addition, the harsher or more negative the language ("I can't stand

hurtful messages
Messages that criticize, tease, reject, or otherwise cause an emotional injury to another.

the sight of you"), the more painful the message is likely to be (Tracy, Van Dusen, & Robinson, 1987). By contrast, when a hurtful message is framed in a humorous manner it is perceived as less harsh, and recipients experience less intense feelings and less hurt than when a message is offered seriously (Young & Bippus, 2001).

Finally, the context in which the message is delivered can impact the recipient's feelings of injury. Hurtful speech that occurs when the dyad is alone may be painful, but if it occurs when others are present, that pain and discomfort often is intensified (Miller & Roloff, 2005). Hurtful comments, by definition, are attacks on the recipient's identity, so the presence of an audience can worsen the feeling of being denigrated plus add feelings of embarrassment.

Despite how painful they can be, at times we need to convey negative messages to our friends and romantic partners. Sometimes friends break rules we see as fundamental to a friendship, and we must address the issue to maintain our closeness. At other times we need to terminate a relationship with our romantic partner. Although it is unlikely that one could find a way to convey these messages painlessly, there are better and worse ways to communicate them. If you need to offer negative feedback in a close relationship, it is best to think through what you are going to say and how you are going to say it. Your message is likely to cause some hurt, but you can minimize its degree by following the guidelines in *Did You Know? Delivering Potentially Hurtful Messages*.

If, however, you have accidentally blurted out something, misspoken, or made a teasing remark that was not received well, you should consider attempting to repair the situation. Typically, apologies or justifications have some success at repairing a relationship after one makes a hurtful comment (Dunleavy, Goodboy, Booth-Butterfield, & Sidelinger, 2007). You can apologize for speaking without thinking or for attempting a joke that fell flat. You also can justify or explain your intentions and behavior. You can explain that you were trying to be funny, but weren't successful; that what you said didn't express what you meant to say; or that you were angry, stressed, or distracted so you didn't think carefully. Perhaps surprisingly, research suggests that justifications (which often place the blame outside the speaker) are more successful in romantic relationships than in professional ones (Dunleavy et al., 2007).

Journal Prompt 9.6: Hurtful Messages
Consider the following questions: What are some examples of hurtful messages? What are five things to consider when delivering hurtful messages?

DID YOU KNOW?
Delivering Potentially Hurtful Messages

Think of a time when you needed to tell someone something that might hurt his or her feelings. How did you handle the situation? Are there ways in which you might have handled it better?

Occasionally, almost everyone has to deliver a message that has the potential to cause the recipient emotional pain. Though you might not be able to avoid delivering such messages, you can learn how to minimize others' pain. To help you accomplish this, we offer the following guidelines for how to deliver hurtful messages more effectively:

1. Convey your message in private. Don't offer it in front of other people. Doing so in private will decrease feelings of hurt and embarrassment for the recipient and make it easier for him or her to respond without being defensive.

2. Use less intense and kinder language. You want to avoid: saying "always" and "never;" using harsh words (e.g., "you look ridiculous"), and using extreme language (e.g., "I hate it when you do that"). Instead, mitigate your statements ("Sometimes you . . ."); use softer language (e.g., "I worry that others won't see how wonderful you are"), and select more reasonable word choices (e.g., "I prefer it when . . .). Overall, be polite.

3. Express your intentions. You should express your concern, caring, and desire to help the other person. Let them know that you are making the comment because you want to help or bring out the best in him or her.

4. Offer fewer rather than more criticisms. Everyone finds friends and partners to be less than ideal. However, instead of offering frequent critiques, save your potentially hurtful comments for when they are most needed.

5. Use humor, if it is appropriate. Do not make fun of the other person, but if offering the comment humorously softens the blow, consider doing so.

SUMMARY

9.1 Describe the importance of close relationships.

- Close relationships are important because they affect our health and emotional well-being.

9.2 Explain five communication theories of relationship development.

- Attraction theory explains the influence of three factors—proximity, physical attractiveness, and similarity—on individuals likelihood of forming a relationship with another person.

- Two theories—uncertainty reduction theory and predicted outcome theory—explain how communication serves to increase or decrease intimacy and commitment in relationships.

- Two theories—social exchange theory and equity theory—explain how individuals evaluate their relationships based on the costs and rewards they accrue. Social exchange theory focuses on individuals' desire to maximize rewards and minimize costs in their relationships while equity theory argues that people are more satisfied in relationships they perceive as fair—where their costs are balanced by their rewards.

9.3 Identify tactics for initiating, maintaining, and terminating friendships and romantic relationships.

- Strategies for initiating relationships include opening with impersonal questions, listening attentively, being polite, expressing approval, and asking open-ended follow-up questions.

- Relationship maintenance strategies and behaviors include being open, expressing positivity, and offering assurances.

- The relationships termination strategies people are likely to use include negative identity management, positive tone strategies, justification, and de-escalation strategies.

9.4 Explain the role that society plays in the formation and maintenance of interpersonal relationships.

- Societal laws and norms influence whom we marry or befriend, how we communicate with relational partners, and how we communicate with the rest of the world about these relationships

9.5 Explain how to ensure that interactions with close others are authentic.

- Authentic communication requires that one: is open to others' communication efforts, open in one's own communication, takes responsibility for what one says, and respects the rights of others to speak.

9.6 Articulate how to deliver hurtful messages effectively.

- One can deliver hurtful messages more effectively by delivering them in private, using kinder and less intense language, expressing one's intentions, offering fewer rather than more criticisms, and using humor when appropriate.

KEY TERMS

APPLY WHAT YOU KNOW

1. **Maintaining Friendships and Romantic Relationships**

   Interview two people and ask them how they maintain their closest friendship. What conscious, deliberate strategies do they use to ensure they will stay close with their good friends? Also, what routine behaviors do they use to maintain closeness (for example, using nicknames, emailing funny stories)? Then interview two people and ask them the same questions about how they maintain their current romantic relationship. Finally, compare the four sets of responses. Do your interviewees use similar or different strategies for maintaining their friendships and their romances?

2. **Societal Influences on Relationships**

   Choose six popular magazines from your local grocery store. Be sure to select a wide range of magazines, including those directed toward men and women as well as some focused on political, social, and health issues. Skim through the magazines, first looking at the advertisements. What can you tell about the way friendships and romances are viewed in the United States? As you look through the magazines, ask yourself these questions:

   a. To what degree do the people in the ads "match" by ethnicity, age, attractiveness, height and weight, and other factors?

   b. How many of the romantic couples are gay or lesbian?

   c. How many of the friendship pairs depicted are female? Male?

   d. In the ads depicting friends, what are female friends doing? What are male friends doing?

   e. How many ads picture people who are overweight? Physically unattractive? What products are they advertising?

   f. What population of readers does the magazine target?

   After answering these questions, look for patterns that exist within magazines by their target audience. What does this reveal about society's views of friendships and romantic relationships?

EXPLORE

1. Go to the *Psychology Today* (or similar website) and locate the page on relationship self-tests and take a jealousy quiz. If possible, choose the quiz that describes your sexual orientation and gender (e.g., gay male, straight female) and complete it. Do your results agree with how you see yourself? What scenarios made you feel most jealous? If you rated in high in jealousy, what can you do to moderate your feelings or responses?

2. Go to a reputable marriage research site, such as John Gottman's (Dr. Gottman is the foremost scholar of marital relationships) or LiveSciene's webpage *Six Scientific Tips for a Successful Marriage*. Read through the strategies that the site you choose provides for how to have a successful marriage. Which of the various strategies and recommendations would you find most helpful? Most realistic? What can you do to maintain your romantic relationship (if you have one) more effectively?

Small Group Communication

LEARNING OBJECTIVES

10.1 Identify four reasons for learning about small group communication.

10.2 Define *small group communication*.

10.3 Identify and give examples of task, relational, and individual small group roles.

10.4 Describe five theories of group leadership.

10.5 Describe the characteristics of communication that occur during the four phases of small group decision making and the role of technology in small group processes.

10.6 Discuss how diversity influences small group processes.

10.7 Give three types of guidelines for communicating more ethically in your small group communication.

10.8 Discuss ways to improve your own small group communication skills.

CHAPTER TOPICS

The Importance of Small Group Communication

What Is Small Group Communication?

Small Group Communication and the Individual: Roles

Small Group Communication and the Individual: Leadership

Effective Small Group Communication

The Individual, Small Group Communication, and Society: Power and Diversity

Ethics and Small Group Communication

Improving Your Small Group Communication Skills

> *"The quality of a group depends on the contributions
> of individual members."*

Charee had an interesting group experience in her Business Communication class. One of the assignments involved working in teams with students from another campus. Each team had six students (half from her campus and half from the other campus). As a group, they were assigned to select one team on a TV show (either reality or staged—for example, judges on *Dancing with the Stars* or *Top Chef*, teams on *Amazing Race*, family salespeople on *Pawn Stars*). Using concepts learned in class, they evaluated the effectiveness of the group communication on the chosen show. They had to show their analysis in a multimedia presentation to be posted on a course Facebook page.

Charee enjoyed the project because her group could select a show that most group members were interested in and use creativity in the analysis and presentation. Most of the group members worked well together; they exchanged messages on Facebook or Twitter or used the course discussion forum, and some actually became friends. All but one of the group members completed the tasks on time, helped each other, and always knew what the other members were doing. However, there was one member who never posted his work on time, rarely communicated with others, and in general didn't do a good, thoughtful job. He never knew what was going on because he never communicated with other group members. Charee and her team members found that part of the project frustrating even though they tried to work around him.

Charee's group experience illustrates many of the issues we will discuss in this chapter. First, almost any job these days involves teamwork—and often working in virtual teams—where members rarely or never work face to face, which holds special challenges. Second, as she discovered, group work can be productive and even enjoyable when group members are motivated and get along. However, it can be frustrating if one or more group members communicate poorly, or as in Charee's group, fail to participate altogether. It is easy to imagine that their group presentation would have been better if the entire group had worked together as assigned.

In this chapter, we begin by discussing reasons for studying small group communication; we explain what a small group is and define small group communication. We then identify the benefits and challenges of small group work, some of which are illustrated in Charee's experience, and discuss the various communication roles and behaviors that help make groups effective and satisfying for group members. Next, we turn to a discussion of group leadership and describe decision-making processes in a common type of group: problem-solving groups. Finally, we discuss the impact of society on small group communication, addressing the issues of power, cultural diversity, and technology in small group communication. We conclude the chapter with suggestions for how you can communicate more effectively and ethically in small groups.

The Importance of Small Group Communication

10.1 Identify four reasons for learning about small group communication.

Small groups seem to be an integral part of life. You probably belong to a number of groups—social groups, course project groups, work teams at your job, or perhaps support or interest groups in your community. However, you might be surprised to discover that learning how to communicate better in groups can actually enhance your academic and professional achievements. Let's see why this is so.

Reasons to Study Small Group Communication

There are at least four reasons to study small group communication: small groups are a fact of life, they enhance your college performance, your career success, and your personal life.

A Fact of Life   If you have mixed feelings about working in small groups, you are not alone. In fact, a term exists, **grouphate**, which describes the distaste and aversion that some people feel toward working in groups (Keyton, Harmon, & Frey, 1996). As one of our students told us, "I would rather just do the whole group project myself than try to get together with a group of students I don't know and might not trust to do a good job." A recent study found that students (in a small group communication course) who reported an active dislike for working in groups (grouphate) also reported experiencing less group cohesion, consensus, and relational satisfaction in their group work (Myers & Goodboy, 2005). Thus, it is possible that by actively disliking group work, students are negatively influencing how they experience working with a group.

Regardless of how you feel about working in groups, groups are everywhere. Social groups, many online, fill an important function and there are as many groups as there are interests: skateboarding, salsa dancing, book clubs, etc. The purpose of these groups is simply to socialize and enjoy each other's company, whether face to face or online.

However, this chapter's focus is on groups that meet principally to solve problems or achieve goals, such as support groups or work groups. These groups can involve long-term commitments, as in the case of support groups that meet regularly for months or even years. Long-term work groups also include standing committees in business and civic organizations. However, probably most common are short-term project groups; for example, groups that students belong to in various classes, as well as work groups in business organizations. Increasingly, most of these groups accomplish their work online, which we'll discuss later in the chapter.

Enhanced College Performance   Considerable research indicates that college students who study in small groups perform at higher intellectual levels, learn better, and have better attitudes toward subject matter than those who study alone (Allen & Plax, 2002). This is probably because studying with others allows you to encounter different interpretations and ideas. As we'll see in the next section, group work can also lead to higher-quality thinking and decision making. Thus, learning how to interact more effectively in groups and seeking out learning groups to participate in can lead to enhanced college performance.

Enhanced Career Success   According to a recent *Forbes* article, the top skills employers say they seek are the ability to work in a team structure, and the ability to make decisions and solve problems (Adams, 2014).These skills are particularly important in today's global workplace—where you may be working, face to face or virtually, with people from different countries/cultural backgrounds. Whether you are in business or another profession, organizations tend to hire and promote those who have proven they can work well with others (Hansen, 2011; Phadnis & Caplice, 2013). Thus, your career advancement prospects could very well depend on your success in a collaborative work environment.

Enhanced Personal Life   Most people also participate in at least some small groups outside work. For one thing, most people communicate with family and friends on a regular basis. In addition, many people serve on committees in religious or political organizations, and increasing numbers of people join support groups to deal with crises, life transitions, or chronic health conditions. So learning how to communicate better in small group settings can serve you personally, academically, and professionally. Despite its prevalence and importance, group work has both advantages and disadvantages.

grouphate
The distaste and aversion that people feel toward working in groups.

Advantages and Disadvantages of Group Work

Working in small groups brings many advantages in addition to those already described. Research shows that groups often make more creative and higher quality decisions than do individuals (Blinder & Morgan, 2000). First, a group can produce more innovative ideas than can an individual working alone. The small group discussion itself actually stimulates creativity as research shows that people tend to work harder and do better when others are around, particularly if the work group is cohesive and other group members are modeling effective group behavior (Park & Shin, 2015).

Second, some evidence indicates that small group work can promote critical thinking, leading to better decisions. A group of people offers more collective information, experience, and expertise than any single person can (Casari, Zhang, & Jackson, 2012). For example, if a group member offers an opinion or makes a claim, collectively, other group members may offer evidence that supports or refutes it; they may also contribute alternative opinions or suggestions. However, some experts caution that critical thinking and cognitively complex ideas are not automatic consequences of small group discussion. Rather, it may take some leadership to elicit diverse ideas and to then facilitate the type of discussion described previously that promotes critical analysis, interpretation, and critiquing (Jobidon et al., 2016).

Of course, group work also has disadvantages: it can be time consuming because group decisions take more time than do individual ones; it can lead to too much

ALTERNATIVE VIEW

Hate Teamwork? You're Not Alone

Do you think of yourself as a team player or more of an individual performer? The results of a recent study show that while employees acknowledge the value of teamwork in the workplace, they would rather go it alone. Do you agree? Why or why not?

In two recent articles, business writer Chad Brooks describes the results of a survey and his interviews with business leaders, both attesting to the importance of teamwork skills in the workplace, as well as the aversion that most employees have toward it.

Brooks reports that many business leaders insist that, when set up correctly, teamwork has great benefit. As it turns out, many employees agree. Brooks reports that a recent survey of more than 1,000 employees found that 95 percent of those surveyed (who had ever worked on a team) thought that teamwork serves a critical function in today's workplace. More than 60 percent surveyed also agreed that collaboration and team building, conflict resolution, and team management are required skills for students looking to join today's workforce.

However, 85 percent of these same employees said that working on teams in the office is difficult and that they would rather work on their own than participate in team efforts. They gave many reasons for their dislike of teamwork; two of the most frequently mentioned were that teamwork goes against the cherished "in-it-for-one's-self" mentality in the workplace, and a lack of clearly defined roles often contributes to team failures.

Other frequently given reasons were that their workload was too heavy, not allowing for enough time to work on team projects, and much of the resistance to teamwork resulted from a lack of proper preparation and training in how to work effectively in teams.

Finally, some of the employees' dislike about working in teams seem to come from previous negative teamwork experiences and having been part of a dysfunctional team. These negative experiences included verbal confrontations among team members, arguments that turned physical, team members blaming each another for things that went wrong in the team, and working with team members who started rumors about one another.

The results of the survey, as well as the interviews with business leaders, seem to suggest that to be successful in today's workplace, acquiring good teamwork skills is a must—even though it might not be a favorite part of the job!

SOURCES: Brooks, C. (2013, January 16). Why employees hate teamwork. *Businessnewsdaily.com*. Retrieved February 22, 2017, from http://www.businessnewsdaily.com/3769-employees-prefer-to-go-it-alone-research-finds.html.

Brooks, C. (2013, October 16). Hate teamwork? You're not alone. *Businessnewsdaily.com*. Retrieved February 22, 2017 from http://www.businessnewsdaily.com/5281-employees-hate-teamwork.html.

closeness and agreement, resulting in premature decisions; and it can silence divergent opinions—particularly from minority group members (Hampton et al., 2014).

Finally, a fourth disadvantage is that group discussion can be less than satisfying when some group members dominate or withdraw, as happened with Charee's group in our opening vignette. Such communication behaviors can cause frustration and conflict, preventing members from working productively (Adams & Galanes, 2003) and cohesively. Given these disadvantages, one can admit that teamwork has limits, as business writer Chad Brooks describes in *Alternative View: Hate Teamwork? You're Not Alone*.

Given that most of us need to work in small groups from time to time and that learning how to communicate better in small groups can enhance critical thinking as well as lead to academic and professional success, what do you need to know to be a successful group member? To answer this question, we first must clarify what we mean by *small group communication*.

Journal Prompt 10.1: Studying Small Group Communication
Consider the following questions:
What do you think is the most important reason for you to learn about group communication? Why?

What Is Small Group Communication?

10.2   Define *small group communication*.

To acquire a clear idea of what we'll be discussing in this chapter, let's consider two types of groups: (1) a group of people waiting in line for a movie and (2) a group of students working on a semester-long research project. The first type of group is not the focus of this chapter, whereas the second is. We define **small group communication** as "communication among a small number of people who share a common purpose or goal, who feel connected to each other, and coordinate their behavior" (Arrow, McGrath, & Berdahl, 2000, p. 34). Let's look more closely at who the small group in this definition is.

small group communication
Communication among a small number of people who share a common purpose or goal, who feel connected to each other, and who coordinate their behavior.

A Small Number of People

Most experts agree that three is the fewest number of people that can constitute a small group and that five to seven people is the optimum upper limit for working groups. This general guideline may vary depending on whether the small group is working face-to-face or in virtual teams. In general, small groups of three (whether working in direct contact or virtually) experience better communication in terms of openness and accuracy than do larger groups of six. As group size increases, people may feel more anonymous, and discussions can become unwieldy and unfocused as members tend to break into smaller groups. However, size seems to have less impact on groups that are working virtually (Lowry, Roberts, Romano, Cheney, & Hightower, 2006). Under this portion of our definition, people waiting in line for a movie would not likely be considered a small group because any number of people can wait for a movie.

A Common Purpose

Although a group of people waiting for a movie fulfills the second requirement of our definition—they share a purpose—that purpose is rather limited. Here we focus on communication in small groups that are working together toward a common purpose. Sometimes the purpose may be assigned by an instructor or employer—a semester-long course project, completing a marketing research study for a client, or working together to recommend a candidate for a job. Having a clear purpose or goal is important and is directly (positively) related to group productivity and increased team performance (Crown, 2007).

A Connection with Each Other

People waiting for the movie don't generally feel any sense of group connection, nor do they need to. In contrast, people in work groups need to experience a group identity and recognize their interdependence because—as we saw in Charee's experience—when members do not feel a sense of connection, the group won't function as it should. The challenge for the small group is to find ways to create a sense of group identity for all members, and communication is often the key to making this happen.

An Influence on Each Other

Members of small groups need to coordinate their behavior, and in doing so, they may exert influence on each other. People waiting for a movie do not need to exert influence on each other, but members of a work group do. This influence can be positive or negative, and each group member contributes to the success or failure of the whole group. Most groups aren't successful without the positive contribution of all members. In Charee's experience, the negative influence of one member detracted from the success of all.

In sum, a collection of people waiting in line for a movie rarely constitutes a small group because they typically don't influence one another, they don't feel connected to each other or develop a shared identity, and they share a common purpose only in the most limited way. We should note that the word *team* is sometimes used interchangeably with the word *group*, but experts distinguish the two in that a work team is a special type of group: a self-managed group that works on specific tasks or projects within an organization (Engleberg & Wynn, 2010, pp. 11–12) and shares responsibility for specific outcomes for the organization (Landy & Conte, 2010, p. 587). With these features of small groups in mind, in the next section we will look at individual communication in small groups.

▲ We define small group communication as "communication among a small number of people who share a common purpose or goal, who feel connected to each other, and who coordinate their behavior."

Critical Thinking Prompt
Think about all the groups you belong to. Which could help you be more successful personally? Academically? Professionally?

Journal Prompt 10.2: Defining Small Group Communication
Consider the following questions:
What is a definition of small group communication? How does a small group, as defined in this chapter, differ from a group of individuals waiting in line at a bank?

Small Group Communication and the Individual: Roles

10.3   Identify and give examples of task, relational, and individual small group roles.

The quality of a group depends on the contributions of individual members—so much so that one reason for ineffective groups is the poor communication skills of individual members (Li, 2007; Oetzel, 2005). Lack of communication among group members can even be disastrous. Poor communication between pilot and co-pilot has been cited as the primary cause of several deadly airplane crashes. Fortunately, poor teamwork doesn't usually have such disastrous consequences; nevertheless, communication scholar Lawrence Frey (1994) points out that "communication *is* the lifeblood that flows through the veins of groups" (p. x).

To better understand communication processes in small groups, it is helpful to think of its two primary dimensions: task communication and relational communication. Task communication focuses on getting the job done and solving the problem at hand; for example, requesting information or asking for clarification. Relational communication focuses on group maintenance and interpersonal relationships, such as offering encouragement or mediating disagreement. These two types of communication are thoroughly mixed during group interaction; in fact, one statement can fill both functions. When a group is getting bogged down in discussion, one member might encourage the group *and* focus on the task by saying something like, "All of these ideas show how creative we are. Which do you think would be the most useful in helping us solve our problem?"

To help you understand how individuals can contribute to (or detract from) the performance of task and relationship communication, we explore the various communication roles that members of small groups perform. We then discuss another important ingredient of small groups—leadership; and in so doing, we present several important theories of leadership. Finally, we'll look at principles and processes that can make small groups effective.

Types of Communication Roles

group roles

The shared expectations group members have regarding each individual's communication behavior in the group.

Every group member plays a variety of roles within a group. **Group roles** describe the shared expectations group members have regarding each individual's communication behavior in the group. These roles can involve task communication or relational communication, or both. When you join an established group, you learn these expectations through communication with current members. If all members are new to the group, they rely on their perceptions and beliefs, as well as their group skills and previous group experience, as they work out various role behaviors (Riddle, Anderson, & Martin, 2000).

For example, our friend Mitchell works for a software company. Although the employees of this company are scattered across the country and primarily work at home, they must work together to design software that meets a client's specific needs. Because Mitchell is the expert at writing software programs, he assumes that role. Similarly, Mitchell and Giuliana make sure to follow the advice of Bob, the market researcher who has studied the client's market needs. In this case, each group member knows his or her roles; they have developed this understanding based on their individual and collective experiences in groups.

Although group roles often evolve as the team works together, sometimes roles are assigned as part of a job description. For example, LaKresha, the chair of her community's Animal Welfare League, always leads the group's discussions because this is one of her responsibilities as chair. Kristie, as secretary of the organization, always takes notes because that is her role. Effective group members contribute by filling roles that are of interest to them and compatible with their skills, but they also fill roles that the group needs at a particular time. Thus, successful small group work depends on task and relational communication, which in turn depends on individuals' effective performance of task and relational roles (Benne & Sheats, 1948). In addition, small group members may perform a third, less productive type of role, which is referred to as an **individual role**. Let's look at these three types of roles and how they contribute to, or detract from, effective group communication.

individual role

Role that focuses more on individuals' own interests and needs than on those of the group.

task roles

Roles that are directly related to the accomplishment of group goals.

Task Roles **Task roles** are directly related to the accomplishment of group goals; they include behaviors such as leading the discussion and taking notes. These communication roles often involve seeking, processing, and evaluating information. A list of task roles is provided in Table 10.1.

Let's explore how task roles function within a group using a case study. Lenore and Jaime were part of a campus task force working to improve campus safety. Their small group of seven members met twice a month for several months and discussed the problem and possible solutions. During the discussions, group members filled the various task roles, depending on their particular strengths and interests and the needs of the group, changing roles as needed.

For example, Karin tended to serve as initiator-contributor, proposing new ideas and suggesting that the group look at several dimensions of the problem, such as personal security and the protection of private property. Information seekers, in particular John

Table 10.1 Small Group Task Roles

Task Role	Description	Example
Initiator–contributor	Proposes new ideas or approaches to group problem solving	"How about if we look at campus safety as issues of personal security *and* protection of private property?"
Information seeker	Asks for information or clarification	"How many instances of theft occur on our campus each year?"
Opinion seeker	Asks for opinions from others	"How do you feel about charging students a fee that would pay for extra police protection?"
Information giver	Provides facts, examples, and other relevant evidence	"My research showed that other campuses have solved similar problems by increasing numbers of campus police and improving lighting."
Opinion giver	Offers beliefs or opinions	"I'm often concerned about my personal safety when I walk to certain campus parking lots at night."
Elaborator	Explains ideas, offers examples to clarify ideas	"If the university had increased security patrols, my bike might not have been stolen last month."
Coordinator	Shows relationships among ideas presented	"Installing new light fixtures might improve personal safety and reduce thefts on campus."
Orienter	Summarizes what has been discussed and keeps group focused	"We've now discussed several aspects of personal safety; maybe it's time to turn our attention to issues of protection of private property."
Evaluator–critic	Judges evidence and conclusions of group	"I think we may be overestimating the problem of theft."
Energizer	Motivates group members to greater productivity	"Wow! We've gotten a lot accomplished this evening, and we only have a few more points to discuss."
Procedural technician	Performs logistical tasks—distributing paper, arranging seating, etc.	"If all four of us sit on the same side of the table, we'll be able to read the diagrams without having to pass them around."
Recorder	Keeps a record of group activities and progress	"We have 10 more minutes; let's see if we can get through our agenda in time to review any questions."

SOURCE: Benne, K. D., & Sheats, P. (1948). Functional roles of group members. *Journal of Social Issues, 4*, 41–49.

and Ralph, often asked for clarification of facts or information. Opinion seekers, such as Eliza and Wen Shu, asked how other group members felt about various proposals—say, the potential expense that would be incurred by implementing suggested solutions. In addition, opinion givers responded by sharing how they felt about the expense.

As information givers, several members provided statistics about the security problem so that the group could know the extent of the problem. They also provided information on how other campuses had solved similar problems—by installing better lighting, and having volunteer "security teams" patrol campus. Serving as elaborator, Lenore told about having her bike stolen and suggested that having an increased number of campus police might have prevented the theft. Jaime often served as coordinator and orienter, showing how various ideas related to each other, whereas other members filled the role of evaluator-critic, carefully evaluating various ideas. The procedural technician made sure that everyone had paper and pens, and a designated recorder took notes and one member often served as the energizer, infusing interest into the group when attention and focus lagged.

Not every group has members who can fill each of these roles, and certainly not with the same level of skill. But the more effectively these roles are filled, the better the group will function and the more likely it is that goals will be met.

Relational Roles   In contrast with task roles, **relational roles** help establish a group's social atmosphere (see Table 10.2). Members who encourage others to talk or mediate disagreements are filling relational roles. Group members can fill both task and

relational roles
Roles that help establish a group's social atmosphere.

Table 10.2   Small Group Relational Roles

Role	Description	Example
Encourager	Offers praise and acceptance of others' ideas	"That's a great idea; tell us more about it."
Harmonizer	Mediates disagreement among group members	"I think you and Ron are seeing two sides of the same coin."
Compromiser	Attempts to resolve conflicts by trying to find an acceptable solution to disagreements	"I think both of you have great ideas. Let's see how we can combine them."
Gatekeeper	Encourages less talkative group members to participate	"Maria, you haven't said much about this idea. How do you feel about it?"
Expediter	Tries to limit lengthy contributions of other group members	"Martin, you've told us what you think about most of the ideas. Why don't we hear from some of the other members?"
Standard setter	Helps to set standards and goals for the group	"I think our goal should be to submit a comprehensive plan for campus safety to the dean by the end of this semester."
Group observer	Keeps records of the group's process and uses the information that is gathered to evaluate the group's procedures	"We completed a similar report last semester. Let's refer to it before we spend time working on this new one."
Follower	Goes along with the suggestions and ideas of group members; serves as an audience in group discussion and decision making	"I like that idea. That's a really good point."

SOURCE: Benne, K. D., & Sheats, P. (1948). Functional roles of group members. *Journal of Social Issues, 4*, 41–49.

relational roles, depending on the needs of the group. For example, in Lenore and Jaime's group, one member sent out emails to get the group organized (task role), and he also sent congratulatory emails after the group did a presentation to the student governing council (relational role).

During their discussion of campus safety, some members served as encouragers (praising and accepting others' ideas). Others served as harmonizers (mediating disagreement) or compromisers (attempting to find solutions to disagreements). As communication majors, Lenore and Jaime paid close attention to how the discussion was going, and when necessary, served as gatekeepers, encouraging participation from less talkative members, or as expediters, gently limiting the contributions of more talkative members. Overall, the group met its goal of addressing the problems of campus security partly because members effectively filled both task and relational roles as needed.

How can you apply this information to improve your own skills as a group member? First, try to keep these roles in mind during your own group work, noting who is playing which roles and whether some essential role is missing. Once you've made this assessment you can try to fill in the missing role behaviors. For example, if a group seems "stuck" and keeps rehashing the same ideas, you might try the role of initiator-contributor or information giver. Or if one person in the group is dominating the discussion and talking constantly, you might assume the expediter or gatekeeper role and try to balance out the contributions of the various members.

Individual Roles   The individual role tends to be dysfunctional to the group process (see Table 10.3). Group members serving in individual roles focus more on their own interests and needs than on those of the group. Thus, they tend to be uninvolved, negative, aggressive, or constantly joking. A group member who consistently assumes one or more negative individual roles can undermine the group's commitment to goals and its sense of cohesion—ultimately resulting in decreased group performance and productivity. This is why it is so important for other group members to be aware of effective task and relational behaviors and to demonstrate them (Wellen & Neale, 2006).

A common individual role is the joker. When another member contributes, the joker always has to "one up" the comment with a joke or a story, constantly moving the group off-task. Here, a member filling the orienter role can help the group refocus on the task

Table 10.3 Small Group Individual Roles

Role	Description	Example
Aggressor	Attacks other group members, tries to take credit for someone else's contribution	"That's a stupid idea. It would never work."
Blocker	Is generally negative and stubborn for no apparent reason	"This whole task is pointless. I don't see why we have to do it."
Recognition seeker	Calls excessive attention to his or her personal achievements	"This is how we dealt with campus security when I was at Harvard."
Self-confessor	Uses the group as an audience to report non-group-related personal feelings	"I'm so upset at my boyfriend. We had a big fight last night."
Joker	Lacks involvement in the group's process, distracts others by telling stories and jokes	"Hey did you hear the one about . . . ?"
Dominator	Asserts control by manipulating group members or tries to take over group; may use flattery or assertive behavior to dominate the conversation	"I know my plan will work because I was a police officer."
Help seeker	Tries to gain unwarranted sympathy from group; often expresses insecurity or feelings of low self-worth	"You probably won't like this idea, either, but I think we should consider contracting out our campus security."
Special-interest pleader	Works to serve an individual need, rather than focusing on group interests	"Because I only have daycare on Wednesdays, can we meet on Wednesday afternoons?"

SOURCE: Benne, K. D., & Sheats, P. (1948). Functional roles of group members. *Journal of Social Issues, 4,* 41–49.

at hand. Another individual role that often hinders effectiveness in student projects is the dominator, who insists on doing things his or her way and the blocker, a member who is negative for no apparent reason, as was the case for one of our students (see *It Happened to Me: Tiacko*).

You may also be familiar with the self-confessor, the help seeker, and the special-interest pleader; all these individual roles take up a lot of air time in unproductive conversation. How can you deal with these types of roles? As illustrated by Tiacko's experience, group members can deal with critical group members by assuming a relational communication role–complimenting other group members for their ideas (i.e., encourager role), and counteracting criticism with positive feedback, such as "I have to say I thought Tanya's idea was really intriguing. Let's look at how we

It Happened to Me
Tiacko

In one of my classes, we had to complete a group project. One of our members dominated the discussion and was always very critical. No matter what contributions we made to the project, he always found a way to criticize them. Nothing was good enough for him. Fortunately, we also had some very skilled communicators in our group and they limited his impact on the group by always countering his negative remarks with more positive comments.

might implement it in our project." A single member's criticism has less force when several members note the high quality of a contribution. In general, probably the best strategies to deal with individual roles come from those relational roles that help the group refocus on the task: the gatekeeper and expeditor roles. Several task roles may also prove helpful—for example, the initiator-contributor, who may start a new line of conversation, or the orienter, who helps the group see where they are in accomplishing their task, or the opinion seeker—to solicit other supportive opinions, contradicting some individual roles' negativity.

Any group member may serve in any of these roles at any time. In a successful group, like Jaime and Lenore's task force, members play various roles as needed, with minimal indulgence in the individual roles. Some group members play only to their

Journal Prompt 10.3: Task and Relational Roles
Consider the following questions: What is the difference between task and relational role behaviors in small group communication? How are they related to each other?

Critical Thinking Prompt
Think about group experiences you've had. Which task communication roles do you tend to fill? Which relational communication roles? Which communication roles would you like to fill? How flexible have you been in your ability to fill various task and relational roles?

strengths and consistently serve in one or two particular roles. This is fine as long as all the needed roles are being filled.

Small Group Communication and the Individual: Leadership

10.4   Describe five theories of group leadership.

A group or organization's success is often directly related to the presence of good leadership, online or face-to-face, and leadership should be a concern for all of us because it is not just a quality for those with formal subordinates. Rather, leadership occurs in many forms and contexts; as one expert says, leadership can take place "during a sales call, a customer service response, a family decision or a meeting with friends" (Gollent, 2007). As we describe leadership characteristics and theories, think about the ways in which you may play leadership roles in the various groups and organizations in which you are a member.

Definition of Leadership   Organizational behavior scholar Richard Daft defines leadership as "an influence relationship among leaders and followers who intend real changes and outcomes that reflect their shared purposes" (2015, p. 5). Perhaps the most important element in this definition is the idea of an influence relationship. Influence does not just reside in one person but rather is a process that involves relationships between leaders and followers (Daft, 2015; Northouse, 2012).

The second element in Daft's definition of leadership involves the intention to change; this distinguishes it from the concept of management, which is more about order and stability. In addition, Daft refers to outcomes that reflect the shared purposes and vision of leaders and followers. For example, Martin Luther King Jr. built a shared vision of a society in which people would be judged by their character, not their color; he mobilized his followers to act via nonviolent protest in realizing this vision. Similarly, today's ordinary citizens and students can rally others around a strongly held idea of change.

Leadership experts describe the essence of good leadership as the capacity to "energize" potential followers by *connecting* with people at a personal, sometimes emotional, level so that they become motivated, engaged, and empowered to help achieve the shared vision (Denhardt & Denhardt, 2004; Matha & Boehm, 2008). These elements are exemplified by the story our student tells about her boss in *It Happened to Me: Martha*.

Because followers are individuals with their own differences, and each leadership situation is unique, there is no one "right" way of communicating nor one way of leading. However, researchers have identified five theories that explain effective leaders: trait theory, functional theory, style theory, transformational leadership theory, and servant leadership theory.

trait theory
A theory that assumes leaders are born, not made.

Trait Theory   Probably the oldest theory concerning leadership in the communication field is **trait theory** (Stogdill, 1974). Trait theory suggests that leaders are born. For example, people associate height with leadership ability (Judge & Cable, 2004), some personality traits (extroversion, openness to experience, agreeableness), and intelligence (Judge, Bono, Ilies, & Gerhardt, 2002; Judge, Colbert, & Ilies, 2004).

A more recent advocate of trait theory, leadership expert Fred E. Fiedler, proposed the "Contingency Model" of leadership (Fiedler, 1981; Fiedler & Garcia, 1987). In his view, a

It Happened to Me
Martha

I've worked at several different organizations in different sectors, but I have found that the most important thing that leaders, bosses, or supervisors can do is give their subordinates a sense of empowerment. When you're given a task by your boss, you want her to trust that you'll do a good job—you want her to believe in your abilities and give you the space to succeed. I couldn't work for someone who questioned everything I did or watched my every move.

leader's strength tended either toward relationship or task orientation and he emphasized that each of these two types of traits were effective in particular situations. A task-orientated style is effective under extreme conditions—in natural disasters or in uncertain situations. Relationship-oriented leaders are more effective when leader-member relations are good and members are able to work independently.

Many examples challenge the trait approach to leadership. In recent years, a number of people have developed leadership qualities out of a deep motivation to make the world a better place. For example, undergraduate Sindhura Citineni felt determined to make a difference when confronted by the appalling statistics of world hunger she found while researching on the Internet. Citineni negotiated with her university to sell several simple food items in the cafeteria where part of the revenue went to hunger-relief work—called Hunger Lunch. She then led a group of students who expanded that project into Nourish International, now a nonprofit organization that connects college students from universities around the United States to development projects abroad (http://nourishinternational.org). As you see, although there are some personality characteristics associated with good leadership, most experts now reject the trait theory notion that leaders are born, not made.

It should also be noted that some of the world's most well-known leaders were reserved and rather introverted, including Abraham Lincoln, Eleanor Roosevelt, Mahatma Ghandhi, and Bill Gates. See *Did You Know: Introverts Can Be Leaders Too.*

Functional Theory   A second approach to analyzing leadership, the **functional (situational) theory**, stands in direct contrast to the trait approach. Unlike trait theory,

▲ As an undergraduate, Sindhura Citineni started a campus project to combat world hunger and later led a group of students to form Nourish International, a worldwide nonprofit organization.

DID YOU KNOW?
Introverts Can Be Leaders Too

Conventional wisdom holds that leaders should be outgoing and extroverted, enjoy meeting new people and making new friends. However, a recent book by author Susan Cain questions this view. What do you think? Do you think extroverts make better leaders? Have you encountered an effective leader who seemed introverted? Which category do you tend to fall into? Take the quiz at http://www.thepowerofintroverts.com/quiet-quiz-are-you-an-introvert/ to find out.

In a recent book, *Quiet: The Power of Introverts in a World That Can't Stop Talking*, author Susan Cain argues that the belief that only extroverts make good leaders reflects a historical shift in early-twentieth-century society—from a culture of character to a culture of personality. She suggests that this belief is changing, and that now, half the population—introverts—are viewed much more positively. In fact, she points out that the traits associated with extroversion sometimes lead to unproductive behaviors and poor leadership: risk taking, dominance, and thoughtless behavior. She encourages extroverts to tone it down a little and learn to listen, suggesting that everyone should "embrace the power of quiet." Business experts, building on her suggestions, note that some of the most influential leaders have been introverts: Abraham Lincoln, Eleanor Roosevelt, Warren Buffet, and Bill Gates. They suggest that introverts and extroverts can learn from each other, each contributing their strengths to make a stronger workforce. Introverted workers bring thoughtfulness and critique to issues, and they are more likely to listen to others and apply suggestions made by others, but they need time and quiet spaces to process. Extroverts are good at inspiring otherwise uninspired workers and need opportunities to mix it up with others.

SOURCES: Cain, S. (2013). *Quiet: The power of introverts in a world that can't stop talking.* New York: Broadway Books.

Moore, K. (2012). Introverts no longer the quiet followers of extroverts. Forbes.com. Retrieved February 22, 2017, from http://www.forbes.com/sites/karlmoore/2012/08/22/introverts-no-longer-the-quiet-followers-of-extroverts/.

functional (situational) theory
A theory that assumes that leadership behaviors can be learned.

shared (collaborative or distributed) leadership
A type of leadership style in which functional leadership is extended to an organizational level; all members are equal partners and share responsibility for the work of the group.

style theory
Theory that asserts that a leader's manner or style determines his or her success.

authoritarian leader
Leader who takes charge, makes all the decisions, and dictates strategies and work tasks.

democratic leader
Leader whose style is characterized by considerable input from group members.

laissez-faire
A leadership style characterized by complete freedom for the group in making decisions.

▼ Rick Pitino is the first coach in NCAA history to lead three different basketball teams to the Final Four (Providence, Kentucky, and Louisville). As a leader, he has to make split-second decisions during basketball games.

which assumes leadership is innate, this theory assumes that leadership behaviors can be learned, even by group members who are not "leadership types." Functional theory assumes that whatever the group needs at a particular time can be supplied by a set of behaviors any group member can contribute (Benne & Sheats, 1948; Pavitt, 1999). Thus, this theory argues that the leader can change from time to time, depending on the changing needs of the group.

According to functional theory, a group does not need a designated leader; rather, any group member can serve as the leader at any particular time by filling the required role. For example, the leader can fill task roles when the group needs direction, then step into relational roles when group members understand the task but need encouragement. Occasionally, no leadership is needed, such as when the short- and long-term purpose is clear and group members are working well independently.

A related notion is **shared leadership**, also called *collaborative* or *distributed leadership*. Here the functional leadership approach is extended to an organizational level where team relationships become more of a partnership in an organization (MacNeil & McClanahan, 2005). This style of leadership can occur either as an explicitly stated objective or may simply emerge if the designated leader is too passive or simply refuses to provide leadership (Kramer, 2006). However it occurs, the requirements for this kind of leadership are a balance of power in which:

all members are equal partners;

all share a common purpose or goal;

all share responsibility for the work of the group (take an active role and are accountable for completing their individual contribution); all have respect for the person—and skills and ideas that each brings to the team; and

all work together in complex, real-world situations.

Style Theory   A third approach to analyzing leadership asserts that a leader's manner or **style** of leading a group determines her or his success. Further, this theory describes three common styles of leadership: authoritarian, democratic, and laissez-faire.

An **authoritarian leader** takes charge and has a high level of intellect and expertise, making all the decisions and dictating strategies and work tasks (Lewin, Lippit, & White, 1939). This type of leadership is appropriate in military, sports, or crisis situations, or when time for discussion is short or when the stakes are high. For example, military organizations have a highly authoritarian structure, and in battle, the chain of command must be rigorously followed because there's no time for discussion or trial and error. Similarly, medical teams in an emergency department generally follow authoritarian leadership—one person, the doctor, directs the others in what needs to be done.

Democratic leadership is the style we are most familiar with, and the one that seems to work best in many group situations. A **democratic leader's** style is characterized by a great deal of input from group members; the qualities of this leader are best summarized by Lao-tse (550 B.C.E.): "A good leader is one who talks little; when his work is done, his aim fulfilled, they will all say 'We did this ourselves'" (cited in Foels, Driskell, Mullen, & Salas, 2000, p. 677). In this style, group discussion determines all policies, strategies, and division of labor. Members are free to assume a variety of roles, to contribute when appropriate, and to share leadership.

In contrast, some small group situations call for a **laissez-faire** style. This style is characterized by complete freedom for the group in making decisions. The leader participates minimally and may supply materials and information when asked, but he or she makes no attempt to evaluate or influence the discussion. The laissez-faire style may work

Table 10.4 Transformational and Charismatic Leaders

Transformational	Charismatic
Strong Vision	Strong Vision
High Expectations for Followers	High Expectations for Followers
Builds Relationships	Relies on Strong Personality
Creates Loyalty to Organization	Creates Loyalty to Self
Enduring Inspiration	Leadership May Be Short-Lived

well when little is at stake, as in some social groups like book clubs or gourmet clubs (Barge, 1989).

Transformational Leadership Theory   A relatively new theory, **transformational leadership** theory, emphasizes the importance of relationships in leadership and group cohesion. That is, such leaders recognize unique strengths and capabilities of followers and coach and empower them to develop their full potential and work beyond standard expectations (Jung & Sosik, 2002). Transformational leaders also have high moral and ethical standards, a strong vision for the future, challenge the status quo and encourage innovation (Bono & Judge, 2004).

> **transformational leadership**
> A leadership style that empowers group members to work independently from the leader by encouraging group cohesion.

Transformational leadership is sometimes confused with **charismatic leadership**, a style proposed by scholars in political science and religious studies. Like transformational leaders, charismatic leaders have a strong belief in their vision. They are also extremely self-confident and able to inspire great dedication and loyalty in their followers. Followers of charismatic (and transformational) leaders are often willing to set high (sometimes unrealistic) objectives and often make tremendous sacrifices, ultimately achieving more than was expected or deemed possible (Rowold & Heinitz, 2007).

> **charismatic leadership**
> A leadership style in which extremely self-confident leaders inspire unusual dedication to themselves by relying on their strong personalities and charm.

As you might imagine, strong communication skills (pleasant vocal style, listening skills, ability to motivate and persuade) are central to both charismatic and transformational leadership. (Levine, Muenchen, & Brooks, 2010). However, as shown in Table 10.4, there are important differences between charismatic and transformational leaders. Specifically, charismatic leaders rely on their strong personalities and charm to create loyalty to themselves, whereas transformational leaders build relationships and strive to create loyalty to the group or organization, not to the individual leader. Thus, when a transformational leader exits the group, the organization is more likely to thrive because member commitment is to the group. When charismatic leaders leave, the group may falter because the individuals' commitment is to the leader, not to one another. And unlike transformational leaders who manage to inspire their followers for a long time, charismatic leadership may be relatively short-lived because they may also be autocratic and self-serving, and followers may become disillusioned (Daft, 2015; Pavitt, 1999). In fact, charismatic leadership can have disastrous results: Hitler and Mussolini, for example, were charismatic leaders. Although such leaders inspire trust, faith, and belief in themselves, there is no guarantee that their vision or mission will be correct, ethical, or successful.

Servant Leadership Theory   The idea of **servant leadership** was introduced to organizations through Robert Greenleaf's 1970 essay, "The Servant as Leader." The concept was further popularized by writers such as Stephen Covey, whose 1989 bestseller *The Seven Habits of Highly Effective People* made a major impact in the business world.

> **servant leadership**
> A leadership style that seeks to ensure that other people's highest priority needs are being served to increase teamwork and personal involvement.

According to Greenleaf, a servant leader must excel at 10 characteristics.

- awareness
- listening
- empathizing
- persuasion
- conceptualization

Critical Thinking Prompt
Consider the definition of leadership provided in this chapter. In which of your relationships and everyday activities do you provide leadership? In which contexts (school, home, extracurricular activities) are you most likely to provide leadership?

Journal Prompt 10.4: Group Leadership
Consider the following question: What is the definition of group leadership, and why is leadership important in small group communication?

- foresight
- stewardship
- healing
- commitment to the growth of others
- building community

You will notice that most of these 10 characteristics are communication skills. Servant leadership emphasizes collaboration, trust, and the ethical use of power. The theory proposes that at heart, the individual is a servant first and makes a conscious decision to lead to better serve others, not to increase his or her own power. The objective is to enhance the growth of individuals in the organization and to increase teamwork and personal involvement (Greenleaf, 1970/1991, 2002).

Effective Small Group Communication

10.5 Describe the characteristics of communication that occur during the four phases of small group decision making and the role of technology in small group processes.

Now that we have described the important role of communication in effective leadership, and various theories of group leadership, we are ready to ask the question: What communication behaviors are necessary for effective small group interaction? The answer seems to be that effective groups maintain a balance of task and relational communication, and the sequence of each appears to be more important than the relative amount of each. For example, after an intense period of task talk, group members might defuse their tension with positive social, or relational, talk and then return to task talk (Pavitt, 1999).

Effective Small Group Communication Practices

What types of communication lead to effective sequencing of task and relational communication? And how can members best use these skills when the primary goal of a small group is to solve a particular problem? Experts find that the following four communication processes lead to task effectiveness and member satisfaction (relational effectiveness) in small groups in many situations—whether a team project in a *Fortune* 500 company, a fund-raising committee for a charity organization, or a small group assignment in a communication course (Oetzel, 1998, 2001, 2005).

1. *Equal participation*: The fact is that if everyone participates, the group can consider a wider variety of ideas, attend to more aspects of the topic, and thus make better decisions. Furthermore, group members who do not contribute feel less commitment to the group outcomes and implementation, and may ultimately sabotage the group effort (Lewis, Isbell, & Koschmann, 2010). It is especially important to encourage participation in online teamwork because quiet or silent members can go unnoticed and the cause of the nonparticipation may be the result of many different reasons. As a group member, you can monitor the participation of all members, playing the expeditor role to prevent talkative or domineering members from talking too much and the gatekeeper role in drawing out those nonparticipating members.

2. *A consensus decision-making style*: Members participate in and agree with the decisions made by the group. Although it is not always possible to have every group member agree with every decision, nonparticipating members and members who disagree with group decisions can have negative impacts on group outcomes—as described previously. Therefore, it is in the best interests of the group to get buy-in from as many members as possible. As a group member, you can facilitate agreement by encouraging participation of all members, by showing how ideas are related (coordinator role), and by encouraging a cooperative conflict style.

3. *A cooperative conflict style*: The group manages conflict by integrating all parties' interests. As we will see, some conflict is an inevitable part of small group discussion, and when handled well, it can be productive in sharpening issues and getting out various positions. For now, let's just say that effective groups approach conflict in a cooperative rather than a competitive, divisive manner. This means that the goal in a cooperative approach is to try to turn the conflict into a communal problem that all members can work on to their mutual benefit. A little later in the chapter, we will provide more specific strategies for dealing with group conflict in a cooperative manner.

4. *A respectful communication style*: Group members demonstrate that other members are valued and important. How is this accomplished? Most often, members show respect by communicating a sense of mutual support and acceptance. This means using the verbal and nonverbal strategies that strengthen interpersonal relationships—described in other chapters in this book.

How can members best use these skills when the primary goal of a small group is to solve a particular problem? One of the great communication challenges for groups is to pinpoint the problem and all its possible solutions. In this section, we'll first describe a five-step agenda that problem-solving groups have found useful. Second, we'll examine how decision making occurs in small groups, including a negative group process—groupthink. Finally, we'll describe the characteristics of discussions in small groups whose members are separated geographically, and in particular, the role technology can play in them.

Dewey Sequence of Problem Solving   A danger in problem-solving groups is jumping immediately to a solution (Broome & Fulbright, 1995). One useful tool for avoiding a premature and incomplete solution is to develop and follow a sequence or agenda, one of the best known is "Dewey's Reflective Thinking Model," which was developed by educator John Dewey (Cragan & Wright, 1999, p. 97). Two points are central to using an agenda effectively, and at first they may sound contradictory. First, researchers have found that most problem-solving groups have less conflict and a more consistent focus when they follow formal procedures (Klocke, 2007). Second, successful groups do not necessarily solve all problems in strict sequential order; they may take a variety of paths (Schultz, 1999). In general, then, groups benefit from keeping the agenda in mind, but members should realize that they may have to cycle back and forth between phases before reaching a solution.

We previously discussed the example of a campus task force working to improve campus safety. Let's return to that example and see how that group might follow the five-step problem-solving agenda and the recommendations for effective communication at each step.

Step 1. *Define and Delineate the Problem.*   The first step in solving a problem is to make sure that everyone in the group understands it in the same way. After all, the problem can't be solved unless group members know what it is (and is not). On the campus security task force case study, the group members were successful in part because they agreed on the definition of the problem. They decided their problem was twofold: (1) the personal security of students in dorms and while walking on campus and (2) the protection of students' personal property. They

▼ If you were a member of this problem-solving group, what communication roles might you use to improve the group's effectiveness?

decided that they would not address the security of classroom and office equipment because they were primarily a student group. This helped them narrow the focus and set limits for the discussion of solutions.

Step 2. *Analyze the Problem.*In some ways, this is the most important phase of the agenda because it determines the direction of potential solutions (Hirokawa & Salazar, 1999). Group members must look at all sides of the problem. To do so, they answer questions such as, Who is affected by the problem? How widespread is it? In the case of the campus security team, the group had to gather data on the exact nature of security problems—the frequency of burglaries, rapes, assaults, and robberies on campus; where and when these incidents were occurring; and what consequences the incidents had. However, a word of caution is in order. In some cases, too much analysis can result in **analysis paralysis** and prevent a group from moving toward a solution (Rothwell, 1995). Our campus security group, for example, could continue to gather statistics, interview people about the problem, and discuss the problem—and never move on to possible solutions.

Step 3. *Identify Alternative Solutions.*   One challenge at this stage is to avoid rushing to premature solutions; instead, the group should consider several possible solutions. One way to make sure that many solutions are considered is to **brainstorm**, generating as many ideas as possible without critiquing them. By brainstorming, the campus security group put forth a wide range of possible solutions, including putting up more lighting, increasing the number of campus police, and helping students to register their private property (bikes, computers, stereo equipment, and so on) so that stolen property could be traced. Some solutions were more unusual, including suggestions to eliminate foliage where assailants could hide, to sell wristband tracking devices to students, to place guard dogs in dormitories, and to have 24/7 volunteer security details in the dorms.

Step 4. *Evaluate Proposed Solutions.*   Evaluating proposed solutions involves establishing evaluation criteria. The campus security task force, for example, identified three criteria for its solutions: They had to be economically feasible, logistically feasible, and likely to solve the problem of campus security. With these criteria in mind, the task force had a basis for evaluating each solution. This stage is critical, but it can be difficult. If members are tired or frustrated by all the work they've already done, they may jump to conclusions. However, if they keep to the agenda and carefully consider each alternative, they will quickly reject some solutions and find others attractive. According to one study, a strong positive relationship exists between a group's decision-making performance and members' satisfaction with alternatives chosen (Hirokawa & Salazar, 1999).

Step 5. *Choose the Best Solution.*   Although this step may seem redundant, choosing the best solution(s) is not the same as evaluating all proposed solutions. Here it is especially important that everyone participates and buys into the solution, and decision-making procedures are most critical.

The problem-solving agenda is a specific format or set of guidelines that task groups can follow to ensure high-quality solutions. As groups progress through the stages, however, they will need to make multiple decisions. For example, during stage four, the evaluation stage, the group will need to decide what the appropriate criteria are for evaluating proposed solutions, whether they will evaluate all, or just some, of the proposed solutions, and how they will manage differences of opinion regarding the value of proposed solutions. To help you understand the decision-making process that occurs throughout the problem-solving agenda, we explore the *process* of decision making in the next section.

Decision-Making Phases   How do small groups arrive at good decisions? Are there specific communication processes that can lead to good decisions? What are some warning signs of unproductive decision making? Is conflict a necessary part of the group decision-making process, or should it be avoided? These are questions we'll tackle in this section. As you can imagine, there is no one recipe for effective decision making. However, there are several phases that seem to represent the communication that occurs

analysis paralysis

Potential pitfall in small group interaction; occurs when excessive analysis prevents a group from moving toward a solution.

brainstorm

To generate as many ideas as possible without critiquing them.

in effective problem-solving groups: orientation, conflict, emergence, and reinforcement (Fisher & Ellis, 1993; Wheelan, Davidson, & Tilin, 2003).

Before describing these phases, we should note that most groups do not proceed through them in an orderly, linear fashion. Rather, they may cycle through the first phase twice before moving to the next phase, or they may revert back to the conflict phase after reaching the final, emergence phase (Poole, 1983). With these thoughts in mind, let's look at the four phases individually.

Phase 1. *Orientation.* During this phase of decision making, group members usually orient themselves to the problem and to each other (if they have just met). Uncertainty at this stage is common and is referred to as **primary tension**. For example, as a group member, you might wonder how the group is going to function.

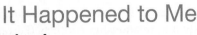

It Happened to Me
Kirstin

Being the only communication major in our group, I immediately noticed some problems. The nonverbal cues from two members contradicted their verbal messages. They rolled their eyes or turned their bodies away from the group when they were asked to do a task. When someone asked what was wrong, those two replied "nothing." I knew this did not bode well for the group, so I shared some of my communication skills and knowledge. I encouraged the two nonparticipating members to contribute and asked them if anything was wrong. They told us they were worried because they'd had a bad experience in an earlier group project. We talked about how we all needed to pull together. I was kind of a cheerleader for the group. So we got through this, and the group arrived at a decision and completed the task without any major conflict.

You may have questions about the relational aspect of the group processes: Are you going to like the other members? Will you all get along, or will you clash? You may also experience uncertainty about the task you are to undertake: Will everyone contribute equally? Will the work get done efficiently and on time? In *It Happened to Me: Kirstin*, one of our students describes a relational problem that emerged at the beginning of her group project and that contributed to the tension the group felt as they began their talk. As you can see, she played an important relational role as a gatekeeper in encouraging the nonparticipating members to communicate and as a harmonizer in helping the group members work through a situation that seemed well on its way to becoming a conflict situation.

Communication at this phase is generally polite, tentative, and focused on reducing uncertainty and ambiguity through clarification and agreement. The importance of the orientation phase is that many relational and task norms are set for the future. Fortunately for Kirstin's group, she realized the importance of group communication and got the group off to a good start.

Regardless of norms that they establish, groups often experience recurring primary tension if they meet over an extended period. For example, at the beginning of each meeting, group members may need to spend time reconnecting and reviewing their views on the task. In response, then, a group member filling the orienter role might summarize what has been accomplished at the most recent meetings, and the recorder could read back minutes or notes from the last meeting.

Phase 2. *Conflict.* The conflict phase in decision making is characterized by **secondary (recurring) tension**. This phase usually occurs after group members become acquainted, after some norms and expectations are set, and when decision alternatives are to be addressed.

As members become more relaxed, this phase of their communication becomes more animated and honest. Members may interrupt each other, talk loudly, and try on group roles. Some may try to dominate, push their own agendas, and form coalitions in an effort to increase their influence; others may engage in side conversations as they lose their focus on the decision at hand. It is especially important at this time to follow the suggestions for effective group communication mentioned previously: equal participation, consensus decision making, and respectful communication. In fact, experts

primary tension
The uncertainty commonly felt in the beginning phase of decision making.

secondary (recurring) tension:
Conflict or tension found in the second or conflict phase of the decision-making process.

suggest assigning members explicit roles such as "decision-maker advisor," someone who monitors and encourages information giving (van Swol, 2009).

We should note here that concerning conflicts in a virtual team, the online environment is a double-edged sword. On the one hand, virtual teams tend to experience less bad relationship conflict because members are usually more focused on their work and less on interpersonal relationships. However, because of the lack of face-to-face conflict—that helps to build trust and empathy—task-related conflict can deteriorate quickly into relationship conflicts (Ferrazzi, 2012). For this reason, the owner of Mitchell's (software) company (described earlier) flies everyone out to Los Angeles periodically so they can work together face-to-face and build trusting relationships (Martinic, Fertalj, & Kalpic, 2012). As we will discuss in Chapter 14, people seem to have less restraint in their online communication, and we've all probably experienced nasty exchanges on Facebook and Twitter that would not occur in face-to-face interaction.

Of course, all groups experience some conflict, and a certain amount of conflict can be both healthy and functional because it can increase member involvement (Klocke, 2007) and even lead to more innovating thinking. For example, innovation often comes about when the majority accepts an opinion advanced by a numerical minority (one group member), which only happens, it turns out, under certain conditions. For example, the minority innovator needs to be confident, consistent, and perceived as knowledgeable (Moscovici, Mugny, & Avermet, 1985; Thameling & Andrews, 1992, 1999).

One productive way to handle group conflict is through using a cooperative conflict style that is open to minority opinion and integrates all members' interests (Oetzl, 2005; Poole & Garner, 2006).

emergence phase

The third phase of the decision-making process; occurs when group members express a cooperative attitude.

Phase 3. *Emergence.* In the **emergence phase**, the group has worked through the primary and secondary tensions, and members express a cooperative attitude. In successful groups, coalitions dissipate, and group members are less tenacious about holding their positions. Comments become more favorable as members compromise to reach consensus, discuss their problem at length, consider possible alternatives, and eventually generate a group decision). This is the longest phase. For various procedures that can help groups reach agreement, see *Did You Know? Procedures That Help Groups Agree.*

DID YOU KNOW?
Handling Conflicts in Virtual Teams

Good news/Bad news: The good news is that bad relationship conflicts don't occur as often because virtual team members are typically focused more on their work and less on interpersonal issues and office politics. But the bad news is that, because of the lack of face-to-face contact, which helps to accelerate empathy and trust, task-related disputes can more quickly devolve into interpersonal conflict. Here are some ground rules for reducing conflict:

- Clarify expectations.
- Adhere to the agenda.
- Make sure everyone participates.
- Respond in timely manner to teammates (understand when things are urgent and need a response).
- Adhere to commitments and invest in relationships with other team members.
- When conflicts do arise, virtual team expert Keith Ferrazzi suggests that having an online discussion board can be effective: It provides an immediate opportunity to discuss minor

issues, so they don't fester. Others can read and take time to reflect and then respond. Transparency builds trust when issues are dealt with openly and in a timely manner. To be most effective:

- Make the discussion board the team's primary focus—a shared workspace.
- Assign a "point person" for a particular issue—that person keeps track and summarizes and then submit for an agenda item.
- "Diverge and then converge"—after all pros and cons are solicited, schedule a real-time discussion (e.g., teleconference) to select a course of action.

SOURCES: *Trends in Global Virtual Teams: Virtual Teams Survey Report 2016.* RW³ Culture Wizard. Retrieved March 2, 2017, from http://cdn.culturewizard.com/PDF/Trends_in_VT_Report_4-17-2016.pdf.

Ferrazzi, K. (2012, November 19). How to Manage Conflict in Virtual Teams. *HBR Blog Network.* Retrieved March 1, 2017 from http://blogs.hbr.org/2012/11/how-to-manage-conflict-in-virt/.

DID YOU KNOW?
Procedures That Help Groups Agree

List some advantages and disadvantages to each of these procedures. Do some of them promote deeper agreement than others? How so?

- *Voting:* simultaneous (raised hands, vocal), sequential (round robin), or secret (written)
- *Decision rule:* predetermined level of support needed to reach agreement (for example, two-thirds majority, simple majority, or unanimity)
- *Straw poll:* nonbinding voting method that allows the group to get a sense of members' preferences while still allowing them to change preferences

- *Concession:* agreement to eventually agree, despite individual preferences
- *Problem-centered leadership:* procedure in which the leader acts as facilitator, guiding group toward agreement
- *Negotiating:* reaching agreement through series of trade-offs

Adapted from: Sunwolf & Seibold, D. R. (1999). The impact of formal procedure on group processes, members, and task outcomes. In L. R. Frey, D. S. Gouran, & M. S. Poole (Eds.), *Handbook of group communication theory and research* (p. 401). Thousand Oaks, CA: Sage.

Recurring and sustained bouts of secondary tension or conflict can be problematic. In response, members can fill relational roles that promote trust (assuring members that they can rely on each other to put forward their best effort) and cohesion (expressing a desire to remain in the group). Members can also reduce tension by articulating a positive attitude or feeling about their group, the task, or other members and by emphasizing group identity and pride in the group's effort. In short, strong relational bonds within a group promote high-quality decisions and problem solving (Keyton, 1999, 2000), and groups with high trust have fewer relationship conflicts (Peterson & Behfar, 2003).

Phase 4. *Reinforcement.* During the **reinforcement phase**, members reach consensus, the decision solidifies, and members feel a sense of accomplishment and satisfaction. If a small majority makes the decision, they spend phase four convincing other members of its value. In successful groups, members unify and stand behind the solution. Comments are almost uniformly positive.

reinforcement phase

The final phase of the decision-making process when group members reach consensus, and members feel a sense of accomplishment.

Preventing Groupthink

One common and potentially disastrous group process is **groupthink**. This happens when groups arrive at a premature decision, before all alternatives have been realistically assessed. What are the symptoms? Groupthink happens when members feel pressure to conform and do not speak up; or they reject new information and may even react negatively to any information that contradicts the group decisions. Other symptoms are evidenced when group members have an illusion of invulnerability or unanimity. These symptoms produce pressure on group members to go along with the favored group position, assuming not only that the group preferences will be successful but also are just and right (Henningsen & Henningsen, 2006). This phenomenon can have disastrous consequences. The term was coined in an analysis of several foreign policy fiascoes, such as the Bay of Pigs Invasion in 1961 and the U.S. decision to invade Iraq in 2003.

Another example of the disastrous consequences of groupthink was the *Challenger* space shuttle explosion on January 28, 1986. Experts concluded that the contributing cause was a flawed decision-making process at NASA. Specifically, it was the unwillingness of individuals to step outside their roles and question those in authority and ask important questions, even though they had info about the danger of going ahead with the launch (e.g., after the decision was made to launch, NASA supervisors asked if there were any objections from engineers, but no one spoke up). Pressure to meet launch deadlines led to poor communication skills and an unwillingness to risk disagreement that ultimately led to catastrophe and undermined the respect for prior achievements of the space agency (Forrest, 2005; Gouran, Hirokawa, & Martz, 1986).

groupthink

A negative, and potentially disastrous, group process characterized by "excessive concurrence thinking."

What causes people to engage in groupthink? One reason may be a high level of cohesiveness. Although group cohesion is usually viewed as a positive thing, too much of it can lead to premature agreement. The same is true about conflict; too much can result in an ineffective group, but some dissent can help prevent groupthink. Leadership can also promote groupthink: either strong leadership, where one dominating person promotes only one idea, or the opposite—a lack of leadership, leaving the group without direction. Groupthink can also result from a failure to set norms for decision making or from a failure to follow a problem-solving agenda. Finally, extreme homogeneity in the backgrounds of group members may also lead to rushed solutions rather than careful examination of alternatives (Henningsen & Henningsen, 2006).

Groupthink can be prevented in several ways. First, following an established procedure and making sure adequate time is spent in discussion before reaching a decision are both helpful. Second, playing "devil's advocate" and arguing an opposing view to the majority opinion can play a legitimate role in thwarting and derailing the impulse to form a consensus too quickly without considering the alternatives. We discussed previously the important role that minority opinion can play in resolving conflict and producing innovative thinking. Minority opinions can also play an important role in preventing groupthink; this suggests that individual critiques of the majority point of view still need to be carefully considered and answered before the group treats an issue as settled. Third and perhaps most important, group members should be aware of the causes and consequences of groupthink and encourage critical evaluation (at the appropriate time) of ideas and some dissension to prevent premature decisions.

Technology and Group Communication

Technology is playing an increased role in group work, a topic we will address in more detail in Chapter 14. Some researchers assert that technology enhances positive outcomes in a diverse workforce because communication technologies reduce the cues that often lead to stereotypes and prejudice. That is, in virtual teams, members cannot see the gender, skin color, or age of their colleagues, which may equalize contributions and facilitate discussion (Bergiel, Bergiel, & Balsmeier, 2008).

For example, Marek, one of our students, works for an international pharmaceutical company and often collaborates on projects with group members whom he has never met. Members of his team are scattered around the globe in multiple time zones. Thus, he may be online with Luc in Montreal, Caroline in London, Liana in Buenos Aires, Ahmed in Riyadh, Setsuko in Osaka, and Giles in Melbourne. Although he may not have met his group members face-to-face, their tasks are well defined, and this enables the group to complete their projects with few problems. Moreover, their diverse cultural backgrounds enhance the group's ideas and produce a stronger product.

Teams like these that are separated by time or distance rely on a variety of technologies. A recent global business report found that corporate teams are now almost entirely virtual (or distributed); 85 percent of the 1,500 respondents reported working on virtual teams and almost 50 percent never meet in person (*Trends in Global Virtual Teams*, 2016). A virtual work team is similar to the definition of a small (task-oriented) group defined at the beginning of this chapter. They are a group of people identified as a team by their organization (defined and limited membership), function interdependently, and are jointly responsible for outcomes. However, the unique characteristics of the *virtual* team are two: the members are geographically dispersed, and they communicate electronically substantially more than they do face-to-face (Berry, 2011). Additionally, this virtual team phenomenon is changing the way people and businesses develop ideas using Internet collaboration (see *Communication in Society: COINs: Innovation Now*).

COMMUNICATION IN SOCIETY
COINs: Innovation Now

One kind of virtual team phenomenon has changed the way people and businesses develop ideas—through collaboration on the Internet. What are the communication challenges of working in these types of virtual teams compared with face-to-face teams?

Peter A. Gloor, a research scientist at Massachusetts Institute of Technology, and his colleagues have been studying the Internet phenomenon of Collaborative Innovation Networks, or COINs. Gloor defines a COIN as "a cyberteam of self-motivated people with a collective vision, enabled by the web to collaborate in achieving a common goal by sharing ideas, information and work" (2006, p. 4). These inspired individuals, working together spontaneously as a virtual team, often at great distances, are not motivated by financial gain. Rather, they collaborate because of their shared passion for innovation and a commitment to common goals or causes. Gloor describes their collaboration as "swarm creativity." As they spontaneously "swarm" together in cyberspace, they create an environment that promotes dynamic and innovative collaborative thinking.

The results of these virtual collaborations have been astounding. As Gloor notes, the Internet itself is an example of a successful COIN. It was started by a group of people working at a physics research lab, then developed and fine-tuned by various groups of students, researchers, and computer scientists, crossing conventional organizational structures and hierarchies. The rest, as they say, is history. Other examples of more recent COIN successes are Wikis, as well as Linux and other open-source software products and a number of other lesser-known commercial innovations. Gloor and colleagues stress that for COINs to be successful, the team members not only need to share a passion for the products they're developing but also need a certain level of trust in fellow team members, balanced communication, and a shared code of ethics guiding their collaboration.

SOURCES: Gloor, P. A. (2006). *Swarm creativity: Competitive advantage through collaborative innovative networks*. Oxford: Oxford University Press.

Gloor, P. A., Heckman, C., & Makedon, F. (2004, April 14–16). Ethical issues in virtual communities of innovation. Ethicomp 2004, the 7th International Conference on the Social and Ethical Impacts of Information and Communication Technologies, Syros, Greece. Retrieved February 27, 2017 from http://ccs.mit .edu/pgloor%20papers/COIN4Ethicomp.pdf.

Gloor, P. A., Paasivaara, M., Schoder, D., & Willems, P. (2008). Finding collaborative innovation networks through correlating performance with social network structure. *Journal of Production Research*, 46(5).

There are four different types of virtual teams, using different types of communication technologies, with differing degrees of virtualness:

1. Same-time, same-place interactions—instead of face-to-face interaction, these use technology-assisted communication, for example, email across an office

2. Same-time, different-place interactions—use instant messaging, videoconferencing, or telephone technologies

3. Different-time, same-place interactions—use a dedicated chat room on a network; and/or discussion board

4. Different-time, different-place interactions—voicemail, email, online discussion boards, or an intra-organizational social networking service such as Yammer may be used

These categories show how almost any team is virtual to some extent (Berry, 2011, p. 180).

This continuum can also be used to illustrate the importance of using different technologies at different phases of a team project (Gareis, 2006). Many experts suggest that face-to-face or same-time, different-place types of communication technologies (videoconferencing) are best at the beginning, planning stage of a project to establish trust, build solid relationships, and set clearly specified expectations and work assignments. When these are established, then there can be different-time, different-place technologies (e.g., email, other asynchronous communication such discussion boards) (*Trends in Global Virtual Teams*, 2016).

Some experts say that the communication problems between virtual team members are related to the number of time zones that separate them. If only a few time zones apart, members can come to work earlier or later and still have overlapping workdays. If members are separated by many time zones, it becomes a much bigger challenge,

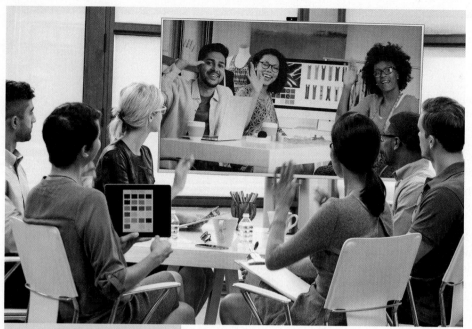

▲ Teams separated by time or distance rely on a variety of technologies, including videoconferencing.

particularly on Fridays and Mondays, but most teams find a way to work with the geographical distance and time differences. For example, one company with team members in the United States and Australia (a difference of 15 time zones) has a policy that members from each country take turns getting up at 2 A.M. once a month for videoconferencing with members from the other country. The rest of the time, they rely on voice-mail and email. Other challenges are the inability to read nonverbal cues, leading to difficulty in establishing rapport and trust, cultural/language differences, and a sense of isolation (*Trends in Global Virtual Teams*, 2016).

How can virtual teams work together most effectively? There seem to be several guidelines—all centered on effective communication: Establish clear rules and expectations about project goals, division of labor, and timelines and choose the appropriate technology for the task at hand (see *Did You Know? The Ultimate List of Virtual Team Technology Tools*). One other element, leadership, is particularly important in virtual

DID YOU KNOW?
The Ultimate List of Virtual Team Technology Tools

Hassan Osman, a Senior Program Manager, has compiled a comprehensive list of communication technologies that can assist virtual teams in scheduling, planning, collaborating and sharing. Which of these have you used? If you have participated in a virtual team, did any of the tools listed here facilitate the team's work? Can you think of other tools a virtual team could use that are not listed here?

1. **Collaboration Tools:** Tools for team collaboration through a central hub for sharing information:
   Slack, Sqwiggle, Grape, Campfire, ActiveCollab, Huddle, Goplan, Podio, Scadaplan, Lighthouse, Blackboard Collaborate, HiveDesk

2. **Project Management Tools:** Tools that help you manage projects with your team through task assignments and scheduling
   Microsoft Project, Basecamp, Primavera, Smartsheet, Workfront, Wrike, Projecturf, Apollo, Brix, Teamwork

3. **Document Storage/File Sharing Tools:** Tools that help you store and share your files securely among team members
   Dropbox, Google Drive, SharePoint, Box, Onehub, Zoho Docs

4. **Meeting Tools:** Tools for web conferencing and collaboration
   WebEx, GoToMeeting, Google Hangouts, Adobe Connect, Anymeeting, MeetingBurner, iMeet

5. **Video & Audio Conferencing Tools:** Tools for meeting through video and audio conferencing
   Skype, Speek, Join Me, Bluejeans, Zoom

   High End-High definition: Cisco Telepresence, Polycom Telepresence, Logitech LifeSize

6. **Instant Messaging Tools:** Tools for real-time chats among team members
   Google Hangouts (was Google Talk), Skype for Business (was Microsoft Lync), Jabber, Sametime, HipChat

7. **Document Co-Creation Tools:** Tools for co-creating and co-editing documents or visuals in real time
   Google Docs (part of Drive), Prezi, Conceptboard, Scribblar

8. **Social Network Tools:** Tools for collaborating and interacting with your team members
   Yammer, Chatter, Jive

9. **Scheduling Tools:** Tools for scheduling common meeting times with team members
   Doodle, Timebridge, ScheduleOnce, TimeandDate

SOURCE: Thecouchmanager.com. (June, 2016). Retrieved February 20, 2017, and adapted from http://www.thecouchmanager.com/the-ultimate-list-of-virtual-team-technology-tools/.

teams: the effective leader needs to ensure that expectations are set and understood (combating the *out of sight/out of mind* problem of virtual work (Berry, 2011) and more importantly, because of the lack of nonverbal cues and face-to-face interaction, a leader of a virtual team needs to pay particular attention to the relationship aspect of group processes. Specifically, leaders need to find ways to establish effective and high-quality relationships with their team members, by showing concern and empathy, encouraging each team member's development and self-expression, and encouraging consensus and a shared team cohesion (Heller et al., 2010; Jawadi, Daassi, Favier, & Kalika, 2013).

A recent study compared the effectiveness of face-to-face and online focus groups working on an evaluation of a leadership program (Abrams et al., 2015). The group discussions were recorded and transcribed and then analyzed for task and social topics. It turns out that the FTF groups generated richer data—more task talk than the online groups— and had less distracting social talk. The virtual teams spent more time socializing than the FTF groups, perhaps because they felt the need to establish a social presence and personality that would be otherwise communicated through tone of voice, facial expression, and so on and their task talk was less rich (fewer words). Other studies have shown that online groups produce higher quality discussions (more evidence of critical thinking) and more equal levels of participation (Dietz-Uhler & Clark, 2001; Guiller et al., 2008; Li, 2007).

In sum, it seems that virtual teams—whether in business, academic, or social contexts—may be most useful for tasks that do not require lots of relational work and require less rich information, but their work could be enhanced by frequent communication and even face-to-face meetings when possible. We'll discuss computer-mediated communication further in Chapter 14.

Journal Prompt 10.5:
Effective Small Group
Communication
Consider the following questions:
What are the four elements of effective small group communication? What are the five steps in the problem-solving agenda? What is a virtual team, and in what circumstances are virtual teams most effective?

The Individual, Small Group Communication, and Society: Power and Diversity

10.6 Discuss how diversity influences small group processes.

Small group communication, like all communication, is influenced by societal forces. The world outside influences this form of communication in two important respects: (1) the way power is used inside and outside groups, and (2) the role cultural diversity plays.

Power and Group Communication

Small groups function within the influences of the societal forces we have discussed throughout this book: political, economic, and historical. People communicating in small groups bring with them their identities and the hierarchical meanings associated with those identities (see Chapter 3). Those group members who hold the values and follow the communication rules of the dominant group in society may more easily contribute to the group and dominate it, which may cause resentment among those who feel marginalized in society generally (Oetzel, 2005).

Groups also establish a power structure. For example, a group member may be elected or appointed to lead a group, which allows that person to wield *legitimate* power (French & Raven, 1959). Much of an individual's power is derived from his or her society/social status and standing. For example, when an individual is appointed to lead a group, this usually occurs because of his or her position within the social hierarchy of the organization.

These power arrangements come with benefits and drawbacks. On the one hand, productive uses of power can facilitate group processes (Sell, Lovaglia, Mannix, Samuelson, & Wilson, 2004). On the other hand, leaders or group members may turn legitimate power into *coercive* power, or threats, to get others to do what they want. For example, they may threaten to withdraw or undermine the process if group members don't do what they want, as experienced by one of our students in *It Happened to Me: Sarah*. In dealing with this dominating member, Sarah's group might have tried some relational roles such as expediter or harmonizer to prevent the dominator from derailing the group discussions.

The use of coercive power is usually unproductive because, as you can see in Sarah's experience, group members resent the threats and may reciprocate by using coercive power when they get the chance. Thus, too much power or a struggle for power can

It Happened to Me
Sarah

We had one girl in our group who was headstrong, but very nice. She wanted to do the project "her way." She insisted that we follow her suggestions. If we didn't, she refused to participate and made comments that undermined the group work. If we did listen to her, then she was sweet and cooperative, and everything went fine. Some members wanted to try to please her; others resented her manipulation, and this situation caused a lot of conflict in the group.

lead to resentment and poor decision making (Broome & Fulbright, 1995). In contrast, researchers find that groups whose members share power equally exhibit higher quality communication. When everyone participates and contributes to the discussion equally, power will more likely be distributed equally. In contrast, the unequal power of social hierarchies often occurs in the small group situation because members bring their identities and experiences to the group. Thus, members' cultural identities, which fall along a power hierarchy, can impact small group work.

Cultural Diversity and Small Group Communication

Given the changing demographics in the United States and abroad, small groups will increasingly include members whose backgrounds differ. As we discussed in Chapter 8, cultural backgrounds influence communication patterns, and small group communication is no exception (Crown, 2007). For example, people from countries where a collectivistic orientation dominates may be most concerned with maintaining harmony in the group, whereas members with an individualistic orientation may be more assertive and competitive in groups, and team members from countries where direct communication style is preferred seem to have an easier time working in virtual teams. These differences can lead to challenges in accomplishing group goals.

How does cultural diversity affect small group processes? Does it result in poor communication, more conflict, lower productivity, and less satisfaction? Or can diverse groups, with their various viewpoints, make better, more effective, and more creative decisions?

Research indicates that even though interactions might be more complex, especially in the early stages of group work, diversity can lead to positive and productive outcomes. Let's look at how diversity influences four aspects of group communication: innovation, efficacy, group processes, and group enjoyment.

Innovation   Decades of research by organizational scientists, psychologists, sociologists, economists, and demographers show that socially diverse groups (that is, those with a diversity of race, ethnicity, gender, and sexual orientation) are more innovative than homogeneous groups (Phillips, 2014). For example, in one study, diversity in education and gender was found to be positively related to the likelihood of introducing an innovation (Ostergaard, Timmermans, & Kristinsson, 2011). Another study of 122 manufacturing firms showed that diverse top management teams (TMT) had a strong impact on new product innovativeness (and ultimately enhanced performance) (Talke, Salomo, & Rose, 2010).

This makes sense, because having different perspectives means also having a variety of information sources to apply to a problem or issue. This variety of information broadens people's views and their ability to evaluate, as one researcher noted "Diversity jolts us into cognitive action in ways that homogeneity simply does not" (Phillip, 2014). So, ultimately, a diverse workforce operating in a rapidly changing world is better able to monitor, identify, and respond quickly and innovatively to external problems than a homogeneous one. What are the implications for you, as a potential group/team member in professional, academic, or social settings? If the group is a diverse one, know that the potential is there for innovative work. But also remember that for maximum innovation and effectiveness, you and other team members need to encourage equal participation.

Performance (Efficacy) Some research studies report that diverse groups work more effectively. For example, a study of 177 bank executives concluded that increases in racial diversity were clearly related to enhanced financial performance (Richard et al., 2003). However, other studies report the opposite (Caya, Mortensen, & Pinsonneault, 2013). This isn't surprising, given the many types of diversity and the

▲ Because diverse groups can outperform homogeneous groups, it is often wise to seek out opportunities to work with people who are different from you.

fact that each group develops communication and processes that may help or hinder performance. Communication in diverse groups may be more challenging at the onset, so that cultural differences in attitudes and communication styles may lead to early conflict (Poole & Garner, 2006). However, if group members handle these differences well, the outcome may be as good or better than in homogeneous groups (Larson, 2007).

There are several ways to accomplish this. One is by focusing the group's attention on the goal of the group, something shared by all, rather than on individual cultural differences (Crown, 2007; Poole & Garner, 2006). A second strategy is to explore commonalities among group members—for example, shared interests, activities, or experiences. In a college course, group members may discover that they are enrolled in other courses together as well or that they participate in the same extracurricular sport or social activity. In a business setting, the team members may find that they have shared professional experiences or hobbies. Some discussion of these commonalities helps solidify relationships, leading to enhanced group cohesion.

It seems that building early group cohesion in diverse groups smoothes the way to managing differences in later discussions (Oetzel, 2005). As a group member, you can help a diverse group perform more productively by facilitating cohesion early on in the team effort.

Group Processes As we discussed in Chapter 8, one way that individuals differ across cultures is in their preference for individualism or collectivism, and these preferences have an impact on **group processes**. To understand these preferences, one group of researchers used a method quite similar to the study we described previously. They randomly assigned students to task groups so that each group had varying degrees of age, gender, and ethnic diversity. Their group task was a course assignment in which they analyzed conversations using various theories presented in class. The students then filled out a questionnaire measuring their communication processes in the group (e.g., participation rate, listening, respect, and conflict management), their own individualistic–collectivist tendencies, and their satisfaction with the group work (Oetzel, 1998).

Interestingly, ethnic, gender, and age diversity in this study had little effect on the communication process, but those who preferred more interdependent or collectivistic interaction participated more and cooperated more in the group, thus having a more positive impact on group processes. Group members who convey respect and participate in a cooperative manner are also likely to put forth substantial effort toward completing a task and to encourage the contributions of others. Why? Effective communication by some may reduce isolation and encourage effort of all group members. Not surprisingly,

group processes
The methods, including communication, by which a group accomplishes a task.

those members who participated more were more satisfied with the group outcome. Other studies have found that collectivistic values and group member interdependence also stimulates creativity—probably because group members feel encouraged to speak up in this positive group climate (Choi et al., 2016; Van der Vegt & Janssen, 2003).

These studies suggest that groups that are diverse in terms of race, ethnicity, and gender don't necessarily experience more difficult processes. Moreover, because people are diverse and different in so many ways, one can't make assumptions about any collection of individuals based on physical attributes like age, race, or gender.

Group Enjoyment Although diverse groups may be more innovative and effective, are they more enjoyable? To explore this question, another study examined the experience of college students who worked in groups that were composed of either (1) mostly whites or (2) mostly ethnic minorities (Asians, Asian Americans, African Americans, Hispanics, and others of mixed ethnicity). The researchers found that minorities and white students all preferred minority-dominated teams to white-dominated teams. How can one explain these findings? The researchers suggest that some level of collectivism may have been working in the minority-oriented groups, and whether or not it was, members of these groups were more attentive to relational harmony (Paletz, Peng, Erez, & Maslach, 2004).

What are the implications to be drawn from all these studies that have examined the effect of diversity on group work, whether working online or face-to-face? First, it seems there are two types of diversity: demographic diversity (age, gender, ethnicity, and race) and deeper cultural differences in attitudes and values (individualism and collectivism preferences) that also play an important role. Second, culturally diverse groups *may* produce more innovative ideas, *may* be more enjoyable, and *can* be as productive as homogeneous groups. However, enjoyment and productivity do not occur automatically in these groups; they depend largely on the communication skills of the group members, which do not always come naturally. "Many people believe that good communication skills are 'common sense.' Contrary to expectations, the problem with common sense is that it is not all that common" (Oetzel, 2005, p. 366). Thus, leaders of culturally diverse groups need to focus on helping all team members, including reticent ones, learn to participate fully and to communicate respectfully in a way that promotes collaboration, group cohesion, and consensus building (Caya et al., 2013).

These findings suggest that organizations need to develop policies and programs allowing for and valuing the unique characteristics of each group, whether working face-to-face or online. Further, with proper education and development, diverse teams have the potential to experience higher levels of satisfaction and lower turnover. Supporting this idea is the finding that groups with high diversity but without proper education in group process are associated with high turnover and more conflict (Poole & Garner, 2006; Sargent & Sue-Chan, 2001).

To summarize, communicating in groups occurs within societal structures—whether the groups are teams working in a small business, task forces in a nonprofit organization, or small problem-solving groups in a college course. These social structures establish power relations and status hierarchies that in turn come into play in group interaction. The cultural backgrounds of group members also influence group communication, and if handled well, cultural diversity can enhance group innovation, performance, communication processes, and enjoyment. However, the bottom line is that effective group work flows from effective and ethical communication skills, the topics we turn to next.

Critical Thinking Prompt
Think about a small group experience you've had recently. What did other group members say that made you (and others) feel a part of the group? What was said that made you (and others) feel excluded from the group?

Journal Prompt 10.6: Power in Small Groups
Consider the following question: What is the difference between legitimate and coercive power in small groups?

Ethics and Small Group Communication

10.7 Give three types of guidelines for communicating more ethically in your small group communication.

Ethical communication in small groups is especially important because the success of the group and the task depend on it. One might argue that being in a group carries additional ethical responsibilities because one's individual actions can affect how people think about and react to other members of the group and their ideas. In short, in groups, you are no longer responsible only for yourself but for other members as well. Consider three types of ethical guidelines: (1) those aimed at strengthening group relationships, (2) those dealing with specific communication practices, and (3) those related to group decisions.

Relational ethics involve demonstrating commitment to the group. For example, an ethical small group member attends group meetings and participates. As we've discussed, equal participation, buy-in, and establishing trust are all important aspects of group success that cannot be achieved when members are absent from or silent in group discussions. Another relational ethic involves doing your fair share of the group work because equal participation extends to sharing equally in the responsibilities for completing the tasks. A third ethical guideline to strengthen small-group relationships is to maintain open channels of communication (maintaining contact with other group members, contacting others when needed, and responding to others in a timely manner).

In considering ethical communication practices in small groups, it might be helpful to think about the ethical guidelines discussed in Chapter 1 and consider how they might apply to a small group context. First, being truthful in your communication is particularly important because you are making contributions that affect larger collective decisions (Hargrove, 1998). Truthfulness also includes being accurate and avoiding exaggeration. For example, if you were reporting facts about crime on campus, you would offer statistics, not just say "I found out that crime is really a huge problem." Although you should strive for accuracy and honesty in your language, there may be times when you should not say everything you know—for example, when you should respect the confidentiality of others, including group members. If your friend has been raped and you know this information might be helpful to your group discussion about campus security, you should ask for your friend's permission before divulging this information. Similarly, group members may disclose personal information in the group discussion that they may not wish repeated outside the group.

Secondly, ethical group members also work toward communicating authentically, as discussed in Chapter 1. Why is authentic communication essential? As we noted previously, group cohesion and trust are important to the performance and success of groups. Authentic communication that is open and free from pretense and language that is inclusive and not hurtful to others go a long way in promoting the kind of group cohesion necessary for group effectiveness. Finally, as a receiver, you must listen with an open mind while also evaluating others' contributions. Doing so will enhance the quality of discussions and help prevent groupthink, in which groups jump to premature conclusions and decisions.

A third area of small group ethics concerns the collective actions of the group members. For example, what if you find a project paper on the Internet that closely resembles the project you've been working on? Your group is running out of time at the end of the semester and it would be easy to copy portions of the paper, making only a few minor changes. What ethical guidelines apply here? Perhaps the ethics of fairness and taking responsibility for one's own actions apply. Submitting someone else's work instead of your own is not fair to other students in the course who did their own work, and taking responsibility for poor time management as a group is a more ethical action than using someone else's work.

Journal Prompt 10.7: Ethics in Small Groups
Consider the following questions: What are three areas of ethical guidelines for small group work? Which guidelines do you think are most important and why?

Improving Your Small Group Communication Skills

10.8 Discuss ways to improve your own small group communication skills.

Although no strategies will work in every group communication situation, two strategies can help you be more effective in many of them.

First, cultivate an interdependent or collectivist attitude, a "we" orientation instead of a "me" orientation, and work toward collaborative communication, whether working face to face or online (Lewis et al., 2010). This means that you must sacrifice some of your personal ambition, needs, and wants in favor of the group's needs and work to ensure buy-in from all group members. People who are extremely individualistic may find this difficult. Yet those with a more collectivist attitude can influence group processes toward more effective communication, more participation, and more satisfaction of all members (Oetzel, 2005).

In addition to cultivating an interdependent attitude, striving for cohesion is also important in successful small group relationships and task accomplishment. Cohesion occurs when team members trust each other. Further, group success depends on the participation of each member, but members are unlikely to give their best to the group if they can't trust other members to do the same. Trust is particularly important in virtual teams, where members have less face-to-face interaction that might otherwise provide important cues to the intent or attitude of fellow group members. Several strategies build trust and cohesion:

- Focus on the strengths of all group members, and recognize their contributions to group goals. Be sure to acknowledge all group achievements.
- Remind the group of common interests and background experiences. Doing this can help build cohesion, prevent unnecessary conflict, and strengthen group identity.
- Be observant and notice when a member might be feeling unappreciated or uninvolved in the group. Encourage that person to participate. People gain trust and become more trusting as they participate, especially if their participation is encouraged. Fortunately, more trust leads to more cohesion and stronger group identity, which in turn leads to better communication, more satisfaction, and more cohesion.

In sum, the effectiveness of a small group depends in large part on the communication and the relationships established among the members. As a group member, you can promote (or inhibit) the productive communication needed. We believe that using the tools discussed in this chapter will not only make your small group work more effectively but will also make it more enjoyable.

Journal Prompt 10.8: Improving Small Group Communication

Consider the following questions:
What are two general strategies for improving your small group communication? Why is cohesion so important in small group communication? What is a collectivist perspective and how does it enhance small group work?

SUMMARY

10.1 Identify four reasons for learning about small group communication.

- Small group communication is a fact of life, and learning to be a better small group communicator can enhance your academic performance, your career achievement, and your personal success.

10.2 Define *small group communication*.

- Small group members share a common purpose, are interdependent, and exert influence on each other.
- The primary benefit of small groups is that they are more productive and creative than individuals working alone.
- The disadvantages are that decisions take longer; groups can silence minority opinions, get distracted, and make poor decisions; and relational problems and conflicts can make the experience less than satisfying.

10.3 Identify and give examples of task, relational, and individual small group roles.

- Twelve task and eight relational roles are required for effective group work. In effective groups, individuals fill these roles as needed at any given time during group work. Eight individual roles also exist that group members may fill; these roles, however, tend to be dysfunctional and unproductive.

10.4 Describe five theories of group leadership.

- A group's or organization's success is often directly related to the presence of good leadership.
- Leadership is defined as an influence relationship among leaders and followers who intend changes and outcomes that reflect their shared purposes.
- Five theories of leadership—trait, style, functional, transformational, and servant—explain leadership effectiveness.

10.5 Describe the characteristics of communication that occur during the four phases of small group decision making and the role of technology in small group processes.

- Successful problem-solving groups tend to follow agendas. The most common is a five-stage agenda: (1) defining the problem, (2) analyzing the problem, (3) identifying alternative solutions, (4) evaluating the proposed solutions, and (5) choosing the best solution.
- Related to the five-stage agenda are the four phases of decision making that most groups complete in every stage of the problem-solving agenda: orientation and primary tension, conflict and secondary tension, emergence, and reinforcement.
- Although group cohesion is generally beneficial, too much of it can lead to groupthink.
- Technology plays an increasing role in small group work, as we touched on here. We'll discuss it in more depth in Chapter 14.

10.6 Discuss how diversity influences small group processes.

- Societal forces impact small group processes via the role of power in small group work and through cultural diversity.
- Although cultural diversity can present challenges for group processes, it can also produce innovative, efficient, and enjoyable group experiences if handled appropriately. Building cohesion and trust in early stages of group work is particularly important in diverse groups.

10.7 Give three types of guidelines for communicating more ethically in your small group communication.

- There are three types of ethical guidelines that should guide small group work: (1) those aimed at strengthening group relationships, (2) those dealing with specific communication practices, and (3) those related to group decisions.

10.8 Discuss ways to improve your own small group communication skills.

- Skills for achieving effective group communication include cultivating an interdependent attitude and striving for trust and cohesion.

KEY TERMS

APPLY WHAT YOU KNOW

1. *Group Roles Activity* Think of a recent group experience you've had. Look at the lists of task, relational, and individual role behaviors in Tables 10.1 through 10.3. Record all behaviors and roles that you filled. Which behaviors (if any) were missing in your group? Which other roles might you have filled?

2. *Groupthink Exercise* Consider experiences you've had in group work. Answer the following questions concerning groupthink. After answering the questions, meet with several classmates and compare answers. Then, as a group, come up with suggestions for ensuring against groupthink.

   - Have you ever felt so secure about a group decision that you ignored all the warning signs that the decision was wrong? Why?
   - Have you ever applied undue pressure to members who disagreed to get them to agree with the will of the group?

   - Have you ever participated in a "we-versus-they" feeling—that is, depicting those in the group who are opposed to you in simplistic, stereotyped ways?
   - Have you ever served as a "mind guard"—that is, have you ever attempted to preserve your group's cohesiveness by preventing disturbing outside ideas or opinions from becoming known to other group members?
   - Have you ever assumed that the silence of the other group members implied agreement?

   For more information about how to spot and prevent groupthink, see https://www.mindtools.com/pages/article/newLDR_82.htm.

Communicating
in Organizations

LEARNING OBJECTIVES

11.1 Explain the importance of understanding communication in organizations.

11.2 Define organizations and explain their communication functions and structures.

11.3 Understand the types of communication that occur among coworkers and explain their functions.

11.4 Discuss current social influences on organizations and organizational communication.

11.5 Distinguish between individual and communal perspectives on organizational ethics.

11.6 Identify four steps involved in a strategic approach to conflict management.

CHAPTER TOPICS

The Importance of Organizational Communication

Defining Organizational Communication

Organizational Communication and the Individual

The Individual, Organizational Communication, and Society

Ethics and Organizational Communication

Improving Your Organizational Communication Skills

"Much of our success within organizations is connected to our communication abilities."

Charee's first assignment in her organizational communication class was to list all the organizations she interacted with for one day. As she went through her day—buying a cup of coffee at Starbucks, interviewing for a job, listening to class lectures, ordering lunch at Chipotle, and tutoring at a community center—she had a realization. Almost every interaction she had that day either occurred with representatives of organizations or within organizations.

We live in a society of organizations. You may not realize it, but organizations shape your life in many ways. For example, legislative bodies and law enforcement agencies implement formal codes—such as traffic laws—that constrain your daily behavior. Educational institutions shape what counts as knowledge, such as when schools determine whether evolutionary theory, intelligent design, or both will be taught in science classes. In addition, religious groups influence popular moral beliefs about issues such as gay marriage or abortion rights.

Business corporations also are major players in shaping our society. Some argue that because they control vast economic resources, huge transnational corporations have become even more powerful than governments, and thus heavily influence government personnel and policy, educational content and practices, and international relations (Deetz, 1992). Corporations also affect our lifestyle desires and choices. For instance, why do consumers want and purchase new, "improved" cell phones, tablets, and televisions when their current ones work perfectly well (Deetz, 1992)?

Even though organizations cast a strong influence on individuals, individuals also affect organizations—as consumers, as supporters, and participants in religious and civic institutions, and as individuals who work for, or against, specific organizations. Although living in an organizational society generally means you can't escape the influence of organizations, you can have a profound effect on them, just as they do on you. For example, in 2017 Uber instituted their surge pricing during a taxicab driver one-hour work stoppage at JFK airport. The drivers were protesting the federal government's immigration and travel ban on seven predominantly Muslim countries. Protestors viewed Uber's behavior as an attempt at "strike breaking." Consequently, tens of thousands of customers expressed their dissatisfaction with Uber by deleting their Uber apps. Uber's management quickly apologized for what they described as a misunderstanding, donated $3 million to a legal defense fund to help drivers with immigration and translation services, and their CEO resigned from President Trump's advisory team. Thus, individuals can influence organizational behavior; however, your ability to have this effect depends on your understanding of organizations and your skills communicating with and within them.

In this chapter, we explain what we mean by organizational communication and explore the types of communication that commonly occur within organizations. First, we look at how individuals communicate within organizations. Then we broaden the discussion to examine the ways society impacts the interactions between individuals and organizations as well as how organizations influence society and individuals. We wrap up with a discussion of ethical issues associated with communication in and by organizations and offer ways to improve your ability to manage conflict more effectively within organizations.

The Importance of Organizational Communication

11.1 **Explain the importance of understanding communication in organizations.**

Because you participate in organizations regularly, you will benefit from understanding how to communicate more effectively with and within them. Doing so will enhance your professional success, allow you to ask more informed questions about everyday organizational practices, and help you decide what organizations you wish to frequent and support.

Much of your success within organizations is connected to your communication abilities. For example, if you want an organization to hire you, you must first display good interviewing skills. If you want a promotion, it may be essential to understand your boss's goals and beliefs (Eisenberg, Monge, & Farace, 1984). And if you seek public or civic office, you must have strong public-speaking and social-influence skills to gain support from your political party and endorsements from influential organizations.

In addition to enhancing your professional success, understanding organizational communication will help you ask more informed questions about everyday organizational practices, such as how the corporation you work for determines pay raises, how a nonprofit charity you support can become a United Way organization, or how you can influence legislation in your community. Knowing what questions to ask and how to ask them will improve your ability to accomplish your goals. Finally, given that a wide variety of religious, corporate, and community organizations exist, there is a limit to how many you can support. Understanding how to question organizations and how to interpret their responses and policies can help you make informed choices regarding which ones to embrace. For example, you might decide not to purchase products or services from for-profit organizations that force their employees to work mandatory overtime at the expense of their home lives. Or you might decide that you are better off working for an organization whose goals and beliefs you support strongly because your agreement with those goals likely will influence your career success.

In sum, organizational communication is central to a person's ability to navigate successfully the myriad legal, educational, religious, corporate, and civic organizations one confronts across a lifetime.

Journal Prompt 11.1: Organizational Communication
Consider the following question: What are the benefits of studying organizational communication?

Defining Organizational Communication

11.2 **Define organizations and explain their communication functions and structures.**

Next, we define what we mean when we say *organization*, and we explain the role communication plays in it. As part of this definition, we focus on two aspects common to all organizing efforts: communication functions and structures. We then conclude this section by examining the role of communication in establishing organizational cultures.

Organizations from a Communication Perspective

Scholars from a variety of fields, including sociology, economics, psychology, and business management, are interested in understanding organizational life. However, communication scholars bring a particular focus to the study of organizations. From their perspective, communication is not just another variable of organizational life. Thus, it is not merely the oil that lubricates other parts of the machine or the glue that binds parts together. Put bluntly, without communication, they argue, there are no "parts"; there is no "machine."

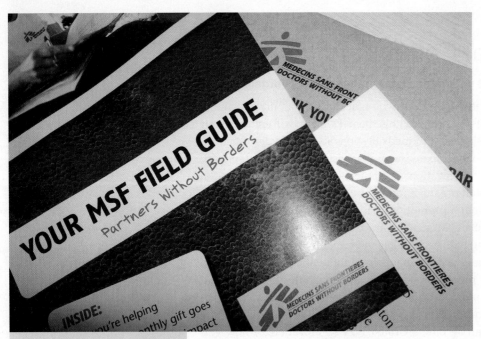

▲ Individuals join organizations such as Doctors without Borders because they can accomplish their goals more effectively if they work with others.

organizations

The set of interactions that members of purposeful groups use to accomplish their individual and common goals.

Consider the organization of a college classroom, for instance. Communication scholars argue that it is in the *process of interacting* as student and teacher—giving and listening to lectures, taking and grading exams—that the meaning of these abstract roles becomes real. In this view, then, communication is the process that calls organizations into being. Thus, communication scholars argue that *communication constitutes organizations*. It enables or creates them.

From this perspective, then, **organizations** are defined as the set of interactions that members of groups use to accomplish their individual and common goals (Taylor & Van Every, 1993). Two parts of this definition are important: that organizations are composed of group members' interactions and that organizational members pursue goals.

In Chapter 9, we explained how a dyad (a pair of individuals) creates and maintains a relationship through communication; this same process occurs within organizations. As individuals in organizations maintain, or alter, their communication practices, they influence the organization itself. For example, if a new store manager is hired who encourages employees to be more courteous in their interactions with each other as well as with customers, the nature of the organization is likely to change. Employee turnover may be reduced, employees may feel more positively about their jobs and therefore work harder, and the more positive interactions with clients could increase sales. Thus, just changing an organization's communication interactions can significantly affect the organization and its members.

In addition to being composed of communication interactions, our definition indicates that organizations are purposeful. Organizations are not random groupings of people; organizational members come together to accomplish individual and collective goals. For example, organizations such as Greenpeace, Doctors without Borders, and Habitat for Humanity exist because their individual members want to make positive changes in the world, and they can do so more effectively if they work together.

Communication Function and Structure

function

The goals and effects of communication.

production

A function of organizational communication in which activity is coordinated toward accomplishing tasks.

maintenance

A function of organizational communication in which the stability of existing systems is preserved.

Organizational communication is interaction that organizes purposeful groups, and it generally exhibits several properties—two of which are especially relevant here. The first we will call **function**, by which we mean the goals and effects of communication. Traditionally, scholars recognized three major functions of organizational communication (Daniels, Spiker, & Papa, 1996). **Production** refers to communication that coordinates individuals' activities so they can accomplish tasks. For example, when a manager creates a set of store opening and closing procedures, informs employees of monthly sales goals, or develops a standardized process for assembling products, she allows employees to accomplish various tasks. The **maintenance** function of organizational communication serves to maintain existing aspects of the organization. Consider, for example, awarding an employee-of-the-month plaque, conducting a performance review, and clarifying a vague set of workflow procedures—all of which enforce the status quo and keep the system running smoothly. A third function is **innovation**, which involves communication that encourages change in the organization. Examples might include suggestion boxes, restructuring and retraining, policy revisions, and the like.

You may have noticed that in most of these examples the three traditional functions overlap considerably. Let's take performance reviews as an illustration. As a manager, you may hope to reinforce the status quo (maintenance) by providing an employee with positive feedback, but you may also hope to instigate change (innovation) in that employee's behavior by offering suggestions for improvement. Also, most performance reviews involve other goals not adequately captured by the three-function model, such as negotiating trust, flexing egos, and so forth. With closer examination, you may see that at least some of these performance review goals are at odds with one another. In fact, most organizational communication serves multiple, even competing, functions.

▲ The maintenance function of organizations serves to preserve existing systems, such as providing high performers with recognition to ensure that workers continue to strive for excellence.

The second major property of organizational communication is **structure**. Traditionally, communication structure referred to lines of communication, or a system of pathways through which messages flow. Such a conduit model of communication emphasizes *direction*: **downward communication**, with subordinates, **upward communication** with superiors, and **horizontal communication**, with peers (Putnam, Phillips, & Chapman, 1996). Note that direction-based metaphors presume **hierarchy**, a kind of power structure in which some members exercise authority over others. A more contemporary way to define structure is as *recurring patterns of interaction among members* (Monge & Contractor, 2001). Rather than treating messages as literal objects moving through conduits, this newer definition points to communication networks that emerge among members. It recognizes that such networks may be hierarchical, though other possibilities exist.

Another important distinction exists between **formal structure** and **informal structure**. Formal structure refers to the officially designated channels of communication, whereas informal structure refers to unspoken but understood channels (Blau & Meyer, 1987; Roy, 1995). As an analogy, think of sidewalks on your campus as the official walkway (formal structure), whereas footprints worn in the grass represent the shortcuts and detours people take from the path they are given (informal structure). Thus, formal structures are explicit or desired patterns of interaction (that is, what the organization suggests we do). Informal structures are patterns of interaction that develop spontaneously. Most organizational members use both formal and informal structures, for example, following corporate procedures for requesting a leave of absence (formal) and asking a friend in a position of power to recommend their leave request to the boss (informal).

Of the many features of organizational communication we might choose to discuss, we highlight function and structure because they have surfaced continually in scholarly visions of organizational communication.

innovation
A function of organizational communication by means of which systems are changed.

structure
Recurring patterns of interaction among organizational members.

downward communication
In a traditional conduit model of communication, communication with subordinates.

upward communication
In a traditional conduit model of communication, communication with superiors.

horizontal communication
In a traditional conduit model of communication, communication with peers.

hierarchy
A power structure in which some members exercise authority over others.

Organizational Culture

In addition to structure and function, each organization also develops a distinct organizational culture. **Organizational culture** refers to a pattern of shared beliefs, values, and

formal structure
Officially designated channels of communication, reflecting explicit or desired patterns of interaction.

informal structure
Unspoken but understood channels of communication, reflecting patterns that develop spontaneously.

organizational culture
A pattern of shared beliefs, values, and behaviors.

behaviors, or "the system of meanings and behaviors that construct the reality of a social community" (Cheney, G., Christensen, L. T., Zorn, T. E., Jr., & Ganesh, S. (2004). Organizational communication in an age of globalizations: Issues, reflections, practices. Prospect Heights, IL: Waveland.). More informally, organizational culture can be thought of as the "personality" of an organization (McNamara, 2008). As these definitions suggest, organizational cultures are created as people act and interact with one another.

Organizational cultures are composed of the artifacts, languages, rites and rituals, ceremonies, stories, beliefs, and habits enacted by members of that group.

Languages in this sense refer to the types of phrases and words used to describe and talk about the organization and its relationships with others. For example, all of the authors of this book worked at Arizona State University (ASU). Here are some examples of languages used in the university: administrators routinely refer to ASU as "the new American University;" the football stadium is called "Sun Devil Stadium;" the university's mascot is "Sparky;" and its archrival in sports is the University of Arizona (UofA). As you can imagine, the UofA has its own mascots, stadium names, and university catchphrase as well. All organizations develop these specific names, words and phrases to describe common practices, experiences, and members in their workplaces.

Ceremonies are preplanned events that can be formal or informal. Generally, they serve a practical purpose as well as a symbolic one (Martin, 2012). For example, universities have graduate ceremonies that serve to recognize the work and success of the year's students who have completed their coursework. These events are largely symbolic in that most universities don't actually hand out diplomas to students during the ceremony. (In case you didn't know, usually students receive diploma covers at graduation and their actual diplomas arrive in the mail.) But they also serve a practical purpose in bringing together students, faculty, and staff as well as students' families so they can celebrate this achievement together.

The terms rites and rituals are often used interchangeably. Ceremonies are composed of rites and rituals; having faculty march into the auditorium at graduation as well as singing the school song, and having students move their graduation cap tassels from the right to the left are all examples of rites and rituals. But rites and rituals can occur during everyday activity as well. Some organizations, for instance, have specific rituals for how they celebrate employee birthdays, how they mark an employee's retirement, or how they recognize outstanding employee performance. Rites and rituals reinforce the organization's values through members' participation in them.

Habits refer to behaviors that people regularly perform at work but that are not part of the organization's formal or informal policies. Rather, habits are voluntary, casual actions that are accepted, ignored, or least not commented on. For example, at some organizations, employees routinely arrive a few minutes late in the morning or when returning from lunch. Such behavior certainly is not part of a company's policies, but it may be tolerated. Because habits are informal behaviors that are implicitly agreed on by a company's membership, they adapt and change as new employees are hired—and especially as management of the organization changes.

Finally, stories are members' recounting of their experiences as a way of dramatizing organizational life. People tell three types of stories at work: personal, collegial, and corporate. Personal stories are ones that individuals tell about themselves; typically they are used to support a positive portrayal of oneself and may include a hint of bragging. Collegial stories are those that employees tell about others. They can be amusing or harrowing, but they tend to reveal how people feel about the organization. Finally, corporate stories represent how managers see the organization and are often used to justify organizational policy or to endorse behaviors they prefer. Stories offer a simple and entertaining way for people to express their beliefs and attitude about the organization (Pacanowsky & Trujillo, 1983).

Participating in an organization's culture is important to one's sense of belonging; consequently, at universities newcomers, students, faculty, and staff become familiar with and integrated into their organizations as they learn the specific languages, attitudes, stories, and so on enacted by that organization.

Organizational cultures develop as a result of organizations' attempts to integrate, or assimilate, new members and as they respond to internal and external feedback. Thus, organizational culture is not static but changes over time. The television show *Mad Men*, for example, was engaging, in part, for its depic-

▲ The television show *Mad Men* was engaging, in part, because it depicted the organizational culture of an advertising agency in the 1960s.

tions of a specific organizational culture that no longer exists—an ad agency in the 1960s. As *Mad Men* reveals through its depictions of male–female work relationships and employee drinking and smoking practices, organizational culture reflects larger cultural values as well as the beliefs, attitudes, and practices of the specific organizations, which can and do change over time.

Each organization develops its own culture, though some organizations may share similar cultural characteristics. One cultural characteristic that is common to a variety of organizations is gender. That is, organizational cultures often are classified as masculine or feminine based on the values they embrace. For instance, fire stations, law enforcement groups, and the military all share a "masculine culture" that values risk taking, courage, and bodily strength (Highgate & Upton, 2005; Prokokos & Padavik, 2002; Thurnell & Parker, 2008). By contrast, "feminine cultures" such as Mary Kay Cosmetics and nursing are described as sharing a value of family-friendly policies, open communication, and participative and egalitarian decision making (Everbach, 2007).

Nonetheless, organizations can be of a similar type or serve a similar function but still have aspects of their culture that differ considerably. Thus, although they are all restaurants, the organizational cultures of McDonald's, Applebee's, and Hooters differ. If you were to assess their cultural differences, you might think about who the employees are, the type of clothing employees wear, how they interact with patrons and each other, and what type of qualities are rewarded and valued. Even a brief visit to these establishments quickly reveals cultural differences.

The discussion thus far may suggest that organizational cultures are viewed positively by their members; however, that is not always the case. Some, many, or even most of the members of an institution may dislike their organization's culture. **Organizational climate** is the term used to describe how people feel about, or experience, organizational cultures (Schneider, Ehrhart, & Ehrhart, 2005). If you have ever worked at a place you detested, it is likely that the organization had a culture you disagreed with or felt uncomfortable in. Often when managers refer to whether or not a job candidate is a good "fit," they are describing whether they believe the person will like and participate in the company's culture.

Now that you have been introduced to the basic features of organizations, in the following section we discuss how individuals become members of organizations and the important role communication serves in supervisor–subordinate and coworker relationships.

organizational climate
How organizational members feel about, or experience, the organization's culture.

Journal Prompt 11.2: Defining Organizational Structure
Consider the following questions: What is the contemporary definition for organizational structure? How does it differ from the previous description of organizational structure?

DID YOU KNOW?
Comparing Corporate Cultures

What type of organizational culture do you think you would find most compatible? Are you aware of any current organizations whose culture sounds appealing to you? When looking for a job, how can you find out about the corporate culture of an organization you're interested in?

One of the most spectacular merger failures on record was in large part due to the differences in corporate cultures. When German auto company Daimler-Benz bought U.S. American Chrysler Company in 1998, the CEOs of both companies hailed it as "a merger of equals," economies of scale and sharing of technology would bring huge savings and higher profits. But the difference in their corporate cultures became quickly evident.

Daimler's corporate culture was formal and hierarchical, with a clear chain of command and respect for authority, although the executives all ate in the same dining room as the workers. Executives and managers preferred to develop detailed plans and implement them carefully. They came to meetings with a detailed agenda they expected to follow.

In contrast, the corporate culture at Chrysler was more relaxed and egalitarian, although executives ate in an executive dining room. Creativity, innovation, and efficiency were emphasized; input from employees was valued and a trial-and-error method of problem solving was acceptable. They expected freewheeling discussions during meetings, using an agenda only as a guideline.

Daimler employees thought Chrysler's operating style was chaotic and careless, and Chrysler employees found Daimler stifling and rigid. Not surprisingly, employee satisfaction (and profits) soon plummeted. In 2007, Daimler sold Chrysler.

SOURCE: Appelbaum, S.H., Roberts, J., & Shapiro, B.T. (2009). Cultural strategies in M&As: Investigating ten case studies, *Journal of Executive Education, 8*(1), 33–58.

Organizational Communication and the Individual

11.3 Understand the types of communication that occur among coworkers and explain their functions.

If you wish to influence the organizations you interact with, you need to understand some of the basic types of communication that help create organizations and organizational life. It is important to be familiar with guidelines for how you might perform these types of communication most successfully. Although all the communication skills and abilities we examine in this book will definitely make you a better communicator in organizational contexts, here we focus on three types of communication that are integral to organizations: assimilation, supervisor–subordinate communication, and coworker communication. We also explore three types of organizational dilemmas or tensions that employees must manage.

Assimilation

assimilation

The communicative, behavioral, and cognitive processes that influence individuals to join, identify with, become integrated into, and (occasionally) exit an organization.

In the organizational context, **assimilation** refers to the communicative, behavioral, and cognitive processes that influence individuals to join, identify with, become integrated into, and (occasionally) exit an organization (Jablin & Krone, 1987). When you join an organization, you usually don't become an accepted member of the group automatically, nor do you immediately identify with the organization and its members. Instead, over time you go through a process in which you and others begin to see you as an integral and accepted part of the organization. The pledge process for sororities and fraternities is one highly ritualized form of assimilation.

Assimilation is a common experience for individuals who join any type of organization, whether it is a business, a religious group, or a social group. However, you probably most often think of assimilation as occurring when you begin a new job. Assimilation is similar to the process of cultural adaptation experienced when individuals enter a new culture, as we discussed in Chapter 8.

Organizational identification is a stage of assimilation that occurs when an employee's values overlap with the organization's values (Bullis & Tompkins, 1989). For example, Arizona Public Service (a utility company) values community involvement, encourages its employees to volunteer, and even provides time off for workers to do so. Some new hires, however, may not inherently value volunteerism, and others may even resist the corporation's attempt to influence their behavior outside work. However, over time, some of these new hires will begin to identify more strongly with the organization and its values, and their attitudes will change. Those who had not given much thought to volunteering may now see it as a corporate responsibility, and those who were opposed may come to see time off for community service as a benefit.

▲ When these soldiers joined the U.S. Army, they were not immediately integrated. As they learned about the organizational culture and its rules, they became assimilated.

Of course, not every new employee experiences organizational identification. Some employees never come to accept their organization's values. For instance, if an employee values an environment in which coworkers become friends and socialize frequently, he or she likely will never identify with a highly competitive sales organization in which employees work independently and socialize only rarely. Such employees often leave their jobs, or if they remain, they never come to see themselves as part of the organization.

organizational identification
The stage of assimilation that occurs when an employee's values overlap with the organization's values.

Over time, most people do identify with the organizations they join, and they become increasingly integrated. If they leave such organizations, they go through a process of decoupling their identities from the organization and move from being seen as insiders to once again being viewed as outsiders. This leaving process can be difficult, especially if one does not have a new identity and organizational affiliation. For example, people who retire often feel sad and disconnected because they have lost an important identity.

The communication process most central to assimilation is information seeking, a reciprocal process in which individuals seek out information that helps them adapt to the organization and the organization attempts to convey information that will assist in this process. Two organizational communication scholars, Vernon Miller and Fred Jablin (1991), developed a typology of the information-seeking tactics that newcomers use to ascertain organizational roles, rules, and norms. These strategies take the same forms as other types of uncertainty-reduction techniques (see Chapter 9) and include active, passive, and interactive strategies (Berger, 1979).

The passive strategies new members use include observation and surveillance. These strategies involve watching others' communication and behavior or interpreting stories about past communication and behavior so that one can infer the rules and norms of the organization. For example, if you wonder what time employees typically arrive for work, you could go to work quite early one day and observe who arrives at what time, or you might attend to stories about people who arrived consistently late to work and what happened to them.

Active strategies include overt questioning, indirect questioning, disguising conversations, and questioning third parties. In these instances, the employee tries to discern organizational expectations by acquiring information from others. For example, a new employee might directly ask a more experienced coworker, "Are we expected to stay after 5 P.M.?" or she might pose the question more indirectly by saying, "How often do most employees stay past 5 P.M.?" Or she could engage in a disguising conversation by complaining about how late she had to stay in her previous job, to see how her colleague responds. In addition, she might ask a third party (a secretary) rather than a primary source (her supervisor) whether employees at her level are expected to stay past 5 P.M.

Finally, new employees seek information through the interactive strategy of "testing limits." A newcomer tests limits by seeing how far he or she can push specific boundaries. For instance, an employee might determine whether leaving at 5 P.M. is acceptable by leaving consistently at that time and then noting how people respond. (To see a different perspective on organizational assimilation, see *Alternative View: What Is a "Real Job"*?).

The communication strategies that employees use to assimilate to their workplaces often set the tone for how they will interact with the organization. Another type of communication that influences how employees' interact act at work is supervisor–subordinate communication.

Critical Thinking Prompt
Which assimilation strategies do you think would be the most effective for a new employee to use?

Supervisor–Subordinate Communication

Supervisor–subordinate communication occurs when one person has the formal authority to regulate the behavior of another. In hierarchical organizations, virtually

---

ALTERNATIVE VIEW
What Is a "Real Job"?

How would you define what a "real job" is? What types of jobs do you think of as not being "real jobs"? Where have you heard the term real job, and who taught you its meaning?

In Robin Clair's work *The Political Nature of a Colloquialism, "A Real Job": Implications for Organizational Assimilation* (1996), she critiques current models of organizational assimilation, such as Miller and Jablin's, for assuming that any work that occurs prior to or aside from working for an organization is not "real" work. To help us understand how individuals become socialized outside the context of organizations and to understand what constitutes work, she studied the popular expression real job by asking undergraduate students to write an essay about a time they encountered the term. She did so to examine what students mean by the term real job as well as to understand who was socializing them into a belief about what a real job looks like.

In their essays, Clair's respondents identified five dominant characteristics of a "real job":

- The money (i.e., one is well paid)
- Utilizes one's education
- Is enjoyable
- Requires 40 hours of work per week/8 hours per day
- Advancement is possible

Specific jobs that were identified as *not* being real jobs included serving in volunteer organizations such as the Peace Corps, working in a fast-food restaurant, working for one's family, or not making enough money to provide for a family. Overall, the respondents suggested that people with a college degree do not belong in unskilled labor positions, which for them did not constitute real jobs.

A number of respondents did acknowledge that the concept of a real job was a social construction and some even rejected it. But even those who embraced jobs that others might consider not a real job continued to compare their own work to the societal standard and felt the need to justify their choices.

When asked who shaped their perceptions of what constitutes a real job, respondents pointed to family members (particularly fathers), friends, and coworkers. As Clair also points out, however, socialization is not a linear process in which society socializes young people into a particular belief about what constitutes a real job. Instead, she argues, those who are being socialized also serve to socialize themselves and others by the ways they talk about their own and others' employment plans and desires.

SOURCE: Clair, R. (1996). The political nature of a colloquialism, "A real job": Implications for organizational assimilation. *Communication Monographs, 63,* 249–267.

all employees engage in supervisor–subordinate communication, even CEOs—who must report upward to boards of directors (their supervisors) and downward to other organizational members (their subordinates).

When organizational hierarchies exist, subordinates frequently attempt to please their supervisors to keep their jobs, receive raises and promotions, or perhaps even to become supervisors themselves someday. By the same token, successful supervisors must motivate and manage their subor-dinates. These sets of needs and goals impact how supervisors and subordinates communicate. At times, a supervisor and subordi-nate's needs can be such that they communicate in ways that create misunderstandings and prob-lems. An example of this is called semantic-information difference.

Semantic-information distance describes the gap in information and understand-ing between supervisors and subordinates on specific issues (Dansereau & Markham, 1987).

It Happened to Me
Yoshi

Upward distortion creates difficulties and makes it impossible to fix a lot of organizational problems. I usually have a conversation with my coworker about problems in our depart-ment on a weekly basis. When we talk, he blows off steam and tells me exactly what the problem is and how it can be fixed; however, when he talks to our manager, he tends to simplify the problem and makes it seem like it is due to his own shortcomings instead of the operation's. This in turn makes it almost impossible to really get the problem fixed. I think that one big cause of this upward distortion is the fact that most managers have the attitude that they don't want excuses, they just want results. How can we address a problem with our manager if he doesn't want to hear anything negative?

What causes this gap? Behaviors of both subordinates and supervisors contribute, but we'll look at the subordinate side first. See *It Happened to Me: Yoshi* for an employee's view on this communication gap.

When subordinates are hesitant to communicate negative news and present informa-tion in a more positive light than is warranted, they engage in a behavior called **upward distortion** (Dansereau & Markham, 1987). Why do subordinates do this? Employees natu-rally edit the information they send upward because not everything is relevant to their bosses and because they can manage many issues without the supervisor's interven-tion. However, when workers withhold or alter important information, supervisors may be making decisions based on distorted and inadequate information. This can impair their ability to perform their own jobs successfully. For example, if an employee knows that an important production deadline is looming, he or she may be reluctant to tell the supervisor that the deadline can't be met for fear of reprisals or blame. Fear of negative repercussions is probably the most important reason that employees distort information as they communicate with their supervisors.

Supervisors, too, may communicate a more positive image than they actually per-ceive. For example, even though a manager may suspect her company is struggling, she may not let her employees know. Why? She may do so in part because she needs to moti-vate employees and to create and maintain their satisfaction as the organization seeks to recover. Employee satisfaction is central to the supervisor–subordinate relationship and, ultimately, to the supervisor's ability to influence subordinates and impact their perfor-mance. Employee satisfaction has been linked to decreased absenteeism and decreased turnover as well as increased productivity (Richmond, McCroskey, & Davis, 1986).

Although the reasons for it make intuitive sense, semantic-information distance can cause problems in supervisor–subordinate relationships. Supervisors need accurate, honest information to perform successfully. Therefore, when they become aware that employees have been distorting information, they are unlikely to trust or reward those employees. Of course, supervisors also need to communicate clearly so subordinates have the information they need to perform their jobs competently.

What can supervisors do to minimize semantic-information distance as well as increase employees' (as well as their own) satisfaction and success? As you might imagine, we suggest that they engage in effective communication. Although many

semantic-information distance
Describes the gap in information and understanding between supervisors and subordinates on specific issues.

upward distortion
Occurs when subordinates present information to superiors in a more positive light than is warranted.

Critical Thinking Prompt
Think about supervisors you have had. What was it about their communication strategies that you liked or disliked? Which of the strategies we've mentioned here did they use?

communication strategies contribute to supervisor success, we highlight four: openness, supportiveness, motivation, and empowerment.

openness

Sharing ideas as well as listening to others in a way that avoids conveying negative or disconfirming feedback.

Openness occurs when communicators are willing to share their ideas and listen to others in a way that avoids conveying negative or disconfirming feedback (Cheney, 1995; Jablin, 1979). When supervisors are open, they create an environment of trust that decreases the likelihood that upward communication will be distorted.

Even though openness is a desirable characteristic, one can engage in *too much* openness. For example, if an employee is on leave to undergo rehabilitation for addiction, a supervisor typically should not share that information directly, or even indirectly, with others because doing so would be inappropriate. In addition, sometimes supervisors need to shield their employees from information. For example, informing subordinates of a possible layoff before the decision is final could cause unnecessary stress and panic.

supportiveness

Providing subordinates with access to information and resources.

Supportive supervisors provide their subordinates with access to information and resources. Thus, supportive supervisors explain roles, responsibilities, and tasks to those they manage; they also take the time to answer employees' questions. Further, managers are supportive when they give their subordinates the tools, skills, education, and time they need to be successful. Overall, supervisors who help their employees solve problems, listen actively, provide feedback, and offer encouragement are not only supportive, but they are also successful (Whetton & Cameron, 2002).

motivation

Feeling personally invested in accomplishing a specific activity or goal.

Productive and successful supervisors are able to motivate their subordinates. Workers experience **motivation** when they feel personally invested in accomplishing a specific activity or goal (Kreps, 1991). Many U.S. American supervisors and organizations focus on creating extrinsic or external motivators, such as pay raises, bonuses, promotions, titles, and benefits. However, supervisors who can instill intrinsic motivation in their subordinates are more successful. Intrinsic motivation occurs when people experience satisfaction in performing their jobs well, find their jobs to be enriching, and are, therefore, dedicated to their organizations or professions (Cheney et al., 2004).

empowerment

Feeling capable of performing a job and having the authority to decide how to perform it well.

Supervisors can create intrinsic motivation by setting clear and specific goals that are challenging but attainable and by engaging workers in the creation of those goals. In addition, they need to provide frequent and specific feedback, including praise, recognition, and corrections. Positive feedback is especially important because it encourages job satisfaction, organizational identification, and commitment (Larson, 1989). Finally, intrinsic motivation thrives in a positive work environment that stresses camaraderie or social relationships.

▼ Positive communication between supervisors and their subordinates is characterized by openness, supportiveness, and the empowerment of subordinates.

Empowerment, the fourth characteristic that improves communication, relates to the supervisor's ability to increase employees' feelings of self-efficacy. He or she does this by instilling the feeling that the subordinate is capable of performing the job and has the authority to decide how to perform it well (Chiles & Zorn, 1995). In general, supervisors who empower their subordinates function more like coaches than traditional managers. They encourage employees to be involved in decision making, to take responsibility for their tasks, and to provide suggestions for improving their own

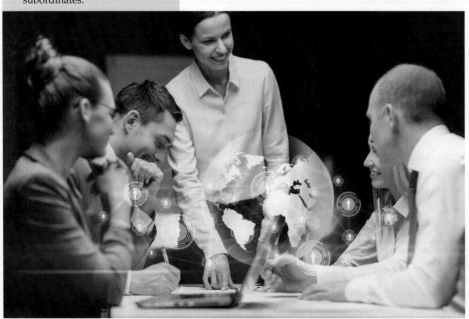

and the organization's performance. Employees who feel empowered are more likely to develop intrinsic motivation and to communicate openly with their supervisors.

Communication is also central to subordinates' success on the job. Subordinates who get along with their supervisors are much more likely to be satisfied and successful. Consequently, subordinates use a variety of means to manage and maintain the quality of their relationships with their supervisors. Studies of subordinate communication tactics determined that employees who use three specific upward communication tactics—ingratiation, assertiveness, and rationality—were most likely to positively affect their manager's perceptions of them (Dockery & Steiner, 1990; Wayne & Ferris, 1990).

Ingratiation refers to behavior and communication designed to increase liking. It includes friendliness and making one's boss feel important. Of course, one can be too ingratiating and come off as being insincere, but genuine respect and rapport can be effective. **Assertive** subordinates who can express their opinions forcefully without offending or challenging their bosses also tend to engender liking and approval. In addition, subordinates who can argue **rationally**—meaning that they communicate with their bosses through reasoning, bargaining, coalition building, and assertiveness—are often adept at managing their supervisors. Finally, employees who understand their bosses' professional and personal goals as well as their strengths and weaknesses, and who can adapt to their preferred communication styles, can create positive working relationships.

ingratiation
Behavior and communication designed to increase liking.

assertiveness
Expressing one's opinions forcefully without offending others.

rationality
The ability to communicate through reasoning, bargaining, coalition building, and assertiveness.

Communicating with Coworkers

Along with assimilation and supervisor–subordinate communication, communication with coworkers is fundamental to organizations and their employees. Sometimes the communication that occurs among coworkers or peers is described as *horizontal* because it is directed neither upward (to superiors) nor downward (to subordinates). No matter how they are described, workplace relationships are distinctive interpersonal relationships that influence both the individuals within them and the organization as a whole (Sias, 2005).

Employees become friends with their colleagues for many of the same reasons they develop other types of interpersonal relationships—proximity, attraction, and similarity. Some people, especially those who live alone, may spend more time with their colleagues than they do with anyone else. Even people who live with others may spend as much—or more—time with coworkers as they do with their families or housemates. However, unlike other interpersonal relationships, friendship development at work is affected by an additional dimension—how supervisors treat individual employees. If supervisors are perceived to treat some employees more favorably and this treatment is perceived as undeserved, coworkers may dislike and distrust favored employees. On the other hand, if a manager is seen as treating a subordinate more negatively than others and the treatment is perceived as unwarranted, it can increase employee interaction and cohesiveness (Graen & Graen, 2006; Sias & Jablin, 1995).

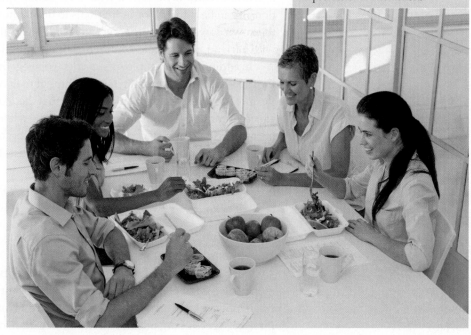

▼ Coworkers engage in informal-personal as well as formal-professional interactions.

Coworkers in organizations engage in both formal–professional and informal–personal interactions. The formal–professional category includes communication about tasks, solving problems, making plans, and influencing one another's beliefs and decisions (Kram & Isabella, 1985). In addition, coworkers engage in considerable informal, or personal, interaction. In fact, adults draw many of their friends from the pool of people at work, and approximately 50 percent of employees state that they have engaged in a romance at work (Vault, 2003). Coworkers also can serve as an important source of emotional and social support (Rawlins, 1994).

The professional and the personal aspects of coworker communication and relationships are not distinct. Rather, professional interactions influence coworkers' personal relationships, and vice versa. Sias and Cahill (1998) found that more talk about more topics among coworkers not only resulted from increased closeness in their relationships but also contributed to it. Thus, coworkers who also are friends tend to communicate more intimately and about more topics, both professionally and personally, than those who are not (Sias, Smith, & Avdeyeva, 2003). As you might expect, being isolated from employee networks can result in isolation from quality work-related information (in addition to loneliness) and cause one to be at an information disadvantage relative to one's colleagues (Sias, 2005). Research indicates that this information disadvantage has important consequences. Poor coworker communication and lack of access to information have been found to predict lower job satisfaction and commitment.

The presence of friendly relationships among coworkers has positive consequences for individuals and organizations. When employees feel connected to their colleagues, they provide each other with support and assistance that can increase their success. Such relationships also intensify workers' loyalty to the company and increase job satisfaction and organizational identification, which can help minimize job turnover (Kram & Isabella, 1985).

Despite the ease, attractiveness, and advantages of forming close relationships at work, such relationships can require careful navigation. Friendship, by its nature, is egalitarian, but power differences often occur among coworkers. Even employees at the same level in the organization may have different levels of informal power, and the situation can become increasingly problematic if one of them receives a promotion and thereby acquires greater formal power in the organization. In addition, coworkers may find themselves torn between their loyalty to the organization and their loyalty to a friend. For example, how should one respond if a friend engages in unethical behavior at work, decides to become a whistleblower, or quits in protest over a denied promotion? It can be difficult for individuals to decide how to respond in a way that protects their own as well as their friends' interests. Finally, it can be more difficult to be objective with a friend, to withhold confidential information, and to provide honest feedback.

In addition, other employees can develop negative perceptions and interpretations of the friendships and courtship relationships of their colleagues. Coworkers may question the motives of the partners, may believe that the individuals involved are conspiring to affect corporate policy, or may perceive that the relationship partners treat others unfairly in comparison. For instance, if two salespeople become close, their coworkers may perceive that they are sharing information or client lists that permit them to be more successful than those outside the relationship. In addition, because of the potential for trouble and bad feelings, some organizations have explicit policies that discourage "affectional" relationships, which may include friendships but most certainly include romances.

Organizational Dilemmas

Although organizations can provide many benefits to an individual, including status, money, a sense of belonging, and even a significant part of one's identity, they also can create physical and psychological distress. Thus, in addition to being proficient at the three key types of organizational communication, members of organizations may have to communicatively manage and respond to three types of organizational dilemmas: emotion labor, stress and burnout, and work–life conflict.

Emotion Labor   As we discussed previously, employees learn a variety of norms for organizational behavior during assimilation. Some of these norms pertain to emotion display rules (Scott & Myers, 2005). Emotion display rules are the explicit or implicit rules that organizations have for what emotions can be appropriately displayed and how those emotions should be communicated. For example, firefighters learn early in the assimilation process that they should not express strong negative emotions such as fear, disgust, and panic (Scott & Myers, 2005). Instead, they learn to speak in calm tones, to offer verbal assurances, and to suppress any comments that might distress the public. Similarly, the employees at the local grocery store have learned to show cheerfulness and helpfulness toward customers, even if they actually feel irritation, anger, or frustration.

It Happened to Me
Sonya

For a year, I worked on a cruise line as an assistant cruise director. My job was to organize activities and help entertain the passengers. I helped with bingo games, organized costume contests, and participated in various games with the passengers. In addition, I was expected to dance with the passengers in the evening at the nightclub. Unfortunately, I often had to deal with passengers who had had a few drinks and wanted to "get friendly" or invite me back to their rooms. No matter how the passenger behaved, I was expected to be polite, pleasant, and friendly without, of course, ever actually becoming involved with one! It was really difficult sometimes. I would be so angry, upset, or embarrassed at how a passenger behaved, but I could never show it. This is one of the major reasons I did not sign up again after my first year on the ship.

When the organization expects or requires workers to display particular feelings, employees are engaging in emotion labor (Hochschild, 1983). Typically, organizations ask employees to alter their emotional behavior in three ways. First, they may ask employees to heighten or increase their expressions of joy (i.e., cruise ship and other tourism employees), to appear mean or indifferent (debt collectors and law officers, on occasion), or to convey "a vaguely pleasant professional demeanor" (nurses and receptionists; Cheney et al., 2004, p. 68). For one student's experience with emotion labor, see *It Happened to Me: Sonya.*

Some scholars believe that performing emotion labor benefits employees. They argue that when workers perform emotions they do not actually feel, they can better cope with stress (Conrad & Witte, 1994), and they are more able to interact in emotionally satisfying ways with their clients (Shuler & Sypher, 2000). These scholars suggest that social workers, emergency medical personnel, and other employees in the social services find their work easier and more meaningful when they perform emotion labor.

Others believe it can be harmful (Tracy, 2000; Waldron, 1994), especially when it is required and when it benefits the organization but not the employee. For example, Sarah Tracy (2005), an organizational communication scholar, studied correctional officers' emotion labor and its consequences. She found that the officers often were expected to manage contradictory emotional displays—for example, showing respect for inmates but not trusting them, or nurturing them while also being tough. She discovered that performing these contradictory emotions led some of the officers to experience withdrawal, paranoia, stress, and burnout. Thus, consistently having to perform emotion labor, especially when the requirements are ambiguous and contradictory, may cause psychological and physical harm to some workers.

Stress and Burnout   As you just read, correctional officers often experience stress and burnout. But they are not the only employees who suffer in this way; stress and burnout have become widespread in the U.S. workplace, and the terms have become common in everyday speech. However, **burnout** includes a specific set of characteristics, including exhaustion, cynicism, and ineffectiveness (Maslach & Leiter, 1997; Maslach, 2003). It is a chronic condition that results from the accumulation of daily stress, where

Critical Thinking Prompt
Do you believe that performing emotion labor is beneficial or detrimental to employees? Why? Could it be beneficial in some jobs but not others? Why?

burnout
A chronic condition that results from the accumulation of daily stress, which manifests itself in a specific set of characteristics, including exhaustion, cynicism, and ineffectiveness.

stress is defined as a common response to important and consequential demands, constraints, or opportunities to which one feels unable to respond (McGrath, 1976).

Exhaustion, which is a core characteristic of burnout, can include physical, emotional, or mental exhaustion. It expresses itself as physical fatigue, loss of affect (or emotion), and an aversion to one's job. Employees who are emotionally exhausted may try to reduce the emotional stress of working with others by detaching from them, a behavior called depersonalization, which is related to the second characteristic of burnout—cynicism. Cynicism is manifested as an indifferent attitude toward others. A person with a cynical attitude may view others as objects or numbers and may also express hostility and harsh criticism toward them. Employees might feel ineffective, the third characteristic of burnout, which occurs when workers negatively evaluate their own performance. Ineffectiveness may result in absenteeism, decreased effort, and withdrawal (Richardsen & Martinussen, 2004).

Burnout arises as a result of a combination of personality factors (e.g., how well one manages ambiguity and stress) and organizational stressors. Organizational stressors are aspects of one's job that create strain. Some of the more significant organizational stressors include work overload; confusion, conflict, and ambiguity related to job roles; being undermined by a supervisor (Westman & Etzion, 2005); and low levels of social support (Koniarek & Dudek, 1996).

Workload refers to the amount of work an individual is expected to perform. Work overload occurs when employees feel they have more work than they can accomplish, and this is a major contributor to feelings of exhaustion. Despite expectations that technology, and especially computer technology, would lessen the burden for workers in the United States, people today are working longer hours and dealing with heavier workloads than before the advent of these technologies. In addition, workers frequently find that now they are never "away" from the job because they are instantly and constantly available through mobile devices. The resulting work pressures are having an increasingly negative effect on individuals, families, and organizations (Glisson & Durick, 1988).

Work overload also is related to our second major organizational stressor—role confusion, conflict, and ambiguity. Role ambiguity occurs when employees do not understand what is expected of them. This is most likely to occur when one begins a new job, but it also occurs when organizations undergo change (Chambers, Moore, & Bachtel, 1998). Because today's workers are faced with continual change resulting from budget cuts, reorganizations, and new technologies, they frequently experience role ambiguity (Chambers et al., 1998).

To give some perspective on the role ambiguity and confusion play as work stressors, consider this. As recently as 20 years ago, newly hired engineers primarily needed to communicate with other engineers, most of whom were born in the United States and were native speakers of English. Since that time, however, U.S. companies have hired more engineers from other countries and have expanded their operations around the world. Consequently, many engineers now need to communicate with and supervise others who do not share their native culture and background. They have been required to develop intercultural communication skills they never expected would be necessary and to become conversant with cultures outside the United States. Some long-term employees are unsure of their ability to respond appropriately. Employees in many industries face similar challenges as organizations respond to changing market conditions, globalization, and new technology. Unfortunately, uncertainty about one's job duties and one's ability to perform those duties creates considerable stress for workers.

Role conflict arises when employees find it difficult to meet conflicting or incompatible job demands (Igbaria & Guimaraes, 1993). For example, the correctional officers we mentioned in our discussion

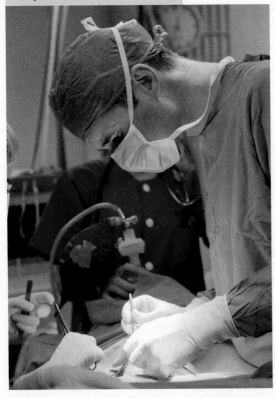

▼ Job stress tends to be high for healthcare workers because of the highly consequential demands inherent in the job and the fact that, in some cases, even the most highly skilled professionals are unable to save a patient's life.

of emotion labor experienced considerable role conflict. On the one hand, they were expected to act like social workers whose job it was to treat prisoners with respect, to nurture them, and to facilitate their well-being and rehabilitation; on the other hand, they were expected to function as paramilitary agents whose job it was to maintain order and safety, to mistrust the prisoners, and to be tough. Similarly, when managers are told to treat their employees fairly and humanely but also to meet tight production deadlines, they suffer from role conflict. Research indicates that being asked to perform such incompatible tasks on the job gives rise to considerable stress and ill effects (Rizzo, House, & Lirtzman, 1970). For example, role conflict and ambiguity can cycle into burnout, leading workers to experience feelings of ineffectiveness in their jobs.

To complete our discussion of organizational stressors and burnout, we focus squarely on communication issues. When employees feel undermined by their supervisors, whether through having information withheld, being denied the resources they need to do their jobs, or being treated unfairly, they are more likely to experience cynicism and a lack of efficacy (Maslach & Leiter, 1997). They may feel they cannot accomplish their work because they lack the resources to do so, and they may believe that even if they do perform well, they will not be rewarded.

Communication with coworkers can contribute to burnout when one's colleagues are unable to provide the social support one needs to cope with organizational stressors. Feelings of burnout then may spread from one employee to his or her colleagues. This fact, combined with the faster pace of most organizations, can lead to a breakdown of community within the organization and disconnect coworkers from one another (Maslach & Leiter, 1997).

Interestingly, research has established that communication itself can be an important moderator of employee burnout. Findings show that supervisor communication that includes active listening, effective feedback, participative decision making, and supportiveness can decrease the severity of subordinate burnout (Casey, 1998; Golembiewski, Boudreau, Sun, & Luo, 1998). Similarly, communication with coworkers that conveys warmth and support and reaffirms the meaning of one's work can help employees cope with burnout (Casey, 1998).

If you would like to see if you are experiencing burnout, go to www.mindtools.com/pages/article/newTCS_08.htm and take the Burnout Self-Test.

Work–Life Conflict   A third type of organizational dilemma that workers face is **work–life conflict**, defined by the difficulties individuals and families face as they try to balance job and home responsibilities. Since the 1990s, work–family balance has become an issue of concern and another type of role conflict, especially for dual-career couples (Kirby & Krone, 2002). As more women have entered the workforce and more families have become reliant on two incomes, people are finding it difficult to manage their competing demands. The pervasiveness of communication technologies such as email, cell phones, instant messaging, and pagers has made it difficult for some workers to ever get away from work and focus on the other aspects of their lives.

work–life conflict
Difficulty balancing job and home responsibilities.

In response to these concerns, organizations began to develop family-friendly policies, such as flextime, family leave, and dependent-care benefits (Morgan & Milliken, 1992). However, studies have shown that many employees do not take advantage of these benefits (Kirby & Krone, 2002; Rapoport & Bailyn, 1996). The reality is researchers have found that some employees are discouraged from taking advantage of these benefits or are not informed about their existence. For example, managers may indirectly communicate that employees should not use the available benefits because it causes problems for them, their departments, and the organization (Rapoport & Bailyn, 1996).

A study of Corning, Xerox, and Tandem Computers determined that employees who used such benefits experienced negative career consequences (Rapoport & Bailyn, 1996). Once employees discovered that their coworkers suffered when they used the company's family leave or flextime benefits, they simply stopped requesting them. Kirby and

▲ The widespread use of technology in many jobs has increased the conflicts people have in maintaining separation between their work lives and private lives.

Krone (2002) conducted another study whose title aptly describes this organizational policy: "The Policy Exists, But You Can't Really Use It." The irony is that some organizations receive credit for being family friendly while not having to actually implement their policies (Jenner, 1994; Solomon, 1994). However, when workers are not able to balance the many demands in their lives, they, their families, and society at large suffer the consequences.

Although both men and women must manage work–life issues, much of the research on work–life conflict has focused on the difficulties working women face as they try to manage paid and unpaid labor. Men are perceived to work as hard as or harder at paid work than women, but research indicates that women contribute at least twice as much unpaid labor to their families, resulting in high levels of work–life conflict (Alberts, Tracy, & Trethewey, 2011).

To summarize, communication is central to an individual's life within an organization, and individuals face many communication-related issues as they navigate organizations. Such challenges involve assimilation as well as communication with supervisors, subordinates, and coworkers. Inevitably, conflicts arise, as do a variety of potential organizational dilemmas, including emotion labor, stress and burnout, and work–life conflict. Thus, successful individuals are those who are able to communicate effectively as they negotiate the challenges, conflicts, and dilemmas of organizational life. However, as you've seen throughout this book, if you only consider individual forces or factors, you can't understand the whole picture. Individuals and organizations both are subject to numerous societal forces, the topic we turn to next.

Journal Prompt 11.3: Supervisor Communication
Consider the following question: What four communication strategies contribute to supervisors' success?

The Individual, Organizational Communication, and Society

11.4 Discuss current social influences on organizations and organizational communication.

In this section, we explore how organizations and the societies in which they are located exert influence on each other and the individuals within them. First, we examine two of the most significant societal forces that impact organizational communication—history and globalization. Next, we discuss three important recent organizational practices that influence individuals and society, including the development of a new social contract between organizations and employees, the rise of urgent organizations, and the blurring of boundaries between home and work. Finally, we examine power relations within organizations and their impact on employees. We address these topics to explicate how each has influenced beliefs about organizational communication and its performance.

Societal Influences on Organizations

Organizations are shaped in part by the societies in which they are located. As societies change over time, so do the organizations within them. In addition, as organizations spread their operations into new cultures, they must change and adapt to those cultures to be successful. In the next section, we focus on these two societal influences on organizations: (1) social change and its impact on organizations and the communication within them, and (2) globalization and its effects on organizations and organizational communication.

Historical Forces   Prevailing beliefs about work, individuals, and knowledge creation have influenced what people expect of organizations as well as how they are expected to act within them. For example, until the early 1900s, popular talk about organizational techniques took a moral tone. Journalists, novelists, clergy, and other prominent figures often described business owners as men of superior character, which they were obligated to model for the betterment of the lower, working class (Barley & Kunda, 1992). During this time, managers' and owners' opinions and communication were considered important, whereas those of the working classes were not.

By the 1930s, a major change in thinking about organization and communication occurred. Resulting from cultural changes as well as researchers such as Mary Parker Follett (1942), people began to question the absolute right of managers to command and control employees and began to focus, instead, on the human relations function of organizations. That is, management began to be seen as needing to educate (through teaching and persuading), to interact with employees (by seeking input), and to integrate everyone's input. Thus, for the first time, organizational theorists and managers came to believe that workers needed to have a voice in the organization.

A variety of developments around the 1960s prompted another shift in thinking about organizations and communication (Barley & Kunda, 1992) toward what we might call a *systems mentality*. Military operations research began to find a home in industry, and the rise of computers fostered interest in organizational communication processes. Across many academic disciplines, researchers began a quest for general, even universal, theoretical principles. Biologist Ludwig von Bertalanffy (1968), for instance, developed a highly influential **general systems theory** that, he believed, applied as well to the social sciences as it did to the life and physical sciences. Many organization scholars agreed. They saw organizations as systems not only composed of many subsystems but also embedded in larger systems. Hence, they sought to develop strategies for communication that occur within the units or subsystems of the organization as well for communication that occurs between the organization and its environment.

Today, one of the most important societal factors to impact organizations, and the individuals who work within them, is globalization. **Globalization** refers to the increasing connectedness of the world in economic, political, and cultural realms (Cheney et al., 2004). Although we typically think of globalization in economic terms, it also describes the ways in which political and cultural events affect people around the world. For example, terrorist attacks in Europe and the Middle East influence tourists' travel plans as well as governments' political alliances. From an economic perspective, conflict in the Middle East leads to fears that oil production will suffer and that higher energy costs will occur in the United States and other countries reliant on this source of oil. Because of globalization, people in the United States are connected intimately to other parts of the world; as a result, decisions and events in far-removed places can affect them.

Although many scholars and experts agree on what globalization *is*, considerable disagreement exists concerning whether globalization, specifically economic globalization, is a positive or negative force in individuals' lives. Proponents believe that globalization leads to decreased trade barriers that result in increased prosperity and economic development across societies (Krugman, 2002). Critics, however, argue that globalization leads to a growing gap between the rich and the poor because transnational organizations can operate without oversight by national and international institutions that protect the interests of individuals (Ganesh, Zoller, & Cheney, 2005). More specifically, these critics maintain that this lack of oversight leads to

general systems theory
Theory that organizations are a system composed of many subsystems and embedded in larger systems, and that organizations should develop communication strategies that serve both.

globalization
The increasing connectedness of the world in economic, political, and cultural realm.

▼ Starbucks is one of many global organizations.

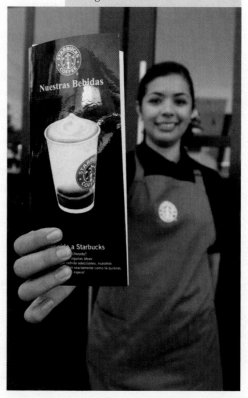

companies attempting to profit by ignoring worker safety, not providing fair compensation, and exploiting the environment.

What are the communication implications of globalization? First, it means that more people and businesses have intercultural contact and that they need to learn how to communicate more effectively across cultures, as we noted in Chapter 10. Many categories of individuals need to interact with support personnel around the world, even in their nonwork lives, and increasingly workers in multinational organizations must communicate and work with people from diverse cultures. Second, global forces such as market deregulation may have leveling or homogenizing effects on organizational practices all over the world. Learn more about this issue in *Communication in Society: Case Study: Antiglobalization Protests*.

Influence of Organizations on Individuals and Society

Not only are organizations influenced by society and cultures, but they also influence them and the individuals who comprise them. In this section, we explore three trends in contemporary organizations and the ways in which they impact society and individuals' lives. These trends include the new social contract, urgent organizations, and blurred boundaries between work and life.

The New Social Contract   Over the past 25 years, a fundamental change has occurred in the relationship between individuals and their employers (Chilton & Weidenbaum, 1994; Jablin & Sias, 2001). Until recently, employees expected to spend years, if not their entire working lives, with a single company and to be rewarded for their service and loyalty with job security and good retirement benefits (Eisenberg, Goodall, & Trethewey, 2010). This is no longer the case. Along with globalization, an increase in organizations'

COMMUNICATION IN SOCIETY
Case Study: Antiglobalization Protests

Do you think economic globalization, on the whole, improves individuals' lives in the United States and elsewhere? Why or why not? What terms would you use to refer to those in the movement opposing globalization? What do you predict the future of corporations and other organizations will be like with regard to globalization?

Most Americans first became aware of the so-called antiglobalization movement in 1999, when protests erupted in Seattle outside the meeting of the World Trade Organization (WTO); hundreds of demonstrators were arrested and thousands were injured. In subsequent years, antiglobalization demonstrations were organized in United States and foreign cities outside meetings of the International Monetary Fund (IMF), World Bank, Group of Eight (G8), and other high-level global economic institutions.

Activists in the movement argue that "antiglobalization" is a misnomer because they are not against globalization as such. Instead, they use terms such as antiplutocracy and anticorporate. Many consider themselves proponents of a global justice movement. In 2001, they organized the first World Social Forum in Porto Alegre, Brazil, as a counterevent to the World Economic Forum, which was taking place in Davos, Switzerland, at the same time.

The loosely organized global social justice movement includes a wide variety of organizations and individuals, among them Nobel Prize–winning economists Amartya Sen and Joseph E. Stiglitz. In general, what they oppose is "corporate personhood" and the unbridled capitalism inherent in "free trade" under agreements such as the North American Free Trade Agreement (NAFTA) and the Association of Southeast Asian Nations Free Trade Area (AFTA). They also oppose what they see as the exploitation of workers in free-trade zones (FTZ) such as the maquiladora zone in Mexico along the U.S. border—manufacturing centers, located primarily in developing countries, where raw goods can be imported, manufactured into finished goods, and reexported without having to pass through normal international trade barriers such as customs inspections.

The antiglobalization movement has been criticized for lacking a coherent set of goals. Critics also point to data indicating that poverty has decreased in developing countries since the early 1990s, when the globalization trend began. They argue that U.S. workers have benefited from increased opportunities to export goods to developing countries.

willingness to lay off workers during economic downturns and corporate restructuring have led to a **new social contract** between employers and employees. Under this "new social contract," loyalty is not expected by workers or organizations and job security rarely exists (Eisenberg et al., 2010). This means that if it is deemed profitable, companies are quick to sell or merge with other corporations, and employees are willing to jump ship if the right opportunity arises.

A number of individuals have argued that the financial crisis of 2007–2009 led to a greater imbalance in the social contract between companies and employees. They argue that organizations used the crisis as an excuse to engage in hiring practices that benefit organizations at great cost to employees. Although not everyone agrees, it is true that during the "Great Recession" approximately 7 million people lost their jobs (Zuckerman, 2011), and the number of Americans working part-time because full-time work was not available doubled between 2005 and 2010 to 9.2 million people (Coy, Conlin, & Herbst, 2010). The rise of the sharing economy, including companies such as Lyft, Airbnb, and Uber, likely is tied to this increase of unemployed workers who are willing to be contingent employees (Roose, 2014).

This change in the employee–employer relationship has resulted in job holders feeling more fearful of or unable to change jobs, so the unemployed now are willing to settle for low wages or no benefits. It also has led to an increase in job and career shifting as well as to an increase in the employment of contingent workers—workers who do not have a long-term commitment to their organizations nor their employers to them.

Competitiveness and Urgent Organizations   Another significant change is the rise of **urgent organizations**. Urgent organizations are companies that attempt to "shorten the time in which they develop new products and respond to customer demands" (Eisenberg et al., 2010, p. 17). Urgent organizations occur because of the intense time pressures related to global competition and the subsequent consumer demand for innovation and immediate fulfillment of wants and needs. Apple and other technology companies manifest many of the behaviors typical of urgent organizations. For example, the first iPhone was sold to the public in June 2007, and then just 10 weeks later its price was dropped $200 in response to customer demand (although doing so infuriated those "early adopters" who bought the phone in June and July). In July 2008, just one year later, the iPhone 3G was released, with the price once again reduced, this time by half. Similarly, Walmart attempts to compete globally by requiring all of its suppliers to abide by a policy that requires every vendor to either lower the price or increase the quality of each product every year (Fishman, 2006).

Urgent companies evolve and thrive because they are successful. Speed and quick response times provide them with an edge; companies that release products first tend to attract the most media and consumer attention, and clients and consumers are more likely to patronize companies that respond quickly to their requests for services and products.

Organizations, Communication, and Power

Organizations in the United States historically have been hierarchical, meaning that power, decision-making authority, and control have been held by a relatively small percentage of people within the organization, including managers, vice presidents,

▲ Google and other technology companies manifest many of the behaviors typical of urgent organizations.

new social contract
Assumes that loyalty is not expected by workers or organizations and that job security is unlikely.

urgent organizations
Companies that try to shorten the time it takes to develop new products and respond to customer demands.

presidents, and CEOs. To a great extent this is still true today. Although a hierarchical structure seems natural and normal to most of us, it can lead to power differences and to communication behavior that negatively affects those workers who hold little or no power. In the discussion that follows, we examine three of the communication problems that can result from large power differences.

bullying

Repeated hostile behaviors that are or are perceived to be intended to harm parties who are unable to defend themselves.

Bullying Organizational **bullying** refers to repeated, hostile behaviors that occur in the workplace over an extended period and that are intended, or are perceived as intended, to harm one or more parties who are unable to defend themselves (Lutgen-Sandvik, Tracy, & Alberts, 2005). Although interpersonal conflict is common in organizations, and perhaps necessary, bullying is not necessary. Bullying differs from conflict in that conflict can be constructive and positive. In addition, intent to harm may not be present in typical interpersonal conflict, and the parties in an interpersonal conflict often are relatively equal in power. However, in bullying, the intent to harm is a defining element, and power differences are important. Bully targets lack the ability to defend themselves and have limited strategies with which to respond. During interpersonal conflict, participants both act and are acted on. In contrast, in bullying interactions, one party (or group) is the actor or perpetrator and one (or more) person(s) is the target.

You may wonder why we bring up the issue of bullying, since it may not seem like a prevalent problem. However, it probably is more common than you think. A 2014 study found that 27 percent of 1,000 respondents claimed that they had been bullied at some point in their careers (Namie, Christiansen, & Phillips, 2014). Seven percent revealed that they had been bullied in just the past year. In addition, bullying is important because, fundamentally, it is a communication issue (Alberts, Lutgen-Sandvik, & Tracy, 2005). Of the 22 behaviors used to enact bullying, seventeen of them involve verbal interaction, such as ridicule, rumors, false allegations, insults, and threats of violence (Alberts et al., 2005).

A different type of bullying that is occurring in the workplace is cyberbullying. Cyberbullying occurs when perpetrators attack targets with harmful, degrading, threatening, or sexually explicit messages or photographs through texting, email, social media, and personal profiles, among others (Madan, 2014). As mentioned, bullying in the physical workspace typically is related to the bully's organizational power; however, with cyberbullying this is not necessarily so. Because individuals can remain anonymous when targeting others, people with low power in the organization are able to engage in cyberbullying that they likely would not attempt if they were physically present with the target or had to make their real names known. We know relatively little about the frequency of cyberbullying at work, but one study of manufacturing firm found that 34 percent of the organizations employees had experienced face-to-face bullying, whereas 10.7 percent had experienced cyberbullying. It is important to note that all of the respondents who were cyberbullied indicated that they also were bullied face to face (Privitera & Campbell, 2009). Thus, we don't currently know how many people in the workplace are only bullied online.

It Happened to Me
Bob

I still can't believe it happened to me. About a year ago, I was transferred to a new branch of my credit union. Within a few months, my supervisor began to criticize everything I did and make sarcastic and mean comments about me in front of other people. I tried to talk to her about it, but she just told me I was too thin-skinned. I don't know if it was because I was one of only a few males in the office or what. Finally, it got so bad that I asked for a meeting with my supervisor and her supervisor. During our meeting, I became so upset that I started having chest pains. I thought I was having a heart attack and had to go to the hospital by ambulance. It turns out it was a panic attack. When I got back to work a few days later, my supervisor started ridiculing me for having a panic attack. I have asked for a transfer, but I am also looking for another job.

Because bullying does occur regularly and typically is related to one's power in the organization, scholars have sought to determine strategies that can help targets respond. However, because targets typically have low power in the organization, their options are limited. For example, a problem-solving approach involves discussing the issue and seeking resolution. It requires that all parties be able to participate openly. This is

COMMUNICATION IN SOCIETY
Employer Responses to Workplace Bullying

Have you ever been bullied at work or known someone who was bullied at work? How did others in your workplace respond? How do you think employers should respond when an employee makes a complaint about bullying?

Many U.S. organizations still do not treat workplace bullying as a serious issue according to a recent survey. The 2014 Workplace Bullying Institute survey of workplace bullying found that 72 percent of employers responded to complaints about bullying by either ignoring it or explicitly condoning it, whereas less than 20 percent took actions to address it. See the chart to examine how respondents indicated their employers responded. Please note that responses highlighted in blue are considered inappropriate or negative ways to respond to reports of workplace bullying.

SOURCE: Namie, G., Christiansen, D., & Phillips, D. (2014). *The 2014 WBI U. S. workplace bullying survey.* Retrieved July 15, 2014, from http://www. workplacebullying.org/wbiresearch/wbi-2014-us-survey/.

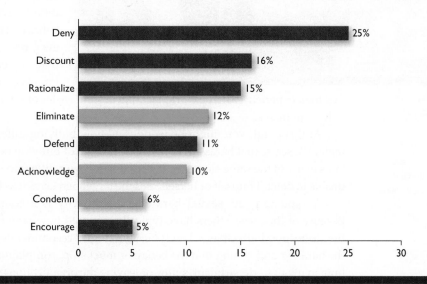

rarely true for the target of bullying. Similarly, compromising can occur only if one has leverage within the organization, meaning that each party must be able to offer something in return for a change in the other's behavior, which a low-power person may not possess. Obliging, or accommodating to the bully's demands, may be the only strategy if one wishes to remain in the organization. Withdrawing may be an option if one is willing to leave, and targets report that leaving the organization was the most effective, and often only, solution to the problem. Competing typically is not a useful strategy; it only intensifies the bully's abusive behavior. For a student's account of organizational bullying, see *It Happened to Me: Bob.*

Sexual Harassment   Sexual harassment describes unwanted sexual attention that interferes with an individual's ability to do his or her job or behavior that ties sexual favors to continued employment or success within the organization (Equal Employment Opportunity Commission, 1980). Federal law recognizes two types of sexual harassment, quid pro quo and hostile work environment (Roberts & Mann, 2000). **Quid pro quo** is the request for sexual favors as a condition of getting or keeping a job or benefit. ("You do what I ask, and I'll help you advance in the organization.") A **hostile work environment** results when a coworker or supervisor engages in unwelcome and inappropriate, sexually based behavior and creates an intimidating, hostile, or offensive atmosphere. Indulging in inappropriate verbal and nonverbal behaviors; repeatedly asking someone for a date; calling coworkers or subordinates by affectionate names (e.g., honey, sweetie); touching, patting, and stroking; and displaying posters and objects of a sexual nature can all constitute acts of sexual harassment.

quid pro quo

Requests for sexual favors as a condition of getting or keeping a job or benefit.

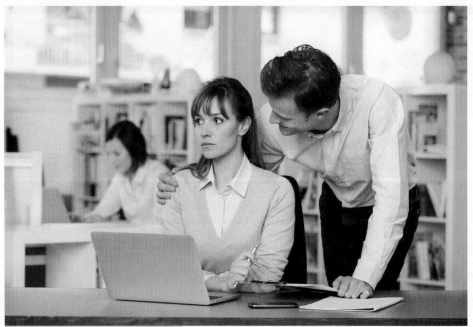

▲ Sexual harassment is primarily a communicative behavior.

hostile work environment
An intimidating, hostile, or offensive workplace atmosphere created by unwelcome and inappropriate sexually based behavior.

Even with this list of criteria, however, people could differ over what constitutes a hostile work environment. As a guideline, the U.S. Court of Appeals (Aeberhard-Hodges, 1996) ruled that sexual harassment should be examined from the perspective of what a "reasonable woman," not a "reasonable person," would find offensive. This led some to this central question: If a reasonable woman standard prevailed, would men, even "reasonable men," ever be sure how to behave? The court's ruling, however, rests on the understanding that women are the most frequent targets of sexual harassment and that their experiences in the workplace and around issues of sexuality often differ markedly from men's.

At this point, you might be wondering how bullying differs from sexual harassment. We see sexual harassment as a specific type of bullying behavior because it contains many of the same elements: It is rooted in power differences, the target typically is unable to defend himself or herself, and the target perceives it as hostile and intentional.

As you can see, sexual harassment primarily is a communicative behavior. Because of this, researchers have typically explored how targets can use communication to respond effectively. The typical strategies recommended include confronting the harasser and stating that the behavior must stop, complaining to one's boss or the human relations department, suing, or leaving the organization (Sigal, Braden-Maguire, Patt, Goodrich, & Perrino, 2003).

However, the majority of female targets of sexual harassment (in fact, 95 percent or more) do not respond assertively by confronting the harasser or reporting the harasser to a supervisor or the organization (Gruber & Smith, 1995; Rudman, Borgida, & Robertson, 1995). Why not? Sexual harassment typically occurs between people of unequal power, so confronting the harasser may not be an option. Targets risk losing their jobs, seeing the harassment intensify, or losing out on promotions and raises.

Complaining to a third party does sometimes work, particularly in organizations that have a clearly articulated sexual harassment policy and in which the human resources department has been empowered to handle sexual harassment cases effectively. However, some organizations do not wish to deal with these issues, or do not see them as important, so complaining to a third party does not always result in a benefit. Of course, suing the harasser and the organization that allows harassment is possible, but not every case is settled to the target's satisfaction, and the process can be long, painful, and ultimately unrewarding.

Finally, although leaving the organization does tend to resolve some aspects of the problem, some employees lack the option of leaving or find that leaving takes considerable time and effort. In addition, leaving one's job may resolve the physical/behavioral aspect of the harassment, but it does not help targets manage the long-term physical or psychological effects of harassment, does not address the impact of the harassment on the target's career, and does not result in changes in the perpetrator or the organization.

None of this means that targets should tolerate inappropriate behavior, but it does mean that they should carefully consider their options before committing to a response strategy. Targets should consider what response will be most effective in their specific situations. To do so, targets of sexual harassment (or bullying) might consider the following options. First, a target should consider responding assertively the first time the harassment occurs. This strategy is most likely to be successful when the perpetrator and target have equal power or a relationship of trust. If direct confrontation does not seem to be an option or has not been successful, then the target should consider approaching his or her supervisor, human resources department, or an organizational ombudsperson. Many organizations want to and will respond to such complaints, recognizing that the organization as a whole is harmed by such behavior.

If confrontation and appealing to authorities have not succeeded, targets must assess their needs and options carefully. They might consider seeking social support from family and friends, seeking assistance from a counselor or therapist to help them manage the emotional distress, developing strategies to avoid the perpetrator (if possible), or requesting a transfer or another job.

Unfortunately, the most common strategy targets select is to do nothing. This is not a response that, in the long run, benefits the individual *or* the organization. Moreover, doing nothing is especially problematic if the target has not even determined what other options exist. Too often, targets assume their efforts will be unsuccessful before they even make an attempt. If you do become a target, we encourage you not to make this assumption.

In conclusion, organizations experience significant impact from the society and the historical time period in which they exist. Two societal factors currently influencing corporations in the United States are globalization and changing power relations in the workplace. Globalization has meant that many jobs have been transferred from the United States to other countries, and both consumers and employees now must increase their contact with workers around the world. This change has been accompanied by an increased focus on power relationships at work and their impact on employees. This tendency to critique organizational uses of power has also led to more discussion of organizational ethics, which we examine next.

> **Journal Prompt 11.4:**
> **Globalization and**
> **Communication**
> **Consider the following questions:**
> What is globalization? What are the communication implications of globalization?

Ethics and Organizational Communication

11.5   Distinguish between individual and communal perspectives on organizational ethics.

As a result of organizational behavior such as providing bonuses to CEOs who lead failing financial companies and the Volkswagen emissions scandal, U.S. Americans are paying more attention to business ethics than perhaps ever before (Matthews & Gandel, 2015) However, observers don't agree on where responsibility for ethical behavior and communication rests within the organization. For example, who should be held accountable for the elaborate systems Volkswagen used to get around EPA pollution controls? Should only the engineers who designed the systems be prosecuted? Should the managers of the company

▼ When corporations dump toxic and dirty water into rivers and lakes, who should be held responsible?

be accountable? How about CEO Matthias Muller? Is he responsible for the ethical standards within his company? When attempting to determine the ethical choices and decisions organizations should make, people usually view the process either from the *individual perspective* or the *communal perspective* (Brown, 1989).

Many U.S. Americans take an individualistic perspective, viewing ethical failures as resting on the shoulders of specific individuals within the organization. From this outlook, each person in the corporation is responsible for his or her own behavior. In the case of Volkswagen, then, only the engineers themselves as well as others who knew about their behavior but did not "blow the whistle" are accountable. In the communal view, however, individuals are considered to be members of a community and are all partially responsible for the behavior of its members. The assumption here is that the ethical standards within an organization are created by and should be monitored and reinforced by all of its members. From this perspective, everyone within the Volkswagen organization, especially the managers and CEO, is responsible, because they had a duty to create and maintain high ethical standards within the company.

When ethics is discussed in organizational contexts, the focus typically is on the rights of the individual—such as the rights to free speech or privacy—and policies and behaviors that infringe on these rights are seen as unethical. However, a communal approach focuses on the "common good," or what is in the best interests of the entire community. Thus, the morality of an action is assessed based on its consequences for the group. In an individualistic approach, the responsibility for Volkswagen's erroneous emissions readings lies with the engineers who directly created the software. From a communal approach, the consequences of this deception are harmful to the organization as well as society, and the people responsible for that harm are the members of the organization collectively, that is, the organization itself.

Problems exist with both approaches. When we view individuals alone as responsible, they alone are punished, whereas the organization is left essentially unchanged. Yet, when we view corporations in a completely communal way and hold them responsible for their unethical practices, no individual may be held accountable or liable. Consequently, those responsible for the decision to engage in unethical and often illegal practices may not suffer any consequences—and may be free to continue these practices.

How should we balance these two approaches? Most likely, we need to hold both the organization and the individuals who lead them responsible for their practices— just as political leaders are tried in war courts for crimes against humanity, even though their subordinates performed the atrocities. At the same time, corporate leaders need to consider the impacts of their decisions on both individuals and society.

How is communication a factor in organizational ethics? Communication figures in organizational ethics in two ways (Cheney et al., 2004). First, many of the ethical issues in organizations revolve around communication. For example, organizations have to decide when to tell employees of impending layoffs, they develop advertising campaigns that communicate the identity of their corporation and

It Happened to Me
Nichole

The chapter on organizational communication helped me better understand a problem I encountered with Residential Life at my college. It wasn't about drinking or drugs, or letting in strangers, or any of the usual problems that students have with the dorm; it was about my Resident Assistant, who now is my boyfriend.

Just to clarify, there were no rules stated that I could not date my RA, and he was never told he couldn't date his residents. Plus, there is actual love involved, not just random friends-with-benefits hookups, and we really feel as though we have met the right person. But, Residential Life has a huge problem with our relationship, and they called us into a meeting. We both felt as though it was a violation of our privacy. We had the meeting, he quit his job, and we are still dating, ten months strong!

Now, though, when I look at the relationship through the eyes of the school, I can see their problems with it. What would have happened if an employee of the college got me pregnant? Also, he lived in my hall and his duty was to keep us in line, but there was huge preferential treatment going on. I mean, would my boyfriend really write me up for anything? So now I see that they had a point. But I don't understand why nothing was ever said about this practice being against the rules.

its products to consumers, and they must decide how to communicate information regarding their profits and losses to shareholders and Wall Street. Second, the ways in which an organization defines, communicates about, and responds to ethical and unethical behavior shape how individuals within the organization behave. If corporate policy and organizational leaders are vague on the issue of ethics, or worse yet, fail to address it, employees may believe that ethics are not a central concern of the organization and may behave accordingly. For example, in 2005, *Esquire* magazine published an article about the alleged ethical violations of military recruiters. The military personnel interviewed for the article claimed that despite written policies that encouraged ethical behavior, their communication with their superiors revolved only around their success or failure at meeting their recruitment goals and never about *how* they met those goals. Thus, they concluded that recruiting ethically was a secondary, or perhaps even an unnecessary, consideration. To read about one student's experience with organizational ethics, see *It Happened to Me: Nichole*.

Journal Prompt 11.5: Organizational Ethics
Consider the following questions: How do the individual and communal approaches to organizational ethics differ? What role does communication play in organizational ethics?

Improving Your Organizational Communication Skills

11.6 Identify four steps involved in a strategic approach to conflict management.

Much of the time, if not most, people are only willing to engage in conflict when they are angry or emotional. How often have you been involved with, or observed others engaging in, highly emotional conflict at work? As you probably have noted, this style of conflict engagement typically doesn't resolve anything and may cause long-lasting damage to one's relationships with others.

A better way to manage conflict with coworkers is to use a strategic approach to conflict management. People who use a strategic approach prepare for their conflicts and engage in **strategy control** (Canary & Lakey, 2012). When behaving strategically, one assesses the available information and options, which increases one's understanding of the conflict and the other party. In turn, these behaviors help people choose conflict behaviors that are responsive to the partner's as well as their own needs and increase the possibility for cooperation, collaboration, and compromise.

strategy control
Assessing the available information and options to increase one's understanding of the conflict and the other party.

When using a strategic approach, before you even initiate a discussion over an issue in conflict, you should know what you want to occur as a result of the interaction. If you wish to confront your coworker about not doing his fair share of a joint project, you should first decide what your goal is. Do you want your colleague to apologize? To stay late until the report is finished? To complete the project by himself? To take the lead on the next joint project? Or do you desire some combination of these outcomes? You will be far more successful and satisfied with your conflict interactions if you go into them knowing what you want.

Second, decide if the issue is worth confronting—or worth confronting now. You may know what you want, but do you have a reasonable chance of accomplishing your goals? That is, how likely is your coworker to apologize or to successfully take the lead on your next joint project? If the answer truly is "highly unlikely," you may choose not to engage in the conflict or to seek other solutions. For example, you might decide to ask your supervisor to assign someone else to work with you. Alternatively, you may decide you do want to have the conversation, but perhaps not right now, because both of you are hungry and tired.

If you decide that the conflict is worth confronting, you next want to try to understand the other party's goals, that is, what he or she wants. What, for example, do you think your coworker's goal is? Does he want to receive credit for the work without having to do it? Does he want assistance with parts of the project he doesn't

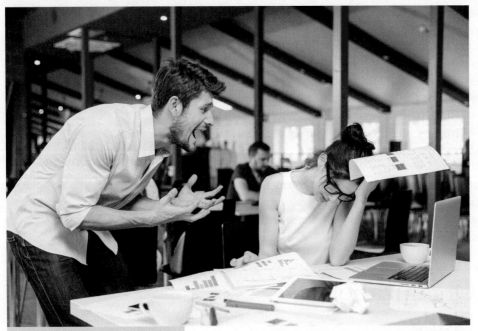

▲ People often are only willing to engage in conflict when they are angry or emotional.

Journal Prompt 11.6: Strategic Conflict Management

Consider the following questions: What is meant by "a strategic approach" to managing conflict? What are the four steps to the "strategic approach" to conflict management?

feel competent to complete? Is he busy with other projects and wants more time to finish the project? Depending on your understanding of his goals and interests, you will likely suggest different solutions. Please remember, however, the tendency for each of us to attribute negative motivations to others' behavior. If you are upset, you will be particularly likely to believe your colleague's goal is to avoid work but receive the rewards of it. Recognize that your attributions may be incorrect and that you probably will need to talk with your coworker to determine what his motivations really are.

You have one more step to complete before you are ready to talk with your colleague; you need to plan the interaction. More specifically, you should think about when and where the conversation should take place and what tactics you believe will be most effective. Typically, you will want to choose a time when neither you nor your coworker is angry, rushed, or stressed. In addition, you should probably have the conversation in private. If others are around, one or both of you may behave more competitively or avoid the interaction entirely because you are embarrassed to be observed by others. Finally, you should think through how you will explain your dissatisfaction with the current state of affairs neutrally and how you will frame your suggested solutions. Once you have done all of this, you are ready to talk with your colleague and discuss calmly what the two of you can do to reduce your feeling that you alone are working on the project.

SUMMARY

11.1 Explain the importance of understanding communication in organizations.

- Understanding how to communicate in organizations will enhance your professional success, allow you to ask more informed questions about everyday organizational practices, and help you decide what organizations you wish to frequent and support.

11.2 Define organizations and explain their communication functions and structures.

- Organizations are composed of interactions that members use to accomplish their individual and common goals.
- Organizational communication functions include production, maintenance, and innovation.
- Organization communication structures include formal structure and informal structure.

11.3 Understand the types of communication that occur among coworkers and explain their functions.

- Assimilation describes the processes that influence individuals to join, identify with, and become integrated into an organization.
- Supervisor–subordinate communication refers to communication that occurs when one person has the formal authority to regulate the behavior of another
- Coworker communication is composed of the formal-professional and informal-personal interactions employees have with one another.

11.4 Discuss current social influences on organizations and organizational communication.

- Two of the most significant societal forces that impact organizational communication are history and globalization.
- Three recent practices that influence organizations are the development of a new social contract between organizations and employees, the rise of urgent organizations, and the blurring of boundaries between home and work.
- Two power relations that influence organizations are workplace bullying and sexual harassment.

11.5 Distinguish between individual and communal perspectives on organizational ethics.

- An individual perspective views ethical failures as resting on the shoulders of specific individuals
- A communal perspective of ethical failures argues individuals are considered to be members of community and are all partially responsible for the behavior of its members.

11.6 Identify four steps involved in a strategic approach to conflict management.

- Decide what you want to occur as a result of the conflict interaction.
- Decide if the issue is worth confronting—or worth confronting now.
- Try to understand the other party's goals.
- Plan the interaction.

KEY TERMS

APPLY WHAT YOU KNOW

1. **Understanding Emotion Labor** Think of five jobs that require employees to engage in emotion labor and delineate the emotions that these employees are "expected" to display. What emotions are they expected to suppress? What contradictory emotions and behaviors are they expected to perform? Which of the five jobs that you listed appears to have the heaviest emotion labor load?

2. **Understanding Relationships at Work** Form a group with one or more of your classmates. Assume that you are a work group that has been charged with developing a fraternization policy for your job. Develop a policy about the types of relationships that are appropriate in your workplace and how people who have these relationships should communicate and behave while at work.

EXPLORE

1. Go to the *Psychology Today* website and locate the page on workplace Self Tests. Select two self-tests (such as the Entrepreneurial Personality Profile or the Leadership Style test) and complete them. After completing the tests, analyze your score. Does the score you received reflect your understanding of yourself and your work life? Which of you answers surprised you? How can this information help you in your future career?

2. Go to a job interviewing website, such as the U.S. Labor's Job Interview Tips or About.com's Job Interview Tips, and read the suggestions offered for how to interview for a job effectively. Afterward, develop a short checklist of helpful hints for interviewing that you can keep on hand for future job interviews.

3. Locate a website devoted to exploring work–life issues, such as the Center for Work-Life Policy site or the Canadian Center for Occupational Health and Safety's Work/Life page, and read at least one essay on work–life issues. After reading the essay, write a brief summary of it that you could share with your classmates.

Rhetorical Communication

 LEARNING OBJECTIVES

12.1 Describe some of the key issues in rhetorical communication.

12.2 Identify cultural and social influences on the development of rhetoric.

12.3 Identify and define the three artistic proofs of ethos, pathos, and logos.

12.4 Explain four functions of rhetoric: reaffirming cultural values, increasing democratic participation, securing justice, and promoting social change.

12.5 Understand the ethical issues facing rhetors and audience members.

12.6 Identify the basic steps in preparing a speech.

CHAPTER TOPICS

The Importance of Rhetoric

What Is Rhetoric? A Broader View

The Rhetor: Rhetoric's Point of Origin

The Individual, Rhetoric, and Society

Ethics and Rhetoric

Using Your Rhetorical Skills: Speaking in Public

"Rhetoric is essential to a vital democracy."

Charee is familiar with the debates about immigration reform and deportations that are going on in the United States. She listens to speeches at rallies, as well as political discussions on television, and she reads the discussions online. In all of these communication contexts, she is swimming in rhetorical communication from various perspectives that attempt to persuade her (and others) to their view on these issues. She knows that she needs to wade through the various arguments and emotional pleas coming from these other perspectives before she can decide how she feels. As the daughter of an immigrant, how does that influence her political views on this issue? What evidence does she believe? Who has more credibility: Someone speaking at a rally? Or someone who is anonymous and posting messages online? Which news sources are more reliable and accurate? Although it may feel overwhelming, Charee wants to have a reasonable way to guide herself through the ocean of rhetorical messages and make smart choices about how to do so.

rhetoric

Communication that is used to influence the attitudes or behaviors of others; the art of persuasion.

Charee recognized the power of rhetorical communication to persuade and motivate people to action. **Rhetoric** is communication that influences the attitudes or behaviors of others; it is also called the art of persuasion. All of the messages that Charee is confronting—whether in person, in media outlets, or on the Internet—are rhetorical in that they are designed to influence how listeners and readers view immigration reform and deportation. On other occasions, communicators might use rhetoric to influence people to vote a particular way, to raise awareness about domestic violence, or to participate in a Walk for the Cure for breast cancer.

All of these rhetorical messages serve important cultural and personal functions, and gaining insight into such functions is, by itself, an important reason to study the art of rhetoric. But people study rhetoric, which comes from the ancient Greek word for speaking, for a variety of other important reasons as well, which we will explore throughout this chapter. Because most of us spend more time as receivers of rhetorical communication, this chapter also focuses on how to be a responsible rhetorical critic.

In this chapter, we explore rhetoric as it informs the study of communication today. We will first consider the definition and functions of rhetoric. We next examine how characteristics of public speakers, or *rhetors*, make them credible, influence what they say, and impact how they relate to their audiences. We then turn our focus to a broader topic, the intersection of society and rhetoric. And before providing a guide for preparing a rhetorical presentation, we consider the merits of being a rhetorical critic.

The Importance of Rhetoric

12.1 Describe some of the key issues in rhetorical communication.

The rhetorical tradition lies at the heart of communication studies. Since the days of Aristotle in ancient Greece, rhetoric has been considered the art of persuasion. Among the many ways that communication operates, the Greeks felt that the ability to influence how others view the world on various issues was paramount. Rhetoric's practice is contingent on culture, political arrangements, and social contexts and conventions. For example, how might courtroom rhetoric differ among people who believe in magic, witches, and the presumption of guilt from a courtroom rhetoric among people who believe in DNA, forensic science, and the presumption of innocence? Or in a political system with a dictator versus one with elected officials? We'll look at the changing notions of rhetoric as cultures and societies have differed. First, let's look at how rhetoric functions in our society.

Rhetoric's Functions in Society

Rhetorical communication serves at least three important social functions. First, as you may have surmised, rhetoric is essential to a vital democracy. For people to make informed decisions (and vote) about a range of issues, they must consume rhetorical messages critically and then advocate with care. By advocating for one's perspective and engaging with the perspectives of others, people can make decisions together regarding the common good. Hence, rhetoric can strengthen democratic society, and speeches or other types of communication to the public can serve important political and social functions.

Sometimes congressional representatives hold town hall meetings to listen to the concerns of their constituents and many people attend those and express their concerns on a variety of issues. But formal government outlets are only one of the many ways that people use the Internet to engage in activism. Activism can be speeches at rallies and more, but it can also be online as in the case of change.org. Claiming to be "the world's largest petition platform," change.org says: "We live in an amazing time, when the opportunity to make a difference is greater than ever before. Gathering people behind a cause used to be difficult, requiring lots of time, money, and a complex infrastructure. But technology has made us more connected than ever" (https://www.change.org/about). Yet, not everyone is convinced of the rhetorical power of online activism. For example, at its peak, the Save Darfur campaign "was one of the largest on the social network" (meaning activist social networking sites) but of the online activists (who numbered more than one million), "less than 3,000" moved on to contribute about $90,000 total to the cause. This level of engagement reflects "pitiful statistics compared to the wider Darfur campaign, which raised over $1m in 2008 alone" (Tostevin, 2014). What do you think about social media and the Internet more generally as a platform for rhetorical messages and democratic engagement?

Second, rhetoric helps people seek justice. Probably one of the most obvious sites of this rhetorical function is the courtroom. Not only lawyers but also jurors need rhetorical skills; they need to listen carefully and critically not only to what is said, but also how it is said, and they must be able to persuade other jurors of the proper verdict. Speakers also use rhetoric to persuade others to pursue social justice, for example, to support a moratorium on the death penalty or treat animals more ethically.

Justice can also be sought outside of the courtroom. If people do not feel that justice is found in the courtroom, they can use social media and other outlets to try to persuade others that an injustice occurred. During and after the trial of Brock Turner, the former Stanford University athlete who was found guilty of sexual assault, some people felt that the relatively short prison sentence did not result in justice and tried to persuade others to their view. More recently Black Lives Matter has highlighted a number of cases of police shootings of African Americans as unjust. In response, the *Washington Post* has posted an interactive webpage about the 963 people killed by police in 2016 at https://www.washingtonpost.com/graphics/national/police-shootings-2016/. On this webpage, you can get more information about each of these shootings. In these cases and in many others, people use the Internet to help shape how we view justice and injustice and actions that we can take to make things right that we are persuaded are wrong.

Third, rhetoric helps people clarify their own beliefs and actions. For example, after the largest mass murder by a single shooter in U.S. history at a gay nightclub in Orlando, Florida, in June 2016, many people, like our student in *It Happened to Me: Lance*, were not sure what to believe about why this happened and how they should respond or behave. Therefore, they turned to experts and national leaders,

It Happened to Me
Lance

I was stunned, shocked and saddened to hear about the mass murder at Pulse Nightclub in Orlando, Florida. I am familiar with antigay hatred but I never thought it would go this far. I turned to President Obama's words for comfort and understanding what this means for us as Americans and our cultural values.

such as the president, to gather information that could help them clarify their beliefs and understanding. In his speech in response to the June 2016 Orlando shooting, President Obama told the national and the world that "this is a sobering reminder that attacks on any American—regardless of race, ethnicity, religion or sexual orientation—is an attack on all of us and on the fundamental values of equality and dignity that define us as a country. And no act of hate or terror will ever change who we are or the values that make us Americans" (Washington Post staff, 2016).

The Advantages of Studying Rhetoric

In addition to serving important functions in society, rhetoric is also an important area of academic inquiry. Studying rhetoric as a field of scholarship is useful for four reasons. First, the study of public communication generates findings that help people understand the range of viewpoints on social issues. For example, if you wanted to understand the reasoning behind the U.S. immigration policy, you could examine the rhetoric of people who are attempting to influence that policy. You might listen to the president's speeches on immigration; you could examine the Catholic Church's views on pending immigration legislation; you could review the public comments of various members of Congress, some of whom are themselves the children or grandchildren of immigrants; and you could listen to interviews and speeches of other people who support various changes to immigration policy. You can find many of these viewpoints online and in more traditional outlets, such as the *Congressional Record* and newspapers. By examining the rhetoric of these individuals and groups, you would be better able to understand how U.S. immigration policies respond to these varied perspectives, as well as think through what you believe is the best course of action. It may also help you understand the barriers to immigration reform.

Second, the study of rhetoric helps people better understand culture. Both consciously and unconsciously, through listening to and analyzing public communication, people learn the expectations of their own cultures—what it means to be a good parent, how to present oneself, how to decorate one's home, and much more. Debates about same-sex marriage led to arguments about what marriage means and how it should be defined. You may find yourself drawn more to one vision and definition of marriage than another based on the rhetoric that you have heard. People can study and understand other cultures, too, by being attuned to how public communication sustains patterns of social life.

Third, studying rhetoric can help people critically evaluate messages designed to influence them, such as advertising. Other rhetoric tries to persuade people to support particular policies or to vote for or against certain politicians or propositions. As receivers of these persuasive messages, people can learn to listen critically, analyze these messages, and respond appropriately.

Finally, the study of public communication helps us to become better public communicators or to understand what makes specific public communicators effective or ineffective. We can learn much about public speaking by analyzing instances of public speech. In addition, we can determine why some speakers are more successful or persuasive than others by comparing their public communication. We can also learn why some web postings are more persuasive than others and why we find them more persuasive and believable.

rhetorical critic
An informed consumer of rhetorical discourse who is prepared to analyze rhetorical texts.

Becoming a Rhetorical Critic   The term **rhetorical critic** refers to an informed consumer of rhetorical discourse who is prepared to analyze rhetorical texts. You may think that a critic's job is simply to be negative about whatever is under analysis. However, everyone is a critic in everyday life, and we have an ethical duty to think critically about the rhetorical texts we encounter. Although some people reserve the term *rhetorical critic* for those who work in academia, we see it differently. We consider anyone who pursues sustained and detailed analyses of rhetorical discourse to be a rhetorical critic.

We hope that you and your fellow citizens all become more attuned to the sensitivities of rhetorical discourse and that you become strong analysts of it because it has tremendous influence on the ways you conduct your everyday life and the way society functions. To give just one example, rhetorical discourse likely shapes your understanding of what it means to be a good parent. Do you think that good parents have to sacrifice everything for their children? Pay for their college educations? Their weddings? Do good parents expect their children to take care of them in their old age? Or should good parents do everything possible to avoid being a burden on their children? Are good parents married? What is the right way for good parents to deal with divorce? Of course, no "right" answer exists for any of these questions. But it's important to be aware that you do have some ideas about what constitutes good parenting. It's also important to be aware that these ideas came from a barrage of rhetorical messages from newspaper reporters, magazine writers, psychologists, religious organizations, movies, television shows, blogs, and others. Understanding how these messages rhetorically frame parenting can help you better understand how you have shaped your own vision of good parenting. Becoming more aware of your opinions and where they come from can make you a more effective rhetorical critic.

Being an informed rhetorical critic can also help one appreciate the artistic aspects of discourse (Darsey, 1994), as well as what makes a particular rhetorical message effective or persuasive. When you read the excerpt from a famous antislavery speech in *Did You Know? Frederick Douglass*, consider what makes it effective. What are the artistic aspects of this speech? Why didn't Douglass simply say, "Slavery is wrong"?

DID YOU KNOW?
Frederick Douglass

When Frederick Douglass began to speak out against slavery, many White Americans did not believe he had really been a slave, or that he was African American. In her biography of Douglass, Sandra Thomas explains: "People gradually began to doubt that Douglass was telling the truth about himself. Reporting on a lecture that he gave in 1844, the Liberator wrote that many people in the audience refused to believe his stories: 'How a man, only six years out of bondage, and who had never gone to school could speak with such eloquence—with such precision of language and power of thought—they were utterly at a loss to devise.'" Unfortunately, this response to minority speakers may not be unusual.

Here is a famous excerpt from a speech Douglass gave about the Fourth of July. How do the artistic proofs used in this speech help to move an audience?

▲ Frederick Douglass was a powerful rhetor who spoke out against slavery in the United States.

What, to the American slave, is your 4th of July? I answer; a day that reveals to him, more than all other days in the year, the gross injustice and cruelty to which he is the constant victim. To him, your celebration is a sham; your boasted liberty, an unholy license; your national greatness, swelling vanity; your sounds of rejoicing are empty and heartless; your denunciation of tyrants, brass-fronted impudence; your shouts of liberty and equality, hollow mockery; your prayers and hymns, your sermons and thanksgivings, with all your religious parade and solemnity, are, to Him, mere bombast, fraud, deception, impiety, and hypocrisy—a thin veil to cover up crimes which would disgrace a nation of savages. There is not a nation on the earth guilty of practices more shocking and bloody than are the people of the United States, at this very hour.

SOURCES: Douglass, F. (1852, July 5). The meaning of July Fourth for the Negro. Retrieved June 26, 2006, from http://www.pbs.org/wgbh/aia/part4/4h2927t.html.

Thomas, S. (n.d.). From slave to abolitionist/editor. Retrieved June 26, 2006, from http://www.history.rochester.edu/class/douglass/part2.html.

Rhetorical criticism is a method for generating knowledge about historical sources of contemporary social problems, especially those that generate a significant amount of discourse. Through attentiveness to how rhetoric has functioned and continues to function in various contexts, you can build an understanding of your culture, society, and the ideas that predominated during a given period. Hence, an analysis of any one rhetorical message should be seen as part of a much larger and ongoing dialogue.

A variety of approaches to rhetorical criticism exist. We cannot cover all the major approaches to rhetorical criticism in this introductory course. There are many courses and textbooks that focus on rhetorical criticism. Instead we hope to teach you to listen carefully to how rhetoric functions every day and to analyze what purposes it serves. As you listen to rhetoric from presidents, governors, mayors, church leaders, or others, ask yourself, how does this message reinforce the status quo? How does it argue for change? What ideas are mentioned and what ideas are absent? How and why is it persuasive, and how might it influence the public in making public policy decisions?

Because you can only consume a limited amount of the rhetoric generated, and because the rhetorical environment is always changing, the ways in which you understand and think about the world will always be changing as well. By adopting a critical approach, you can empower yourself to better understand the messages and the issues at hand.

Truth and Rhetoric

Since the fifth century B.C.E., teachers and scholars of rhetoric have argued over its fundamental purpose. Does it help speakers and listeners discern truth, or is it only concerned with what an audience can be persuaded to believe? If persuasion is the goal, then truth plays a smaller, perhaps even nonexistent, role.

The first people to teach persuasive speaking skills in the Greek city-states were called **sophists**. Their approach to rhetoric was practical; they believed rhetoric's purpose was to persuade, especially on matters of urgency. Therefore, they taught speakers to adjust their notions of right or wrong, true or untrue, depending on their speaking situation, their audience, and their goals. Today sophistry is often associated with a focus on the ends justifying the means; in other words, use whatever means are expedient to get the desired results. Because anyone might use deception, invented "facts," and other problematic ways to persuade others, sophistry is largely seen as unethical in today's rhetorical environment. At the same time, sophistication is seen as a value in some speech contexts. So the debate between the sophists and Plato is ongoing two millennia later.

Some contemporaries disagreed with the sophists. One of the more prominent of these was Plato (429–347 B.C.E.), who strongly opposed a relativistic approach to speechmaking. In his well-known dialogue, *Gorgias,* he disparagingly compared sophistic rhetoric to "cookery," in which a set of elements (or ingredients) were "mixed together" to create the final speech (or dish) for the sake of pleasure and not of the good, or health, of the body. Plato insisted that speakers only speak in favor of universal principles of truth and that these truths should then influence society's behavior for the better. Plato's position implies that access to universal truth is possible.

But there is reason to believe that Plato was not as critical of rhetoric as he was of sophistical rhetoric. In fact, Plato wrote dialogues, not philosophical treatises. Evidently, he thought that the best way to search for truth was through oral dialogue. In an eloquently written dialogue, the *Phaedrus,* Plato argued for a philosophical rhetoric based on truth and a philosophical truth spoken rhetorically (Conley, 1994; Infante, Rancer, & Womack, 1990). Whether he was critical or supportive, the irony between Plato's rhetorical choices and criticisms about sophists still captivates modern audiences. Looking back, some will judge President Obama's terms not as much by which policies he passed, but as by hope that his rhetoric engendered in an upcoming generation. Persuasion, meaning the sweetness of words, evidently means that pleasure can sometimes have good effects.

Critical Thinking Prompt
How do you view the sophists' relativistic approach to rhetoric? Have you ever been in a situation in a class or debate where you were required to argue for a position that clashed with your personal values? How did it feel to make the argument?

sophists
The first group to teach persuasive speaking skills in the Greek city-states.

Not unlike students today, Plato's student Aristotle (384–322 B.C.E.) challenged his teacher's arguments. He did not agree with Plato's insistence on the relationship of absolute truth to rhetoric; instead he believed speakers needed to learn skillful persuasion so they could defend truth and justice. As you might guess, his position was more relativistic than Plato's, but less so than the sophists'. However, some rhetorical historians argue that Aristotle could strike a middle-of-the-road position because he wrote about oratorical practices as theoretical. Theorizing practices into definitions as he did narrows the avenues future speakers take to express themselves. In effect, Aristotle's permutation of the Sophists and Plato organizes a plurality of styles by prescriptions of what kinds of speech techniques are more effective than others (Haskins 2006; 2013).

Aristotle defined rhetoric as "the art of discovering all the available means of persuasion in a given situation" (Aristotle, 1991, p. 42). With this perspective in mind, he sought to create general rules of rhetoric that could be applied to a variety of circumstances and occasions. He was so successful that his text, *The Rhetoric*, has been used as a handbook for public speaking for more than 2,000 years.

When the Romans conquered the Greeks in 146 B.C.E., they incorporated the writings of Greek rhetoricians into Roman education. Cicero (106–43 B.C.E.), a prominent advocate and politician, is often considered the greatest Roman **orator**, or public speaker, and the most influential theorist of ancient rhetoric. Cicero believed speakers should use rhetoric for the public good and that eloquence without wisdom was feeble and even dangerous.

orator
A public speaker.

Cicero offered guidelines for organizing speeches and was a master of style; in fact, his speeches are still appreciated today for their rhetorical force. He is known best for identifying the three purposes or goals of public speaking: to instruct, to please, and to win over. Modern public speaking courses require mastery of these three types of speeches, which we now refer to as speeches to inform, to entertain, and to persuade.

As the Roman Empire declined, the Catholic Church replaced secular educational institutions as the leading disseminator of knowledge in the West. Once again, the issue of truth's relationship to rhetoric became important. First, because rhetoric had developed from a non-Christian tradition, concerns arose about its relevance and appropriateness to Christianity. The most prominent thinker and writer of this era was Augustine of Hippo (354–430 C.E.), whom you may know as St. Augustine. He was a professor of rhetoric before converting to Christianity, and he struggled to reconcile his rhetorical background with his religious beliefs. Augustine's view of truth was close to Plato's— that truth exists in an absolute way—and he promoted the idea that rhetoric could impart the divine truth (Conley, 1994). From this perspective, ethical decisions were not situation specific; choices were always right or wrong, good or evil.

Journal Prompt 12.1: Study of Rhetoric
Consider the following question: What are some of the ways that the study of rhetoric has been influenced by its historical context?

What Is Rhetoric? A Broader View

12.2   Identify cultural and social influences on the development of rhetoric.

When you think of rhetoric, you may think about overblown statements, exaggerations, or even outright lies and misstatements—as in, "Oh, that's just a bunch of political rhetoric." Unfortunately, this dismissive view of rhetoric is all too common today. However, as we saw in the preceding section, rhetoric has a rich history, and it serves important functions in a democratic society. As you saw in the opening example about debates regarding immigration reform and deportations, rhetoric in its truest sense refers to communication that is used to influence others. Thus, rhetoricians would not view the president's communication following September 11th as simply an attempt to provide information, but also as an attempt to guide U.S. Americans to view this topic in a way that suits his particular goals. In both the historical and the contemporary sense, rhetoric focuses primarily on public communication or messages designed to influence large audiences.

More than 50 years ago, communication professor Douglas Ehninger suggested that throughout history people have had different ideas of what rhetoric is and the purposes it serves (1967). Ehninger's thinking sparked interest in connecting rhetoric to the cultural, social, and historical forces that exist in any particular time and in exploring how these forces shape rhetoric. Therefore, scholars began to research the ways that rhetoric serves social needs in societies around the world. For example, they looked at how the uses of rhetoric in a religious state may differ from those in a secular one. In addition, their research showed that the methods and reasons that people speak out in public depend on how such communication is received. Although Ehninger focused on the European tradition, his argument stirred interest in understanding how non-Western cultures developed their own rhetorical traditions (Lucaites, Condit, & Caudill, 1999).

The European rhetorical tradition is only one of many in the world, and public communication functions in different ways in other places. It can, however, be difficult to research and study rhetoric historically or globally because the word *rhetoric* is not used in all cultures to describe that which is called "rhetoric" in the European tradition. The term comes to the English language from the Greek word *rhetorike*, the Greek *rhetor* was in use, indicating that the concept of "rhetoric" can likewise exist in non-Greek cultures whether or not a synonym for the specific word exists in respective languages. A **rhetor** is a person or institution that addresses the public. Public address can happen without reference to the public speech forums of Greek democracy and Roman republicanism. George Kennedy, a scholar of the ancient world, focuses less on the word and more on the concept itself: "Rhetoric is apparently a form of energy that drives and is imparted to communication. . . . All communication carries some rhetorical energy" (1998, p. 215). In this sense, rhetoric is not a cultural phenomenon unique to the West, but it is a facet of communication across cultures; it is the motive for communicating.

Culturally, the social position of the rhetor often determines his or her right to speak or to access civic speaking spaces. In some cultures, it is important that the rhetor is an elder or that he be male or come from a high-status family. In others, everyone is able to speak. These cultural differences influence who has the ability to speak and who needs to study rhetoric to be the most capable communicators.

To understand how these social positions differ across cultures, it is important to seek out the structures of different cultures and societies. In some cultures, people rise to leadership positions by being democratically elected, whereas in other cultures leaders gain and hold onto power through financial prowess, political intrigue, or military force. Religious leaders sometimes hold the most powerful positions. Some cultures are led by a group instead of a single leader. Relationships to certain families, credentials from certain schools, or even one's physical attractiveness can lead to empowerment (or disempowerment). Yet, how one's rhetoric is received is dependent on one's social position.

Some rhetorical critics have strategically located rhetoric in spaces traditionally disassociated from civic forums. For example, the kitchen, and kitchen table talk specifically, has been a domestic site of transformative dialogue for many women. This was especially so during America's twentieth-century civil activist history. Today, many black feminist scholars feature the kitchen table as a metaphor for a place where rhetoric is in action. Even if it is not a location for legislation, women who have been excluded from public domains

rhetor

A person or institution that addresses a large audience; the originator of a communication message but not necessarily the one delivering it.

▼ Different cultures assign power to people based on different factors.

of political action have debated political issues and spread word about community at their hearths. In this way, rhetorical criticism can analyze classical modes of rhetoric by changing where we think rhetoric takes place.

As you think about the role of rhetoric around the world, consider how decisions are made in different societies. You might also contemplate how our own culture is changing as we take part in public debates over such far-reaching topics as same-sex marriage, immigration reform, retirement and pension plans, and more.

Journal Prompt 12.2:
The Rhetor
Consider the following question:
What is a rhetor, and how does the rhetor's social status and culture influence the ability to speak?

The Rhetor: Rhetoric's Point of Origin

12.3 Identify and define the three artistic proofs of ethos, pathos, and logos.

It is conventional to think about a rhetor as a specific public speaker; for example, when the president speaks to the nation, the president is a rhetor. As notions of rhetoric have expanded over time, however, corporations, organizations, and governments have also come to be thought of as rhetors. Thus, a rhetor is the originator of a communication message, not necessarily the person delivering it.

Like other areas of communication studies, the study of rhetoric acknowledges the relationship between individual forces and societal forces. In this segment of the chapter, we look at the individual forces that make for more or less effective rhetors. These forces include the rhetor's artistic proofs, position in society, and relationship to the audience.

Ethos, Pathos, and Logos

In the *Art of Rhetoric*, Aristotle argued that there are three **artistic proofs**, or means through which a rhetor gains the trust of an audience and designs credible messages.

They are: ethos, pathos, and logos.

artistic proofs
Artistic skills of a rhetor that influence effectiveness.

Ethos Aristotle considered **ethos**—usually translated as "character"—the most important of the three artistic proofs. Aristotle emphasized that rhetors create ethos, or a sense of their character, by displaying to their audience good sense, moral character, and goodwill. He also included family background, attractiveness, and athletic ability as valuable assets in persuasion through ethos. Advertising commonly exploits this aspect of ethos, using famous family names, attractive models, and celebrated athletes to promote products.

ethos
The rhetorical construction of character.

To communicate a certain aspect of their ethos, a rhetor can create and project a *persona*. **Persona** is related to the notion of identity that we discussed in Chapter 3. It describes the identity one creates through one's public communication efforts. A speaker's public persona may be quite different from his or her private one. In contrast, a speaker's social identities, such as race, ethnicity, age, and nationality, remain unchanged from situation to situation and are not under the speaker's control. The public persona a speaker projects can enhance his or her ethos if audiences find the persona credible, informed, or intelligent; it can diminish his or her ethos if audiences perceive the persona to be untrustworthy, deceitful, unintelligent, or misinformed.

persona
The identity one creates through one's public communication efforts.

Interpretations of ethos are influenced not only by how a speaker presents herself or himself but also by social factors such as stereotypes and assumptions. For example, sometimes people hear accents that increase or decrease their perceptions of the speaker's intelligence. British accents tend to increase credibility in the United States, whereas Southern accents may have the opposite effect, especially in the northern United States.

Critical Thinking Prompt
What characteristics do you think are important to a speaker's credibility, or ethos? Which of Aristotle's list apply today? Which characteristics are most important to you?

Pathos **Pathos** refers to the rhetorical use of emotions to affect audience decision making. Speakers often use emotion to influence the audience to identify with a particular perspective. In a court case, the prosecuting lawyer may reenact the crime to help the jury see the case from the victim's point of view. An effective reenactment may influence the jury to emotionally identify, and thus side, with the prosecution rather than the defense.

pathos
The rhetorical use of emotions to affect audience decision making.

There are many different emotional appeals that can be made. Emotional appeals have been used many times throughout history. Fear can get people to support government actions that they otherwise would not, such as the USA PATRIOT Act, Transportation Security Administration (TSA) screening procedures, and other measures instituted in reaction to fears of terrorism.

Emotional appeals are often more subtle. For example, the athletic and alumni websites of many universities incorporate pathos to invite participation in their events and support for their organizations. Some of these emotional appeals may involve feelings of pride by associating with the university, as well as positive memories that alumni may have about their student days. You may have similar feelings some day.

logos

Rational appeals; the use of rhetoric to help the audience see the rationale for a particular conclusion.

Logos   Although the word **logos** looks like "logic," it is not as narrowly defined. Rather, *logos* refers to reasoning or argumentation more generally. As an artistic proof, logos refers to how rhetors construct arguments or present evidence so that audiences reach a particular conclusion. For example, a lawyer may use evidence such as fingerprints to build a case and explain how a crime occurred, or a politician may point to her voting record to establish her credibility as a conservative.

Aristotle felt that combining ethos, pathos, and logos was more effective than relying on only one kind of proof. For example, if a rhetor wanted to address the problem of obesity, it would be important to use ethos appeals to establish goodwill, avoiding mockery or mean-spiritedness. Logos, in turn, could offer the rationale for losing weight. Combining these appeals with the pathos-based approach of television shows like *The Biggest Loser* might enhance the impact on waistlines. The three artistic proofs work best synergistically.

Sometimes, the speaker may select to emphasize or subordinate one of the three artistic proofs. In early 2017, President Trump found a way to subordinate his usual high intensity emotional performance. Instead of focusing on emotional grandstanding, the President gave what the *Washington Post* called his "most presidential speech." In it, he calmly described which policies his administration has pursued in his first 100 days. Although he subordinated pathos to logos, emotion did punctuate in the middle of the address. When the President honored U.S. Navy Special Operator, Senior Chief William "Ryan" Owens, the camera panned to Senior Chief Owens' widow. Forty-eight million Americans watched members of Congress give her a recordbreaking stand of ovation as she cried. Later, CNN political analyst Van Jones argued that President Trump's speech had achieved the unprecedented. In part, it was because he had mitigated his direct appeal to pathos. Instead, he presided over an emotional connection between Congress and a citizen.

Social Position and Relationship to Audiences

Related to the concept of ethos is the social position from which a rhetor speaks. Aristotle noted that those who came from noble families were better positioned as rhetors. Yet **social position** refers to more than the prestige of one's family. One's social position comes from the way society is structured. Everyone is located in more than one position in the social structure as she or he speaks—as a student, a customer, a friend, a voter, and so on. As a receiver of public communication, you should always consider the position or positions from which the rhetor is speaking.

social position

Place in the social hierarchy, which comes from the way society is structured.

What aspects of social position might help or hinder a speaker's ability to advocate a point of view? The answer is that it depends on the society and the situation. We expect certain people to speak in certain situations, such as family members at a funeral or the governor after a natural disaster. In these cases, the rhetor's authority comes from a combination of her or his position and the audience members' expectations. Yet these social positions are also hierarchical, meaning that some positions have more power than others. For example, if you, as a student, were to speak out about U.S. immigration policies, you would be less influential than the president when he speaks about the same topic. Even if you spoke well, you could not make up for the difference in social positions between a student and a president. Social positions and positions of power are deeply intertwined because social positions gain their power from the society that supports the structure. This power structure allows certain rhetors to be more effective than others in promoting a message.

In societies that have strong caste systems, such as India, lower castes have few rhetorical mechanisms for changing the rules that guide their lives. Compared with higher castes, fewer of them have access to the Internet, they are less able to garner media coverage of their issues, and they therefore have fewer opportunities to be heard by those in power. Furthermore, in her study of the use of Native Americans as sports mascots, Janis King (2002) concluded that Native Americans have few opportunities to change the use of these mascots, as "team owners and the majority of the fans are White. And it is these individuals who have the power to eliminate the mascots, clothing and actions" (p. 211). More recently, the controversy has been focused on the Washington Redskins, but they are not the only team with controversial mascots.

Social institutions, also considered rhetors according to our definition, have distinct social positions that contribute to the effectiveness or persuasiveness of their public messages. For example, when the U.S. Supreme Court issues a ruling, it sends a public message that—coming from its position of power within our social structure—has tremendous implications for the ways in which we live. Other social institutions, including those involved in medicine, religion, the military, and education, also exercise their power through rhetoric.

Just as different rhetors wield different amounts of influence, so do audiences differ in terms of cultural, social, and political assumptions and perspectives. For example, in the aftermath of Hurricane Katrina, polls showed that Whites and African Americans had different views on the role of race in the response to this disaster. A Pew Research Center Survey found that 66 percent of African Americans felt that the response would have been faster if the victims were White, whereas only 17 percent of Whites felt that way (Pew Research Center for People and the Press, 2005). One common mistake of speakers is to think only of the dominant culture, overlooking minorities who may also be part of the audience. The wide disparity in the ways racial groups viewed the government's response to Katrina serves as an important reminder of the range of opinions that may be represented in any audience.

Who, then, is the rhetorical audience for any particular message? Rhetorical scholar Lloyd Bitzer (1968) argued that only those people who could take the appropriate action are part of the **rhetorical audience**. In other words, if a candidate for president of the United States wants to persuade a group of people to vote for her, only those people in the audience who are U.S. citizens and registered voters are part of the rhetorical audience. Although citizens of other nations or minors may be physically present for the campaign pitch, because they cannot vote for this candidate, they would not be part of the rhetorical audience. Thinking about the audience in this way may help the speaker design an appropriate, appealing, and potentially persuasive message.

Yet, this perspective on audience is quite narrow. As you may have noticed from following presidential elections, not all citizens who can vote do. In 2016, the United States saw the lowest voter turnout "in two decades" (Wallace, 2016) with only about 55 percent of the American electorate participating. But this does not necessarily mean that nonvoters weren't part of the rhetorical audience, especially those who understood their nonvote as a vote against an electoral system. Furthermore, U.S. citizens are not the only people who pay attention to campaign

rhetorical audience
Those people who can take the appropriate action in response to a message.

▼ If this officer were to testify against you in court, how might your different social positions influence how the officer's testimony and your testimony are heard?

rhetoric. People around the world are also quite interested in who is elected and which policies—economic, military, cultural—this president will pursue. We live in a global environment in which the actions of the United States affect others around the world. Thus, the presidential candidate can use rhetoric to construct the desired rhetorical audience, perhaps including non-U.S. citizens and even people living in other countries.

In addition to being broader than a speaker might initially think, audiences are also fragmented. French theorist Michel Maffesoli (1996) has suggested that society consists of multiple "tribes," or identity groups, with their own ways of seeing the world. These groups are often marked by how they consume products, wear clothing, or participate in certain activities. These tribes might include NASCAR dads, soccer moms, or goths. This tribe theory can help illuminate the complexity of audiences and how rhetoric works in differing contexts with various groups. Much more work needs to be done on the use of specific rhetorical devices among diverse cultural audiences so that we can better understand their complex functions.

In summary, a rhetor's effectiveness depends on a configuration of characteristics such as artistic proofs—ethos, pathos, and logos—as well as social position and relationship to audiences. Many factors contribute to our impression that one speaker is more charismatic and powerful than another. Audience members may not always agree on which speaker is the best, but most can say which one moves them and which leaves them cold—or drowsy! Considering individual rhetor characteristics gives us only a partial view of rhetoric. In the next section, we will broaden our focus to examine the relationship between rhetoric and society and the roles rhetoric plays in giving meaning to major events, fulfilling democratic functions, and bringing about justice and social change.

Journal Prompt 12.3:
Characteristics of Rhetors
Consider the following questions:
What are the most important characteristics of individual rhetors? What characteristics do you find most effective in some speakers vs. others?

The Individual, Rhetoric, and Society

12.4 Explain four functions of rhetoric: reaffirming cultural values, increasing democratic participation, securing justice, and promoting social change.

Because rhetoric always arises within a specific social context, its functions can vary considerably. The distinct cultural forces that influence a particular society should be considered when studying its rhetoric. In the United States today, rhetoric serves four important democratic functions that form the basis of how we come to decisions and work together collectively. We will look at these four functions next.

Reaffirming Cultural Values

rhetorical event

Any event that generates a significant amount of public discourse.

The term **rhetorical event** refers to any event that generates a significant amount of public discourse. Such "explosions" of rhetoric give insight into the ways meaning is constructed and rhetoric and cultural values are affirmed. For example, unusual weather or natural disasters incite a great deal of rhetorical discourse that attempts to explain what has occurred. Some of the discourse usually comes from scientists, who provide scientific explanations about the event. Other discourse may come from political commentators, who try to connect such natural disasters to a larger political or religious meaning. For example, after the devastating earthquake and tsunami that hit Japan in March 2011, some political commentators connected the events to Japan's careful and meticulous recycling practices. They used this tragedy to criticize environmentally friendly policies and practices. By connecting this tragedy to environment practices, they attempted to advance their own criticism and view of recycling and other practices as misguided. This affirmation, as well as negation, of cultural values is known as **epideictic rhetoric**.

epideictic rhetoric

The type of rhetoric that reaffirms cultural values through praising and blaming.

Part of the function of rhetorical events, then, is to reaffirm cultural values. Every four years, for example, the United States inaugurates a president, and the speeches given, particularly the president's inaugural speech, highlight important national values along with that president's goals. Holidays, sports events, weddings, funerals, retirement parties, campaign speeches, declarations of war, and protest marches are also rhetorical events. Such occasions often include speakers who celebrate cultural values relevant to, and that resonate with, their respective audiences.

Increasing Democratic Participation

As noted, among the ancient Greeks and Romans, rhetoric was valued for its use in civic life. The belief that advocating for one's ideas is in the best interests of society is a cornerstone of democracy. Not all societies are democracies, of course, and in those nondemocratic societies rhetoric has served different purposes. For our discussion we will examine aspects of rhetorical communication that influence citizen participation, which is a key part of the democratic process.

Deliberative rhetoric, the type of rhetoric used to argue what courses of action a society should do in the future, is deeply embedded in the democratic process. When legislators argue about raising taxes to pay for new roads or increasing funding for education, they are engaged in deliberative rhetoric. A speaker's ability to advocate effectively drives the open discussion and debate about what society should or should not do.

deliberative rhetoric
The type of rhetoric used to argue what courses of action a society should take in the future.

Also essential to a democracy is citizens' ability to evaluate the many important arguments they hear. In 2003, the United States argued in front of the United Nations Security Council that Saddam Hussein had weapons of mass destruction, and therefore, military intervention was needed. In hindsight, both government officials and citizens can see the errors made in arguments for the invasion. However, at the time, social position played an important role in the persuasiveness of the argument to go to war. Because Secretary of State Colin Powell was well respected nationally and internationally, he spoke from a position of power and credibility. Donald Rumsfeld, as Secretary of Defense, also spoke in favor of invading Iraq, as did President George W. Bush. In this instance, however, as well as in many others, citizens in a democracy benefit from listening to a variety of arguments and evaluating them based on the evidence available—without the undue influence of social position.

Another important area of inquiry within rhetorical studies as it relates to democracy focuses on the public sphere. The **public sphere** is the arena in which deliberative decision making occurs through the exchange of ideas and arguments. For example, legislative bodies such as Congress are places where decisions are made about a wide range of issues. Protests against the World Trade Organization, underground and alternative magazines and newspapers, and performance art that critiques social issues also constitute types of public sphere rhetoric, but are sometimes referred to as *counterpublics* because they occur outside the mainstream media and institutions. This type of rhetoric is also central to the functioning of a democratic society because it typically includes the voices of marginalized or less powerful individuals and groups.

public sphere
The arena in which deliberative decision making occurs through the exchange of ideas and arguments.

Bringing about Justice

As we noted previously in this chapter, a specific type of rhetoric is used in courts of law to bring about justice. Called **forensic rhetoric**, this form addresses events that happened in the past, as in "Where were you on the night of April 24?" The goal of forensic rhetoric is to set things right after an injustice has occurred. Another function of rhetoric in the context of justice is to allow citizens to exchange and negotiate ideas about what constitutes "just" and "unjust." As we look back over U.S. history, we can see how notions of justice have changed. In 1692, people in Salem, Massachusetts, felt that justice was served when they hanged nineteen people and jailed hundreds more for practicing witchcraft. Today, we see those trials as examples of injustice. In 1872, Susan B. Anthony, along with a number of other women, voted in an election in Rochester, New York. Anthony was arrested and convicted of violating laws that prevented women from voting. Today, most people view her actions as not only just but also courageous.

forensic rhetoric
Rhetoric that addresses events that happened in the past with the goal of setting things right after an injustice has occurred.

As these examples illustrate, laws and court judgments can only determine what is just and unjust within specific situations at particular moments in history. For example, Dred Scott was a nineteenth-century slave who tried to buy freedom for himself and his wife, but when the owner refused, he sought freedom through the court system. The U.S. Supreme Court ultimately ruled that he was neither a citizen—and therefore could not bring a case in federal court—nor entitled to his freedom because he was someone's personal property. Today, we would be shocked at this kind of Supreme Court ruling. As a nation, we have decided that slavery is an injustice, but coming to this decision involved considerable public communication, or rhetoric, about slavery. It also involved a bloody civil war. Nevertheless, debates about citizenship and racial restrictions on who was eligible to be a U.S. citizen continued well into the twentieth century.

Hindsight makes it easy to see that slavery or the denial of rights to women or Blacks is unjust. In many cases, however, considerable disagreement exists about what is just. For example, the U.S. military has been grappling with cases of torture, the most notorious being those committed at Abu Ghraib prison in Iraq in 2003. Visual images of the atrocities at Abu Ghraib were studied by communication scholars to understand how they functioned as rhetoric (Smith & Dionosopoulos, 2008; Solaroli, 2011). How do the images shape how we think about what happened? See *Did You Know? Visual Rhetoric.* Should we focus on the role of U.S. foreign policy or was this the work of a few rogue military personnel? Some of the photographs of tortured prisoners at Abu Ghraib were broadcast on television. What is the just response to this set of events? As the discussion about justice ensues, some will argue that these soldiers were under orders from their superiors and thus not responsible, whereas others will argue that each person is

DID YOU KNOW?
Visual Rhetoric

As you consider the following image of former First Lady Michelle Obama and former President George W. Bush, consider how the image stirred forensic elements about how the country can heal after past injustices. Can images take on rhetorical functions? What are the differences and similarities between verbal and visual rhetorics?

This image, originally taken at the opening of the National Museum of African American History and Culture, went viral on social media outlets like Twitter. Many commented on the image as a moment of hope and healing; others saw it as a moment of bipartisanship.

SOURCE: Coleburn, C. (2016, September 25). The hug felt around the country: Michelle Obama and George W. Bush embrace at museum opening. *NBC News.* Retrieved March 29, 2017 from: http://www.nbcnews.com/news/us-news/hug-felt-around-country-michelle-obama-george-w-bush-embrace-n654091.

responsible for her or his own acts. Lawyers are generally at the forefront of these discussions, at least in the courtroom, but the public, the press, and politicians also weigh in.

In the effort to find justice, Ameneh Bahrami, an Iranian woman, asked that Islamic law be imposed on a man who threw acid on her face, disfiguring and blinding her. This man had wanted to marry Bahrami, but she declined his marriage proposal. Recently, "an Iranian court ordered that five drops of the same chemical be placed in each of her attacker's eyes, acceding to Bahrami's demand that he be punished according to a principle in Islamic jurisprudence that allows a victim to seek retribution for a crime" (Erdbrink, 2008, p. A1). In late July 2011, she pardoned her attacker so that he did not end up being blinded (Dehghan, 2011). Although recognizing cultural and religious differences, is this justice? How do we determine what is just and what is unjust, except through public discussion and deliberation? As you contemplate these types of questions you will undoubtedly realize that many different kinds of punishments were (and are) acceptable in different periods and places. Questions of justice are neither easily settled nor universally agreed on, and they are negotiated rhetorically. Through our public discussions, we try to build a more just society.

Prompting Social Change

As you can see from the Dred Scott case and others, laws do not always ensure justice for all. Thus, people who want to bring about social change and promote their views of justice often use rhetoric to mobilize large numbers of people. If a mobilization succeeds, it can lead to a **social movement**, which is a mass movement of people motivated to create social change. Scholars have studied the public messages of social movements, such as the movement to abolish slavery, the women's suffrage movement, and the anti–Vietnam War movement. Social movement scholars also have tried to understand opposition to such movements and to evaluate the persuasiveness of that opposition.

Other social movements that have received attention from rhetoricians include the Chicano movement (Delgado, 1995), the environmental movement (DeLuca, 1999), and the gay/lesbian movement (Darsey, 1991). In this latter study, Darsey tracked the changing arguments of gay rights activists over time in relation to the changing contexts of sexual liberation, antigay legislation, and AIDS. The goals of his study and other similar ones are to understand the arguments that activists in social movements make, the social and historical context in which they put forth these arguments, the events that spark the emergence of social movement discourse, the resistance to the arguments, and why arguments on both sides are or are not persuasive.

As you can see, public messages are deeply embedded in the culture of their times. In past eras, debates and speeches about slavery, women's suffrage, and U.S. involvement in the Vietnam War permeated the daily life of Americans. Today, far more rhetoric focuses on terrorism, Iraq, and gay marriage. As people perceive wrongs that need to be corrected, social movements emerge, and people use rhetoric to argue for the desired changes. Because a social movement is typically controversial, those who prefer to maintain the status quo will oppose it and also use rhetoric to argue against change. (See *Alternative View: Uptalk/Vocal Fry*). This has been the case in every social movement mentioned.

Today, the uses of rhetoric extend far beyond the traditional medium of public speaking. People who desire to change our society use every available means of communicating. This means that rhetoric is a part of our everyday lives, relayed via advertising, blogs, emails, texts, television programming, and newspapers. Rhetoric is embedded in all manner of communicative media, which are themselves the topic of the next chapter. Various aspects of communication often overlap.

social movement
A large, organized body of people who are attempting to create social change.

▼ In 2016, British voters decided to leave the European Union, which has been called "Brexit." Rhetoric was used by both those who wanted to leave the European Union and those who wanted to stay in the European Union.

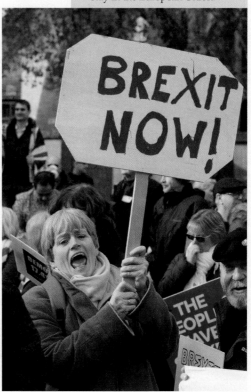

ALTERNATIVE VIEW
Uptalk/Vocal Fry

NPR produced a special series on "The Changing Lives of Women," in which they reported on recent efforts to overcome a micro-aggressive resistance to women's changing voices. Studies show that typical listeners—both men and women—perceive less authority in higher pitched voices. However, a voice consistently dropped to a lower vocal pitch than is its natural range sounds fried. According to Dr. Penny Eckert, author of *Language and Gender,* vocal fry and up-speak are conjoined examples of a dilemma: women are discounted or judged whether they sound childlike, high-pitched, or grating on the one hand; or inauthentic, low-pitched, or masculine on the other. Accordingly, some studies show that listeners do not trust women whose voices fry.

Are we "resistant to change or are there problems with how women speak?" asks Terri Gross in the opening of her *Fresh Air* episode. What follows is a conversation that resistance to change sometimes creates social movements. Some feminists are now speaking up about uptalk. They find that women's voices are being policed, especially in rhetorical contexts, where we internally or externally attribute negative traits to a woman's voice. Easing our resistance to changing sources of authority in this case is a change.

SOURCES: "Changing Lives of Women" http://www.npr.org/sections/health-shots/2014/10/24/357584372/video-what-women-get-flak-for-when-they-talk.

"From Upspeak To Vocal Fry" http://www.npr.org/2015/07/23/425608745/from-upspeak-to-vocal-fry-are-we-policing-young-womens-voices.

**Journal Prompt 12.4:
Rhetoric and Society**
Consider the following questions:
Why is rhetoric important in a democratic society? How can rhetoric bring about justice and social change?

In sum, rhetoric plays an important role in a society. It can provide meaning and shape our thoughts about major events. It can also serve democratic functions in the political life of a society. Furthermore, rhetoric can bring about justice and provide momentum for major social changes, as it has in historical movements and as it continues to do today. But how can you use these ideas about rhetoric to become more ethical? This is the topic of the next section.

Ethics and Rhetoric

12.5   Understand the ethical issues facing rhetors and audience members.

Concerns about ethics and rhetoric have been a mainstay in rhetorical studies since the origins of rhetoric. From ancient Greeks to contemporary thinkers, rhetoricians have wrestled with the best ways to be ethical in using and consuming rhetorical messages. There have been many debates over what is ethical and unethical in attempting to persuade others to view the world as the rhetor does. Although most would agree that the use of outright deception or lying would be unacceptable, there is no set list of rules that are universally agreed on to guide your ethical choices. In building a rhetorical case advocating a particular way of viewing a topic—for example, death penalty, abortion, financial reform—be aware of the choices that the rhetor is making. Is the best available evidence being used? Is the message adapted to the audience?

It is important to be aware of the language that is used. Obviously, pejorative terms for members of various cultural groups should be avoided because it is unethical to dismiss entire groups of people with negative terms. Sometimes rhetors demean or disparage particular social groups, either overtly or subtly. When someone engages in this communication behavior, much of the audience may turn against the rhetor. For example, Robert Copeland, the police commissioner of Wolfeboro, New Hampshire, said that "he wouldn't apologize for calling President Barack Obama the N-word" (Salahi, 2014). He later resigned his position.

Aside from such obvious choices, you should also consider your use of what rhetorician Richard Weaver described as "god terms" and "devil terms" (1985). These terms too easily lead (or mislead) people without critical reflection. God terms are words such as "freedom," "equality," and so on. Devil terms are similar but negative, such as "communist," "nazi" and so on. God terms and devil terms must be used carefully because they can serve more as propaganda than rhetoric, and when we hear those terms, we should carefully consider what the rhetor is trying to persuade us to think or do.

Rhetorical ethics are also focused on the ends or goals of the rhetorical messages. For example, if someone is trying to convince people that we should undertake the genocide of a particular cultural group, does it matter if he or she does not lie or fabricate any evidence in making the argument? So, ethics in rhetoric include a consideration of the goals of the rhetoric. What do these rhetorical messages encourage us to do or to think?

Social media present new challenges to the need to think through how we attempt to persuade others to view the world as we do (and vice versa). The Internet not only reproduces and reflects larger social issues, but it can also shape the ways that the rhetorical discussions take place (Nakamura & Chow-White, 2012). You may have encountered many problematic comments online. This phenomenon is interesting in that it creates a space for people to try to align others to their worldviews. For example, Leslie Jones faced tremendous online racist and sexist hatred in 2016 (Brown, 2016). Jones was in a remake of *Ghostbusters,* which seemed to provoke these postings. One of these provocateurs, Milo Yiannopoulos, was a major participant in these hateful messages. Twitter eventually banned him (Ohlheiser, 2016). The racist and sexist messages posted online deflected attention away from the movie, as well as highlighting the problem of racism and sexism. Although racist and sexist discourse is not unique to the online environment, online comments are an important part of our rhetorical environment because they are public.

Using what you know about rhetoric, then, what can you do to become an ethical receiver of rhetorical communication? Here are some guidelines:

- Be willing to listen to a range of perspectives on a particular topic. Although you may not initially agree with a particular rhetor, you should consider her or his perspective (Makau, 1997), including why you do or do not agree.

- Be willing to speak out if you know that a rhetor is giving misinformation or deceiving an audience.

- Don't be silenced by information overload. If a speaker gives too much information, focus on the main points and be critical of this kind of presentation.

- Listen critically to the rhetor; don't accept the arguments presented at face value.

- Be willing to speak out publicly if a rhetor communicates in a way that dehumanizes or demeans others (Johannesen, 1997).

- Listen to and fairly assess what you hear, which may require that you postpone judgment until you hear the entire message.

- Be willing to change your mind as more evidence becomes available.

**Journal Prompt 12.5:
Ethical Rhetoric**
Consider the following question:
What are some of the major ethical issues facing rhetors and audiences?

Using Your Rhetorical Skills: Speaking in Public

12.6 Identify the basic steps in preparing a speech.

Throughout this chapter, we have discussed rhetoric primarily from the viewpoint of the receiver or critic. But we can also be rhetors by writing for an audience, by using other media such as video to reach audiences, and by practicing the art of public speaking. Becoming an effective rhetor is important because speaking in public is a cornerstone of our participatory democracy in the United States. Citizens need to become adept public speakers so that they can advocate for what they think is best (Gayle, 2004). Learning to speak up for your interests can also improve your satisfaction from participating in student organizations, as well as in local organizations such as a city council or a volunteer group. Public speaking skills are also important for success in most jobs. Increasingly, businesses want employees who can speak well in meetings and in public settings outside the organization (Osterman, 2005).

In the following sections, we introduce the basic elements of speech preparation. We'll look at the range of communication events in which people may be called to speak, the importance of understanding audiences, and the basics of constructing, organizing, and delivering a speech. These elements supply the foundations for effective public speaking.

Understanding the Communication Event: The Synergetic Model

Recall from Chapter 1 that the Synergetic Model of Communication depicts communication as a transactional process that is influenced by individual, societal, and cultural factors. It is easy to see how this model applies to public speaking. Far from being a one-way communication in which the rhetor delivers a speech to the audience, effective public speaking is a transaction between the rhetor and the audience. You as an individual bring yourself to the speech—speaking is self-presentation as well as being the presentation of a message. A good speaker also relates to audience members as individuals, giving each listener the sense that the speaker is "talking to me." Finally, every speech event is influenced by the societal and cultural contexts in which it takes place.

In this section, we will examine the steps in understanding the communication event: identifying your general purpose, understanding your audience, selecting your topic, and identifying a specific purpose for your speech.

Identifying Your General Purpose   The great Roman orator Cicero identified three objectives for public speaking: to inform, to persuade, and to entertain. These three types of speeches are still taught in most public speaking courses today (McKerrow, Gronbeck, Ehninger, & Monroe, 2003; O'Hair, Stewart, & Rubenstein, 2004). However, the objective "to entertain" has been broadened to "to evoke feeling," which is a more accurate description of what this type of speech can do. For example, a half-time locker room speech does not aim to be entertaining but inspiring. Of course, inspiration motivates the team to win, so it remains a kind of persuasion, albeit indirect. For reference, watch Tony D'Amato, Al Pacino's character in *Any Given Sunday*, deliver a moving football half-time locker room speech. D'Amato doesn't have to persuade his team to win. They already want to win but their morale is low. Sometimes, stirring emotion is the key to goading people to persevere and perhaps achieve their goals. We will refer to this third type as the *evocative speech*.

The *informative speech* explains, instructs, defines, clarifies, demonstrates, or teaches. The *persuasive speech* attempts to influence, convince, motivate, sell, preach, or stimulate action. Finally, the purpose of the *evocative speech* is to entertain, inspire, celebrate, commemorate, or build community (Sprague & Stuart, 2005, p. 65). A common type of evocative speech, including the wedding toast, celebrates aspects of a person or topic. Sometimes evocative speeches are also known as **special-occasion speeches**, and they include speeches given at retirement dinners, award ceremonies, weddings, graduations, and funerals.

Obviously, the three general purposes do not function in isolation. Speakers often persuade others by informing them about something, or they inform audiences by entertaining them. A speech by a politician might primarily aim to persuade voters to adopt a particular point of view, but it might also be informative and evocative. Of the three, the one that is dominant in a given speech is known as the **general purpose** of that speech. Once you identify your general purpose, you are ready to begin the next step of developing your presentation by focusing on your audience.

Understanding Your Audience   Because the speaking event is a transactional process between you and your audience, it is important to learn as much as possible about your audience as you develop your speech. In public speaking this is called **audience analysis**. Understanding and relating to your audience are crucial aspects of public speaking because, regardless of purpose or goals, the success of your presentation depends on its appropriateness for your audience.

special-occasion speeches
Evocative speeches intended to entertain, inspire, celebrate, commemorate, or build community.

general purpose
Whichever of three goals—to inform, persuade, or entertain—dominates a speech.

audience analysis
The process of determining what an audience already knows or wants to know about a topic, who they are, what they know or need to know about the speaker, and what their expectations might be for the presentation.

Audience analysis involves learning as much as you can in response to the following four questions.

1. What does the audience already know about your topic? What do they want to know?

2. What do your listeners know about you? What do they need to know about you?

3. What expectations do your listeners have for the presentation?

4. Who are your audience members in terms of identity characteristics such as age, gender, race and ethnicity, education, socioeconomic status, and group membership? These characteristics are known as audience demographics, and the process of investigating them is known as **demographic analysis**.

▲ Audiences can be complex groups of people who may share some interests but differ on others. Demographic information can be helpful, but avoid playing into stereotypes.

demographic analysis
The portion of an audience analysis that considers the ages, races, sexes, sexual orientations, religions, and social classes of the audience.

Although it may seem difficult to obtain answers to these questions, it is easy to see that if your audience consists of people you have already met—such as fellow students in your class—you may already be able to provide many answers. You can also ask them about various aspects of these audience analysis questions, either in informal conversations or by developing an audience analysis questionnaire. If you are speaking to an unfamiliar group of listeners and do not have an opportunity to meet them before the speech, ask the person who invited you to speak. Like most facets of public speaking, audience analysis is a rich topic in itself, but we hope these essentials will enable you to approach the task effectively.

Selecting Your Topic   Selecting a topic can be the most interesting and the most difficult part of any speech presentation. Assuming that the topic is not already determined for you, here are some guidelines to help you choose:

- Consider the communication event. What are the expectations for your presentation? What types of topics would be appropriate to speak about?

- Consider your interests. Take a personal inventory. What are some unusual experiences you've had? What subjects do you know a lot about? What topics do you feel strongly about? What would you like to learn more about?

- Consider your relationship to the communication event. Why are you being asked to speak? Do you have a special relationship to someone—for example, the bride at a wedding or the deceased at a funeral? If so, you may have special insight into topics the audience would consider appropriate and effective. Have you been chosen because you are an expert in a particular area? If so, the audience will expect you to demonstrate that expertise and to answer questions effectively.

We'll return to the development of speech topics when we guide you through the important process of narrowing a broad topic to an appropriately focused one.

Critical Thinking Prompt
If you had to give a speech today to the graduating class of the high school you attended, what topics might you consider for your speech?

Identifying a Specific Purpose   Once you know the general purpose of your speech and have selected your speech topic, you can begin focusing on the specific purpose of your speech. As discussed previously, your general purpose may be to inform, persuade, or evoke a certain feeling from your audience. Your **specific purpose** focuses on what you would like to inform or persuade your audience about, or what type of

specific purpose
What a speaker wants to inform or persuade an audience about, or the type of feelings the speaker wants to evoke.

feelings you want to evoke. Identifying your specific purpose helps you focus your topic and establish your organizational structure.

The specific purpose of your speech should be a "nutshell" summary of what you want your audience to take away. Here are some examples of specific purposes for informative, persuasive, and evocative speeches.

- My specific purpose is to inform my audience about the cost of private preschools in our local area.
- My specific purpose is to inform my audience about the history of immigration at Ellis Island.
- My specific purpose is to persuade my audience that our public school system should raise taxes to institute a universal preschool program.
- My specific purpose is to persuade my audience to donate money to the Ellis Island Museum.
- My specific purpose is to evoke a humorous mood regarding parents' anxiety over their children's performance in preschool interviews.
- My specific purpose is to evoke nostalgia with the story of my great-grandfather's immigration experience at Ellis Island.

Once you have a specific purpose, you need to research your topic, gather evidence for your claims, and organize your speech. We will turn to those steps next. But first, to make sure you've obtained all the preliminary "nuts and bolts" information you need to prepare your speech, refer to *Communication in Society: Communication Event Checklist*.

Researching and Organizing Your Presentation

Once you have laid the foundation for developing your speech, you are ready to craft your thesis statement, locate supporting materials, and decide how to organize your message.

thesis statement
A statement of the topic of a speech and the speaker's position on it.

Crafting Your Thesis Statement By rephrasing your specific purpose as a **thesis statement**, you create a statement of your topic and your position on it. The thesis statement is important because it is the foundation on which you construct your presentation. For example, if your specific purpose is to argue that voting should be mandatory, you might articulate your thesis statement this way: "Voting should be mandatory in the United States." This is an effective thesis statement because it clearly sets out the proposition to be considered. Each of the main points you want to convey should clearly connect to and develop your thesis statement.

supporting materials
Information that supports the speaker's ideas.

Finding Supporting Materials Some topics require extensive research, particularly those on which you are not an expert. However, all speech preparations should include some research to find **supporting materials** that support your ideas.

COMMUNICATION IN SOCIETY
Communication Event Checklist

What other details might you need to know for a particular speaking event?

_____ 1. When will you speak (date and time), and how long is your speech supposed to last?

_____ 2. Where will you speak (address, directions), and what will the size and physical layout of the room be?

_____ 3. What is the general purpose of your speech? The specific purpose?

_____ 4. What do you know about your audience?

_____ 5. Have you arranged for any computer or audiovisual equipment you will need?

_____ 6. Do you have the name and phone number of a person in charge whom you can contact in case a question or emergency arises?

Supporting materials are available from at least three sources: electronic, print, and personal. You can start with the electronic card catalog in your library, accessing databases and online journals. You will also want to search the Internet, which is increasingly an excellent and acceptable source for research, even scholarly studies. One caution about Internet sources, however: You must evaluate them carefully, as you should any source. Referring to credible sources is especially important for informative and persuasive speeches.

Print sources include books, magazines, and newspapers. Again, evaluate the source. Newspapers such as *The Wall Street Journal* or *The Washington Post* are considered highly reliable on certain topics. Note that some print materials (e.g., *The New American, The Nation, Ms. Magazine*) have a specific point of view. You may use such sources to support your point, but you should acknowledge their viewpoint or bias in your speech. You can find magazines that address every topic imaginable—from general news (e.g., *Newsweek*) to specific hobbies (e.g., *Model Railroader, Scrapbooking, Sky and Telescope*). Use Internet databases such as EBSCO or NexisLexis® to help you locate print magazine articles that address your speech topic. In addition to newspapers and magazines, there are encyclopedias and other reference works (e.g., *Statistical Abstract of the United States, People's Almanac, Guinness Book of World Records*) that offer a wealth of information on a variety of topics.

A final source of supporting materials can be personal interviews. You might want to interview people who can give you facts, opinions, and background information on your topic. In addition, you can use interviews to find leads to other sources, including the faculty at your college or university. Most professors have a wealth of information in several areas of expertise and enjoy sharing that information, including where you might do further research. Before any interview, be sure to prepare well. Know what kind of information you're looking for, contact potential interviewees in advance to make appointments, and be able to explain why you chose them (this shows you've done some homework).

As you identify and use any of these kinds of sources, take careful notes because you may need to refer to them. Moreover, some instructors require that references be submitted with a speaking outline. We'll discuss different types of outlines when we discuss organizing speeches.

Once you have a collection of relevant sources, what kinds of material do you look for within them? Statistics, examples, and personal narratives can all be useful in bolstering your points. Visual aids also provide effective support, especially when a topic is complex. Let's look at the uses for each of these types of support materials.

Statistics   Statistics can highlight the size of a problem and help the audience understand a contrast or comparison. However, they can be overwhelming or confusing if they are too complex for the audience to follow. If you are dealing with large numbers, it is often best to round them off. For example, according to the U.S. Census Bureau, 5,220,579 people in the United States were counted as American Indian and Alaska Natives in the 2010 census (U.S Census Bureau, 2012). Your audience is more likely to remember this statistic if you round it off and say that there are slightly more than 5.2 million American Indians and Alaska Natives in the United States.

When citing statistics, however, be careful about attributing meaning to them because the reasons for statistical differences are not always apparent or reported with the statistical data. For example, the Pew Research Center (Smith & Martinez, 2016) came out with a preliminary report on who voted for Donald Trump vs. Hillary Clinton in the 2016 election based on race and religion. They report that white Catholics voted for Trump 60 percent to 37 percent, whereas Hispanic Catholics voted for Clinton 67 percent to 26 percent. Mormons voted for Trump 61 percent to 25 percent for Clinton, while Jewish voters supported Clinton 71 percent to 24 percent for Trump. Those who are unaffiliated or without religious identity voted for Clinton 68 percent to 26 percent for Trump. The numbers do not add up to 100 percent as people may have voted for someone else or chose not to answer. Although this is interesting information that may be useful in supporting a point you want to make about religion in the United States, it is important to be aware that the Pew survey did not attribute any causes to these percentages. We don't know why the survey respondents answered as they did, so you would not want to mislead your audience by adding attributions of your own unless you clearly state that such attributions are your own opinion.

Examples   A second type of supporting material, examples, can also add power to a presentation. A speaker might give a brief example to illustrate a point in passing or use a more extended example, woven throughout a speech. Examples provide a concrete and realistic way of thinking about a topic and clarifying it. If you were to speak about nonfiction television programming, for example, your audience may better understand your point if you name specific programs, such as *60 Minutes, Nova*, or *Monday Night Football*. Without these examples, some audience members might think you are referring to reality television programs, such as *Survivor, Amazing Race*, and *Big Brother*.

Personal Narratives   A third kind of support for your presentation—personal narratives and testimony of others—can give your speech a human touch. For example, if you are speaking about non-English languages in the United States and you describe your own family's struggle to retain its non-English language, your story adds emotional texture to the issue. See *It Happened to Me: Lisa* to read how a personal narrative can influence your audience.

Visual Aids   As a student in elementary school, you may have used visual aids in show-and-tell speeches. In these speeches, the visual aid—perhaps a favorite toy, gift, or souvenir—was at the center. As part of your college coursework, your instructors may also require that you use visual aids in speeches. Even if you are not required to do so, you should consider whether visual aids would enhance the clarity of your presentation or make it more memorable or more interesting. **Visual aids** are any audiovisual materials that help you reach your speech goals. Some of the most common kinds are video or audio clips, photographs and drawings, charts and graphs, and PowerPoint slides.

visual aids
Audiovisual materials that help a speaker reach intended speech goals.

Always select and incorporate visual aids carefully, remembering that their purpose is to augment and enhance your presentation, not to detract from your presentation. They are also not a substitute for content, as Edward Tufte instructs in *Alternative View: PowerPoint Is Evil: Power Corrupts. PowerPoint Corrupts Absolutely*.

To determine whether a visual aid is going to augment or detract, ask yourself why you are using it and how it will support your speech goals. Here are some tips for handling visual aids effectively:

1. Prepare visual aids in advance.
2. Make sure your visual aids are easy for all audience members to see.
3. Make sure the equipment you need will be available when you speak.
4. Make sure your speech can stand on its own in case of a technology failure.

In using a visual aid during your speech, follow these three steps: (a) introduce the visual aid to your audience members by explaining what they will see, (b) point to the parts of the visual aid that you want them to focus on, and (c) reaffirm the major point of the visual aid, thus pointing audience members to the conclusion you want them to draw.

Organizing Your Message
Once you have gathered enough information and evidence to build your speech, you need to organize the presentation in a clear manner. Organizing an effective presentation means

It Happened to Me
Lisa

We once had a speaker in class who told us about her family's struggle with diabetes. I had never really thought about diabetes before, and the statistics about diabetes didn't impact me as much as her story. I didn't know that some diabetics had to have their feet amputated, but now that I know, I am much more sensitive to the struggles of diabetics.

ALTERNATIVE VIEW
PowerPoint Is Evil: Power Corrupts. PowerPoint Corrupts Absolutely

Have you ever sat through a horrible PowerPoint presentation? PowerPoint is a tool that can be very helpful and effective in presentations, but—like any tool—it can be used in ways that are counterproductive. Bad PowerPoint presentations can turn audiences away from the presentation and sometimes turn against the presenter. We've all been subjected to bad PowerPoint presentations, but you can avoid making one by following some important tips.

1. Do not put your text on the slides and then read to the audience. Audiences can often read faster than you can read aloud and you risk losing the audience. They may read the slides and then, while you continue reading to them, they may check their smartphones, send text messages, daydream and so on.
2. Think about the number of slides that you use. While it is often easy to include a lot of slides, audiences can get overwhelmed by a large number of slides. Keep the focus of the presentation on your content.
3. Be careful not to overload your audience with too much information. Much of the information in a presentation does not need to be reflected on PowerPoint slides.

4. Don't forget the affective or emotional aspects of your presentation, especially if your goal is to persuade as in a sales talk. Emotions can be powerful motivators and PowerPoint slides may draw away from those emotional appeals.
5. Consider what the strengths of PowerPoint are and how you can best use this tool. For example, a PowerPoint slide can show an image that would be much more difficult to explain verbally. Images can also help audiences spark emotional responses of childhood, family, home and more which you can then use to draw your audience toward the direction that you wish to take them.

Overall, remember that PowerPoint is a tool to help you with your presentation. It should not overwhelm or distract the audience away from your talk. Keep your talk at the center of the presentation and use the PowerPoint to assist you in the goals of the presentation. PowerPoint should never be a substitution for your presentation. An audience should never feel that they would have been better off if you had just printed out your PowerPoint slides and distributed them.

---

choosing and following a pattern that is compatible with your topic and that will make sense to your audience. It also involves creating an outline that can serve as the framework for your material. To anchor your organizational structure, you will develop an introduction, a conclusion, and transitions.

Organizational Patterns   In most cases, a speech should be organized around three to five main points. If you have fewer than three points, you may not yet have sufficiently thought about or researched your topic. Once you have identified your main points, divide them into subpoints. These subpoints should all clearly relate to their corresponding main points. Once you have all your main points and subpoints, you need to consider how to arrange them. Speakers generally follow one of five organizational patterns: chronological, spatial, topical, problem–solution, or cause–effect.

A **chronological pattern** follows a timeline; for example, a speech on the life of a famous person lends itself well to a chronological outline.

Here is an example of a chronological pattern:

Topic: Life of Susan B. Anthony

chronological pattern
An organization that follows a timeline.

▼ Visual aids can be helpful in explaining ideas and instructions. In this photo, students receive hands-on training in CPR.

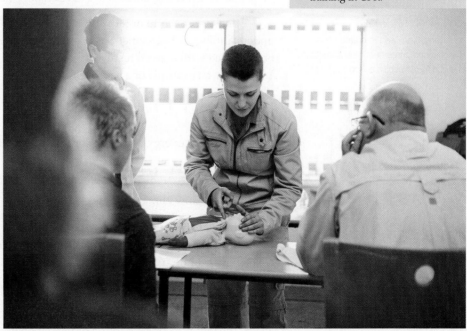

I. Her birth and formative years (1820–1840)
II. Her fight to end slavery (1840–1860)
III. Her fight for women's rights (1860–her death in 1906)

spatial pattern

An organization that arranges points by location and can be used to describe something small.

A **spatial pattern** arranges points by location and can be used to describe something small (for example, parts of a flower—moving from the edge to its center) or something large (for example, the immigration center buildings at Ellis Island—moving along a central hallway).

Here is an example of a spatial pattern:

Topic: A Tour of Ellis Island

I. The Baggage Room
II. The Registry Room
III. The Hearing Room
IV. The Bunk Room

topical pattern

An organization that has no innate organization except that imposed by the speaker.

A **topical pattern** of organization, the most common, is used when your main points have no innate pattern except the one you impose on them. This situation requires more thinking because the points have no predetermined relationship, and you will need to find the scheme that is most logical and will work best for your audience.

Here is an example of a topical pattern:

Topic: MERS (Middle Eastern Respiratory Syndrome)

I. What is MERS?
II. Who is most at risk?
III. How can you prevent MERS?

problem–solution pattern

An organization in which the speaker describes various aspects of a problem and then proposes solutions.

In the **problem–solution pattern**, you describe various aspects of a problem and then propose solutions; it is frequently used in persuasive speeches.

Here is an example of a problem–solution pattern:

Topic: Childhood obesity

I. Problem: Increasing obesity rates in U.S. children
II. Solution: Eat healthier foods and drink water
III. Solution: Increase amount of exercise, sports activities, and general physical activity

cause–effect pattern

An organization used to create understanding and agreement, and sometimes to argue for a specific action.

A final approach to organization, the **cause–effect pattern**, is often used to create understanding and agreement or to argue for a specific action in light of the cause that is associated with a given result.

Here is an example of a cause–effect pattern:

Topic: Climate Change

I. Causes
   Subpoints: energy consumption, overpopulation, increasing consumption
II. Effects
   Subpoints: extreme weather events, rising sea levels, melting ice caps
III. How to slow climate change

Outlining your Speech   Once you have selected your pattern, you will have a good idea of the order in which you want to present your points. Thus, you are ready to create your outline. You are probably already familiar with how to outline. In the past, you may have used outlining chiefly to organize your written compositions. However, outlining also is useful in organizing a public-speaking presentation. An outline should be considered a working document, so you shouldn't hesitate to change it again and again. The idea is to create a sound organizational structure and a road map from which you can best build your presentation.

Introduction, Body, and Conclusion   After you have developed your outline, arranging your points and subpoints according to the pattern you have chosen, you will need to develop this skeleton into a full-bodied presentation. In doing so, you will pay special attention to your introduction and conclusion. Audiences usually remember much more about these opening and closing elements than they do about the body of the speech.

From your **introduction**, audience members gain a first impression of your speech's content and of you as the speaker, so both the content and presentation of the introduction are important. You'll want to start with a bang, not a whimper. To do this, your introduction should: (1) gain audience attention, (2) focus their attention on your topic by relating it to them, (3) give them an overview of your organizational pattern, and (4) help them understand your thesis.

You can gain audience attention with a snappy quotation, a startling fact, a personal example, or a shocking statistic connected to your speech topic.

Once you have gotten the audience's attention, you need to focus it on your specific topic. Your next task is to present your thesis statement so the audience understands the point of the speech. In the final part of your introduction, you would preview the overall organization of the presentation.

Moving on to the body of your speech, you will want to insert transitions to help your audience understand your organization as you progress from main point to main point, and from subpoint to subpoint. These transitions, called **signposts**, tell the audience where you are in the overall organization, thus making it easier for them to follow along and stay oriented. Common signposts include phrases such as, "my second point is" or "a second stage of the" or "in addition." These devices are not merely mechanical. You can use them in an artful way to help your words and ideas flow together gracefully.

The transition into your conclusion needs to be marked by a major signpost so that the audience knows you are preparing to end your speech. The **conclusion** should accomplish several goals. First, it should review the three to five main points in the body of your presentation. Second, if you are giving a persuasive speech, during the conclusion, you will challenge the audience to act. Actions may include finding out more about the topic or becoming more involved in the issue—for example, by registering to vote, donating blood, or signing a petition. As you formulate this challenge, or call the audience to action, consider how you want your presentation to impact their lives. Do you want them to vote a particular way? Change their eating habits? Use sunscreen? Finally, the conclusion should leave the audience with a positive view of you and your topic.

Whatever closing technique you choose, remember that public speaking is an art that requires artistic judgment. There is no one right or wrong way to do it, only more effective and less effective ones. See Figure 12.1 for an outline of the basic speech structure that has just been described.

Rehearsing and Delivering Your Speech

After you have developed, researched, and organized your materials, you are ready to consider the presentation of your speech. Many people think of public speaking as being all about delivery, but delivery is, as we hope you have seen, only one aspect of the entire process. In the context of public speaking, **delivery** refers to the presentation of the speech you have researched, organized, outlined, and practiced. Delivery *is* important, of course, because it is what is most immediate to the audience. In this section, we focus on three important aspects of delivery: being aware of time, developing a speaking persona, and finally, putting your speech into action.

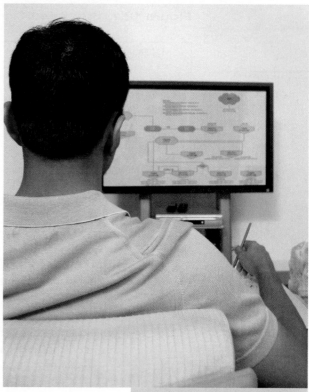

▲ Outlining your speech is a very important part of the public-speaking process. Your outline will form the basis of your speaking notes.

introduction

Opening material of a speech from which the audience members gain a first impression of the speech's content and of the speaker.

signposts

Transitions in a speech that help an audience understand the speaker's organization, making it easier for them to follow.

conclusion

Closing material of a speech where the speaker reviews the main points, may challenge the audience to act, and leaves the audience with a positive view of speaker and topic.

delivery

The presentation of a speech before an audience.

Figure 12.1 Basic Speech Structure

I. Introduction
  A. Attention-getting step
  B. Connection to audience
  C. Thesis statement
  D. Preview of main points
  E. Transition to first point
 	
II. First Main Point
 	
  A. Signpost your first point.
  B. Make your point (include supporting material).
  C. Transition to your next point.
	III. Second Main Point
	  A. Signpost your second point.
	  B. Make your point (include supporting material).
	  C. Transition to your next point.
	
	IV. Third Main Point
	  A. Signpost your third point.
	  B. Make your point (include supporting material).
	  C. Transition to conclusion.
	
	V. Conclusion
	  A. Review main points.
	  B. Connect back to audience.
	  C. Create a memorable conclusion.

Being Aware of the Time   In the United States, we often think about time as absolute, a phenomenon that can be broken down into clearly measurable units: seconds, minutes, and hours. Yet, communication scholars have repeatedly shown that notions of time are relative. Many public speakers experience this relative nature of time, feeling like they have been speaking for a long time, whereas their audience may feel that they have heard only a short speech, or vice versa.

Knowing for how long to speak is an important aspect of the art of public speaking. The length of any speech should be guided by audience expectations in a particular context as well as by the content of your message. In some instances, the guidelines are rather loose, such as speeches at weddings and retirements. In other cases, the time limits are strict, and you may be cut off before you finish. For example, a citizen advocating a position in city council meetings often faces strict time limits. In classroom speech situations, you are often told how long to speak, and your audience will expect you to stay within those limits.

If your speech is significantly longer than expected, your audience may become restless, impatient, or even hostile. On the other hand, if your speech is significantly shorter than the time expected, your audience may leave feeling disappointed or shortchanged because they may have made a significant effort to attend your presentation. If your speech is part of a larger program, the planners will be depending on you to fill a particular time slot.

One way to make sure you comply is to time yourself when you practice. Doing this will ensure that you know how long your speech runs and whether you need to adjust it. If you have prepared, practiced, and timed your speech, you should have no problem meeting your time requirement.

Projecting a Persona   Developing a persona, or the image a speaker conveys, is one of the most artistic aspects of public speaking. If you have seen Ellen DeGeneres on her talk show, you know that she projects a down-to-earth, almost naïve persona. She dresses casually and jokes with her audience. Her nonverbal communication is informal and relaxed. She makes direct eye contact with her audience and the television camera; she sometimes slouches in the chair and even does a little dance at the beginning of every show. These elements together contribute to her public persona.

As you create your public persona, consider a few factors that shape it. First, the speed at which you speak will shape your persona and how people perceive you. There is no one ideal speaking rate; it should vary to fit your message. For example, speaking slowly and deliberately can be effective if you want to highlight the gravity of a situation. At other times, you may wish to speak more quickly, particularly for a light, humorous presentation. You may also vary your speed as you move from point to point, slowing down, perhaps, to emphasize one item in particular.

Eye contact is another important element of creating your persona. Making **eye contact** is one of the most direct ways to show your engagement with your

eye contact
Looking directly into the eyes of another.

audience, and it can lend credibility to your presentation. If you watch *Law & Order: SVU* on television, you may have noticed that the lawyers make direct eye contact with the jury in their closing remarks. Gestures and movement also contribute to one's persona. One of the best ways to ensure that your gestures and movement are smooth and natural-looking is to practice them along with your speech.

Finally, although you may think that your delivery begins when you stand up to speak, you begin to present your persona well before that. In some cases, for example, speakers are part of a panel, seated at a table in front of the audience, or a single speaker is introduced by someone else. In both cases, the speakers are constructing their personas while they wait to speak. Fidgeting, rolling the eyes, yawning, chewing gum, being late, and displaying other unflattering nonverbal behaviors will detract from the persona you want to project. Assume that you are "on stage" from the moment you walk into the room until the moment you leave.

Rehearsing your Speech   One of the best ways to become an effective public speaker is to practice. However, going over the points silently in your head does not count as practice. Practice means giving your speech out loud, standing up and speaking as if you were in front of an audience. In fact, it is ideal to practice in front of an audience— ask one or two of your friends to watch, listen, and give you feedback. To see yourself as others will see you, it is helpful to practice in front of a mirror or to record yourself with audio or video equipment. Do this as many times as necessary to ensure that you are familiar with your speech and feel comfortable delivering it.

Rehearsing will enable you to identify and avoid any distracting nervous mannerisms you may have, and to improve your signposting, your speaking rate, and your eye contact. In other words, you can work on projecting the type of public persona you desire. Each time you practice your speech, you can focus on a different aspect—one time on your gestures, one time on clear enunciation, and so on—until you feel comfortable with the persona and style you have developed. See *It Happened to Me: Tamara* to learn how one speaker approaches practice.

Although you may practice your speech many times, your goal is not to memorize it. A memorized speech often sounds like a recording rather than a real human being. In addition, if you

> ## It Happened to Me
> ### Tamara
>
> I have had to deliver several speeches this year, and I discovered that I like to practice the beginning of my speech a little bit more than the middle or end. Why? I've learned that if I do well at the beginning, after a few minutes, I feel confident, I get into the rhythm, and I even relax a bit.

work strictly from memory and you stumble over a word or phrase, you may lose your place and find it difficult to recover. Instead, during practice, focus on a delivery that is enthusiastic, vibrant, and engaging. Each time you practice, you will come out with different phrasing, different wording, and different movements. When the time comes to give your speech "for real," yet another version may appear, but this time, it will likely be a version that you are comfortable presenting.

Speech Delivery and Overcoming Anxiety   When the day comes for you to give your speech, be sure to arrive early enough to check out the room and any audiovisual or computer equipment you have arranged for. Have alternative plans in mind in case anything goes wrong with your equipment.

It's likely that you will be nervous, but if you have prepared well, you will be able to speak confidently despite any apprehension you may feel. In fact, seasoned performers depend on nerves for an extra boost of energy when they are in front of an audience. Remember that your listeners want you to do well. Focus on the faces in the audience who look friendly and who may be smiling or nodding in agreement. The peak anxiety time for most speakers is the first moment of confronting the audience (Behnke & Sawyer, 1999, 2004). Receiving positive reinforcement early on is an excellent way to

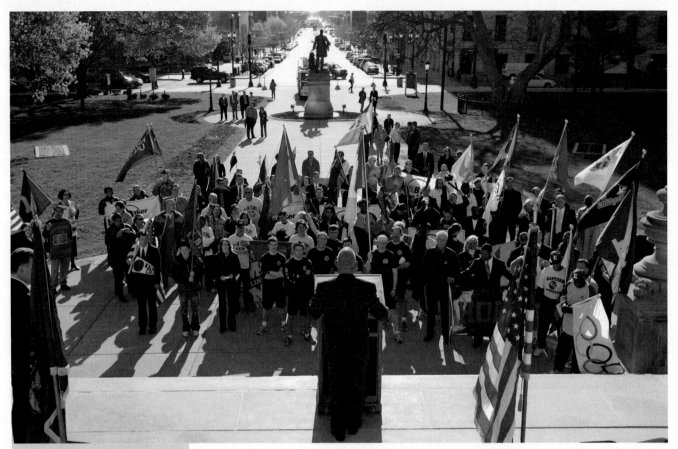

▲ With practice, you can develop a delivery style that is enthusiastic, vibrant, and engaging.

get over this initial anxiety. Before you know it, your speech will be over and you'll be beaming as the audience applauds.

If you are troubled by performance anxiety, you may want to try using relaxation techniques just before speaking. Although the fear may be in your head, it manifests itself in physiological changes in your body: Your muscles tense, your breathing becomes shallow, and adrenaline pumps through your system (Behnke & Sawyer, 2004). Effective relaxation techniques for such situations include taking several deep, even breaths; yawning once or twice to relax your throat; smiling, shaking hands and talking with attendees; taking sips of water (avoid caffeine); and looking at your notes. Visit the Great Speaking Center's "Stage Fright Strategies" at http://www.antion.com/articles/stagefright.htm for many more suggestions. Although you may feel nervous, your inner anxiety is not often easy for your audience members to see. Do not assume they see how nervous you feel, and it's best not to mention it. Project confidence, and you will feel more confident as you speak.

Finally, the strategy most public speaking instructors and students use to overcome anxiety is to take the opportunity to give lots of speeches (Levasseur, Dean, & Pfaff, 2004). Public speaking becomes easier and easier with each speech. As one seasoned speaker said, "Learning to become a confident speaker is like learning to swim. You can watch people swim, read about it, listen to people talk about it, but if you don't get into the water, you'll never learn" (Sanow, 2005). Take opportunities to hone your public-speaking skills. Volunteer to give speeches or become a member of Toastmasters International or a local group of public speakers.

The public speaking process involves a lot of preparation and practice. We hope that these guidelines will help you become a more effective rhetor.

Journal Prompt 12.6: Purposes for Public Speaking

Consider the following questions: Identify three general purposes in public speaking. How is the general purpose different from the specific purpose? Provide some examples.

SUMMARY

12.1 Describe some of the key issues in rhetorical communication.

- Rhetoric is important in our society for at least three reasons: it is vital to the functioning of a democracy; it plays an important role in finding justice; and it helps us understand our world.

12.2 Identify cultural and social influences on the development of rhetoric.

- Rhetoric is tied intimately to the social, cultural, and historical environment in which it functions.
- It has been defined differently in different societies, cultures, and historical eras.

12.3 Identify and define the three artistic proofs of ethos, pathos, and logos.

- Characteristics of rhetors play an important role in effective public communication.
- These include use of ethos, pathos, and logos; position in society; and relationship to the audience.
- Organizations, institutions, and corporations can also be rhetors. Rhetoric gives meaning and shape to public thinking about major events, and it can serve vital democratic functions. Rhetoric also can bring about justice and provide momentum for major social changes.

12.4 Explain four functions of rhetoric: reaffirming cultural values, increasing democratic participation, securing justice, and promoting social change.

12.5 Understand the ethical issues facing rhetors and audience members.

- To be an ethical receiver of rhetoric, one should be willing to: listen with an open mind, speak out when one disagrees, and change one's mind based on persuasive evidence.

12.6 Identify the basic steps in preparing a speech.

- One can become a more effective rhetor by practicing the art of public speaking.
- Effective rhetors understand the communication event, have focused their topics and purpose with the audience in mind, have researched and organized their speeches, and have practiced their delivery to be aware of the time, project a persona, and overcome anxiety.

KEY TERMS

APPLY WHAT YOU KNOW

1. **Create a List of Ten Speakers You Have Heard**
   This list might include politicians such as Hillary Clinton, Paul Ryan, Rand Paul, or Barack Obama, entertainers such as Margaret Cho, Jon Stewart, or Oprah Winfrey, and so on. Put these speakers in order of most to least effective and powerful, and be clear about your reasons for ranking them in this way. Then without revealing your order, exchange lists with a classmate. Rank each other's speakers and see how your rankings compare. If they differ, discuss your reasons. Think about the criteria that you are using.

2. **Research the Characteristics of a Particular Kind of Speech**
   Ask your family and friends what they might expect from a speaker who is giving a eulogy, a graduation speech, or a retirement speech. How long would they expect the presentation to be? What level of formality do they expect? Do the people you ask differ in their opinions? What did you learn from this exercise? Compile your findings in a presentation to your class, following the steps outlined in this chapter.

3. **Watch a Videotape of Someone You Consider to Be a Good Speaker**
   Possibilities include Barack Obama, Oprah Winfrey, Ken Burns, Alec Baldwin, Janet Yellen, or Sonia Sotomayor. Analyze the speech, the style, and the delivery. How do your favorite speakers organize their speeches? Do they project a particular persona or use a particular style? Take notes as you watch them and compile your notes into a report that identifies some public-speaking skills that you would like to incorporate.

4. **Research Some Ways That Public Speaking Functions in Other Cultures**
   How might culture influence how we speak in public?

Mass Media and Communication

LEARNING OBJECTIVES

13.1 Identify the issues facing mass media.

13.2 Identify the main forms of mass media.

13.3 Describe various models of media.

13.4 Understand five issues in media studies: social identities, understanding the world, media events, media violence, and media economics.

13.5 Identify five ethical issues with mass media.

13.6 Describe three ways to be a more effective consumer of media messages.

CHAPTER TOPICS

The Importance of Mass Media

What Are Mass Media?

The Individual and Mass Media

The Individual, Mass Media, and Society

Ethics and Mass Media

Becoming a More Effective Media Consumer

> *"The economics of media production shapes mass communication and gives it a unique and powerful role in our society."*

Charee loves to watch television shows, especially if her favorite stars are in them. Sometimes she watches shows just to "veg out" or escape from her work. Although she often watches a lot of shows on television, she also watches some shows online. She recently bought a smart TV so that she can watch a lot of the new shows with her subscriptions to video streaming services. Charee has to make a lot of choices in deciding which shows to watch and when. Some shows she wants to see when they are broadcast because she is devoted to them, but other shows are available online only or she doesn't mind watching online later after the episodes are broadcast. Much of her decision making depends on what else is going on in her life, as well as her mood.

Charee's experience with television is not unique; many television viewers are devoted to a favorite show and don't want to miss a single episode. When you think about this behavior on the individual level, you probably view it as a matter of choice or taste. When communication scholars analyze television viewing on the social level, however, they examine the influence media have on individuals and how media messages exert influence. In 2010, *Law & Order: SVU* ran an episode that highlighted the backlog of untested rape kit samples (Rubin, 2010). Rape kits store the evidence collected after a reported rape to help convict suspected rapists. Actress Mariska Hargitay, who plays a detective on that show, testified before a House committee about this issue (Dwyer & Jones, 2010). Although her television character is fictional, Hargitay uses her image to be an advocate. In 2013, she received a star on the Hollywood Walk of Fame, and Dick Wolf, creator of *Law & Order: SVU*, noted that she "has a role and an influence beyond her on-screen TV persona" (Scott, 2013). She has gone on to found the Joyful Heart Foundation to help "survivors of sexual assault, domestic violence and child abuse" (Scott, 2013). Television programs, like other types of mass media from radio to film, can influence people's lives in important ways.

In this chapter, we first look at the importance of media in everyday life. We then briefly examine the major forms of mass media. Next, we investigate how individuals use media and the influence that media messages have on individuals. Then we consider media usage within the context of the societal framework and explore the influence media have on society overall. Finally, we discuss media activism as a means for individuals to express media ethics, and we introduce guidelines for becoming more effective consumers of media. Although the Internet is also a type of media, we address that topic in Chapter 14, where we will focus on the role of interactive mediated communication.

The Importance of Mass Media

13.1 Identify the issues facing mass media.

Media hold an important place in our society. As an indication of their importance to you, consider these questions. If you met someone who did not watch television shows, see or rent movies, or listen to the radio, would you be surprised? What if the same person never heard of Lady Gaga, Stephen Colbert, Oprah Winfrey, Lebron James, or J. Lo? Would knowing this change your interaction with that person? What topics could you and couldn't you discuss? If you concluded that many topics would be off limits, you can see that media messages serve important social functions. For example, they help people bond with others who like or dislike the same shows, movies, advertisements, singers, or actors. Media messages and images also help shape how people view the world and what they understand—and perhaps misunderstand—about events

▲ Smart TVs are increasing the choices for viewers. Is it making television even more important in our lives?

around the globe. Because people are so deeply immersed in this media environment, however, they rarely think about their participation in it. Nevertheless, it is indeed an interaction because individuals participate in the communication process by selecting certain programs and agreeing or disagreeing with what they hear or see.

Why are media studies important? To begin with, U.S. Americans watch an enormous amount of television, although the exact number of hours is difficult to pin down. In 2016, Nielsen reported that U.S. adults spent a little over 32 hours per week watching television, followed by over 15 hours per week on their smartphones. When combining television, radio, PCs, TV-connected devices (e.g., DVDs, game consoles), tablets and smartphones, adults spend about 74.5 hours per week using these various media (Nielsen, 2017).

People turn to communication media both for information and entertainment. For example, most U.S. Americans turned to television to learn the results of the 2016 presidential elections. 84 percent turned to television, while 48 percent used online platforms and a smaller number, 21 percent, turned to social media, such as Facebook and Twitter. The numbers add up to more than 100 percent because many people used more than one media. Thirty-seven percent used both television and the Internet to learn about the election results (Anderson, 2016). Although more people are turning to the Internet, it is important to recognize that television remains the primary information source. Of course, not all people turn to television. People at work may not have access to television but can check frequently for news on the Internet while working at their computers. People traveling by car rely on radio for their information.

Media scholars today recognize that they work during an era of rapid media change and development. For example, communication scholars Jennings Bryant and

Dorina Miron (2004) identified six kinds of changes that are currently affecting and being affected by mass communication:

1. new form, content, and substance in mass communication;
2. new kinds of interactive media, such as the Internet;
3. new media ownership patterns in a global economy;
4. new viewing patterns and habits of audiences;
5. new patterns in family life; and
6. new patterns of interactive media use by youth.

Because of the rapid pace of these changes, measuring and studying their influence can be a challenge.

We live in an age when media consumers have more options than ever. In the United States, the average household in 2016 had 206 television channels, which is the highest ever recorded. Despite the increase in choices, the average U.S. viewer only watches 20 of them, about 10 percent of the total channels (Nielsen, 2016). So more choices do not necessarily mean that consumers are becoming more fragmented in their viewing.

Nielsen also recognizes that we are becoming increasingly diverse demographically, as well as in the ways we are consuming media. In another report, Nielsen reports, "Changes in the population are creating a younger, more diverse, more tech-savvy consumer base. But connecting with them has become more complicated due to an exploding number of viewing options" (Nielsen, 2014, May 12). The rise of the Internet and the many choices that we now have has led some to discuss the "end" of mass media; some going so far as to claim, "The mass-media era now looks like a relatively brief and anomalous period that is coming to an end" ("Coming full circle," 2011). Some claim that the economic model for mass media is no longer viable and that spells the end of mass media (Greenslade, 2016), but others do not agree.

In contrast, others are seeing the Internet as another way for consumers to continue to consume even more television programming in many more places at many more times than ever before. Jeff Bewkes, CEO of Time Warner, has even claimed television is taking over the Internet, as TV programming is now available online (Rosenbaum, 2014). Services like Hulu and Amazon Prime are becoming popular as ways that more people can watch television programming. The Internet is an important way that traditional broadcasting corporations are reaching wider audiences. Instead of killing the traditional broadcasting corporations, the Internet is seen by some as an increasingly important medium for traditional broadcasters to reach more audiences.

We see this influence, for example, when we look at Netflix, which many people view as a provider of movies. Ted Sarandos, the chief content officer at Netflix, tells us that "About 70 percent of the total watching on Netflix is television shows in their previous season models" (Stelter, 2014). Although some of this television programming is created by Netflix (e.g., *Orange is the New Black, House of Cards*), these are all destined for a mass audience who can watch it whenever they wish, wherever they wish. Netflix is also internationalizing U.S. television offerings by adding TV "series from Argentina, Britain, Canada, Japan, Mexico, South Korea, Spain and Turkey to its American offerings" (Hale, 2017).

The coming years will reveal what happens to mass media. Will audiences become further fragmented as more choices become available across a range of platforms? Or will media consumption be driven by popularity among audiences so that television programming continues to draw mass audiences—although not all people are watching at the same time or on the same screens? Or will different media take different paths with the Internet?

Although it is difficult to measure the precise power of media messages, these messages surround and influence people every day. The importance of media in our everyday lives and in our society has been rapidly increasing. The rise of the Internet, cell phones, and other "new media" has led to a distinction being made between "mass media" and "new media." In this chapter, we will focus on mass media, and in

Chapter 14, we explore interactive media. To help you to understand the term *mass media*, we discuss this topic next.

What Are Mass Media?

13.2   Identify the main forms of mass media.

Mediated communication refers to communication that is transmitted through a channel, such as television, film, radio, and print. We often refer to these channels of communication more simply as media.

The word **media** is the plural form of *medium*. Television is one communication medium; others include film, radio, magazines, advertisements, and newspapers. When you pick up the telephone to speak to someone, you are using yet another communication medium. When you write a letter, your communication is mediated by the form of letter writing. Even the voice and the body can be considered media of communication.

For all the complexity and variety of media studies, its focus typically falls on **mass media**, or mediated communication intended for a large audience. Mass-mediated messages are usually produced and distributed by large organizations or industries in the business of mass communication. Mass media businesses are also known as **culture industries** because they produce television shows, made-for-television movies, video games, and other cultural products as an industry. The creation of these cultural products is not driven by individual artists, but by large groups of workers in for-profit (and some nonprofit) organizations.

The study of media is often a moving target because changes in media continually occur. Part of understanding the influence of media on our everyday lives entails understanding the changes that have occurred and what media were available in other time periods. Historically, communication has been framed by the media available during a given time. Let's now look at some of these industries and the media texts they produce.

One of the first media addressing a large public was newspapers. During the nineteenth century, many newspapers grew in distribution and readership as the cost of mass printing declined. As expansion westward continued in the United States, the newspaper played a critical role in community building. Newspapers flourished during this period in staggering numbers. For example, "Before the end of 1867, at least four newspapers had been published in Cheyenne, a town that still had a population well under 800, in the Wyoming Territory" (Boorstin, 1965, p. 131). These numbers are all the more impressive in view of today's decline in newspaper readership. As you can see, different eras embraced different communication media.

Today, when most people think of newspapers, they first think of large-circulation papers in large metropolitan areas, such as the *New York Times, Washington Post*, and *Los Angeles Times.* They might also think about smaller, local papers, including the *Corvallis Gazette-Times*, the *Nome Nugget*, and the *Knoxville News Sentinel*. Because large-circulation newspapers serve different needs from local papers, many readers subscribe to both. Other newspapers target specific demographic groups, such as immigrant communities, ethnic and racial communities, gay and lesbian communities, or retirees. Some are bilingual. Others are referred to as the "alternative" press. These alternative-press newspapers attempt to present perspectives and voices that may not be heard in the mainstream press. Examples of alternative papers include the *Seattle Stranger*, the *San Francisco Bay Guardian*, and New York City's *Village Voice.*

Another development that followed the lowered cost of mass printing was the development of the magazine. Magazines are produced weekly, monthly, bimonthly, or quarterly. Some, such as *Time, Harper's, Reader's Digest*, and *Smithsonian*, target broad, general audiences. Other magazines focus on more limited audiences—*Ebony, Latina, Men's Health*, and *Woman's World*, for example—and still others on specific topics, as shown by the titles *Gourmet Magazine, Hot Rod Magazine*, and *Rhode Island Magazine*. Like newspapers,

Journal Prompt 13.1: Mass Media and Change
Consider the following question: What are six kinds of changes currently affecting or being affected by mass media?

media
The plural form of *medium*; a channel of communication.

mass media
Mediated communication intended for large audiences.

culture industries
Large organizations in the business of mass communication that produce, distribute, or show various media texts (cultural products) as an industry.

magazines offer important forums for political discussions, but they also address distinct interests, such as crafts, hobbies, or travel. Like newspapers, magazines have generally seen declining revenue in their print formats and have been moving increasingly to online digital formats. However, the Pew Research Center reports that "2013 and early 2014 brought a level of energy to the news industry not seen for a long time. Even as challenges of the past several years continue and new ones emerge, the activities this year have created a new sense of optimism—or perhaps hope—for the future of American journalism" (Mitchell, 2014). Newspapers and magazines are adjusting to the new digital world and feeling more optimistic about their future as new revenues are coming in to digital news platforms. Investors sense that digital formats will bring a positive return on their investments. Even after President Trump tweeted that the *New York Times* was "fake news" and its subscribers "dwindling," the newspaper reported that it added 276,000 digital and 25,000 print subscribers in the fourth quarter of 2016 (Pallotta, 2017).

Popular books are another medium addressed to a large audience. Sometimes called **mass-market paperbacks**, these books include romance novels, self-help books, and comic books, as well as other genres that are produced in large numbers and distributed widely. **E-books** (electronic books) constitute a recent development in mass media. E-books are books read on a computer screen instead of a printed page. Currently, it is not clear how important a form of media this will become. Although e-reader devices are becoming increasingly user-friendly, many readers still say they prefer the printed page.

Motion pictures, first shown commercially in the 1890s, flourished throughout the twentieth century. Although today people can make movies relatively cheaply with digital video, high-quality productions that draw large audiences cost millions of dollars to produce, distribute, and advertise. Therefore, movie studios with adequate resources dominate the motion picture industry. Although some documentary movies do become popular, such as *March of the Penguins, Fahrenheit 9/11*, and *Supersize Me*, most best-selling movies are purely entertainment-oriented, such as the *Star Wars* movies, *Deadpool, The Incredibles 2*, and *Avengers: Infinity War*. Typically, large-budget films receive the widest distribution and the most publicity, but small-budget films can also reach audiences and sometimes offer alternative views of important social issues.

Like movies, radio technology emerged in the late nineteenth century. At first, it had important applications at sea, but in the 1920s stations sprang up all over the United States. As journalism professor Jane Chapman notes, "Radio's take-off was swift, and public enthusiasm for it peaked during the 'golden age' of the 1930s and 1940s" (2005, p. 147). Radio programming included not only news and commentary but also quiz shows, dramas, and situation comedies. With the rise of television, the Internet, and other competing media, radio broadcasting has become much more specialized, with radio stations serving specific audiences by broadcasting classical music, jazz, country music, news, sports, or other focused content. Audiences for these specialized programs are often targeted based on identities, such as age, socioeconomic class, race and ethnicity, or language. Today, radio is also broadcast over the Internet, via satellite, and through podcasts. And although commercial enterprises dominate radio in the United States, nonprofit radio, such as National Public Radio and Pacifica, also exists.

Popular music, another form of mass media, existed long before radio, and people listened to it live in public and private venues and, later, on gramophones and record players. Popular music now also plays on television and via other communication media, such as CDs, DVDs, and MP3 players. Streaming music services are increasingly how many people listen to music, and yet the digital turn in streaming music has still not necessarily led to profitability. Spotify, for example, had thirty million paying subscribers in March 2016 and that number jumped to 50 million by March 2017 ("Number of paying," 2017). Spotify has been criticized by "musicians who say it's hurting the record industry" (Luckerson, 2013), and Spotify has responded with its "Spotify for Artists" page to explain how royalties are paid. Some musicians are critical of Spotify, and the different payout for signed versus unsigned artists can be stark (Arria, 2015). In

---

mass-market paperbacks
Popular books addressed to a large audience and widely distributed.

e-books
Electronic books read on a computer screen instead of a printed page.

Critical Thinking Prompt
Should consumer-created media such as blogs, Twitter, and video sites like YouTube and Vimeo be considered mass media? Why or why not? In what ways are their functions similar to, or different from, those of mass media created by larger organizations?

▲ Some magazines offer important forums for political discussions. Others address distinct interests, such as sports, travel, beauty, and fashion.

contrast, when Ed Sheeran released his album, ÷, in March 2015, he earned $5 million in a week on Spotify (Newman, 2017).

Television is among the most familiar forms of communication media. Early in its development, in the mid-twentieth century, networks such as ABC, CBS, and NBC dominated because they were the only providers of content. The rise of cable television, with its multiple specialized channels, has taken significant market share away from the networks, yet they remain important and continue to draw large audiences. Since its inception, cable television has expanded to include pay channels such as HBO, Showtime, and Cinemax. In addition, satellite television is challenging cable television. Because television programming is expensive, the medium is dominated by commercial enterprises; however, the United States also has nonprofit television stations, many of which belong to the Public Broadcasting network or to the satellite network Deep Dish TV. In addition, cable TV stations are required to provide public, educational, and government-access channels.

All told, these many forms of mass media saturate our world and penetrate deeply into our individual consciousness, yet we still have some choices regarding which messages to accept. Let's see how this works.

Journal Prompt 13.2: Common Mass Media
Consider the following question: What are some of the most common forms of mass media?

The Individual and Mass Media

13.3 Describe various models of media.

Media scholars are interested in the impact media messages have on individuals, but they are also interested in how individuals decide which media messages to consume or avoid. Marketers and media producers especially want to know how they might predict and characterize individuals' choices so that they can more effectively influence

active agents

Seekers of various media messages and resisters of others.

consumer choice. In this section, we'll explore both aspects of individual media consumption—how media messages influence us and how we become **active agents**, or active seekers, of various media messages and resisters of others. With the term *active agent*, we stress that even though people inhabit a densely media-rich environment, they need not be passively bombarded by media messages.

How Media Messages Affect the Individual

One approach to studying the influence of media messages relies on the linear model. Recall that in Chapter 1 we described how early models conceived of communication as a linear process involving the transfer of information without feedback from one person to another. Similarly, when it comes to media, there is a traditional linear model that portrays communication as a process that occurs in a linear fashion—for example, on a path from the television to the viewer (see Figure 13.1). In this traditional approach, scholars focus on the sender, the medium, the audience, and the effect of the message. This model views media communication as a process that moves from one source to many receivers. Although researchers who use this approach recognize that people are not passive viewers or consumers of media messages, they are interested only in measuring the influence of media messages on the individual, not vice versa.

By understanding the effects of media messages, communication scholars in the linear tradition hope to assist public policy debates about media regulation. For example, their research findings might be used in debates about the effects on viewers of violence or sexuality in the media. So, on a societal level, research based on the linear model often influences public policy decision making. On an individual level, this kind of research may help you select the types of television shows you watch or the movies you allow your children to see.

As an analytic tool, the linear model of media analysis has its limits. For example, critics argue that its simplicity cannot account for the multiple ways people respond to media messages (Sproule, 1989). Viewers are neither merely passive receivers of messages, these critics say, nor do the viewers necessarily believe or imitate everything they watch or read. Those who watched *Modern Family*, for example, did not necessarily model their family behaviors on the show's characters. Nor did everyone who watched the trial of Casey Anthony, accused of murdering her daughter Caylee, agree with the jury's verdict (Hightower & Sedensky, 2011).

On the other hand, the linear model does highlight the power and influence of media messages. Some people did try to imitate the antics of Johnny Knoxville on the MTV television show *Jackass*, resulting in serious injuries despite televised warnings against trying to imitate the stunts. And in a classic example, a mass panic was set off when thousands of listeners to Orson Welles's 1938 Halloween radio broadcast, *War of the Worlds*, believed that Martians were landing in New Jersey.

mass media effects

The influence that media have on people's everyday lives.

Scholars who study media influence work in an area called **mass media effects**. The study of mass media effects has undergone significant changes over the years, as researchers have disagreed about how much effect a particular media message has on people's everyday lives (McQuail, 1987). In the 1930s, Paul Lazarsfeld and his colleagues studied radio's effect on listeners and, in particular, its effect on voting behavior. This study, titled *The People's Choice* (Lazarsfeld, Berelson, & Gaudet, 1948), argued that media had limited effects because they found that radio tended to reinforce preexisting beliefs rather than shape new ones.

Figure 13.1 The Linear Model

The linear model emphasizes the effect of media messages on the individual. Communication in this model is largely (although not entirely) one way.

Today, the focus on effects remains important in media research. For example, contemporary researchers have examined media images of beautiful bodies and how those images influence people's perceptions of their own bodies and their resultant behavior in response to those images, including dieting, working out, taking diet pills, and undergoing cosmetic surgery. An early influential book, *The Beauty Myth* by Naomi Wolf, argued that these images of beauty are unattainable and are used against women. Originally published in 1991, it has remained a best seller; a new edition was released in 2002. In their study of the effects of entertainment television and sports media, Kimberly Bissell and Peiqin Zhou (2004) found a high correlation between images of thin women's bodies that appear repeatedly in entertainment television and eating disorders among college-age women who watched those shows.

Another area of inquiry among media-effects scholars involves media images of violence. In their study of media usage among middle-school children in ten regions in the United States, Michael Slater and his colleagues found that aggressive young people seek out violent media and that exposure to media violence can predict aggression (Slater, Henry, Swaim, & Anderson, 2003). Thus, they see media violence and aggression as mutually reinforcing and call their model a *downward spiral model* to describe the powerful, negative influence the interaction has on youth. Those youth who are prone to violent behaviors seek out violent media that reinforce more violent behavior. More recently, Bushman and Gibson (2011) have also found that aggression continues long after engaging with violent video games.

Promoting health through media messages is another significant area of inquiry among scholars seeking to understand media effects. In a recent study on antidrug advertisements for adolescents, Hunyi Cho and Franklin J. Boster (2008) compared antidrug messages framed around the costs of using drugs (loss) versus the benefits of avoiding them (gain). The study found that framing loss rather than gain was more effective among adolescents who had friends who used drugs. There was no difference among adolescents whose friends did not use drugs. To engage the most effective communication messages to promote public health, media effects scholars are also trying to better understand how media messages can be more effective.

How Individuals Choose Media Messages

Advertisers, political campaign strategists, and communication scholars all want to understand which groups of people consume which media texts. They want to know who watches *Grey's Anatomy*, who reads the *New York Times*, and who reads *People* magazine. As you might guess, this type of information enables advertisers to target their messages more accurately toward certain consumers. It also enables campaign strategists to focus their message to attract more votes. But why would media scholars be interested in this information?

Media scholars need this information so that they can correctly target their research. For example, if scholars want to study the effect of a particular **media text**—for example, a television show, advertisement, or movie—they need to know which audience group to study. If they want to know how people interpret a particular media text, they need to know the audience of that text. Or if scholars want to know about the economic influence of particular media texts, they need to know which audience groups advertisers target with these messages.

media text
A television show, advertisement, movie, or other media event that a media scholar isolates for study.

As an individual, you are constantly faced with media choices, and your choices have increased considerably in the past decade as a result of the increased predominance of online news and blogging as well as instant downloads of movies and TV episodes. Researchers are interested in not only *what* we choose but *how* we choose. See how one of our students considers this in *It Happened to Me: Kevin.*

Although Kevin doesn't mention it explicitly, both what people choose and how they choose are related to their identities. And, as we noted in Chapter 3, identities are not fixed; they are dynamic across time and situations. With them, media choices change as well. For example, as a child, Kevin may have been a fan of Saturday morning cartoons or *Sesame Street*, but as an adult, perhaps he prefers *Monday Night Football* or HBO's *Game of Thrones*. Kevin's age and the ages of his friends likely influence the television shows and movies he selects. But age is only one aspect of identity, and perhaps one of the simplest factors that influence media choices. Other aspects, such as regional identity, might also have an effect, but they are more difficult to correlate with media tastes.

It Happened to Me
Kevin

I'm not a fan of musicals and musical comedies and so I didn't go to see *La La Land*. I might watch it later on Netflix or some other streaming service, but I didn't want to pay to see it in a movie theater. I prefer to see movies based on real events, such as *Hacksaw Ridge* or *Hidden Figures*, as well as more dramatic movies, so I went to see *Fences* and *Moonlight*. If I'm in the right mood, I like some comedies and action films, but it depends a lot on which actors are in the movies and what I've heard about the films from my friends. We don't always like the same movies, but they know what types I enjoy.

Selective Exposure   Selective exposure theories help us

selective exposure

The idea that people seek media messages or interpret media texts in ways that confirm their beliefs and, conversely, resist or avoid messages that challenge their beliefs.

understand how identity plays a role in media tastes and preferences. These theories are based on the idea that people seek media messages and interpret media texts in ways that confirm their beliefs—and, conversely, that they resist or avoid messages that challenge their beliefs. Depending on their personal and political beliefs, some people enjoyed watching the inauguration of President Trump.

COMMUNICATION IN SOCIETY
Watching or Not Watching *12 Years a Slave*

12 Years a Slave is a 2013 movie that is based on the slave narrative of a free man, Solomon Northrup, who was sold into slavery in the 1840s. It won a number of awards, including three Oscars (Academy Awards), notably Best Picture. Given the widespread attention that this film received, what were the most important reasons that you decided to watch or not to watch it? What might be reasons that influenced others' decisions to watch or not watch this film? Do you think that racial identities may have influenced some people's decisions? Let's take a look at some of the discussions about watching or not watching this film.

Despite the critical acclaim that it received, the box office receipts for the film did not match those of other films, such as *Captain Phillips, Gravity*, and *Frozen*. A film critic for the *Los Angeles Times* explains why this film may not have drawn the audiences that other films did: "The racial legacy we struggle with today lives inside '12 Years a Slave.' Slavery on our soil is painful to remember, painful to admit, difficult to discuss, almost unbearable to watch—and that is why so many choose not to. It will take more than an Oscar win on Sunday to change that" (Sharkey, 2014).

The racial history that envelopes all of us led one woman to struggle with whom to go to see the movie: "I'm not a racist. But I do have a race problem. I finally owned up to it as I was anticipating seeing *12 Years a Slave*. In the weeks leading up to its opening in my state of North Carolina, I tried to think of whom among my friends I could see this film with. I have a number of racially and ethnically diverse friends and acquaintances who would love to see it, and yet, I knew I could only see this movie alone or with another dark-skinned person" (Okoro, 2013). In the end, she went to see the movie alone because she didn't want to have to engage in explaining or discussing anything in the film.

One of the controversies that arose in relation to the Academy Awards is that some of the voting members did not watch the film. One of these voting members admitted that the film was too difficult to watch. There are many painful scenes in this film, and many people chose not to subject themselves to the violent and disturbing scenes in the film. Some people felt that they already knew about the ugly history of slavery in the United States and did not need to subject themselves to the film. Everyone is an active consumer of mass media and some people are willing to watch films that others are not willing to watch.

As you can see, there are many complex reasons why people decided to watch or not watch this film. As you think about media consumption, it is important to remember that we are active agents who are consciously making decisions about what or what not to watch, and with whom to watch it.

SOURCES: Feinberg, S. (2014, March 2). Brutally honest Oscar voter ballot no. 7. *The Hollywood Reporter.* Retrieved June 9, 2014, from http://www.hollywoodreporter.com/race/brutally-honest-oscar-voter-ballot-684839.

Okoro, E. (2013, November 27). Why I wouldn't see *12 Years a Slave* with a white person. *The Atlantic.* Retrieved June 9, 2014. from http://www.theatlantic.com/entertainment/archive/2013/11/why-i-wouldnt-see-em-12-years-a-slave-em-with-a-white-person/281883/.

Sharkey, B. (2014, February 27). Oscars 2014: For many, "12 Years a Slave" is too hard to watch. *Los Angeles Times.* Retrieved June 9, 2014, from http://articles.latimes.com/2014/feb/27/entertainment/la-et-mn-12-years-a-slave-notebook-20140227/2.

Others chose not to watch the inauguration. (See *Communication in Society: Watching or Not Watching* 12 Years a Slave.)

One television show that was studied heavily in terms of selective exposure is *The Cosby Show*, a prime-time situation comedy that ran from 1984 to 1992. According to selective exposure theory, if someone believes racism no longer exists, then she or he is likely to interpret media messages as confirming or reinforcing this perception. In a study of *The Cosby Show*, Sut Jhally and Justin Lewis (1992) set up focus groups. Twenty-six of these focus groups were composed of White viewers of the show, and 23 were composed of African American viewers. In analyzing the White focus group responses, Jhally and Lewis found that Whites were more likely to think that *The Cosby Show* proved Black people can succeed; therefore, they said, African Americans who did not succeed were to blame for their own failure. In other words, as the White focus groups saw it, personal failings, rather than discrimination or racism, were what blocked success. In contrast, Black respondents saw *The Cosby Show* as a "cultural breakthrough" in terms of positive portrayals of Black culture (p. 121). Thus, they expressed far more concern about the pervasive negative images of African Americans in media and the influences of those images on viewers. As you can see, although both racial groups were watching the same television show, their interpretations were different.

▲ According to selective exposure theories, people seek out media that confirm what they already believe. What political views might be different among viewers of different channels?

ALTERNATIVE VIEW
Hostile Media Effect

In what ways do you selectively expose yourself to media messages? Do you generally listen to the same news commentators rather than seeking alternative voices? Do you watch the same shows your friends watch, or do you look for something different?

Selective exposure theories tell us that people tend to consume media that reinforce or support their own views. Yet, some media researchers counter this idea. Why? Researchers have found that people on both sides of an issue can be exposed to the same media coverage, and when asked what they thought of the coverage, both groups say that it was biased against their views. If both sides find the same coverage biased, it may undermine the idea that people only seek messages that confirm their views. Thus, the researchers concluded that although bias in media news stories surely does occur, another kind of bias rests with the viewer—a phenomenon called the "hostile media effect" because it reflects a general hostility toward media.

In their study, Albert C. Gunther and Kathleen Schmitt (2004) used the controversy over genetically modified foods to understand the hostile media effect. In part, their study found that regardless of respondents' position on genetically modified

foods, they viewed news media stories as biased against them. However, when respondents saw the same information in a student essay format, the hostility tended to be absent or at least minimal. The researchers conclude, then, that the hostile media effect is created by the perception that a media message has the potential to influence large numbers of people for or against a particular viewpoint.

If the selective exposure theory is correct, and people tend to select media messages that support their own views, then why would they interpret these messages to be biased against them? There is no easy answer, but perhaps questions of bias and media selection need to be thought about in more complicated ways. When charges of bias arise against a media source, how often do we consider that the bias may be our own?

SOURCE: Gunther, A. C., & Schmitt, K. (2004). Mapping boundaries of the hostile media effect. *Journal of Communication, 54,* 55–70.

Selective exposure theories point to the ways that both groups interpret the show to confirm their own beliefs and views. Those who subscribe to selective exposure theory argue that people rarely inhabit a media environment that challenges their social identities, including their religious and political beliefs, notions about gender, or ideas about race. Not all scholars subscribe to this theory, however: see *Alternative View: Hostile Media Effect.*

uses and gratifications

The idea that people use media messages and find various types of gratifications in some media texts rather than in others.

Another line of media research, called **uses and gratifications** studies, explores how people use media messages and what types of gratifications they find in some media texts rather than others. Working within this approach, researchers might want to know why viewers watch *The Bachelor* instead of *Dancing with the Stars, Chicago PD* instead of *Chicago Med,* or *48 Hours* instead of *60 Minutes.* For example, a researcher might want to know why some people enjoy watching *Saturday Night Live* during the Donald Trump presidency. What parts of the show satisfy particular needs or wants? What is satisfying about the portrayals of President Trump, Press Secretary Sean Spicer, and other administration officials? Denis McQuail and his colleagues (1972) suggested four general uses and gratifications that audiences have for media texts:

- information
- personal identity
- integration and social interaction
- entertainment

The first motivation, information seeking, is straightforward: audiences want to learn from some media presentations, as in the case of a news event. The second motivation, personal identity, refers to the idea that viewers may use media messages to affirm some aspect of their personal identity—for example, as mothers, consumers, or political conservatives. The third motivation, integration and social interaction, underscores the role that media can play in helping people connect with others, as they do when discussing sports or the events on a soap opera. Finally, the entertainment motivation refers to the use of media for pleasure, or the desire simply to be entertained. Of course, these motivations can overlap, so that we can watch a program for information while at the same time using it as a topic for conversation with others, which would fit within McQuail's third motivation.

Cultural Values in Media Consumption   Understanding why some groups choose one program over another highlights the cultural values at work in the consumption of media. In his study of television preferences among Israeli adults, Jonathan Cohen (2002) examined viewing habits and choice. He found that factors influencing media selection included loyalty to particular channels, preferences for certain types of shows, and even the language of the programs, because programming in Israel is available in Hebrew, English, and other languages. His conclusion was that "Most Israeli viewers seem to prefer native programming, whether due to language problems or to cultural resonance" (p. 218). Cohen suggests that Israeli audiences use television not only for entertainment but also to affirm their Israeli identities and as a context for social interaction with other Israelis.

Determining why people seek specific media texts and not other texts is important from an economic perspective. After all, a media corporation does not want to spend a lot of money on a television show or magazine if it is going to fail. However, it is notoriously difficult to predict which media texts will become popular and which will not. *This Is Us*, for example, was described as "the more surprising show that looks as if it's going to be a hit" (Yahr, 2016). Despite major investments in market research, there is no completely foolproof way to predict audience response.

Of course, the inability to accurately predict audience response does not mean that media producers have no information on trends. In certain eras, viewers are more interested in Westerns or police dramas, reality shows, or evening soap operas than they are during other periods. Today, reality shows are quite popular. Furthermore, advertisers know that some groups prefer to consume certain kinds of media. For example, the advertising that appears during televised football games or *Dancing with the Stars* reveals what advertisers have learned about those audiences through careful market research and analysis.

How Individuals Resist Media Messages

Although media messages bombard people every day, individuals do not necessarily, or even easily, accept all that they receive. In addition, people actively resist certain media texts. For example, some people sought out and watched the *X-Men* films, *Ghostbusters, Moonlight* and *Beauty and the Beast*. Others actively avoided them. Why? We resist media texts every day for many reasons, including something as hard to quantify as individual taste and something as personal as what we see as negative portrayals of our political, moral, or religious views; our interests, age, or level of education; or our gender, sexuality, and racial and ethnic identities. Other far less political reasons can create consumer resistance as well, as our student reveals in *It Happened to Me: Emma.*

Resisting media messages entails much more than simply whether we go to a particular movie or watch a particular video. It is also about how we resist the power of media to shape our identities. For example, in one study, Meenakshi Gigi Durham (2004) interviewed South Asian immigrant teenage girls living in the United States. She explored the question of how these girls dealt with traditional Indian notions of female gender expectations in the context of available media. She found that the only mainstream U.S. show they liked to watch was *Friends*, which they found to be funny, and they disliked *Dawson's Creek*, which they thought was unrealistic. In general, they distanced themselves from mainstream U.S. media. In contrast, they consumed large amounts of media (films, popular music) from India, which they rented from Indian grocery stores and restaurants, borrowed from others, and watched or downloaded from the Internet. They particularly identified with the narratives in *Mississippi Masala, Bend It Like Beckham*, and *American Desi*, which are three Indian films with narratives involving "taboo relationships between Indian girls and men of different racial/cultural backgrounds" (p. 154). Durham concludes that these adolescent girls use media to create new identities, and that these identities do not conform to stereotypes of either Asian Indian women or U.S. American women.

It Happened to Me
Emma

My boyfriend really wanted to watch *127 Hours*. Although I do like James Franco, I just couldn't imagine sitting through a long movie watching someone suffering and cutting his arm off. So, I said no anyway, even though he mentioned it four or five times. He was unhappy that I wouldn't watch this movie, but I just didn't want to sit through that kind of emotional drama.

In another example, it has been reported that former President Obama refuses to watch any of the videos showing U.S. Americans being beheaded that are posted by the Islamic State of Iraq and Syria (ISIS). His decision not to watch these videos is explained by his desire to avoid playing into the propaganda of ISIS ("Has Obama Seen," 2014). Given his social and political position as president of the United States, his avoidance and resistance to this type of media is very public and has important implications for how we interpret and deal with these media messages. All of us must make decisions about media consumption and resistance that are based on our many identities.

As you have seen through our discussion, communication researchers are interested in all aspects of the relationship between individuals and the media messages that surround them. First, they wonder what effect media messages have on individuals; and second, they explore how individuals choose, resist, and interpret these messages. Research has revealed that the answers to both questions involve complex processes related to individual identity, individual needs, and individual taste. Audiences respond to and interpret texts based on both their individual and social identities, and therefore, different social groups can consume the same text while being affected by it differently and interpreting it differently. However, all individual responses and choices occur in a larger social context. Thus, to provide a more complete picture, we now shift our attention to the role of media at the societal level.

**Journal Prompt 13.3:
Selecting Mass Media**
Consider the following questions:
What strategies do media consumers use to select and reject media texts? Why might audiences prefer to watch media texts that affirm the values and beliefs they already hold?

The Individual, Mass Media, and Society

13.4   Understand five issues in media studies: social identities, understanding the world, media events, media violence, and media economics.

Why do media play such an important role in society? One reason is that they often serve as the voice of the community. In this way, media offer people a means of thinking about themselves, their places in the world, and the societal forces around them. As individuals, we can only choose from among the media choices available. Societal forces, including the government, economics, media organizations, and advertisers, largely determine which media options are available. In the following section, we'll look at three important roles that media play in society: confirming social identities, helping people understand the world, and helping individuals understand important public events. And finally, because no discussion of media and society would be complete without a discussion of media violence and media economics, we will conclude with these topics.

Confirming Social Identities

As we've noted, media representations influence our understanding of social identities, such as gender or age identity, as well as the identities of others. This is one of the functions of media usage we examined as we discussed uses and gratifications. For example, images we see on television and in films, magazines, and newspapers shape our sense of what it is to be a man or woman. These views generally create or enforce a hierarchy of identities, often portraying men as more powerful than women. Thus, media messages not only shape the way we understand social identities; they also show us which social identities are valued. For example, as Associated Press reviewer Christy Lemire (2005) noted in her review of the film *Deuce Bigalow: European Gigolo*, "Making fun of homosexuality seems to be the one area of humor that has yet to be ruled off-limits by political correctness; such jokes also appeared in the far superior *Wedding Crashers* earlier this summer." If Lemire's analysis is correct, this "permission" to joke about one particular social identity can reinforce a hierarchy in which heterosexuality is valued over homosexuality.

content analysis
Approach to understanding media that focuses on a specific aspect of the content of a text or group of texts.

One approach to understanding how and what media communicate about various social identities is content analysis. **Content analysis** focuses on some specific aspect of a text's content. Bernard Berelson (1952/1971), a behavioral scientist, explains that content analysis took off during the late 1930s, with the work of Harold Laswell and his colleagues (see Chapter 2), who were concerned with "propaganda and public opinion and the emergence of radio as a great mass medium of communication."

▼ Content analysis can provide data on factors such as media representation of various groups, media violence, and the kinds of topics covered and the way in which they are covered in the media.

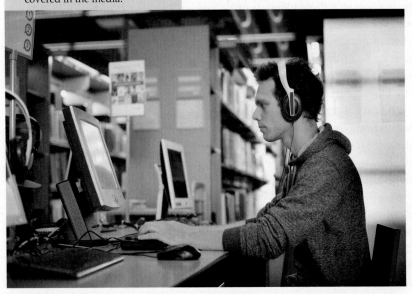

How does content analysis work? To begin, a researcher might want to know how many non-White characters appear on the television show *NCIS: Los Angeles*, a show set in a city where Whites are a minority population. The researcher would thus watch a number of episodes, count the number of non-White characters, note the kinds of roles they play and which characters are central, and finally, draw conclusions based on these data. Recently, actress Geena Davis became quite concerned about the imbalance between males and females in media representations. In two large studies on television programs and films, males outnumbered females by 70 percent to 30 percent (Belkin, 2010). To try to understand these content differences and their impact on children, she founded the Geena Davis Institute on Gender and Media (https://seejane.org). Further, researcher Caroline Aoyagi (2004) conducted a content analysis of TV shows set in the state of Hawaii and concluded the following:

> No one can blame the big television networks for their love affair with the beautiful islands of Hawaii, but as several new shows are set to launch or are already on air, the lack of Asian Pacific Americans in the shows' casts have many wondering: what Hawaii is this?
>
> In a state where Asian Pacific Islander Americans [APIA] make up more than 80 percent of the population and whites are considered the minority, a look at the new line-up of shows for FOX, the WB network, and NBC show no APIA lead actors and only one or two APIAs in supporting roles. (p. 1)

A content analysis of television shows, thus, can provide data on racial representation in media. Content analysis also can reveal the kinds of topics that arise most often, the way episodes and conflicts are resolved most frequently, the number and types of conflicts that occur, and many other issues. In their study of television news in Los Angeles and Orange County, California, Travis Dixon and Daniel Linz (2002) employed content analysis to determine whether correlations existed between pretrial publicity and race. Using the American Bar Association's definition of potentially prejudicial information, they found that "Blacks and Latinos are twice as likely as Whites to have prejudicial information aired about them, and Latinos are three times more likely than Whites to have prejudicial information aired when they victimize Whites" (p. 133). Through content analysis, then, these two scholars were able to show a strong correlation between the race of the accused and the reporting of prejudicial information in the news. Moreover, they found that reporting of prejudicial information dramatically increased when the crime victim was White.

Similarly, Cheryl Law and Magdala Peixoto Labre (2002) conducted a content analysis of images of male bodies in thirty years of popular magazines, specifically *GQ, Rolling Stone*, and *Sports Illustrated.* They found that "the images of men in popular magazines became more lean and muscular from 1967 to 1997, and that the V-shaped male figure also became more prevalent over time" (p. 705). As the researchers report, "this content analysis suggests that the new ideal seen in the mass media does not represent the body type most men have" (p. 706), and they speculate on the effect these images have on men's behavior, for example, their use of steroids, diets, and workouts. Because this was a content analysis and not a media-effects study, the researchers did not survey male readers of these magazines to find out whether they actually went on diets, used steroids, and so on. Instead, the point of the study is to highlight what media messages communicate to men (and women) about the ideal male image and male social identity.

Content analysis by itself does not reveal why viewers choose to watch particular television shows or consume other kinds of media messages. Collecting demographic information about an audience's racial, ethnic, or age composition may give some insight as to which groups are drawn to what kind of content, but, again, this is not the primary purpose of content

▼ Images of male beauty are socially constructed.

analysis. For example, the study we mentioned previously by Dixon and Linz did not try to explain whether or why southern Californians preferred pretrial television news coverage with prejudicial information about minorities, or why the television news industry produces this kind of news. What their data do confirm, however, is that Blacks and Latinos are represented more negatively in news programs.

Some studies use a more detailed analysis of media messages than content analysis does, and this approach can help us better understand which social identities are being confirmed and elevated. Such studies, which rely on textual analysis, typically focus on fewer media texts than content analyses do. Researchers who conduct textual analyses of media messages take an approach similar to literary critics when they explore meanings in a literary work. However, in textual analysis, any kind of media image can be considered a text. For example, in her study of the news coverage of Freaknik, a spring break event that used to draw African American college students to Atlanta, Marian Meyers (2004) looked closely at the news reports of sexual violence against African American women perpetrated by African American men. "In essence," she wrote, "the news criminalized Black men primarily with respect to property damage while decriminalizing them concerning their abuse of women. The safety of Black women appears of less consequence than that of property" (p. 113). Thus, these news reports confirmed an identity of Black men as criminals while undermining the identity of Black women as crime victims.

In her study of masculinity, Helene Shugart (2008) focused on the media construction of the "metrosexual" in the context of commercialism. Metrosexuals are men who are meticulous about their appearance—not only their physiques, but also their clothing, hair styles, and so forth. In her textual analysis of the metrosexual, Shugart found that metrosexuality "bore all the hallmarks of a fad or a trend" (p. 295), but metrosexuality also "served a vital and strategic rhetoric function as part of a much larger and ongoing cultural discourse about masculinity(ies)" (p. 295). Because commercialism has threatened traditional masculinity by insisting on enhancing masculinity through the purchase of various products, metrosexuality helped to reconcile the contradiction between the commercial masculinity and a more traditional or normative masculinity.

Thus, what people see, hear, and read in the media can confirm identities, but so can their media choices. Although our social identities are not absolute predictors of media choices, trends do emerge if we look at the correlations between media consumption and various social identities. Nielsen Media Research has studied the most popular television shows among all U.S. Americans and among African Americans as a subgroup, revealing that their choices are similar in some respects and different in others, and thus, that racial identities do somewhat correlate with media consumption.

In addition, people often choose media images that not only confirm their identities but also help them deal with the various issues involved in any identity. For example, some African American women are drawn to the ABC shows *How to Get Away with Murder* and *Scandal*, which feature strong women characters—one working as a law professor and attorney and the other as a media consultant—who work in male-dominated environments. These characters help women envision how they can operate successfully in white, masculine environments and retain their gender and racial identities.

How does media coverage favor some identities over others? The amount of coverage, as revealed by content analysis, is sometimes the controlling factor. For example, in their study of the Salt Lake City Olympics in 2002, Billings and Eastman (2003) found that NBC devoted more time to reporting on male athletes and White athletes than on other groups. The potential effect of this imbalance is that the identities of particular viewers are reinforced, while the identities of other viewers are undermined. Remember, however, that more extensive coverage can also have the opposite effect. For example, if an identity is portrayed with great frequency in a negative way, that identity can be undermined, as Dixon and Linz (2002) found in their analysis of pretrial coverage in southern California.

As you learned in Chapter 3, social identities help shape individuals' outlook on the world; at the same time, individuals interpret media texts from their identity positions. Media critics have been instrumental in bringing to the public's attention these issues of identity confirmation and media bias in portraying identities. As a result, many with identities that media portray less positively have come to recognize their exclusion. The effect can be anger or disengagement when few, if any, images exist of one's own social group acting in positive ways.

Understanding the World

Media play a key role in helping people understand the world. Most people will never travel to the Ukraine, North Korea, Iraq, Palestine, Rwanda, Indonesia, Somalia, or Brazil, but they can learn something about these places through media. They may see these distant regions on the Travel Channel or in *National Geographic* magazine, or they may see news about them on CNN, MSNBC, or other news channels.

However, the texts that media organizations produce can distort the images of faraway places as well as enhance them, especially if viewers have never been to the parts of the world represented. In her study of AP wire photographs of Afghan women—both during and after the Taliban regime—Shahira Fahmy (2004) found that "1 percent of [published] AP photographs portrayed women revealing their face and hair." Thus, even after the fall of the Taliban, Afghan women are depicted wearing their burqas—despite the fact that many photos exist that portray "images of Afghan women removing their burqas as a sign of liberation" (p. 110). In this study, Fahmy brings to light the discrepancy between the pool of available AP photographs and the ones selected for publication in the United States, noting that the ones that editors select shape and sometimes distort our impressions of the subject.

As another example of the media's power to shape knowledge and understanding, prior to the current Syrian Civil War, there had been little U.S. news coverage of Syria. Many U.S. Americans did not know the difference between Aleppo and Raqqa and the involvement of Al Qaeda, ISIS, and the government of Bashir al-Assad. In contrast, media provide U.S. audiences with extensive detail on the British royal family, as well as international celebrities, such as Shakira and Ed Sheeran. As you can see, by choosing what to cover and how extensively, media shape audience understanding of what is and isn't important in the world.

Agenda-Setting Capacity

This power of media coverage to influence individuals' view of the world is referred to as its **agenda-setting capacity**. Thus, in agenda-setting research, scholars focus on audience perceptions of reality and attempt to discover how or whether media coverage correlates with these audience perceptions. For example, Lowry, Nio, and Leitner (2003) studied correlations between crime rates, news coverage on crime, and public attitudes about crime from 1978 to 1998. Existing data indicated that in March 1992, only 5 percent of the public thought that crime was the most important problem. By August 1994, however, 52 percent felt that way. What accounted for this jump? By correlating the amount of television news coverage with the crime rates, the researchers found that the amount of news coverage was far more influential than actual crime rates in this change in public perception. By focusing so much attention on crime reporting, the theory goes, media set the public agenda for what was important. Agenda-setting studies often look at long time periods, as the crime-coverage study did, to correlate media coverage to changes in audience perceptions.

In another study using an agenda-setting perspective, Jochen Peter (2003) focused on the issue of 14 European nations and their integration into the European Union (EU). Here, however, he did not find a simple correlation between more news coverage of EU integration and public attitudes about the importance of this issue. Instead he found that when political elites agreed about integration, public involvement or interest in the issue declined. Coverage of disagreement among political elites over EU integration did correlate, though, with increased public involvement in the issue. Thus, controversy and the degree of exposure does play a role in setting the public's agenda.

agenda-setting capacity
The power of media coverage to influence individuals' view of which topics are more salient than others.

cultivation theory

The idea that long-term immersion in a media environment leads to "cultivation," or enculturation, into shared beliefs about the world.

Cultivation Theory   Media messages also play a critical role in acculturating individuals. **Cultivation theory** proposes that long-term immersion in a media environment leads to "cultivation," or enculturation, into shared beliefs about the world. Unlike other approaches that focus on specific media messages, television programs, movies, or other kinds of text, "Cultivation analysis is concerned with the more general and pervasive consequences of cumulative exposure to cultural media" (Morgan & Signorielli, 1990, p. 16). Initiated by George Gerbner (2002) and his colleagues, cultivation analysis seeks to uncover how television, in particular, influences those who are heavy viewers. Those who watch television news, the theory goes, will share certain beliefs or distortions about the world. Moreover, this theory argues that media coverage shapes attitudes about one's own society and the issues it faces. For example, although crime rates have gone down overall in recent years, many U.S. Americans feel more insecure than ever. In their study on fear of crime, Daniel Romer, Kathleen Hall Jamieson, and Sean Aday (2003) surveyed 2,300 Philadelphia residents. Within that population group, they found a relationship between the widespread belief that crime is a significant problem and the amount of local television news coverage of crimes. The point of the study is that Philadelphia media coverage cultivates attitudes and beliefs that shape everyday life in the city, with a key element of daily life being an exaggerated fear of crime.

In a recent cultivation study, Jeff Niederdeppe and his colleagues (2010) studied the ways that local television news covers cancer prevention because the "sheer volume of news coverage about cancer causes and prevention has led to broad speculation about its role in promoting fatalistic beliefs" (p. 231), Niederdeppe and colleagues developed three hypotheses comparing local television news coverage with local newspaper coverage of various cancer issues, and their fourth hypothesis focused on the relationship between local TV news viewing and fatalistic beliefs about cancer prevention. They found that there is "a tendency for local TV news to focus on aspects of cancer that are likely to cultivate the beliefs that everything causes cancer or that there are too many recommendations about cancer prevention" (p. 246). It creates the fatalistic sense that nothing can be done to avoid cancer. In both these studies, then, immersion in the television environment shaped, or cultivated, a particular view of the world.

hegemony

The process by which we consent to social constructions, rather than having them imposed on us.

Media Hegemony   A different way of explaining how media influence how we understand the world is through **hegemony**. Hegemony refers to the process by which people consent to particular understandings as reflected in media representations. For instance, we come to understand what "mother" means through often idealized images of mothers on television programs, films, and other media. Although there are no laws that regulate what a "mother" must do, we consent to these images of motherhood and we expect mothers to engage in certain behaviors, such as throwing birthday parties for their children. In contrast, our hegemonic understanding of "fathers" does not include that kind of activity. Fathers can, of course, throw birthday parties for their children, but it is not part of the hegemonic construction of fatherhood.

Masculinity, as represented in media content, has been a rich site for investigating how hegemony functions. For example, in his work on hegemony, communication scholar Nick Trujillo

▼ Cultivation theory has been used to emphasize the role of news coverage of crime in the perceptions of crime rates.

(1991) studied the media representations of Nolan Ryan, a baseball pitcher, to show how masculinity is constructed. He found five features of how Ryan was portrayed: (1) male athletic power, (2) ideal image of the capitalist worker, (3) family patriarch, (4) White rural cowboy, and (5) symbol of male (hetero)sexuality. Trujillo asks that we consider the negative consequences of this construction of masculinity. Additionally, in his study of the television show *thirtysomething*, Hanke (1990) analyzes the way that hegemonic masculinity shifts slightly to focus on men "who are more open to domestic concerns and interpersonal relationships" (p. 245). His analysis focuses on hegemony as a process in which masculinity shifts to respond to changing social needs. Hegemony is a process by which we all participate in the social construction of ourselves and others. If we violate these hegemonic notions, we risk alienation. This approach to the study of media content helps us better understand the contours and limits of how we might present ourselves and interpret others because hegemony outlines what is acceptable, normal, or even ideal.

Interpreting Media Events

The term **media event** applies to those occasions or catastrophes that interrupt regular programming. Like rhetorical events, which we discussed in the previous chapter, media events create vast numbers of media messages. Examples include the funeral of John F. Kennedy, the Olympics, Princess Diana's funeral, or the attacks of September 11, 2001. Media scholars are interested in the coverage of such events because such coverage can shape viewers' understanding of what has occurred and create powerful responses. For example, Daniel Dayan and Elihu Katz (1992) found that media events bring society closer together. As a new form of "high holidays of mass communication" (p. 1), these events both reinforce and celebrate national identity.

media event
Occasions or catastrophes that interrupt regular programming.

Some media events are staged by public relations officers to garner media attention on a particular issue. When the president of the United States calls a press conference, for example, he is creating a media event. Then, of course, the representatives of various news media are present to report what he says. In these cases, the president and his public relations staff carefully control many aspects of the conference—where it will be staged, what kinds of issues will be raised, who will be present, what video images will be shown, and so on. Other politicians, movie stars, and lawyers in high-profile cases also commonly create media events to bring attention to themselves or their causes.

Not everyone, however, can attract this kind of media attention. People seeking media attention who lack notoriety or celebrity must use other measures. For example, during the World Trade Organization meetings in Seattle in 1999, protestors used the Internet and alternative newspapers to plan a large march in downtown Seattle. The violence that erupted between police and some protesters drew considerable media attention and was broadcast widely (DeLuca & Peeples, 2002). More recently, when President Donald Trump signed a travel ban on people from some Middle East countries, protests took place at airports around the United States which drew media attention. Following the inauguration of President Trump, the Women's March took place in January 2017 and a number of other protests followed. These public protests drew crowds that made them media events.

Media events often focus on important rituals while promoting a variety of less obvious messages, or subtexts. Examples of rituals include royal marriages, state funerals, and presidential inaugurations. These events, media observers say, go well beyond the occasion to promote important cultural values through media coverage. For example, in their analysis of the British queen's Golden Jubilee, Claire Wardle and Emily West (2004) concluded that the British press framed the event not simply as an anniversary celebration for the queen, but as a sign of British national strength, thus converting it to a nationalistic celebration.

Media events are filled with messages that shape one's view of the world and invite one to view the world in a particular way. The funerals of Yasser Arafat and Ronald Reagan, the inaugurations of Barack Obama and Donald Trump, and many other media events are worthy of examination for the underlying assumptions and meanings they communicate beyond reporting the facts. For example, in addition to explaining what occurred, such events can stimulate nationalistic feelings, celebrate a nation's history or values, or reinforce specific political beliefs and positions. Another example of a powerful media event was the 2010 earthquake in Haiti and the 2011 earthquake and tsunami in Japan. Media played a key role in bringing attention to these human tragedies, which in turn prompted huge numbers of people to make donations to relief organizations.

Monitoring Media Violence

media violence
Representations of violent acts in media.

Representations of violent acts in media are common and are an increasingly important area of research, as well as a concern among parents and other groups. As you might surmise, our society is ambivalent about **media violence**, as indicated by the range of responses to it. On the one hand, a large number of people must be entertained by it, or why would there be so many violent books, movies, and video games? On the other, media producers and editors make intentional decisions to keep certain violent images out of the public view (beheadings, coffins, bodies). In addition, we are inventing tools such as parental control devices for television to protect certain members of society from witnessing violence. These conflicting trends reveal tensions between the principles of censorship, freedom of the press, and protection of children.

Although no clear-cut definition of violence exists, most people generally consider shootings, stabbings, and other kinds of killings and attempted killings to be violent. Slapping, hitting, and fighting of all types also constitute violence. Most of the concern about media violence focuses on its impact on children. The American Academy of Pediatrics, for example, is particularly concerned about the influence of media violence on children under eight years of age; they have concluded that media violence has the following effects on children:

- increased aggressiveness and antisocial behavior,
- increased fear of becoming victims,
- less sensitivity to violence and to victims of violence, and
- increased appetite for more violence in entertainment and in real life.

These concerns are not new. People, especially parents, began to worry about media violence in television almost as soon as broadcasting began in 1946. Also, as we noted previously, numerous studies have shown that "media violence contributes to a more violent society" (Anderson & Bushman, 2002, p. 2377). Research has also demonstrated that although cartoons are far more violent than prime-time television, an intervention by parents and adults can influence how children respond to those violent images. For example, in her study of five- to seven- and ten- to twelve-year-old children, Amy Nathanson (2004) found that when parents and other adults simply discussed the production techniques of a program, this either had no effect on children or it increased the influence of the violent images. In contrast, when parents underscored the fictional nature of a program's characters, the children were better able to deal with the violence and were less afraid.

V-chip
Device that identifies television program ratings by content and can block programming designated by the owner.

In response to concerns about children and television content, in 1998 the Federal Communications Commission (2003) mandated that half of all new televisions 13 inches or larger manufactured after July 1, 1999, and *all* sets 13 inches or larger manufactured after January 1, 2000, must have a **V-chip** installed. A V-chip identifies program ratings by content and can block programming that is designated by the owner, typically the parent(s). For example, a parent who does not want a child to watch programs with TV-14 ratings can block such programs from being shown. Similar systems have been developed to block access to certain kinds of websites on the Internet and other media.

Of course, not all violent images presented in media are fictional. Television news journalists must decide what is and is not too horrifying to broadcast. Internet broadcasts of hostages in Iraq being beheaded in 2014–2015 were not shown on U.S. network television. Images of people leaping to their deaths from the World Trade Center towers on September 11, 2001, also were considered too troubling to broadcast.

The Federal Communications Commission has oversight of the appropriateness of television programming, but it focuses more on the major network channels than on cable channels. Moreover, the commission can fine broadcasters for presenting inappropriate materials, but these fines are typically for indecency rather than violence. Sometimes broadcasters warn audiences that an upcoming image may not be suitable for all audiences— one approach to dealing with extremely violent images. For example, some television newscasters provided such warnings before showing the numerous bodies of victims of the 2004 Indian Ocean tsunami. Some offer similar warnings before showing fatal shootings, or material that some parents may not want their children to see. Cable broadcasts, particularly pay-per-view, have more leeway in their programming because the assumption is that viewers have actively sought out and paid for a particular type of programming.

▲ Parents play an important role in their children's media viewing, as well as the way in which their children interpret the programs they watch.

Critical Thinking Prompt
How well does the V-chip serve its intended purpose? What measures do you think society should take to limit children's exposure to inappropriate media content?

Analyzing Media Economics

Mass communication today is dominated by the large corporations that produce and distribute media messages. Thus, the economics of media production shapes mass communication and gives it a unique and powerful role in our society. No individual can easily compete with a multinational corporation in producing and distributing media messages. Therefore, these huge media corporations determine which messages are available, and this ownership can have consequences for society in important ways. The Walt Disney Company, one of the world's largest media conglomerates, owns several television networks as well as TV and movie production and distribution companies; these, together with its publishing and merchandising divisions and Disney character licensing, give the company enormous influence on the messages that fill the media environment. An equally wide-reaching media conglomerate is News Corporation, headed by Australian-born entrepreneur Rupert Murdoch (see *Alternative View: Murdoch and the News Corporation Fallout*).

In the area of media studies concerned with economic issues, scholars focus on **political economy**, or the ways in which media institutions produce texts in a capitalist system and the legal and regulatory frameworks that shape their options for doing so. Political economists also examine how these media products are marketed to understand what they reveal about our society. This approach is an extension of the work of Karl Marx, the influential nineteenth-century socialist thinker, and it emphasizes the economics of media, rather than its messages or audiences, although all those components are interrelated. An example of this theory's application can be seen in one researcher's analysis of the recent decision by ABC to cease broadcasting the Miss America pageant. After all, the researcher noted, "a little more than a decade ago [this pageant] had copped about 27 million viewers; last month it drew a record-low 9.8 million" (de Moraes, 2004). With a small viewing audience, the demand for and price of advertising during the pageant also dropped. Thus, the theory goes, economic factors largely determine what media content people are exposed to.

political economy

The ways in which media institutions produce texts in a capitalist system and the legal and regulatory frameworks that shape their options for doing so.

ALTERNATIVE VIEW
Murdoch and the News Corporation Fallout

How much attention should we pay to media ownership and the power of the media, especially in relation to politicians and other government officials? Can media organizations become too powerful?

News Corporation—popularly known as News Corp.—originated from an Australian newspaper company that Rupert Murdoch inherited from his father in the 1950s; it grew to become "one of the world's largest media conglomerates. Created and controlled by Rupert Murdoch, the company once owned *Fox News*, *The Wall Street Journal*, *The New York Post*, and *20th Century Fox* film studio among other assets. The company also owned influential newspapers in Britain like *The Times of London* and *The Sun*" (News Corporation, 2011). In addition, in the United States, its vast holdings included the *Fox Network*, *Dow Jones*, *HarperCollins US*, *FX*, and *National Geographic Channel*, among many others.

As News Corp. expanded into more and more countries and media markets, concerns were raised about the consolidation of these media industries and the political power it could exert. Among these concerns were allegations that News Corp. reporters had obtained information for news stories through unethical and possibly illegal means. In particular, allegations and investigations into phone hacking had been aimed at News Corp.'s British tabloid newspaper, *News of the World*. By July 2011, a scandal broke out over the hacking into voicemail messages left on phones of prominent public figures, victims of the 2005 London subway bombing, British soldiers killed in action, and—the example that truly outraged the public—a 13-year-old schoolgirl named Milly Dowler who had been kidnapped and later found dead. Evidence of bribing police for tips on stories also emerged. The anger over these breaches of journalistic ethics led to the closure of *News of the World*, the withdrawal of News Corp.'s bid to buy British Sky Broadcasting, the arrests of a number of News Corp. employees, the resignations of police officials, and further investigations into News Corp.'s activities.

In the wake of the scandal, News Corp split into two separate companies, under "pressure from shareholders and UK politicians" (Douglas, 2012). The entertainment part of the old News Corp was spun off under the name 21st Century Fox and the publishing part kept the name News Corp. Rupert Murdoch serves as "chairman and chief executive of 21st Century Fox, as well as executive chairman of News Corp" ("News Corp officially splits," 2013).

In July 2016, Roger Ailes, former Chairman and CEO of Fox News resigned in the wake of sexual harassment accusations. In the aftermath of this latest scandal, including payouts, "here we are again," as it seems "eerily similar terrain" (Rutenberg, 2016). The power of this media corporation may have insulated it, but "executives at 21st Century Fox indicate [. . .] that profits will no longer suspend the basic rules of modern corporate life" (Rutenberg, 2016). It will be interesting to see what happens to this media corporation in the future, as Mr. Murdoch remains in his leadership position.

Broader concerns, which should interest us as students of communication, focus on the organizational culture of News Corp. that may encourage unethical and illegal activities in pursuit of organizational goals: "Time and again in the United States and elsewhere, Mr. Murdoch's News Corporation has used blunt force spending to skate past judgment, agreeing to payments to settle legal cases and, undoubtedly more important, silence its critics" (Carr, 2011). At issue here is the power of media conglomerates, such as News Corp., and the influence they may have on society, politics, and everyday life. Some are now questioning whether transnational, capitalist media organizations are in the best interests of any nation-state, or only in the best interests of the corporation.

SOURCES: Douglas, T. (2012, June 28). News Corp confirms plan to split the media giant. *BBC.* Retrieved March 23, 2017, from http://www.bbc.com/news/business-18621949.
News Corp officially splits in two. (2013, June 28). *BBC.* Retrieved March 23, 2017, from http://www.bbc.com/news/business-23104822.
News Corporation. (2011, September 20). *New York Times.* Retrieved October 5, 2011, from http://topics.nytimes.com/top/news/business/companies/news_corporation/index.html.
Rutenberg, J. (2016, August 14). Fox News turmoil recalls News Corp. phone hacking scandal. *New York Times.* Retrieved March 23, 2017, from https://www.nytimes.com/2016/08/15/business/fox-news-turmoil-recalls-news-corpphone-hacking-scandal.html?_r=0.

Previously in this chapter, we introduced the term *culture industries* to refer to organizations that produce, distribute, or show various media texts. In the United States, these culture industries most often are media corporations or media industries that operate for profit. In some other countries, however, culture industries are more like U.S. public television—meaning that they are nonprofit media organizations—and this economic structure affects content and programming. Consider for a moment how a nonprofit media organization might develop programming as compared with a for-profit organization. What factors might guide their decision making? PBS, for example, needs to please the public and the government, both of which fund it. President Trump has proposed ending all federal funding for public broadcasting which is not the first time such a proposal has been made (Stelter, 2017). In contrast, for-profit networks need to please shareholders and advertisers by drawing large audiences.

Although television networks have historically been identified with specific nations—for example, CBC with Canada and BBC with Britain—globalization has recently sparked and sustained transnational television networks. Many media corporations with significant financial backing are moving in this direction. Though initial attempts at transnational broadcasting in the early 1980s to mid-1990s faced many difficulties and most did not survive (Chalaby, 2003), today, transnational television networks are growing, and some of these include U.S.-based networks such as CNN International and MTV. Some are European-based, such as BBC World, Deutsche Welle, Euronews, France24, and Skynews. More studies need to be done to determine how this global flow of information and entertainment may be influencing societies.

In China, another kind of change has been occurring in the mass media system, related in part to globalization. As the Chinese economy has moved toward a capitalist or free-enterprise model, the state-owned mass media system has experienced changes, including the "rise of semi-independent newspapers and broadcasting stations, the proliferation of private Internet content providers and unlicensed cable networks, and increasing cross-investment by the media into other commercial enterprises, including joint ventures with international media giants" (Akhavan-Majid, 2004, p. 553). In her study of these new Chinese media, Akhavan-Majid argues that "non-state actors (e.g., citizens, journalists, entrepreneurs)" (2004, p. 554) have used loopholes in official Chinese policies to creatively open new media opportunities. As you can see, changes in political and economic structures can be intimately intertwined with changes in mass media.

Political economists also analyze the mergers and acquisitions that occur in the media industry as a way of understanding changes in programming. For example, when NBC acquired the Bravo channel (2001), it added performing arts and art films to its roster, as well as some riskier programs, including *Boy Meets Boy* (2003), *Queer Eye for the Straight Guy* (2003–2007) and *Girl* (2008). In a news release related to this sale, Bob Wright, Vice Chairman of General Electric and Chairman and CEO of NBC, noted that "Bravo, with its desirable demographic, is a perfect strategic addition to our portfolio, providing a particularly good fit with NBC's network and cable viewers" (Cablevision, 2000). In analyzing these developments, a political economist might focus on the economic reasons behind this acquisition and the potential future revenues to be generated by appealing to this desirable demographic group ("desirable" typically refers to an audience with the size and demographic profile to bring in high advertising revenues). As Bravo continues to search for desirable audiences, the network has moved to new television programming, including *Top Chef, Vanderpump Rules, Below Deck,* the *Million Dollar Listing* franchise, and *The Real Housewives* franchise.

Another desirable demographic are Millennials. As the largest generational group, Millennials are expected to become an important market for advertisers. In order to capture this market, it's important to understand what they are watching, as well as how they are watching media texts. In 2017, Nielsen released a report, "Millennials on millennials (Nielson, 2017)," that looked at their media consumption. Traditional TV viewing still dominates the media consumption of Millennials, but less than older generations. Millennials have migrated to other screens, for example, tablets, smart phones, and other digital streaming devices to watch various media. They also tend to multitask while watching programs, change the channel less often and remember fewer of the advertisements. These viewing habits are important for advertisers to understand, as they try to make money selling to this generation.

Of course, political economists cannot predict the kinds of media texts that will emerge from any specific merger. They know that television stations seek viewers who are more affluent so they can attract more advertisers, but political economists do not know (nor does anyone) what kinds of shows will attract affluent viewers. Although television production companies try to create—and television networks try to buy— television programs that will draw large audiences, they do not always succeed. Political economists cannot and do not predict such successes, either. Instead, they focus on the ways that corporate media influence the information we get, the consequences of capitalist media corporations on society, and the demands that this political and economic structure places on journalists, broadcasters, and other media workers.

In the context of the 2003 Federal Communications Commission's decision to relax restrictions on ownership of media, understanding and unraveling the complex relationships among media economics, media ownership, and media content can be crucial. For example, because news is sold for profit, the profit motive shapes what readers consider "news." This commercial pressure influences the work of journalists as well as the way media organizations are run. One leading scholar in this area, Robert McChesney (1998), raised this alarm more than a decade ago:

> The American media system is spinning out of control in a hyper-commercialized frenzy. Fewer than 10 transnational media conglomerates dominate much of our media; fewer than two dozen account for the overwhelming majority of our newspapers, magazines, films, television, radio, and books. With every aspect of our media culture now fair game for commercial exploitation, we can look forward to the full-scale commercialization of sports, arts, and education, the disappearance of notions of public service from public discourse, and the degeneration of journalism, political coverage, and children's programming under commercial pressure. (p. 4)

By focusing on the political and economic structures in which media industries operate, political economists offer a unique perspective on the influence of media in our lives. Their analysis of areas that many people ignore reveals the potential consequences of the business of media on all of us.

Societal issues very much influence individuals' interactions with media. Moreover, both personal and social identities are important to one's interactions with media and how one interprets media violence. Given the profits to be made, media economics ensures that media violence will remain pervasive as long as people continue to purchase products with violent content.

Journal Prompt 13.4: Mass Media Issues

Consider the following question: What are five issues in the study of mass media and how do each of these relate to the individual and to society at large?

Ethics and Mass Media

13.5   Identify five ethical issues with mass media.

Because media messages are so powerful, they can generate powerful responses. One potential response is **media activism**, or the practice of organizing to communicate displeasure with certain media images and messages, as well as to advocate for change in future media texts. The issues that media activists address are important because they highlight many significant ethical questions surrounding mediated communication. Media activism, of course, is not limited to the United States. Media activist groups have mobilized around the world to express ethical concerns about media coverage on a range of issues.

Voicing ethical concerns through media activism is not a recent phenomenon. People have been concerned about media content and images for centuries. The notions of freedom of speech and freedom of the press articulated in the U.S. Constitution reflect one response to media control. In the early twentieth century, as silent movies became popular entertainment, concerns about their racy content and the transition to talking movies led to calls for government regulation of media. In an attempt to avoid government regulation, Hollywood established the Hays Office to create its own system of regulation. The **Hays Code**, which was published in 1930, established strict rules for media content with the goal of wholesome entertainment. Some of the Hays regulations still apply today, such as the ban on exposing children's sex organs. Other regulations, however, have become outdated, such as the ban against portraying sexual relationships between interracial couples or using vulgar expressions or profanity, which the code specified as including the words "God, Lord, Jesus, Christ (unless used reverently); cripes; fairy (in a vulgar sense)."

The Hays code came about because of media activism in the 1920s, and it continued to set industry standards until the late 1960s, when the Motion Picture Association of America (**MPAA**) devised its rating codes. The MPAA represents the six major Hollywood studios. These codes have changed slightly since then, but most people are familiar with the G, PG, PG-13, R, and NC-17 ratings.

media activism

The practice of organizing to communicate displeasure with certain media images and messages, as well as to force change in future media texts.

Hays Code

Self-imposed rules for Hollywood media content instituted in 1930 with the goal of creating "wholesome entertainment."

MPAA

Motion Picture Association of America is a film sector industry representing the six major Hollywood studios.

Today, media activism has concentrated largely on the ethics of five areas: children's programming, representations of cultural groups, bias in news reporting, alternative programming, and the use of media as an activist strategy. Let's look at each of these in turn.

The first area of ethical focus of media activism is the concern over the impact of media images on children. Complaints about content in television shows and its influence on children led to the creation of the **TV Parental Guidelines** (TV Parental Guidelines Monitoring Board, n.d.), which are a self-regulating system of the television industry. These guidelines rate programs in terms of appropriateness for particular age groups. You have probably noticed the rating codes in the upper-left corner of the television screen. (An explanation of the ratings is available at www.tvguidelines.org/ratings.htm.) This kind of rating system is voluntary, so unless an adult activates the V-chip or an adult is present to change the channel or turn off the television, the rating system may not work as it was intended.

The second ethical focus of media activists has been distortions perpetrated or reinforced by media. The concern here is that such portrayals create stereotypes and misunderstandings. Minority groups, in particular, have had such concerns, as we can see in the number of media activist groups focused on media representations of racial and sexual minorities. On record with *Newsweek*, Martin Reynolds of the Maynard Institute for Journalism Education, a nonprofit that promotes diversity in the newsroom, has asserted that: "The black press and the ethnic press as a whole have consistently maintained far more credibility in their communities than their mainstream counterparts" (Celis, 2017). Yet that is not to say that minority groups have the same alternative viewpoints about mainstream news.

Media activism has recently taken on more meaning since the "fake news" phenomenon which has been causing confusion among Americans (Barthel et al., 2016). Media activism has traditionally been understood as alternative outlets using media to spark and sustain social movements. But in a world where journalists are no longer the exclusive "gatekeepers" of information, mainstream media channels are increasingly seeing themselves as activists. Media activism, then, now refers to media owners repurposing what it means to disseminate news to the public (Ward, 2015). In fact, some media insiders increasingly see themselves as activists against privately disseminated fake news.

These activists argue that when people have limited contact with minority groups, they are likely to gain false impressions from media misrepresentations. In turn, these distorted images may lead to hate crimes or discriminatory government policies, such as racial profiling. Media activist groups that monitor media producers and challenge them to create responsible and accurate images include Media Action Network for Asian Americans (MANAA) and Gay and Lesbian Alliance Against Defamation (GLAAD) as well as organizations that have broader goals but that include a media activist focus, such as the National Organization for Women (NOW) and the League of United Latin American Citizens (LULAC).

A third category of activist groups has focused on structural issues in media industries and the consequences for how news content is constructed and broadcast to consumers. Within a profit-making environment, does making money influence what stories are covered, how and for wealthier consumers? For example, organizations such as Fairness and Accuracy in Reporting [FAIR], the Annenberg Public Policy Center's factcheck.org, the Arthur W. Page Center for Integrity in Public Communication, and the National Public Radio program *On the Media* are some of the organizations that focus on the news media and their accuracy and fairness in reporting various issues and the inclusion of diverse viewpoints.

TV Parental Guidelines
A self-regulating system of the television industry that rates programs in terms of appropriateness for particular age groups.

▼ The GLAAD Media Awards is an annual event that honors responsible and accurate media images of lesbians, gays, transgendered individuals, and bisexuals. Laverne Cox attended the 2016 event.

The fourth ethical focus of media activists has been to find and provide media texts that offer alternatives to mainstream sources. Many newspapers, radio programs, and Internet sites are available for those who want alternatives to mainstream news media coverage so that they can hear a diversity of voices and opinions. Previously, we discussed the alternative press, but there is also alternative radio programming, such as the Progressive Radio Network, and other alternative media outlets, such as Amy Goodman and Juan Gonzalez's daily television program *Democracy Now!* Other alternative views are expressed as humor in print, online in *The Onion*, and on television on *The Daily Show* and *Last Week Tonight with John Oliver*. Alternative media outlets are not the same as fake news, in that they do not present false facts, but focus more on alternative interpretations of facts and report news that is not covered in mainstream media outlets.

Finally, some activists use media to communicate specific ethical concerns and messages to a wide audience. Thus, despite the fact that they lack the backing of huge media conglomerates, activists have used media to educate or influence audiences regarding cruelty to animals; the situations in Palestine, Guantánamo, and Afghanistan; violence against women; anti-Semitism; genocide; racism; and more. To get their messages out, these groups set up websites and webcasts, solicit funds to run advertisements on television or in mainstream newspapers or magazines, and sometimes organize demonstrations at strategic times and places.

As new media outlets develop (for example via the Internet, cable TV, and satellite radio) and the world continues to confront new challenges, new ethical issues and new ways of communicating will continue to emerge. We cannot forecast the future, but we do know that the ongoing process of change in the media environment shows no signs of abating. Media activists will continue to try to shape the media messages we receive, while at the same time, media producers will continue to try to sell what people are interested in purchasing. And so, bombarded as you are by media and the messages of a range of media activists, how can you become a responsible media consumer? Let's explore this topic next.

Journal Prompt 13.5: Mass Media Ethics
Consider the following question:
\What are the five ethical focuses in mass media?

Becoming a More Effective Media Consumer

13.6 Describe three ways to be a more effective consumer of media messages.

As a potential consumer of practically nonstop messages coming from radio, television, newspapers, magazines, advertisements, movies, and so on, you need strategies for dealing with this complex media environment. The solution cannot be boiled down to a set of simple guidelines, of course, but here are some ideas to consider when interacting with media. To become more effective in your media consumption, be an active agent in your media choices, be mindful of the media choices you make, and speak out if you find media content offensive.

Be an Active Agent

How can you become an active consumer of media? First, don't just watch or read whatever is available. Make deliberate choices about media you expose yourself to so that you can better control the effect that media messages have on you. As you become more selective, you express a set of media-related values, which in turn indicates to media providers what type of media programming they should be providing.

As an active agent, then, seek out those media that meet your needs and avoid or resist others. To be a truly active agent, however, you have to think about the basis for your media choices. Are you avoiding some media messages simply because they challenge your beliefs? If so, this probably is not the best way to navigate through the media environment. Sometimes, you can benefit from being open-minded about the views and perspectives of others.

Broaden Your Media Horizons

People often live within the confines of a particular media environment and, like a fish in water, can't see the limits. With the vast possibilities now available via the Internet, in libraries, and through other media outlets, you have access to practically the whole world. Even if your only language is English, you have many media options available to you.

As you work to broaden your horizons, obtain a range of views on world events. Try to understand why other people view the world the way they do, no matter how different their views are from your own. Try to understand the rising anti-Americanism coming from around the world. You may disagree with what you hear, or even find it offensive, but by seeing the complexity of issues involved you can gain a better understanding of the world we live in.

Overall, being a responsible and effective consumer of media is not easy. It certainly extends far beyond lounging around watching whatever is on television. Becoming an active partner in this complex communication process is a challenge, one we hope you will take up.

Talk Back

You can benefit from talking back or challenging the messages you receive via news commentators, politicians, reporters, or even characters in television programs. In other words, if you hear something you disagree with or that sounds wrong, point this out, even if only to yourself. For example, suppose you hear a reporter covering a natural disaster refer to "innocent victims." What, you might ask yourself, is a "guilty victim" in the context of an earthquake, or in any context for that matter? Noticing and questioning these kinds of empty phrases makes you a more active consumer of media. As you watch or listen, you might also consider why one news story is given more time than another one, or why a particular story is reported at all, and what that prioritizing and selection communicates about what is and isn't valued.

Talking back also includes being attentive to the ethical implications of media to which you are exposed, particularly if it promotes some social identities at the expense of others. More specifically, be aware of the ways that, for example, women and racial minorities, sexual minorities, and religious minorities are portrayed and what influences these images may have on the groups depicted. If you watch movies that mock particular cultural or religious groups, that denigrate women, or that misrepresent the experiences of certain individuals, consider the implications. You not only ratify this depiction by your attendance, but you also encourage the production of more of this type of media with your dollars.

Talking back, however, can involve much more than talking to the images that come to you in media or making choices about which images to support or resist. If you find something particularly objectionable, you can contact the television station, magazine, or newspaper that has offended you. For example, if you believe that specific programs manipulate or attempt to unfairly influence children, use the "contact us" information on the station's website to let the producers of those programs, and the companies that advertise in that medium, know exactly how you feel. Or you can complain to the Federal Communications Commission, the federal agency that regulates radio, television, wire, cable, and satellite. On the other hand, if you believe specific media have a positive influence and should be more widely produced or distributed, let advertisers and media companies know that as well. Certainly, praising a job well done is as important a form of talking back as raising objections.

In general, few consumers are sufficiently deliberate about the media messages they select. But because media messages have such a powerful impact on consumers, and because you can have some influence on the availability of specific types of media, you benefit society when you become an active and critical media consumer.

▲ As an active media consumer, you can talk back to your television as well as discuss media messages with family and friends.

Critical Thinking Prompt
How can media consumers find a range of media outlets from which to get news and information? How would you define an adequate and well-balanced "diet" of media consumption?

Journal Prompt 13.6: Mass Media Activism
Consider the following questions: How do media activists respond to media messages they find objectionable? What are some concerns that contemporary media activists have raised?

SUMMARY

13.1 Identify the issues facing mass media.

- Media influence how we see ourselves and the world around us.
- *Mediated communication* are mediated, or transmitted, through a channel, such as television, film, radio, or print.
- Mass media communication refers to communication that is directed at a mass audience.
- Individuals choose what types of media texts to watch, read, listen to, purchase, or avoid.

13.2 Identify the main forms of mass media.

- The main forms of mass media are: newspapers, magazines, mass market paperbacks and e-books, motion pictures or movies, radio, popular music, and television.

13.3 Describe various models of media.

- The linear model focuses on media effects.
- Selective exposure theory emphasizes how people choose media that confirm their views and avoid media that challenge those beliefs.
- Uses and gratifications studies focus on how people use media to satisfy their need for information, personal identity, social interaction, and entertainment.
- People also resist media, as they are active agents.

13.4 Understand five issues in media studies: social identities, understanding the world, media events, media violence, and media economics.

- Media confirm our social identities, help us understand the world, help us understand important media events, and shape the images of real and imagined violence.
- Media are influenced by and function within a capitalist economic system.

13.5 Identify five ethical issues with mass media.

- Media activism is one way that people express their ethical views and respond to objectionable media messages and powerful media corporations.
- Media activists are concerned about children's programming.
- Media activism is also focused on how cultural groups are represented or stereotyped.
- Media activism is also concerned about news reporting and fake news.
- Media activism can also produce alternative programming.

13.6 Describe three ways to be a more effective consumer of media messages.

- Be an active agent and aware of your own media consumption habits.
- Broaden your media horizons and be active in making your choices.
- Talk back when media content is offensive or problematic.

KEY TERMS

media p. 319
mass media p. 319
culture industries p. 319
mass-market paperbacks p. 320
e-books p. 320
active agents p. 322
mass media effects p. 322
media text p. 323

selective exposure p. 324
uses and gratifications p. 326
content analysis p. 328
agenda-setting capacity p. 331
cultivation theory p. 332
hegemony p. 332
media event p. 333
media violence p. 334

V-chip p. 334
political economy p. 335
media activism p. 338
Hays Code p. 338
MPAA p. 338
TV Parental Guidelines p. 339

APPLY WHAT YOU KNOW

1. Research a popular media text—for example, a magazine, television show, or newspaper—that targets an identity group different from your own. What elements differ from a text targeted at one of your identity groups?

2. Select and study a media event such as the Super Bowl, Miss America Pageant, or a famous murder trial, and identify the rituals that surround this event. How does the media event affirm U.S. cultural values?

3. Select a media activist group to study. Go to their webpage and identify their concerns about media. What strategies do they use to promote their messages? Who is their audience? How do they plan to change media in the ways that concern them?

Communicating through Social and Other Interactive Media

LEARNING OBJECTIVES

14.1 Identify two reasons for learning about interactive media.

14.2 Identify and describe interactive media.

14.3 Describe the dimensions of interactive media and how these dimensions combine into a framework for understanding the use of interactive media.

14.4 Describe issues that can arise in identity and relationship development when using interactive media.

14.5 Understand the role of power and privilege in interactive media use.

14.6 Identify and describe four ethical challenges involving interactive media use.

14.7 Discuss ways to improve your own mediated communication skills.

CHAPTER TOPICS

The Importance of Interactive and Social Media

What Are Interactive Media?

How Does Interactive Media Use Affect Our Communication Choices?

Interactive Media and the Individual

The Individual, Communication Technology, and Society

Ethics and Interactive Media

Improving Your Mediated Communication Skills

> *"Experts predict the Internet will become 'like electricity'—less visible, yet more deeply embedded in people's lives for good and ill."*
>
> —Digital Life in 2025, *Pew Report, 2014* —*J. G. Ballard*

Charee just heard that a friend's mother has been diagnosed with a serious illness. Charee would like to contact her friend, but she's not sure how best to get in touch. Should she call her? Send a message through Facebook? Contact her with a text message? She started to think about all the communication choices she has every day and the impacts of those choices. For example, her mother got offended when she just sent a text message on Mother's Day instead of phoning her. Her grandmother refuses to text, so Charee has to talk with her on the phone, which she really doesn't like. Most of her friends communicate on Snapchat.

Charee's thinking about her communication choices illustrates a number of issues we will address in this chapter. For example, given the many choices we have to connect with people in our daily lives, how do we decide which is the most appropriate? How do people use technology to communicate in different contexts and with different people? How has the pervasiveness of technology impacted the way we communicate with others? And how does the constant "connectivity" to others affect our identities and our interpersonal relationships?

In the previous chapter, we focused on mass media—The focus of mass media is one-way mediated communication produced by large industries intended for a large audience, such as television, radio, and films. In this chapter, we focus on **interactive media**, or mediated communication, which relies on technologies such as the Internet and mobile phones and other devices. First, we describe how interactive media play an important role in our lives and define what we mean by interactive media. As you'll see, social media is the largest group of interactive media—which is why it is included in the title of this chapter. However, as we will explain later, interactive media also include text messaging and email, which are not technically social media. Then we examine individuals' use of interactive media, including identity issues and impacts on personal and work relationships. We then shift the focus to societal forces—examining how gender, race/ethnicity, and socioeconomic class impact interactive media use and who does (and does not) have access to these and other communication technologies. Finally, we discuss ethical issues related to interactive media use and conclude with suggestions for improving your own skills in using communication technologies.

interactive media
A collection of mediated communication technologies that are digital and converging and tend to be mobile.

The Importance of Interactive and Social Media

14.1 Identify two reasons for learning about interactive media.

Interactive media are a constant reality in our lives and affect our daily activities in multiple ways. This pervasiveness provides the first and primary reason for learning more about this topic. A second reason is that understanding interactive media and having good media skills will help you be more successful personally and professionally.

First, we say that interactive media are pervasive because most of us interact with these communication technologies almost constantly. As shown in Figure 14.1, digital technologies have grown exponentially in the last 15 years and now almost 90 percent of Americans use the Internet, almost 80 percent own a smartphone, and almost 70 percent use social media (Smith, 2017). While Twitter, Pinterest, Instagram, and LinkedIn are popular, Facebook remains the most popular social media platform; 8 in 10 Americans now use it not only to connect with friends and family but also as a source of news, to

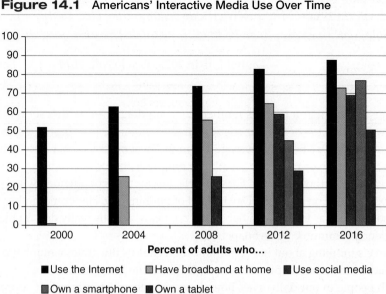

Figure 14.1 Americans' Interactive Media Use Over Time

take a break on the job, or seek employment, and most report that they visit the site on a daily basis (Greenwood et al., 2016). More than 40 percent of U.S. Americans ages 18 to 34 use the Snapchat app, which increasingly functions like a social media platform, and more than half of all new users are older than 25 (Benner, 2016; Stern, 2017). Although all these communication technologies are a huge boon for many people around the globe, it presents challenges to communication researchers (and textbook authors) in trying to understand and study the implications of these interactive mobile media for our daily lives. Communication technologies come and go at a rapid rate. By the time researchers design a study, the particular technology may have lost prominence (your parents may remember MySpace, pagers, car phones, Xanga?), and the study results can then seem irrelevant. In addition, it's difficult to predict which technologies will be important in the future or how we will use current ones differently. For example, Facebook—a commercial behemoth that reaches deep into so much of our daily activities—is now a far cry from its 2004 beginning as a website for Harvard students (and later anyone with an email address) to simply connect with each other (La Monica, 2016).

That said, we have to start somewhere to describe the role of interactive media in our everyday lives, and most experts agree that we currently use communication technologies primarily for (1) connecting with others and (2) consuming content (verbal and visual). These interactive media offer many ways to stay connected, and as Charee discovered, present many communication choices. Our friends can know immediately what books we're reading, what brand of sunscreen we've purchased, the restaurant where we're eating, films we're watching, and help us to connect with others in the same physical location (e.g., Meetup) to potential sexual or romantic relationships (e.g., Grindr, Tinder, Blendr, Hinge, Tastebuds, Bumble, etc.). Of course, different social media platforms have different audiences that require different approaches. What you would post on LinkedIn, for example, is different from what you post on Facebook or Pinterest or Twitter. We are constantly making choices about which information we want to share with which friends/acquaintances/colleagues and in which medium. Throughout this chapter, we will examine how this pervasive connectivity can affect our communication choices as well as our sense of identity, personal privacy, and romantic, work, and acquaintance relationships.

Another important interactive media activity is searching for information/consuming content (visual and verbal). Some activities may be less interactive (e.g., getting directions, movie/restaurant reviews, stock quotes, weather reports, news headlines, watching funny cat videos), but others are quite interactive—reading and commenting on political/news/opinion blogs, posting your own opinion on restaurant reviews, or sending that funny cat video to a friend with a message about your own cat experiences.

Crowdsourcing, a combination of the words crowd + outsourcing, refers to using services from internal and external providers, or to gathering input from the general public, using search engines or social media networks. Deciding where to search for information presents another set of decisions. In searching for information, when do you use a search engine (e.g., Google, Bing) and when do you use your social network on Facebook or Twitter? How do you decide? A group of researchers investigated this topic and found that people carefully choose their platform based on the nature of the question they are looking to answer and the audience they're interested in sourcing (Oeldorf-Hirsch, Hecht, & Morris, 2014). For example, people used Facebook status message questions 20 percent of the time when they wanted opinions from their friends, were seeking very specific information, or asking friends to supplement info from a search engine. They tended to use Twitter when they needed a broader audience or were seeking information they thought inappropriate (too sensitive or too controversial) for Facebook friends. They used search engines when very specific information was needed and they didn't think their FB friends would have the answer or for a topic that was too sensitive for social media. In addition to openly asking questions as a status message, Facebook is full of locally based groups. They can be especially helpful when relocating to a new city or country, and you want to find your favorite brand of honey or buy secondhand furniture. When asking for more abstract or philosophical information, and you're looking for a variety of answers beyond your personal social network, it's helpful to go to platforms that are built for question asking, such as quora.com or askreddit.com, the equivalent to the help section of an online bulletin board. In addition to asking questions, Quora allows users to follow certain topics, bookmark answers, and upvote or downvote responses.

Interacting with others around information on Twitter also offers opportunities for closer access to political leaders (e.g., President Trump) and celebrities (e.g., Justin Bieber, Katy Perry) and this group of "mega tweeters" has upset the traditional role of political and celebrity journalists by communicating directly with their followers and fans (Berg, 2015). But social media such as Twitter also presents opportunities for civic engagement and political activism. For example, a Facebook post and then a tweet (#blacklivesmatter) after the murder of Trayvon Martin and Michael Brown by white police officers gathered momentum that led hundreds, then thousands of protesters from around the country to protest against perceived injustices and institutionalized racism and ultimately provoked and shaped public debates about race, policing, governance, and justice (Day, 2015; Jackson & Welles, 2015).

Some experts worry about our overreliance on interactive media for information and identify three issues:

1. Reduction in memory, intuition, or critical thinking skills. We don't need to remember anything, we're never lost or need to take risks or figure things out because there's an app for everything: "Apps reinforce the idea that people, information, services, and products are always and immediately available. There is no work involved in obtaining, researching, or thinking about how they came to be. Apps provide immediate gratification" (Gardener & Davis, 2013).

2. "Echo chamber syndrome." As with mass media selective exposure discussed in Chapter 13, we (and social media platform administrators) often tailor the material we access on interactive media to conform to our particular tastes and opinions, cutting ourselves off from a range of views and opinions (Oremus, 2016).

3. Challenges in evaluating the information we access. According to recent reports by Pew Research Center, most young Americans get their news from social media and many believe that fake news on social media is "sowing confusion" (Barthel, Mitchell & Holcomb, 2016; Gottfried & Shearer, 2016). For example, when minority students at the University of Missouri protested racist incidents on campus, hashtags #Mizzou and #PrayForMizzou spread false Twitter reports that the University of Missouri police were complicit with the Ku Klux Klan and that crosses were being burned on the university lawn—messages originating from

crowdsourcing
The practice of engaging a 'crowd' or group online for a common goal—often for information or problem solving.

hate groups apparently trying to show that overly sensitive anti-racist protesters will believe anything, thus diminishing their effectiveness. Twitter banned the username, but the damage had been done (Hawkes, 2016).

Communication professor Jonathon Albright found that fake news sites are "colonizing the digital space" by millions of hyperlinks around choice subjects such as Muslims, women, Jews, and black people, which are skewing Google's PageRank system (Maquire, 2017). Once on a front page, the cycle is perpetuated: the more people who see these links, the more traffic fake news sites get, the more links they'll accumulate and the more impressive they'll seem.

Google itself claims not to be biased. However, it's important not to blindly trust everything that comes up on that first page of a Google search results. In 2006, if you only typed certain categories of people into the search bar and pressed enter, such as "are Jews," the first result that appeared was "look out for these awful Jews who are ruining your life." When you typed in a category that included almost half the human race ("women are"), Google offered "evil" as an automated choice, and if you pressed enter, the top results included entries such as "every woman has some degree of prostitute in her" (Guarino, 2016).

Currently, results have improved. As of 2017, when you type in "are women," the first 10 results yield a variety of headlines from "Why are women in combat?" and "Why are women always cold?" (temperature-wise), to statistics such as "women make up 40 percent or more of workforce." They appear side by side with headlines that show vestiges of 2006, such as "are women really promiscuous?" and even "are women people?" based on issues raised during the 2016 presidential election.

Now that we've discussed the pervasiveness and related challenges of interactive media in our lives, let's examine the second reason for studying about interactive media: the fact that an understanding of these media and good digital skills can help ensure personal and professional success. As we'll see later in the chapter, understanding the sometimes complex role that interactive media play in interpersonal relationships and employee–employer relationships is essential. In addition, recent research shows a strong relationship between professional success and active use of social media such as LinkedIn and Twitter. Active users reported significant gains in useful professional information as well as strategic networking benefits (Utz, 2016).

Interpersonally, knowing about the specific characteristics of various media and their effects on relationships is crucial. You may not choose a career in social media (e.g., social influencer, digital marketer), but knowing how to use social media effectively to find and secure a job or using social media and other communication technologies in whatever career will enhance your chances of professional success. Perhaps most important, understanding organizational rules and practices involving interactive media, including surveillance, privacy concerns, and "netiquette," will serve you well. There are frequent news stories about employees who lost their jobs or were penalized as a result of not understanding the informal or formal rules about media behavior in the workplace (e.g., tweeting about low pay, to joking about stealing cocaine from the evidence room as a cop, to making racist jokes) (Sun, 2017). Twenty-eight percent of employers report that they've fired people for using the Internet for nonwork-related activity (such as shopping online or checking out Facebook) during the workday and 18 percent have dismissed employees because of something they posted on social media (Rapacon, 2016).

Before looking at how these media forms affect our everyday communication, our identity, and our relationships, let's discuss what we mean by the term interactive media.

Journal Prompt 14.1: Professional Communication Skills
Consider the following question:
Why is it important to have communication technology skills in professional contexts?

▼ Interactive media are a constant reality in our lives and affect our daily activities in multiple ways.

What Are Interactive Media?

14.2   Identify and describe interactive media.

We define interactive media as a collection of mediated communication technologies that are digital and converging and tend to be mobile, all accessed on a variety of devices, from desktop and laptop computers, smartphones, tablets, and other mobile devices. Let's unpack this definition a little further and distinguish interactive media from mass media—the topic covered in Chapter 13. In contrast to face-to-face (FtF) communication, both mass media and interactive media are mediated forms of communication, meaning that the messages are carried through an *intervening* system of **digital** electronic storage before being transmitted between two or more people.

In contrast to mass media, in which messages are generally one-to-many, interactive media messages converge, meaning that they can be sent one to one, one to many, or many to many. Also in contrast to mass media, they are interactive, meaning that communication goes both ways and permits individuals to connect and interact with others. So what are examples of interactive media? There are many, but the easiest description is: Interactive media is **social media** *plus text messages and email*. Social media is "a group of Internet-based, web applications that allow the creation and exchange of user-generated content" (Kaplan & Haenlein, 2010, p. 61).

Business scholars Andreas Kaplan and Michael Haenlein (2010) identify six categories of social media: (1) blogs, (2) Social Networking Sites (SNSs) such as Facebook, (3) Virtual social worlds such as Surreal VR (described as an immersive Second Life), (4) Collaborative projects such as wikis, (5) Content communities like YouTube, and Pinterest, and (6) **Massively Multiplayer Online Role-Playing Games (MMORPGs)** such as Legends of Aria, which are increasingly incorporating virtual reality technology. These categories are not set in stone. Twitter, for example, is an SNS but is also categorized as a microblog. Snapchat is a messaging app but functions like a social media platform. Remember, in addition to social media, interactive media also include mobile messaging and email.

One of the characteristics of interactive media is new versions are always emerging. It is a dynamic form of communication, and increasingly mobile. Distinctions between mass and new media are becoming more and more blurred. For example, some mass media forms like television reality shows viewed on mobile devices incorporate audience reaction and participation. And some media, like podcasts, may not allow interaction, functioning in a way that is similar to traditional mass media. For the purposes of this chapter, we focus on the *interactive* elements of new media, where the "real give and take of social life" in cyberspace occurs (Walther & Parks, 2002, p. 3).

How does this mobility and constant connection with others and information sources through interactive media affect our communication choices? Before addressing this question, we need to understand how various communication technologies differ from each other and from FtF communication—the topic we turn to next.

digital

Information that is transmitted in a numerical format based on only two values (0 and 1).

social media

Group of Internet-based applications that allow the creation and exchange of user-generated content.

Massively Multiplayer Role-Playing Online Games (MMORPGs):

Text-based "virtual reality" games in which participants interact with enrichments, objects, and other participants.

Journal Prompt 14.2: Defining Interactive Media
Consider the following question: What is the definition of interactive media?

How Does Interactive Media Use Affect Our Communication Choices?

14.3   Describe the dimensions of interactive media and how these dimensions combine into a framework for understanding the use of interactive media.

Because interactive media are rapidly changing forms of communication, it is difficult to arrive at definitive conclusions about their exact role in everyday life. Researching these forms of communication can be like trying to hit a moving target. Still, with a basic understanding of what interactive media are, and some of the ways they can differ, we can get some sense of their increasingly important role.

To begin, consider this question that Charee faced: How should she decide whether to communicate a message by text, Facebook post, phone, or in person? Like Charee, perhaps you have had an issue to discuss with a friend or acquaintance and were unsure what the most effective mode of communication would be. If so, you had good reason to feel unsure. Interactive media differ in important ways, and these differences can affect the outcome of your conversation.

One way to understand these differences is to show how interactive media vary along two dimensions, employing two sets of theories and ideas about communication theories: (1) Media characteristics: media richness and social presence and (2) social processes: self presentation and self disclosure.

Media Characteristics   There are two characteristics that differentiate various interactive media. First, some forms of communication technologies lack the capability to carry nonverbal cues. Second, some are also asynchronous in nature—which means a delay may occur between the time the message is sent and when it is responded to. As we discussed in Chapter 6, nonverbal cues play an important role in understanding the totality of a person's message. When we speak face-to-face, we see the other person's gestures, facial expressions, and attire, we hear their sighs, accent, or dialect; these are just a few of the many cues we use to fully understand what a person means. Some interactive media, however—like mobile messages and tweets—eliminate all of those cues that help us to determine what is being communicated.

Another variation in interactive media forms is the degree to which the exchange of messages is synchronous or asynchronous. FtF communication and media like the telephone/Facetime and Skype chats are **synchronous**; that is, messages are sent and received at the same time. However, blog/FB/Instagram posts and tweets are **asynchronous**; that is, messages may be received at a later time. The distinction between synchronous and asynchronous messages can be blurred. Mobile messaging may be synchronous or not, depending on how quickly the other person acknowledges or responds to the message. In some instances, one can choose to make a media interaction asynchronous (e.g., sending phone calls directly to voicemail, saving Snapchats). It seems that people increasingly prefer asynchronous messages and phone calls are now considered intrusive. Experts suggest that this is because we can now be reached anywhere, at possibly a very inconvenient time (having a romantic dinner, middle of class, dentist appointment). This requires us to draw some boundaries around our "constant connectivity." If we need to talk with someone we may choose to schedule the voice call through an asynchronous mobile message (Paule, 2016). Or, as some experts suggest, our preference for asynchronous messages reflects an increasing lack of desire for real human connection and intimacy (see *Alternative View: Alone Together*)?

When you send a mediated message through an asynchronous medium, it is almost impossible to know if the other person has received your message because you don't receive any "in the moment" response. A challenge in mobile messaging is when to respond. What do silences mean in interactive media? In FtF interaction, silences can be meaningful and are usually interpreted by nonverbal cues to mean hesitation, reflection, or perhaps anger. But silence after posting a new Facebook status or sending a Snap might mean anything, ranging from lack of interest to the receiver being unable to respond (for whatever reason) or a technology glitch. Yet, the implications for relationships can be important.

Two theories can help us understand the impact of lack of and presence of nonverbal cues and degree of synchronicity in various interactive media: media richness theory and social presence theory. **Media richness theory** describes the potential information-carrying capacity of a communication medium (Daft & Lengel, 1984, 1986). According to this theory, FtF communication is the richest medium for communicating because you can see facial expressions and body gestures, as well as hear the tone, speed, and quality of a person's voice. All these factors relay a tremendous amount of information and allow you to interpret and respond to messages more accurately. You not only hear

synchronous
Communication in which messages are sent and received at the same time.

asynchronous
Communication in which messages are sent and received at different times.

media richness theory
Theory that describes the potential information-carrying capacity of a communication medium.

ALTERNATIVE VIEW
Alone Together

Do you agree with Turkle's premise that pervasive connectivity actually makes us less connected to other people? Why or why not?

In her recent book, media expert Sherry Turkle challenges us to reexamine our assumptions about technology being the answer to intimacy and connections. She thinks that, although we are constantly in contact with each other—*tethered* to our technology—we sometimes choose technologies that merely substitute for human intimacy and that the technology is taking us "places we don't want to go." She offers as proof that adults would rather email, coworkers would rather leave voicemail messages, and teenagers would rather text. These technologies give us control over our relationships and actually distance us from others; as she puts it, "Technology makes it easy to communicate when we wish and to disengage at will" (2011, p. 13). A 13-year-old tells her that she hates the phone and never listens to voicemail but finds texting just right. Texting puts us in touch, but not too close.

Turkle describes the story of Ellen, working in Paris, who used Skype to connect with her grandmother in Philadelphia. Twice a week they would talk for an hour. But, unbeknownst to her grandmother, Ellen was multitasking during the conversation—typing away on her keyboard answering emails. So it wasn't a *real* connection because Ellen wasn't really present. And Ellen reportedly felt guilty about her actions.

Later, in a TED (Technology Entertainment Design) talk, Turkle gives another example. She describes the creation of furry stuffed animal-like social robots designed to be with and comfort lonely older people. Dr. Turkle thinks this is proof that we're abdicating our human responsibility and what makes us human: the ability to care for others in intimate ways. We substitute technology for intimacy.

Turkle concludes that we should continually examine the benefits and challenges of our "connectivity culture," always asking "how we got to this place and whether we are content to be here" (2011, p. 2).

SOURCES: Turkle, S. (2011). *Alone together: Why we expect more from technology and less from each other.* New York: Basic Books.

Turkle, S. (2012, February). *TED talk: Connected, but alone?* Retrieved May 25, 2014, from http://www.ted.com/talks/sherry_turkle_alone_together#t-755215.

the words, or the content of the message, but you also receive the relational messages that are being sent nonverbally and that reveal how that person feels about you. If the other person is smiling, leaning toward you, and maintaining eye contact, you probably infer that the person is happy or glad to talk with you. If the person is scowling and avoiding eye contact, you might infer that she or he is angry or unhappy with you.

According to media richness theory, some types of mediated communication do allow for a certain amount of richness. Consider video/audio communication, or Skype. When you communicate using a webcam, you might miss some immediate context cues, such as body posture or gestures, but you have the benefit of seeing some of the nonverbal behaviors of the person you're communicating with. The telephone is a less rich medium, revealing some paralinguistic cues (for example, tone of voice), but no facial expression, eye gaze, or gestures.

The least-rich media, according to media richness theory, are text-based messages—email, mobile messaging, and tweets. But nonverbal cues aren't completely absent here, either. Some relational/nonverbal information *can* be communicated in these text-based media, with emojis or abbreviations. Messages can also be made "richer" by altering the

▼ Emojis and and video/photo features convey emotions and increase the social presence and media richness of social media messages.

font color, using animation, icons or particular punctuation, or by emphasizing particular words in a sentence or by repetition.

social presence
Degree of psychological closeness or immediacy engendered by various media.

social presence theory
Theory that suggests face-to-face communication is generally high in social presence, and that media vary in the amount of social presence they convey.

Social presence refers to the feelings of psychological closeness or immediacy that people experience when they interact with each other (Short, Williams, & Christie, 1976). This closeness is communicated through nonverbal cues, such as smiling, leaning forward, and relaxed body posture, and through synchronous communication. **Social presence theory** suggests that FtF communication is generally high in this kind of social presence, and that media vary in the amount of social presence they convey. For example, talking on the telephone conveys less social presence than FtF interaction, but more than email communication—where all nonverbal cues are eliminated. The implication is that media low in social presence (such as texting, emailing, and tweets) may seem more impersonal, less "relationship-focused."

One challenge is how to make good communication choices in a social media environment where there is, on the one hand, constant connectivity and on the other, communication that is mostly text-based—low in media richness, low in social presence and often asynchronous. This seems to present great potential for misunderstanding and relational difficulties. However, social media innovations often respond to users' communicative needs. For example, Snapchat may have evolved as a way to approximate the immediacy and social presence of a face-to-face conversation by affording synchronicity and the ephemeral element of conversation (the message "disappears" with no permanent record like face-to-face conversations) as well as providing emoji and video/photo features, also increasing the social presence and media richness of the text based messages. Are these similarities to FtF conversations part of the reason for Snapchat popularity? And do these characteristics influence your choices about interactive media use? These are questions that communication researchers are just starting to investigate. There is another concept—social processes—and a framework that can help guide our decision-making.

Social Processes   A second way that interactive media can vary is in the type of self-presentation and self-disclosure allowed. These are not specific theories, but are important notions in the field of communication. As we discussed in Chapter 3, we are motivated to control the impressions others have of us (self-presentation)—to influence them to think of us in the ways we want and also to create an image that is consistent with our self-concept and our personal identity. So when you create your Facebook profile, change your FB status, or post photos of your travels during Spring Break on Instagram, you are engaging in and controlling your self-presentation—what others think of you. If, in a given social media platform, you want others to see you as a serious professional, you will post information that is consistent with this self-concept. If you want to present yourself as a fun-loving party animal, you will probably post other information.

One of the important aspects of self-presentation is self-disclosure. And as we noted in Chapter 9, mutual self-disclosure is a crucial step in the development of relationships. The more we disclose to others, the more others tend to self-disclose to us, which in turn strengthens relationships. One way that we can understand the variation in social media is the degree of self-disclosure it requires and the type of self-presentation it allows. So when you create your Facebook or LinkedIn profile, you are required to disclose some information about yourself (you also have the opportunity to disclose a lot more); when playing online games you disclose much less.

Combining these two dimensions—media richness characteristics (richness/social presence) and social processes (self-disclosure/self-presentation)—results in the framework presented in Figure 14.2—and helps us understand how these interactive media vary and the options they present in making communication choices. Concerning media richness/social presence, blogs are the lowest as they are text-based and do not allow for synchronous interaction; the same is true for email and mobile messaging—depending on how quickly the receiver responds. SNSs are higher in that they allow for photos and some "richer" communication, and virtual social worlds are the highest as

Critical Thinking Prompt
Think of a recent conflict you had and describe how it might have been different if the communication media had been different. How might it have gone over the telephone? Face to face? Mobile messaging?

Figure 14.2   Interactive media characteristics

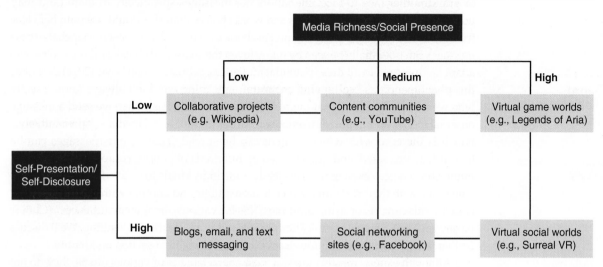

SOURCE: Adapted from Kaplan & Haenlein, 2010, p. 62.

encounters there are synchronous. On the self-presentation/self-disclosure dimensions, collaborative projects are low because they are mostly text based (few photos or videos can be posted) and allow for simple exchanges and relatively little self-disclosure; content communities and SNSs enable more self-disclosure than collaborative projects. Finally, the highest level of self-presentation/self-disclosure is a virtual social world.

This framework can be useful in at least two ways: First, it shows the tremendous number and variation of communication opportunities we have in our everyday lives. Second, this framework can be used to think through and guide our communication choices—in terms of how much to disclose, how to present ourselves to others, and how much social presence or media richness we desire. Individuals make many different choices every day. In the opening vignette, Charee was trying to decide how to communicate with her friend about her mother's illness. In this case, she might decide that social presence/media richness was necessary for that interaction, and so would phone her. By contrast, when she wanted to ask her professor about a course requirement, she assumed that social presence or synchronicity was not required, so emailing would be a fine choice. A person may choose to switch media in the same conversation, depending on the topic. Our student Rosemary started getting into an argument with a friend on Facebook through posts and comments and then switched to private messaging to continue the discussion.

In addition to considering the content and context of a particular communication message, it is also helpful to consider carefully the other communicator in a mediated asynchronous lean message environment. How do you interpret a message that isn't responded to? Or a cryptic message from a friend after you send a message that you're feeling bad and you assume she knows you want some FtF time? How do you communicate to a romantic partner that you don't want to be in the relationship anymore? Or that you don't want so much "together time"? Perhaps the tried and true rhetorical guideline of "know your audience" is useful here. For example, Youngju knows that one of her friends is always on Facebook and that's the best way to contact her and she'll respond quickly to Youngju's post; another friend is a single mom, is rarely on FB but responds quickly to text messages. She has another friend who just doesn't respond very quickly to any messages. It can be several days before she responds to one of Youngju's messages. Knowing her audience helps her make decisions about interpreting and sending interactive media messages.

Another complicating issue of some interactive media is that your communication can potentially be seen and received by many different audiences. In FtF encounters, you

collapsing contexts

In social media, not knowing exactly who is reading one's posts.

spreadability

The ease with which content can be spread on social media.

know who you are addressing your message to. When Charee is talking to her mother or grandmother face-to-face, she tailors her messages specifically to them (and may use different communication styles and word choices than she would use with her close friends). However, when she posts on Facebook or sends a Tweet or she Snapchats, these messages can potentially be seen by many (even the snaps and chats), and she can't easily adapt her message to all these potential audiences. Scholar danah boyd (2014) describes this phenomenon as "**collapsing contexts**"—meaning we don't always know exactly who we are speaking to (what the communication context is) when we send a message on social media, and this leads to another characteristic of social media—"**spreadability**," which is the ease with which content can be spread. That is, our messages can be forwarded, retweeted, and quickly seen by hundreds of people, complicating our communication choices even more! This leads some individuals to create different Facebook pages, one with their real name which is more public and another with a name that only close friends can see, or using multiple SNSs for various "imagined audiences" (Choi & Bazarova, 2015). Our communication choices today are clearly challenging. We'll discuss further the topic of these communication choices in the next section on identity.

Although experts mostly agree on these characteristics of various media, they do not always agree on the specific impacts these characteristics have on our communication choices and relationships. Some experts point to the positive and some point to the negative aspects of interactive media. Some experts suggest that the digital future is only bright—bringing more connectivity, maximizing human potential, more civic engagement, democracy, and equality. Others point to the downside, and researchers even identity two types of digital stressors encountered by young people: (1) common forms of relational hostility now online (mean personal attacks, public shaming and humiliation, and impersonating someone else in order to harass them), and (2) stressful challenges in forming and maintaining intimacy (feeling smothered, pressure to provide access to accounts or nude photos, and breaking and entering into digital accounts and devices) (Weinstein & Selman, 2016).

However, seeing social media and technology in general as all good or all evil for human interaction is too simplistic. What is clear is that they play an increasingly important role in our lives and that people use multiple media in addition to FtF interactions to fit their social needs and lifestyles. It seems more useful to view interactive media through a dialectical lens. As we described in Chapters 8 (Communication Across Cultures) and 9 (Close Relationships), a dialectical perspective emphasizes simultaneous contradictory truths, recognizing that things may be "both/and"—both good and bad, strong and weak—and that we each have to navigate this media landscape, making the best choices we can. And this complexity of choice should not be a surprise, considering the pace of technology development and how much we still have to learn about interactive media capacities. With these thoughts in mind, let's look at a related topic—how personal identity is performed and managed in interactive media use.

Journal Prompt 14.3: Interactive Communication
Consider the following questions: What are key differences among various interactive media and face-to-face communication? What is the dialectical perspective on the benefits and challenges of interactive media?

Interactive Media and the Individual

14.4 Describe issues that can arise in identity and relationship development when using interactive media.

Clearly, interactive media use presents us with a range of choices, and those choices can have a powerful impact on communication between individuals in terms of identity, and in turn, personal relationships. Let's examine the way this works.

Managing Identity

The range of communication choices in interactive media has profound implications for how we manage our identity online. Social media provides many opportunities to be seen and admired and to self-disclose. At the same time, some media (Twitter, Internet forums) allow us to control the amount of information we disclose about ourselves. All these options provide a fluidity to our identities that we don't have in FtF communication. As we noted in Chapter 3, one's identity or self-concept is developed and expressed through communication with others. From the framework presented in the previous section, we can see that identity/self-presentation/self-disclosure would be most relevant to communication on blogs and SNSs. How do you present yourself and manage impressions that others have of you on these sites, given the characteristics and range of possibilities discussed in the previous section?

Self-Presentation Online   In using interactive media, you often make decisions about what kind of information to reveal about yourself. There seem to be three (overlapping) types of information that can be disclosed:

1. Standard information (for example, name, gender, profile picture);
2. Sensitive personal information—details that could be used to locate/identify or to threaten or harm (for example, email address, birthday, birth year, employer, job position, profile picture, photo albums);
3. Potentially stigmatizing information—information that could result in stigmatization within society (for example, religious views, political views, birth year, sexual orientation, photos).

An important question in deciding how much and what type of information to disclose: Who are your intended/"imagined" audiences? Some students see their Facebook profile/page as a professional platform, almost like a resume, where potential employers can read about their academic achievements and intern experiences. Others see it as a place to hang out with good friends and discuss the latest partying activities.

For young people working out issues around their sexual identity or sexual practices, participation in interactive media can be tricky. On the one hand, it can provide communities of support where they can develop identities consistent with their desires. For example, Jen a 21—year-old midwest transgender woman with a disapproving parent—appreciated the hundreds of transgender-themed websites and online forums and YouTube videos where she could access other transgender individuals talking about their transitions and their daily lives (e.g., how to shop in the boy's section instead of men's as a petite transgender woman). She created a Facebook page with her evolving female identity and photos and found spaces to vent and relax that were safer than the places she went in public with her support group, where people would gawk and make hateful comments (Cavalcante, 2016). On the other hand, for LGBT individuals, interactive media, especially given collapsing contexts, exposes them to potential discrimination or reactions from people they may not want to see certain aspects of their identity development (Dhoest & Szulc, 2016).

Perhaps one of the biggest challenges in how to present yourself and manage your online identity is that you don't know exactly who might be listening or reading. You may discover that your intended audience is not who is responding. For example, one student described his frustration when he posts messages about playing his latest favorite retro video game (Legend of Zelda) and his cousins make fun of his "lame" interest and mock him. Even worse, his sister also annoys him by responding to his posts intended for his friends ("fell asleep in boring Mr. K.'s class") when she plays the older sister role in her posts ("hey bro, you shouldn't do that, should be paying attention"). This shows the challenge of trying to control one's self-presentation online (Boyd, 2014). It's easier on some social media than others. Relatively speaking, your Facebook and Snapchat audiences are more known to you than your Twitter audience, so you're probably more careful about your self-disclosure and self presentation on Twitter than other media.

Sometimes young people have their intended self-presentation sabotaged by others—when friends tag them in photos or post photos of them engaging in activities they'd rather not have others see. Or they have been embarrassed (often intentionally) by their parents on their SNSs—who post inappropriate photos and/

lurkers

People who read, observe, but do not actively participate in online communities/sites.

or comments (Hindman, 2016). Another consequential audience is the **lurkers**, people who see and read material posted on SNSs but don't comment. Most lurkers are harmless, but underage users should remember that accepting "followers" they don't know could result in their photos and videos ending up on pedophile websites, especially given that Facebook has made it easier to search for public content (Barrett, 2015).

Some decisions about what to reveal on SNSs may be related to a person's age, with younger people disclosing more. One long-time Facebook user bemoaned her earlier days of FB postings, her four-year-long "lapse of judgment" following high school. She describes photos of herself where she was:

> sticking out my tongue, flopping on couches, stuffing my face with food, wearing too-short tops . . . attempting to show I was having an amaaaaazing time (whoooo!!!!), all in all, trying much, much too hard. There was an album titled, I'm cringing even now, "Bro'ing and Ho'ing out—Spring Break 07". (Bosker, 2014)

She goes on to say that her (millennial) generation seems less inclined now to make their lives an open book, are more selective in what they post on Facebook and opt for less public sharing—preferring Snapchat, private Picasa albums, and the one-on-one WhatsApp. When Facebook users were asked what they disliked about Facebook, the number-one response was people sharing too much information about themselves (Smith, 2014b). Oversharing can also have negative professional impacts; as we noted in Chapter 1, potential employers and college admissions officers can access your (and your friends') profile information, and many employers and admission committees admit to dismissing a candidate from consideration because of what they found on social networking sites (e.g., profanity, illegal/questionable behavior).

Interestingly, one recent study found a "privacy paradox," that although online users said they were concerned about privacy, their behaviors didn't seem to mirror those concerns because they reported revealing quite a bit of personal and sensitive information, especially if their friends and acquaintances also shared (Taddicken, 2014). This may reflect the widespread public assumption that privacy has been abandoned on the Internet, although some experts persuade us that choices can and should be made about online privacy (James, 2016). How do you make decisions about what to disclose? In addition to considering your "imagined audience," you might think about the impact of the information of others. One colleague complains about humblebragging and the disheartening feeling she has when she reads Facebook humblebrags (see *Did You Know: Humblebrag*).

humblebrag

Subtly letting others know about how fantastic your life is while undercutting it with a bit of self-effacing humor.

Disclosing information on SNSs is also related to other factors. For example, perhaps not surprisingly, people with low self-esteem tend to accept friend requests from people they don't know well, reveal more information about themselves, and present exaggerated information. For example, someone might say he plays in a band, when in reality his older brother plays in a band and he gets to play occasionally with them when they practice. In contrast, popular users tend to disclose information strategically to further enhance their popularity—for example, changing their profile picture often to show them having fun at parties, public events, and traveling and changing their Facebook profiles often to note new activities or interests (Tazghini & Siedlecki, 2012; Zywica & Danowski, 2008). Additionally, single people tend to reveal more demographic and personal information, probably because they feel that information is needed to attract partners (Nosko, Wood, & Molema, 2010).

Another aspect of self-presentation is listing friendship links, and on SNSs, "friends" can be used to provide context—to remind users of the imagined audiences they hope to interact with. But adding too many friends can have the opposite effect—raising doubts about one's popularity and desirability (Jarrett, 2015). Fascination with fame and celebrity is associated with more frequent Facebook and Twitter use, for example, following celebrities and trying to integrate them into their own social networks (Greenwood, 2013).

Critical Thinking Prompt

How many personal details do you think people should disclose on their SNS pages? Is there any information that you think should be routinely disclosed? Never disclosed? How much do you disclose? Why?

DID YOU KNOW?
Humblebrag

The term 'humblebrag,' first coined by comedian Harris Wittels, an NBC writer for the series "Parks and Recreation," made its way into the urban dictionary in May of 2011. How do you react to humblebrags? with humor? Distain? Why do people humblebrag? What effect are they aiming for?

In the *New York Times*, Henry Alford (2012) contrasts the humblebrag with outright bragging as angling for sympathy in addition to awe, as opposed to just plain awe. He also categorizes humblebrags into three recurring themes of self-promotion, branding oneself as: "'I have too much work'; 'I am an idiot/impostor'; or 'I have firsthand knowledge of the gritty gilt to be found inside the gilded cage.'" Some examples:

> Too much work: Broadway actress Kerry Butler ("I've been signing so many autographs lately, that I was writing a card to my dad and started to write my last name!!")

> Idiocy: Joe Jonas ("Totally walked down the wrong escalator at the airport from the flashes of the cameras ... Go me")

> Gilded cage: Comedian Dane Cook, a megatweeter: "Being famous and having a fender bender is weird. You want to be upset but the other driver's just thrilled & giddy that it's you."

Not only famous people humblebrag. Every person reading this probably has more than a handful of friends who humblebrag from time to time about accomplishments or forward strides. The danger now is to assume that every publicly shared piece of good news has an element of the humblebrag within it. The truth is that if we really know our Facebook or Instagram friends, we'll know the spirit behind a post that can easily be read differently from a random person. We'll want to laugh at silly mishaps even when a friend is doing better than us, and we'll want to help celebrate when good news is shared that puts them ahead of us. Why should we have to choose just one emotion to feel toward someone?

Since 2011, Wittels has turned his term into a book entitled "Humblebrag: The Art of False Modesty," while there are multiple online Humblebrag Halls of Fame, and some people have even begun countering this phenomenon with the anti-humblebrag, or the 'underbrag,' where they post about genuine failures, like face-plants in mud.

Source: Alford, H. (Nov. 30, 2012). If I Do Humblebrag So Myself.

Anonymity and Psuedoanonymity   When you communicate via Twitter or in an online forum, or post a comment on YouTube, others may not know your age, gender, race, nationality, or many of the other cues that affect perceptions of individuals. However, it seems that there is increasingly less opportunity for anonymity online as more and more of our lives and information about our "real" selves is posted, persistent, and available for searching. The old adage of "There are no erasers on the Internet" is still very true. Getting rid of information once it's out on the Internet can be difficult, if not impossible. For example, if you deactivate your Facebook account, the information remains stored on the website. To entirely delete your Facebook account (not just deactivate it), you have to complete a form and it may take up to 90 days for Facebook to delete everything associated with your account and you will not be able to reaccess it (Curtis, 2017).

The degree to which people should be able to remain anonymous online has been vigorously debated. When Facebook founders instituted a "real name policy" in 2014, saying that real names allow people to better connect to their offline friends, there was vigorous opposition from various groups including the ACLU of California, Human Rights Watch, and others. For example, drag queens, locked out of their Facebook accounts for using "fake" names, protested that forcing them and other "gender non-normative people" to use their legal names was discriminatory. Likewise, victims of abuse, stalking, or bullying use aliases to hide from perpetrators (MacAulay & Moldes, 2016). In response, Facebook relaxed their policy in 2015 (Holpuch, 2015).

There are at least three issues in the complex relationship between anonymity and identity in online communication. The first has to do with the informative aspect of the identity. On the one hand, knowing something about the person sending information gives a context for judging his or her messages. If you know, for example, that the person answering your medical question online is a doctor, that person seems more credible than a person who does not have a medical degree. On the other hand, because information on age, gender, and race can form the basis for stereotyping and prejudice, some anonymity presents the possibility of interactions somewhat free of prejudice.

A second issue regarding anonymity is its capacity to liberate speech. For example, without knowing who has issued a statement, the legal restrictions on speech are difficult to enforce. So if someone is misrepresenting oneself online and makes racist or libelous statements, it is almost impossible to implement legal sanctions. On the other hand, anonymity can give people courage to express unpopular opinions or question conventional wisdom, which they might be afraid to do in FtF interaction (e.g., websites such as 4Chan and Yik Yak;) (van der Nagel & Frith, 2015). Some young people find anonymity gives a sense of freedom that they don't have on SNSs where parents or other authority figures are always watching, or even on sites or online games where they construct a pseudo identity (boyd, 2014).

The third and final issue related to anonymity is that in some ways, the freedom that people feel as a result of their anonymity may lead them to be less responsible communicators. Five of these irresponsible behaviors are discussed below: trolling, spam messages, phishing, cuberbullying, and deceptive message. For example, anonymity can lead to irresponsible and destructive online behavior, like **trolling** (Fichman & Sanfilipo, 2016). Recent examples include how male online players denigrate, harass, and drive off female would-be gamers, and how anti-Chinese racism is expressed in hostile in-game interactions and in YouTube rants (Cisneros & Nakayama, 2015; Nakayama, 2017; Reagle, 2015). In addition, anonymity facilitates email rumors and hoaxes (e.g., the suggestion that swallowing active dry yeast before drinking alcohol prevents you from getting drunk) and fake news stories (e.g., that Hillary Clinton was linked to a secret underground human trafficking ring or that the Pope endorsed Donald Trump for president). These stories were eventually traced to fake publishers in a small town in Macedonia called Veles, where apparently 140 fake news sites are based (Ritchie, 2016). For information about evaluating these types of messages, check out Snopes.com.

Also annoying are the millions of spam messages (unwanted commercial messages and advertisements sent through email), which might be greatly reduced if addresses or spammers' identities were easier to trace. **Phishing**—the practice of trying fraudulently to get consumer banking/credit card or other personal information, such as usernames, passwords, Social Security numbers—is another problem for interactive media users. Ever increasing numbers of fake emails are "warning" users that their account information needs to be updated and then pointing to websites that ask the user to enter personal or financial information (King, 2016). Although technology companies and banks aggressively pursue those who send spam and phishing messages, apprehending and prosecuting them is difficult (Kleinman, 2014). This leads to a good reason to be careful about how much personal information to disclose on SNSs; spammers have used freely accessible profile data from SNSs to craft phishing schemes that appear to originate from a friend on the network. Targets are much more likely to give away information to this "friend" than to a perceived "stranger."

Another form of bad behavior online is **cyberbullying**—"the deliberate and repeated misuse of communication technology by an individual or group to threaten or harm others" (Roberto & Eden, 2010, p. 198). Cyberbullying differs from traditional bullying partly because it is anonymous, it can occur anywhere (through voice, text, picture, or video messages on cell phones and through social networking sites, chat rooms, and so on), and an infinite number of viewers can observe or participate. Research shows that cyberbullying can have many negative consequences for victims, ranging from psychological problems such as depression, anxiety, and low self-esteem to disastrous consequences, as in the tragic case of Tyler Clementi, who committed suicide after being harassed by his roommate, who used a webcam to spy on his trysts with another man and then sent tweets with info about how others could watch the hookups (Boyle, 2012). Some experts report that approximately 25 percent of minors are victims of

trolling
Posting Internet messages meant to intentionally anger or frustrate in order to provoke reactions from others.

phishing
The practice of trying fraudulently to get consumer banking and credit card information.

cyberbullying
The deliberate and repeated misuse of communication technology by an individual or group to threaten or harm others.

cyberbullying and about 15 percent admit that they cyberbullied others, leading many schools to implement cyberbullying prevention programs. Communities are also beginning to seriously enforce anticyberbullying laws (Ferman, 2014; Patchin, 2014). Students, who are gay, lesbian, bisexual, transgender, or queer (LGBTQ), are often the targets of bullies, and some experts suggest that bullying is not always just aggressive behavior, but often reflects the socially accepted norm of marginalizing those outside the norm. They propose rethinking intervention programs to include challenges to the culturally accepted and perpetuated inequities regarding gender, racial, ethnic, and sexual identities (Payne & Smith, 2013). An example of online antibully support is the "It Gets Better" campaign, a collection of video messages by adult LGBTQ individuals offering stories of support to young gay teens suffering from homophobic bullying (Gal et al., 2015).

▲ Players of MMORPGs invent new identities by creating avatars.

The final form of bad online behavior related to anonymity is deception. If you have represented yourself as something you are not on a Facebook or other social media profile, you are not alone. Many people say they put false information on their social networking sites and they give many reasons for doing so. In some cases, it's a strategy for projecting a more positive image (e.g., lying about one's salary, weight, achievements), or for some, it's about achieving privacy because they become more and more aware of the consequences of having their posted information taken out of context. Fabricating data on these sites may protect from unwanted advances from strangers, but for young people, it can also shield them from the watchful eyes of their parents (boyd, 2014), or be a strategy for finding out what "friends" think of them by starting an online conversation about oneself, using a false identity.

However, some children are lying about their age to create accounts on SNSs, and engaging in other risky online behaviors leaving them open to fraud and predators (Byrne, Katz, Linz, & Mcilrath et al., 2014; Notten & Nikken, 2016), although some experts think the media focus on online risks to children is misplaced. They say that children and teens who engage in risky behavior online are often struggling offline (with unsafe home environments, addicted parents, etc.) and that in fact technology can often help keep children safe (boyd, 2014).

Beyond anonymity is the phenomenon of **pseudoanonymity**, or projecting a "false" identity. For example, people can invent identities through acceptable means, for example, in online sites (e.g., Reddit) where users create a screen name that follows them across the site or on MMORPG virtual worlds where they create **avatars**. These sites afford people the opportunity to construct alternate identities, different from those in their offline world of school and work. There are rarely negative consequences because this "deception" is expected.

To summarize, interactive media technologies afford many possibilities for performing and managing identities, but these possibilities should be balanced with consideration of safety and ethical concerns, as well as impression management concerns. Let's now turn our attention to how relationships develop and are maintained through interactive media.

pseudoanonymity
Projecting a false identity.

avatars
Digital alter egos or versions of oneself, used in MMORPGs.

Relationship Development

You probably have some relationships that exist only online, such as with acquaintances you met in an online course or on an SNS, although it appears that people use SNSs less to make new friends and more to strengthen relationships with their existing friends. Let's consider the impact of mediated communication on three types of relationships: friendships, romantic relationships, and relationships in the workplace.

Friendships   Although online and offline relationships have much in common, interactive media can affect our relational development in at least a couple significant ways. First, you can come into contact with many more people online than you ever would in person, so online relationships may offer many more potential partners than offline life.

Second, relationships that are initiated or maintained through interactive media also overcome limits of time and space. You do not have to (ever) be in close proximity to these people and you do not (ever) have to exchange messages at the same time, and you can stay in close contact almost 24/7. What are the implications of these characteristics for these relationships?

There has been much debate about whether social media in particular yield overall positive or negative effects on relationships. A summary of recent research suggests that social media have a range of positive psychological outcomes, providing greater feelings of belonging and keeping up with friends and providing shy students with a sense of social support (Jarrett, 2015). This suggests that SNS communication does not replace intimacy or FtF communication. However, users also reported more loneliness than nonusers, especially males; so maybe heavy SNS use also increases feelings of isolation and loneliness (Brandtzaeg, 2012).

It is clear that we cannot assume that interactive media has all positive (or negative) effects on communication or relationships. For this reason, we prefer a dialectical view of interactive media's affect on relationships and assume that *interactive media BOTH strengthens AND weakens relationships.*

The lack of nonverbal cues on some media can weaken relationships. Not being able to see the expression on your friend's face while she texts about a problem she's having might result in you not realizing how unhappy she is. However, media scholars also point out that the reduced nonverbal cues can have a positive effect on communication because these cues (such as appearance or accent) can sometimes trigger stereotypes. For example, viewing tweets or mobile messages, we may not be able to determine someone's race, gender, age, ability–disability and so are less likely to show prejudice or discrimination in social media communication.

Similarly, asynchronicity may weaken personal relationships because the notion of friendship includes shared experiences, feelings, and activities. So, when you receive terrific news that you want to share with your best friend, telling him or her through a delayed message (if your friend does not immediately respond to your chat) does not have the same impact that a FtF conversation or phone call would.

However, media scholars also point out that the asynchronicity of mediated messages can have positive effects on relationships. For example, it can give people time to formulate a message, which can be helpful for shy people and others as well (Baker & Oswald, 2010). In fact, in one study, young people explained that although there were often misunderstandings, they preferred mobile messaging over other forms of communication partly because it gave them more time to reflect and think about what they were trying to express (Coyne, Stockdale, Busby, Iverson, & Grant, 2011). Asynchronicity, allowing the time to formulate thoughts into words, can also be useful when communicating in a foreign language (Thompson & Ku, 2005).

Online relationships may be both more durable and fragile. An example of the greater durability of online relationships is that if you have a relationship that is strictly online and you relocate to a faraway place, the relationship may not be affected. By contrast, digital relationships can be somewhat more fragile, partly because they require some skepticism.

As we discussed previously, deception frequently occurs in the initial stages of digital relationships. There are also people who drop out because they find the pressures of social media "performance" too stressful (agonizing over how to present themselves, which photos to post, whether their photos and music picks are "cool" enough, and so on) (Turkle, 2011). Or sometimes because discussions become too politically contentious, causing damage to their relationships. As one FB user posted after the 2016 presidential election:

> "The election was the last straw for me. In the days after, all I saw was hate. From both sides. . . . I decided that day to get rid of my original Facebook and create my 'new' Facebook . . . full of running, bikes, breweries, cat videos, satire, art, music, hiking, food, and good people. . . . (Selyukh, 2016)

How can you effectively navigate social networking sites, for example, where online relationships are developed? Because the information you post on SNSs is potentially accessed by hundreds or thousands of people, you should consider carefully how much and what type of information you post. It's useful to ask yourself: Do you know who has access to the information? Do you know how it will be used? How much information do you want to share with others?

Romantic Relationships   Who becomes involved in online romantic relationships, and how does online romance differ from in-person romance? According to one survey, the number of online dating sites/and e apps (especially by young adults) has tripled since 2013 (Smith & Anderson, 2016b). Many online romance sites feature a scientific approach, which often includes compatibility and personality testing and seems to cover all ages and income levels (Match, OkCupid, eHarmony, Coffee meets Bagel, Hinge, and Bumble). Some focus more on hook-ups than dating per se (e.g., Tinder), specialize in niche marketing focusing on religion (Jewish, Catholic, Christian), race/ethnicity (interracial, Black, Latino), or age (OurTime for singles older than 50). Others use matching activities, such as music (Tastebuds) or social gaming (Tagged), or as mentioned previously, physical location (Tinder, Happn; Digital Trends Staff, 2017).

There are several benefits of online romantic relationships: the ease of finding similar others and of achieving intimate exchanges—as there is already information known about the other (physical characteristics, hobbies, political and religious attitudes, etc.) prior to meeting. However, developing online relationships poses dangers and can provide opportunities for deception (as described in *It Happened to Me: Jacqueline*). One study found that older daters were more likely to misrepresent age, and men were more likely to misrepresent personal assets and interests, attributes, and relationship goals. Women were more likely to misrepresent weight (Hall, Park, Song, & Cody, 2010). However, online daters also report that they usually assume some deception and learn to "correct" for it: "One woman mentioned that if a profile said a man was 5'11" she would assume he was probably 5'9"; a man said that if a woman said she was 'average' body type, he would assume she was slightly heavy" (Heino, Ellison, & Gibbs, 2010).

And as noted previously, more serious deception can occur with the practice of **catfishing**—creating an intentionally deceptive social media profile, sometimes even

catfishing
Creating an intentionally deceptive social media profile.

She knew that her online boyfriend would be just as sensitive in person.

including fake photos, bios, friends, and so on, often with the goal of making a romantic connection. Of course, the person who is catfishing needs to avoid any offline contact with the intended target and the motivation may be a search for a close relationship, or the satisfaction of manipulating another (D'Costa, 2014). More sinister, even criminal motives are increasingly prevalent; many people have been swindled out of money by someone who poses as a potential suitor and asks for money after gaining the trust and interest of a dating partner (Flacy, 2014). Despite the potential risks, people can and do form close, lasting relationships online. Many of the same things that make offline romantic relationships work are important in online relationships, like intimacy, trust, and communication satisfaction. *In fact*, it appears that interactive media and constant connectivity *can* strengthen romantic relationships. Although not replacing FtF expressions of affection, a quick mobile message to say "I luv u :)" or a phone call while doing routine errands enables couples to continue expressing affection throughout the day. Interestingly, in one study married heterosexual couples used a larger variety of media (phone, social networking, blogs, and webcams) than dating couples (Coyne, 2011).

It Happened to Me
Jacqueline

My first year in college I met a guy in one of my online courses—we were on the same team for our group project. We seemed to have a lot in common. We had the same major, film studies, and we talked a lot about our favorite (obscure) movies and traded recommendations for movie watching. He said he wasn't on Facebook, which seemed a little odd to me, but we mostly communicated through text messages and some phone conversations. We lived about 50 miles apart and finally did get together a few times. Finally, I found out (through another student in the class) that he did have a Facebook page—using his middle name—and a wife and two kids! I felt betrayed and was much more cautious after that about forming friendships in online courses.

However, there are also downsides to the constant connectivity of new media in maintaining romantic relationships. Experts have found that the use of Facebook is associated with increased jealousy in romantic relationships and relational dissatisfaction (Elphinston, 2011). For example, one young woman describes how her boyfriend reads all her messages when she's not looking. Similarly, the connectedness of mobile messaging can be seen as stifling or even as harassing if one partner insists on constant communication: "So my boyfriend is constantly txting me every minute of everyday . . . he's becoming really clingy with it. what should i do???" (Weinstein & Selman, 2016). And some individuals (more than 40 percent of respondents in one study!) complain that their partners are too distracted by cellphones. Others argue about the amount of time their partners spend on particular online activities (Lenhart & Duggan, 2014).

Terminating romantic relationships, given all the communication choices, can be particularly challenging. In one study, researcher Illana Gershon (2010) interviewed college students about their media choices in breaking up with a romantic partner. Although almost all said that face-to-face was the most appropriate way to end a relationship, they often chose interactive media for various stages of breakup. The particular communication form chosen varied a great deal, and they believed the particular choice affected the message that was sent but didn't always agree on the particular effect (e.g., some saw texting as intimate because the phone is always with you, whereas others saw it as distancing because of message length limit), which often complicated the relationship negotiation. Some used a variety of media, initiating the breakup by text, then talking on the phone and finishing by face-to-face. A few ended relationships by changing their Facebook status, because they didn't want to deal with the partner's reaction over the phone or face-to-face.

Now, after a breakup, it's much more difficult to digitally disconnect from a former partner in every sense. This is probably why around 2014, clauses called "social media clauses" began appearing in prenuptial agreements, protecting exes from potentially embarrassing aftermaths with belated releases of demeaning photographic or textual data (Rothenburg, 2014). Unflattering disclosures aside, navigating media waters can almost turn into digital posturing and mind games, where articles from thrillist.com and GQ advise readers how not to let an ex "win," in the "get the better of your sanity" sense. Tips include publicly posting evidence of postbreakup outings, even if it's just getting ice cream, and unfollowing, instead of unfriending, an ex on social media platforms. Now, what used to be a private ritual of trashing that shoebox of mementos becomes public when you delete every former photo or album with an ex. A certain amount of postbreakup stalking is to be expected, so online advisors to men and women alike tell readers not to show how much they're hurting by artificially trying to erase history. GQ author Ella Ceron even advises her male readers to strategically ask friends to post photos of them and tag them, not to look too obvious. The question is, if you are devoting this much mental energy to stage your life postbreakup, then are you going to truly move forward? (Ceron, 2015; King, 2015).

Work Relationships   Most workers report that communication technologies have improved their ability to do their job, share ideas with coworkers, and work in a flexible way. For example, one software company has seventeen employees at three locations: Phoenix, Arizona; Cape Cod, Massachusetts; and Philadelphia, Pennsylvania. All their documents are in cloud storage; they communicate regularly through Yammer. They have monthly video conference meetings and meet face-to-face from time to time. These inter-active technologies mean that none of the employees had to relocate when they were hired, and through media technologies, they stay connected and productive. Although interactive technologies generally have positive effects on work relationships, some con-cerns exist. According to a recent study, many workers think that these technologies result in longer hours and increased stress levels because they sometimes are expected to read email and be available for phone calls after work [note: France recently passed a law estab-lishing workers "right to disconnect"—requiring companies with more than 50 employees to denote hours when employees must refrain from sending or answering work emails (Morris, 2017)]. The impact of technology on work varies, however, depending on the type of relationship—whether it is a superior–subordinate relationship or a peer relationship.

Superior–Subordinate Communication   At least three areas of concern center on interactive media in the workplace: status and boundary issues, surveillance issues, and confidentiality issues. A major impact of online communication in the workplace is its status-leveling effect. With email, anyone can have instant access to superiors and this status leveling can raise boundary issues: How much online interaction is appropriate between boss and employees? Should you ask to friend your boss on Facebook? Should a supervisor request to friend a subordinate? Most experts say not—because it blurs the work–personal relationships in unproductive ways (Calderon, 2013). However, at least one CEO disagrees. David Kalt, CEO of Reverb.com, says he always does just that–friends all new employees on Facebook. His reasoning is that this virtual connec-tion "paves the way for a better real-life connection," and most employees, especially millennials, want purpose at work, to feel connected to their coworkers and to be heard by others, including their CEO. He does admit that this strategy can backfire—exposing CEOs to unwanted inappropriate info but he still thinks it's worth it (Kalt, 2017).

Communication technologies also give superiors a way of checking up on subor-dinates. Messages sent through email may be stored forever on company servers, so management can monitor employees' correspondence. Also, if you are Facebook friends with an employee, you can check his or her account and see if it is used during the day when they are at work!

Technological surveillance occurs in many ways in the workplace. In fact some "monitoring" happens prior to being hired. According to one report, 52 percent of companies now check job applicants' social media profiles before hiring them (Kumar, 2015). However, they must be careful about accessing certain information (e.g, any legally protected characteristics including age, disability, pregnancy, race, religion, and so on that would not otherwise be apparent in a face-to-face interview) as an applicant could claim that a decision not to hire was based on that characteristic (Choi, 2014).

Many companies monitor employee email and Internet usage, and web-based security cameras are increasingly common. Also, technologies such as GPS and employee badges with radio frequency identification (RFID) tags provide an even higher level of employee monitoring. These tracking systems can record, display, and archive the exact location of any employee—both inside and outside the office—at any time. Other software allows employers to see every photo, text message, or email sent from employees and also monitor their social media use. These monitoring policies are somewhat controversial. Some say that keeping an eye on employees (including employees' social media use) helps companies protect themselves, as disgruntled employees can easily go on social media and criticize customers, harass subordinates, damaging a company's reputation. Others say no, that monitoring is too often a fishing expedition that wastes important time and resources (i.e., employees, especially millennials, are experts at controlling and manipulating their online presence) and should only be done when there is a solid reason to suspect employee wrongdoing (Kumar, 2015). Some employees view surveillance as a violation of privacy, and one study showed that workers who were electronically monitored reported higher levels of job boredom, psychological stress, depression, anger, and fatigue (Brustein, 2013).

Another issue concerns decisions about what should be handled in person or online. Just as in romantic relationships, bad news (termination, negative job performance reviews) should probably be communicated in person. By contrast, communicating electronically gives workers the opportunity to think carefully about their communication before sending it, but it can result in misunderstandings.

Peer Communication   Although interactive media may make the communication between workers more efficient and effective, access to certain kinds of information often decreases when one relies on online communication. For example, in FtF work contexts, you can observe colleagues in the next office during meetings and talk with them in the halls or mailroom, but if you communicate online with a coworker at a different location, you have little information about them. This lack of information increases uncertainty as well as the potential for disagreements and misunderstanding, as one of our students describes in *It Happened to Me: Mei-Lin*. As we discussed in Chapter 10, to minimize these misunderstandings and build trust among personnel, some employers try to arrange periodic FtF meetings or even promote social networking communication among coworkers.

To summarize, interactive media provides opportunities and challenges for relationship development and maintenance, and each type of relationship, whether a friendship, a romance, or a work relationship, has unique challenges. When we expand the frame of reference beyond individuals, as we do in the next section, we encounter a new set of new media-related issues and challenges—those posed by societal forces.

It Happened to Me
Mei-Lin

I sent an urgent email to a colleague requesting information for a report I was writing. He didn't respond, and I became very irritated at his lack of response. A few days later, I found out that his child had been in a serious accident, and he missed work for several days. If we had been located in the same office, I would have known immediately what was wrong, would have responded more appropriately to his absence, and could have gotten the information I needed in some other way.

Journal Prompt 14.4: Anonymity Concerns
Consider the following questions: What are three identity concerns that result from the anonymity afforded by some new media forms? How do these concerns relate to staying safe when using social media?

The Individual, Communication Technology, and Society

14.5   Understand the role of power and privilege in interactive media use.

All media activities—whether for fun, socializing, or information seeking—are enacted by humans within a social context and the larger society. These activities both reflect and influence larger societal norms. For example, some of the same social hierarchies that exist in the larger society also exist in the realm of interactive media. When we sort people out by various identities (for example, gender, ethnicity, or race), we find differences not only in how many of them use communication technologies, but also in how they are perceived to use these media. In this section, we'll first look at how various identities influence technology use and then examine some of the inequalities in communication technologies use.

Gender, Age, Ethnicity, and Technology Use

Does technology use vary with gender, along traditional gender roles—with men being more action oriented and females more interpersonally oriented? The answer, it turns out, is somewhat. Males are more likely than females to play online games and to play a larger variety of games, although female players are increasing in numbers (Galarneau, 2014). Hacking also seems to be a predominantly male activity and most computer code is written by males (Humphreys & Vered, 2014). Men participate more in online political activities than women (Wei, 2012). Not surprisingly, more men than women tend to major in and pursue careers in computer science or other technology-related fields (Vitores & Gil-Juárez, 2016).

Women tend to email more and are more likely to use and access social networking sites in general (Greenwood et al., 2016). This is particularly true of Pinterest; women are almost three times as likely as men to access Pinterest, and also access Facebook and Instagram at slightly higher rates than men. Nevertheless, some of the conventional stereotypes about gender are unfounded. For example, some evidence shows males and females having equal levels of computer skills (Cheong, 2008), and it seems that both genders are equally likely to shop online and take online courses. Taken together, then, this evidence suggests that the use of communication technologies only partially reflects and reinforces gender roles and stereotypes.

It should be noted, however, that while gender inequality in uses has lessened, societal norms about what is acceptable or inacceptable online behavior vary greatly, especially when it comes to sexting and related activities. Focus group studies show that young men's sharing digital photos of their own nudity, their bodily functions or even sharing female friends' nude photos without permission are often viewed as funny, daring, even part of male bonding, and with little negative consequence. In contrast, young women engaging in the same behaviors are labeled "attention sluts" or whores and are socially shamed and humiliated (Salter, 2016).

How do other identities—such as age—interact with interactive media use? As one might expect, young people are still more comfortable with new technologies than older folks, and they tend to use communication technologies in more and different ways (Smith 2014c; Wei, 2012). The younger you are, the more likely you are to use a variety of social media (Facebook, Instagram, Twitter) and messaging apps, (WhatsApp or Kik) and especially those apps that are auto deleting and anonymous (Snapchat, Wickr) than are older people (Greenwood et al., 2016). Young people are also more likely to not use Internet at home but depend on smartphone for most Internet activities, for example, shopping (Mobile Fact Sheet, 2017; Smith & Anderson, 2016a). However, the stereotype of older people avoiding technology is somewhat inaccurate. Although older folks do tend to use interactive media less, the number of older people (age 50 and older) who visit SNSs has increased significantly in the last few years (Greenwood et al., 2016).

Social media use also varies somewhat with race. It turns out that the Black American presence on Twitter is significant, and several communication experts have studied the "Black Twitter" phenomenon (Wortham, 2016). It seems that many Blacks (not all!) seem to use Twitter differently than other racial/ethnic groups. They form tighter clusters on the network; that is, they follow one another more readily, retweet each other more often, and more of their posts are @-replies (directed at other users). While much tweeting is playful, much is focused on political activism, feeding a loop of online and offline actions and demonstrations. There was the #BlackLivesMatter topic mentioned earlier in the chapter and also #OscarsSoWhite in 2015, protesting the complete lack of any person of color in four major acting categories, which led to national visibility, and eventually some actors boycotting the Oscar event (Brock, 2012; Wotham, 2016). Some experts suggest that

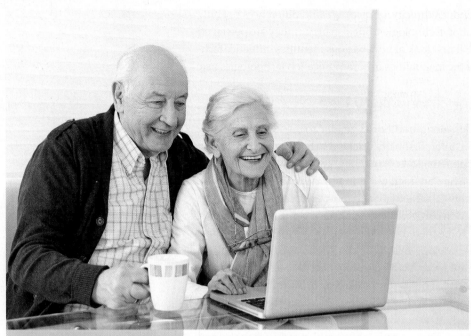

▲ The number of older people who visit SNSs has increased significantly in the last few years.

Twitter is particularly conducive to the strong participative oral traditions within many Black communities—the "call and response" between minister and congregation or the "playin' the dozens," which are playful back and forth insults (Brock, 2012; Florini, 2014).

Concerning race and gender in online gaming—the gaming population is more diverse now because smartphones and tablets make gaming more accessible and the population of gamers worldwide includes female gamers, people of different racial and cultural backgrounds, and gamers of varying ages (Anderson, 2015; Cheong & Gray, 2011). However, Hispanics are more likely than whites or blacks to categorize themselves as gamers and Blacks generally hold more positive views about video games than Whites or Hispanics (Anderson, 2015). Stereotypes of ethnic, racial, and gender groups still persist somewhat online. Studies show that characters in video games are overwhelmingly White and male. Outside of sports video games, only a few Black characters exist, and they are mostly portrayed as sidekicks, athletes, rappers, and gangsters. Latinos and Native Americans are extremely underrepresented as video game characters; female characters are more likely to be represented by partially nude avatars of an unrealistic body type (Ong, 2016). However, almost half of American adults surveyed in one report (regardless of race or ethnicity) said they were unsure whether video games portray minority groups poorly. However, this may be because gaming has not been subject to racial and gender bias scrutiny like other popular culture produces and this lack of publicity could explain why a typical video game player might not think of these issues when thinking of video games (Anderson, 2015).

As you can see, people use social media in different ways and not everyone is equally represented in the communication technology revolution, nor does everyone have equal access to digital life and cyberspace, which is perhaps the most important way that societal forces affect interactive media use.

Power, Access, and Digital Inequalities

It would be a mistake to think that the United States is the most technologically advanced country. For example, South Koreans did their banking by mobile phone years ago and have more mobile phones per capita than in almost any other country; it's not uncommon in Singapore and other Asian cities for restaurant goers to order their food from their own tableside computer tablet menu, or tourists to be provided a smartphone during their stay for easy access to web info and for texting, phone calls, and so on (Avanti, 2015; Woodhouse, 2015). On the highways in the Gauteng urban region in South Africa, overhead electronic camera tracking (e-tolling) monitors individual motorists (through e-tags on license plates) and eliminates toll booths and related traffic slowdowns. However, in many other countries, only a tiny fraction of the population has access to computers and the Internet, and according to a recent Pew Internet and American Life Project report, about 15 percent of Americans are not online at all—unchanged since 2013 (Anderson & Perrin, 2017).

The inequality of access between the technology "haves" and the "have nots"—once referred to as the **digital divide**—is probably more accurately viewed now as a continuum of digital inequalities rather than a divide (Wei, 2012). These inequalities exist within the United States and also on a global scale. Although there is high Internet access and mobile connectivity in Western Europe, North America, and East Asia, usage in developing countries—especially in Africa—is sparse. In Africa, mobile Internet connectivity is 29 percent, compared with 80 percent in East Asia, 17 percent in South Asia, 70 percent in Southeast Asia, 32 percent in Central Asia; 64 percent in the Middle East, 47 percent in Latin America, 75 percent in South America, 97 percent in Western Europe, 93 percent in Oceania (Australia, New Zealand), and 95 percent in North America (Digital Trends, 2017). Many developing countries lack landline services, but their mobile phone usage is growing exponentially; it's estimated that 95 percent of the world's population now owns a cellphone and even in Africa, 81 percent of the population has mobile connectivity (Global Digital Statistics, 2017), allowing people to connect in ways never possible before (James, 2014).

▲ Cultural capital includes the knowledge enabling people to make use of interactive media.

Why do differences in digital access and use matter? In a global information society, information is an important commodity that everyone needs to function. In addition, to function effectively in society, people need **cultural capital** (Bourdieu, 1986), or certain bodies of cultural knowledge and cultural competencies. Those with the most power in a society decide what constitutes cultural capital, and it is passed down from parents to children, just as economic capital is.

In the United States and much of the world, cultural capital includes the ability to use communication technologies in appropriate ways, and digital exclusion is one of the most damaging forms of exclusion in our increasingly digitized world. What hinders people from acquiring **technocapital**, that is, access to technological skills and resources? Without these skills and knowledge, one can feel disconnected from the center of society (Wei, 2012). For example, a researcher told of a man who had little experience with computers. When the man went for a haircut, he was told to check in online, either with his phone or on the computer at the counter. He was too embarrassed to admit not knowing how to do this, so he left the shop without getting a haircut. Why is this man on the far side of the digital inequalities continuum? What factors keep him, and others, from having digital technocapital?

Who Has Access to Interactive Media?   Inequalities in digital access and usage is decreasing in some ways. For example, gender differences in digital access—once a feature underlying the digital divide in the United States—have all but disappeared, and cellphone ownership is almost universal. Racial and ethnic disparities are also shrinking for some media use, especially the more recent technologies. However, some experts say that disparities based on race, income, education, and physical ability persist. Let's look more closely at what they mean by this statement.

Although all smartphone users can access the Internet by phone, Blacks and especially Latinos are more likely than Whites to rely *only* on mobile phones because they are less likely to have access to a computer or broadband Internet at home, therefore being

digital divide

Inequity of access between the technology "haves" and "have nots."

cultural capital

Cultural knowledge and cultural competencies that people need to function effectively in society.

technocapital

Access to technological skills and resources.

▲ Gender, race, ethnicity, and age influence technology use to varying degrees.

multimodality

The range or breadth of Internet activities.

crowdfunding

The process of raising money online—often many small amounts from a large number of people.

"smartphone dependent." The same is true for less educated and lower-income and disabled Americans in all ethnic and racial groups—people who make less than $30,000 and people with less than a high school education) (Mobile Fact Sheet, 2017). What are the implications? It is difficult or impossible to accomplish some important activities with a smartphone, such as updating a résumé and conducting a job search online. In addition, they are more likely than other users to run up against data-cap limits and more frequently have to cancel or suspend service due to financial constraints (Horrigan & Duggan, 2015). Thus, these ethnic and socioeconomic groups are at a disadvantage, which illustrates the new configuration of digital inequalities; it has to do with how one *uses* interactive media. Communication scholar Lu Wei suggests that to understand digital inequalities, we should measure the number of online activities one engages in (**multimodality**), not just whether one has access to the Internet or a particular media device (like a smartphone). That is, the more digital activities one pursues (e.g., check email, log on to Facebook, write on Twitter, share a video on YouTube, post a picture on Tumblr, move money from one account to another on a banking site, and update and post a resume on LinkedIn), the more digitally empowered one is.

In addition, interactive media have been used successfully by advocates of social change, enabling organizers to reach many people quickly to recruit people, organize collective action, raise money, and increase communication with decision makers. For example, social media played an especially prominent role in the millions of dollars raised for amyotrophic lateral sclerosis (ALS) research during the "Ice Bucket Challenge" in summer 2014. Participants who were nominated (usually via social media like Facebook, Twitter, Instagram) were filmed (and posted on social media) having a bucket of ice water poured on their heads and then nominating others to do the same. When nominated, participants usually had 24 hours to comply or forfeit by way of a charitable financial donation.

Similar efforts are often realized through **crowdfunding** (closely related to crowdsourcing, discussed earlier), where users can raise money from a variety of donors in small increments for projects as diverse as making baby-kits for refugees to funding personal yoga trips. GoFundMe raised the most funds in 2014, $470 million, and to date, has raised over $3 billion for personal fundraisers. Kickstarter and Indiegogo are two other popular platforms, although Kickstarter distinguishes itself by only funding creative, group projects. There are also crowdfunding sites such as Kiva that enable people from third world countries who cannot afford bank loans to crowdfund temporary loans. However, other evidence suggests that new media technologies primarily benefit wealthy Western nations, promoting their cultural values and technology and enriching their countries. Evidence here includes the fact that Western countries control and profit from the majority of new media hardware and software.

Globalization and Digital Inequalities

Compared with those in the United States, even larger digital inequalities exist on a global scale. The issues of who does and does not have technocapital and whose culture dominates it are relevant in our current global economy. Why? Some activists and policymakers hope that a world facilitated by new communication technologies, economic globalization—meaning increased mobility of goods, services, labor, and capital—can lead to a more democratic and equitable world. And some evidence supports this hope. For example, outsourcing American jobs to overseas locations has provided income opportunities for many in English-speaking countries such as India. And, despite some governments' attempts to limit their citizens' access to new media, the Internet provides information, world news, and possibilities for interpersonal communication that were not available previously.

Reducing Digital Inequalities: What Keeps People Offline?   To understand how to reduce these digital inequalities we need to better understand why some people lack technocapital. Thirteen percent of Americans have never been online and are categorized as the "truly disconnected." They are more likely to be older (65 and older), have no high school degree, and have an annual income of less than $30,000 (Anderson & Perrin, 2016).

As we've seen, there are other groups that are digitally connected but less so than other groups. Experts have conducted a number of studies and advanced several theories to explain these inequalities. One theory that explains why some people accept new technologies and others don't is the diffusion of innovations, which was developed by Everett Rogers (2003). The theory suggests that for people to accept a new technology such as a computer or a smartphone, they have to see it as useful and compatible with their values and lifestyle. Moreover, if people important to the individual (e.g., an adolescent's peers) adopt the innovation first, then the individual is more likely to adopt it. So although giving people access to computers and mobile devices is an important first step, it is not enough to eliminate the digital inequalities.

Another theory—which is similar to the diffusions of innovations theory—is proposed by Dutch sociologist Jan van Dijk (2004) and addresses strategies for reducing digital inequalities. Van Dijk, like researcher Wei (2012), emphasizes that access to computer hardware or mobile devices is only one part of exclusion from the digital world. To survive and thrive in the digitized world people must have access to four levels of access to technocapital: mental, material, skills (or **digital readiness**), and usage. Furthermore, each level builds on the previous one.

digital readiness
People's preparedness and comfort in using digital tools for learning.

1. **Mental access.** The first and perhaps most important level of technocapital, and perhaps the easiest to overcome, relates to motivation and acceptance of new media as meaningful, and probably most people now believe that digital skills are important. However, older people and some poor people still do not see the benefit for themselves and more effort needs to be directed to overcoming these mental-access barriers.

▼ Suneet Tuli, CEO of DataWind, discusses how DataWind's technology will bring Internet access to low-income populations across Guatemala.

2. **Material access to digital hardware.** Most public policy currently focuses in this area. For example, one U.S. federal program uses telephone taxes to pay for Internet connections in elementary schools; state and local funds are used to pay for Internet connections at public libraries; and companies donating computer and technical training are given tax incentives. On a more global scale, computer hardware and software developers have been working for years on inexpensive sturdy laptops and tablets for developing countries markets. For

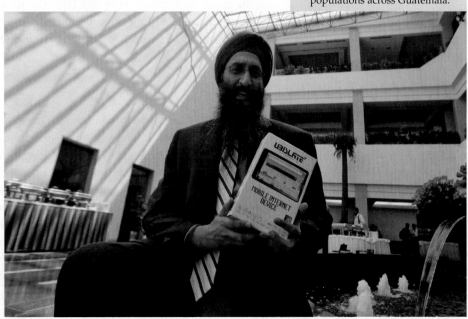

example, DataWind, a Canadian/Indian startup has developed a low-cost Ubislate 3G7 tablet, selling for about $20 (cheaper than a smartphone) and hopes to have distributed 5 million tablets in India by 2017. The company has recently partnered with an Internet provider in Guatemala, offering the tablet bundled with one year of web browsing (World's most affordable tablet computers launched . . . , 2016). Clearly, access to hardware and Internet connections is necessary for acquiring technocapital.

3. **Skills access.** Many nonusers view lack of training and lack of user-friendly technology, or lack of digital readiness as barriers, and frustration levels can be significant. Digital readiness involves confidence in using computers, facility with getting new technology to work, use of digital tools for learning, and ability to determine the trustworthiness of online information. To facilitate skills access, hardware and software developers must better understand the minds of users, taking into consideration their diverse cultural communication norms and practices (Horrigan, 2016). We need "technology that can think like the user" and that can think like users from many cultural backgrounds.

4. **Knowledge of computer applications.** Finally, usage access means knowing how to use a variety of computer applications. For example, learning to build a website or navigate social media or conduct online banking takes more know-how than using the computer to play games or send email. More important, those who are at the high end of multimodality use the computer in ways that are professionally and personally enhancing; for example, they visit sites that provide useful information about national and international news, health and financial information, government services, and product information (Büchi, et al., 2016). Even if people have computers, their lack of technological proficiency and social resources may frustrate them in high-tech societies. Older, poorer, and less-educated people use the Internet for limited basic applications, which, experts point out, are also associated with less political communication and participation (Wei, 2012).

Journal Prompt 14.5:
Digital Inequalities
Consider the following questions:
What is digital inequality? What
are the most important factors that
determine digital inequalities?

Ethics and Interactive Media

14.6 Identify and describe four ethical challenges involving interactive media use.

One message we hope you take from this chapter is that interactive media are not good or bad in themselves, nor better or worse than offline communication. They are simply different. However, these differences can allow for irresponsible, thoughtless, or even unethical communication. How can you become an ethical user of social media?

There are at least four areas of ethical consideration: (1) presentation of identity online, (2) privacy issues, (3) posting ethical messages, and (4) building online relationships.

Ethics and Online Identity

As we discussed previously, the issue of identity and ethics online is complex, and one can take various positions on the issue. An extreme position would be that one should never misrepresent oneself. By contrast, some interactive media (e.g., MMORPGs) clearly offer legitimate opportunities to take on a new identity or pseudo-identity, and in some cases, social media users have good reasons to mask their true identity (for example, victims of cyberbullying, domestic abuse, or online harassment). It's fairly common to assume a pseudonym/handle on Tumblr or Twitter, that reflects your interests, or because your preferred nickname may be already taken. Perhaps a more challenging issue is deciding when to set up a second Facebook page or another SNS with a pseudo-identity because you don't want all your posts to be seen by all your potential audiences, or you want to post opinions that may be unaccepted by some of your friends/acquaintances. One general principle might be "Do no harm." As described earlier in *It Happened to Me: Jacqueline*, in the example of Jacqueline's online friend, who pretended not to be married, the behavior was clearly deceitful.

Communication, of course, is interactive and reciprocal; it takes two people to engage in any interaction, and both have responsibility. Among the receiver's responsibilities is the duty to harbor a certain amount of skepticism for messages that may be questionable. In the case of interactive media, skepticism should focus on how people present their identity—particularly in certain contexts (e.g., in SNSs, online forums, or other interactive media sites).

Privacy Issues

A second ethical issue concerns online privacy, and the general guideline of doing no harm can also apply here. Specifically, ethical interactive media use includes respecting others' privacy and not snooping around Facebook or text messages that are not intended for you. There is increasing opportunity for privacy violation as we own more mobile devices (tablet, phones, and so on).

Finally, if you accidentally access private information, you should consider carefully the consequences of sharing this information with others—would the owner of the information want this information to be shared? Will others be harmed by sharing the information? Of course, the harm could be mild (sharing news about a friend that she or he would not want shared) to much more drastic consequences (sharing personal identity information that could result in cyberbullying or identity theft).

Respecting others' privacy extends to making others' private lives public without their permission. This includes posting pictures of others on social media sites and tagging them on platforms such as Facebook without their permission. Photos that can seem harmless to the person posting about her bachelorette party may be incriminating for others. For example, a picture of a teacher consuming alcohol could have negative repercussions on his or her credibility. Even without explicit tags, facial recognition systems can also be at play.

Posting Ethical Messages

A third ethical issue is the incivility of messages posted on SNSs, blogs, and especially Twitter. When bloggers disclose their feelings and opinions, they become vulnerable to personal attacks via comments left by readers. Women seem to be frequent targets of vulgar or insulting comments—from death threats to manipulated photos (Humphries & Vered, 2014). It can be tempting to retweet or repost a link that will give you lots of likes or retweets. With the prevalence of media in our lives today, the news that we post has the potential to impact hundreds or thousands of strangers, depending on our networks. This gives us a responsibility to double-check the authenticity of a news story so that we don't contribute to the spreading of nonsense or fake news. In a deeper sense, it is also worth taking a moment to think about the impact we will have on people's days with the content that we share. It doesn't take more than a moment to ask yourself, "Am I spreading mostly negative stories, or a balance of critical, thought-provoking, and uplifting stories?" If you retweet an opinion piece that claims that students don't need to go to class in university like they did in high school, what are you hoping to accomplish by spreading this, besides gathering likes?

Some website and software developers have suggested that a set of guidelines for conduct be created and implemented to "bring civility to the web" (Bryson, 2013). Some progress is being made as bloggers control if and when they will allow anonymous comments by strangers, and they often make explicit which behaviors they will (and will not) tolerate. However, an ethical stance is a balanced one. Some bloggers become so obsessed with policing comments that their blogs cease to become anything but an echo chamber because any dissenting comment is labeled as a violation of the rules of the blog. Discussion needs to be civil, but when disagreement of any kind is labeled as offensive trolling, then discussion becomes impossible.

Building Ethical Mediated Relationships

The first step in building ethical relationships is to remember the characteristics of interactive media—the variations in media richness, social presence, opportunities for anonymity, deception, and so on. First, present yourself as honestly and truthfully as you can and behave as you would in real life. How you act online may be the most direct way that people—including potential employers as well as love interests—will perceive you. You also need to give recipients of your message enough information to discern the "tone" of your message. For example, you may have to explain in words (or emojis) the humorous tone that in person you would communicate with facial expressions or gestures.

It Happened to Me
Cruzita

My boss writes novels, so I picked up her most recent mystery book and read it over the weekend. One of the characters—Amy—goes missing and is never found. On Monday morning, I emailed her in all capital letters, "WHAT HAPPENED TO AMY?," thinking she would immediately get the reference and have a good laugh. Unfortunately, I forgot that we work with an Amy. My boss called Amy to find out what was wrong only to learn Amy was totally fine. She then called me and I had to backtrack and explain the whole situation. It was very embarrassing.

A second step is to consider which form of communication is appropriate for your message. Here, relevant factors are your relationship with the receiver and the purpose of the message. For example, in a work context, a lean email message can convey essential information. However, personal messages may be better delivered in person, especially if miscommunication is likely and you need immediate feedback to make sure you are understood.

A final thought about ethical digital behavior. Based on extensive interviews with young people, media scholar Carrie James (2014) identifies three ways to approach online privacy, property, and participation: *self-focused thinking*, concerned mostly about consequences for herself; *moral thinking*, concerned about the consequences for people one knows; or *ethical thinking*, concerned about unknown individuals and larger communities. James offers a vision of *conscientious connectivity*, which involves ethical thinking skills but, perhaps more important, is marked by sensitivity to the dilemmas posed by online life, a motivation to wrestle with them, and a sense of moral agency that supports socially positive online actions.

Journal Prompt 14.6: Ethical Self-Presentation
Consider the following question: Which of these ethical guidelines do you think is most important in presenting *your* identity online?

Improving Your Mediated Communication Skills

14.7 Discuss ways to improve your own mediated communication skills.

What should you take from this chapter that can help you be a better communicator? First, you can strive to communicate more politely, following guidelines for interactive media etiquette. Second, you can use social media effectively in job hunting.

Interactive Media Etiquette

Just as we have norms of courtesy for traditional, FtF communication, we also have etiquette for computer-mediated communication. Let's look at several interactive media forms and the challenges they pose for communicating politely.

Email Because email is still prevalent in work and school contexts (for example, contacting professors), it is worth considering how to increase its effectiveness. The most important guideline is to think before writing a message and hitting the send button. Remember that what you put in writing can never be unwritten and that others besides the intended recipient may see it. Here are a few specific suggestions:

- **Write a specific subject line.** Give your email a context. Don't just write "FYI" or "Hi" in the subject field; let the recipient know specifically what you're writing about. This is especially important in work contexts. Because of the status-leveling effects of email, people get many more messages now than they ever did by telephone, so they want to know the subjects of those messages.

- **Address the recipient appropriately.** If the recipient is your professor, address him or her by title unless you are securely on a first-name basis. It's always better to err on the formal side rather than the informal. Abruptly starting with "Hey!," "Hi there," or "I need to talk with you about my grade" is not respectful.

- **Mind the time.** Although professors or professionals may set not policies about not replying to emails after a certain hour, the reality is that most people operate with a smartphone, remain connected to the Internet during most of their waking hours, and have settings where they are notified each time they receive a new email. This is perhaps the reason that France has recently passed a law barring email after work hours—noted earlier. Think about this before emailing a professor or a boss. Just because s/he doesn't respond at 11:30 P.M. doesn't mean that the notification on his or her phone doesn't go off. Try writing the email draft when an idea comes to you and waiting to send it out during normal working hours.

- **Check your spelling carefully.** Sending emails full of typos and grammar mistakes or written like a text message communicates a lack of respect for yourself and the recipient.

- **Analyze your audience.** Does a certain person usually reply to emails within the same day, or within several days? What is your relationship to that person? Before sending a follow-up email, consider these aspects if you can.

Mobile Phones Research shows that although most users think they have good phone manners, in one study 92 percent said they wished people practiced better etiquette in public places (New Intel Survey, 2011).

Here are some tips for cell-phone use:

- **Be safe.** Using your phone while driving is not worth risking your life. According to the National Safety Council (2014), drivers using phones are four times as likely to be involved in a crash as other drivers. If you must talk on the phone (if it's legal in your state), keep calls short, even if you're using your Bluetooth. There's no difference in accident

▼ Surveys report that loud cell-phone conversations in public places are one of the top complaints about bad manners with regard to digital mobile communication.

statistics between drivers using hand-held versus hands-free phone devices. Texting while walking is almost as dangerous. According to the Pew Research Center, 53 percent of adults have either bumped into someone while on their phones or been bumped into by someone on a phone (Smith, 2014a). At best, it's annoying for others to have to move out of the way while you're walking with your head down and your eyes on your phone. If there's no one around, you risk tripping, falling, running into objects, or not being aware of surroundings that can make you vulnerable.

- **Respect your company.** Put your phone away when you're with friends or loved ones. They came to be with you, not to watch you talk with others on your phone. Don't keep your headphones in while you're with other people. It's hard to tell if you're talking to them, someone on the phone, or an invisible friend. If you absolutely need to text, step away from the group and keep it short.

- **Respect the servers.** Don't use your phone while ordering in a restaurant. One study showed that food takes longer to get to the table now because servers have to wait for diners to finish talking on the phone call/texting before ordering.

- **Respect shared spaces.** Don't talk on the phone in confined spaces (doctor's office, elevator) and don't use the speakerphone. Talking loudly is annoying and very disruptive. If you have to talk or text in a restricted area, leave the room, finish your conversation or text message, turn off your phone, and return to your seat.

- **Turn your ringer off.** Not everyone appreciates hearing your favorite song or ringtone when you're at work or on public transportation. Turn your ringer off or keep your phone on vibrate when you're not at home.

- **Use your camera sparingly.** At public events, like concerts and weddings, limit your mobile photography accordingly. Don't view the event solely through a lens.

Twitter   As microblogging services such as Twitter have grown in popularity, they pose etiquette challenges of their own. Here are some suggestions:

- **Follow others selectively.** Be thoughtful about who you follow. Don't feel obligated to follow every user who follows you, and conversely, don't expect those you follow to follow you.

- **Don't overuse hashtags.** Hashtags are used to aggregate data about trending topics (https://support.twitter.com/articles/49309). They can be used to join a discussion or research a topic, but they are not meant to be used in excess. Twitter recommends using no more than two hashtags per tweet.

- **Watch your language.** As with any online dialogue, you want to maintain a respectful and dignified tone. Respect your followers as you want to be respected. Additionally, use good grammar. Bad grammar reduces the effect of your message so take a minute to proof your tweet before sending.

- **Tweet with purpose.** Your tweets should add value to an ongoing conversation—don't copy others' words, and don't over-tweet (more than 20 times per day).

- **Don't overshare.** Share only information that you don't mind making public.

- **Mind your privacy settings.** Public tweets can be viewed by anyone, from your future employer to your communication professor. If your account isn't private, tweet like your grandmother is reading.

As you can see, the overarching principle here is to be considerate of others' time and convenience. Put yourself in the place of the person receiving your message and ask yourself, "Would I appreciate the way this message has been worded and transmitted?" If the answer is yes, you are probably doing all right.

Using Social Media in Job Hunting

Social media are playing an increasingly important role in job searches for both employers and job applicants. How can you use mediated messages effectively in searching for employment?

First of all, network. Get the word out that you're looking (but, of course, be discreet if you don't want your current employer to know). Use as many media forms as possible—Facebook, Twitter, LinkedIn (which allows you to search by people, jobs, and companies; you can also join groups related to your industry and participate in job-related discussions). Create relevant profiles for yourself that include your job history. In general, the more visible you are, the more likely you are to make the contacts that will lead to a job while meeting a lot of professionals who share your same career aspirations. And you never know where *the* contact might happen.

Turn over the virtual rocks to find job postings: Simply Hired, CareerBuilder, Monster, Indeed. Be thoughtful and considerate in contacting and following up with potential employers. After a meeting or interview, it's good to follow up with a short thank-you email. Similarly, be sure to thank anyone who helps you by giving you leads or recommendations. However, don't continue to try to get in touch after that. If you push too hard, you'll look like a stalker rather than an eager applicant.

A final suggestion is to remember to help others. Be known as a resource. In your job search, you may come across information or contacts that may not be relevant to your search but might be helpful to a friend, colleague, or online acquaintance. What goes around comes around—the person you help today may be in a position to do you a favor next week or next year.

Interactive media are deeply imbedded in the way we do business and research and in the ways we socialize and connect with others. Clearly, we have much to think about as we use these tools in every context to communicate responsibly, ethically, equitably, and with social awareness.

Journal Prompt 14.7:
Interactive Media Etiquette
Consider the following question: What are some guidelines for improving your interactive media etiquette?

SUMMARY

14.1 Identify two reasons for learning about interactive media.

- Interactive media is pervasive and constant in our daily lives.
- Understanding and having good media skills will help you be more successful personally and professionally.

14.2 Identify and describe interactive media.

- Interactive media are defined as a collection of mediated communication technologies that are digital and converging and tend to be interactive.
- Interactive media include social media, email, and text messaging and present us with many communication choices in our everyday lives.
- These media are neither good nor bad, but better viewed through a dialectical lens—as having potentially both beneficial and harmful impacts.

14.3 Describe the dimensions of interactive media and how these dimensions combine into a framework for understanding the use of interactive media.

- Interactive media vary in two ways, in media characteristics (media richness and social presence) and social processes (self-presentation and self-disclosure).
- These yield four communication dimensions that help us understand how the various communication forms impact our choices.

14.4 Describe issues that can arise in identity and relationship development when using interactive media.

- Interactive media choices have implications for how we present ourselves online (self-presentation, anonymity, and pseudoanonymity).

- Interactive media afford access to many more potential relationships, and these relationships are not bound by time or space. Interactive media impact friendships, as well as romantic and work relationships.
- Using a dialectical lens, interactive media can strengthen and weaken interpersonal relationships as they are both durable and fragile.

14.5 Understand the role of power and privilege in interactive media use.

- Digital inequalities—differential access and knowledge about interactive media—often vary along income, educational, ethnic/racial, and national lines.
- Power also comes into play in digital in equalities, as it does in other parts of society because the most powerful are the ones who develop and define computer literacy and expertise—sometimes excluding those from less powerful groups.
- Two theories are proposed to help us understand and reduce these inequalities: diffusion of innovation and four levels of technocapital.

14.6 Identify and describe four ethical challenges involving interactive media use.

- The four challenges include ethics and online identity, ethics and privacy issues, posting ethical messages, and building ethical online relationships.

14.7 Discuss ways to improve your own mediated communication skills.

- Follow appropriate etiquette when using email, mobile phones, and Twitter.
- Use social media effectively when job hunting.

KEY TERMS

spreadability p. 354
lurkers p. 356
humblebrag p. 356
trolling p. 358
phishing p. 358

cyberbullying p. 358
pseudoanonymity p. 359
avatars p. 359
catfishing p. 361
digital divide p. 367

cultural capital p. 367
technocapital p. 367
multimodality p. 368
crowdfunding p. 368
digital readiness p. 369

APPLY WHAT YOU KNOW

1. Don't use any interactive media for 24 hours and then answer the following questions. To what extent did you miss these forms of communication? What did you miss most and least? What might you conclude about the role interactive media play in *your* everyday life and relationships? How do you view those who have limited access to new communication technologies?

2. Select any personal webpage from the Internet and describe the identity you think the person is trying to project. Describe the elements that contribute to this identity. What kind of information is presented? What information is missing?

Glossary

absolutism The belief that there is a single correct moral standard that holds for everyone, everywhere, every time.

action-oriented listening style Listening style that reflects a preference for error-free and well-organized speaking.

active agents Seekers of various media messages and resisters of others.

adaptors Gestures used to manage emotions.

African American Vernacular English A version of English that has its roots in West African, Caribbean, and U.S. slave languages.

age identity A combination of self-perception of age along with what others understand that age to mean.

agenda-setting capacity The power of media coverage to influence individuals' view of which topics are more salient than others.

analysis paralysis Potential pitfall in small group interaction; occurs when excessive analysis prevents a group from moving toward a solution.

androcentrism The use of male experience as normative for humanity and female experience as emphasizing gender difference.

appropriateness Following the rules, norms and expectations for specific situations or relationships.

artifacts Physical objects including cars, clothing, and other material items.

artistic proofs Artistic skills of a rhetor that influence effectiveness.

assertiveness Expressing one's opinions forcefully without offending others.

assimilation The communicative, behavioral, and cognitive processes that influence individuals to join, identify with, become integrated into, and (occasionally) exit an organization.

asynchronous Communication in which messages are sent and received at different times.

attraction theory Theory that explains the primary forces that draw people together.

attractiveness The appeal one person has for another, based on physical appearance, personalities, or behavior.

attribution theory Explanation of the processes we use to judge our own and others' behavior.

attributional bias A cognitive bias that refers to the systematic errors made when people evaluate or try to find reasons for their own and others' behaviors.

audience analysis The process of determining what an audience already knows or wants to know about a topic, who they are, what they know or need to know about the speaker, and what their expectations might be for the presentation.

authoritarian leader Leader who takes charge, makes all the decisions, and dictates strategies and work tasks.

avatars Digital alter egos or versions of oneself, used in MMORPGs.

avoiding Stage of romantic relational dissolution in which couples try not to interact with each other.

behavioral de-escalation Avoiding the partner.

behaviorism The focus on the study of behavior as a science.

border dwellers People who live between cultures and often experience contradictory cultural patterns.

brainstorm To generate as many ideas as possible without critiquing them.

bullying Repeated hostile behaviors that are or are perceived to be intended to harm parties who are unable to defend themselves.

burnout A chronic condition that results from the accumulation of daily stress, which manifests itself in a specific set of characteristics, including exhaustion, cynicism, and ineffectiveness.

categorization A cognitive process used to organize information by placing it into larger groupings of information.

catfishing Creating an intentionally deceptive social media profile.

cause–effect pattern An organization used to create understanding and agreement, and sometimes to argue for a specific action.

channel The means through which a message is transmitted.

charismatic leadership A leadership style in which extremely self-confident leaders inspire unusual dedication to themselves by relying on their strong personalities and charm.

chronemics The study of the way people use time as a message.

chronological pattern An organization that follows a timeline.

circumscribing Stage of romantic relational dissolution in which couples discuss safe topics.

cisgender Someone whose gender identity matches their biological sex.

cocultural group A significant minority group within a dominant majority that does not share dominant group values or communication patterns.

cocultural theory Explores the role of power in daily interactions.

code switching The practice of changing language or dialect to accommodate to the communication situation.

cognitive complexity The degree to which a person's constructs are detailed, involved, or numerous.

cognitive representation The ability to form mental models of the world.

cohort effect The process by which historical events influence the perceptions of people who grew up in a given generation and time period.

cohort effect The influence of shared characteristics of a group that was born and reared in the same general period.

collectivistic orientation A value orientation that stresses the needs of the group.

communicating information Using nonverbal behaviors to help clarify verbal messages and reveal attitudes and motivation.

communication competence The ability to adapt one's communication to achieve one's goals.

communication ethics The standards of right and wrong that one applies to messages that are sent and received.

conclusion Closing material of a speech where the speaker reviews the main points, may challenge the audience to act, and leaves the audience with a positive view of speaker and topic.

confirming communication   Comments that validate positive self-images of others.

congruent   Verbal and nonverbal messages that express the same meaning.

connotative meaning   The affective or interpretive meanings attached to a word.

constructive marginal people   People who thrive in a border-dweller life, while recognizing its tremendous challenges.

constructs   Categories people develop to help them organize information.

content analysis   Approach to understanding communication that focuses on specific aspects of the content of a text or group of texts.

content analysis   Approach to understanding media that focuses on a specific aspect of the content of a text or group of texts.

content meaning   The concrete meaning of the message and the meanings suggested by or associated with the message, as well as the emotions triggered by it.

content-oriented listening style   A listening style that reflects an interest in detailed and complex information, simply for the content itself.

contradicting   Verbal and nonverbal messages that send conflicting messages.

critical approach   An approach used not only to understand human behavior but ultimately to change society also.

critical listening   Listening skills that are useful in a wide variety of situations—particularly those involving persuasive speaking.

crowdfunding   The process of raising money online—often many small amounts from a large number of people.

crowdsourcing   The practice of engaging a 'crowd' or group online for a common goal—often for information or problem solving.

cultivation theory   The idea that long-term immersion in a media environment leads to "cultivation," or enculturation, into shared beliefs about the world.

cultural capital   Cultural knowledge and cultural competencies that people need to function effectively in society.

cultural communication   Communication patterns within a specific community.

cultural values   Beliefs that are so central to a cultural group that they are never questioned.

culture   Learned patterns of perceptions, values, and behaviors shared by a group of people.

culture industries   Large organizations in the business of mass communication that produce, distribute, or show various media texts (cultural products) as an industry.

culture shock   A feeling of disorientation and discomfort as a result of the lack of familiar environmental cues.

cyberbullying   The deliberate and repeated misuse of communication technology by an individual or group to threaten or harm others.

de-escalation strategies   A broad category that includes promising some continued closeness and suggesting that the couple might reconcile in the future.

deception   Concealment, distortion, or dishonesty in communication.

decoding   Receiving a message and interpreting its meaning.

defensive communication   Behavior that occurs when an individual perceives threat or anticipates threat from another individual.

deliberative rhetoric   The type of rhetoric used to argue what courses of action a society should take in the future.

delivery   The presentation of a speech before an audience.

demand touching   A type of touch used to establish dominance and power.

demand-withdrawal   An interaction pattern in which one partner criticizes or tries to change the other partner, who responds by becoming defensive and/or then disengaging—either psychologically or physically.

democratic leader   Leader whose style is characterized by considerable input from group members.

demographic analysis   The portion of an audience analysis that considers the ages, races, sexes, sexual orientations, religions, and social classes of the audience.

denotative meaning   The dictionary, or literal, meaning of a word.

dialect   A variation of a language distinguished by its vocabulary, grammar, and pronunciation.

dialectical approach   Recognizes that things need not be perceived as "either/or," but may be seen as "both/and."

diaspora   The movement, migration, or scattering of a people away from an established or ancestral homeland.

dichotomous thinking   Thinking in which things are perceived as "either/or"—for example, "good or bad," "big or small," "right or wrong."

differentiating   Stage of romantic relational dissolution in which couples increase their interpersonal distance.

digital   Information that is transmitted in a numerical format based on only two values (0 and 1).

digital divide   Inequity of access between the technology "haves" and "have nots."

digital readiness   People's preparedness and comfort in using digital tools for learning.

disability identity   Identification with physical or mental impairment that substantially impact everyday life.

disconfirming communication   Comments that reject or invalidate a positive or negative self-image of our conversational partners.

downward communication   In a traditional conduit model of communication, communication with subordinates.

e-books   Electronic books read on a computer screen instead of a printed page.

effectiveness   Achieving one's goals successfully.

ego-defensive function   The role prejudice plays in protecting individuals' sense of self-worth.

emblems   Gestures that stand for a specific verbal meaning.

emergence phase   The third phase of the decision-making process; occurs when group members express a cooperative attitude.

empowerment   Feeling capable of performing a job and having the authority to decide how to perform it well.

enacting identities   Performing scripts deemed proper for particular identities.

encapsulated marginal people   People who feel disintegrated by having to shift cultures.

encoding   Converting ideas into messages.

epideictic rhetoric   The type of rhetoric that reaffirms cultural values through praising and blaming.

equity   Perception that one's costs (or inputs) are balanced by one's rewards (or outputs).

equity theory   Theory that argues that people are more satisfied in relationships they perceive as fair, that is, where their costs are balanced by their rewards.

establishing social control Using nonverbal communication to exercise influence over other people.

ethnic identity Identification with a particular group with which one shares some or all of these characteristics: national or tribal affiliation, religious beliefs, language, and/or cultural and traditional origins and background.

ethnocentrism The tendency to view one's own group as the standard against which all other groups are judged.

ethnographic Relating to studies in which researchers actively engage with participants.

ethos The rhetorical construction of character.

evaluating Assessing your reaction to a message.

experimenting Stage of romantic relational development in which both people seek to learn about each other.

expressing and managing intimacy Using nonverbal behaviors to help convey attraction and closeness.

eye contact Looking directly into the eyes of another.

feedback The response to a message.

field of experience The education and experiences that a communicator possesses.

forensic rhetoric Rhetoric that addresses events that happened in the past with the goal of setting things right after an injustice has occurred.

formal structure Officially designated channels of communication, reflecting explicit or desired patterns of interaction.

frame Assumptions and attitudes that we use to filter perceptions to create meaning.

friendship touch Touch that is more intimate than social-polite touch and usually conveys warmth, closeness, and caring.

function The goals and effects of communication. A function of organizational communication in which activity is coordinated toward accomplishing tasks.

functional (situational) theory A theory that assumes that leadership behaviors can be learned.

functional touch The least intimate type of touch; used by certain workers such as dentists, hairstylists, and hospice workers, as part of their livelihood; also known as *professional touch.*

fundamental attribution error The tendency to attribute others' negative behavior to internal causes and their positive behaviors to external causes.

gender fluid Someone whose gender identity is not fixed, but is dynamic and changes in different contexts, at different times.

gender identity How and to what extent one identifies with the social construction of masculinity and femininity.

general purpose Whichever of three goals—to inform, persuade, or entertain—dominates a speech.

general systems theory Theory that organizations are a system composed of many subsystems and embedded in larger systems, and that organizations should develop communication strategies that serve both.

generalized other The collection of roles, rules, norms, beliefs, and attitudes endorsed by the community in which a person lives.

gestures Nonverbal communication made with part of the body, including actions such as pointing, waving, or holding up a hand to direct people's attention.

globalization The increasing connectedness of the world in economic, political, and cultural realm.

grammar The structural rules that govern the generation of meaning in a language.

group processes The methods, including communication, by which a group accomplishes a task.

group roles The shared expectations group members have regarding each individual's communication behavior in the group.

grouphate The distaste and aversion that people feel toward working in groups.

groupthink A negative, and potentially disastrous, group process characterized by "excessive concurrence thinking."

haptics The study of the communicative function of touch.

hate speech Use of verbal communication to attack others based upon some social category.

Hays Code Self-imposed rules for Hollywood media content instituted in 1930 with the goal of creating "wholesome entertainment."

hearing The stage when listeners pick up the sound waves directed toward them.

hegemony The process by which we consent to social constructions, rather than having them imposed on us.

heterogeneous Diverse.

heuristic Use of language to acquire knowledge and understanding.

hierarchy A power structure in which some members exercise authority over others.

homogeneity High degree of similarity.

horizontal communication In a traditional conduit model of communication, communication with peers.

hostile work environment An intimidating, hostile, or offensive workplace atmosphere created by unwelcome and inappropriate sexually based behavior.

human communication A transactional process in which people generate meaning through the exchange of verbal and nonverbal messages in specific contexts, influenced by individual and social forces, and embedded in culture.

human–nature value orientation The perceived relationship between humans and nature.

humanism A system of thought that celebrates human nature and its potential.

humblebrag Subtly letting others know about how fantastic your life is while undercutting it with a bit of self-effacing humor.

hurtful messages Messages that criticize, tease, reject, or otherwise cause an emotional injury to another.

hypothesis A supposition or proposed explanation.

identity Who a person is; composed of individual and social categories a person identifies with, as well as the categories that others identify with that person.

illustrators Signals that accompany speech to clarify or emphasize the verbal message.

imaginative Use of language to express oneself artistically or creatively.

immediacy How close or involved people appear to be with each other.

individual role Role that focuses more on individuals' own interests and needs than on those of the group.

individualistic orientation A value orientation that respects the autonomy and independence of individuals.

indulgence versus restraint orientation A value orientation that reflects a subjective feeling of happiness. The indulgence orientation emphasizes relatively free gratification of basic and natural human drives related to enjoying life and having fun. Restraint emphasizes suppressing gratification of needs and regulates it by means of strict social norms.

informal structure   Unspoken but understood channels of communication, reflecting patterns that develop spontaneously.

informational listening   Listening skills that are useful in situations requiring attention to content.

informative   Use of language to communicate information or report facts.

ingratiation   Behavior and communication designed to increase liking.

initiating   Stage of romantic relational development in which both people behave so as to appear pleasant and likeable.

innovation   A function of organizational communication by means of which systems are changed.

instrumental   Use of language to obtain what you need or desire.

integrating   Stage of romantic relational development in which both people portray themselves as a couple. Stage of romantic relational development characterized by public commitment.

intensifying   Stage of romantic relational development in which both people seek to increase intimacy and connectedness.

interactional   Use of language to establish and define social relationships.

interactive media   A collection of mediated communication technologies that are digital and converging and tend to be mobile.

intercultural communication   Communication that occurs in interactions between people who are culturally different.

interpersonal violence   Physical violence against a partner or child.

interpretation   The act of assigning meaning to sensory information.

interpretive approach   Contemporary term for humanistic (rhetorical) study.

intimate distance   (zero to eighteen inches) The space used when interacting with those with whom one is very close.

introduction   Opening material of a speech from which the audience members gain a first impression of the speech's content and of the speaker.

jargon   The specialized terms that develop in many professions.

jealousy   A complex and often painful emotion that occurs when a person perceives a threat to an existing relationship.

justification strategies   Providing a reason or excuse for ending the relationship.

kinesics   Nonverbal communication sent by the body, including gestures, posture, movement, facial expressions, and eye behavior.

Knapp's stage model   Model of relationship development that views relationships as occurring in "stages" and that focuses on how people communicate as relationships develop and decline.

label   A name assigned to a category based on one's perception of the category.

laissez-faire   A leadership style characterized by complete freedom for the group in making decisions.

lexical choice   Vocabulary.

listening   The process of receiving, constructing meaning from, and responding to spoken and/or nonverbal messages.

listening style   A set of attitudes, beliefs, and predispositions about the how, where, when, who, and what of the information receiving and encoding process.

logos   Rational appeals; the use of rhetoric to help the audience see the rationale for a particular conclusion.

long-term orientation   A value orientation in which people stress the importance of virtue.

long-term versus short-term orientation   The dimension of a society's value orientation that reflects its attitude toward virtue or truth.

looking-glass self   The idea that self-image results from the images others reflect back to an individual.

love-intimate touch   The touch most often used with one's romantic partners and family.

lurkers   People who read, observe, but do not actively participate in online communities/sites.

Machiavellian tactics   Having a third party convey one's unhappiness about a relationship.

maintenance   A function of organizational communication in which the stability of existing systems is preserved.

mass media   Mediated communication intended for large audiences.

mass media effects   The influence that media have on people's everyday lives.

mass-market paperbacks   Popular books addressed to a large audience and widely distributed.

Massively Multiplayer Role-Playing Online Games (MMORPGs):   Text-based "virtual reality" games in which participants interact with enrichments, objects, and other participants.

matching hypothesis   The tendency to develop relationships with people who are approximately as attractive as we are.

media   The plural form of *medium*; a channel of communication.

media activism   The practice of organizing to communicate displeasure with certain media images and messages, as well as to force change in future media texts.

media event   Occasions or catastrophes that interrupt regular programming.

media richness theory   Theory that describes the potential information-carrying capacity of a communication medium.

media text   A television show, advertisement, movie, or other media event that a media scholar isolates for study.

media violence   Representations of violent acts in media.

member-checking   Obtaining feedback from respondents to help improve the accuracy of research results.

messages   The building blocks of communication.

methods   The specific ways that scholars collect and analyze data, which they then use to support, prove, or disprove their theoretical claims.

monochronically   Engaging in one task or behavior at a time.

monotheistic   Belief in one god.

motivation   Feeling personally invested in accomplishing a specific activity or goal.

MPAA   Motion Picture Association of America is a film sector industry representing the six major Hollywood studios.

multimodality   The range or breadth of Internet activities.

multiracial identity   One who self-identifies as having more than one racial identity.

mutable   Subject to change.

national identity   A person's citizenship.

naturalistic   Relating to everyday, real-life situations, such as a classroom, café, or shopping mall.

negative identity management   Communicating in ways that arouse negative emotions to make the other person upset enough to agree to break off the relationship.

new social contract   Assumes that loyalty is not expected by workers or organizations and that job security is unlikely.

noise Any stimulus that can interfere with, or degrade, the quality of a message.

nominalists Those who argue that any idea can be expressed in any language and that the structure and vocabulary of the language do not influence the speaker's perception of the world.

nonverbal behavior All the nonverbal actions people perform.

nonverbal codes Distinct, organized means of expression that consists of symbols and rules for their use.

nonverbal communication The sending and receiving of information through appearance, objects, the environment, and behavior.

openness Straightforwardly explaining why the relationship is ending.

openness Sharing ideas as well as listening to others in a way that avoids conveying negative or disconfirming feedback.

orator A public speaker.

organization The process by which one recognizes what sensory input represents.

organizational climate How organizational members feel about, or experience, the organization's culture.

organizational culture A pattern of shared beliefs, values, and behaviors.

organizational identification The stage of assimilation that occurs when an employee's values overlap with the organization's values.

organizations The set of interactions that members of purposeful groups use to accomplish their individual and common goals.

overattribution Selecting an individual's most obvious characteristic and using it to explain almost anything that person does.

overbenefitted Overbenefitted people perceive that their rewards exceed their costs.

paradigm Belief system that represents a particular worldview.

paralinguistics All aspects of spoken language except for the words themselves; includes rate, volume, pitch, and stress.

participants The people interacting during communication.

particular others The important people in an individual's life whose opinions and behavior influence the various aspects of identity.

passing away Process by which relationships decline over time.

pathos The rhetorical use of emotions to affect audience decision making.

peacebuilding Working toward stability in a region to prevent conflicts from escalating into war.

people-oriented listening style A listening style that is associated with friendly, open communication and an interest in establishing ties with others.

perception A sense-making procedure in which we attempt to understand our environment so we can respond to it appropriately.

performance of identity The process or means by which we show the world who we think we are.

persona The identity one creates through one's public communication efforts.

personal distance (eighteen inches to four feet) The space used when interacting with friends and acquaintances.

personal language Use of language to express individuality and personality.

phishing The practice of trying fraudulently to get consumer banking and credit card information.

phonology The study of the sounds that compose individual languages and how those sounds communicate meaning.

political economy The ways in which media institutions produce texts in a capitalist system and the legal and regulatory frameworks that shape their options for doing so.

polychronically Engaging in multiple activities simultaneously.

polytheistic Belief in more than one god.

positive tone strategies Communicating concern for the rejected partner and trying to make the person feel better.

posture and movement Kinesics behaviors that communicate messages by how immediate or relaxed they are.

power distance A value orientation that refers to the extent to which less powerful members of institutions and organizations within a culture expect and accept an unequal distribution of power.

pragmatics Field of study that emphasizes how language is used in specific situations to accomplish goals.

predicted outcome theory Theory that attempts to explain how reducing uncertainty can lead to attraction or repulsion.

preferred personality A value orientation that expresses whether it is more important for a person to "do" or to "be."

prejudice Experiencing aversive or negative feelings toward a group as a whole or toward an individual because she or he belongs to a group.

primacy effect The tendency to form a judgment or opinion based on the first information received.

primary tension The uncertainty commonly felt in the beginning phase of decision making.

problem–solution pattern An organization in which the speaker describes various aspects of a problem and then proposes solutions.

professional touch Type of touch used by certain workers, such as dentists, hairstylists, and hospice workers, as part of their livelihood; also known as *functional touch*.

prototype A representative or idealized version of a concept.

proxemics The study of how people use spatial cues, including interpersonal distance, territoriality, and other space relationships, to communicate.

proximity How physically close one is to others.

pseudoanonymity Projecting a false identity.

public distance (twelve to twenty-five feet) The distance used for public ceremonies such as lectures and performances.

public sphere The arena in which deliberative decision making occurs through the exchange of ideas and arguments.

qualitative methods Methods in which researchers study naturally occurring communication rather than assembling data and converting it to numbers.

quantitative methods Methods that convert data to numerical indicators, which are then analyzed using statistics to establish relationships among the concepts.

quid pro quo Requests for sexual favors as a condition of getting or keeping a job or benefit.

racial identity Identification with a particular racial group.

rationality The ability to communicate through reasoning, bargaining, coalition building, and assertiveness.

recency effect The tendency to form a judgment or opinion on the most recent information received.

reflected appraisals The idea that people's self-images arise primarily from the ways that others view them and from the many messages they have received from others about who they are.

regulating interaction Using nonverbal behaviors to help manage conversational interaction.

regulators   Gestures used to control conversations.

regulatory   Use of language to control or regulate the behaviors of others.

reinforcement phase   The final phase of the decision-making process when group members reach consensus, and members feel a sense of accomplishment.

relational maintenance   Behaviors that couples perform that help maintain their relationships.

relational roles   Roles that help establish a group's social atmosphere.

relational trajectory models   Relationship development models that view relationship development as more variable than do stage models.

relationship meaning   What a message conveys about the relationship between the parties.

relativism   The belief that moral behavior varies among individuals, groups, and cultures and across situations.

relativists   Those who argue that language serves not only as a way for us to voice our ideas but "is itself the shaper of ideas, the guide for the individual's mental activity."

relaxation   The degree of tension displayed by the body.

religious identity   Aspect of identity defined by one's spiritual beliefs.

responding   Showing others how you regard their message.

reverse culture shock/re-entry shock   Culture shock experienced by travelers on returning to their home country.

rhetor   A person or institution that addresses a large audience; the originator of a communication message but not necessarily the one delivering it.

rhetoric   Communication that is used to influence the attitudes or behaviors of others; the art of persuasion.

rhetorical analysis   Used by researchers to examine texts or public speeches as they occur in society with the aim of interpreting textual meaning.

rhetorical audience   Those people who can take the appropriate action in response to a message.

rhetorical critic   An informed consumer of rhetorical discourse who is prepared to analyze rhetorical texts.

rhetorical event   Any event that generates a significant amount of public discourse.

role expectations   The expectation that one will perform in a particular way because of the social role occupied.

Sapir-Whorf hypothesis   Idea that the language people speak determines the way they see the world (a relativist perspective).

schemas   Cognitive structures that help us organize information.

script   A relatively fixed sequence of events that functions as a guide or template for communication or behavior.

secondary (recurring) tension   Conflict or tension found in the second or conflict phase of the decision-making process.

selection   The process of choosing which sensory information to focus on.

selective attention   Consciously or unconsciously attending to just a narrow range of the full array of sensory information available.

selective exposure   The idea that people seek media messages or interpret media texts in ways that confirm their beliefs and, conversely, resist or avoid messages that challenge their beliefs.

self-concept   The understanding of one's unique characteristics as well as the similarities to, and differences from, others.

self-esteem   Part of one's self-concept; arises out of how one perceives and interprets reflected appraisals and social comparisons.

self-fulfilling prophecy   When an individual expects something to occur, the expectation increases the likelihood that it will, as the expectation influences behavior.

self-presentation   Influencing others' impressions by creating an image that is consistent with one's personal identity.

self-respect   Treating others, and expecting to be treated, with respect and dignity.

self-serving bias   The tendency to give one's self more credit than is due when good things happen and to accept too little responsibility for those things that go wrong.

semantic-information distance   Describes the gap in information and understanding between supervisors and subordinates on specific issues.

semantics   The study of meaning.

servant leadership   A leadership style that seeks to ensure that other people's highest priority needs are being served to increase teamwork and personal involvement.

service-task functions   Using nonverbal behavior to signal close involvement between people in impersonal relationships and contexts.

setting   The physical surroundings of a communication event.

sexual coercion   Physically nonviolent pressure to engage in unwanted sex.

sexual identity   Which of the various categories of sexuality one identifies with.

shared (collaborative or distributed) leadership   A type of leadership style in which functional leadership is extended to an organizational level; all members are equal partners and share responsibility for the work of the group.

short-term orientation   A value orientation that stresses the importance of possessing one fundamental truth.

signposts   Transitions in a speech that help an audience understand the speaker's organization, making it easier for them to follow.

similarity   Degree to which people share the same values, interests, and background.

small group communication   Communication among a small number of people who share a common purpose or goal, who feel connected to each other, and who coordinate their behavior.

social class identity   An informal ranking of people in a culture based on their income, occupation, education, dwelling, child-rearing habits, and other factors.

social distance   (four to twelve feet) The distance most U.S. Americans use when they interact with unfamiliar others.

social exchange theory   Theory that explains the development and longevity of relationships as a result of individuals' ability to maximize the rewards and minimize the costs of their relationships.

social media   Group of Internet-based applications that allow the creation and exchange of user-generated content.

social movement   A large, organized body of people who are attempting to create social change.

social penetration theory   Theory that proposes relationships develop through increases in self-disclosure.

social position   Place in the social hierarchy, which comes from the way society is structured.

social presence   Degree of psychological closeness or immediacy engendered by various media.

social presence theory   Theory that suggests face-to-face communication is generally high in social presence, and that media vary in the amount of social presence they convey. In social media, not knowing exactly who is reading one's posts.

social role The specific position or positions one holds in a society.

social science approach Contemporary term for the behaviorist approach.

social-polite touch Touch that is part of daily interaction in the United States; it is more intimate than professional touch but is still impersonal.

sophists The first group to teach persuasive speaking skills in the Greek city-states.

soundscape The everyday sounds in our environments.

spatial pattern An organization that arranges points by location and can be used to describe something small.

special-occasion speeches Evocative speeches intended to entertain, inspire, celebrate, commemorate, or build community.

specific purpose What a speaker wants to inform or persuade an audience about, or the type of feelings the speaker wants to evoke.

speech act theory Branch of pragmatics that suggests that when people communicate, they do not just say things, they also *do* things with their words.

spreadability The ease with which content can be spread on social media.

stagnating Stage of romantic relational dissolution in which couples try to prevent change.

stereotype threat Process in which reminding individuals of stereotypical expectations regarding important identities can impact their performance.

stereotyping Creating schemas that overgeneralize attributes of a specific group.

strategy control Assessing the available information and options to increase one's understanding of the conflict and the other party.

structure Recurring patterns of interaction among organizational members.

style theory Theory that asserts that a leader's manner or style determines his or her success.

sudden death Process by which relationships end without prior warning for at least one participant or due to a betrayal.

supporting materials Information that supports the speaker's ideas.

supportive listening Listening skills focused not only on understanding information but also "listening" to others' feelings.

supportiveness Providing subordinates with access to information and resources.

symbol Something that represents something else and conveys meaning.

synchronous Communication in which messages are sent and received at the same time.

Synergetic Model A transactional model that emphasizes how individual and societal forces, contexts, and culture interact to affect the communication process.

syntax The rules that govern word order.

task roles Roles that are directly related to the accomplishment of group goals.

technocapital Access to technological skills and resources.

terminating Stage of romantic relational dissolution in which couples end the relationship.

textual analysis Similar to rhetorical analysis; used to analyze cultural "products," such as media and public speeches.

theory A set of statements that explains a particular phenomenon.

thesis statement A statement of the topic of a speech and the speaker's position on it.

time-oriented listening style A listening style that prefers brief, concise speech.

topical pattern An organization that has no innate organization except that imposed by the speaker.

trait theory A theory that assumes leaders are born, not made.

transformational leadership A leadership style that empowers group members to work independently from the leader by encouraging group cohesion.

transgender Someone whose gender identity does not match their biological sex.

trolling Posting Internet messages meant to intentionally anger or frustrate in order to provoke reactions from others.

truth bias The tendency to not suspect one's intimates of deception.

turning point model Model of relationship development in which couples move both toward and away from commitment over the course of their relationship.

TV Parental Guidelines A self-regulating system of the television industry that rates programs in terms of appropriateness for particular age groups.

uncertainty reduction theory Theory that argues relationship development is facilitated or derailed by participants' efforts to reduce their uncertainty about each other.

underbenefitted Underbenefitted people perceive that their costs exceed their rewards.

understanding Interpreting the messages associated with sounds or what the sounds mean.

upward communication In a traditional conduit model of communication, communication with superiors.

upward distortion Occurs when subordinates present information to superiors in a more positive light than is warranted.

urgent organizations Companies that try to shorten the time it takes to develop new products and respond to customer demands.

uses and gratifications The idea that people use media messages and find various types of gratifications in some media texts rather than in others.

V-chip Device that identifies television program ratings by content and can block programming designated by the owner.

value-expressive function The role played by prejudice in allowing people to view their own values, norms, and cultural practices as appropriate and correct.

view of human nature A value orientation that expresses whether humans are fundamentally good, evil, or a mixture.

visual aids Audiovisual materials that help a speaker reach intended speech goals.

vocalizations Uttered sounds that do not have the structure of language.

voice qualities Qualities such as pitch, rhythm, vocal range, and articulation that make up the "music" of the human voice.

withdrawal/avoidance Friendship termination strategy in which friends spend less time together, don't return phone calls, and avoid places where they are likely to see each other.

work–life conflict Difficulty balancing job and home responsibilities.

References

Chapter 1

Alberts, J. K., Yoshimura, C. G., Rabby, M. K., & Loschiavo, R. (2005). Mapping the topography of couples' daily interaction. *Journal of Social and Personal Relationships, 22*, 299–323.

Andersen, P. A., Lustig, M. W., & Andersen, J. F. (1990). Changes in latitude, changes in attitude: The relationship between climate and interpersonal communication predispositions. *Communication Quarterly, 38*, 291–311.

A year and a day for Lil' Kim. (July 7, 2005). *CNN.com.* Retrieved March 10, 2014, from http://www.cnn.com/2005/LAW/07/07/ctv.lilkim/

Barnlund, D. C. (1962). Consistency of emergent leadership in groups with changing tasks and members. *Speech Monographs, 29*, 45–52.

Buck, R., & Van Lear, C. A. (2002). Verbal and nonverbal communication: Distinguishing symbolic, spontaneous and pseudo-spontaneous nonverbal behavior. *Journal of Communication, 52*, 522–541.

Burgoon, J. K., Buller, D. B., & Woodall, W. G. (1996). *Nonverbal communication: The unspoken dialogue.* New York: Harper & Row.

Christians, C., & Traber, M. (Eds.) (1997). *Communication ethics and universal values.* Thousand Oaks, CA: Sage.

Cupach, W., Canary, D., & Spitzberg, B. (2009). *Competence in interpersonal conflict.* Prospect Heights, IL: Waveland Press.

DePaulo, B. (2011, September 6). Who lies? Frequent liars. What kinds of people lie most often? *Psychology Today.* Retrieved March 11, 2014, from http://www.psychologytoday.com/blog/living-single/201109/who-lies

Dickens, T. E. (2003). General symbol machines: The first stage in the evolution of symbolic communication. *Evolutionary Psychology, 1*, 192–209.

Diener, M. (2002, January). Fair enough: To be a better negotiator, learn to tell the difference between a lie and a *lie. Entrepreneur Magazine.* Retrieved March 16, 2006, from http://www.Entrepreneurmagazine.com/article/47442

Dixon, M., & Duck, S. W. (1993). Understanding relationship processes: Uncovering the human search for meaning. In S. W. Duck (Ed.), *Understanding relationship processes, Vol. 1: Individuals in relationships* (pp. 175–206). Newbury Park, CA: Sage.

Duck, S. (1994). *Meaningful relationships: Talking, sense and relating.* Newbury Park, CA: Sage.

Eisenberg, E. M., Goodall, H. L., Jr., & Trethewey, A. (2010). *Organizational communication: Balancing creativity and constraints.* New York: St. Martin's.

Emanuel, R. (2007). Humanities: Communication's core discipline. *American Communication Journal, 9*(2). Retrieved March 11, 2009, from http://www.acjournal.org/holdings/vol9/summer/articles/discipline.html

Friedrich, G. W. (1994). Essentials of speech communication. *SCA Rationale Kit: Information supporting the speech communication discipline and its programs* (pp. 9–12). Annandale, VA: Speech Communication Association.

Gergen, K. J. (1982). *Toward transformation in social knowledge.* New York: Springer.

Johannesen, R. (1990). *Ethics in human communication.* Prospect Heights, IL: Waveland.

Kant, I. (1949). *Fundamental principles of the metaphysic of morals.* (T. K. Abbott, Trans.). Indianapolis: Bobbs-Merrill. (Original work published 1785)

Laswell, H. D. (1948). The structure and function of communication in society. In L. Bryson (Ed.), *The Communication of Ideas.* New York: Harper.

Martin, J. N., & Nakayama, T. K. (2005). *Experiencing intercultural communication* (2nd ed.). Boston: McGraw-Hill.

McCabe, D. L., & Trevino, L. K. (1996). What we know about cheating in college: Longitudinal trends and recent developments. *Change, 28*, 28–33.

McCornack, S. A., & Parks, M. R. (1986). Deception detection and relationship development: The other side of trust. In M. L. McLaughlin (Ed.), *Communication Yearbook 9* (pp. 377–389). Newbury Park, CA: Sage. Retrieved March 16, 2006, from http://www.natcom.org/policies/External/EthicalComm

Mead, G. H. (1934). *Mind, self, and society.* Chicago: University of Chicago Press.

National Communication Association, (2003). What is communication? *Pathways.* Retrieved October 24, 2008, from http://www.natcom.org/nca/Template2.asp?bid=339

Nolen-Hoeksema, S., Wisco, B., & Lyumbomirski, S. Rethinking rumination. (2008). *Perspectives on Psychological Science, 3*, 400–424.

Passer, M. W., & Smith, R. E. (2004). *Psychology: The science of mind and behavior* (2nd ed.). New York: McGraw-Hill.

Paul, R., & Elder, L. (2008). *The miniature guide to critical thinking concepts and tools.* Dillon Beach, CA: Foundation for Critical Thinking Press.

Robinson-Smith, G. (2004). Verbal indicators of depression in conversations with stroke survivors. *Perspectives in Psychiatric Care, 40*, 61–69.

Rogers, E. M., & Chafee, S. H. (1983). Communication as an academic discipline: A dialogue. *Journal of Communication, 3*, 18–30.

Sartre, J. P. (1973). *Existentialism and humanism* (P. Mairet, Trans.) London: Methuen Ltd. (Original work published 1946.)

Schirato, T., & Yell, S. (1996). *Communication & cultural literacy: An introduction.* St. Leonards, Australia: Allen & Unwin.

Shannon, C. E., & Weaver, W. (1949). *A mathematical model of communication.* Urbana: University of Illinois Press.

Warren, S. F., & Yoder, P. J. (1998). Facilitating the transition to intentional communication. In A. Wetherby, S. Warren, & J. Reichle (Eds.), *Transitions in Prelinguistic Communication*, (pp. 39–58). Baltimore: Brookes Publishing.

Watzlawick, P., Beavin, J., & Jackson, D. D. (1967). *Pragmatics of human communication.* New York: W. W. Norton.

Wokutch, R. E., & Carson, T. L. (1981). The ethics and profitability of bluffing in business. In Lewickis, Saunders, & Minton (Eds.), *Negotiation: Readings, exercises, and cases* (pp. 341–353). Boston: Irwin/McGraw-Hill.

Chapter 2

Arkowitz, H., & Lilienfeld, S. O. (2009). Lunacy and the full moon: Does a full moon really trigger strange behavior? *Scientific American.* Retrieved from https://www.scientificamerican.com/article/lunacy-and-the-full-moon/

Arkowitz, H., & Lilienfeld, S. O. (2017). *Facts and fictions in mental health.* Malden, MA: John Wiley & Sons.

Becker, J. A. H., Ellevold, B., & Stamp, G. H. (2008). The creation of defensiveness in social interaction II: A model of defensive communication among romantic couples. *Communication Monographs, 75*(1), 86–110.

Birditt, K. S., Brown, E., Orbuch, T. L., & McIlvane, J. M. (2010). Marital conflict behaviors and implications for divorce over 16 years. *Journal of Marriage and Family, 72*(5), 1188–1204.

Borda, J. L. (2002). The woman suffrage parades of 1910–1913: Possibilities and limitations of an early feminist rhetorical strategy. *Western Journal of Communication, 66*, 25–52.

Burrell, G., & Morgan, G. (1988). *Sociological paradigms and organizational analysis.* Portsmouth, NH: Heinemann.

Campbell, K. K. (1994). *Women public speakers in the United States, 1925–1993: A bio-critical sourcebook.* Westport, CT: Greenwood.

Carbaugh, D. (2007). Cultural discourse analysis: Communication practices and intercultural encounters. *Journal of Intercultural Communication Research, 36*(3), 167–182.

Carbaugh, D., & Berry, M. (2001). Communicating history, Finnish and American discourses: An ethnographic contribution to intercultural communication inquiry. *Communication Theory, 11,* 352–366.

Carbaugh, D., & Cerulli, T. (2013). Cultural discourses of dwelling: Investigating enviornmental communication as a place-based practice. *Environmental Communication: Journal of Nature and Culture, 7,* 1–20.

Christians, C. G. (2011). Ethics and politics in qualitative research. In N. K. Denzin & Y. S. Lincoln (Eds.), *The Sage Handbook of Qualitative Research* (pp. 61–80). Thousand Oaks, CA: Sage.

Craig, R. T. (2013). Constructing theories in communication research. In P. Cobley & P. J. Schulz (Eds.), *Theories and models of communication* (pp. 39–57). (Handbooks of communication science, HOCS 1.) Berlin/Boston: De Gruyter Mouton.

Davis, O. I., & Marsiglia, F. F. (2011, June). *Cultural catalysts for community dialogues: Black barbers as interventionists in cardiovascular health of African American men.* Poster presented at the annual meeting of the Society for Prevention Research, Washington, DC.

Eldridge, K. A., & Christensen, A. (2002). Demand-withdraw communication during couple conflict: A review and analysis. In P. Noller & J. A. Feeney (Eds.), *Understanding marriage: Developments in the study of couple interaction* (pp. 289–322). Cambridge: Cambridge University Press.

Dunn, M. J., & McLean, H. (2015). Jealousy-induced sex differences in eye gaze in text messages. *Cyberpsychology, Behavior, and Social Networking, 18*(1), 37–40.

Ellis, C. (2007). Telling secrets, revealing lives: Relational ethics in research with intimate others, *Qualitative Inquiry, 13*(1), 3–29.

Fox, J., Warber, K. M., & Makstaller, D. C. (2013). The role of Facebook in romantic relationship development: An exploration of Knapp's relational stage model. *Journal of Social and Personal Relationships, 30*(6), 771–794.

Glaser, B. G., & Strauss, A. (1967). *Discovery of grounded theory: Strategies for qualitative research.* Chicago: Aldine de Gruyter.

Hargittai, E., & Sandvig, C. (2015). *Digital research confidential: The secrets of studying behavior online.* Cambridge, MA: The MIT Press.

Hasinhoff, A. A. (2015). *Sexting panic: Rethinking criminalization, privacy, and consent.* Urbana, IL: University of Illinois Press.

Humphreys, S., & Vered, K. O. (2014). Reflecting on gender and digital networked media. *Television & New Media, 15*(1), 3–13.

Jones, H. A. (2016). New media producing new labor: Pinterest, yearning, and self-surveillance. *Critical Studies in Media Communication, 33*(4), 352–365.

Kraybill, D. B., Nolt, S. M., & Weaver-Zercher, D. L. (2010). *Amish grace: How forgiveness transcended tragedy.* San Francisco: John Wiley.

Krog, A. (2011). In the name of human rights: I say (how) you speak (before I listen). In N. K. Denzin & Y. S. Lincoln (Eds.), *The Sage Handbook of Qualitative Research* (pp. 381–387). Thousand Oaks, CA: Sage.

Lindlof, T. R., & Taylor, B. C. (2011). *Qualitative communication research methods* (3rd ed.). Thousand Oaks, CA: Sage.

Macapagal, K., Coventry, R., Puckett, J., Phillips, G., & Mustanski, B. (2016). Geosocial networking app use among men who have sex with men in serious romantic relationships. *Archives of Sexual Behavior, 45*(6), 1513–1524.

Markham, A. (2012). Fabrication as ethical practice. *Information, Communication & Society, 15*(3), 334–353.

McGinn, M. M., McFarland, P. T., & Christensen, A. (2009). Antecedents and consequences of demand/withdraw. *Journal of Family Psychology, 23*(5), 749–757.

Meriam-Webster Collegiate Dictionary (11th ed.). (2017). Springfield, MA; Meriam-Webster Inc.

Mumby, D. (1997). Modernism, postmodernism, and communication studies: A rereading of ongoing debates. *Communication Theory, 7,* 1–28.

Mumby, D. (2005). Theorizing resistance in organization studies: A dialectical approach. *Management Communication Quarterly, 19*(1), 19–44.

Palmer-Mehta, V. (2016). A "suitably dead" woman: Grieving Andrea Dworkin. *Communication and Critical/Cultural Studies, 13*(3), 287–304. http://dx.doi.org/10.1080/14791420.2015.1119291

Ruppel, E. K. (2016). Use of communication technologies in romantic relationships: Self-disclosure and the role of relationship development. *Journal of Social and Personal Relationships, 32*(5), 667–686.

Rybas, N. (2012). Producing the self at the digital interface. In P. H. Cheong, J. N. Martin, & L. P. Macfadyen (Eds.), *New media and intercultural communication: Identity, community and politics,* (pp. 93–108). New York: Peter Lang.

Simonson, R., Peck, J., Craig, R. T., & Jackson, J. (2013). *The handbook of communication history.* New York: Routledge.

Sponcil, M., & Gitimu, P. (2013). Use of social media by college students: Relationship to communication and self-concept. *Journal of Technology Research, 4,* 1–14.

Strauss, A., & Corbin, J. (1998). *Basics of qualitative research: Techniques and procedures for developing grounded theory* (2nd ed.). Newbury Park, CA: Sage.

Tanno, D. (1997). *Communication and identity across cultures.* Thousand Oaks, CA: Sage.

Thompson, C. M., & Vangelisti, A. L. (2016). What happens when the standard for openness goes unmet in romantic relationships? Analyses of stress, coping, and relational consequences. *Journal of Social and Personal Relationships, 33*(3), 320–343.

Tracy, S. J. (2013). *Qualitative research methods: Collecting evidence, crafting analysis, communicating impact.* Hoboken, NJ: Wiley-Blackwell.

Traywick, C. (2008, July 31). Art and performance as healing. *AHD Connection, 1*(1), pp. 1–3. Retrieved from http://www.azdhs.gov/documents/prevention/health-systems-development/health-disparities/newsletters/newsletter-issue1-july08.pdf

Turnage, A. (2013). Technological resistance: A metaphor analysis of Enron e-mail messages. *Communication Quarterly, 61*(5), 519–538.

Turnage, A. (2016). Electronic discourse, agency, and organizational change at Enron corporation. *Western Journal of Communication, 80*(2), 204–219.

Venzo, P., & Hess, H. (2013) "Honk Against Homophobia": Rethinking relations between media and sexual minorities, *Journal of Homosexuality, 60*(11), 1539–1556.

Weaver, R., Ferguson, C., Wilbourn, M., & Salamonson, Y. (2014). Men in nursing on television: Exposing and reinforcing stereotypes. *Journal of Advanced Nursing, 70*(4), 833–842.

Yang, C., Brown, B. B., & Braun, M. T. (2014). From Facebook to cell calls: Layers of electronic intimacy in college students' interpersonal relationships. *New Media & Society, 16*(1), 5–23.

Zaeske, S. (2002). Signature of citizenship: The rhetoric of women's antislavery petitions. *Quarterly Journal of Speech, 88,* 147–168.

Chapter 3

Abrams, J., O'Connor, J., & Giles, H. (2002). Identity and intergroup communication. In W. B. Gudykunst & B. Mody (Eds.), *Handbook of international and intercultural communication* (2nd ed., pp. 225–240). Thousand Oaks, CA: Sage.

Adams, T. E., & Berry, K. (2013). Size matters: Performing (il)logical male bodies on *FatClub.com. Text and Performance Quarterly, 33*(4), 308–325.

Allen, B. (2004). *Difference matters: Communicating social identity.* Long Grove, IL: Waveland.

Americans with Disabilities Act of 1990, as amended with Amendments of 2008. Retrieved May 13, 2011, from http://www.ada.gov/pubs/adastatute08.htm

Arana, M. (2008, November 30). He's not black. *Washington Post.* Retrieved December 31, 2008, from http://www.washingtonpost.com/wp-dyn/content/article/2008/11/28/AR2008112802219.html

Bailey, C. (2016, November 14). Hundreds of hate crimes reported since election: SPLC. *NBC News.* Retrieved from http://www.nbcnews.com/news/us-news/hundreds-hate-crimes-reported-election-splc-n683761

Baker, C. (2003, November 30). What is middle class? *The Washington Times.* Retrieved January 16, 2005, from http://www.washtimes.com/specialreport/200311291058557412r.htm

Bennett-Haigney, B. (1995, August). Faulkner makes history at the Citadel. *NOW Newsletter.* Retrieved March 1, 2006, from http://www.now.org/nnt/08-95/citadel.html

Blumer, H. (1969). *Symbolic interactionism: Perspective and method.* Englewood Cliffs, NJ: Prentice Hall.

Bock, G. (1989). Women's history and gender history: Aspects of an international debate. *Gender & History, 1*(1), 7–30.

Brian Boitano: I never intended to reveal I'm gay. (2014, January 10). *CBS News.* Retrieved March 3, 2014, from http://www.cbsnews.com/news/brian-boitano-i-never-intended-to-reveal-im-gay/

Bourdieu, P. (1984). *Distinction: A social critique of the judgment of taste.* (R. Nice, Trans.). London: Routledge & Kegan Paul.

Butler, J. (1990). *Gender trouble: Feminism and the subversion of identity.* New York: Routledge.

Butler, J. (1993). *Bodies that matter: On the discursive limits of "sex."* New York: Routledge.

Campbell, H. A. (Ed.). (2013). *Digital religion: Understanding religious practice in new media worlds.* New York: Routledge.

Carbaugh, D. (2007). Cultural discourse analysis: Communication practices and intercultural encounters. *Journal of Intercultural Communication Research, 36*(3), 167–182.

Cardillo, L. W. (2010). Empowering narratives: Making sense of the experience of growing up with chronic illness or disability. *Western Journal of Communication, 74*(5), 525–546.

Cooley, C. H. (1902). *Human nature and the social order.* New York: Scribner's.

Corey, F. C. (2004). A letter to Paul. *Text and Performance Quarterly, 24,* 185–190.

Corey, F. C., & Nakayama, T. K. (2004). Introduction: Religion and Performance. [Special issue]. *Text and Performance Quarterly, 24,* 209–211.

Cornell University. (2004). Fear factor: 44 percent of Americans queried in Cornell national poll favor curtailing some liberties for Muslim Americans. *Cornell News.* Retrieved December 6, 2006, from http://www.news.cornell.edu/releases/Dec04/Muslim.Poll.bpf.html

Creighton, J. (2014, January 30). Digging into the "Hot or Not" app: What's it all about? *Information Space.* Syracuse University. Retrieved March 2, 2014, from http://infospace.ischool.syr.edu/2014/01/30/digging-into-the-hot-or-not-app-whats-it-all-about/

Croizet, J., & Claire, T. (1998). Extending the concept of stereotype threat to social class: The intellectual underperformance of students from low socioeconomic backgrounds. *Personality and Social Psychology, 24*(5), 588–594.

Daigle, K. (2011, February 12). India's census counts "third gender." *Edge Boston.* Retrieved March 22, 2011, from http://www.edgeboston.com/?116206

Davies, R., & Ikeno, O. (Eds.). (2002). *The Japanese mind: Understanding contemporary culture.* Boston: Tuttleman.

Edwards, R. (1990). Sensitivity to feedback and the development of the self. *Communication Quarterly, 38,* 101–111.

Fassett, D. L., & Morella, D. L. (2008). Remaking (the) discipline: Marking the performative accomplishment of (dis)ability. *Text and Performance Quarterly, 28*(1–2), 139–156.

Foucault, M. (1988). *History of sexuality* (R. Hurley, Trans.). New York: Vintage Books.

Fussell, P. (1992). *Class: A guide through the American status system.* New York: Touchstone.

Guzmán, I. M., & Valdivia, A. N. (2004). Brain, brow, and booty: Latina iconicity in U.S. popular culture. *Communication Review, 7,* 205–221.

Hacker, A. (2003). *Two nations: Black and white, separate, hostile, unequal.* New York: Scribner.

Harwood, J. (2006). Communication as social identity. In G. J. Shepherd, J. St. John, & T. Striphas (Eds.), *Communication as . . . : Perspectives on theory* (pp. 84–90). Thousand Oaks, CA: Sage.

Hecht, M. L. (1993). 2002—A research odyssey. *Communication Monographs, 60,* 76–82.

Hecht, M. L., Jackson R. L., III, & Ribeau, S. A. (2003). *African American communication: Exploring identity and culture.* (2nd ed.). Mahwah, NJ: Lawrence Erlbaum Associates.

Henderson, B., & Ostrander, R. N. (2008). Introduction to special issue on disability studies/performance studies. *Text and Performance Quarterly, 28*(1–2), 1–5.

Hirschman, C. (2003, May). *The rise and fall of the concept of race.* Paper presented at the annual meeting of the Population Association of America, Minneapolis, MN.

Horn, D. (2013, April 14). Middle class a matter of income, attitude. *USA Today.* Retrieved March 2, 2014, from http://www.usatoday.com/story/money/business/2013/04/14/middle-class-hard-define/2080565/

Johnson, A. G. (2001). *Privilege, power and difference.* Boston: McGraw-Hill.

Jones, N. A., & Smith, A. S. (2001). The two or more races population. *Census 2000 Brief (U.S. Census Bureau Publication No. C2KBR/01-6).* Washington, DC: U.S. Government Printing Office.

Kimel, S., & Kunst, J. (2016, May 26). Can DNA ancestry testing make you more racist? Scientific American. Retrieved from https://blogs.scientificamerican.com/guest-blog/can-dna-ancestry-testing-make-you-more-racist/"

Kimmel, M. S. (2005). *The history of men: Essays in the history of American and British masculinities.* Albany: State University of New York Press.

Koshy, S. (2004). *Sexual naturalization: Asian Americans and miscegenation.* Stanford, CA: Stanford University Press.

Kraybill, D. B. (1989). *The riddle of Amish culture.* Baltimore: Johns Hopkins University Press.

Lagarde, D. (2005, September 22–28). Afghanistan: La loi des tribus. *L'Express International,* 30–37.

Lindemann, K. (2008). "I can't be standing up out there": Communicative performances of (dis)ability in wheelchair rugby. *Text and Performance Quarterly, 28*(1–2), 98–115.

Lerner, M. (2008, November 18). Minnesota disciplines four doctors, two for inappropriate contact. *Star-Tribune.* Retrieved May 3, 2011, from http://www.startribune.com/lifestyle/34691559.html?page=all&prepage=1&c=y#continue

Loden, M., & Rosener, J. B. (1991). *Workforce America: Managing workforce diversity as a vital resource.* Homewood, IL: Business One Irwin.

Lucas, K. (2011). Socializing messages in blue-collar families: Communication pathways to social mobility and reproduction. *Western Journal of Communication, 75*(1), 95–121.

Lum, Z.-A. (2017, February 2). Joël Lightbound urges no more silence over Islamophobia after Quebec City mosque attack. Huffington Post Canada. Retrieved from: http://www.huffingtonpost.ca/2017/02/02/joel-lightbound-quebec-shooting_n_14575968.html

Manczak, D. W. (1999, July 1). Raising your child's self-esteem. *Clinical Reference Systems,* 1242.

Marshall, G. A. (1993). Racial classification: Popular and Scientific. In S. G. Harding (Ed.), *The "racial" economy of science: Toward a democratic future* (pp. 116–127). Bloomington: Indiana University Press.

Martin, J. N., & Harrell, T. (1996). Reentry training for intercultural sojourners. In D. Landis & R. S. Bhagat (Eds.), *Handbook of intercultural training* (2nd ed., pp. 307–326). Thousand Oaks, CA: Sage.

McGlone, M. S., & Aronson, J. (2006). Stereotype threat, identity salience, and spatial reasoning. *Journal of Applied Development Psychology, 27*(5), 486–493.

McHugh, M. (2013, August 23). It's catfishing season! How to tell lovers from liars online, and more. *Digital Trends.* Retrieved March 3, 2014, from http://www.digitaltrends.com/web/its-catfishing-season-how-to-tell-lovers-from-liars-online-and-more/#ixzz2uvnrrkOx

Mead, G. H. (1934). *Mind, self, and society.* Chicago: University of Chicago Press.

Mikkelsen, E. G., & Einarsen, S. (2001). Bullying in Danish work-life: Prevalence and health correlates. *European Journal of Work and Organizational Psychology, 10,* 393–413.

Negley, C. (2014, February 17). Hockey creates patriotic hashtag. *Sporting News.* Retrieved March 2, 2014, from http://www.sportingnews.com/olympics/story/2014-02-17/2014-sochi-olympics-usa-hockey-creates-patriotic-hashtag-america-dawnsearlylight

Next UK census may ask about sexuality and gender identity. (2016, May 23). *The Guardian.* Retrieved April 23, 2017, from https://www.theguardian.com/uk-news/2016/may/23/next-uk-census-may-ask-about-sexuality-and-gender-identity

Office for National Statistics. (2012, December 11). *Ethnicity and national identity in England and Wales.* Retrieved March 2, 2014, from http://www.ons.gov.uk/ons/dcp171776_290558.pdf

Online Glossary. (2005, January). Prentice Hall. Retrieved January 16, 2005, from www.prenhall.com/rm_student/html/glossary/a_gloss.html

Palladino, G. (1996). *Teenagers: An American history.* New York: Basic Books.

Papalia, D. E., Olds, S. W., & Feldman, R. D. (2002). *A child's world: Infancy through adolescence*. New York: McGraw-Hill.

Philipsen, G. (1992). *Speaking culturally: Explorations in social communication*. Albany: State University of New York Press.

Rawls, J. (1995). Self-respect, excellence, and shame. In R. S. Dillon (Ed.), *Dignity, character, and self-respect* (pp. 125–131). New York: Routledge.

Razavi, M. (2013). *Navigating new national identity online: On immigrant children, identity & the internet*. Master's Thesis. Georgetown University, Washington, DC. Retrieved March 2, 2014, from https://repository.library.georgetown.edu/bitstream/handle/10822/558243/Razavi_georgetown_0076M_12273.pdf?sequence=1

Roland, C. E., & Foxx, R. M. (2003). Self-respect: A neglected concept. *Philosophical Psychology*. 16(2), 247–288.

Rosenblith, J. F. (1992). *In the beginning: Development from conception to age two*. Newbury Park, CA: Sage.

Sanders, W. B. (1994). *Gangbangs and drive-bys: Grounded culture and juvenile gang violence*. New York: Aldine de Gruyter.

Shih, M., Pittinsky, T. L., & Ambady, N. (1999). Stereotype susceptibility: Identity salience and shifts in quantitative performance. *Psychological Science*. 10(1), 80–83.

Sloop, J. M. (2004). *Disciplining gender: Rhetoric of sex identity in contemporary U.S. culture*. Amherst: University of Massachusetts Press.

Smith, J. L., & White, P. H. (2002). An examination of implicitly activated, explicitly activated, and nullified stereotypes on mathematical performance: It's not just a women's issue. *Sex Roles*, 47(3–4), 179–191.

Steele, C. M., & Aronson, J. (1995). Stereotype threat and intellectual test performance of African Americans. *Journal of Personality and Social Psychology*, 69(5), 797–811.

Sullivan, H. S. (1953). *The interpersonal theory of psychology*. New York: Norton.

Sullivan, T. A., Warren, E., & Westbrook, J. (2001). *The fragile middle class: Americans in debt*. New Haven: Yale University Press.

Taylor, J. (2005, June 6). Between two worlds: How many Americans really attend church each week? [Web log post]. Retrieved January 30, 2006, from http://theologica.blogspot.com/2005/06/how-many-americans-really-attend.html

Ting-Toomey, S. (1999). *Communicating across cultures*. New York: Guilford.

Trethewey, A. (2001). Reproducing and resisting the master narrative of decline: Midlife professional women's experiences of aging. *Management Communication Quarterly*, 15, 183–226.

Van Meter, J. (2013, April 10). Anthony Weiner and Huma Abedin's post-scandal playbook. *New York Times*. Retrieved March 3, 2014, from http://www.nytimes.com/2013/04/14/magazine/anthony-weiner-and-huma-abedins-post-scandal-playbook.html?pagewanted=all&_r=0

Vevea, N. (2008). *Body Art: Performing Identity Through Tattoos and Piercing*. Paper presented at the annual meeting of the NCA 94th Annual Convention, TBA, San Diego, CA Online. Retrieved March 11, 2011, from http://www.allacademic.com/meta/p258244_index.html

Waters, M. C. (1990). *Ethnic options: Choosing identities in America*. Berkeley: University of California Press.

Wax, E. (2005, September 26–October 2). Beyond the pull of the tribe: In Kenya, some teens find unity in contemporary culture. *Washington Post*, National Weekly Edition, 22(49), 8.

Weber, P. (2014, February 21). Confused by all the new Facebook genders? Here's what they mean. *Slate*. Retrieved March 2, 2014, from http://www.slate.com/blogs/lexicon_valley/2014/02/21/gender_facebook_now_has_56_categories_to_choose_from_including_cisgender.html.

Yan, H., Squeglia, K., & Walker, K. (2016, December 22). "Make America White Again": Hate speech and crimes post-election. CNN. Retrieved from: http://www.cnn.com/2016/11/10/us/post-election-hate-crimes-and-fears-trnd/

Chapter 4

Applegate, J. (1982). The impact of construct system development on communication and impression formation in persuasive contexts. *Communication Monographs*, 49, 277–289.

Bradbury, T. N., & Fincham, F. D. (1988). Individual difference variables in close relationships: A contextual model of marriage as an integrative framework. *Journal of Personality and Social Psychology*, 54, 713–721.

Braithwaite, C. (1990). Communicative silence: A cross-cultural study of Basso's hypothesis. In D. Carbaugh (Ed.), *Cultural communication and intercultural contact* (pp. 321–327). Hillsdale NJ: Lawrence Erlbaum Associates.

Brislin, R. (2000). *Understanding culture's influence on behavior* (2nd ed.). Belmont, CA: Wadsworth.

Burgoon, J. K., Berger, C. R., & Waldron, V. R. (2000). Mindfulness and interpersonal communication. *Journal of Social Issues*, 56, 105–127.

Burleson, B. R., & Caplan, S. E. (1998). Cognitive complexity. In J. C. McCroskey, J. Daly, & M. M. Martin (Eds.), *Communication and personality: Trait perspectives*. Cresskill, NJ: Hampton.

Chaiken, S. (1986). Physical appearance and social influence. In C. P. Herman, M. P. Zanna, & E. T. Higgins (Eds.), *Physical appearance, stigma, and social behavior: The Ontario symposium* (Vol. 3, pp. 143–144). Hillsdale, NJ: Erlbaum.

Chapin, J. (2001). It won't happen to me: The role of optimistic bias in African American teens' risky sexual practices. *Howard Journal of Communication*, 12, 49–59.

Classen, C. (1990). Sweet colors, fragrant songs: Sensory models of the Andes and the Amazon. *American Ethnologist*, 14, 722–735.

Cox, W. T. L., Abramson, L. Y., Devine, P. G., & Hollon, S. D. (2012). Stereotypes, prejudice, and depression: The integrated perspective. *Perspectives on Psychological Science* 7(5), 427–449. doi:10.1177/1745691612455204

Croy, I., Buschhüter, D., Seo, H. S., Negoias, S., & Hummel, T. (2010). Individual significance of olfaction: Development of a questionnaire. *Eur Arch Otorhinolaryngol*, 267(1), 67–71. doi : 10.1007/s00405-009-1054-0

Dean, J. (2014). Intriguing types of synesthesia: Tasting words, seeing sounds and hearing colors. *PsyBlog*. Retrieved December 15, 2014, from http://www.spring.org.uk/2014/05/6-intriguing-types-of-synesthesia-tasting-words-seeing-sounds-hearing-colours-and-more.php

Deutsch, F. M., Sullivan, L., Sage, C., & Basile, N. (1991). The relations among talking, liking, and similarity between friends. *Personality and Social Psychology Bulletin*, 17, 406–411.

Dijk, T. A., van. (1977). *Text and context: Explorations in the semantics and pragmatics of discourse*. London: Longman.

Dillard, J. P., Solomon, D. H., & Samp, J. A. (1996). Framing social reality: The relevance of relational judgments. *Communication Research*, 23, 703–723.

Douthat, R. (2005, November). Does meritocracy work? *Atlantic*, 120–126.

Durfeel, J. (2006). "Social change" and "status quo" framing effects on risk perception: An exploratory experiment. *Science Communication* 27(4), 459–495. doi : 10.1177/1075547005285334

Ehrenreich, B. (2001). *Nickel and dimed: On (not) getting by in America*. New York: Metropolitan Books.

Estroff, H. (2004, September/October). Cupid's comeuppance. *Psychology Today*. Retrieved March 15, 2006, from www.psychologytoday.com/articles/pto-20040921-000001.html

Everyday fantasia: The world of synesthesia. *American Psychological Association*. Retrieved December 15, 2014, from http://www.apa.org/monitor/mar01/synesthesia.aspx

Fehr, B., Baldwin, M., Collins, L., Patterson, S., & Benditt, R. (1999). Anger in close relationships: An interpersonal script analysis. *Personality and Social Psychology*, 25(3), 299–312. **doi : 10.1177/0146167299025003003**

Goldstein, E. B. (2010). *Encyclopedia of perception* (8th ed.). Thousand Oaks, CA: Sage Publications.

Granello, D. H. (2010). Cognitive complexity among practicing counselors: How thinking changes with experience. *Journal of Counseling and Development*, 88(1), 92–100. doi : 10.1002/j.1556-6678.2010.tb00155

Greenough, W. T., Black, J. E., & Wallace, C. S. (1987). Experience and brain development. *Child Development*, 58, 539–559.

Griffin, E. (1994). *A first look at communication theory*. New York: McGraw-Hill.

Goldstein, E. B. (2010). *Sensation and Perception* (9th ed.). Belmont, CA: Wadsworth.

Gueguen, N., & De Gail, M. (2003). The effect of smiling on helping behavior: Smiling and good Samaritan behavior. *Communication Reports*, 16(2), 133–140.

Hacker, A. (2003). *Two nations: Black and white, separate, hostile, unequal.* New York: Scribner.

Harvey, P., & Martinko, M. J. (2010). Attribution theory and motivation. In N. Borkowski (Ed.), *Organizational behavior in health care* (2nd *ed.*, pp. 147–164). Boston: Jones and Bartlett.

Hehman, E., Carpinella, C. M., Johnson, K. L., Leitner, J. B., & Freeman, J. B. (2014). Early processing of gendered facial cues predicts the electoral success of female politicians. *Social Psychology and Personality Science, 5*(7), 815–824.

Heider, F. (1958/2013). *The psychology of interpersonal relations.* New York: Wiley.

Heine, S. J., & Lehman, D. R. (2004). Move the body, change the self: Acculturative effects on self-concept. In A. Schaller & C. Crandall (Eds.), *The psychological foundations of culture* (pp. 305–331). Hillsdale, NJ: Erlbaum.

Herz, R. S., & Inzlicht, M. (2002). Sex differences in response to physical and social factors involved in human mate selection: The importance of smell for women. *Evolution and Human Behavior, 23,* 359–364.

Holmstrom, A. J., & Burleson, B. R. (2010). An initial test of a cognitive-emotional theory of esteem support messages. *Journal of Counseling and Development, 88*(1), 92–100.

Hummel T., Kobal G., Gudziol H., Mackay-Sim, A. (2007). Normative data for the "Sniffin' Sticks" including tests of odor identification, odor discrimination, and olfactory thresholds: An upgrade based on a group of more than 3,000 subjects. *European Archives of Otorhino-laryngology, 264*(3), 237–43.

Hurley R. W., & Adams, M. C. B. (2008). Sex, gender and pain: An overview of a complex field. *Anesthesia and Analgesia. 107,* 309–17.

Kanizsa, G. (1979). *Organization in vision.* New York: Praeger.

Kellerman, K. (2004). A goal-direct approach to compliance-gaining: Relating differences among goals to differences in behavior. *Communication Research, 31,* 345–347.

Kelley, H. H. (1973). The processes of causal attribution. *American Psychologist, 28,* 107–128.

Kim, M. S. (2002). *Non-Western perspectives on human communication.* Thousand Oaks, CA: Sage.

Korneliussen, I. (2012). Women smell better than men. *Science Nordic.* Retrieved May 14, 2014, from http://sciencenordic.com/women-smell-better-men

Kirouac, G., & Hess, U. (1999). Group membership and the decoding of nonverbal behavior. In R. S. Feldman & P. Philippot (Eds.), *The social context of nonverbal behavior* (pp. 182–210). New York: Cambridge University Press.

Krivonos, P. D., & Knapp, M. L. (1975). Initiating communication: What do you say when you say hello? *Central States Speech Journal, 26,* 115–125.

Lakoff, G. (1987). *Women, fire, and dangerous things: What categories reveal about the mind.* Chicago: University of Chicago Press.

Langer, E. J. (1978). Rethinking the role of thought in social interaction. In J. H. Harvey, W. Ickes, & R. F. Kidd (Eds.), *New directions in attribution research* (Vol. 2, pp. 3–58). New York: Wiley.

Levinthal, D., & Gavetti, G. (2000, March). Looking forward and looking backward: Cognition and experiential search. *Administrative Science Quarterly,* 1–9.

Link, B. G., & Phelan, J. C. (2001, August). Conceptualizing stigma. *Annual Review of Sociology, 27,* 363–385.

Lupfer, M. B., Weeks, M., & Dupuis, S. (2000). How pervasive is the negativity bias in judgments based on character appraisal? *Personality and Social Psychology Bulletin, 26,* 1353–1366.

Maccaby, E. E., & Jacklin, C. N. (1978). *The psychology of sex differences.* Palo Alto, CA: Stanford University Press.

Manusov, V., & Spitzberg, B. (2008). Attributes of attribution theory: Finding good cause in the search for a theory. In D. O. Braithwaite & L. A. Baxter (Eds.), *Engaging theories in interpersonal* (pp. 37–49). Thousand Oaks, CA: Sage.

Markus, H. R., Mullally, P. R., & Kitayama, S. (1997). Selfways: Diversity in modes of cultural participation. In U. Neisser & D. A. Jopling (Eds.), *The conceptual self in context* (pp. 13–59). Cambridge, UK: Cambridge University Press.

McCoy, N. L., & Pitino, L. (2002). Pheromonal influences on sociosexual behavior in young women. *Physiology and Behavior, 75,* 367–375.

Middle of the Class (July 14, 2005). [Special report: America]. *Economist.* Retrieved March 10, 2006, from http://www.economist.com/displayStory.cfm?Story_id=4148885

Morgan, M. J. (1977). *Molyneux's question: Vision, touch and the philosophy of perception.* New York: Cambridge University Press.

Neale, M. A., & Bazerman, M. H. (1991). *Cognition and rationality in negotiation.* New York: Free Press.

Olivier, C., Leyens, J.-P., Yzerbyt, V. Y., & Walther, E. (1999). Judgeability concerns: The interplay of information, applicability, and accountability in the over-attribution bias. *Journal of Personality and Social Psychology, 76*(3), 377–387. doi : 10.1037/0022-3514.76.3.377

Operario, D., & Fiske, S. T. (2003). Stereotypes: Content, structures, processes, and contexts. In R. Brown & S. L. Gaertner, (Eds.) *Blackwell Handbook of Social Psychology: Intergroup Processes* (pp. 22–44). Malden, MA: Blackwell.

Pearce, W. B. (1994). *Interpersonal communication: Making social worlds.* New York: HarperCollins.

Pew Research Center for People and the Press. (2005, September 8). *Two-in-three critical of Bush's relief efforts: Huge racial divide over Katrina and its consequences.* Retrieved June 1, 2006, from http://people-press.org/reports/pdf/255.pdf

Planalp, S. (1993). Communication, cognition, and emotion. *Communication Monographs, 60,* 3–9.

Putnam, L. L., & Holmer, M. (1992). Framing, reframing and issue development. In L. L. Putnam & M. E. Roloff (Eds.), *Communication and negotiation* (pp. 128–155). Newbury Park, CA: Sage.

Rothenberg, P. S. (1992). *Race, class, and gender in the United States.* New York: St. Martin's Press.

Samter, W., & Burleson, B. R. (1984). Cognitive and motivational influences on spontaneous comforting behavior. *Human Communication Research, 11,* 231–260.

Schwarz, N. (2006). Attitude research: Between Ockham's razor and the fundamental attribution error. *Journal of Consumer Research, 33,* 19–21.

Scollon, R., & Wong-Scollon, S. (1990). Athabaskan-English interethnic communication. In D. Carbaugh (Ed.), *Cultural communication and intercultural contact* (pp. 259–287). Hillsdale, NJ: Erlbaum.

Seligman, M. (1998). *Learned optimism.* New York: Simon & Schuster.

Sherwood, B. (2009). *The survivor's club.* New York: Grand Central Publishing.

Shore, B. (1996). *Culture in mind: Cognition, culture and the problem of meaning.* New York: Oxford University Press.

Sillars, A. L., Roberts, L. J., Leonard, K. E., & Dun, T. (2000). Cognition during marital conflict: The relationship of thought and talk. *Journal of Social and Personal Relationships, 17,* 479–502.

Sillars, A. L., Roberts, L. J., Leonard, K. E., & Dun, T. (2002). Cognition and communication during marital conflicts: How alcohol affects subjective coding of interaction in aggressive and nonaggressive couples. In P. Noller & J. A. Feeney (Eds.), *Understanding marriage: Developments in the study of couples' interaction* (pp. 85–112). Cambridge, UK: Cambridge University Press.

Singh, D., & Bronstad, P. M. (2001). Female body odour is a potential cue to ovulation. *Proceedings of the Royal Society: Biological Science, 268,* 797–801.

Siu, W. L. W., & Finnegan, J. R. (2004, May). *An exploratory study of the interaction of affect and cognition in message evaluation.* Paper presented at the International Communication Association Convention, San Francisco, CA.

Smith, S. W., Kopfman, J. E., Lindsey, L., Massi, Y. J., & Morrison, K. (2004). Encouraging family discussion on the decision to donate organs: The role of the willingness to communicate scale. *Health Communication, 16,* 333–346.

Snyder, M. (1998). Self-fulfilling stereotypes. In P. S. Rothenberg (Ed.), *Race, class and gender in the U.S.: An integrated study* (pp. 452–457). New York: St. Martin's Press.

Stephan, C., & Stephan, W. (1992). Reducing intercultural anxiety through intercultural contact. *International Journal of Intercultural Relations, 16,* 89–106.

Than, K. (2005). Rare but real: People who feel, taste and hear color. *LiveScience.* Retrieved December 15, 2014, from http://www.livescience.com/169-rare-real-people-feel-taste-hear-color.html

Ting-Toomey, S. (1999). *Communicating across cultures.* New York: Guilford.

National Research Council. (1989). *Improving risk communication.* Committee on risk perception and communication. Washington, DC: National Academy Press.

Weick, K. (1995). *Sensemaking in organizations*. Thousand Oaks, CA: Sage.

Wilson, G., & Nias, D. (1999). Beauty can't be beat. In J. A. DeVito & L. Guerrero, (Eds.), *The nonverbal communication reader: Classic and contemporary readings* (2nd ed., pp. 92–132). Prospect Heights, IL: Waveland Press.

Chapter 5

Académie française. (2017, February 2). Self-service. Retrieved February 20, 2017, from http://www.academie-francaise.fr/self-service

American Civil Liberties Union. (1994). Free speech: Hate speech on campus. Retrieved March 16, 2014, from http://www.aclu.org/free-speech/hate-speech-campus

Anderson, J. F., Beard, F. K., & Walther, J. B. (2010). Turn-taking and the local management of conversation in a highly simultaneous computer-mediated communication system. *Language@Internet*. Retrieved March 7, 2014, from http://www.languageatinternet.org/articles/2010/2804

Arana, G. (2013 January 10). Creaky voice: Yet another example of young women's linguistic ingenuity. *Atlantic.com*. Retrieved March 16, 2014, from http://www.theatlantic.com/sexes/archive/2013/01/creaky-voice-yet-another-example-of-young-womens-linguistic-ingenuity/267046/

Austrian woman convicted under law that makes Holocaust denial illegal. *Jewish Telegraphic Agency*. Retrieved April 23, 2017, from http://www.jta.org/2017/02/19/news-opinion/world/austrian-woman-convicted-under-law-that-makes-holocaust-denial-illegal

Aylor, B., & Dainton, M. (2004). Biological sex and psychological gender as predictors of routine and strategic relational maintenance. *Sex Roles: A Journal of Research, 50*, 689–697.

Bippus, A. M., & Young, S. L. (2005). Owning your emotions: Reactions to expressions of self versus other-attributed positive and negative emotions. *Journal of Applied Communication Research, 33*, 26–45.

Bowen, S. P. (2012). Jewish and/or woman: Identity and communicative styles. In A. González, M. Houston, & V. Chen. (Eds.), (5th ed., pp. 47–52). New York: Oxford University Press.

Boxer, D. (2002). Nagging: The familial conflict arena. *Journal of Pragmatics, 34*, 49–61.

Burrell, N. A., Donohue, W. A., & Allen, M. (1988). Gender-based perceptual biases in mediation. *Communication Research, 15*, 447–469.

Caughlin, J. P. (2002). The demand/withdraw pattern of communication as a predictor of marital satisfaction over time: Unresolved issues and future directions. *Human Communication Research, 28*, 49–85.

Chomsky, N. (1957). *Syntactic Structures*. The Hague/Paris: Mouton.

Cohen, R. (2014, March 12). In defense of *I can't even*. *Slate.com*. Retrieved March 16, 2014, from http://www.slate.com/blogs/lexicon_valley/2014/03/12/language_i_can_t_even_is_just_the_newest_example_of_an_old_greek_rhetorical.html

Crystal, D. (2003). *The Cambridge encyclopedia of the English language*. New York: Cambridge University Press.

Dance, F. E. X., & Larson, C. E. (1976). *The functions of human communication*. New York: Holt, Rinehart, & Winston.

Deutscher, G. (2010). *Through the language glass: Why the world looks different in other languages*. New York: Metropolitan Books.

Duke, M. P., Fivush, R., Lazarus, A., & Bohanek, J. (2003). *Of ketchup and kin: Dinnertime conversations as a major source of family knowledge, family adjustment, and family resilience* [Working Paper #26]. Retrieved March 16, 2014, from http://www.marial.emory.edu/research/

Duncan, J. (October 21, 2016). Thug, 37, smashed a plank of wood in a Spanish man's face and screamed 'speak English' at him in a racist attack. *Daily Mail*. Retrieved April 23, 2017, from http://www.daily-mail.co.uk/news/article-3859032/Thug-37-smashed-plank-wood-Spanish-man-s-face-screamed-speak-English-smirked-shown-pictures-injuries.html

Edwards, J. V. (2004). Foundations of bilingualism. In T. K. Bhatia & W. C. Ritchie (Eds.), *The handbook of bilingualism* (pp. 7–31). Malden, MA: Blackwell.

Ellis, A., & Beattie, G. (1986). Variations within a language. *The psychology of language and communication*. (pp. 109–114). East Sussex, UK: Psychology Press.

Fromkin, V., & Rodman, R. (1983). *An introduction to language*. New York: Holt, Rinehart, and Winston.

Gamp, O. (2017, February 12). Online giant Amazon facing pressure over Holocaust denial books. *International Business Times*. Retrieved April 23, 2017, from http://www.ibtimes.co.uk/online-giant-amazon-facing-pressure-over-holocaust-denial-books-1606130

Gong, G. (2012). When Mississippi Chinese talk. In A. González, M. Houston, & V. Chen (Eds.), *Our voices: Essays in culture, ethnicity, and communication* (5th ed., pp. 104–111). New York: Oxford University Press.

Gray, J. (2012). *Men are from Mars, women are from Venus* (20th anniversary ed.). New York: HarperCollins.

Hannah, A., & Murachver, T. (2007). Gender preferential responses to speech. *Journal of Language and Social Psychology, 26*(3), 274–290.

Hecht, M. L., Jackson, R. L., II, & Ribeau, S. A. (2003). *African American communication*. Mahwah, NJ: Lawrence Erlbaum Associates.

Hegarty, P., & Buechel, C. (2006). Androcentric reporting of gender differences in APA journals: 1965–2004. *Review of General Psychology, 10*(4), 377–389.

Heilman, M. E. (2001). Description and prescription: How gender stereotypes prevent women's ascent up the organizational ladder. In "Gender, hierarchy and leadership," Ed. L. Carli & A. Eagly. *Journal of Social Issues, 57*(4), 657–674.

Heilman, M. E., Caleo, S., & Halim, M. L. (2010). Just the thought of it! Effects of anticipating computer-mediated communication on gender stereotyping. *Journal of Experimental Social Psychology, 46*(4), 672–675.

Hess, A. (2016, March 29). Who's 'they'? *New York Times*. Retrieved April 23, 2017 from https://www.nytimes.com/2016/04/03/magazine/whos-they.html

Hoijer, H. (1994). The Sapir-Whorf hypothesis. In L. Samovar & R. E. Porter (Eds.), *Intercultural communication: A reader* (pp. 194–200). Belmont, CA: Wadsworth.

Holmes, S. (2017, February 12). Dozens of books claiming the Holocaust was a HOAX are available on Amazon for as little as 99 p." *Daily Mail*. Retrieved April 23, 2017, from http://www.dailymail.co.uk/news/article-4216568/Dozens-books-claiming-Holocaust-hoax-Amazon-buy.html

Hudson, R. A. (1983). *Sociolinguistics*. London: Cambridge University Press.

Hyde, J. S. (2006). Gender similarities still rule. *American Psychologist, 61*(6), 641–642.

Jany, L. (2016, November 22). Man punched for speaking Somali on Metro Transit bus, charges say. *Star Tribune*. Retrieved April 23, 2017, from http://www.startribune.com/man-charged-with-racially-motivated-assault-aboard-metro-transit-bus/402503115/

Kikoski, J. F., & Kikoski, C. K. (1999). *Reflexive communication in the culturally diverse workplace*. Westport, CT: Praeger.

Kim, M. S. (2002). *Non-Western perspectives on human communication*. Thousand Oaks, CA: Sage.

Kohonen, S. (2004). Turn-taking in conversation: Overlaps and interruptions in intercultural talk. *Cahiers, 10.1*, 15–32.

Kubany, E. S., Bauer, G. B., Muraoka, M., Richard, D. C., & Read, P. (1995). Impact of labeled anger and blame in intimate relationships. *Journal of Social and Clinical Psychology, 14*, 53–60.

Labov, W. (1980). The social origins of sound change. In W. Labov (Ed.), *Locating language in time and space* (pp. 251–265). New York: Academic Press.

Labov, W. (Ed.). (2005). *Atlas of North American English*. New York: Walter De Gruyter.

Leaper, C., & Ayres, M. M. (2007). A meta-analytic review of gender variation in adults' language use: Talkativeness, affiliative speech, and assertive speech. *Personality and Social Psychology Review, 11*(4), 328–363.

Liptak, A. (2008). Hate speech or free speech? What much of West bans is protected in U.S. *New York Times*. Retrieved March 16, 2014, from http://www.nytimes.com/2008/06/11/world/americas/11iht-hate.4.13645369.html

Martin, J. N., Krizek, R. L., Nakayama, T. K., & Bradford, L. (1999). What do white people want to be called? A study of self-labels for white Americans. In T. K. Nakayama & J. N. Martin (Eds.),

Whiteness: The communication of social identity (pp. 27–50). Thousand Oaks, CA: Sage.

Media Awareness Network (n.d.). Online hate and free speech. Retrieved March 16, 2014, from http://mediasmarts.ca/online-hate/online-hate-and-free-speech

Mehl, M. R., & Pennebaker, J. W. (2003). The sounds of social life: A psychometric analysis of students' daily social environments and natural conversations. *Journal of Personality and Social Psychology, 84,* 857–70.

Mey, J. L. (2001). *Pragmatics: An introduction* (2nd ed.). Oxford, UK: Blackwell Publishing.

Mulac, A., Bradac. J. J., & Gibbons, P. (2001). Empirical support for the gender-as-culture hypothesis: An intercultural analysis of male/female language differences. *Human Communication Research, 27,* 121–152.

Nofsinger, R. (1999). *Everyday conversation*. Prospect Heights, IL: Waveland.

Orbe, M. P. (1998). *Constructing co-cultural theory: An explication of culture, power, and communication*. Thousand Oaks, CA: Sage.

Paramasivam, S. (2007). Managing disagreement while managing not to disagree: Polite disagreement in negotiation discourse. *Journal of Intercultural Communication Research, 36*(2), 91–116.

Park, J. E. (2016). Turn-taking in Korean conversation. *Journal of Pragmatics, 99,* 62-77.

Pennebaker, J. W., & Stone, L. D. (2003). Words of wisdom: Language use across the life span. *Journal of Personality and Social Psychology, 82,* 291–301.

Philips, S. U. (1990). Some sources of cultural variability in the regulation of talk. In D. Carbaugh (Ed.), *Cultural communication and intercultural contact* (pp. 329–344). Hillsdale, NJ: Erlbaum.

Piaget, J. (1952). *The origins of intelligence in children*. New York: International Universities Press.

Pinker, S. (2007). *The stuff of thought: Language as a window into human nature*. New York: Viking.

Pinto, D., & Raschio, R. (2007). A comparative study of requests in heritage speaker Spanish, L1 Spanish, and L1 English. *International Journal of Bilingualism, 11*(2), 135–155.

Preston, D. R. (2003). Where are the dialects of American English at anyhow? *American Speech, 78,* 235–254.

Ramírez-Esparza, N., Gosling, S. D., Benet-Martínez, V., Potter, J. D., & Pennebaker, J. W. (2006). Do bilinguals have two personalities? A special case of cultural frame switching. *Journal of Research in Personality, 40,* 99–120.

Reid, S. A., Keerie, N., & Palomares, N. A. (2003). Language, gender salience, and social influence. *Journal of Language and Social Psychology, 22,* 210–233.

Ruben, D. L. (2003). Help! My professor (or doctor or boss) doesn't talk English! In J. N. Martin, T. K. Nakayama, & L. A. Flores (Eds.). *Readings in intercultural communication* (2nd ed., pp. 127–138). Boston: McGraw-Hill.

Sacks, H., Schegloff, E., & Jefferson, G. (1978). A simplest systematics for the organization of turn-taking for conversation. In J. Schenkein (Ed.), *Studies in the organization of conversational interaction* (pp. 7–55). New York: Academic Press.

Sagrestano, L. M., Heavey, C. L., & Christensen, A. (1998). Theoretical approaches to understanding sex differences and similarities in conflict behavior. In D. J. Canary & K. Dindia (Eds.), *Sex differences and similarities in communication: Critical essays and empirical investigations on sex and gender in interaction* (pp. 287–302). Mahwah, NJ: Erlbaum.

Sauerbrey A. (2013, September 25). How do you say "blog" in German? *New York Times.* Retrieved March 6, 2014, from http://www.nytimes.com/2013/09/26/opinion/how-do-you-say-blog-in-german.html?_r=0

Sbisa, M. (2002). Speech act in context. *Language & Communication, 22,* 421–436.

Schegloff, E. A. (2000). Overlapping talk and the organization of turn-taking for conversation. *Language in Society, 29,* 1–63.

Scheibel, D. (1995). Making waves with Burke: Surf Nazi culture and the rhetoric of localism. *Western Journal of Communication, 59*(4), 253–269.

Sedivy, J. (2012, March 28). Votes and vowels: A changing accent shows how language parallels politics. *Discover.* Retrieved March 7, 2014, from http://blogs.discovermagazine.com/

crux/2012/03/28/votes-and-vowels-a-changing-accent-shows-how-language-parallels-politics/#.UxoiICifNiF

Sellers, J. G., Woolsey, M. D., & Swann, J. B. (2007). Is silence more golden for women than men? Observers derogate effusive women and their quiet partners. *Sex Roles, 57*(7–8), 477–482.

Shutiva, C. (2012). Native American culture and communication through humor. In A. González, M. Houston, & V. Chen (Eds.), *Our voices: Essays in culture, ethnicity, and communication* (5th ed., pp. 134–138). New York: Oxford University Press.

Social Mobility Commission. (2017, January 26). New research uncovers 'class pay gap' in Britain's professions. Retrieved from https://www.gov.uk/government/news/new-research-uncovers-class-pay-gap-in-britains-professions

Stavans, I. (2017, January 30). Trump, the Wall and the Spanish Language. *The New York Times.* Retrieved from https://www.nytimes.com/2017/01/30/opinion/trump-the-wall-and-the-spanish-language.html?_r=0

U.S. Department of Health and Human Services. (n.d.). *What is cyberbullying?* Retrieved March 7, 2014, from: http://www.stopbullying.gov/cyberbullying/what-is-it/

Walker, J. L. (2010). *"You are an African American, so why are you talking like a white person?"* Omaha, NE: P.T.C.E, Inc.

Weger, H., Jr. (2005). Disconfirming communication and self-verification in marriage: Associations among the demand/withdraw interaction pattern, feeling understood, and marital satisfaction. *Journal of Social and Personal Relationships, 22,* 19–31.

Willsher, K. (2016, February 5). Not the oignon: Fury as France changes 2,000 spellings and drops some accents. *The Guardian.* Retrieved from https://www.theguardian.com/world/2016/feb/05/not-the-oignon-fury-france-changes-2000-spellings-ditches-circumflex

Wood, J. T. (2002). *Gendered lives: Communication, gender and cultures.* Belmont, CA: Wadsworth.

Chapter 6

Abu-Ghazzeh, T. M. (2000). Environmental messages in multiple family housing: Territory and personalization. *Landscape Research, 25,* 97–114.

Als, H. (1977). The newborn communicates. *Journal of Communication, 2,* 66–73.

Axtell, R. (1993). *Do's and taboos around the world.* New York: Wiley.

Becker, F. D. (1973). Study of special markers. *Journal of Personality and Social Psychology, 26,* 429–445.

Birdwhistell, R. L. (1985). *Kinesics and context: Essays in body motion communication.* Philadelphia: University of Philadelphia Press.

Boone, R. T., & Cunningham, J. G. (1998). Children's decoding of emotion in expressive body movement: The development of cue attunement. *Developmental Psychology, 34,* 1007–1016.

Briton, N. J., & Hall, J. A. (1995). Beliefs about female and male nonverbal communication. *Sex Roles, 32,* 79–90.

Burgoon, J. K., & Guerrero, L. K. (1994). Nonverbal communication. In M. Burgoon, F. G. Hunsaker, & E. J. Dawson (Eds.), *Human communication* (pp. 122–171). Thousand Oaks, CA: Sage.

Burgoon, J. K., & Hale, J. L. (1988). Nonverbal expectancy violations: Model elaboration and application to immediacy behaviors. *Communication Monographs, 55,* 58–79.

Burgoon, J. K., & Le Poire, B. A. (1993). Effects of communication expectancies, actual communication, and expectancy disconfirmation on evaluations of communicators and their communication behavior. *Human Communication Research, 20*(1), 67–96.

Burgoon, J. K., Buller, D. B., & Woodall, W. G. (1996). *Nonverbal communication: The unspoken dialogue.* New York: Harper & Row.

Capella, J. (1985). The management of conversations. In M. L. Knapp & G. R. Miller (Eds.), *Handbook of interpersonal communication* (pp. 393–435). Beverly Hills, CA: Sage.

Carvajal, D. (2006, February 7). Priming for the cameras in the name of research. *New York Times.* Retrieved February 23, 2006, from http://www.nytimes.com/2006/02/07/business/07hair.html?ex=1139979600&en=f5f94cb9d81a9fa8&ei=5070&emc=eta1

Chartrand, T. L., & Bargh, J. A. (1999). The chameleon effect: The perception-behavior link and social interaction. *Journal of Personality and Social Psychology, 76,* 893–910.

Chiang, L. H. (1993, October). *Beyond the language: Native Americans' nonverbal communication.* Paper presented at the annual meeting of the Midwest Association of Teachers of Educational Psychology, Anderson, IN: October 1–2.

Cicca, A. H., Step, M., & Turkstra, L. (2003, December 16). Show me what you mean: Nonverbal communication theory and application. *ASHA Leader, 34*, 4–5.

Dié, L. (2008, November 9). Obama: Speech patterns analyzed. *News Flavor: U. S. Politics.* Retrieved May 31, 2011, from http://newsflavor.com/category/politics/us-politics/

Dijksterhuis, A., & Smith, P. K. (2005). What do we do unconsciously? And how? *Journal of Consumer Psychology 15*(3), 225–229.

Duke, L. (2002). Get real! Cultural relevance and resistance to the mediated feminine ideal. *Psychology and Marketing, 19*, 211–234.

Eibl-Eibesfeld, I. (1972). Similarities and differences between cultures in expressive movement. In R. A. Hinde (Ed.), *Nonverbal communication* (pp. 297–314). Cambridge: Cambridge University Press.

Ekman, P. (2003). *Emotions revealed: Recognizing faces and feelings to improve communication and emotional life.* New York: Times Books.

Ekman, P., & Friesen, W. V. (1969). The repertoire of nonverbal behavior: Categories, origins, usage and coding. *Semiotica, 1*, 49–98.

Ekman, P., & Friesen, W. V. (1986). A new pan-cultural expression of emotion. *Motivation and Emotion, 10*(2), 159–168.

Elfenbein, H. A. (2006). Learning in emotion judgments: Teaching and the cross-cultural understanding of facial expressions. *Journal of Nonverbal Communication, 30*, 21–36.

Elfenbein, H. A., Maw, D. F., White, J., Tan, H. H., & Aik, V. C. (2007). Reading your counterpart: The benefit of emotion recognition accuracy for effectiveness in negotiation. *Journal of Nonverbal Behavior, 31*, 205–223.

Eskritt, M., & Lee, K. (2003) Do actions speak louder than words? Preschool children's use of the verbal-nonverbal consistency principle during inconsistent communication. *Journal of Nonverbal Behavior, 27*, 25–41.

Field, T. (2002). Infants' need for touch. *Human Development, 45*, 100–104.

Fussell, P. (1992). *Class: A guide through the American status system.* New York: Touchstone Books.

Givens, D. B. (2005). *The nonverbal dictionary of gestures, signs, and body language cues.* Spokane, WA: Center for Nonverbal Studies Press.

Grammer, K., Fink, B., Joller, A., & Thornhill, R. (2003). Darwinian aesthetics: Sexual selection and the biology of beauty. *Biological Reviews, 78*, 385–408.

Guerrero, L. K., & Andersen, P. A. (1991). The waxing and waning of relational intimacy: Touch as a function of relational stage, gender, and touch avoidance. *Journal of Social and Personal Relationships, 8*, 147–165.

Guerrero, L. K., & Andersen, P. A. (1994). Patterns of matching and initiation: Touch behavior and touch avoidance across romantic relationship stages. *Journal of Nonverbal Behavior, 18*, 137–153.

Guerrero, L. K., & Ebesu, A. S. (1993, May). While at play: An observational analysis of children's touch during interpersonal interaction. Paper presented at the annual conference of the International Communication Association, Washington, DC.

Gundersen, D. F. (1990). Uniforms: Conspicuous invisibility. In J. A. Devito & M. L. Hecht (Eds.), *The nonverbal communication reader* (pp. 172–178). Prospect Heights, IL: Waveland.

Hall, E. T. (1966). *The hidden dimension.* New York: Doubleday.

Hall, E. T. (1983). *The dance of life.* Garden City, NY: Doubleday.

Hall, E. T., & Hall, M. R. (1987). *Hidden differences: Doing business with the Japanese.* Garden City, NY: Anchor.

Hall, E. T., & Hall, M. R. (1990). *Understanding cultural differences: Germans, French and Americans.* Yarmouth, ME: Intercultural Press.

Hanzal, A., Segrin, C., & Dorros, S. M. (2008). The role of marital status and age on men's and women's reactions to touch from a relational partner. *Journal of Nonverbal Behavior, 32*, 21–35.

Isaacson, L. A. (1998). Student dress codes. *ERIC Digest, 117.* Retrieved June 15, 2006, from http://eric.uoregon.edu/publications/digests/digest117.html

Johnson, A. G. (2001). *Privilege, power, and difference.* Boston: McGraw-Hill.

Jones, S. E., & LeBaron, C. D. (2002). Research on the relationship between verbal and nonverbal communication: Emerging integration. *Journal of Communication, 52*, 499–521.

Kemmer, S. (1992). Are we losing our touch? *Total Health, 14*, 46–49.

Knapp, M. L., & Hall, J. A. (1992). *Nonverbal communication in human interaction* (3rd ed.). New York: Holt, Rinehart and Winston.

Knapp, M. L., & Hall, J. A. (2001). *Nonverbal communication in human interaction.* Belmont, CA: Wadsworth.

Koerner, A., & Fitzpatrick, M.A. (2002). Nonverbal communication and marital adjustment and satisfaction: The role of decoding relationship relevant and relationship irrelevant affect. *Communication Monographs, 68*(1), 33–51.

Kraus, M., & Keltner, D. (2009). Signs of socio-economic status: A thin-slicing approach. *Psychological Science, 20*, 99–106.

Lord, T. L. (2009). *The relationship of gender-based public harassment to body image, self-esteem, and avoidance behavior.* (Unpublished dissertation). Ann Arbor, MI:Indiana University of Pennsylvania.

Manusov, V. (1995). Reacting to changes in nonverbal behaviors: Relational satisfaction and adaptation patterns in romantic dyads. *Human Communication Research, 21*, 456–477.

Manusov, V., & Patterson, M. (2006). *Handbook of nonverbal communication.* Thousand Oaks, CA: Sage.

Mast, M. S., & Hall, J. A. (2004). Who is the boss and who is not? Accuracy of judging status. *Journal of Nonverbal Behavior, 28*, 145–165.

Matsumoto, D. (2006). Culture and nonverbal behavior. In V. Manusov & M. Patters (Eds.), *Handbook of nonverbal communication* (pp. 219–235). Thousand Oaks, CA: Sage.

Mehrabian, A. (1971). *Nonverbal communication.* Chicago: Aldine-Atherton.

Mehrabian, A. (2007). *Nonverbal communication.* Chicago, IL: Aldine de Gruyter.

Mehrabian, A., & Weiner, M. (1967). Decoding of inconsistent communication. *Journal of Personality and Social Psychology, 6*, 109–104.

Meltzoff, A. N., & Prinz, W. (2002). *The imitative mind: Development, evolution, and brain bases.* Cambridge: Cambridge University Press.

Montepare, J. M., Goldstein, S. B., & Clausen, A. (1987). The identification of emotions from gait information. *Ethology and Sociobiology, 6*, 237–247.

Newport, F. (1999). Americans agree that being attractive is a plus in American society. *Gallup Poll Monthly, 408*, 45–49.

Parasuram, T. V. (2003, October 23). Sikh shot and injured in Arizona hate crime. *Sikh Times.* Retrieved February 24, 2006, from http://www.sikhtimes.com/news_052103a.html

Patterson, M. L. (1982). A sequential functional model of nonverbal exchange. *Psychological Bulletin, 89*, 231–249.

Patterson, M. L. (1983). *Nonverbal behavior.* New York: Springer.

Patterson, M. L. (2003). Commentary. Evolution and nonverbal behavior: Functions and mediating processes. *Journal of Nonverbal Behavior, 27*, 201–207.

Phillips, J. (1998). Personal space in a virtual community. In Carat, C. M., & Lund, A. (Eds.), *Summary of the Conference in Human Factors in Computing Systems,* (347–348). New York: ACM.

Richards, V., Rollerson, B., & Phillips, J. (1991). Perceptions of submissiveness: Implications for victimization. *Journal of Psychology, 125*(4), 407–411.

Richeson, J. A., & Shelton, J. N. (2005). Brief report: Thin slices of racial bias. *Journal of Nonverbal Behavior, 29*, 75–86.

Samovar, L., & Porter, R. (2004). *Communication between cultures.* Thomson, Wadsworth.

Schwartz, L. M., Foa, U. G., & Foa, E. B. (1983) Multichannel nonverbal communication: Evidence for combinatory rules. *Journal of Personality and Social Psychology, 45*, 274–281.

Segerstrale, U., & Molnár, P. (Eds.). (1997). *Nonverbal communication: Where nature meets culture* (pp. 27–46). Mahwah, NJ: Erlbaum.

Shelp, S. (2002). Gaydar: Visual detection of sexual orientation among gay and straight men. *Journal of Homosexuality, 44*, 1–14.

Tiedens, L., & Fragale, A. (2003). Power moves: Complementarity in dominant and submissive nonverbal behavior. *Journal of Personality and Social Psychology, 84*, 558–568.

Trost, M. R., & Alberts, J. K. (2006). How men and women communicate attraction: An evolutionary view. In D. Canary & K. Dindia (Eds.), *Sex, gender and communication: Similarities and differences* (2nd ed., pp. 317–336). Mahwah, NJ: Lawrence Erlbaum.

Watson, O., & Graves, T. (1966). Quantitative research in proxemic behavior. *American Anthropologist, 68*, 971–985.

Wise, T. (2005, October 23). Opinions on NBA dress code are far from uniform. *Washington Post,* p. A01. Retrieved February 24, 2006, from http://www.washingtonpost.com/wp-dyn/content/article/2005/10/22/AR2005102201386.html

Wolburg, J. M. (2001). Preserving the moment, commodifying time, and improving upon the past: Insights into the depiction of time in American advertising. *Journal of Communication, 51*, 696–720.

Young, R. L. (1999). *Understanding misunderstandings*. Austin: University of Texas Press.

Zezima, K. (2005, December 3). Military, police now more strict on tattoos. *The San Diego Union-Tribune*. Retrieved February 22, 2006, from http://www.signonsandiego.com/uniontrib/20051203/news_1n3tattoo.html

Chapter 7

Ala-Kolterman, S., & Isotelus, P. (2015). Professional listening competence promoting well-being at work in the legal context. *International Journal of Listening, 29*(1), 30–49.

Barker, L., & Watson, K. (2000). *Listen up: How to improve relationships, reduce stress, and be more productive by using the power of listening*. New York: St. Martin's Press.

Battell, C. (2006). *Effective listening*. Alexandria, VA: ASTD Press.

Beall, M. L. (2010). Perspectives on intercultural listening. In A. D. Wolvin (Ed.), *Listening and human communication in the 21st century* (pp. 232–238). Malden, MA: Wiley-Blackwell.

Beard, D. (2009). A broader understanding of the ethics of listening: Philosophy, cultural studies, media studies and the ethical listening subject. *The International Journal of Listening, 23*(1), 7–20.

Bodie, G. D. (2010). Treating listening ethically. *International Journal of Listening, 24*(3), 185–188.

Bodie, G. D., & Fitch-Hauser, M. (2010). Quantitative research in listening: Explication and overview. In A. D. Wolvin (Ed.), *Listening and human communication in the 21st century* (pp. 46–93). Malden, MA: Wiley-Blackwell.

Bodie, G. D., & Jones, S. M. (2012). The nature of supportive listening II: The role of verbal person centeredness and nonverbal immediacy. *Western Journal of Communication, 76*(3), 250–269.

Bodie, G. D., & Worthington, D. L. (2010). Revisiting the Listening Styles Profile (LSP-16): A confirmatory factor analytic approach to scale validation and reliability estimation. *International Journal of Listening, 24*(2), 69–88.

Bodie, G. D., Vickery, A. J., & Gearhart, C. C. (2013). The nature of supportive listening, I: Exploring a relation between supportive listeners and supportive people. *The International Journal of Listening, 27*(1), 39–49.

Bodie, G. D., Worthington, D., Imhof, M., & Cooper, L. (2008). What would a unified field of listening look like? A proposal linking past perspectives and future endeavors. *The International Journal of Listening, 22*, 103–122.

Brownell, J. (2012). *Listening: Attitudes, principles and skills* (5th ed.). Boston: Pearson.

Cheong, P. H., Shuter, R., & Suwinyattichaiporn, T. (2016). Managing student digital distractions and hyperconnectivity: Communication strategies and challenges for professorial authority. *Communication Education, 65*(3), 272–289.

Clark. A. (2005). Listening to and involving young children: A review of research and practice. *Early Child Development and Care, 175*(6), 489–505.

Cooper, L. O., & Buchanan, T. (2010). Listening competency on campus: A psychometric analysis of student listening. *International Journal of Listening, 24*(3), 141–163.

Crawford, K. (2009). Following you: Discipline of listening in social media. *Continuum: Journal of Media & Cultural Studies, 23*(4), 525–535.

Deprez-Sims, A-S., & Morris, S. B. (2010). Accents in the workplace: Their effects during a job interview. *International Journal of Psychology, 45*(6), 417–426.

Diamond, L. E. (2007). *Rule #1: Stop talking! A guide to listening*. Cupertino, CA: Listeners Press.

Emanuel, R., Adams, J., Baker, K., Daufin, E. K., Ellington, C., Fitts, E., . . . & Okeowo, D. (2008). How college students spend their time communicating. *The International Journal of Listening, 22*(1), 13–28.

Ferrari-Bridgers, F., Vogel, R., & Lynch, B. (2017). Fostering and assessing critical listening skills in the speech course. *International Journal of Listening, 31*(1), 19–32.

Floyd, J. (2010). Provocation: Dialogic listening as reachable goal. *International Journal of Listening, 24*(3), 170–173.

Floyd, K. (2014). Empathic listening as an expression of interpersonal affection. *International Journal of Listening, 28*, 1–14.

Fowler, K. (2005). *Mind tools on active listening*. Retrieved December 7, 2009, from http://www.mindtools.com/CommSkll/Mind20Tools20Listening.pdf

Froemming, K. J., & Penington, B. A. (2011). Emotional triggers: Listening barriers to effective interactions in senior populations. *The International Journal of Listening, 25*, 113–131.

Fujii, Y. (2008). You must have a wealth of stories: Cross-linguistic differences between addressee support behaviour in Australian and Japanese. *Multilingua, 27*(4), 325–370.

Genette, J., Olson, C. D., & Linde, J. (2017). *Hot topics, cool heads: A handbook on Civil Dialogue®*. Dubuque, IA: Kendall Hunt.

Gottfried, J., & Shearer, E. (2016). News use across social media platforms 2016. Pew Research Center Report. Retrieved February 17, 2017, from http://www.journalism.org/2016/05/26/news-use-across-social-media-platforms-2016/

Greenwood, S., Perrin, A., & Duggan, M. (2016). *Social Media Update 2016*. Pew Research Report. Retrieved February 17, 2017 from http://www.pewinternet.org/2016/11/11/social-media-update-2016/

Imhof, M. (2001). How to listen more efficiently: Self-monitoring strategies in listening. *The International Journal of Listening, 5*, 2–19.

Imhof, M. (2004). Who are we as we listen? Individual listening profiles in varying contexts. *The International Journal of Listening, 18*, 39–44.

Imhof, M. (2010). Listening to voices and judging people. *International Journal of Listening, 24*(1), 19–33.

Imhof, M., & Janusik, L. A. (2006). Development and validation of the Imhof-Janusik listening concepts inventory to measure listening conceptualization differences between cultures. *Journal of Intercultural Communication Research, 35*, 79–98.

International Listening Association. (1995, April). An ILA Definition of Listening. *ILA Listening Post, 53*, 1–4.

Itzchakov, G., Kluger, A. N., Emanuel-Tor, M., & Gizbar, H. K. (2014). How do you like me to listen to you? *International Journal of Listening, 28*(3), 177–185.

Janusik, L. A. (2010). Listening pedagogy: Where do we go from here? In A. D. Wolvin (Ed.), *Listening and human communication in the 21st century* (pp. 193–224). Malden, MA: Wiley-Blackwell.

Janusik, L. A., & Wolvin, A. D. (2009). 24 hours in a day: A listening update to the time studies. *International Journal of Listening, 23*(2), 104–120.

Johnson-Curiskis, N. (2012). Hearing screening. *International Journal of Listening, 26*(2), 71–74.

Johnston, M., Weaver, J., Watson, K., & Barker, L. (2000). Listening styles: Biological or psychological differences? *International Journal of Listening, 14*(1), 32–46.

Jones, S. M. (2011). Supportive listening. *International Journal of Listening, 25*, 85–103.

Kluger, A. N., & Zaidel, K. (2013). Are listeners perceived as leaders? *International Journal of Listening, 27*(2), 73–84.

Lacey, K. (2013). *Listening Publics: The Politics and Experience of Listening in the Media Age*. Cambridge: Polity.

Lloyd, K. J., Boer, D., Kluger, A. N., & Voelpel, S. C. (2015). Building trust and feeling well: Examining intraindividual and interpersonal outcomes and underlying mechanisms of listening. *International Journal Of Listening, 29*(1), 12–29.

Lynch, J. J. (1985). *Language of the heart: The body's response to human dialogue*. New York: Basic Books.

Mooney, D. (1996) *Improving your listening skills*. Retrieved December 7, 2009, from http://suicideandmentalhealthassociationinternational.org/improvlisten.html

National Institute on Deafness and Other Communication Disorders (NIDCD). (2016, December 15). *Quick statistics about hearing*. Retrieved February 24, from https://www.nidcd.nih.gov/health/statistics/quick-statistics-hearing

Nichols, M. P. (2009). *The lost art of listening* (2nd ed.). New York: The Guilford Press.

Olson, C. D., Genette, J., & Linde, J. (n.d.). *Civility in urban spaces: The use of Civil Dialogue® in urban controversies*. Available at http://www.civil-dialogue.com/civil-dialogue-in-urban-controversies.html

Pasupathi, M., & Billitteri, J. (2015). Being and becoming through being heard: Listener effects on stories and selves. *International Journal of Listening, 29*(2), 67–84.

Pearce, C. G., Johnson, I. W., & Barker, R. T. (2003). Assessment of the Listening Styles Inventory: Progress in establishing reliability and validity. *Journal of Business and Technical Communication, 17*(1), 84–113.

Robertson, K. (2005). Active listening: More than just paying attention. *Australian Family Physician, 34*(12), 1053–1055.

Rosenfeld, L. B., & Berko, R. (1990). *Communicating with competency.* Glenview, IL: Scott, Foresman/Little.

Shafir, R. Z. (2003). *The Zen of listening* (2nd ed). Wheaton, IL: Quest Books.

Shotter, J. (2009). Listening in a way that recognizes/realizes the world of "the other." *The International Journal of Listening, 23*(1), 21–43.

Stoltz, M. (2010). Response: Choice and ethics in listening situations. *International Journal of Listening, 24*(3), 177–178.

Tannen, D. (1994). *Talking from 9 to 5.* New York: William Morrow.

Villaume, W. A., & Bodie, G. D. (2007). Discovering the listener within us: The impact of trait-like personality variables and communicator styles on preferences for listening style. *International Journal of Listening, 21*(2), 102–123.

Watson, K. W., Barker, L. L., & Weaver, J. B. (1995). The Listening Styles Profile (LSP-16): Development and validation of an instrument to assess four listening styles. *Journal of the International Listening Association, 9,* 1–13.

Welch, S. A., & Mickelson, W. T. (2013). A listening competence comparison of working professionals. *International Journal of Listening, 27*(2), 85–99.

Williams, M.C., Garcia, A., & Jensen, T. (2017, January 22). *When your loved ones voted the other way.* Retrieved February 20, 2017, from https://www.nytimes.com/video/us/politics/100000004881605/family-conversations-on-trump.html

Wolvin, A. (2013). Understanding the listening process: Rethinking the 'one size fits all' model. *International Journal of Listening, 27*(2), 104–106.

World Health Organization Media Center. (2014, February). *Deafness and hearing loss: Fact sheet.* Retrieved February 17, 2017, from http://www.who.int/mediacentre/factsheets/fs300/en/

Chapter 8

Allen, B. (2011). *Difference matters: Communicating social identity* (2nd ed). Long Grove, IL: Waveland Press.

Allison Nafziger Travel Blog. Reprinted by permission of Allison Nafziger.

American Indians by the Numbers (From the U.S. Census Bureau 2010). Retrieved March 17, 2014, from: http://www.infoplease.com/spot/aihmcensus1.html

Barboza, T. (2013, May 7). Water war between Klamath River farmers: tribes poised to erupt. *LA Times.* Retrieved March 17, 2014, from http://articles.latimes.com/2013/may/07/local/la-me-klamath-20130507

Bellah, R. N., Madsen, R., Sullivan, W. M., Swidler, A., & Tipton, S. M. (2007). *Habits of the heart: Individualism and commitment in American life, with a new preface.* Los Angeles: University of California Press.

Bennett, J. M. (1998). Transition shock: Putting culture shock in perspective. In M. J. Bennett (Ed.), *Basic concepts in intercultural communication: Selected readings* (pp. 215–224). Yarmouth, ME: Intercultural Press. First published in 1977, in N. C. Jain (Ed.), *International and Intercultural Communication Annual, 4,* 45–52.

Bernal, V. (2005). Eritrea on-line: Diaspora, cyberspace, and the public sphere. *American Ethnologist, 32,* 660–675.

Bhatia, S. (2008). 9/11 and the Indian diaspora: Narratives of race, place and immigrant identity. *Journal of Intercultural Studies, 29*(1), 21–39.

Bond, M. (1991). *Beyond the Chinese face.* Hong Kong: Oxford University Press.

Bond, M. (Ed.). (2010). *The Oxford handbook of Chinese psychology.* New York: Oxford University Press.

Braskamp, L. A., Braskamp, D. C., Merrill, K. C. (2009). Assessing progress in global learning and development of students with education abroad experiences. *Frontiers: The Interdisciplinary Journal of Study Abroad, 13,* 101–118.

Broome, B. J. (1991). Building shared meaning: Implications of a relational approach to empathy for teaching intercultural communication. *Communication Education, 40*(3), 235–249.

Broome, B. J. (2004). Building a shared future across the divide: Identity and conflict in Cyprus. In M. Fong and R. Chuang (Eds.), *Communicating ethnic and cultural identity* (pp. 275–294). Lanham, MD: Rowman and Littlefield, Publishers.

Broome, B. J. (2013). Building cultures of peace: The role of intergroup dialogue. In J. G. Oetzel & S. Ting-Toomey (Eds.), *Sage handbook of conflict communication: Integrating theory, research, and practice* (2nd ed., pp. 737–762). Los Angeles: Sage.

Broome, B. J. (2014). Dialogue across the divide: Bridging the separation in Cyprus. In N. Haydari & P. Holmes (Eds.), *Case studies in intercultural dialogue* (pp. 39–54). Dubuque, IA: Kendall Hunt Publishers.

Broome, B. J. (2015). Empathy. In J. M. Bennett (Ed.), *The SAGE Encyclopedia of Intercultural Competence.* (pp. 287–291). Thousand Oaks, CA: SAGE Publications, Inc.

Broome, B. J., & Collier, M. J. (2012). Culture, communication, and peacebuilding: A reflexive multi-dimensional contextual framework. *Journal of International and Intercultural Communication, 5*(4), 245–269.

Broome, B. J., & Jakobsson, H. A. (2006). Building peace in divided societies: The role of intergroup dialogue. In J. Oetzel and S. Ting-Toomey (Eds.), *Handbook of conflict communication* (pp. 627–662). Thousand Oaks, CA: Sage Publications.

Chinese Culture Connection. (1987). Chinese values and the search for culture-free dimensions of culture. *Journal of Cross-Cultural Psychology, 18,* 143–164.

Colby, S. L., & Ortman, J. M. (2015). *Projections of the size and composition of the U.S. population: 2014-2060.* U.S. Census Bureau. Retrieved February 18, 2017, from https://www.census.gov/content/dam/Census/library/publications/2015/demo/p25-1143.pdf

Cooper, M. (2012, December 13). Census officials, citing increasing diversity, say U.S. will be a 'Plurality Nation.' *New York Times,* p. A20.

Cowan, G. (2005). Interracial interactions of racially diverse university campuses. *Journal of Social Psychology, 14,* 49–63.

Custer, C. (2015, May 20). The 3 biggest reasons foreign companies fail in China. *Techinasia.com.* Retrieved February 6, 2017, from https://www.techinasia.com/3-biggest-reasons-foreign-companies-fail-china

De La Garza, A. T., & Ono, K. (2015). Retheorizing adaptation: Differential adaptation and critical intercultural communication. *Journal of International & Intercultural Communication, 8*(4), 269–289.

DeTurk, S. (2001). Intercultural empathy: Myth, competency, or possibility for alliance building? *Communication Education, 50*(4), 374–384.

DiAngelo, R. (2011). White fragility. *International Journal of Critical Pedagogy, 3*(3), 54–70.

Djamba, Y. K., & Kimuna, S. R. (2014). Are Americans really in favor of interracial marriage? *Journal of Black Studies, 45*(6), 528–544.

Dunbar, R. A. (1997). Bloody footprints: Reflections on growing up poor white. In M. Wray & A. Newitz (Eds.), *White trash: Race and class in America* (pp. 73–86). New York: Routledge.

Dyson, M. E. (2009). An American man, an American moment. *Ebony, 64*(3), 90–94.

Eagle aviary allows American Indians to continue heritage. (2005, March 3). *Newswise.com.* Retrieved March 22, 2014, from http://www.newswise.com/articles/eagle-aviary-allows-american-indians-to-continue-heritage

Engen, D. (2012). Invisible identities: Notes on class and race. In A. González, M. Houston, & V. Chen (Eds.), *Our voices: Essays in culture, ethnicity and communication* (5th ed., pp. 223–239). New York: Oxford University Press.

Fantz, A., & Brumfield, B. (2015, November 19). More than half the nation's governors say Syrian refugees not welcome. *CNN.com.* Retrieved Feb 6, 2017, from http://www.cnn.com/2015/11/16/world/paris-attacks-syrian-refugees-backlash/

Flores, L. A. (1996). Creating discursive space through a rhetoric of difference: Chicana feminists craft a homeland. *Quarterly Journal of Speech, 82,* 142–156.

Geeraert, N., Demoulin, S., & Demes, K. A. (2014). Choose your (international) contact wisely: A multilevel analysis on the impact of intergroup contact while abroad. *International Journal of Intercultural Relations, 38*(2014), 86–96

Guéguen, N., Lourel, M., Charron, C., Fischer-Lokou, J., & Lamy, L. (2009). A web replication of Snyder, Decker, and Bersheid's (1977) experiment on the self-fulfilling nature of social stereotypes. *Journal of Social Psychology, 149*(5), 600–602.

Hall, B. J. (1997). Culture, ethics and communication. In F. L. Casmir (Ed.), *Ethics in intercultural and international communication* (pp. 11–41). Mahwah, NJ: Erlbaum.

Halualani, R. T. (2008). How do multicultural university students define and make sense of intercultural contact? A qualitative study. *International Journal of Intercultural Relations, 32*, 1–16.

Hanasono, L. K., Chen, L., & Wilson, S. R. (2014). Identifying communities in need: Examining the impact of acculturation on perceived discrimination, social support, and coping amongst racial minority members in the United States. *Journal of International and Intercultural Communication 7*(3), 216–237.

Hecht, M., Sedano, M., & Ribeau, S. (1993). Understanding culture, communication, and research: Application to Chicanos and Mexican Americans. *International Journal of Intercultural Relations, 17*, 157–165.

Hecht, M. L., Jackson, R. L., II, & Ribeau, S. (2002). *African American Communication: Exploring identity and culture* (2nd ed.). Hillsdale, NJ: Erlbaum.

Hegde, R. S. (1998). Swinging the trapeze: The negotiation of identity among Asian Indian immigrant women in the United States. In D. V. Tanno & A. González (Eds.), *Communication of identity across cultures* (pp. 34–55). Thousand Oaks, CA: Sage.

Hegde, R. S. (2012). Hybrid revivals: Ethnicity and South Asian celebration. In A. González, M. Houston, & V. Chen (Eds.), *Our voices: Essays in culture, ethnicity and communication* (5th ed., pp. 158–163). New York: Oxford University Press.

Ho, M. K., Rasheed, J. M., & Rasheed, M. N. (2004). *Family therapy with ethnic minorities* (2nd ed). Thousand Oaks, CA: Sage.

Hofstede, G. (1998). *Masculinity and femininity*. Thousand Oaks, CA: Sage.

Hofstede, G., Hofstede, G. J., & Minkov, M. (2010). *Cultures and organizations: Software of the mind* (3rd ed.). Boston: McGraw-Hill.

Hulse, E. (1996). Example of the English Puritans. *Reformation Today, 153*. Retrieved June 13, 2006, from http://www.puritansermons.com/banner/hulse1.htm

Institute of International Education. (2016). *Open Doors 2016: International Education.* Retrieved February 6, 2017 from http://www.iie.org/Research-and-Publications/Open-Doors/Data/US-Study-Abroad/Infographic and from http://www.iie.org/Research-and-Publications/Open-Doors/Data/International-Students#.WJgAg_krLSF

Jaret, C. (1999). Troubled by newcomers: Anti-immigrant attitudes and action during two eras of mass immigration to the United States. *Journal of American Ethnic History, 18*(3), 9–40.

Johnson, A. J. (2017). Privilege, power and difference (2nd ed.). Thousand Oaks, CA: Sage.

Johnson, B. R., & Jacobson, C. K. (2005). Context in contact: An examination of social settings on whites' attitudes toward interracial marriage. *Journal of Social Psychology, 68*, 387–399.

Kayne, E. (2013, June 13). White majority in U.S. gone by 2043. *NBCNews.com.* Retrieved February 6, 2017 from https://usnews.newsvine.com/_news/2013/06/13/18934111-census-white-majority-in-us-gone-by-2043?lite

Kim, Y. Y. (2005). Adapting to a new culture: An integrative communication theory. In W. B. Gudykunst (Ed.), *Theorizing about intercultural communication* (pp. 375–400). Thousand Oaks, CA: Sage.

Kim, Y. Y., & McKay-Semmler, K. (2013). Social engagement and cross-cultural adaptation: An examination of direct and mediated interpersonal communication activities of educated non-natives in the United States. *International Journal of Intercultural Relations, 37*, 99–112.

Kluckhohn, F., & Strodtbeck, F. (1961). *Variations in value orientations.* Chicago: Row, Peterson & Co.

Koinova, M. (2010). Diasporas and secessionist conflicts: The mobilization of the Armenian, Albanian, and Chechen diasporas. *Ethnic and Racial Studies, 34*, 333–356.

Lee, J. J., & Rice, C. (2007). Welcome to America? International student perceptions of discrimination. *Higher Education, 53*, 381–409.

Lightblau, E. (2016, November 14). U.S. hate crimes surge 6%, fueled by attacks on Muslims. *New York Times.* Retrieved February 7, 2017, from https://www.nytimes.com/2016/11/15/us/politics/fbi-hate-crimes-muslims.html?_r=0

Loewen, J. W. (2010). *Teaching what really happened.* New York: Teachers College, Columbia University.

Mahapatra, L. (2013, August 14). Prisoners per 100,000: U.S. has highest incarceration rate in the world. *International Business Times.* Retrieved March 17, 2014, from http://www.ibtimes.com/prisoners-100000-us-has-highest-incarceration-rate-world-chart-1384305

Martin, J. N., & Nakayama, T. K. (2014). *Experiencing intercultural communication: An introduction* (4th ed.). Boston: McGraw-Hill.

Massey, D. S. (2016). Residential segregation is the linchpin of racial stratification. *City & Community, 15*(1), 3–7.

Matsumoto, D. (2007). *The new Japan: Debunking seven cultural stereotypes.* London, ME: Nicholas Brealey.

McGoldrick, M., Giordano, J., & Garcia-Preto, N. (Eds.). (2005). *Ethnicity and family therapy* (3rd ed.). New York: Guilford Press.

Moon, D. G. (2016). "Be/coming" white and the myth of white ignorance: Identity projects in white communities. *Western Journal Of Communication, 80*(3), 282–303.

Newport, F. (2013, July 5). In U.S., 87% approve of black-white marriage, vs. 4% in 1958. *Gallup.com.* Retrieved April 10, 2017 from http://www.gallup.com/poll/163697/approve-marriage-blacks-whites.aspx

Orbe, M. P. (1998). *Constructing co-cultural theory: An explication of culture, power, and communication.* Thousand Oaks, CA: Sage.

Orbe, M., & Roberts, T. L. (2012). Co-cultural theorizing: Foundations, applications, and extensions. *Howard Journal of Communications, 23*(4), 293–311.

Parker, J., Morin, R., Horowitz, J. M., Lopez, M. H., & Rohal, M. (2015). *Multiracial in America: Proud, diverse and growing in numbers.* Retrieved February 6, 2017, from http://www.pewsocialtrends.org/files/2015/06/2015-06-11_multiracial-in-america_final-updated.pdf

Pendery, D. (2008). Identity development and cultural production in the Chinese diaspora to the United States, 1850–2004: New perspectives. *Asian Ethnicity, 9*(3), 201–218.

Phillips, K. W. (2014, October 1). How diversity makes us smarter. *Scientificamerican.com.* Retrieved February 6, 2017 from http://www.scientificamerican.com/article/how-diversity-makes-us-smarter/

Pitts, M. J. (2016). Sojourner reentry: A grounded elaboration of the integrative theory of communication and cross-cultural adaptation. *Communication Monographs, 83*(4), 419–445.

Porter, T. (2002). The words that come before all else. *Native Americas, 19*, 7–10.

Reiter, M. J., & Gee, C. B. (2009). Open communication and partner support in intercultural and interfaith romantic relationship: A relational maintenance approach. *Journal of Social and Personal Relationships, 25*(4), 539–599.

Root, M. P. P. (2001). *Love's revolution: Interracial marriage.* Philadelphia: Temple University Press.

Rosenstone, R. A. (2005). My wife, the Muslim. *Antioch Review, 63*, 234–246.

Rothman, L. (2012, July 8). Essence Fest 2012: Is reality TV still not diverse enough? *Time.com.* Retrieved March 22, 2014, from: http://entertainment.time.com/2012/07/08/essence-reality-tv-family-panel/

Sahagun, L. (2014, February 24). Northern spotted owls are being ousted by barred owl invaders. *LA Times.* Retrieved March 17, 2014, from http://www.latimes.com/science/sciencenow/la-sci-sn-barred-owl-invasion-20140224,0,4292055.story

Sanchez-Burks, J., Lee, F., Choi, I., Nisbett, R., Zhao, S., & Koo, J. (2003). Conversing across cultures: East-West communication styles in work and nonwork contexts. *Journal of Personality and Social Psychology: Personality Processes and Individual Differences, 85*(2), 363–372.

Scott, K. D. (2013). Communication strategies across cultural borders: Dispelling stereotypes, performing competence, and redefining black womanhood. *Women's Studies in Communication, 36*, 312–329.

Scott, B. (2016, May 19). America's schools are still segregated by race and class. That has to end. *The Guardian.* Retrieved February 7, 2017, from https://www.theguardian.com/commentisfree/2016/

may/19/america-schools-segregation-race-class-education-policy-bobby-scott

Shim, Y. J., Kim, M. S., & Martin, J. N. (2008). *Changing Korea: Understanding culture and communication.* New York: Peter Lang.

Smith, S. (2017, February 3). *Young people less likely to view Iraqi, Syrian refugees as major threat to the U.S.* Retrieved February 6, 2017, from http://www.pewresearch.org/fact-tank/2017/02/03/young-people-less-likely-to-view-iraqi-syrian-refugees-as-major-threat-to-u-s/

Sobré-Denton, M. (2011). The emergence of cosmopolitan group cultures and its implications for cultural transition: A case study of an international student support group. *International Journal of Intercultural Relations, 35,* 79–91.

Teixeira, R., Frey, W. H., & Griffin, R. (2015, February 24). 10 big trends that are transforming America. *Center for American Progress.com.* Retrieved March 8, 2016, from https://www.americanprogress.org/issues/progressive-movement/report/2015/02/24/107261/states-of-change/

The PEW Charitable Trusts. (2013, November). *Moving on up: Why do some Americans leave the bottom of the economic ladder, but not others?* Retrieved March 22, 2014, from http://www.pewstates.org/uploadedFiles/PCS/Content-Level_Pages/Reports/2013/Moving_On_Up.pdf

Ting-Toomey, S. (1999). *Communicating across cultures.* New York: Guilford.

Ting-Toomey, S. (2010). Applying dimensional values in understanding intercultural communication. *Communication Monographs, 77*(2), 169–180.

Torres, L. (2009). Latino definitions of success: A cultural model of intercultural competence. *Hispanic Journal of Behavioral Sciences, 31,* 576–593.

Townsend, M., Walters, J., & Otten, C. (2017, January 28). Global fury as Donald Trump's ban on migrants takes effect. *The Guardian.* Retrieved February 6, 2017, from https://www.theguardian.com/us-news/2017/jan/29/global-fury-donald-trump-us-ban-immigration-muslim-countries

Triandis, H. C. (1995). *Individualism & collectivism.* Boulder, CO: Westview Press.

Trompenaars, F., & Hampden-Turner, C. (2012). *Riding the waves of culture: Understanding diversity in global business* (3rd ed.). Boston: McGraw-Hill.

United Nations High Commissioner for Refugees. (2016). *Figures at a glance.* Retrieved February 6, 2017, from http://www.unhcr.org/en-us/figures-at-a-glance.html

United Nations Tourism Organization. (2016, November 7). *Close to one billion international tourists in first nine months of 2016.* Retrieved February 6, 2017, from http://media.unwto.org/press-release/2016-11-07/close-one-billion-international-tourists-first-nine-months-2016

Ward, C. (2008). Thinking outside the Berry boxes: New perspectives on identity, acculturation and intercultural relations. *International Journal of Intercultural Relations, 32,* 105–114.

Waterston, A. (2005). Bringing the past into the present: Family narratives of holocaust, exile, and diaspora: The story of my story: An anthropology of violence, dispossession, and diaspora. *Anthropological Quarterly, 78,* 43–61.

Woodard, C. (2012). *American nations: A history of the eleven rival regional cultures of North America.* New York: Penguin Books.

Yako, R. M., & Biswas, B. (2014). "We came to this country for the future of our children. We have no future": Acculturative stress among Iraqi refugees in the United States. *International Journal of Intercultural Relations, 38,* 133–141

Yamato, G. (2001). Something about the subject makes it hard to name. In M. L. Andersen & P. H. Collins (Eds.), *Race, class, and gender: An anthology* (4th ed., pp. 90–94). Belmont, CA: Wadsworth.

Chapter 9

Aboud, F. E., & Mendelson, M. J. (1996). Determinants of friendship selection and quality: Developmental perspectives. In W. M. Bukowski, A. F. Newcomb, & W. W. Hartup (Eds.), *The company they keep: Friendship in childhood and adolescence* (pp. 87–112). New York: Cambridge University Press.

Alberts, J., Yoshimura, C., Rabby, M., & Loschiavo, R. (2005). Mapping the topography of couples' everyday interaction. *Journal of Social and Personal Relationships, 22,* 299–322.

Allan, G. (1977). Class variation in friendship patterns. *British Journal of Sociology, 28,* 389–393.

Altman, I., & Taylor, D. (1987). Communication in interpersonal relationships: Social penetration theory. In M. E. Roloff & G. R. Miller (Eds.), *Interpersonal processes: New directions in communication research* (pp. 257–277). Newbury Park, CA: Sage.

Altman, I., & Taylor, D. A. (1973). *Social penetration: The development of interpersonal relationships.* New York: Holt, Rinehart, & Winston.

Altman, I., Vinsel, A., & Brown, B. B. (1981). Dialectic conceptions in social psychology: An application to social penetration and privacy regulation. In L. Berkowitz (Ed.), *Advances in experimental social psychology* (Vol. 14, pp. 107–160). New York: Academic Press.

American Psychological Association. (1996). *Violence and the family: Report of the American Psychological Association presidential task force on violence and the family.* Retrieved June 15, 2006, from http://www.apa.org/pi/viol&fam.html

Andersen, P., Eloy, S. V., Guerrero, L. K., & Spitzberg, B. H. (1995). Romantic jealousy and relational satisfaction: A look at the impact of jealousy experience and expression. *Communication Reports, 8,* 77–85.

Anglin, K., & Holtzworth-Munroe, A. (1997). Comparing the responses of maritally violent and nonviolent spouses to problematic marital and nonmarital situations: Are the skills deficits of physically aggressive husbands and wives global? *Journal of Family Psychology, 11,* 301–313.

Argyle, M., & Henderson, M. (1984). The rules of friendship. *Journal of Social and Personal Relationships, 1,* 211–237.

Aune, K. S., & Comstock, J. (1991) Experience and expression of jealousy: Comparison between friends and romantics. *Psychological Reports, 69,* 315–319.

Balsam, K., Beauchaine, T., & Rothblum, E. (2005). Victimization over the lifespan: Comparison of lesbian, gay, bisexual and heterosexual siblings. *Journal of Consulting and Clinical Psychology, 73,* 477–487.

Baxter, L. A. (1982). Strategies for ending relationships: Two studies. *Western Journal of Speech Communication, 46,* 233–242.

Baxter, L. A. (1988). A dialectical perspective on communication strategies in relationship development. In S. W. Duck, D. F. Hay, S. E. Hobfoll, W. Ickes, & B. Montgomery (Eds.), *Handbook of personal relationships* (pp. 257–273). London: Wiley.

Baxter, L. A. (1991). Gender differences in the heterosexual relationship rules embedded in break-up accounts. *Journal of Social and Personal Relationships, 3,* 289–306.

Baxter, L. A., & Bullis, C. (1986). Turning points in developing romantic relationships. *Human Communication Research, 12,* 469–493.

Becker, J. A. H., Johnson, A. J., Craig, E. A., Gilchrist, E., Haigh, M. M., & Lane, L. L. (2009). Friendships are flexible not fragile: Turning points in geographically-close and long-distance friendships. *Journal of Social and Personal Relationships, 26*(4), 347–369.

Benhold, K. (2012, June 12). Equality and the end of marrying up. *New York Times.* Retrieved August 27, 2014, from http://www.nytimes.com/2012/06/13/world/europe/13ihtletter13.html?pagewanted=all&_r=0

Berg, J. H., & Piner, K. E. (1990). Social relationships and the lack of social relationships. In S. Duck & R. C. Silver (Eds.), *Personal relationships and social support* (pp. 140–158). London: Sage Publications.

Berger, C. R., & Calabrese, R. J. (1975). Some explorations in initial interaction and beyond: Toward a developmental theory of interpersonal communication. *Human Communication Theory, 1,* 99–112.

Berger, C. R., & Kellerman, N. (1994). Acquiring social information. In J. Daly & J. Wiemann (Eds.), *Strategic interpersonal communication* (pp. 1–31). Hillsdale, NJ: Lawrence Erlbaum.

Berscheid, E., & Reis, H. T. (1998). Attraction and close relationships. In D. Gilbert, S. Fiske, & G. Lindzey (Eds.), *Handbook of social psychology* (Vol. 2, 4th ed., pp. 193–281). New York: McGraw-Hill.

Black, M. C., Basile, K. C., Breiding, M. J., Smith, S. G., Walters M. L., Merrick, M. T., . . . & Stevens, M. R. (2011). *The national intimate partner and sexual violence survey, 2010.* Retrieved July 12, 2014, from http://www.cdc.gov/violenceprevention/pdf/nisvs_executive_summary-a.pdf

Bleske-Rechek, A., & Lighthall, M. (2010). Attractiveness and rivalry in women's friendships with women. *Human Nature, 21*(1), 82-97.

Blieszner, R., & Adams, R. G. (1992). *Adult friendship*. Newbury Park, CA: Sage.

Bok, S. (1978). *Lying: Moral choice in public and private life*. New York: Random House.

Bowker, A. (2004). Predicting friendship stability during early adolescence. *Journal of Early Adolescence, 24*, 85–112.

Bradshaw, C., Kahn, A. S., & Saville, B. K. (2010). To hook up or date: Which gender benefits? *Sex Roles, 9–10*, 661–669.

Bramlett, M. D., & Mosher, W. D. (2002). Cohabitation, marriage, divorce, and remarriage in the United States. *National Center for Health Statistics*. Vital Health Stat, 23(22). Retrieved August 27, 2014, from http://www.cdc.gov/nchs/data/series/sr_23/sr23_022.pdf

Bureau of Justice Statistics. (1995, August). *Special report: Violence against women: Estimates from the redesigned survey* (NCJ-154348), 3.

Burgoon, J. K., & Bacue, A. E. (2003). Nonverbal communication skills. In J. O. Greene & B. R. Burleson (Eds.), *Handbook of communication and social interaction skills*. Mawah, NJ: Lawrence Erlbaum.

Burgoon, J. K., Buller, D. B., Ebesu, A., & Rockwell, P. (1994). Interpersonal deception: V. Accuracy in deception detection. *Communication Monographs, 61*(4), 303–325.

Burleson, B. R., & Samter, W. (1996). Similarity in the communication skills of young adults: Foundations of attraction, friendship, and relationship satisfaction. *Communication Reports, 9*, 127–137.

Buss, D. M. (1985). Human mate selection. *American Scientist, 73*, 47–51.

Buss, D. M. (1988). From vigilance to violence: Tactics of mate retention in American undergraduates. *Ethology and Sociobiology, 9*, 291–317.

Buss, D. M. (2003). *The evolution of desire: Strategies of human mating*. New York: Basic Books.

Buss, D. M., Shackelford, T. K., Kirkpatrick, L. A., & Larsen, R. J. (2001). A half century of mate preferences: The cultural evolution of values. *Journal of Marriage and the Family, 63*, 491–503.

Byrne, D. (1997). An overview (and underview) of research and theory within the attraction paradigm. *Journal of Social and Personal Relationships, 14*, 417–431.

Canary, D.J., & Dainton, M. (2002). *Maintaining relationships through communications: Relational, contextual, and cultural variations*. Mahwah, NJ: Erlbaum.

Canary, D. J., & Spitzberg, B. H. (1985). Loneliness and relationally competent communication. *Journal of Social and Personal Relationships, 2*, 387–402.

Canary, D. J., & Stafford, L. (1992a). Relational maintenance strategies and equity in marriage. *Communication Monographs, 51*(3), 342–267.

Canary, D. J., & Stafford, L. (1992b). Managing relationships through strategic and routine interaction. In D. J. Canary & L. Stafford (Eds.), *Communication and relational maintenance* (pp. 3–21). San Diego, CA: Academic Press.

Canary, D. J., & Stafford, L. (1994). Maintaining relationships through strategic and routine interaction. In D. J. Canary & L. Stafford (Eds.), *Communication and relational maintenance* (pp. 3–22). San Diego, CA: Academic Press.

Canary, D. J., Stafford, L., Hause, K. S., & Wallace, L. A. (1993). An inductive analysis of relational maintenance strategies: Comparisons among lovers, relatives, friends, and others. *Communication Research Reports, 10*, 5–14.

Cano, A., & O'Leary, K. D. (1997). Romantic jealousy and affairs: Research and implications for couples' therapy. *Journal of Sex and Marital Therapy, 23*, 249–275.

Cash, T. F., & Derlega, V. J. (1978). The matching hypothesis: Physical attractiveness among same-sex friends. *Personality and Social Psychology Bulletin, 4*, 240–243.

Cauffman, E., Feldman, S., Jensen, L., & Arnett, J. (2000). The (Un)acceptability of violence against peers and dates. *Journal of Adolescent Research, 15*, 652–673.

Center for American Progress. (2011). *Domestic violence in the LGBT community: A fact sheet*. Retrieved August 27, 2014, from http://www.americanprogress.org/issues/lgbt/news/2011/06/14/9850/domestic-violence-in-the-lgbt-community/

Chung, C. (2016, July 21). Why Chinese parents don't say I love you. *The Sydney Morning Herald*. Retrieved March 20, 2017, from http://www.smh.com.au/lifestyle/life-and-relationships/real-life/why-chinese-parents-dont-say-i-love-you-20140304-341ws.html

Child Trends Data Bank. (2014). *Physical fighting by youth*. Retrieved August 2014 from http://www.childtrends.org/?indicators=physical-fighting-by-youth

Cody, M. J. (1982). A typology of disengagement strategies and an examination of the role intimacy, reactions to inequity and relational problems play in strategy selection. *Communication Monographs, 49*, 148–170.

Cordova, J. V., Jacobsen, N. S., Gottman, J. M., Rushe, R., & Cox, G. (1993). Negative reciprocity and communication in couples with a violent husband. *Journal of Abnormal Psychology, 102*, 559–564.

Dainton, M. A., Zelley, E., & Langan, E. (2003). Maintaining friendships throughout the lifespan. In D. J. Canary & M. Dainton (Eds.), *Maintaining relationships through communication* (pp. 79–102). Mahwah, NJ: Erlbaum.

Donaghue, N., & Fallon, B. J. (2003) Gender-role self-stereotyping and the relationship between equity and satisfaction in close relationships. *Sex Roles, 48*, 217–230.

Duck, S. (1991). *Understanding relationships*. New York: Guilford Press.

Duck, S. W. (1982). Social and cognitive features of the dissolution of commitment to relationships. In S. W. Duck (Ed.), *Personal relationships 4: Dissolving personal relationships*, (pp. 51–73). London: Academic Press.

Duck, S. W. (1988). *Relating to others*. Chicago: Dorsey Press.

Dunleavy, K. N., Goodboy, A. K., Booth-Butterfield, M., & Sidelinger, S. B. (2007). Repairing hurtful messages in marital relationships. *Communication Quarterly, 57*(1), 67–84.

Edgell, P. (2003). In rhetoric and practice: Defining the "good family" in local congregations. In M. Dillon (Ed.), *Handbook of the sociology of religion* (pp. 164–178). New York: Cambridge University Press.

Emmers-Sommers, T. M. (2004). The effect of communication quality and quantity indicators on intimacy and relational satisfaction. *Journal of Social and Personal Relationships, 21*(4), 399–411.

Essau, C. A., Conradt, J., & Petermann, F. (1999). Frequency and comorbidity of social phobia and fears in adolescents. *Behavior Research and Therapy, 37*, 831–843.

Fehr, B. (2000). The life cycle of friendship. In C. Hendrick & S. S. Hendrick (Eds.), *Close relationships: A source book* (pp. 71–82). Thousand Oaks: CA: Sage.

Felmlee, D. H. (1995). Fatal attractions: Affections and disaffections in intimate relationships. *Journal of Social and Personal Relationships, 12*, 295–311.

Ferraro, K. (1996). The dance of dependency: A genealogy of domestic violence discourse. *Hypatia, 11*, 72–91.

Fingerhut, A. W. & Peplau, L. A. (2013). Same-sex romantic relationships. In C. J. Patterson & A. R. D'Augelli (Eds.), *Handbook of psychology and sexual orientation* (pp. 165-178). New York: Oxford University Press.

Folkes, V. S. (1982). Communicating the causes of social rejection. *Journal of Experimental Social Psychology, 18*, 235–252.

Galassi, J. P., & Galassi, M. D. (1979). Modifications of heterosexual skills deficits. In A. S. Bellack & M. Hersen (Eds.), *Research and practice in social skills training* (pp. 131–188). New York: Plenum.

Gierveld, J., & Tilburg, T. (1995). Social relationships, integration and loneliness. In C. P. M. Knipscheer, J. Gierveld, T. Tilburg, & P. A. Dykstra (Eds.), *Living arrangements and social networks among older adults* (pp. 95–113). Amsterdam: VU University Press.

Glen, N., & Marquardt, E. (2001). *Hooking up, hanging out, and hoping for Mr. Right*. A report conducted by the Institute for American Values for the Independent Women's Forum. Retrieved May 22, 2011, from http://www.americanvalues.org/Hooking_Up.pdf

Goodwin, R., & Tang, D. (1991). Preferences for friends and close relationships partners: A cross-cultural comparison. *Journal of Social Psychology, 131*, 579–581.

Grotpeter, J. K., & Crick, N. R. (1996). Relational aggression, overt aggression, and friendship. *Child Development, 67*, 2328–2338.

Guerrero, L. K., & Afifi, W. A. (1999). Toward a goal-centered approach for understanding strategic communicative responses to jealousy. *Western Journal of Communication, 63*, 216–248.

Guerrero, L. K., & Andersen, P. A. (1998). Jealousy experience and expression in romantic relationships. In L. K. Guerrero & P. A. Andersen (Eds.), *Communication and emotion: Theory, research and application* (pp. 155–188). San Diego, CA: Academic Press.

Guerrero, L. K., Eloy, S. V., & Wabnik, A. I. (1993). Linking maintenance strategies to relationship development and disengagement: A reconceptualization. *Journal of Social and Personal Relationships, 10,* 273–283.

Haas, S. M., & Stafford, L. (1998). An initial examination of relationship maintenance behaviors in gay and lesbian relationships. *Journal of Social and Personal Relationships, 15,* 846–855.

Hays, R. B. (1988). Friendship. In S. W. Duck (Eds.), *Handbook of personal relationships* (pp. 391–408). New York: Wiley.

Hinsz, V. B. (1989). Facial resemblance in engaged and married couples. *Journal of Social and Personal Relationships, 6,* 223–229.

Holt-Lunstad, J., Birmingham, W., & Jones, B. Q. (2008). Is there something unique about marriage? The relative impact of marital status, relationship quality, and network support on ambulatory blood pressure and mental health. *Annals of Behavioral Medicine, 35,* 239–244.

Holt-Lunstad, J., Smith, T. B., & Layton, J. B. (2010). Social relationships and mortality risk: A meta-analytic review. Retrieved August 27, 2014, from http://www.plosmedicine.org/article/info%3Adoi%2F10.1371%2Fjournal.pmed.1000316

Infante, D. A., Chandler, T. A., & Rudd, J. E. (1989). A test of an argumentative skill deficiency model of interspousal violence. *Communication Monographs, 56,* 163–177.

Janz, T. A. (2000). The evolution and diversity of relationships in Canadian families. *Canadian Journal of Higher Education.* Retrieved June 15, 2006, from http://www.lcc.gc.ca/research_project/00_diversity_1-en.asp

Johnson, A. J. (2000, July). *A role theory approach to examining the maintenance of geographically close and long-distance friendships.* Paper presented at the International Network on Personal Relationships Conference, Prescott, AZ.

Johnson, A. J., Wittenberg, E., Haigh, M., & Wigley, S. (2004). The process of relationship development and deterioration: Turning points in friendships that have terminated. *Communication Quarterly, 52,* 54–68.

Kalmijn, M. (1994). Assortative mating by cultural and economic occupational status. *American Journal of Sociology, 100*(2), 422–452.

Kelley, H. H., Berscheid, E., Christensen, A., Harvey, J., Huston, T., Levinger, G., . . . & Peterson, D. (1983). *Close relationships.* San Francisco: Freeman.

Kenrick, D., & Trost, M. R. (1996). Evolutionary approaches to relationships. In S. Duck (Ed.), *Handbook of personal relationships* (2nd ed.). London: Wiley.

Kimmel, M. S. (2002). Male victims of domestic violence: A substantive and methodological research review. *Violence Against Women, 8*(11), 1332–1363.

Knapp, M. L. (1978). *Social intercourse: From greeting to goodbye.* Boston: Allyn & Bacon.

Knapp, M. L., & Vangelisti, A. (1997). *Interpersonal communication and relationships* (2nd ed.). Boston: Allyn & Bacon.

Knight, K. (September, 2014). Communicating dilemmas in adults' friends with benefits relationships: Challenges to relational talk. *Emerging Adulthood.* Retrieved November 25, 2014, from http://eax.sagepub.com/content/early/2014/09/19/2167696814549598

Knox, D., Schacht, C., Holt, J., & Turner, J. (1993). Sexual lies among university students. *College Student Journal, 27*(2), 269–272.

Kowalski, R., Valentine, S., Wilkinson, R., Queen, A., & Sharpe, B. (2003). Lying, cheating, complaining, and other aversive interpersonal behaviors: A narrative examination of the dark side of relationships. *Journal of Social and Personal Relationships, 20,* 471–490.

Kramer, D., & Moore, M. (2001). Gender roles, romantic fiction and family therapy. *Family Therapy, 12*(24), 1–8.

Kurdek, L. A. (1991). The dissolution of gay and lesbian couples. *Journal of Social and Personal Relationships, 8,* 265–278.

Kurt, J. E., & Sherker, J. L. (2003). Relationship quality, trait similarity, and self-other agreement on personality ratings in college roommates. *Journal of Personality, 71,* 21–40.

LaFollette, H. (1996). *Personal relationships: Love, identity, and morality.* Cambridge, MA: Blackwell Publishers.

Lever, J., Groy, C., Royce, T., & Gillespie, J. (2008). Searching for love in all the "write" places: Exploring internet personals use by sexual orientation, gender, and age. *International Journal of Sexual Health, 20*(4), 233–246.

Little, A. C., Burt, D. M., & Perret, D. I. (2006). Assortative mating for perceived facial personality traits. *Personality and Individual differences, 40,* 973–984.

Lloyd, S. A. (1990). Conflict types and strategies in violent marriages. *Journal of Family Violence, 5,* 269–284.

Lloyd, S. A. (1999). The interpersonal and communication dynamics of wife battering. In X. Arriaga & S. Oskamp (Eds.), *Violence in intimate relationships* (pp. 91–111). Thousand Oaks, CA: Sage.

Lloyd, S. A., & Emery, B. C. (2000). The context and dynamics of intimate aggression against women. *Journal of Social and Personal Relationships, 17*(4–5), 503–521.

McCormick, N. B., & Jones, J. J. (1989). Gender differences in nonverbal flirtation. *Journal of Sex Education and Therapy, 15,* 271–282.

McCornack, S. A., & Parks, M. R. (1986). Deception detection and relationship development: The other side of trust. In M. L. McLaughlin (Ed.), *Communication Yearbook, 9,* 377–389. Newbury Park, CA: Sage.

McCoy, K., & Oelschlager, J. (n.d.) Sexual coercion awareness and prevention. *Florida Institute of Technology.* Retrieved May 17, 2011, from http://www.fit.edu/caps/documents/SexualCoercion_000.pdf

McEwen, W. J., & Greenberg, B. S. (1970). The effects of message intensity on receiver revaluations of source, message, and topic. *Journal of Communication, 20,* 340–350.

McCroskey, L. L., McCroskey, J. C., & Richmond, V. P. (2006). Analysis and improvement of the measurement of interpersonal attraction and homophily. *Communication Quarterly, 54*(1), 1–31.

Menning, C., and Holtzman, M. (2014). Process and patterns in gay, lesbian and bisexual assault: A multmethodological assessment. *Journal of Interpersonal Violence, 29*(6), 1071–1093.

Messman, S. J., Canary, D. J., & Hause, K. S. (2000). Motives to remain platonic, equity, and the use of maintenance strategies in opposite-sex friendships. *Journal of Social and Personal Relationships, 17,* 67–94.

Miller, C. W., & Roloff, M. (2005). Gender and willingness to confront hurtful messages from romantic partners. *Communication Quarterly, 53*(3), 323–337.

Miller, R. S. (1997). We always hurt the ones we love: Aversive interactions in close relationships. In R. M. Kowalski (Ed.), *Aversive Interpersonal Behaviors* (pp. 12–29). New York: Plenum.

Miller, R. S. (2002). Suicidal and death ideation in older primary care patients with depression, anxiety, and at-risk. *American Journal of Geriatric Psychiatry, 10,* 417–427.

Mills, R. S. L., Nazar, J., & Farrell, H. M. (2002). Child and parent perceptions of hurtful messages. *Journal of Social and Personal Relationships, 19,* 731–754.

Mongeau, P. A., Ramirez, R., & Vorell, M. (2003). *Friends with benefits: An initial exploration of a sexual but not romantic relationship.* Paper presented at the Western States Communication Association. Salt Lake, UT.

MSNBC News. (2004, March 8). *Lip-lock could mean lockup in Indonesia.* Retrieved March 8, 2006.

Muehlenhard, C. L., & Hollabough, L. C. (1988). Do women sometimes say no when they mean yes? The prevalence and correlates of women's token resistance to sex. *Journal of Personality and Social Psychology, 54,* 872–879.

Muehlenhard, C. L., & McFalls, M. C. (1981). Dating initiation from a woman's perspective. *Behavior Therapy, 14,* 626–636.

Muehlenhard, C. L., & Miller, E. N. (1988). Traditional and non-traditional men's responses to women's dating initiation. *Behavior Modification, 12*(3), 385–403.

Mullen, P. E., & Maack, L. H. (1985). Jealousy, pathological jealousy, and aggression. In D. P. Farrington & J. Gunn (Eds.), *Aggression and dangerousness* (pp. 103–126). New York: Wiley.

Myers, S. A., Schrodt, P., & Rittenour, C. E. (2006). The impact of parents' use of hurtful messages on adult children's self-esteem and educational motivation. In L. H. Turner & R. West (Eds.), *The family communication sourcebook* (pp. 425–446). Thousand Oaks, CA: Sage Publications.

Nardi, P. M. (1992). That's what friends are for: Friends as family in the gay and lesbian community. In K. Plummer (Ed.), *Modern homosexualities: Fragments of lesbian and gay experience* (pp. 108–120). New York: Routledge.

Nardi, P. M. (2007). Friendship, sex, and masculinity. In M. Kimmel (Ed.), *The sexual self* (pp. 49–60). Nashville, TN: Vanderbilt University Press.

National Coalition Against Domestic Violence. (2015). *National statistics domestic violence fact sheet.* Retrieved March 24, 2017, from www.ncadv.org/learn-more/statistics

Noller, P., & Fitzpatrick, M. A. (1990). Marital communication in the eighties. *Journal of Marriage and the Family, 52,* 832–843.

O'Brien, E., & Foley, L. (1999). The dating game: An exercise illustrating the concepts of homogamy, heterogamy, hyperogamy, and hypogamy. *Teaching Sociology, 27*(2), 145–149.

Owen, W. F. (1987). The verbal expression of love by women and men as a critical communication event in personal relationships. *Women's Studies in Communication, 10,* 15–24.

Payne, E., & Smith, M. (2013). LGBTQ kids, school safety and missing the big picture: How the dominant bullying discourse prevents school professionals from thinking about systemic marginalization or . . . why we need to rethink LGBTQ bullying. *QED: A Journal in GLBTQ Worldmaking, Inaugural issue,* 1–36.

Peplau, A. (2009). Gay, lesbian, and bisexual relationships. In the *Encyclopedia of Human Relationships*. Retrieved July 3, 2014, from http://www.sage-reference.com/humanrelationships/Article_n238.html

Pogrebin, L. C. (1992). The same and different: Crossing boundaries of color, culture, sexual preference, disability, and age. In W. B. Gudykunst & Y. Y. Kim (Eds.), *Readings on communicating with strangers* (pp. 318–336). New York: McGraw-Hill.

Psarska, A. D. (1970). Jealousy factor in homicide in forensic material. *Polish Medical Journal, 9,* 1504–1510.

Rawlins, W. K. (1992). *Friendship matters.* Hawthorne, NY: Aldine de Gruyter.

Reeder, H. (1996). *What Harry and Sally didn't tell you.* (Unpublished Doctoral dissertation). Arizona State University, Tempe, AZ.

Rennison, C. M., & Welchans, S. (2000). *Intimate Partner Violence Special Report,* NCJ 178247. Washington, DC: U.S. Department of Justice.

Rohrbaugh, J. R. (2006). Domestic violence in same-gendered relationships. *Family Court Review, 44,* 287–299.

Romano, T. (May 23, 2014). Amazon is killing my sex life. *Dame Magazine.* Retrieved June 5, 2014, from http://www.damemagazine.com/2014/05/23/amazon-killing-my-sex-life

Root, M. P. (2001). *Love's revolution: Interracial marriage.* Philadelphia, PA: Temple University Press.

Rose, S. M. (1984). How friendships end: Patterns among young adults. *Journal of Social and Personal Relationships, 1,* 267–277.

Roth, M., & Parker, J. (2001). Affective and behavioral responses to friends who neglect their friends for dating partners: Influences of gender, jealousy and perspective. *Journal of Adolescence, 24,* 281–296.

Sabourin, T. C. (1996). The role of communication in verbal abuse between spouses. In D. D. Cahn & S. A. Lloyd (Eds.), *Family violence from a communication perspective* (pp. 199–217). Thousand Oaks, CA: Sage.

Sagarin, B. J., Rhoads, K. L., & Cialdini, R. B. (1998). Deceiver's distrust: Denigration as a consequence of undiscovered deception. *Personality and Social Psychology Bulletin, 24,* 1167–1176.

Schafer, R. B., & Keith, P. M. (1990). Matching by weight in married couples: A life cycle perspective. *Journal of Social Psychology, 130*(5), 657–664.

Segrin, C., & Givertz, M. (2003). Methods of social skills training and development. In J. O. Green & B. R. Burleson (Eds.), *Handbook of communication and social interaction skills* (pp. 135–176). Mahwah, NJ: Erlbaum.

Sias, P. M., & Cahill, D. J. (1998). From coworkers to friends: The development of peer friendships in the workplace. *Western Journal of Communication, 62,* 273–299.

Sollors, W. (Ed.). (2000). *Interracialism: Black and white intermarriage in American history, literature and law.* New York: Oxford University Press.

Spitzberg, B. (1998). Sexual coercion in courtship relationships. In B. Spitzberg & W. Cupach (Eds.), *The dark side of close relationships.* Hillsdale, NJ: Erlbaum.

Sprecher, S. (1998). Insiders' perspectives on reasons for attraction to a close other. *Social Psychology Quarterly, 61,* 287–300.

Sprecher, S. & Hatfield, E. (2009). Matching hypothesis. In H. Reis & S. Sprecher (Eds.) *Encyclopedia of human relationships.* New York: Sage.

Sprecher, S., & Regan, P. (2002). Liking some things (in some people) more than others: Partner preferences in romantic relationships and friendships. *Journal of Social and Personal Relationships, 19,* 463–481.

Stafford, L. (2010). Geographic distance and communication during courtship. *Communication Research, 37*(2), 275–297.

Stiff, J. B., Kim, H. J., & Ramesh, C. N. (1989). *Truth biases and aroused suspicion in relational deception.* Paper presented at the Annual Meeting of the Interpersonal Communication Association (May), San Francisco, CA.

Struckman-Johnson, C. J., Struckman-Johnson, B. L., & Anderson, B. (2003). Tactics of sexual coercion: When men and women won't take no for an answer. *Journal of Sex Research, 40*(1), 76–86.

Sunnafrank, M. (1986). Predicted outcome value in initial conversations. *Communication Research Reports, 5*(2), 169–172.

Surra, C. (1987). Reasons for changes in commitment: Variations by courtship type. *Journal of Social and Personal Relationships, 4,* 17–33.

Thibault, J. W., & Kelley, H. H. (1959). *The Social Psychology of Groups.* New York: John Wiley & Sons.

Times Square Travels. (2004). *Travel in Japan.* Retrieved June 15, 2006, from http://www.taveltst.ca/index.php?tpl=vacation-guides_japan-guide_introduction

Tolhuizen, J. H. (1990). *Deception in developing dating relationships.* Paper presented at the Speech Communication Association Convention, Chicago, IL.

Tracy, K., Van Dusen, D., & Robinson, S. (1987). "Good" and "bad" criticism: A descriptive analysis. *Journal of Communication, 37*(2), 46–59.

Trost, M. R., & Kenrick, D. T. (1993). An evolutionary perspective on interpersonal communication. In S. Petronio, J. K. Alberts, M. Hecht, & J. Buley (Eds.), *Contemporary perspectives on interpersonal communication* (pp. 120–124). Madison, WI: Brown & Benchmark.

Turner, R. E., Edgley, C., & Olmstead, G. (1975). Information control in conversations: Honesty is not always the best policy. *Kansas Journal of Sociology, 11,* 69–89.

U.S. Bureau of the Census. (2012, April 12). *2010 census shows that interracial or interethnic married couples grew by 28% over decade.* Retrieved August 27, 2014, from http://www.census.gov/newsroom/releases/archives/2010_census/cb12-68.html

Vangelisti, A. L. (1994). Messages that hurt. In W. R. Cupach, & B. H. Spitzberg (Eds.), *The dark side of interpersonal communication* (pp. 53–82). Hillsdale, NJ: Erlbaum.

Vangelisti, A. L. (2007). Communicating hurt. In B. Spitzberg, & W. Cupach (Eds.), *The dark side of close relationships* (pp. 121–142). Mawah, NJ: Erlbaum.

Vorauer, J., & Ratner, R. (1996). Who's going to make the first move? *Journal of Social and Personal Relationships, 13,* 483–506.

Walster, E., Berscheid, E., & William. G. (1973). New directions in equity research. *Journal of Personality and Social Psychology, 25*(2), 151–176.

Wang, W. (2012, February 16). *The rise of intermarriage.* Retrieved April 30, 2017, from http://www.pewsocialtrends.org/2012/02/16/the-rise-of-intermarriage/2/

Watson, D., Klohnen, E., Casillas, A., Simms, E., Haig, J., & Berry, D. (2004). Assortative mating in married couples. *Journal of Personality, 72*(5), 1029–1068.

Weber, A. L. (1998). Losing, leaving and letting go: Coping with nonmarital breakups. In B. H. Spitzberg & W. R. Cupach (Eds.), *The dark side of close relationships* (pp. 267–306). Mahwah, NJ: Erlbaum.

White, G. L. (1980). Physical attractiveness and courtship progress. *Personality and Social Psychology, 39,* 660–668.

White, G. L., & Mullen, P. E. (1989). *Jealousy.* New York: Guilford Press.

Willan, V. J., & Pollard, P. (2003). Likelihood of acquaintance rape as a function of males' sexual expectations, disappointment, and adherence to rape-conducive attitudes. *Journal of Social and Personal Relationships, 20,* 637–661.

Wolcott, J. (2004). Is dating dead on college campuses? *Christian Science Monitor.* Retrieved May 25, 2011, from http://www.csmonitor.com/2004/0302/p11s01-legn.html

The World Travel Guide. (2004). *Kuwait travel guide.* Retrieved March 16, 2006, from http://www.worldtravelguide.net/country/141/country_guide/Middle-East/Kuwait.html

Wright, D. E. (1999). *Personal relationships: An interdisciplinary approach.* Mountain View, CA: Mayfield Publishing.

Young, J. E. (1981). Cognitive therapy and loneliness. In G. Emery, S. D. Hollon, & R. C. Bedrosian (Eds.), *New directions in cognitive therapy: A casebook* (pp. 139–159). New York: Guilford Press.

Young, S. L., & Bippus, A. M. (2001). Does it make a difference if they hurt you in a funny way? Humorously and non-humorously phrased hurtful messages in personal relationships. *Communication Quarterly, 49,* 35–52.

Chapter 10

Abrams, K. M., Wang, Z., Song, Y. J., & Galindo-Gonzalez, S. (2015). Data richness trade-offs between face-to-face, online audiovisual, and online text-only focus groups. *Social Science Computer Review, 33*(1), 80–96.

Adams, K., & Galanes, G. J. (2003). *Communicating in groups: Applications and skills.* Boston: McGraw-Hill.

Adoption.com. (n.d.). *Support groups: Do I really need one?* Retrieved April 19, 2014, from http://library.adoption.com/articles/support-groups-.html

Allen, T. H., & Plax, T. G. (2002). Exploring consequences of group communication in the classroom. In L. R. Frey (Ed.), *New directions in group communication* (pp. 219–234). Thousand Oaks, CA: Sage.

Alsop, R. (2003, September 9). Playing well with others. *Wall Street Journal* (Eastern edition), p. R11.

Arrow, H., McGrath, J. E., & Berdahl, J. L. (2000). *Small groups as complex systems.* Thousand Oaks, CA: Sage.

Baldoni, J. (2004). Powerful leadership communication. *Leader to Leader, 32*, 20–21.

Barge, J. K. (1989). Leadership as medium: A leaderless group discussion model. *Communication Quarterly, 37*, 237–247.

Barnard, C. (1938). *The functions of an executive.* Cambridge, MA: Harvard University Press.

Benne, K. D., & Sheats, P. (1948). Functional roles of group members. *Journal of Social Issues, 4*, 41–49.

Bensimon, E. M., & Neumann, A. (1994). *Redesigning collegiate leadership: Teams and teamwork in higher education.* Baltimore, MD: Johns Hopkins University Press.

Bergiel, B. J., Bergiel, E. B., & Balsmeier, P. W. (2008). Nature of virtual teams: A summary of their advantages and disadvantages. *Management Research News, 31*(2), 99–110.

Berry, G. R. (2011). Enhancing effectiveness of virtual teams. *Journal of Business Communication, 48*(2), 186–206.

Blinder, A. S., & Morgan, J. (2000). *Are two heads better than one?: An experimental analysis of group vs. individual decision making.* National Bureau of Economic Research (NBER) Working Paper No. 7909. Retrieved February 27, 2017, from http://www.nber.org/papers/w7909

Bock, W. (2006). Three star leadership. Retrieved March 30, 2011, from http://www.threestarleadership.com/articles/4mistakes.htm

Bonito, J. A., DeCamp, M. H., & Ruppel, E. K. (2008). The process of information sharing in small groups: Application of a local model. *Communication Monographs, 75*, 171–192.

Bono, J. E., & Judge, T. A. (2004). Personality and transformational and transactional leadership: A meta-analysis. *Journal of Applied Psychology, 89*(5), 901–910.

Bormann, E. G. (1975). *Discussion and group methods* (2nd ed.). New York: Harper & Row.

Bowers, C. A., Pharmer, J. A., & Salas, E. (2000). When member homogeneity is needed in work teams: A meta-analysis. *Small Group Research, 31*, 305–327.

Brooks, C. (2013, January 16). Why employees hate teamwork. *Business News Daily.* Retrieved October 5, 2014, from http://www.businessnewsdaily.com/3769-employees-prefer-to-go-it-alone-research-finds.html

Brooks, C. (2013, October 16). Hate teamwork? You're not alone. *Business News Daily.* Retrieved October 5, 2014, from http://www.businessnewsdaily.com/5281-employees-hate-teamwork.html

Broome, B. J., & Chen, M. (1992). Guidelines for computer-assisted problem solving: Meeting the challenges of complex issues. *Small Group Research, 23*, 216–236.

Broome, B. J., & Fulbright, L. (1995). A multistage influence model of barriers to group problem solving: A participant-generated agenda for small group research. *Small Group Research, 26*, 24–55.

Brown, S. (2007, April 12). It's teamwork, not solos, that make for discoveries, research finds. *The Chronicle of Higher Education.* Retrieved April 17, 2011, from http://chronicle.com/article/Its-Teamwork-Not-Solos-That/38549/

Cady, S. H., & Valentine, J. (1999). Team innovation and perceptions of consideration: What difference does team diversity make? *Small Group Research, 30*, 730–750.

Cain, S. (2013). *Quiet: The power of introverts in a world that can't stop talking.* New York: Broadway Books.

Casari, M., Zhang, J., & Jackson, C. (2012). *Working paper no. 504: When do groups perform better than individuals?* (University of Zurich Institute for Empirical Research in Economics, Series ISSN 1424-0459). Retrieved February 27, 2017, from http://www.econ.uzh.ch/static/wp_iew/iewwp504.pdf

Caya, O., Mortensen, M., & Pinsonneault, A. (2013). Virtual teams demystified: An integrative framework for understanding virtual teams. *International Journal of e-collaboration, 9*(2), 1–33.

Choi, H.-S., Cho, S.-J., Seo, J.-G., & Bechtoldt, M. N. (2016). The joint impact of collectivistic value orientation and independent self-representation on group creativity. *Group Processes & Intergroup Relations,* 1–20.

Covey, S. R. (1989). *The seven habits of highly effective people: Restoring the character ethic.* New York: Simon and Schuster.

Cox, T. (1994). *Cultural diversity in organizations: Theory, research and practice.* San Francisco: Berrett-Kochler.

Cragan, J. F., & Wright, D. W. (1999). *Communication in small groups: Theory, process, skills* (5th ed.). Belmont, CA: Wadsworth.

Crown, D. F. (2007). The use of group and groupcentric individual goals for culturally heterogeneous and homogeneous task groups: An assessment of European work teams. *Small Group Research, 38*(4), 489–508.

Daft, R. L. (2015). *The leadership experience* (6th ed.). Stamford, CT: Cengage Higher Education.

Denhardt, R. B., & Denhardt, J. V. (2004). *The dance of leadership.* Armonk, NJ: M. E. Sharpe.

Dietz-Uhler, B., & Bishop-Clark, C. (2001). The use of computer-mediated communication to enhance subsequent face-to-face discussions. *Computers in Human Behavior, 17*, 269–283.

Dubberke, S. (2012, May 4). *Survey reveals global employees not prepared for virtual team work.* Retrieved April 10, 2017, from https://www.rw-3.com/blog/2012/05/survey-reveals-global-employees-not-prepared-for-virtual-teamwork

Engleberg, I. N., & Wynn, D. R. (2010). *Working in groups: Communication principles and strategies* (5th ed.). Boston: Allyn-Bacon.

Eysenbach, G., Powell, J., Englesakis, M., Rizo, C., & Stern, A. (2004). Health related virtual communities and electronic support groups: Systematic review of the effects of online peer to peerinteractions. *BMJ Journal.* Retrieved April 2, 2011, from http://www.bmj.com/content/328/7449/1166.short

Ferrazzi, K. (2012, November 19). How to manage conflict in virtual teams. HBR Blog Network. Retrieved April 22, 2014, from http://blogs.hbr.org/2012/11/how-to-manage-conflict-in-virt/

Fiedler, F. E. (1981). *Leader Attitudes and Group Effectiveness.* Westport, CT: Greenwood Publishing Group.

Fiedler, F. E., & Garcia, J. E. (1987). *New approaches to leadership, cognitive resources and organizational performance,* New York: John Wiley and Sons.

Fisher, B. A. (1970). Decision emergence: Phases in group decision-making. *Speech Monographs, 37*, 53–66.

Fisher, B. A. (1980). *Small group decision making: Communication and the group process* (2nd ed.). New York: McGraw-Hill.

Fisher, B. A., & Ellis, D. G. (1993). *Small group decision making: Communication and the group process.* Boston: McGraw-Hill.

Foels, R., Driskell, J. E., Mullen, B., & Salas, E. (2000). The effects of democratic leadership on group member satisfaction: An integration. *Small Group Research, 31*, 676–701.

Forrest, J., (2005). *The Space Shuttle Challenger disaster: A failure in decision support system and human factors management.* Retrieved March 14, 2014, from http://dssresources.com/cases/spaceshuttlechallenger/

French, J. R., Jr., & Raven, B. H. (1959). The bases of social power. In D. Cartwright (Ed.), *Studies in social power* (pp. 150–167). Ann Arbor, MI: Institute for Social Research.

Frey, L. R. (1994). The call of the field: Studying communication in natural groups. In L. R. Frey (Ed.), *Group communication in context: Studies of natural groups* (pp. ix–xiv). Hillsdale, NJ: Erlbaum.

Gagné, M., & Zuckerman, M. (1999). Performance and learning goal orientations as moderators of social loafing and social facilitation. *Small Group Research, 30*, 524–541.

Gareis, E. (2006). Virtual teams: A comparison of online communication channels. *Journal of Language for International Business, 17*(2), 6–21.

Gladwell, M. (2008). *Outliers*. New York: Little, Brown and Company.

Gloor, P. A. (2006). *Swarm creativity: Competitive advantage through collaborative innovative networks*. Oxford: Oxford University Press.

Gloor, P. A., Heckman, C., & Makedon, F. (2004, April 14–16). Ethical issues in virtual communities of innovation. Ethicomp 2004, the 7th International Conference on the Social and Ethical Impacts of Information and Communication Technologies, Syros, Greece. Retrieved July 19, 2017, from http://citeseerx.ist.psu.edu/viewdoc/download?doi=10.1.1.490.4762&rep=rep1&type=pdf

Gloor, P. A., Paasvaara, M., Schoder, D., & Willems, P. (2007, April). Finding collaborative innovation networks through correlating performance with social network structure. *International Journal of Production Research*. Retrieved July 17, 2011, from http://www.tandfonline.com/doi/abs/10.1080/00207540701224582

Gokhale, A. (1995). Collaborative learning enhances critical thinking. *Journal of Technology Education, 7*, 22–30.

Gollent, M. (2007, June 6). Why are leadership skills important—for everyone? Retrieved March 30, 2011, from http://ezinearticles.com/?why-are-leadership-skills-important—for-everyone?&id=591333

Gouran, D. S., Hirokawa, R., & Martz, A. (1986). A critical analysis of factors related to the decisional processes involved in the *Challenger* disaster. *Central States Speech Journal*, 119–135.

Greenleaf, R. (1970/1991). *The servant as leader* (pp. 1–37). Indianapolis: The Robert K. Greenleaf Center.

Greenleaf, R. K. (2002). *Servant leadership: A journey into the nature of legitimate power and greatness*. 25th anniversary edition. New York: Paulist Press.

Guiller, J., Durndell, A., & Ross, A. (2008). Peer interaction and critical thinking: Face-to-face or online discussion? *Learning and Instruction, 18*(2), 187–200.

Hampton, K., Rainie, L., Lu, W., Dwyer, M., Shin, I., & Purcell, K. (2014, August 26). Social media and the 'Spiral of Silence.' *Pew Research Center Internet, Science & Tech Report*. Retrieved April 10, 2017, from http://www.pewinternet.org/2014/08/26/social-media-and-the-spiral-of-silence/#fn-11806-1

Hansen, R. S. (2011, September 12). 15 quick tips for excelling at work. *Quintzine.com, 12*(9). Retrieved April 19, 2014, from http://www.quintcareers.com/15_excelling_work_tips.html

Hargrove, R. (1998). *Mastering the art of creative collaboration*. New York: BusinessWeek Books.

Haslett, B. B., & Ruebush, J. (1999). What differences do individual differences in groups make? The effects of individuals, culture, and group composition. In L. R. Frey, D. S. Gouran, & M. S. Poole (Eds.), *The handbook of group communication theory and research* (pp. 115–138). Thousand Oaks, CA: Sage.

Heller, R., Laurito, A., Johnson, K., Martin, M., Fitzpatrick, R., & Sundin, K. (2010). Global teams: Trends, challenges and solutions. *Cornell University Center for Advanced Human Resources Studies White Papers*. Retrieved February 27, 2017, from https://est05.esalestrack.com/eSalesTrack/Content/Content.ashx?file=4578f59e-21b3-4a2c-bbfe-63e53af3f5dc.pdf

Henningsen, D. D., & Henningsen, M. L. M. (2006). Examining the symptoms of groupthink and retrospective sensemaking. *Small Group Research, 37*(1), 36–64.

Hirokawa, R. Y., & Salazar, A. J. (1999). Task-group communication and decision-making performance. In L. R. Frey, D. S. Gouran, & M. S. Poole (Eds.), The *handbook of group communication theory and research* (pp. 167–191). Thousand Oaks, CA: Sage.

Ilgen, D. R., Hollenbeck, J. R., Johnson, M., & Jundt, D. (2005). Teams in organizations: From input-process-output models to IMOI models. *Annual Review of Psychology, 56*, 517–543.

Jawadi, N., Daassi, M., Favier, M., & Kalika, M. (2013). Relationship building in virtual teams: A leadership behavioral complexity perspective. *Human Systems Management, 32*(3), 199–211.

Jobidon, M.-E., Turcotte, I., Aubé, C., Labrecque, A., Kelsey, S., & Tremblay, S. (2016). Role variability in self-organizing teams working in crisis management. *Small Group Research, 48*(1), 62–92.

Judge, T. A., & Cable, D. M. (2004). The effect of physical height on workplace success and income: Preliminary test of a theoretical model. *Journal of Applied Psychology, 89*, 428–441.

Judge, T. A., Bono, J. E., Ilies, R., & Gerhardt, M. W. (2002). Personality and leadership: A qualitative and quantitative review. *Journal of Applied Psychology, 87*, 765–780.

Judge, T. A., Colbert, A. E., & Ilies, R. (2004). Intelligence and leadership: A quantitative review and test of theoretical propositions. *Journal of Applied Psychology, 89*, 542–552.

Jung, D. I., & Sosik, J. J. (2002). Transformational leadership in work groups: The role of empowerment, cohesiveness, and collective-efficacy on perceived group performance. *Small Group Research, 33*, 313–336.

Kent, M. V. (1994). The presence of others. In A. P. Hare, H. H. Blumberg, M. F. Davies, & M. V. Kent. *Small group research: A handbook* (pp. 81–106). Norwood, NJ: Ablex.

Keyton, J. (1999). Relational communication in groups. In L. R. Frey, D. S. Gouran, & M. S. Poole (Eds.), *Handbook of group communication theory and research* (pp. 199–222). Thousand Oaks, CA: Sage.

Keyton, J. (2000). Introduction: The relational side of groups. *Small Group Research, 34*, 387–396.

Keyton, J., Harmon, N., & Frey, L. R. (1996, November). *Grouphate: Implications for teaching group communication*. Paper presented at the Annual Meeting of the National Communication Association, San Diego, CA.

King, N., & Anderson, N. (1990). Innovation in working groups. In M. A. West & J. F. Farr (Eds.), *Innovation and creativity at work: Psychological and organizational strategies* (pp. 110–135). Chichester, UK: Wiley.

Klocke, U. (2007). How to improve decision making in small groups: Effects of dissent and training interventions. *Small Group Research, 38*(3), 437–468.

Komives, S. R., Lucas, N., & McMahon, T. (1998). *Exploring leadership for college students who want to make a difference*. San Francisco: Jossey-Bass Publishers.

Kramer, M. W. (2006). Shared leadership in a community theater group: Filling the leadership role. *Journal of Applied Communication Research, 34*(2), 141–162.

Landy, F. J., & Conte, J. M. (2010). *Work in the 21st century: An introduction to industrial & organizational Psychology* (3rd ed.). Hoboken: John Wiley & Sons.

Larson, J. R. (2007). Deep diversity and strong synergy: Modeling the impact of variability in members' problem solving strategies on group problem-solving performance. *Small Group Research, 38*(3), 413–436.

Levine, K. J., Muenchen, R. A., & Brooks, A. M. (2010). Measuring transformational and charismatic leadership: Why isn't charisma measured? *Communication Monographs, 77*(4), 576–591.

Lewin, K., Lippit, R., & White, R. K. (1939). Patterns of aggressive behavior in experimentally created "social climates." *Journal of Social Psychology, 10*, 271–279.

Lewis, L. K., Isbell, M. G., & Koschmann, M. A. (2010). Collaborative tensions: Practitioners' experiences of interorganizational relationships. *Communication Monographs, 77*(4), 462–481.

Li, D. C. S. (2007). Computer-mediated communication and group decision making: A functional perspective. *Small Group Research 38*(5), 593–614.

Littlejohn, S. W. (2002). *Theories of human communication* (7th ed.). Belmont, CA: Wadsworth.

Lowry, P. B., Roberts, T. L., Romano, N. C., Cheney, P. D., & Hightower, R. T. (2006). The impact of group size and social presence on small-group communication: Does computer-mediated communication make a difference? *Small Group Research, 37*(6), 631–661.

MacNeil, A., & McClanahan, A. (2005). *Shared leadership, The Connexions Project*. Retrieved April 19, 2014, from http://cnx.org/content/m12923/latest/

Matha, B., & Boehm, M. (2008). *Beyond the Babble: Leadership communication that drives results*. San Francisco, CA: Jossey-Bass.

Martinic, A., Fertalj, K., & Kalpic, D. (2012). Methodological framework for virtual team project management. *International Journal of Innovation, Management and Technology, 3*(6), 702–707.

McLeod, P. L., Lobel, S. A., & Cox, T. H. (1996). Ethnic diversity and creativity in small groups. *Small Group Research, 27*, 248–264.

Meade, R. (1985). Experimental studies of authoritarian and democratic leadership in four cultures: American, Indian, Chinese and Chinese-American. *High School Journal, 68*, 293–295.

Moore, K. (2012). Introverts no longer the quiet follow-ers of extroverts. *Forbes.* Retrieved April 22, 2014, from http://www.forbes.com/sites/karlmoore/2012/08/22/introverts-no-longer-the-quiet-followers-of-extroverts/

Moore, R. M., III. (2000). Creativity of small groups and of persons working alone. *Journal of Social Psychology, 140,* 143–144.

Moscovici, S., Mugny, G., & Van Avermaet, E. (Eds.). (1985). *Perspectives on minority influence. European studies in social psychology.* Cambridge, UK: Cambridge University Press.

Myers, S. A., & Goodboy, A. K. (2005). A study of grouphate in a course on small group communication. *Psychological Reports, 97*(2), 381–386.

Northouse, P. G. (2012). *Leadership: Theory and practice* (6th ed.). Thousand Oaks, CA: Sage.

Oetzel, J. G. (1998). Explaining individual communication processes in homogeneous and heterogeneous group through individual-collectivism and self-construal. *Human Communication Research, 25,* 202–224.

Oetzel, J. G. (2001). Self-construals, communication processes, and group outcomes in homogeneous and heterogeneous groups. *Small Group Research, 32,* 19–54.

Oetzel, J. G. (2005). Effective intercultural workgroup communication theory. In W. B. Gudykunst (Ed.), *Theorizing about intercultural communication* (pp. 351–371). Thousand Oaks, CA: Sage.

Ostergaard, C., Timmermans, B., & Kristinsson, K. (2011). Does a different view create something new? The effect of employee diversity on innovation. *Research Policy, 40*(3), 500–509.

Paletz, S. B. F., Peng, K., Erez, M., & Maslach, C. (2004). Ethnic composition and its differential impact on group processes in diverse teams. *Small Group Research, 35,* 128–158.

Park, H. S., & Shin, S.-Y. (2015). The role of the star player in a cohesive group. *Small Group Research, 46*(4), 415–430.

Pavitt, C. (1999). Theorizing about the group communication-leadership relationship. In L. R. Frey, D. S. Gouran, & M. S. Poole (Eds.), *Handbook of group communication theory and research* (pp. 313–334). Thousand Oaks, CA: Sage.

Peterson, R. S., & Behfar, K. J. (2003). The dynamic relationship between performance feedback, trust, and conflict in groups: A longitudinal study. *Organizational Behavior and Human Decision Processes, 92,* 102–112.

Phadnis, S., & Caplice, C. (2013). Global virtual teams: How are they performing? *Supply Chain Management Review, 17*(4), 8–9.

Phillips, K. W. (2014, October 1). How diversity makes us smarter. *Scientific American.* Retrieved February 6, 2017 from http://www.scientificamerican.com/article/how-diversity-makes-us-smarter/

Polzer, J. T., Milton, L. P., & Swann, W. B., Jr. (2002). Capitalizing on diversity: Interpersonal congruence in small work groups. *Administrative Science Quarterly, 47,* 296–324.

Poole, M. S. (1983). Decision development in small groups: A study of multiple sequences in decision-making. *Communication Monographs, 50,* 206–232.

Poole, M. S. (1999). Group communication theory. In L. R. Frey, D. S. Gouran, & M. S. Poole (Eds.), *Handbook of group communication theory and research* (pp. 37–70). Thousand Oaks, CA: Sage.

Poole, M. S., & Garner, J. T. (2006). Workgroup conflict and communication. In J. G. Oetzel & S. Ting-Toomey (Eds.), *The Sage handbook of conflict communication* (pp. 267–292). Thousand Oaks, CA: Sage.

Propp, K. M. (1999). Collective information processing in groups. In L. R. Frey, D. S. Gouran, & M. S. Poole (Eds.), *Handbook of group communication theory and research* (pp. 225–250). Thousand Oaks, CA: Sage.

Rauch, C. F., Jr., & Behling, O. (1984). Functionalism: Basis for alternative approach to the study of leadership. In J. G. Hunt, D.-M. H. Hosking, C. A. Schriesheim, & R. Stewart (Eds.), *Leaders and managers: International perspectives on managerial behavior and leadership* (pp. 45–62). New York: Pergamon.

Richard, O., McMillan, A., Chadwick, K., & Dwyer, S. (2003). Employing an innovation strategy in racially diverse workforces. *Group & Organization Management, 28*(1), 107–126.

Riddle, B. L., Anderson, C. M., & Martin, M. M. (2000). Small group socialization scale: Development and validity. *Small Group Research, 31,* 554–572.

Rothwell, J. D. (1995). *In mixed company: Small group communication* (2nd ed.). Fort Worth, TX: Harcourt Brace.

Rowold, J., & Heinitz, K. (2007). Transformational and charismatic leadership: Assessing the convergent, divergent and criterion validity of the MLQ and the CKS. *The Leadership Quarterly, 18,* 121–133.

Salazar, A. J. (1997). Communication effects in small group decision-making: Homogeneity and task as moderators of the communication performance relationship. *Western Journal of Communication, 61,* 35–65.

Sargent, L. D., & Sue-Chan, C. (2001). Does diversity affect group efficacy? *Small Group Research, 32,* 426–450.

Savič, B. S., & Pagon, M. (2008). Individual involvement in health care organizations: Differences between professional groups, leaders and employees. *Stress and Health, 24,* 71–84.

Schultz, B. G. (1999). Improving group communication performance. In L. R. Frey, D. S. Gouran, & M. S. Poole (Eds.), *Handbook of group communication theory and research* (pp. 371–394). Thousand Oaks, CA: Sage.

Scott, C. R. (1999). Communication technology and group communication. In L. R. Frey, D. S. Gouran, & M. S. Poole (Eds.), *The handbook of group communication theory research* (pp. 432–472). Thousand Oaks, CA: Sage.

Sell, J., Lovaglia, M. J., Mannix, E. A., Samuelson, C. D., & Wilson, R. K. (2004). Investigating conflict, power, and status within and among groups. *Small Group Research, 35,* 44–72.

Shepard, J. (2009). *The meaning of Matthew: My son's murder in Laramie and a world transformed.* New York: Penguin Group.

Stogdill, R. M. (1974). *Handbook of leadership: A survey of theory and research.* New York: Free Press.

SunWolf & Seibold, D. R. (1999). The impact of formal procedure on group processes, members, and task outcomes. In L. R. Frey, D. S. Gouran, & M. S. Poole (Eds.), *Handbook of group communication theory and research* (p. 401). Thousand Oaks, CA: Sage.

Support Groups: Do I Really Need One? (n.d.) Adoption.com. Retrieved April 19, 2014, from http://library.adoption.com/articles/support-groups-.html.

Thameling, C. L., & Andrews, P. H. (1992). Majority responses to opinion deviates: A communicative analysis. *Small Group Research, 23*(4), 475–502.

Thameling, C. L., & Andrews, P. H. (1999). Majority perceptions of opinion deviates' interpersonal attractiveness: A communicative analysis. *Small Group Research, 30*(5), 582–607.

The ultimate list of virtual team technology tools. (2016, June). Retrieved February 20, 2017, and adapted from http://www.thecouchmanager.com/the-ultimate-list-of-virtual-team-technology-tools

Trends in Global Virtual Teams: Virtual Teams Survey Report 2016. (2016). Retrieved March 2, 2017, from http://cdn.culturewizard.com/PDF/Trends_in_VT_Report_4-17-2016.pdf

Van der Vegt, G. S., & Janssen, O. (2003). Joint impact of interdependence and group diversity on innovation. *Journal of Management, 29*(5), 729–751.

Van Swol, L. M. (2009). Discussion and perception of information in groups and judge-advisor systems. *Communication Monographs, 76*(1), 99–120.

Talke, K., Salomo, S., & Rose, K. (2010). How top management team diversity affects innovativeness and performance via the strategic choice to focus on innovation fields. *Research Policy, 39*(7), 907–918.

Wellen, J. M., & Neale, M. (2006). Deviance, self-typicality and group cohesion: The corrosive effects of the bad apples on the barrel. *Small Group Research, 37*(2), 165–186.

Wheelan, S. A., Davidson, B., & Tilin, F. (2003). Group development across time: Reality or illusion? *Small Group Research, 34,* 223–245.

Chapter 11

Appelbaum, S.H., Roberts, J., & Shapiro, B.T. (2009). Cultural strategies in M&As: Investigating ten case studies. *Journal of Executive Education, 8*(1), 33–58.

Aeberhard-Hodges, J. (1996). Sexual harassment in employment: Recent judicial and arbitral trends. *International Labor Review, 135*(5), 499–533.

Alberts, J. K., Lutgen-Sandvik, P., & Tracy, S. J. (2005, May). *Bullying in the workplace: A case of escalated incivility. Organizational*

Communication Division. The International Communication Association Convention, New York, NY.

Alberts, J. K., Tracy, S., & Trethewey, A. (2011). An integrative theory of the division of domestic labor: Threshold level, social organizing, and sensemaking. *Journal of Family Communication, 11,* 271–238.

American Management Association. (2005, May 18). *2005 electronic monitoring & surveillance survey: Many companies monitoring, recording, videotaping, and firing employees.* Retrieved June 16, 2006, from http://www.amanet.org/press/amanews/ems05.htm

Barley, S. R., & Kunda, G. (1992). Design and devotion: Surges of rational and normative ideologies of control in managerial discourse. *Administrative Science Quarterly, 37,* 363–399.

Berger, C. (1979). Beyond initial interaction. In H. Giles & R. St. Clair (Eds.), *Language and psychology* (pp. 122–144). Oxford, UK: Basil Blackwell.

Blau, P. M., & Meyer, M. W. (1987). *Bureaucracy in modern society* (3rd ed). New York: Random House.

Brown, M. (1989, Winter). Ethics in organizations. *Issues in Ethics, 2*(1). Retrieved March 15, 2006, from http://www.scu.edu/ethics/publications/iie/v2n1/homepage.html

Bullis, C., & Tompkins, P. K. (1989). The forest ranger revisited: A study of control practices and identification. *Communication Monographs, 56,* 287–306.

Canary, D., & Lakey, S. L. (2012). *Strategic conflict.* New York: Routledge.

Casey, M. K. (1998). *Communication, stress and burnout: Use of resource replacement strategies in response to conditional demands in community-based organizations.* (Doctoral dissertation). Michigan State University, East Lansing, MI.

Chambers, B., Moore, A. B., & Bachtel, D. (1998). *Role conflict, role ambiguity and job satisfaction of county extension agents in the Georgia Cooperative Extension Service.* AERC Proceedings. Retrieved September 15, 2006, from http://www.edst.educ.ubc.ca/aercd1998/98chambers.htm

Cheney, G. (1995). Democracy in the workplace: Theory and practice from the perspective of communication. *Journal of Applied Communication Research, 23,* 167–200.

Cheney, G., Christensen, L. T., Zorn, T. E., Jr., & Ganesh, S. (2004). *Organizational communication in an age of globalizations: Issues, reflections, practices.* Prospect Heights, IL: Waveland.

Chiles, A., & Zorn, T. (1995). Empowerment in organizations: Employees' perceptions of the influences on empowerment. *Journal of Applied Communication Research, 23,* 1–25.

Chilton, K., & Weidenbaum, M. (1994, November). *A new social contract for the American workplace: From paternalism to partnering.* St. Louis, MO: Center for the Study of American Business.

Clair, R. (1996). The political nature of a colloquialism, "a real job": Implications for organizational assimilation. *Communication Monographs, 63,* 249–267.

Conrad, C., & Witte, K. (1994). Is emotional expression repression oppression? *Communication Yearbook, 17,* 417–428.

Coy, P., Conlin, M., & Herbst, M. (2010, January 7). The disposable worker. *Bloomberg Business Week.* Retrieved September 17, 2011, from http://www.businessweek.com/magazine/content/10_03/b4163032935448.htm

Daniels, T. D., Spiker, B. K., & Papa, M. J. (1996). *Perspectives on organizational communication* (4th ed.). Madison, WI: Brown & Benchmark.

Dansereau, F. D., & Markham, S. E. (1987). Superior–subordinate communication: Multiple levels of analysis. In F. Jablin, L. Putnam, K. Roberts, & L. Porter (Eds.), *Handbook of organizational communication* (pp. 343–386). Newbury Park, CA: Sage.

Deetz, S. (1992). *Democracy in an age of corporate colonization: Developments in communication and the politics of everyday life.* Albany, NY: SUNY Press.

DiTecco, D., Cwitco, G., Arsenault, A., & Andre, M. (1992). Operator stress and monitoring practices. *Applied Ergonomics, 23*(1), 29–34.

Dockery, T. M., & Steiner, D. D. (1990). The role of the initial interaction in leader-member exchange. *Group and Organization Studies, 15,* 395–413.

Eisenberg, E., Goodall, H. L., & Trethewey, A. (2010). *Organizational communication: Balance, creativity and constraint.* Boston, MA: Bedford/St. Martin's.

Eisenberg, E. M., Monge, P. R., & Farace, R. V. (1984). Coorientation on communication rules in managerial dyads. *Human Communication Research, 11,* 261–271.

Equal Employment Opportunity Commission. (1980). Guidelines on discrimination because of sex (Sect. 1604.11). *Federal Register, 45,* 74676–74677.

Everbach, T. (2007). The culture of a women-led newspaper: An ethnographic study of the *Sarasota Herald-Tribune. Journalism and Mass Communication Quarterly, 83,* 477–493.

FBI probes Murdoch empire over 9/11 hacking claims. (2011, July 14). *MSNBC.* Retrieved August 9, 2011, from http://www.msnbc.msn.com/id/43750733/ns/world_news-europe/t/fbi-probes-murdoch-empire-over-hacking-claims/

Fishman, C. (2006). *The Wal-Mart effect.* New York: Penguin Press.

Follett, M. P. (1942). *Dynamic administration.* New York: Harper & Row.

Ganesh, S., Zoller, H., & Cheney, G. (2005). Transforming resistance, broadening our boundaries: Critical organization meets globalization from below. *Communication Monographs, 72*(2), 169–191.

Glisson, C., & Durick, M. (1988). Predictors of job satisfaction and organizational commitment in human service organizations. *Administrative Quarterly, 33,* 61–81.

Golembiewski, R. T., Boudreau, R. A., Sun, B. C., & Luo, H. (1998). Estimates of burnout in public agencies: Worldwide how many employees have which degrees of burnout, and with what consequences? *Public Administration Review, 58,* 59–65.

Graen, G., & Graen, J. (2006). *Sharing network leadership.* Greenwich, CT: Information Age Publishing.

Gruber, J. E., & Smith, M. D. (1995). Women's responses to sexual harassment: A multivariate analysis. *Basic and Applied Social Psychology, 17,* 543–562.

Highgate, P., & Upton, J. (2005). War, militarism, and masculinities. In M.S. Kimmel, J. Hearn, & R. W. Connell (Eds.), *Handbook of studies on men and masculinities* (pp. 432–447). Thousand Oaks, CA: Sage.

Hochschild, A. (1983). *The managed heart.* Berkeley: University of California Press.

Howard-Grenville, J. A. (2006). Inside the "black box": How organizational culture and subcultures inform interpretations and actions on environmental issues. *Organization & Environment, 19*(1), 46–73.

Igbaria, M., & Guimaraes, T. (1993). Antecedents and consequences of job satisfaction among information center employees. *Journal of Management Information Systems, 9*(4), 145–155.

Jablin, F. M. (1979). Superior-subordinate communication: The state of the art. *Psychological Bulletin, 86,* 1201–1222.

Jablin, F. M., & Krone, K. J. (1987). Organizational assimilation. In C. R. Berger & S. H. Chafee (Eds.), *Handbook of communication science* (pp. 711–746). Newbury Park, CA: Sage.

Jablin, F. M., & Sias, P. M. (2001). Communication competence. In F. M. Jablin & L. Putnam (Eds.), *The new handbook of organizational communication* (pp. 819–864). Thousand Oaks, CA: Sage.

Jenner, L. (1994). Work-family programs: Looking beyond written programs. *HR Focus, 71,* 19–20.

Kirby, E. L., & Krone, K. J. (2002). "The policy exists but you can't really use it": Communication and the structuration of work-family polices. *Journal of Applied Communication Research, 30,* 50–77.

Koniarek, J., & Dudek, B. (1996). Social support as a barrier in the stress–burnout relationship. *International Journal of Stress Management, 3,* 99–106.

Kram, K. E., & Isabella, L. A. (1985). Mentoring alternatives: The role of peer relationships in career development. *Academy of Management Journal, 28,* 110–132.

Kreps, G. (1991). *Organizational communication: Theory and practice* (2nd ed.). New York: Longman.

Krugman, P. (2002). *The great unraveling: Losing our way in the new century.* New York: W. W. Norton.

Larson, J., Jr. (1989). The dynamic interplay between employees: Feedback-seeking strategies and supervisors' delivery of performance feedback. *Academy of Management Review, 14,* 408–422.

Ludden, J. (2011, June 30). Men now have more "work-life conflict" than women, study says. *National Public Radio.* Retrieved July 14, 2011, from http://www.gpb.org/news/2011/06/30/men-now-have-more-work-life-conflict-than-women-study-says

Lutgen-Sandvik, P., Tracy, S., & Alberts, J. (2005, February). *Burned by bullying in the American workplaces: A first time study of U.S.*

prevalence and delineation of bullying "degree." Paper presented at the Western States Communication Convention, San Francisco, CA.

Madan, A. O. (2014). Cyber aggression, cyber bullying and the dark triad: Effect on workplace behavior and performance. *International Journal of Social, Management, Economics and Business Engineering, 8*(6), 1682–1687.

Martin, J. (2002). *Organizational culture: Mapping the terrain.* Thousand Oaks, CA: Sage.

Martin, J. (2012). That's how we do things around here: Organizational culture (and change) in libraries. Retrieved July 17, 2014, from http://www.inthelibrarywiththeleadpipe.org/2012/thats-how-we-do-things-around-here/

Maslach, C. (2003). Job burnout: New directions in research and intervention. *Current Directions in Psychological Science, 12*(5), 189–192.

Maslach, C., & Leiter, M. (1997). *The truth about burnout: How organizations cause personal stress and what to do about it.* San Francisco: Josey-Bass.

Matthews, C., and Gandel, S. (2015, December 27). The 5 Biggest Corporate Scandals of 2015. *Fortune.* Accessed April 30, 2017, from http://fortune.com/2015/12/27/biggest-corporate-scandals-2015/

McGrath, J. E. (1976). Stress and behavior in organizations. In M. D. Dunnette (Ed.), *Handbook of industrial and organizational psychology.* Palo Alto, CA: Consulting Psychologists Press.

McNamara, C. (2008). *Field guide to leadership and supervision.* Minneapolis, MN: Authenticity Publishing.

Miller, V. D., & Jablin, F. (1991). Information seeking during organizational entry: Influence, tactics and a model of the process. *Academy of Management Review, 16,* 522–541.

Monge, P. R., & Contractor, N. S. (2001). Emergence of communication networks. In F. M. Jablin & L. L. Putnam (Eds.), *The new handbook of organizational communication* (pp. 440–502). Thousand Oaks, CA: Sage.

Morgan, H., & Milliken, F. J. (1992). Keys to action: Understanding differences in organizations' responsiveness to work-and-family issues. *Human Resource Management, 31,* 227–248.

Namie, G., Christiansen, D., & Phillips, D. (2014). *The 2014 WBI U.S. workplace bullying survey.* Retrieved July 15, 2014, from http://www.workplacebullying.org/wbiresearch/wbi-2014-us-survey/

Pacanowsky, M. L., & Trujillo, N. (1983). Organizational communication as organization performance. *Communication Monographs, 50,* 126–147.

Privitera, C., & Campbell, M. A. (2009). Cyberbullying: The new face of workplace bullying. *Cyber Psychology & Behavior, 12*(4), 395–400.

Prokokos, A., & Padavik, I. (2002). "There ought to be a law against bitches": Masculinity lessons in police academy training. *Gender, Work and Organization, 9*(4), 439–459.

Putnam, L. L., Phillips, N., & Chapman, P. (1996). Metaphors of communication and organization. In S. R. Clegg, C. Hardy, & W. R. Nord (Eds.), *Handbook of organization studies* (pp. 375–408). London: Sage.

Rapoport, R., & Bailyn, L. (1996). *Relinking life and work.* New York: Ford Foundation.

Rawlins, W. K. (1994). Being there and growing apart: Sustaining friendships during adulthood. In D. Canary & L. Stafford, *Communication and relational maintenance* (pp. 275–294). San Diego, CA: Academic.

Richardsen, A. M., & Martinussen, M. (2004). The Maslach burnout inventory: Factorial validity and consistency across occupational groups in Norway. *Journal of Occupational and Organizational Psychology, 77,* 1–20.

Richmond, V. P., McCroskey, J. C., & Davis, L. M. (1986). The relationship of supervisor use of power and affinity-seeking strategies with subordinate satisfaction. *Communication Quarterly, 34,* 178–193.

Rizzo, J. R., House, R. J., & Lirtzman, S. L. (1970). Role conflict and ambiguity in complex organizations. *Administrative Science Quarterly, 15,* 150–163.

Roberts, B. S., & Mann, R. A. (2000, December 5). Sexual harassment in the workplace: A primer. *Akron Law Review.* Retrieved September 12, 2006, from http://www3.uakron.edu/lawrev/robert1.html

Roose, K. (2014, April 24). The Sharing Economy Isn't About Trust, It's About Desperation. *New York Magazine.* Accessed April 30,

2017, at http://nymag.com/daily/intelligencer/2014/04/sharing-economy-is-about-desperation.html

Roy, D. F. (1995). Banana time: Job satisfaction and informal interaction. In S. R. Corman, S. P. Banks, C. R. Bantz, & M. E. Mayer (Eds.), *Foundations of Organizational Communication: A Reader* (pp. 111–120). White Plains, NY: Longman.

Rudman, L., Borgida E., & Robertson, B. (1995). Suffering in Silence: Procedural Justice Versus Gender Socialization Issues in University Sexual Harassment Grievance Procedures. *Basic and Applied Social Psychology, 17* (4), 519–541.

Schein, E. H. (2002). *Organizational culture and leadership.* San Francisco, CA: Josey-Bass.

Schneider, B., Ehrhart, K. H., & Ehrhart, M. G. (2005). Organizational climate. In C. L. Cooper (Ed.), *The Blackwell Encyclopedia of Management, XI,* 270–272. Retrieved March 19, 2017, from http://www.blackwellreference.com/public/tocnode?id=g9780631233176_chunk_g978063123536119_ss2-8#citation

Scott, C., & Myers, K. (2005). The emotion of socialization and assimilation: Learning emotion management at the firehouse. *Journal of Applied Communication Research, 33*(1), 67–92.

Shuler, S., & Sypher, B. D. (2000). Seeking emotion labor: When managing the heart enhances the work experience. *Management Communication Quarterly, 14,* 50–89.

Sias, P. M. (2005). Workplace relationship quality and employee information experiences. *Communication Studies, 56*(4), 375–395.

Sias, P. M., & Cahill, D. J. (1998). From coworkers to friends: The development of peer friendships in the workplace. *Western Journal of Communication, 62,* 273–279.

Sias, P. M., & Jablin, F. M. (1995). Differential superior–subordinate relations: Perceptions of fairness, and coworker communication. *Human Communication Research, 22,* 5–38.

Sias, P. M., Smith, G., & Avdeyeva, T. (2003). Sex and sex-composition differences and similarities in peer workplace friendship development. *Communication Studies, 54,* 322–340.

Sigal, J., Braden-Maguire, J., Patt, I., Goodrich, C., & Perrino, C. S. (2003). Effect of coping response, setting, and social context on reactions to sexual harassment. *Sex Roles, 48*(3–4), 157–166.

Solomon, C. (1994). Work/family's failing grade: Why today's initiatives aren't enough. *Personnel Journal, 73*(5), 72–87.

Stanton, J. M., & Julian, A. L. (2002). The impact of electronic monitoring on quality and quantity of performance. *Computers in Human Behavior, 18*(1), 85–113.

Taylor, J. R., & Van Every, J. F. (1993). *The vulnerable fortress: Bureaucratic organizations and management in the information age.* Toronto, Canada: University of Toronto Press.

Thurnell, R., & Parker, A. (2008). Men, masculinities and firefighting: Occupational identity, shop-floor culture and organisational change. *Emotion, Space and Society, 1*(2), 127–134.

Tracy, S. J. (2000). Becoming a character for commerce: Emotion labor, self-subordination and discursive construction of identity in a total institution. *Management Communication Quarterly, 14,* 90–128.

Tracy, S. J. (2005). Locking up emotion: Moving beyond dissonance for understanding emotion labor discomfort. *Communication Monographs, 72,* 261–238.

Trethewey, A., & Corman, S. (2001). Anticipating k-commerce: E-Commerce, knowledge management, and organizational communication. *Management Communication Quarterly, 14,* 619–628.

Vault office romance survey. (2003). Retrieved March 10, 2006, from http://www.vault.com/nr/newsmain.jsp>nr_page=3dch_id=420d.article_id=16513021

von Bertalanffy, L. (1968). *General systems theory.* New York: Braziller.

Waldron, V. R. (1994). Once more, with feeling: Reconsidering the role of emotion in work. In S. Deetz (Ed.), *Communication Yearbook, 17,* 388–416. Thousand Oaks, CA: Sage.

Wayne, S. G., & Ferris, G. R. (1990). Influence tactics, affect and exchange quality in supervisor-subordinate interactions: A laboratory experiment and field study. *Journal of Applied Psychology, 75,* 487–499.

Westman, M., & Etzion, D. (2005). The crossover of work-family conflict from one spouse to the other. *Journal of Applied Social Psychology, 35*(9), 1936–1957.

Whetton, D. A., & Cameron, K. S. (2002). *Developing managerial skills* (6th ed.). Upper Saddle River, NJ: Prentice Hall.

Zuckerman, M. B. (2011, June 20). Why the job situation is worse than it looks. *U.S. News and World Report.* Retrieved September, 17, 2011, from http://www.usnews.com/opinion/mzuckerman/articles/2011/06/20/why-the-jobs-situation-is-worse-than-it-looks

Chapter 12

Aristotle. (1991). *On rhetoric: A theory of civic discourse* (G. A. Kennedy, Trans.). New York: Oxford University Press.

Behnke, R., & Sawyer, C. (1999). Milestones of anticipatory public speaking anxiety. *Communication Education, 48,* 165–173.

Behnke, R., & Sawyer, C. (2004). Public speaking anxiety as a function of sensitization and habituation processes. *Communication Education, 53,* 164–173.

Bitzer, L. (1968). The rhetorical situation. *Philosophy and Rhetoric, 1,* 1–14.

Brown. K. V. (2016, July 19). How a racist, sexist hate mob forced Leslie Jones off Twitter. *Fusion.* Retrieved from http://fusion.net/story/327103/leslie-jones-twitter-racism/

Bush, G. W. (2001, September 12). "Today . . . our very freedom came under attack." *Boston Globe.* Retrieved September 14, 2011, from http://www.boston.com/news/packages/underattack/globe_stories/0912/_Today_our_very_freedom_came_under_attack_+.shtml

Conley, T. (1994). *Rhetoric in the European tradition.* Chicago: University of Chicago Press.

Darsey, J. (1991). From "gay is good" to the scourge of AIDS: The evolution of gay liberation rhetoric, 1977–1990. *Communication Studies, 42,* 43–66.

Darsey, J. (1994). Must we all be rhetorical theorists? An anti-democratic inquiry. *Western Journal of Communication, 58,* 164–181.

Dehghan, S. K. (2011, July 31). Iranian woman blinded by acid attack pardons assailant as he faces same fate. *Guardian.* Retrieved July 31, 2011, from http://www.guardian.co.uk/world/2011/jul/31/iran-acid-woman-pardons-attacker

Delgado, F. (1995). Chicano movement rhetoric: An ideographic interpretation. *Communication Quarterly, 43,* 446–455.

DeLuca, K. M. (1999). *Image politics: The new rhetoric of environmental activism.* New York: Guilford.

Douglass, F. (1852, July 5). The meaning of July Fourth for the Negro. Retrieved June 26, 2006, from http://www.pbs.org/wgbh/aia/part4/4h2927t.html

Ehninger, D. (1967). On rhetoric and rhetorics. *Western Speech, 31,* 242–249.

Erdbrink. T. (2008, December 14). Woman blinded by spurned man invokes Islamic retribution. *Washington Post,* p. A1.

Gayle, B. M. (2004). Transformations in a civil discourse public speaking class: Speakers' and listeners' attitude change. *Communication Education, 53,* 174–185.

Haddix, Marcelle, et al. (2016). At the kitchen table: Black women English educators speaking our truths. *English Education, 48*(4), 380–395. ProQuest. Web. March 2, 2017.

Haskins, E. (2013). On the term 'Dunamis' in Aristotle's definition of rhetoric. *Philosophy & Rhetoric, 46*(2), 234–240. www.jstor.org/stable/10.5325/philrhet.46.2.0234

Haskins, E. (2006). Choosing between Isocrates and Aristotle: Disciplinary assumptions and pedagogical implications. *Rhetoric Society Quarterly, 36*(2), 191–201. www.jstor.org/stable/3886176

Infante, D. A., Rancer, A. S., & Womack, D. F. (1990). *Building communication theory.* Prospect Heights, IL: Waveland.

Johannesen, R. L. (1997). Diversity, freedom, and responsibility in tension. In J. M. Makau & R. C. Arnett (Eds.), *Communication ethics in an age of diversity* (pp. 157–186). Urbana: University of Illinois Press.

Kennedy, G. A. (1998). *Comparative rhetoric: An historical and cross-cultural introduction.* New York: Oxford University Press.

King, J. L. (2002). Cultural differences in the perceptions of sports mascots: A rhetorical study of Tim Giago's newspaper columns. In J. N. Martin, T. K. Nakayama, & L. A. Flores (Eds.), *Readings in intercultural communication: Experiences and contexts* (pp. 205–212). New York: McGraw-Hill.

Levasseur, D. G., Dean, K. W., & Pfaff, J. (2004). Speech pedagogy beyond the basics: A study of instructional methods in the advanced public speaking course. *Communication Education, 53,* 234–252.

Lucaites, J. L., Condit, C. M., & Caudill, S. (1999). *Contemporary rhetorical theory: A reader.* New York: Guilford.

Maffesoli, M. (1996). *The time of the tribes: The decline of individualism in mass society.* Thousand Oaks, CA: Sage.

Makau, J. M. (1997). Embracing diversity in the classroom. In J. M. Makau & R. C. Arnett (Eds.), *Communication ethics in an age of diversity* (pp. 48–67). Urbana: University of Illinois Press.

Mandell, N. (2012, January 13). Scott sisters devastated they weren't on Mississippi Gov. Haley Barbour's pardon list. *New York Daily News.* Retrieved May 18, 2014, from http://www.nydailynews.com/news/national/scott-sisters-devestated-weren-mississippi-gov-haley-barbour-pardon-list-article-1.1005655

McKerrow, R. E., Gronbeck, B. E., Ehninger, D., & Monroe, A. H. (2003). *Principles of public speaking* (15th ed.). Boston: Allyn & Bacon.

Mitchell, M. (2012, March 21). Social media can act as watchdog for injustice. *Chicago Sun-Times.* Retrieved May 18, 2014, from http://www.suntimes.com/news/mitchell/11448870-452/social-media-can-act-as-watchdog-for-injustice.html#.U3j84yifNiE

Nakamura, L., & Chow-White, P. A. (Eds.). (2012). *Race after the internet.* New York: Routledge.

Obama, B. H. (n.d.). *We the people: Your voice in our government.* Retrieved May 18, 2014, from http://www.whitehouse.gov/

O'Hair, D., Stewart, R., & Rubenstein, H. (2004). *A speaker's guidebook* (2nd ed.). Boston: Bedford/St. Martin's.

Ohlheiser, A. (2016, July 21). Just how offensive did Milo Yiannopoulos have to be to get banned from Twitter? *Washington Post.* Retrieved from https://www.washingtonpost.com/news/the-intersect/wp/2016/07/21/what-it-takes-to-get-banned-from-twitter/?utm_term=.9e9235320b04

Osterman, R. (2005, May 23). "Soft skills" top list of what area employers desire. *Sacramento Bee,* D1.

Pew Forum on Religion and Public Life. (2008, December 18). Many Americans say other faiths can lead to eternal life. Retrieved January 7, 2009, from http://pewresearch.org/pubs/1062/many-americans-say-other-faiths-can-lead-to-eternal-life

Pew Research Center for People and the Press. (2005, September 8). Huge racial divide over Katrina and its consequences: Two-in-three critical of Bush's relief efforts. Retrieved June 26, 2006, from http://people-press.org/reports/pdf/255.pdf

Salahi, L. (2014, May 19). Wolfeboro police commissioner resigns following racist comments. *Boston Globe.* Retrieved May 19, 2014, from http://www.boston.com/news/local/massachusetts/2014/05/19/wolfeboro-police-commissioner-resigns-following-racist-comments/j87BzO0UESpKP1ySjcvENO/story.html

Sanow, A. (2005, March 3). How I overcame the fear of public speaking. Retrieved June 26, 2006, from http://www.expertclick.com/NewsReleaseWire/default.cfm?Action=ReleaseDetail&ID=8372&NRWid=1698

Smith, C. M., & Dionosopoulos, G. M. (2008). The Abu Ghraib images: "Breaks" in a dichotomous frame. *Western Journal of Communication, 72*(3), 308–328.

Smith, G. A., & Martinez, J. (2016, November 9). How the faithful voted: A preliminary 2016 analysis. Retrieved from http://www.pewresearch.org/fact-tank/2016/11/09/how-the-faithful-voted-a-preliminary-2016-analysis/

Solaroli, M. (2011). Mediatized conflicts, performative photographs and contested memory: The Abu Ghraib scandal and the iconic struggle over the meanings of the "war on terror." *Global Media and Communication, 7*(3), 245–250.

Sprague, J., & Stuart, D. (2005). *The speaker's handbook.* Belmont, CA: Wadsworth/Thomson.

Students show true colors online after being denied class cancellation. (2014). *The Daily Illini.* Retrieved May 19, 2014, from http://www.dailyillini.com/opinion/editorials/article_cb88c132-87b9-11e3-a571-001a4bcf6878.html

Thomas, S. (n.d.). *From slave to abolitionist/editor.* Retrieved June 26, 2006, from http://www.history.rochester.edu/class/douglass/part2.html

Tostevin, R. (2014, March 14). Online activism: It's easy to click, but just as easy to disengage. *The Guardian.* Retrieved May 18, 2014, from http://www.theguardian.com/

media-network/media-network-blog/2014/mar/14/online-activism-social-media-engage

Tufte, E. (2003, September). PowerPoint is evil. *Wired Magazine*, (pp. 118–119). Reprinted by permission from Edward R. Tufte, *The Cognitive Style of PowerPoint.* Cheshire, CT: Graphics Press.

U.S. Census Bureau. (2003, February 25). *Census 2000. Table 5: Detailed list of languages spoken at home for the population 5 years and over by state.* Retrieved March 27, 2009, from http://www.census.gov/population/www.cen2000/briefs/phc-t20/tab05.pdf

U.S. Census Bureau. (2012). *The American Indian and Alaska Native population: 2010.* Retrieved from https://www.census.gov/prod/cen2010/briefs/c2010br-10.pdf

Wallace, G. (2016, November 30). Voter turnout at 20-year low in 2016. *CNN.* Retrieved from http://edition.cnn.com/2016/11/11/politics/popular-vote-turnout-2016/

Washington Post staff. (2016, June 12). President Obama's complete remarks on Orlando shooting. *Washington Post.* Retrieved from https://www.washingtonpost.com/news/post-politics/wp/2016/06/12/president-obamas-complete-remarks-on-orlando-shooting/?utm_term=.92e859d16221

Weaver, R. (1985). *The ethics of rhetoric.* New York: Routledge.

Chapter 13

Akhavan-Majid, R. (2004). Mass media reform in China: Toward a new analytical perspective. *Gazette: The International Journal for Communication Studies, 66,* 553–565.

Anderson, C. A., & Bushman, B. J. (2002, March 29). The effects of media violence on society. *Science, 295,* 2377–2378. Retrieved May 1, 2006, from http://www.psychology.iastate.edu/faculty/caa/abstracts/2000-2004/02AB2.pdf

Anderson, M. (2016, November 21). *TV still the top source for election results, but digital platforms rise.* Retrieved from http://www.pewresearch.org/fact-tank/2016/11/21/tv-still-the-top-source-for-election-results-but-digital-platforms-rise/

Aoyagi, C. (2004, July 2–15). TV networks' current fascination with Hawaii often doesn't translate into more roles for APAs. *Pacific Citizen, 139,* 1.

Arria, M. (2015, April 8). Spotify exploits musicians: What is an artist to do? *Alternet.* Retrieved from http://www.alternet.org/labor/spotify-exploits-musicians-what-artist-do

Barthel, M., Mitchell, A., & Holcomb, J. (2016, December 15). *Many Americans believe fake news is sowing confusion.* Retrieved from http://www.journalism.org/2016/12/15/many-americans-believe-fake-news-is-sowing-confusion/

Belkin, L. (2010, December 14). Wanted: More girls on screen. *New York Times.* Retrieved July 19, 2011, from http://parenting.blogs.nytimes.com/2010/12/14/wanted-more-girls-on-screen/

Berelson, B. (1952/1971). *Content analysis in communication research.* New York: Hafner Publishing Co.

Billings, A. C., & Eastman, S. T. (2003). Framing identities: Gender, ethnic, and national parity in network announcing of the 2002 Olympics. *Journal of Communication, 53,* 569–586.

Bissell, K. L., & Zhou, P. (2004). Must-see TV or ESPN: Entertainment and sports media exposure and body-image distortion in college women. *Journal of Communication, 54,* 5–21.

Boorstin, D. J. (1965). *The Americans: The national experience.* New York: Random House.

Brustein, J. (2014, May 26–June 1). Streams of tears: Why Spotify—and the streaming music industry—can't make money. *Bloomberg Businessweek,* 70–73.

Bryant, J., & Miron, D. (2004). Theory and research in mass communication. *Journal of Communication, 54,* 662–704.

Bushman, B. J., & Gibson, B. (2011). Violent video games cause an increase in aggression long after the game has been turned off. *Social Psychological and Personality Science, 2,* 29–32.

Cablevision. (2002, November 4). *NBC to acquire Bravo from Cablevision Systems Corporation.* Retrieved June 24, 2006, from http://www.cablevision.com/index.jhtml?id=2002_11_04

Carr, D. (2011, July 17). Troubles that money can't dispel. *New York Times.* Retrieved July 19, 2011, from http://www.nytimes.com/2011/07/18/business/media/for-news-corporation-troubles-that-money-cant-dispel.html?hp

Celis, B. (2017, March 12). The time's right for a new wave of Black media activism. *Newsweek.* Retrieved from http://www.newsweek.com/time-right-new-wave-black-media-activism-565377

Chalaby, J. K. (2003). Television for a new global order: Transnational television networks and the formation of global systems. *Gazette: The International Journal for Communication Studies, 65,* 457–472.

Chapman, J. (2005). *Comparative media history.* Malden, MA: Polity Press.

Cho, H., & Boster, F. J. (2008). Effect of gain versus loss frame antidrug ads on adolescents. *Journal of Communication, 58,* 428–446.

Cohen, J. (2002). Television viewing preferences: Programs, schedules, and the structure of viewing choices made by Israeli adults. *Journal of Broadcasting & Electronic Media, 46,* 204–221.

Coming full circle: The end of mass media. (2011, July 7). Retrieved June 6, 2014, from http://www.economist.com/node/18904158

Dayan, D., & Katz, E. (1992). *Media events: The live broadcasting of history.* Cambridge, MA: Harvard University Press.

DeLuca, K. M., & Peeples, J. (2002). From public sphere to public screen: Democracy, activism, and the "violence" of Seattle. *Critical Studies in Media Communication, 19,* 125–151.

de Moraes, L. (2004, October 21). No more Miss America pageantry for ABC. *Washington Post,* p. C7. Retrieved June 24, 2006, from http://www.washingtonpost.com/wp-dyn/articles/A50114-2004Oct20.html

Dixon, T. L., & Linz, D. (2002). Television news, prejudicial pretrial publicity, and the depiction of race. *Journal of Broadcasting & Electronic Media, 46,* 112–136.

Douglas, T. (2012, June 28). News Corp confirms plan to split the media giant. *BBC.* Retrieved March 23, 2017, from http://www.bbc.com/news/business-18621949

Durham, M. G. (2004). Constructing the "new ethnicities": Media, sexuality, and diaspora identity in the lives of South Asian immigrant girls. *Critical Studies in Media Communication, 21,* 140–161.

Dwyer, D., & Jones, L. (2010, May 20). Rape kit testing backlog thwarts justice for victims. *ABC News.* Retrieved July 14, 2011, from http://abcnews.go.com/Politics/sexual-assault-victims-congress-solve-rape-kit-backlog/story?id=10701295

Fahmy, S. (2004). Picturing Afghan women: A content analysis of AP wire photographs during the Taliban regime and after the fall of the Taliban regime. *Gazette: The International Journal for Communication Studies, 66,* 91–112.

Federal Communications Commission. (2003, July 8). *V-chip: Viewing television responsibly.* Retrieved June 24, 2006, from http://www.fcc.gov/vchip/

Feinberg, S. (2014, March 2). Brutally honest Oscar voter ballot no. 7. *The Hollywood Reporter.* Retrieved June 9, 2014, from http://www.hollywoodreporter.com/race/brutally-honest-oscar-voter-ballot-684839

Gerbner, G. (2002). *Against the mainstream: The selected works of George Gerbner.* M. Morgan (Ed.). New York: Peter Lang.

Greenslade, R. (2016, May 31). Mass media is over, but where does journalism go from here? *The Guardian.* Retrieved from https://www.theguardian.com/media/greenslade/2016/may/31/mass-media-is-over-but-where-does-journalism-go-from-here

Gunther, A. C., & Schmitt, K. (2004). Mapping boundaries of the hostile media effect. *Journal of Communication, 54,* 55–70.

Hale, M. (2017, March 13). On Netflix, the borders remain open. *New York Times.* Retrieved from https://www.nytimes.com/2017/03/13/arts/television/netflix-fauda-nobel-review.html?_r=0

Hanke, R. (1990). Hegemonic masculinity in *thirtysomething. Critical Studies in Mass Communication, 7,* 231–248.

Has Obama Seen ISIS Execution Videos? (2014, September 5). Retrieved December 12, 2014, from http://abcnews.go.com/Politics/video/obama-isis-execution-videos-25258267?utm_source=twitterfeed&utm_medium=twitter

Hightower, K., & Sedensky, M. (2011, July 10). Anger over Casey Anthony verdict pours out online. *USA Today.* Retrieved August 1, 2011, from http://www.usatoday.com/news/topstories/2011-07-09-2575323558_x.htm

Jhally, S., & Lewis, J. (1992). *Enlightened racism: The Cosby show, audiences, and the myth of the American dream.* Boulder, CO: Westview Press.

Law, C., & Labre, M. P. (2002). Cultural standards of attractiveness: A thirty-year look at changes in male images in magazines. *Journalism and Mass Communication Quarterly, 79*, 697–711.

Lazarsfeld, P. F., Berelson, B., & Gaudet, H. (1948). *The people's choice: How the voter makes up his mind in a presidential campaign.* New York: Columbia University Press.

Lemire, C. (2005, August 10). Even trashing "Deuce Bigalow" a tired cliché. *MSNBC.* Retrieved June 24, 2006, from http://msnbc.msn.com/id/8887672

Lowry, D. T., Nio, T. C. J., & Leitner, D. W. (2003). Setting the public fear agenda: A longitudinal analysis of network TV crime reporting, public perceptions of crime and FBI crime statistics. *Journal of Communication, 53*, 61–73.

Luckerson, V. (2013, December 3). Here's how much top musicians are making on Spotify. *Time.* Retrieved June 29, 2014, from http://business.time.com/2013/12/03/heres-how-much-money-top-musicians-are-making-on-spotify/

McChesney, R. (1998). Making media democratic. *Boston Review, 23*, 4–10, 20. Retrieved June 24, 2006, from http://www.bostonreview.net/BR23.3/mcchesney.html

McQuail, D., Blumler, J. G., & Brown, J. R. (1972). The television audience: a revised perspective. In McQuail, D. (ed.), *Sociology of Mass Communication* (pp. 135–165). New York: Penguin.

McQuail, D. (1987). *Mass communication theory: An introduction* (2nd ed.). Newbury Park, CA: Sage Publications.

Meyers, M. (2004). African American women and violence: Gender, race, and class in the news. *Critical Studies in Media Communication, 21*, 95–118.

Millennials on millennials: A look at viewing behavior, distraction and social media stars. (2017, March 2). Retrieved from http://www.nielsen.com/us/en/insights/news/2017/millennials-on-millennials-a-look-at-viewing-behavior-distraction-social-media-stars.html

Mitchell, A. (2014, March 26). State of the news media 2014. *Pew Research Journalism Project.* Retrieved June 11, 2014, from http://www.journalism.org/2014/03/26/state-of-the-news-media-2014-overview/

Morgan, M., & Signorielli, N. (1990). Cultivation analysis: Conceptualization and methodology. In N. Signorielli & M. Morgan (Eds.), *Cultivation analysis: New directions in media effects research* (pp. 13–34). Newbury Park, CA: Sage Publications.

Nathanson, A. (2004). Factual and evaluative approaches to modifying children's responses to violent television. *Journal of Communication, 54*, 321–336.

Newman, M. (2017, March 15). How much has Ed Sheeran's new album made on Spotify? *Forbes.* Retrieved from https://www.forbes.com/sites/melindanewman/2017/03/15/ed-sheerans-new-album-has-made-how-much-on-spotify-already/#b7f840123bdd

News Corporation. (2011, September 20). Retrieved October 5, 2011, from http://topics.nytimes.com/top/news/business/companies/news_corporation/index.html

News Corp officially splits in two. (2013, June 28). Retrieved March 23, 2017, from http://www.bbc.com/news/business-23104822

Niederdeppe, J., Fowler, E. F., Goldstein, K., & Pribble, J. (2010). Does local television news coverage cultivate fatalistic beliefs about cancer prevention? *Journal of Communication, 60*, 230–253.

Nielsen. (2013, December 3). *A look across media: The cross-platform report Q3 2013.* Retrieved June 9, 2014, from http://www.nielsen.com/us/en/reports/2013/a-look-across-media-the-cross-platform-report-q3-2013.html

Nielsen. (2014, May 12). *Advertising and audiences: State of the media.* Retrieved June 6, 2014, from http://www.nielsen.com/us/en/reports/2014/advertising-and-audiences-state-of-the-media.html

Nielsen. (2016, September 26). *Nielsen Total Audience Report: Q2 2016.* Retrieved from http://www.nielsen.com/us/en/insights/reports/2016/the-nielsen-total-audience-report-q2-2016.html

Nielsen. (2017). *The Nielsen comparable metrics report, Q3 2016.* Retrieved March 23, 2017 from http://www.nielsen.com/content/dam/corporate/us/en/reports-downloads/2017-reports/q3-2016-comparable-metrics-report.pdf

Number of paying Spotify subscribers worldwide from July 2010 to March 2017 (in millions). (2017). Retrieved from https://www.statista.com/statistics/244995/number-of-paying-spotify-subscribers/

Okoro, E. (2013, November 27). Why I wouldn't see *12 Years a Slave* with a white person. *The Atlantic.* Retrieved June 9, 2014, from http://www.theatlantic.com/entertainment/archive/2013/11/why-i-wouldnt-see-em-12-years-a-slave-emwith-a-white-person/281883/

Pallotta, F. (2017, February 2). New York Times touts subscriber growth with a jab at Trump. *CNN Money.* Retrieved from http://money.cnn.com/2017/02/02/media/new-york-times-subscribers-trump/

Peter, J. (2003). Country characteristics as contingent conditions of agenda setting: The moderating influence of polarized elite opinion. *Communication Research, 30*, 683–712.

Romer, D., Jamieson, K. H., & Aday, S. (2003). Television news and the cultivation of fear of crime. *Journal of Communication, 53*, 88–104.

Rosenbaum, S. (2014, May 25). Time Warner CEO says tv is taking over the web. *Forbes.* Retrieved June 6, 2014, from http://www.forbes.com/sites/stevenrosenbaum/2014/05/25/time-warner-ceo-says-tv-is-taking-over-the-web/

Rubin, S. (2010, October 6). Rape kit backlog hits primetime on "SVU." *Ms. Magazine.* Retrieved July 14, 2011, from http://msmagazine.com/blog/blog/2010/10/06/rape-kit-backlog-hits-primetime-on-svu/

Rutenberg, J. (2016, August 14). Fox News turmoil recalls News Corp. phone hacking scandal. *New York Times.* Retrieved March 23, 2017, from https://www.nytimes.com/2016/08/15/business/fox-news-turmoil-recalls-news-corp-phone-hacking-scandal.html?_r=0

Scott, D. C. (2013, November 9). Mariska Hargitay: A Hollywood star for an actress—and activist. *The Christian Science Monitor.* Retrieved June 6, 2014, from http://www.csmonitor.com/The-Culture/2013/1109/Mariska-Hargitay-A-Hollywood-star-for-an-actress-and-activist-video

Sharkey, B. (2014, February 27). Oscars 2014: For many, "12 Years a Slave" is too hard to watch. *Los Angeles Times.* Retrieved June 9, 2014, from http://articles.latimes.com/2014/feb/27/entertainment/la-et-mn-12-years-a-slave-notebook-20140227/2

Shugart, H. (2008). Managing masculinities: The metrosexual moment. *Communication and Critical/Cultural Studies, 5*, 280–300.

Slater, M. D., Henry, K. L., Swaim, R. C., & Anderson, L. L. (2003). Violent media content and aggressiveness in adolescents: A downward spiral model. *Communication Research, 30*, 713–736.

Sproule, J. M. (1989). Progressive propaganda critics and the magic bullet myth. *Critical Studies in Mass Communication, 6*, 225–246.

Stelter, B. (2014, June 6). Netflix's tv guru: "Don't make me wait!" *CNN Money.* Retrieved June 6, 2014, from http://money.cnn.com/2014/06/06/media/ted-sarandos-netflix-interview/

Stelter, B. (2017, March 16). PBS and NPR are ready to fight budget cuts—again. *CNN Money.* Retrieved April 23, 2017, from http://money.cnn.com/2017/03/16/media/public-media-pbs-npr-budget-cuts/

Trujillo, N. (1991). Hegemonic masculinity on the mound: Media representations of Nolan Ryan and American sports culture. *Critical Studies in Mass Communication, 8*, 290–308.

TV Parental Guidelines Monitoring Board. (n.d.). *Understanding the TV ratings.* Retrieved June 24, 2006, from http://www.tvguidelines.org/ratings.htm

Ward, B. (2015, September 25). "I can't ever unsee that": Which unforgettable moments should a journalist choose to cover? *Poynter.* Retrieved from https://www.poynter.org/2015/i-cant-ever-unsee-that-which-unforgettable-moments-should-a-journalist-choose-to-cover/374171/

Wardle, C., & West, E. (2004). The press as agents of nationalism in the Queen's Golden Jubilee: How British newspapers celebrated a media event. *European Journal of Communication, 19*, 195–219.

Yahr, E. (2016, October 19). NBC's 'This Is Us' is officially the surprise breakout hit of the fall TV season. *Washington Post.* Retrieved from https://www.washingtonpost.com/news/arts-and-entertainment/wp/2016/10/19/nbcs-this-is-us-is-officially-the-surprise-breakout-hit-of-the-fall-tv-season/?utm_term=.f7a8f9d09aa0

Chapter 14

Alford, H. (2012, November 30). If I do humblebrag so myself. *The New York Times.* Retrieved April 23, 2017, from http://www.nytimes.com/2012/12/02/fashion/bah-humblebrag-the-unfortunate-rise-of-false-humility.html

Anderson, M. (2015, December 17). *Views on gaming differ by race, ethnicity*. Retrieved March 19, 2017, from http://www.pewresearch.org/fact-tank/2015/12/17/views-on-gaming-differ-by-race-ethnicity/

Anderson, M. (2017, March 22). *Digital divide persists even as lower-income Americans make gains in tech adoption*. Retrieved March 22, 2017, from http://www.pewresearch.org/fact-tank/2017/03/22/digital-divide-persists-even-as-lower-income-americans-make-gains-in-tech-adoption/

Anderson, M., & Perrin, A. (2016, September 7). *13% of Americans don't use the internet. Who are they?* Retrieved March 22, 2017, from http://www.pewresearch.org/fact-tank/2016/09/07/some-americans-dont-use-the-internet-who-are-they/

Baker, L. R., & Oswald, D. L. (2010). Shyness and online social networking services. *Journal of Social and Personal Relationships, 27*, 873–889.

Barrett, B. (2015, October 22). Facebook search now finds public posts—so hide yours. *Wired*. Retrieved March 17, 2017, from https://www.wired.com/2015/10/facebook-search-privacy/

Barthel, M., Mitchell, A., & Holcomb, J. (2016, December 15). *Many Americans believe fake news is sowing confusion*. Retrieved April 26, 2017, from http://www.journalism.org/2016/12/15/many-americans-believe-fake-news-is-sowing-confusion/

Benner, K. (2016). How Snapchat is shaping social media. *New York Times*. Retrieved on March 8, 2017, from https://www.nytimes.com/2016/11/30/technology/how-snapchat-works.html?_r=0

Berg, M. (2015). The social 100: Twitters most followed celebrities. *Forbes*. Retrieved March 12, 2017, from https://www.forbes.com/sites/maddieberg/2015/06/29/twitters-most-followed-celebrities-retweets-dont-always-mean-dollars/#632eecaa6c87

Bosker, B. (2014, February 4). The oversharers are over sharing: 10 years on, the Facebook generation is covering up. *The Huffington Post*. Retrieved May 18, 2014, from http://www.huffingtonpost.com/bianca-bosker/facebook-10-anniversary_b_4718871.html

Bourdieu, P. (1986). The forms of capital. In J. G. Richardson (Ed.), *Handbook of theory and research for the sociology of education* (pp. 241–258). Westport, CT: Greenwood.

Boyd, D. (2014). *It's complicated: The social lives of networked teens*. New Haven: Yale University Press.

Boyle, C. (2012, February 23). Trial for Rutgers student accused of cyber-bullying his gay roommate begins Friday. *New York Daily News*. Retrieved May 18, 2014, from http://www.nydailynews.com/news/rutgers-university-student-accused-cyber-bullying-gay-roommate-committed-suicide-begins-friday-imn-new-jersey-article-1.1027771

Brandtzæg, P. B. (2012). Social networking sites: Their users and social implications—a longitudinal study. *Journal of Computer-Mediated Communication, 17*, 467–488.

Brock, A. (2012). From the Blackhand side: Twitter as a cultural conversation. *Journal of Broadcasting & Electronic Media, 56*(4), 529–549.

Bryson, D. (2013, July 23). What is web civility. *Endurance International Group*. Retrieved May 27, 2014, from http://enduranceinternational.com/our-mission/web-civility/what-is-web-civility

Brustein, J. (2013, August 27). Your boss won't stop spying on you (because it works). *Business Week*. Retrieved May 25, 2014, from http://www.businessweek.com/articles/2013-08-27/your-boss-wont-stop-spying-on-you-because-it-works

Büchi, M., Just, N., & Latzer, M. (2016). Modeling the second level digital divide: A five country study of social differences in Internet use. *New Media & Society, 18*(11), 2703–2722.

Byrne, S., Katz, S. J., Linz, D., & Mcilrath, M. (2014). Peers, predators, and porn: Predicting parental underestimation of children's risky online experiences. *Journal of Computer-Mediated Communication, 19*, 215–231.

Calderon, A. (2013, May 28). 16 reasons you should never add your boss on Facebook. *Buzzfeed*. Retrieved May 27, 2014, from http://www.buzzfeed.com/ariellecalderon/16-reasons-you-should-never-add-your-boss-on-facebook

Cavalcante, A. (2016). "I did it all online": Transgender identity and the management of everyday life. *Critical Studies in Media Communication, 33*(1), 109–122.

Ceron, E. (2015). How to mentally survive a breakup on social media. *GQ Magazine*. Retrieved on March 19, 2017, from http://www.gq.com/story/social-media-breakup-guide

Cheong, P. H. (2008). The young and techless? Investigating internet use and problem-solving behaviors of young adults in Singapore. *New Media & Society, 10*(5), 771–791.

Cheong, P. H., & Gray, K. (2011). Mediated intercultural dialectics: Identity perceptions and performances in Virtual Worlds. *Journal of International and Intercultural Communication, 4*(4), 265–271.

Choi, C. (2014). 5 Best practices for lawfully monitoring your employees' social media activities. *Philadelphia Business Journal*. Retrieved on March 9, 2017, from http://www.bizjournals.com/philadelphia/blog/guest-comment/2014/10/5-best-practices-for-lawfully-monitoring-your.html

Choi, Y. H., & Bazarova, N. N. (2015). Self-disclosure characteristics and motivations in social media: Extending the functional model to multiple social network sites. *Human Communication Research, 41*(4), 480–500.

Cisneros, J. D., & Nakayama, T. K. (2015). New media, old racisms: Twitter, Miss America, and cultural logics of race. *Journal of International & Intercultural Communication, 8*(2), 108–127.

Coyne, S. M., Stockdale, L., Busby, D., Iverson, B., & Grant, D. M. (2011). "I luv u :)!": A descriptive study of the media use of individuals in romantic relationships. *Family Relations, 60*, 150–162.

Curtis, S. (2017, January 2). How to permanently delete your Facebook account. *Daily Telegraph*. Retrieved March 17, 2017, from http://www.telegraph.co.uk/technology/0/permanently-delete-facebook-account/

Daft, R. L., & Lengel, R. H. (1984). Information richness: A new approach to managerial behavior and organization design. *Research in Organizational Behavior, 6*, 191–233.

Daft, R. L., & Lengel, R. H. (1986). A proposed integration among organizational information requirements, media richness, and structural design. *Management Science, 32*(5), 544–571.

Day, E. (2015, July 19). #Black lives matter: The birth of a new civil rights movement. *The Guardian*. Retrieved April 10, 2016, from http://www.theguardian.com/world/2015/jul/19/blacklivesmatter-birth-civil-rights-movement

D'Costa, K. (2014, April 25). Catfishing: The truth about deception online. *Scientific American*. Retrieved June 27, 2014, from http://blogs.scientificamerican.com/anthropology-in-practice/2014/04/25/catfishing-the-truth-about-deception

Dhoest, A., & Szulc, L. (2016, October–November). Navigating online selves: Social, cultural and material contexts of social media use by diasporic gay men. *Social Media + Society*, 1–10.

Digital trends 2017: A collection of internet, social media and mobile data from around the world. (2017). *thenextweb.com*. Retrieved March 22, 2017 from https://thenextweb.com/insights/2017/01/24/digital-trends-2017-report-internet/#.tnw_ySq5AHab.

Digital Trends Staff. (2017, February 10). *Start dating more efficiently with one of these 8 apps*. Retrieved March 17, 2017, from http://www.digitaltrends.com/mobile/best-dating-apps/

Elphinston, R. A., & Noller, P. (2011). Time to face it! Facebook intrusion and the implications for romantic jealousy and relationship satisfaction. *Cyberpsychology, Behavior, and Social Networking, 14*(11), 631–635.

Ferman, R. (2014, April 1). Cyber-bullying: Taking on the tormentors. *The Huffington Post*. Retrieved May 18, 2014, from http://www.huffingtonpost.com/risa-ferman/cyberbullying-taking-on-t_b_5064537.html

Fichman, P., & Sanfilippo, M. R. (2016). *Online trolling and its perpetrators: Under the cyberbridge*. Lanham, MD: Roman and Littlefield.

Flacy, M. (2014, January 16). Woman loses $300,000 in Christian Mingle online dating scam. Retrieved May 27, 2014, from http://www.digitaltrends.com/social-media/woman-loses-300000-christian-mingle-online-dating-scam/#!Q9KZ3

Florini, S. (2014). Tweets, tweeps, and signifyin': Communication and cultural performance on "Black Twitter." *Television & New Media, 15*(3), 223–237.

Gal, N., Shifman, L., & Kampf, Z. (2016). "It gets better": Internet memes and the construction of collective identity. *New Media & Society, 18*(8), 1698–1714.

Galarneau, L. (2014, January 16). The top 10 gaming trends. Retrieved August 29, 2014, from http://www.bigfishgames.com/blog/2014-global-gaming-stats-whos-playing-what-and-why/

Gardner, H., & Davis, K. (2013). *The app generation: How today's youth navigate identity, intimacy, and imagination in a digital world*. New Haven, CT: Yale University Press.

Gershon, I. (2010). Breaking up is hard to do: Media switching and media ideologies. *Journal of Linguistic Anthropology, 20*(2), 389–405.

Global Digital Statistics. (2014). Retrieved August 29, 2014, from http://www.slideshare.net/ntdlife/2014-global-digital-overview

Gottfried, J., & Shearer, E. (2016). *News use across social media platforms 2016*. Retrieved April 25, 2017, from http://www.journalism.org/2016/05/26/news-use-across-social-media-platforms-2016/

Greenwood, D. N. (2013). Fame, Facebook, and Twitter: How attitudes about fame predict frequency and nature of social media use. *Psychology of Popular Media Culture, 2*(4), 222–236.

Greenwood, S., Perrin, A., & Duggan, M. (2016, November). *Social media update 2016*. Retrieved April 25, 2017, from http://www.pewinternet.org/2016/11/11/social-media-update-2016/

Guarino, B. (2016, June 10). Google faulted for racial bias in image search results for black teenagers. *The Washington Post*. Retrieved on March 14, 2017, from https://www.washingtonpost.com/news/morning-mix/wp/2016/06/10/google-faulted-for-racial-bias-in-image-search-results-for-black-teenagers/?utm_term=.650a1477e5e9

Hall, J. A., Park, N., Song, H., & Cody, M. J. (2010). Strategic misrepresentation in online dating: The effects of gender, self-monitoring, and personality traits. *Journal of Social and Personal Relationships, 27*, 117–135.

Hawkes, K. (2016, January 5). How the extremist right hijacked 'Star Wars,' Taylor Swift and the Mizzou student protests to promote racism. Retrieved March 8, 2016, from https://www.splcenter.org/hatewatch/2016/01/05/how-extremist-right-hijacked-%E2%80%98star-wars%E2%80%99-taylor-swift-and-mizzou-student-protests-promote

Heino, R. D., Ellison, N. B., & Gibbs, J. L. (2010). Relationshopping: Investigating the market metaphor in online dating. *Journal of Social and Personal Relationships, 27*, 427–447.

Hindman, K. L. (2016, May). 15 parents who embarrassed their kids on social media. Retrieved March 17, 2017, from http://www.thethings.com/15-parents-who-embarrassed-their-kids-on-social-media/

Holpuch, A. (2015, December 15). Facebook adjusts controversial 'real name' policy in wake of criticism. *The Guardian*. Retrieved March 18, 2017, from https://www.theguardian.com/us-news/2015/dec/15/facebook-change-controversial-real-name-policy

Horrigan, J. B. (2016, September 20). *Digital readiness gaps*. Retrieved March 19, 2017 from http://www.pewinternet.org/2016/09/20/digital-readiness-gaps/

Horrigan, J. B., & Duggan, M. (2015, December 21). *Home broadband 2015*. Retrieved March 19, 2017, from http://www.pewinternet.org/2015/12/21/home-broadband-2015/

Humphreys, S., & Vered, K. O. (2014). Reflecting on gender and digital networked media. *Television & New Media, 15*(1), 3–13.

Jackson, S. J., & Welles, B. F. (2015): #Ferguson is everywhere: Initiators in emerging counterpublic networks. *Information, Communication & Society, 19*(3), 1–22.

James, C. (2016). *Disconnected: Youth, new media and the ethics gap*. Cambridge, MA: MIT Press.

James, J. (2014). Mobile phone use in Africa: Implications for inequality and the digital divide. *Social Science Computer Review, 32*(1), 113–116.

Jarrett, C. (2015, January 19). The psychology of Facebook digested. *British Psychological Society Research Digest*. Retrieved March 17, 2017, from https://digest.bps.org.uk/2015/01/19/the-psychology-of-facebook-digested/

Kalt, W. (2017, March 12). Why CEOs should friend their employees on social media. *Wall Street Journal*. Retrieved March 22, 2017, from http://blogs.wsj.com/experts/2017/03/12/why-ceos-should-friend-their-employees-on-social-media/

Kaplan, A. M., & Haenlein, M. (2010). Users of the world, unite! The challenges and opportunities of social media. *Business Horizons, 53*, 59–68.

King, K. (2015). *How to survive on social media after a breakup*. Retrieved on March 19, 2017, from https://www.thrillist.com/sex-dating/nation/how-to-survive-on-social-media-after-a-breakup

King, H. (2016, April 22). Top 5 social media scams to avoid. *CNN*. Retrieved March 17, 2017, from http://money.cnn.com/2016/04/22/technology/facebook-twitter-phishing-scams/

Kleinman, A. (2014, March 18). There's a new scam to steal your Gmail info, and it's hard to catch. *The Huffington Post*. Retrieved May 18, 2014, from http://www.huffingtonpost.com/2014/03/18/gmail-scam-phishing_n_4986510.html

Kumar, S. (2015). Why monitoring employees' social media is a bad idea. *Time Magazine*. Retrieved March 8, 2017, from http://time.com/3894276/social-media-monitoring-work/

La Monica, P. R. (2016). Why Facebook could one day be worth $1 trillion. *CNN*. Retrieved March 12, 2017, from http://money.cnn.com/2016/04/28/investing/facebook-trillion-dollar-market-value/

Lenhart, A., & Duggan, M. (2014, February 11). *Couples, the Internet and Social Media*. Retrieved May 19, 2014, from http://pewinternet.org/Reports/2014/Couples-and-the-internet.aspx

MacAuley, M., & Moldes, M. D. (2016). Queen don't compute: reading and casting shade on Facebook's real names policy. *Critical Studies in Media Communication, 33*(1), 6–22.

Maguire, M., (2017, January 7). Elon professor shedding light on web of fake news. *The News and Observer*. Retrieved March 22, 2017, from http://www.newsobserver.com/news/politics-government/state-politics/article125143304.html

Mix. (2017). Digital trends 2017: 106 pages of internet, mobile, and social media stats. *The Next Web*. Retrieved March 22, 2017, from https://thenextweb.com/insights/2017/01/24/digital-trends-2017-report-internet/#.tnw_ySq5AHab

New Intel survey finds 'mobile etiquette' mishaps are running rampant. (2011, February 24). Retrieved April 26, 2017, from https://newsroom.intel.com/news-releases/new-intel-survey-finds-mobile-etiquette-mishaps-are-running-rampant/

Mobile Fact Sheet. (2017, January 12). Retrieved March 19, 2017, from http://www.pewinternet.org/fact-sheet/mobile/

Mobile Technology Fact Sheet. (2014). Retrieved May 20, 2014, from http://www.pewinternet.org/fact-sheets/mobile-technology-fact-sheet/

Morris, D. Z. (2017). New French law bars work email after hours. *Fortune*. Retrieved March 19, 2017, from http://fortune.com/2017/01/01/french-right-to-disconnect-law/

Nakayama, T. K. (2017) What's next for whiteness and the Internet. *Critical Studies in Media Communication, 34*(1), 68-72.

National Safety Council. (2014, March 24). *NSC releases latest injury and fatality statistics and trends*. Retrieved April 26, 2017, from http://www.nsc.org/NewsDocuments/2014-Press-Release-Archive/3-25-2014-Injury-Facts-release.pdf

Nosko, A., Wood, E., & Molema, S. (2010). All about me: Disclosure in online social networking profiles: The case of Facebook. *Computers in Human Behavior, 26*, 406–418.

Notten, N., & Nikken, P. (2016). Boys and girls taking risks online: A gendered perspective on social context and adolescents' risky online behavior. *New Media & Society, 18*(6), 966–988.

Oeldorf-Hirsch, A., Hecht, B., & Morris, M. R. (2014). *To search or to ask: the routing of information needs between traditional search engines and social networks*. Proceedings of the CSCW 2014, Baltimore, MD.

Ong, S. (2016, October 13). The video game industry's problem with racial diversity. *Newsweek*. Retrieved March 19, 2017, from http://www.newsweek.com/2016/10/21/video-games-race-black-protagonists-509328.html

Oremus, W. (2016, Jan 3). Who controls your Facebook feed. *Slate Magazine*. Retrieved April 25, 2017, from http://www.slate.com/articles/technology/cover_story/2016/01/how_facebook_s_news_feed_algorithm_works.html

Patchin, J. W. (2014, April 9). *Summary of our research (2004–2014)*. Retrieved May 18, 2014, from http://cyberbullying.us/summary-of-our-research/

Paul, F. (2015, September 1). The real reason everyone hates making phone calls today. *Network World*. Retrieved March 16, 2017, from http://www.networkworld.com/article/2978859/mobile-wireless/the-real-reason-everyone-hates-making-phone-calls-today.html

Payne, E., & Smith, M. (2013). LGBTQ kids, school safety and missing the big picture: How the dominant bullying discourse prevents school professionals from thinking about systemic marginalization or . . . why we need to rethink LGBTQ bullying. *QED: A Journal in GLBTQ Worldmaking, Inaugural issue*, 1–36.

Rapacon, S. (2016). How using social media can get you fired. *CNBC*. Retrieved March 14, 2017, from http://www.cnbc.com/2016/02/05/how-using-social-media-can-get-you-fired.html

Reagle, J. M., Jr. (2015). *Reading the comments: Likers, haters, and manipulators at the bottom of the web*. Cambridge, MA: The MIT Press.

Ritchie, H. (2016, December 30). Biggest fake news stories of 2016. *CNBC*. Retrieved March 18, 2017, from http://www.cnbc.com/2016/12/30/read-all-about-it-the-biggest-fake-news-stories-of-2016.html

Roberto, A. J., & Eden, J. (2010). Cyberbullying: Aggressive communication in the digital age. In T. A. Avtgis & A. S. Rancer (Eds.), *Arguments, aggression, and conflict: New directions in theory and research* (pp. 198–216). New York: Routledge.

Rogers, E. M. (2003). *Diffusion of innovations* (5th ed.). New York: The Free Press.

Rothenberg, K. (2014). Prenups evolving to include new 'Social Media Clause.' Fox News. Retrieved on March 19, 2017, from http://www.foxnews.com/us/2014/06/22/prenups-evolving-to-include-new-social-media-clause.html

Salter, M. (2016). Privates in the online public: Sex(ting) and reputation on social media. *New Media & Society, 18*(11), 2723–2739.

Short, J., Williams, E., & Christie, B. (1976). *The social psychology of telecommunications*. New York: Wiley.

Smith, A. (2014, January 2). *More than half of cell owners affected by 'distracted walking.'* Retrieved April 26, 2017, from http://www.pewresearch.org/fact-tank/2014/01/02/more-than-half-of-cell-owners-affected-by-distracted-walking/

Smith, A. (2014, February 3). *6 new facts about Facebook*. Retrieved August 29, 2014, from http://www.pewresearch.org/fact-tank/2014/02/03/6-new-facts-about-facebook/

Smith, A. (2014, April 3). *Older adults and technology use*. Retrieved May 16, 2014, from http://www.pewinternet.org/2014/04/03/older-adults-and-technology-use/

Selyukh, A. (2016, November 20). Postelection, overwhelmed Facebook users unfriend, cut back. *NPR*. Retrieved March 18, 2017, from http://www.npr.org/sections/alltechconsidered/2016/11/20/502567858/post-election-overwhelmed-facebook-users-unfriend-cut-back

Smith, A. (2017). *Record shares of Americans now own smartphones, have home broadband*. Retrieved March 8, 2017, from http://www.pewresearch.org/fact-tank/2017/01/12/evolution-of-technology/

Smith, A., & Anderson, M. (2016, December 19). *Online shopping and purchasing preferences*. Retrieved March 18, 2017, from http://www.pewinternet.org/2016/12/19/online-shopping-and-purchasing-preferences/

Smith, A. & Anderson, M. (2016, February 29). *5 facts about online dating*. Retrieved March 19, 2017, from http://www.pewresearch.org/fact-tank/2016/02/29/5-facts-about-online-dating/

Sun, C. (2016). These social media fails got people fired. Retrieved March 11, 2017, from https://www.entrepreneur.com/article/271823

Stern, J. (2017). What so great about Snapchat anyway? *The Wall Street Journal*. Retrieved March 6, 2017, from https://www.wsj.com/articles/whats-so-great-about-snapchat-anyway-1486133169

Taddicken, M. (2014). The "privacy paradox" in the Social Web: The impact of privacy concerns, individual characteristics, and the perceived social relevance on different forms of self-disclosure. *Journal of Computer-Mediated Communication, 19*, 248–273.

Tazghini, S., & Siedlecki, K. L. (2012). A mixed method approach to examining Facebook use and its relationship to self-esteem. *Computers in Human Behavior, 29*, 827–832.

Thompson, L., & Ku, H. Y. (2005). Chinese graduate students' experiences and attitudes toward online learning. *Educational Media International, 42*(1), 33–47.

Turkle, S. (2011). *Alone together: Why we expect more from technology and less from each other*. New York: Basic Books.

Turkle, S. (2012, February). *Sherry Turkle: Connected, but alone?* [Video file]. Retrieved May 25, 2014, from http://www.ted.com/talks/sherry_turkle_alone_together#t-755215

Utz, S. (2016). Is LinkedIn making you more successful? The informational benefits derived from public social media. *New Media & Society, 18*(11), 2685–2702.

van der Nagel, E., & Frith, J. (2015). Anonymity, pseudonymity, and the agency of online identity. *FirstMonday, 20*(3). Retrieved April 25, 2017, from http://firstmonday.org/article/view/5615/4346)

Vitores, A., & Gil-Juárez, A. (2016) The trouble with 'women in computing': A critical examination of the deployment of research on the gender gap in computer science, *Journal of Gender Studies, 25*(6), 666–680.

Walther, J. B., & Parks, M. R. (2002). Cues filtered out, cues filtered in: Computer-mediated communication and relationships. In M. L. Knapp & J. A. Daly (Eds.), *Handbook of interpersonal communication* (pp. 529–563). Thousand Oaks, CA: Sage.

Wei, L. (2012). Number matters: The multimodality of Internet use as an indicator of the digital inequalities. *Journal of Computer-Mediated Communication, 17*, 303–318.

Weinstein, E. C., & Selman, R. L. (2016). Digital Stress: Adolescents' personal accounts. *New Media & Society, 18*(3), 391–409.

Woodhouse, A. (2015, December 8). Tink labs wants to bring its Handy smartphones to hotel rooms in Europe. *South China Morning Post*. Retrieved April 23, 2017 from http://www.scmp.com/tech/start-ups/article/1886783/tink-labs-wants-bring-its-handy-smartphones-hotel-rooms-europe

World's most affordable tablet computers launched with unlimited free internet access in Guatemala. Retrieved March 19, 2017, from https://globenewswire.com/news-release/2016/11/01/885227/0/en/World-s-Most-Affordable-Tablet-Computers-Launched-with-Unlimited-Free-Internet-Access-in-Guatemala.html

Wortham, J. (2016, September). Black tweets matter. *Smithsonian, 47*(5), 1–4.

Zywica, J., & Danowski, J. (2008). The faces of Facebookers: Investigating social enhancement and social compensation hypotheses: Predicting Facebook and offline popularity from sociability and self-esteem, and mapping the meaning of popularity with semantic networks. *Journal of Computer-Mediated Communication, 14*, 1–34.

Credits

Photo Credits

Chapter 1 Page 1: rawpixel/123RF GB Ltd; **p. 4:** greenstockcreative/ Fotolia; **p. 5:** luckybusiness/Fotolia; **p. 7:** Artem Zaicev/Alamy Stock Photo; **p. 7:** Hugo Félix/Fotolia; **p. 9:** Andres Rodriguez/Fotolia; **p. 13:** ONOKY – Photononstop/Alamy Stock Photo; **p. 18:** George Dolgikh/ Fotolia; **p. 19:** Robert Stainforth/Alamy Stock Photo.

Chapter 2 Page 23: Rawpixel Ltd/Alamy Stock Photo; **p. 25:** MBI/ Alamy Stock Photo; **p. 29:** Junial Enterprises/Shutterstock; **p. 30:** George Impey/Alamy Stock Photo; **p. 32:** Hugo Félix/Fotolia; **p. 35:** Erik Isakson/Blend Images/Alamy Stock Photo; **p. 37:** Drobot Dean/ Fotolia; **p. 37:** ton koene/Alamy Stock Photo; **p. 39:** Odilon Dimier/ PhotoAlto sas/Alamy Stock Photo.

Chapter 3 Page 45: SIBSA/StockImagebank.com/SIBSA Digital Pvt. Ltd./Alamy Stock Photo; **p. 48:** Sergey Novikov/Fotolia; **p. 49:** MIKA Images/Alamy Stock Photo; **p. 50:** pathdoc/Fotolia; **p. 51:** michaeljung/Fotolia; **p. 52:** Jonathan Goldberg/Alamy Stock Photo; **p. 53:** ESB Professional/Shutterstock; **p. 55:** jentzphoto/Alamy Stock Photo; **p. 56:** Stanislaw Tokarski/Alamy Stock Photo; **p. 57:** Colin Hawkins/Cultura Creative (RF)/Alamy Stock Photo; **p. 61:** Alan Wilson/Alamy Stock Photo; **p. 62:** attator/Alamy Stock Photo; **p. 64:** MBI/Alamy Stock Photo ; **p. 65:** Elenathewise/Fotolia; **p. 67:** Eugenio Marongiu/Alamy Stock Photo.

Chapter 4 Page 71: pdtnc/Fotolia; **p. 73:** Dinis Tolipov/123RF; **p. 76:** Marty Bicek/ZUMA Press. Inc./Alamy Stock Photo; **p. 76:** SC Governor's Office/Alamy Stock Photo; **p. 77:** XiXinXing/Shutterstock; **p. 78:** taka/Fotolia; **p. 80:** Image 100/Alamy Stock Photo; **p. 81:** Auremar/ Fotolia; **p. 84:** Berc/Fotolia; **p. 85:** Michael Greenberg/Getty Images; **p. 86:** salvo severino/Alamy Stock Photo; **p. 87:** Michael Simons /123RF GB Ltd; **p. 90:** Radius Images/Alamy Stock Photo.

Chapter 5 Page 94: Laura Doss/AGEFotostock; **p. 95:** Monkey Business/Fotolia; **p. 96:** Sandor Kacso/Fotolia; **p. 100:** Chris Rout/ Alamy Stock Photo; **p. 101:** nyul/Fotolia; **p. 102:** Rob Crandall/ Stock Connection Blue/Alamy Stock Photo; **p. 103:** Vivian Zink/ Bravo/Everett Collection; **p. 108:** WavebreakmediaMicro/Fotolia; **p. 108:** Astrakan Images/Alamy Stock Photo; **p. 109:** EpicStockMedia/ Fotolia; **p. 112:** Hitdelight/Shutterstock; **p. 113:** leungchopan/Fotolia; **p. 115:** Enigma/Alamy Stock Photo.

Chapter 6 Page 121: Alen-D/Fotolia; **p. 123:** denys_kuvaiev/Fotolia; **p. 124:** Claudia Wiens/Alamy Stock Photo; **p. 125:** RAY STUBBLEBINE/ REUTERS/Alamy Stock Photo; **p. 127:** David Madison/Getty Images; **p. 127:** Jasmin Merdan/123RF GB Ltd; **p. 129:** magann/Fotolia; **p. 130:** Burlingham/Fotolia; **p. 133:** Sylvie Bouchard/Fotolia; **p. 135:** arekmalang/123RF GB Ltd; **p. 136:** Jupiterimages/PHOTOS. com>>/Getty Images Plus/Getty Images; **p. 137:** Jandrie Lombard/ Shutterstock; **p. 138:** Lightwave Stock Media/123RF GB Ltd; **p. 139:** HONGQI ZHANG/123RF GB Ltd; **p. 141:** McClatchy-Tribune/ Tribune Content Agency LLC/Alamy Stock Photo; **p. 143:** Otto Greule Jr./Getty Images.

Chapter 7 Page 147: HONGQI ZHANG/123RF GB Ltd; **p. 149:** Fuse/Getty Images; **p. 154:** Riccardo Piccinini/Shutterstock; **p. 155:** Ammentorp Photography/Alamy Stock Photo; **p. 156:** Wavebreak Media Ltd/123RF GB Ltd; **p. 158:** Antonio Guillem/123RF GB Ltd; **p. 159:** Bill Cheyrou/Alamy Stock Photo; **p. 161:** Sean Nel/Alamy Stock Photo; **p. 163:** Rommel Canlas/123RF GB Ltd; **p. 165:** Catchlight Visual Services/Alamy Stock Photo.

Chapter 8 Page 172: Marcin Sadlowski/Fotolia; **p. 174:** Ashwin/ Fotolia; **p. 175:** DNF-Style/Fotolia; **p. 176:** Lisa F. Young/Fotolia; **p. 178:** mast3r/Fotolia; **p. 188:** Monart Design/Fotolia; **p. 167:** Innocenti/Cultura Creative (RF)/Alamy Stock Photo; **p. 172:** Ariel Skelley/ Blend Images/Alamy Stock Photo; **p. 179:** Image Solutions LLC/Alamy Stock Photo; **p. 180:** Anders Ryman/Alamy Stock Photo; **p. 181:** Ashwin/Shutterstock; **p. 182:** Camerique/ClassicStock/Getty Images; **p. 186:** Matthew Micah Wright/ Lonely Planet Images/Getty Images; **p. 187:** McClatchy-Tribune/Tribune Content Agency LLC/Alamy Stock Photo.

Chapter 9 Page 192: Joana Lopes/123RF GB Ltd; **p. 193:** Michaelpuche/ Shutterstock; **p. 194:** CandyBox Images/Shutterstock; **p. 195:** szefei/123RF GB Ltd; **p. 197:** Cathy Yeulet/123RF GB Ltd; **p. 201:** luminastock/123RF GB Ltd; **p. 202:** Wavebreak Media Ltd/123RF GB Ltd; **p. 203:** Andy Dean/Fotolia; **p. 205:** puhhha/123RF GB Ltd; **p. 206:** mavoimage/123RF GB Ltd; **p. 207:** naka-stockphoto/Shutterstock; **p. 208:** Jari Hindström/Fotolia; **p. 209:** Livio Monti/123RF GB Ltd; **p. 210:** Antonio Guillem/123RF GB Ltd; **p. 212:** Peter Bernik/123RF GB Ltd; **p. 213:** vgstudio/Shutterstock; **p. 216:** Roman Samborskyi/ Shutterstock; **p. 217:** Donna Ellen Coleman/Shutterstock; **p. 219:** Cathy Yeulet/123RF GB Ltd.

Chapter 10 Page 224: PhotoAlto/Alamy Stock Photo; **p. 229:** Tony Tallec/ Alamy Stock Photo; **p. 233:** Antonio Gravante/Fotolia; **p. 234:** ysbrandcosijn/Fotolia; **p. 235:** Sindhura Citineni; **p. 236:** Andy Lyons/Staff/Getty Images; **p. 239:** dotshock/123RF GB Ltd; **p. 241:** PhotoMediaGroup/ Shutterstock; **p. 246:** Ariel Skelley/Blend Images/Alamy Stock Photo; **p. 248:** Hugo Félix/Fotolia; **p. 249:** ESB Professional/Shutterstock.

Chapter 11 Page 255: ammentorp/123RF GB Ltd; **p. 258:** Jonny White/ Alamy Stock Photo; **p. 259:** auremar/123RF GB Ltd; **p. 261:** Carin Baer/© AMC/Courtesy: Everett Collection; **p. 263:** Teddy Wade/US Army; **p. 265:** elwynn/Shutterstock; **p. 266:** Syda Productions/Shutterstock; **p. 267:** Wavebreak Media Ltd/123RF GB Ltd; **p. 269:** Jason Stitt/Shutterstock; **p. 270:** Franck Boston/Shutterstock; **p. 272:** Fuse/ Alamy; **p. 273:** LUIS GALDAMEZ/REUTERS/Alamy Stock Photo; **p. 275:** DANIEL MIHAILESCU/AFP/Getty Images; **p. 276:** ZouZou/ Shutterstock; **p. 278:** Ldprod/Shutterstock; **p. 279:** WvdMPhotography/ Shutterstock; **p. 280:** olly/Fotolia; **p. 282:** Dean Drobot/123RF GB Ltd.

Chapter 12 Page 285: KENA BETANCUR/AFP/Getty Images; **p. 287:** Sigrid Olsson/PhotoAlto/Alamy Stock Photo; **p. 289:** Library of Congress; **p. 292:** dbimages/Alamy Stock Photo; **p. 295:** Phil Sears/ The New York Times/Redux; **p. 298:** Pablo Martinez Monsivais/ Associated Press; **p. 299:** Jeff Gilbert/Alamy Stock Photo; **p. 303:** Rido/ Fotolia; **p. 306:** ESB Basic/Shutterstock; **p. 307:** Trevor Adeline/caia image/Alamy Stock Photo; **p. 309:** Image Source/Alamy Stock Photo; **p. 311:** OLJ Studio/Shutterstock; **p. 312:** Al Goldis/AP Images.

Chapter 13 Page 315: Patti McConville/Alamy Stock Photo; **p. 317:** JHPhoto/Alamy Stock Photo; **p. 321:** Megapress/Alamy Stock Photo; **p. 324:** Rimagine Group Limited/Cultura RM/Alamy Stock Photo; **p. 325:** Paul Bradbury/OJO Images Ltd/Alamy Stock Photo; **p. 327:** Samuel Borges Photography/Shutterstock; **p. 328:** anyaberkut/Fotolia; **p. 329:** Bill Aron/PhotoEdit; **p. 332:** Digital Vision/Getty Images; **p. 335:** Eric Audras/ONOKY – Photononstop/Alamy Stock Photo; **p. 339:** Everett Collection Inc/Alamy Stock Photo; **p. 341:** NewStock/ Alamy Stock Photo.

Chapter 14 Page 344: ONOKY – Photononstop/Alamy Stock Photo; **p. 348:** Michael Simons/123RF GB Ltd; **p. 351:** Antonio

Guillem/123RF GB Ltd; **p. 359:** Cathy Yeulet/ 123RF GB Ltd; **p. 361:** CartoonResource/YAY Media AS/Alamy Stock Photo; **p. 362:** Mathias Rosenthal/Fotolia; **p. 364:** ESB Professional/Shutterstock; **p. 366:** stylephotographs/123RF GB Ltd; **p. 367:** Prasit Rodphan/Shutterstock; **p. 368:** Peter Muller/Cultura Creative (RF)/Alamy Stock Photo; **p. 369:** PARIVARTAN SHARMA/REUTERS/Alamy Stock Photo; **p. 372:** ESB Basic/Shutterstock; **p. 373:** BE&W agencja fotograficzna Sp. z o.o./Alamy Stock Photo.

Text Credits

Chapter 1 Page 3: Based on Nolen-Hoeksema, S., Wisco, B., & Lyumbomirski, S. Rethinking rumination. (2008). Perspectives on Psychological Science, 3, 400–424.; **p. 4:** Passer, M. W., & Smith, R. E. (2004). Psychology: The science of mind and behavior (2nd ed.). New York: McGraw-Hill.; **p. 5:** Chelsea; **p. 7:** Alyssa.

Chapter 2 Page 29: Birditt, K. S., Brown, E., Orbuch, T. L., & McIlvane, J. M. (2010). Marital conflict behaviors and implications for divorce over 16 years. Journal of Marriage and Family, 72(5), 1188–1204.; **p. 31:** Adapted from Hasinhoff, A. A. (2015). Sexting panic: Rethinking criminalization, privacy and consent. Urbana, IL: University of Illinois Press.; **p. 33:** Chia-chen Yang, B. Bradford Brown, Michael T. Braun (2014), From Facebook to cell calls: Layers of electronic intimacy in college students' interpersonal relationships. New Media & Society, pp. 5–23; **p. 33:** Fox, J., Warber, K. M., & Makstaller, D. (2013).The role of Facebook in romantic relationship development: An exploration of Knapp's relational stage model. Journal of Social & Personal Relationships, 30, 771-794. doi:10.1177/0265407512468370; **p. 33:** Kathryn Macapagal, Ryan Coventry, Jae A. Puckett, Gregory Phillips, Brian Mustanski (2016). Geosocial Networking App Use Among Men Who Have Sex With Men in Serious Romantic Relationships. Arch Sex Behav 2016 Aug 11;45(6):1513-24.; **p. 36:** Ellis, C. (2007). Telling secrets, revealing lives: Relational ethics in research with intimate others, Qualitative Inquiry, 13(1), 3-29.(p. 5).; **p. 38:** Anna Turnage (2013). Technological Resistance: A Metaphor Analysis of Enron E-Mail Messages. Communication Quarterly Vol. 61. pp. 519-538; **p. 38:** "Engaging through Art and Performance." Retrieved April 20, 2011, from http://community.uui.asu.edu/features/art.asp. Davis, O. I., & Marsiglia, F. F. (2011, June). Cultural catalysts for community dialogues: Black barbers as interventionists in cardiovascular health of African American men. Poster presented at the annual meeting of the Society for Prevention Research, Washington, DC; **p. 39:** Hillary Jones (2016). New media producing new labor: Pinterest, yearning, and self-surveillance. Critical Studies In Media Communication Vol. 33. pp. 352-365.; **p. 40:** Christians, C. G. (2011). Ethics and politics in qualitative research. In N. K. Denzin & Y. S. Lincoln (Eds.), The Sage Handbook of Qualitative Research (pp. 61-80). Thousand Oaks, CA: Sage.; **p. 32:** Ali; **p. 37:** Kenneth; **p. 35:** Palmer-Mehta V. International Journal of Communication 10(2016), 4176–4192; **p. 39:** Hillary Jones (2016). New media producing new labor: Pinterest, yearning, and self-surveillance. Critical Studies In Media Communication Vol. 33. pp. 352-365.

Chapter 3 Page 47: Harwood, J. (2006). Communication as social identity. In G. J. Shepherd, J. St. John, & T. Striphas (Eds.), Communication as . . . : Perspectives on theory (pp. 84–90). Thousand Oaks, CA: Sage.; **p. 49:** Abrams, J., O'Connor, J., & Giles, H. (2002). Identity and intergroup communication. In W. B. Gudykunst & B. Mody (Eds.), Handbook of international and intercultural communication (2nd ed., pp. 225–240). Thousand Oaks, CA: Sage.; **p. 50:** Bianca; **p. 55:** Bailey, C. (2016, November 14). Hundreds of hate crimes reported since election: SPLC. NBC News. Retrieved from: http://www.nbcnews.com/news/us-news/hundreds-hate-crimes-reported-election-splc-n683761; Yan, H. et al. (2016, December 22). "Make America White Again": Hate speech and crimes post-election. CNN. Retrieved from: http://www.cnn.com/2016/11/10/us/post-election-hate-crimes-and-fears-trnd/; **p. 12:** Yan, H. et al. (2016, December 22). "Make America White Again": Hate speech and crimes post-election. CNN. Retrieved from: http://www.cnn.com/2016/11/10/us/post-election-hate-crimes-and-fears-trnd/; **p. 55:** Adams, T. E., & Berry, K. (2013). Size

matters: Performing (il)logical male bodies on FatClub.com. Text and Performance Quarterly, 33 (4): 308–325.; **p. 55:** Adams, T. E., & Berry, K. (2013). Size matters: Performing (il)logical male bodies on FatClub.com. Text and Performance Quarterly, 33 (4): 308–325.; **p. 55:** Vevea, N. (2008) "Body Art: Performing Identity Through Tattoos and Piercing," Paper presented at the annual meeting of the NCA 94th Annual Convention, TBA, San Diego, CA Online. Retrieved March 11, 2011, from: http://www.allacademic.com/meta/p258244_index.html. (p. 22).; **p. 56:** Lerner, M. (2008, November 18). Minnesota disciplines four doctors, two for inappropriate contact. Star-Tribune. Retrieved May 3, 2011, from: http://www.startribune.com/life-sytle/34691559.html?page=all&prepage=1&c=y#continue; **p. 58:** Based on Kimel, S. & Kunst, J. (2016, May 26). Can DNA ancestry testing make you more racist? Scientific American. Retrieved from https://blogs.scientificamerican.com/guest-blog/can-dna-ancestry-testing-make-you-more-racist/; **p. 58:** Marshall, G. A. (1993). Racial classification: Popular and Scientific. In S. G. Harding (Ed.), The "racial" economy of science: Toward a democratic future (pp. 116–127). Bloomington: Indiana University Press.; **p. 59:** Arana, M. (2008, November 30). He's not black. Washington Post, p. B1. Retrieved December 31, 2008, from: www.washingtonpost.com/wp-dyn/content/article/2008/11/28/AR2008112802219.html.; **p. 59:** Cassandra Negley. 2014 Sochi Olympics: USA hockey creates patriotic hashtag. SportingNews.com; **p. 60:** Wax, E. (2005, September 26-October 2). Beyond the pull of the tribe: In Kenya, some teens find unity in contemporary culture. Washington Post, National Weekly Edition, 22(49), 8. p. 18; **p. 60:** Daigle, K. (2011, February 12). India's census counts 'third gender.' Edge Boston. Retrieved March 22, 2011, from http://www.edgeboston.com/?116206; **p. 62:** Weber, P. (2014, February 21). Confused by all the new Facebook genders? Here's what they mean. Slate. Retrieved March 2, 2014, from: http://www.slate.com/blogs/lexi-con_valley/2014/02/21/gender_facebook_now_has_56_categories_to_choose_from_including_cisgender.html.; **p. 62:** Brian Boitano: I never intended to reveal I'm gay, CBS/AP, January 10, 2014, http://www.cbsnews.com/news/brian-boitano-i-never-intended-to-reveal-im-gay/; **p. 62:** Van Meter, J. (2013, April 10). Anthony Weiner and Huma Abedin's post-scandal playbook. New York Times. Retrieved March 3, 2014, from: http://www.nytimes.com/2013/04/14/magazine/anthony-weiner-and-huma-abedins-post-scandal-playbook.html?pagewanted=all&_r=0.; **p. 64:** Horn, D. (2013, April 14). Middle class a matter of income, attitude. USA Today. Retrieved March 2, 2014, from: http://www.usatoday.com/story/money/business/2013/04/14/middle-class-hard-define/2080565/.; **p. 65:** Lucas, K. (2011). Socializing messages in blue-collar families: Communication pathways to social mobility and reproduction. Western Journal of Communication, 75(1), 95-121. p. 95; **p. 65:** Melinda; **p. 65:** Daigle, K. (2011, February 12). India's census counts 'third gender.' Edge Boston. Retrieved March 22, 2011, from: http://www.edgeboston.com/?116206; **p. 65:** Fassett, D. L., & Morella, D. L. (2008). Remarking (the) discipline: Marking the performative accomplishment of (dis)ability. Text and Performance Quarterly, 28(1-2), 139-156. p. 144.; **p. 66:** Henderson, B., & Ostrander, R. N. (2008). Introduction to special issue on disability studies/performance studies. Text and Performance Quarterly, 28(1-2), 1-5. p. 2; **p. 66:** Lindemann, K. (2008). "I can't be standing up out there": Communicative performances of (dis)ability in wheelchair rugby. Text and Performance Quarterly, 28(1-2), 98-115; **p. 66:** Cardillo, L. W. (2010). Empowering narratives: Making sense of the experience of growing up with chronic illness or disability. Western Journal of Communication, 74(5), 525-546. p. 539; **p. 66:** Corey, F. C. (2004). A letter to Paul. Text and Performance Quarterly, 24, 185-190. p. 189; **p. 67:** Based on Lum, Z.-A. (2017, February 2). Joël Lightbound urges no more silence over Islamophobia after Quebec City mosque attack. Huffington Post Canada. Retrieved from: http://www.huffingtonpost.ca/2017/02/02/joel-lightbound-quebec-shooting_n_14575968.html; **p. 67:** Corey, F. C., & Nakayama, T. K. (2004). Introduction. Special issue "Religion and Performance." Text and Performance Quarterly, 24, 209–211.; **p. 67:** Campbell, H. A., ed. (2013). Digital religion: Understanding religious practice in new media worlds. New York: Routledge.; **p. 67:** Elizabeth; **p. 69:** McHugh, M. (2013, August 23) It's catfishing season! How to tell lovers from liars online, and more. Digital Trends. Retrieved March 3, 2014, from: http://www.digitaltrends.com/web/its-catfishing-season-how-totell-lovers-from-liars-online-and-more/#ixzz2uvnrrkOx. Read more: http://www.digitaltrends.com/web/its-catfishing-season-how-to-tell-lovers-from-liars-online-and-more/#ixzz2uvnL1KoP; **p. 58:** Office for National Statistics, (2012, December 11). Ethnicity and national identity in England and Wales. Retrieved March 2, 2014, from: http://www.ons.gov.uk/ons/dcp171776_290558.pdf.; **p. 59:** Cassandra Negley. 2014 Sochi Olympics: USA hockey creates patriotic hashtag. SportingNews.com.

Chapter 4 Page 74: Based on Croy, I., Buschhüter, D., Seo, H. S., Negoias, S., & Hummel, T. (2010) Individual significance of olfaction: Development of a questionnaire. Eur Arch Otorhinolaryngol, 267(1), 67–71. doi: 10.1007/s00405-009-1054-0. Hummel, T., Kobal, G., Gudziol, H., Mackay-Sim, A. (2007). Normative data for the "Sniffin' Sticks" including tests of odor identification, odor discrimination, and olfactory thresholds: An upgrade based on a group of more than 3,000 subjects. Eur Arch Otorhinolaryngol, 264(3), 237–243. Korneliussen, I. (2012). Women smell better than men. Science Nordic. Retrieved May 14, 2014, from: http://sciencenordic.com/women-smellbetter-men. Maccaby, E. E., & Jacklin, C. N. (1978).). The psychology of sex differences. Palo Alto, CA: Stanford University Press.; **p. 78:** Lin Sue; **p. 81:** Danika; **p. 87:** Damien; **p. 87:** Ting-Toomey, S. (1999). Communicating across cultures. New York: Guilford. p. 149.

Chapter 5 Page 96: Cristina; **p. 98:** Chomsky, N. (1957). Syntactic Structures, The Hague/Paris: Mouton.; **p. 99:** Based on Académie française. Exemples de remarques normatives, 9th edition. Retrieved March 6, 2014, from: http://www.academie-francaise.fr/le-dictionnaire-la-9e-edition/exemples-de-remarques-normatives/; Académie française. (2014, March 6). Replay. Retrieved March 6, 2014, from: http://www.academie-francaise.fr/dire-ne-pas-dire; Sauerbrey A. (2013, September 25). How do you say "blog" in German? New York Times. Retrieved March 6, 2014, from: http://www.nytimes.com/2013/09/26/opinion/how-do-you-say-blog-in-german.html?_r=0 "Duflot: 'Appelez-moi Madame la ministre.'" (2012, September 26). Le Figaro. Retrieved March 7, 2014, from: http://www.lefigaro.fr/flash-actu/2012/09/26/97001-20120926FILWWW00677-duflot-appelez-moi-madame-la-ministre.php; **p. 104:** Heilman, M. E. (2001). Description and prescription: How gender stereotypes prevent women's ascent up the organizational ladder. In Gender, hierarchy and leadership, Ed. L. Carli & A. Eagly. Journal of Social Issues, 57(4), 657-674. p. 658 **p. 107:** Sedivy, J. (2012, March 28). Votes and vowels: A changing accent shows how language parallels politics. Discover. Retrieved March 7, 2014, from: http://blogs.discovermagazine.com/crux/2012/03/28/votes-and-vowels-a-changing-accent-shows-how-language-parallels-politics/#.UxoiICifNiF; **p. 107:** Hecht, M. L., Jackson, R. L. II, & Ribeau, S. A. (2003). African American communication. Mahwah, NJ: Lawrence Erlbaum Associates. p. 2; **p. 108:** Jessica; **p. 109:** Hoijer, H. (1994). The Sapir-Whorf hypothesis. In L. Samovar & R. E. Porter (Eds.), Intercultural communication: A reader (pp. 194-200). Belmont, CA: Wadsworth. p. 194; **p. 112:** Bart; **p. 113:** Social Mobility Commission. (2017, January 26). New research uncovers 'class pay gap' in Britain's professions. Retrieved from: https://www.gov.uk/government/news/new-research-uncovers-class-pay-gap-in-britains-professions; **p. 113:** Hiroko; **p. 114:** Stavans, I. (2017, January 30). Trump, the Wall and the Spanish Language. The New York Times. Retrieved from: https://www.nytimes.com/2017/01/30/opinion/trump-the-wall-and-the-spanish-language.html?_r=0; **p. 116:** Based on US Department of Health and Human Services. (n.d.). What is cyberbullying? Retrieved March 7, 2014, from: http://www.stopbullying.gov/cyberbullying/what-is-it/; **p. 115:** http://www.startribune.com/man-charged-with-racially-motivated-assault-aboard-metro-transit-bus/402503115/.

Chapter 6 Page 124: Isaacson, L. A. (1998). Student dress codes. ERIC Digest, 117. Retrieved June 15, 2006, from: http://eric.uoregon.edu/publications/digests/digest117.html.; **p. 124:** Manusov, V., & Patterson, M. (2006). Handbook of nonverbal communication. Thousand Oaks, CA: Sage.; **p. 126:** Birdwhistell, R. L. (1985). Kinesics and context: Essays in body motion communication. Philadelphia:

University of Philadelphia Press. Mehrabian, A. (1971). Nonverbal communication. Chicago: Aldine-Atherton. Mehrabian, A. (2007). Nonverbal communication. Chicago, IL: Aldine de Gruyter.; **p. 127:** Abbad; **p. 130:** Trost, M. R., & Alberts, J. K. (2006). How men and women communicate attraction: An evolutionary view In D. Canary & K. Dindia (Eds.), Sex, gender and communication: Similarities and differences (2nd ed, pp, 317–336). Mahwah, NJ: Lawrence Erlbaum; **p. 132:** Burgoon, J. K., & Hale, J. L. (1988). Nonverbal expectancy violations: Model elaboration and application to immediacy behaviors. Communication Monographs, 55, 58-79. Burgoon, J. K., & Le Poire, B. A. (1993). Effects of communication expectancies, actual communication, and expectancy disconfirmation on evaluations of communicators and their communication behavior. Human Communication Research, 20(1), 67-96.; **p. 133:** Katarina; **p. 134:** Lord, T. L. (2009). The relationship of gender-based public harassment to body image, self-esteem, and avoidance behavior. Unpublished dissertation. Ann Arbor, MI: ProQuest.; **p. 141:** Wise, T. (2005, October 23). Opinions on NBA dress code are far from uniform. Washington Post, p. A01. Retrieved February 24, 2006, from: http://www.washingtonpost.com/wp-dyn/content/article/2005/10/22/AR2005102201386.html.; **p. 139:** Chartrand T. L., & Bargh J. A. (1999). The chameleon effect: The perception-behavior link and social interaction. Journal of Personality and Social Psychology, 76, 893–910. Dijksterhuis, A., & Smith, P. K. (2005). What do we do unconsciously? And how? Journal of Consumer Psychology 15(3), 225–229. Tiedens, L., & Fragale, A. (2003). "Power moves: Complementarity in dominant and submissive nonverbal behavior." Journal of Personality and Social Psychology, 84, 558–568.; **p. 135:** Alondra.

Chapter 7 Page 150: International Listening Association (1995, April). An ILA Definition of Listening. ILA Listening Post, 53, 1-4. p. 4; **p. 151:** Based on Crawford, K. (2009). Following you: Discipline of listening in social media. Continuum: Journal of Media & Cultural Studies, 23(4), 525-535. Lacey, K. (2013). Listening Publics: The Politics and Experience of Listening in the Media Age. Cambridge: Polity.; **p. 152:** Watson, K. W., Barker, L. L., & Weaver, J. B. (1995). The Listening Styles Profiles (LSP-16): Development and validation of an instrument to assess four listening styles. Journal of the International Listening Association, 9, 1-13. p. 2; **p. 152:** Based on Cooper, L. O., & Buchanan, T. (2010). Listening competency on campus: A psychometric analysis of student listening. International Journal of Listening, 24(3), 141–163.; **p. 157:** Based on (2014, February) World Health Organization Media Center Fact Sheet. Retrieved October 5, 2014, from http://www.who.int/mediacentre/factsheets/fs300/en/, National Institute on Deafness and Other Communication Disorders (NIDCD) Quick Statistics. Retrieved October 5, 2014, from http://www.nidcd.nih.gov/health/statistics/pages/quick.aspxdemographics.htm; **p. 158:** Shafir, R. Z. (2003). The Zen of listening (2nd ed) Wheaton, IL: Quest Books; **p. 159:** Genette, J., Olson, C. D. & Linde, J. (2017). Hot topics, cool heads: A handbook on Civil Dialogue®. Dubuque, IA: Kendall Hunt.; **p. 160:** Shafir, R. Z. (2003). The Zen of listening (2nd ed). Wheaton, IL: Quest Books; **p. 160:** Shafir, R. Z. (2003). The Zen of listening (2nd ed). Wheaton, IL: Quest Books; **p. 161:** Danny; **p. 165:** Nichols, M. P. (2009). The lost art of listening (2nd ed.). New York: The Guilford Press.

Chapter 8 Page 189: Scott, K. D. (2013). Communication strategies across cultural borders: Dispelling stereotypes, performing competence, and redefining Black womanhood. Women's Studies in Communication, 36, 312–329.; **p. 188:** Angelina; **p. 184:** Based on Rothman, L. (2012, July 8). Essence Fest 2012: Is reality TV still not diverse enough? Time.com. Retrieved March 22, 2014, from http://entertainment.time.com/2012/07/08/essence-reality-tv-family-panel/; **p. 181:** Nagesh; **p. 176:** Rosenstone, R. A. (2005). My wife, the Muslim. Antioch Review, 63, 234–246.; **p. 174:** Retheorizing Adaptation: Differential Adaptation and Critical Intercultural Communication. Antonio Tomas De La Garza and Kent A. Ono. Journal Of International And Intercultural Communication Vol. 8 , Iss. 4, 2015; **p. 175:** Based on Torres, L. (2009). Latino definitions of success: A cultural model of intercultural competence. Hispanic Journal of Behavioral Sciences, 31, 576-593.; **p. 174:** Yako, R. M., & Biswas, B. (2014). "We came to this country for the future of our children. We have no future": Acculturative stress among Iraqi refugees in the United States. International Journal of Intercultural Relations, 38, 133–141.; **p. 174:** Maham; **p. 172:** Susan; **p. 172:** Broome, B. J., & Collier, M. J. (2012). Culture, communication, and peacebuilding: A reflexive multi-dimensional contextual framework. Journal of International and Intercultural Communication, 5(4), 245–269.; **p. 170:** US Census Bureau projections, 2012; **p. 169:** Allison Nafziger Travel Blog. Reprinted by permission of Allison Nafziger.

Chapter 9 Page 193: Olivia; **p. 198:** Knight, K. (September, 2014). Communicating dilemmas in adults' friends with benefits relationships: Challenges to relational talk. Emerging Adulthood. Retrieved http://eax.sagepub.com/content/early/2014/09/19/2167696814 549598 November 25, 2014; **p. 200:** Buss, D. M. (2003). The evolution of desire: Strategies of human mating. New York: Basic Books. Trost, M. R., & Kenrick, D. T. (1993). An evolutionary perspective on interpersonal communication. In S. Petronio, J. K. Alberts, M. Hecht, & J. Buley (Eds.), Contemporary perspectives on interpersonal communication (pp. 120–124). Madison, WI: Brown & Benchmark.; **p. 201:** Knapp, M. L., & Vangelisti, A. (1997). Interpersonal communication and relationships (2nd ed.). Boston: Allyn & Bacon.; **p. 202:** Baxter, L. A., & Bullis, C. (1986). Turning points in developing romantic relationships. Human Communication Research, 12, 469–493.; **p. 203:** Reeder, H. (1996). What Harry and Sally didn't tell you. Ph.D. diss., Arizona State University, Tempe.; **p. 207:** Laurel; **p. 208:** Canary, D. J., Stafford, L., Hause, K. S., & Wallace, L. A. (1993). An inductive analysis of relational maintenance strategies: Comparisons among lovers, relatives, friends, and others. Communication Research Reports, 10, 5–14.; **p. 208:** Dainton, M. A., Zelley, E., & Langan, E. (2003). Maintaining friendships throughout the lifespan. In D. J. Canary & M. Dainton (Eds.), Maintaining relationships through communication (pp. 79–102). Mahwah, NJ: Erlbaum.; **p. 212:** Kowalski, R., Valentine, S., Wilkinson, R., Queen, A., & Sharpe, B. (2003). Lying, cheating, complaining, and other aversive interpersonal behaviors: A narrative examination of the dark side of relationships. Journal of Social and Personal Relationships, 20, 471–490.; **p. 215:** Struckman-Johnson, C. J., Struckman-Johnson, B. L., & Anderson, B. (2003). Tactics of sexual coercion: When men and women won't take no for an answer. Journal of Sex Research, 40(1), 76–86.; **p. 215:** McCoy, K., & Oelschlager, J. (n.d.) Sexual coercion awareness and prevention. Florida Institute of Technology. Retrieved May 17, 2011, from: http://www.fit.edu/caps/documents/SexualCoercion_000.pdf.; **p. 216:** McCoy, K., & Oelschlager, J. (n.d.) Sexual coercion awareness and prevention. Florida Institute of Technology. Retrieved May 17, 2011, from: http://www.fit.edu/caps/documents/SexualCoercion_000.pdf.; **p. 204:** Adapted from Dwyer, K. (December 9, 2015). The surprising reality of hook-up culture in college. Teen Vogue. http://www.teenvogue.com/story/hookup-culture-myth-dating-college. Retrieved March 22, 2017.

Chapter 10 Page 227: Based on Brooks, C. (2013, January 16). Why employees hate teamwork. Businessnewsdaily.com. Retrieved October 5, 2014, from http://www.businessnewsdaily.com/3769-employees-prefer-to-go-it-alone-research-finds.html, Brooks, C. (2013, October 16). Hate teamwork? You're not alone. Businessnewsdaily.com. Retrieved October 5, 2014, from http://www.businessnews-daily.com/5281-employees-hate-teamwork.html; **p. 228:** Arrow, H., McGrath, J. E., & Berdahl, J. L. (2000). Small groups as complex systems. Thousand Oaks, CA: Sage, p. 34.; **p. 229:** Lawrence. R. Frey (1994). The call of the field: Studying communication in natural groups. In L. R. Frey (Ed.), Group communication in context: Studies of natural groups (pp. ix-xiv). Hillsdale, NJ: Erlbaum. (p. X).; **p. 231:** Benne, K. D., & Sheats, P. (1984). Functional roles of group members. Journal of Social Issues, 4, 41-49; **p. 232:** Benne, K. D., & Sheats, P. (1984). Functional roles of group members. Journal of Social Issues, 4, 41-49; **p. 233:** Benne, K. D., & Sheats, P. (1984). Functional roles of group members. Journal of Social Issues, 4, 41-49; **p. 233:** Tiacko; **p. 234:** Gollent, M. (2007, June 6). Why are leadership skills important - for everyone? Retrieved March 30, 2011, from http://ezinearticles.com/?Why-Are-Leadership-Skills-Important---For-Everyone?&id=591333; **p. 234:** Daft, R. L. (2010). The Leadership experience (5th Ed). Mason, OH:

Thomson Higher Education. p. 5.; **p. 234:** Martha; **p. 235:** Based on Cain, S. (2013). Quiet: The power of introverts in a world that can't stop talking. NYC: Broadway Books. Moore, K. (2012). Introverts no longer the quiet followers of extroverts. Forbes.com. Retrieved April 22, 2014, from http://www.forbes.com/sites/karlmoore/2012/08/22/introverts-no-longer-the-quiet-followers-of-extroverts/; **p. 236:** Foels, R., Driskell, J. E., Mullen, B., & Salas, E. (2000). The effects of democratic leadership on group member satisfaction: An integration. Small Group Research, 31, 676-701. p. 677; **p. 241:** Kirstin; **p. 242:** Based on Trends in Global Virtual Teams: Virtual Teams Survey Report 2016. RW3 Culture Wizard. Retrieved March 2, 2017, from http://cdn.culturewizard.com/PDF/Trends_in_VT_Report_4-17-2016.pdf. Ferrazzi, K. (2012, November 19) How to Manage Conflict in Virtual TeamsHBR Blog Network. Retrieved April 22, 2014, from http://blogs.hbr.org/2012/11/how-to-manage-conflict-in-virt/; **p. 243:** Based on Sunwolf & Seibold, D. R. (1999). The impact of formal procedure on group processes, members, and task outcomes. In L. R. Frey, D. S. Gouran, & M. S. Poole (Eds.), Handbook of group communication theory and research (p. 401). Thousand Oaks, CA: Sage.; **p. 245:** Based on Gloor, P. A. (2006). Swarm creativity: Competitive advantage through collaborative in-innovative networks. Oxford: Oxford University Press. Gloor, P. A., Heckman, C., & Makedon, F. (2004, April 14–16). Ethical issues in virtual communities of innovation. Ethicomp 2004, the 7th International Conference on the Social and Ethical Impacts of Information and Communication Technologies, Syros, Greece. Retrieved July 17, 2011, from https://exchange.asu.edu/exchange/mar22/Drafts/documents/COIN4Ethicomp.pdf Gloor, P. A., Paasvaara, M., Schoder, D., & Willems, P. (2007, April). Finding collaborative innovation networks through correlating performance with social network structure. Journal of Production Research, Taylor and Francis. Retrieved July 17, 2011, from exchange.asu.edu/exchange/mar22/Drafts/documents/Gloor_JPR_3.pdf; **p. 246:** Based on (21 May, 2013.) Thecouchmanager.com. Retrieved May 14, 2014, and adapted from http://www.thecouchmanager.com/2013/05/21/the-ultimate-list-of-virtual-team-technology-tools/; **p. 248:** Sarah; **p. 248:** Katherine W. Phillips (2014). How Diversity Makes Us Smarter. Scientific American; **p. 250:** Oetzel, J. G. (2005). Effective intercultural workgroup communication theory. In W. B. Gudykunst (Ed), Theorizing about intercultural communication (pp. 351-371) Thousand Oaks, CA: Sage, p. 366.

Chapter 11 Page 260: Cheney, G., Christensen, L. T., Zorn, T. E., Jr., & Ganesh, S. (2004). Organizational communication in an age of globalizations: Issues, reflections, practices. Prospect Heights, IL: Waveland.; **p. 262:** Appelbaum, S. H., Roberts, J., & Shapiro, B. T. (2009). Cultural strategies in M&As: Investigating ten case studies, Journal of Executive Education, 8(1), 33–58.; **p. 264:** Clair, R. (1996). The political nature of a colloquialism, "A real job": Implications for organizational assimilation. Communication Monographs, 63, 249–267.; **p. 265:** Yoshi; **p. 269:** Yoshi; **p. 275:** Eisenberg, E., Goodall, H. L., & Trethewey, A. (2010). Organizational communication: Balance, creativity and constraint. Boston, MA: Bedford/St. Martin's.; **p. 280:** Nichole; **p. 276:** Bob; **p. 277:** Namie, G., Christiansen, D., & Phillips, D. (2014). The 2014 WBI US workplace bullying survey. Retrieved July 15, 2014, from: http://www.workplacebullying.org/wbiresearch/wbi-2014-us-survey/.

Chapter 12 Page 287: https://www.change.org/about; **p. 287:** Tostevin, R. (2014, March 14). Online activism: It's easy to click, but just as easy to disengage. The Guardian. Retrieved May 18, 2014, from: http://www.theguardian.com/media-network/media-network-blog/2014/mar/14/online-activism-social-media-engage; **p. 288:** Washington Post staff. (2016, June 12). President Obama's complete remarks on Orlando shooting. Washington Post. Retrieved from: https://www.washingtonpost.com/news/post-politics/wp/2016/06/12/president-obamas-complete-remarks-on-orlando-shooting/?utm_term=.92e859d16221; **p. 003:** Lance; **p. 004:** Based on Douglass, F. (1852, July 5). The meaning of July Fourth for the Negro. Retrieved June 26, 2006, from www.pbs.org/wgbh/aia/part4/4h2927t.html Thomas, S. (n.d.). From slave to abolitionist/editor. Retrieved June 26, 2006, from http://www.history.rochester.

edu/class/douglass/part2.html; **p. 291:** Aristotle. (1991). On rhetoric: A theory of civic discourse (G. A. Kennedy, trans.) New York: Oxford University Press, (p. 42) (Original work written about 350 B.C.E); **p. 292:** George Kennedy, (1998). Comparative rhetoric: An historical and cross cultural introduction. New York: Oxford University Press (p. 215).; **p. 295:** Janis King (2002) Cultural differences in the perceptions of sports mascots: A rhetoric study of Tim Giago's newspaper columns. In J. N. Martin, T. K. Nakayama, L. A. Flores (Eds.), Reading in intercultural communication: Experiences and context (pp. 205-212) New York: McGraw-Hill (p. 211).; **p. 14:** Thomas Erdbrink (2008). Iranian Woman Blinded by Spurned Suitor Persuades Court to Punish Him Similarly. Washington Post; **p. 300:** "Changing Lives of Women" http://www.npr.org/sections/health-shots/2014/10/24/357584372/video-what-women-get-flak-for-when-they-talk; "From Upspeak To Vocal Fry" http://www.npr.org/2015/07/23/425608745/from-upspeak-to-vocal-fry-are-we-policing-young-womens-voices; **p. 300:** Salahi, 2014. Wolfeboro Police Commissioner Resigns Following Racist Comments. Boston Globe Media Partners, LLC; **p. 306:** Lisa; **p. 311:** Tamara; **p. 312:** Sanow, A. (2005, March 3). How I overcame the fear of public speaking. Retrieved June 26, 2006, from http://www.expertclick.com/NewsreleaseWire/default.cfm?Action=ReleaseDetail&ID-8372&NRWid=1698.

Chapter 13 Page 316: Scott, D. C. (2013, November 9). Mariska Hargitay: A Hollywood star for an actress—and activist (+video). The Christian Science Monitor. Retrieved June 6, 2014, from: http://www.csmonitor.com/The-Culture/2013/1109/Mariska-Hargitay-A-Hollywood-star-for-an-actress-and-activist-video.; **p. 318:** Nielsen. (2014, May 12). Advertising and audiences: State of the media. Retrieved June 6, 2014, from: http://www.nielsen.com/us/en/reports/2014/advertising-and-audiences-state-of-the-media.html.; **p. 318:** Coming full circle: The end of mass media. (2011, July 7). The Economist. Retrieved June 6, 2014, from: http://www.economist.com/node/18904158.; **p. 318:** Stelter, B. (2014, June 6). Netflix's tv guru: "Don't make me wait!" CNN Money. Retrieved June 6, 2014, from: http://money.cnn.com/2014/06/06/media/ted-sarandos-netflix-interview/.; **p. 003:** Hale, M. (2017, March 13). On Netflix, the borders remain open. New York Times. Retrieved from: https://www.nytimes.com/2017/03/13/arts/television/netflix-fauda-nobel-review.html?_r=0; **p. 319:** Boorstin, D. J. (1965). The Americans: The national experience. New York: Random House.; **p. 320:** Mitchell, A. (2014, March 26). State of the news media 2014. Pew Research Journalism Project. Retrieved June 11, 2014, from: http://www.journalism.org/2014/03/26/state-of-the-news-media-2014-overview/.; **p. 320:** Chapman, J. (2005). Comparative media history. Malden, MA: Polity Press.; Luckerson, V. (2013, December 3). Here's how much top musicians are making on Spotify. Time. Retrieved June 29, 2014, from: http://business.time.com/2013/12/03/heres-how-much-money-top-musicians-are-making-on-spotify/.; **p. 326:** Cohen, J. (2002). Television viewing preferences: Programs, schedules, and the structure of viewing choices made by Israeli adults. Journal of Broadcasting & Electronic Media, 46, 204–221.: Cohen, J. (2002). Television viewing preferences: Programs, schedules, and the structure of viewing choices made by Israeli adults. Journal of Broadcasting & Electronic Media, 46, 204–221.: Cohen, J. (2002). Television viewing preferences: Programs, schedules, and the structure of viewing choices made by Israeli adults. Journal of Broadcasting & Electronic Media, 46, 204–221.; **p. 323:** Kevin; **p. 324:** Feinberg, S. (2014, March 2). Brutally honest Oscar voter ballot no. 7. The Hollywood Reporter. Retrieved June 9, 2014, from: http://www.hollywoodreporter.com/race/brutally-honest-oscar-voter-ballot-684839. Okoro, E. (2013, November 27). Why I wouldn't see 12 Years a Slave with a white person. The Atlantic. Retrieved June 9, 2014. from: http://www.theatlantic.com/entertainment/archive/2013/11/why-i-wouldnt-see-em-12-years-a-slave-emwith-a-white-person/281883/. Sharkey, B. (2014, February 27). Oscars 2014: For many, "12 Years a Slave" is too hard to watch. Los Angeles Times. Retrieved June 9, 2014, from: http://articles.latimes.com/2014/feb/27/entertainment/la-et-mn-12-years-a-slave-notebook-20140227/2.; **p. 325:** Gunther, A. C., &

Schmitt, K. (2004). Mapping boundaries of the hostile media effect. Journal of Communication, 54, 55–70. Gunther, A. C., & Schmitt, K. (2004). Mapping boundaries of the hostile media effect. Journal of Communication, 54, 55–70. Gunther, A. C., & Schmitt, K. (2004). Mapping boundaries of the hostile media effect. Journal of Communication, 54, 55–70.; **p. 326:** Yahr, E. (2016, October 19). NBC's 'This Is Us' is officially the surprise breakout hit of the fall TV season. The Washington Post. Retrieved from: https://www.washingtonpost.com/news/arts-and-entertainment/wp/2016/10/19/nbcs-this-is-us-is-officially-the-surprise-breakout-hit-of-the-fall-tv-season/?utm_term=.f7a8f9d09aa0; **p. 327:** Emma; **p. 327:** Durham, M. G. (2004). Constructing the "new ethnicities": Media, sexuality, and diaspora identity in the lives of South Asian immigrant girls. Critical Studies in Media Communication, 21, 140–161.; **p. 328:** Lemire, C. (2005, August 10). Even trashing "Deuce Bigalow" a tired cliché. MSNBC. Retrieved June 24, 2006, from: http://msnbc.msn.com/id/8887672.; **p. 329:** Aoyagi, C. (2004, July 2–15). TV networks' current fascination with Hawaii often doesn't translate into more roles for APAs. Pacific Citizen, 139, 1.; **p. 329:** Dixon, T. L., & Linz, D. (2002). Television news, prejudicial pretrial publicity, and the depiction of race. Journal of Broadcasting & Electronic Media, 46, 112–136.; **p. 329:** Law, C., & Labre, M. P. (2002). Cultural standards of attractiveness: A thirty-year look at changes in male images in magazines. Journalism and Mass Communication Quarterly, 79, 697–711.; **p. 330:** Meyers, M. (2004). African American women and violence: Gender, race, and class in the news. Critical Studies in Media Communication, 21, 95–118.; **p. 330:** Shugart, H. (2008). Managing masculinities: The metrosexual moment. Communication and Critical/Cultural Studies, 5, 280–300.; **p. 331:** Fahmy, S. (2004). Picturing Afghan women: A content analysis of AP wire photographs during the Taliban regime and after the fall of the Taliban regime. Gazette: The International Journal for Communication Studies, 66, 91–112.; **p. 332:** Morgan, M., & Signorielli, N. (1990). Cultivation analysis: Conceptualization and methodology. In N. Signorielli & M. Morgan (Eds.), Cultivation analysis: New directions in media effects research (pp. 13–34). Newbury Park, CA: Sage Publications.; **p. 332:** Niederdeppe, J., Fowler, E. F., Goldstein, K., & Pribble, J. (2010). Does local television news coverage cultivate fatalistic beliefs about cancer prevention? Journal of Communication, 60, 230–253.; **p. 333:** Hanke, R. (1990). Hegemonic masculinity in thirtysomething. Critical Studies in Mass Communication, 7, 231–248.; **p. 333:** Dayan, D., & Katz, E. (1992). Media events: The live broadcasting of history. Cambridge, MA: Harvard University Press.; **p. 334:** Anderson, C. A., & Bushman, B. J. (2002, March 29). The effects of media violence on society. Science, 295, 2377–2378. Retrieved May 1, 2006, from: http://www.psychology.iastate.edu/faculty/caa/abstracts/2000-2004/02AB2.pdf.; **p. 335:** Douglas, T. (2012, June 28). News Corp confirms plan to split the media giant. BBC. Retrieved March 23, 2017, from News Corporation. (2011, September 20). New York Times. Retrieved October 5, 2011, from: http://topics.nytimes.com/top/news/business/companies/news_corporation/index.html.; **p. 335:** de Moraes, L. (2004, October 21). No more Miss America pageantry for ABC. Washington Post, p. C7. Retrieved June 24, 2006, from: http://www.washingtonpost.com/wp-dyn/articles/A50114-2004Oct20.html; **p. 337:** Akhavan-Majid, R. (2004). Mass media reform in China: Toward a new analytical perspective. Gazette: The International Journal for Communication Studies, 66, 553–565.; **p. 337:** Akhavan-Majid, R. (2004). Mass media reform in China: Toward a new analytical perspective. Gazette: The International Journal for Communication Studies, 66, 553–565.; **p. 023:** Cablevision. (2000, November 4). NBC to acquire Bravo from Cablevision Systems Corporation. Retrieved June 24, 2006, from: http://www.cablevision.com/index.jhtml?id=2002_11_04.; **p. 338:** McChesney, R. (1998). Making media democratic. Boston Review, 23, 4–10, 20. Retrieved June 24, 2006, from: http://www.bostonreview.net/BR23.3/mcchesney.html.; **p. 339:** Celis, B. (2017, March 12). The time's right for a new wave of Black media activism. Newsweek. Retrieved from: http://www.newsweek.com/time-right-new-wave-black-media-activism-565377; **p. 339:** http://www.tvguidelines.org/ratings.htm.

Chapter 14 Page 345: Digital Life in 2025, Pew Report, 2014 —J. G. Ballard; **p. 348:** Guarino, B. (June 10, 2016). Google faulted for racial bias in image search results for black teenagers. washing-tonpost. com. Retrieved on March 14, 2017 https://www.washingtonpost. com/news/morning-mix/wp/2016/06/10/google-faulted-for-racial-bias-in-image-search-results-for-black-teenagers/?utm_term=.650a1477e5e9; **p. 349:** Kaplan, A. M., & Haenlein, M. (2010). Users of the world, unite! The challenges and opportunities of social media. Business Horizons, 53, 59–68.; **p. 349:** Walther, J. B., & Parks, M. R. (2002). Cues filtered out, cues filtered in: Computer-mediated communication and relationships. In M. L. Knapp & J. A. Daly (Eds.), Handbook of interpersonal communication (pp. 529–563). Thousand Oaks, CA: Sage.; **p. 350:** Turkle, S. (2011). Alone together: Why we expect more from technology and less from each other. New York: Basic Books. Turkle, S. (2012, February). TED talk: Connected, but alone? Retrieved May 25, 2014, from: http://www.ted.com/talks/sherry_turkle_alone_together#t-755215.; **p. 353:** Kaplan, A. M., & Haenlein, M. (2010). Users of the world, unite! The challenges and opportunities of social media. Business Horizons, 53, 59–68.;

p. 353: Bosker, B. (2014, February 4). The oversharers are over sharing: 10 years on, the Facebook generation is covering up. Huffingtonpost. com. Retrieved May 18, 2014, from: http://www.huffingtonpost.com/bianca-bosker/facebook-10-anniversary_b_4718871.html.; **p. 357:** Alford, H. (Nov. 30, 2012). If I Do Humblebrag So Myself.; **p. 358:** Roberto, A. J., & Eden, J. (2010). Cyberbullying: Aggressive communication in the digital age. In T. A. Avtgis & A. S. Rancer (Eds.), Arguments, aggressions, and conflict: New directions in theory and research (pp. 198-216). New York: Routledge.; **p. 361:** Heino, R. D., Ellison, N. B., & Gibbs, J. L. (2010). Relationshopping: Investigating the market metaphor in online dating. Journal of Social and Personal Relationships, 27, 427-447.; **p. 361:** Selyukh, 2016. Postelection, Over-whelmed Facebook Users Unfriend, Cut Back. NPR; **p. 362:** Weinstein, E. C. & Selman, R. L. (2016). Digital Stress: Adolescents' personal accounts. New Media & Society, 18(3), 391-409.; **p. 362:** Jacqueline; **p. 364:** Mei-Lin; **p. 371:** Bryson, D. (2013, July 23). What is web civility. enduranceinternational.com. Retrieved May 27, 2014, from: http://enduranceinternational.com/our-mission/web-civility/what-is-web-civility.; **p. 372:** Cruzita.

Index

A

absenteeism, 265, 270
absolutism, ethical, 18–19
Abu Ghraib, 298–299
academic performance
   listening and, 149
   small group work and, 225, 226
Académie française, 99
accents, 95, 99, 111–112, 113
accommodation, 185
ACLU, 357
action-oriented listening style, 152–153
active agents, 322, 324, 340
activism, 287
   interactive media and, 347
   media, 316, 338–340
Adams, Tony, 54–55
adaptors, 128
Aday, Sean, 332
advertising, 326
Afghanistan, 332
African Americans
   access to interactive media and, 367–368
   health disparities among, 38
   on Hurricane Katrina response, 295
   ideal body type among, 136
   intercultural communication and, 182–183
   language use by, 107–108
   legacy of slavery and, 183
   media choices and, 324–325
   nonverbal behavior interpretation by, 124
   perception of racial bias among, 85
   population of, 170
   preferred personality among, 178–179
   sexual violence among, 330
   stereotype threat and, 52–53
   on TV, 184
African Americans and the Media (Squires), 184
African American Vernacular English, 107–108, 113
age
   cohort effects and, 88–89
   cultural perceptions of, 87
   identity, 63
   interactive media and, 365
   intercultural conflicts and, 178
   listening and, 155–156
   mass media choices and, 323–324
   perception and, 82
   sense of smell and, 74
   verbal communication differences and, 105
agenda-setting capacity, 331–333
agents, active, 322, 340
aggression
   in close relationships, 217–218
   eye gaze in communicating, 130
   in interactive media, 354
   interpersonal violence, 214–215
   jealousy and, 213
   mass media effects on, 323

sexual coercion and, 215–216
social comparisons and, 51
space invasion and, 134
touch and, 136
aggressor role, 233
Ailes, Roger, 336
Airbnb, 275
Akhavan-Majid, R., 337
Albright, Jonathan, 348
Alford, Henry, 357
Alone Together (Turkle), 351
alternative media, 340
alternative press, 319
Amazing Race (TV show), 225
Amazon, 115
Amazon Prime, 318
American Academy of Pediatrics, 334
American Bar Association, 329
American Desi (movie), 327
American Dialect Society, 96–97, 111
American Life Project, 366
American Psychiatric Association, 118
American Psychological Association, 30
Americans with Disabilities Act, 65
Amish, 36
   self-effacement among, 54
   social comparisons and, 51
analysis
   audience, 302–303
   demographic, 303
analysis paralysis, 240
Ancestry DNA, 58
Andes Mountains, sensory models in, 85
androcentrism, 112
Annenberg Public Policy Center, 339
anonymity, online, 357–359
Anthony, Casey, 322
Anthony, Caylee, 322
Anthony, Susan B., 297, 307–308
antiglobalization protests, 274
anti-social behaviors, 208
anxiety, 193
Any Given Sunday (movie), 302
Aoyagi, Caroline, 329
apologies, 221
appearance
   listening and, 161
   nonverbal communication and, 136–137, 140
Appelbaum, S. H., 262
appropriateness, 20
Arafat, Yasser, 333
Arana, Marie, 59
Aristotle, 2, 291, 293, 294
Arizona Public Service, 263
Arizona State University, 260
Arthur W. Page Center for Integrity in Public Communication, 339
artifacts, 136–137, 140
artistic proofs, 293–294
Art of Rhetoric (Aristotle), 293

Asian Pacific Islander Americans, 329
Asians/Asian Americans
   adaptation to US culture by, 175
   census categories and, 58
   cultural values of, 178
   indirect communication and, 101
   labels on, 113
   listening and, 156
   preferred personality among, 178–179
   resistance to media messages by, 327
   stereotype threat and, 52–53
   stereotyping, 78
   turn-taking by, 101
askreddit.com, 347
Assad, Bashir al-, 331
assertiveness, 267
assimilation, 174, 185
   definition of, 262
   organizational communication and, 262–264
   organizational cultures and, 261
Associated Press (AP), 331
Association of Southeast Asian Nations Free Trade Area (AFTA), 274
assurances, 208, 209
asynchronous communication, 350, 360
attention, selective, 74–75
attraction theory, 195
attractiveness, 136–137, 195, 196
   listening and, 161
   mass media images of, 323
attributional bias, 79–80, 282
attribution theory, 79–81
audience
   analysis of, 302–303
   rhetorical, 295–296
audio conferencing tools, 246
Augustine of Hippo, 291
authenticity, 34, 218–220
   in small groups, 251
authoritarian leaders, 236–237
autonomy, 178, 207, 210
avatars, 359
aversive communication behaviors, 212–216
   deception, 212–213
   interpersonal violence, 214–215
   jealousy, 213–214
   sexual coercion, 215–216
avoidance, 208
avoiding, 200, 201
awareness, leadership and, 237–238

B

Baby Boomers, 63, 170
The Bachelor/Bachelorette (TV show), 63
Bahrami, Ameneh, 299
Bailey, Cynthia, 184
Ballard, J. G., 345
Balley, C., 55
Barbershop Hypertension Screening Program, 38

417